ASIAN DEVELOPMENT
OUTLOOK 2022

MOBILIZING TAXES FOR DEVELOPMENT

APRIL 2022

ASIAN DEVELOPMENT BANK

© 2022 Asian Development Bank
6 ADB Avenue, Mandaluyong City, 1550 Metro Manila, Philippines
Tel +63 2 8632 4444; Fax +63 2 8636 2444
www.adb.org

Some rights reserved. Published in 2022.

ISBN 978-92-9269-456-2 (print); 978-92-9269-457-9 (electronic); 978-92-9269-458-6 (e-book)
ISSN 0117-0481 (print), 1996-725X (electronic)
Publication Stock No.FLS220141-3
DOI: http://dx.doi.org/10.22617/FLS220141-3

Notes:
In this publication, "$" refers to US dollars.
ADB recognizes "Hong Kong" as Hong Kong, China; "China" as the People's Republic of China; "Korea" and "South Korea" as the Republic of Korea; and "Vietnam" as Viet Nam.

Cover design by Anthony Victoria.

Cover artwork by Demosthenes Campos/2017.

CONTENTS

PART 1

Recovery continues amid global headwinds   1

PART 2

Mobilizing taxes for development   77

PART 3

Economic trends and prospects in developing Asia   151

FOREWORD

The significant progress being made in COVID-19 vaccine rollouts bodes well for the continued resilience of developing Asia's economies. 66% of the region's population is now fully vaccinated. Increased immunity and the less severe health impacts of the Omicron variant are allowing economies to stay open and perform better than during previous outbreaks. This will support developing Asia's continued return to normality. This year's *Asian Development Outlook* forecasts the region's growth at a buoyant but steady 5.2% in 2022 and 5.3% in 2023.

The welcome return to a more stable pattern of growth comes with caveats. Developing Asia is still recovering from the social and economic impacts of a pandemic that is by no means over. Indeed, the rapid spread of the Omicron variant earlier this year was a reminder that public health risks continue to endanger the region. The Russian invasion of Ukraine has heightened geopolitical risks, confounding the outlook for the world economy. Monetary tightening by the United States Federal Reserve is complicating the policy environment. And adverse developments, including rising inflationary pressures and supply disruptions, are intensifying global uncertainty.

Moreover, developing Asia's recovery remains incomplete, and progress on its development agenda must accelerate. Public spending to counter the harsh effects of the COVID-19 pandemic has narrowed fiscal space for the region's economies—even as greater spending is needed to meet the Sustainable Development Goals.

A difficult challenge for policy makers will be mobilizing sufficient revenue to sustain development. Tax revenue was gradually rising in the region before COVID-19, but the levels were comparatively low. Fiscal resources will need to increase if fiscal sustainability is to be restored once the pandemic passes. Our theme chapter focuses on ways to achieve this. Recommendations include minimizing tax expenditure (foregone taxes), increasing green and health taxes, and improving value-added tax collection, especially from the expanding digital economy. Strengthening personal income and property taxes also can raise additional revenue and make tax systems more progressive.

This year's *Asian Development Outlook* continues the Asian Development Bank's commitment to provide comprehensive policy analysis and sound policy advice. The report shines a light on possible interventions and solutions to help Asian economies navigate their way out of the COVID-19 pandemic and through the current geopolitical turmoil. Whatever the challenges, we at the Asian Development Bank remain committed to helping advance sustainable, resilient, and inclusive growth across developing Asia.

MASATSUGU ASAKAWA
President
Asian Development Bank

ACKNOWLEDGMENTS

Asian Development Outlook 2022 was prepared by staff of the regional departments and resident missions of the Asian Development Bank (ADB) under the guidance of the Economic Research and Regional Cooperation Department (ERCD). Representatives of these departments met regularly as the Regional Economic Outlook Task Force to coordinate and develop consistent forecasts for the region.

ERCD economists, led by Abdul Abiad, director of the Macroeconomics Research Division, coordinated the production of this report, assisted by Edith Laviña and Priscille Villanueva. Shiela Camingue-Romance, Cindy Castillejos-Petalcorin, David Keith De Padua, Rhea Manguiat Molato, Nedelyn Magtibay-Ramos, Pilipinas Quising, Dennis Sorino, and Priscille Villanueva provided technical and research support. Emmanuel Alano, Jesson Pagaduan, Reizle Jade Platitas, Rene Cris Rivera, and Michael Timbang did additional research. Economic editorial advisors Robert Boumphrey, Eric Clifton, Joshua Greene, Srinivasa Madhur, Richard Niebuhr, and Reza Vaez-Zadeh made substantial contributions to the country chapters and regional outlook.

The support and guidance of ADB Chief Economist Albert Park and Deputy Chief Economist Joseph E. Zveglich Jr. is gratefully acknowledged.

Authors who contributed the sections are bylined in each chapter. The subregional coordinators were Kenji Takamiya and Fatima Catacutan for Central Asia, Akiko Terada-Hagiwara for East Asia, Rana Hasan and Lani Garnace for South Asia, James Villafuerte and Dulce Zara for Southeast Asia, and Rommel Rabanal, Cara Tinio, and Remrick Patagan for the Pacific.

In addition to the contributors named in the bylines and the authors of the background papers, the theme chapter benefitted from inputs from the ADB Governance Thematic Group of the Sustainable Development and Climate Change department. Steven Sheffrin reviewed the background papers and Margarita Debuque-Gonzales gave editorial advice on the theme chapter.

Peter Fredenburg and Alastair McIndoe advised on ADB style and English usage. Alvin Tubio did the typesetting and graphics, assisted by Heili Ann Bravo, Elenita Pura, and Rhia Bautista-Piamonte. Art direction for the cover was by Anthony Victoria, with artwork from Demosthenes Campos. Kevin Nellies designed the landing page for *Asian Development Outlook 2022*. Fermirelyn Cruz provided administrative and secretarial support. A team from the Department of Communications, led by David Kruger and Terje Langeland, planned and coordinated the dissemination of *Asian Development Outlook 2022*.

DEFINITIONS AND ASSUMPTIONS

The economies discussed in *Asian Development Outlook 2022* are classified by major analytic or geographic group. For the purposes of this report, the following apply:

- **Association of Southeast Asian Nations** (ASEAN) comprises Brunei Darussalam, Cambodia, Indonesia, the Lao People's Democratic Republic, Malaysia, Myanmar, the Philippines, Singapore, Thailand, and Viet Nam. The ASEAN-5 are Indonesia, Malaysia, the Philippines, Thailand, and Viet Nam.

- **Developing Asia** comprises the 46 members of the Asian Development Bank listed below by geographic group.

- **Caucasus and Central Asia** comprises Armenia, Azerbaijan, Georgia, Kazakhstan, the Kyrgyz Republic, Tajikistan, Turkmenistan, and Uzbekistan.

- **East Asia** comprises Hong Kong, China; Mongolia; the People's Republic of China; the Republic of Korea; and Taipei,China.

- **South Asia** comprises Afghanistan, Bangladesh, Bhutan, India, Maldives, Nepal, Pakistan, and Sri Lanka.

- **Southeast Asia** comprises Brunei Darussalam, Cambodia, Indonesia, the Lao People's Democratic Republic, Malaysia, Myanmar, the Philippines, Singapore, Thailand, Timor-Leste, and Viet Nam.

- **The Pacific** comprises the Cook Islands, the Federated States of Micronesia, Fiji, Kiribati, the Marshall Islands, Nauru, Niue, Palau, Papua New Guinea, Samoa, Solomon Islands, Tonga, Tuvalu, and Vanuatu.

Unless otherwise specified, the symbol "$" and the word "dollar" refer to US dollars.

A number of assumptions have been made for the projections in *Asian Development Outlook 2022*: The policies of national authorities are maintained. Real effective exchange rates remain constant at their average from 13 January to 9 March 2022. The average price of oil is $107/barrel in 2021 and $93/barrel in 2022. The 6-month London interbank offered rate for US dollar deposits averages 0.5% in 2022 and 1.3% in 2022, the European Central Bank refinancing rate averages 0.0% in 2022 and 0.5% in 2023, and the Bank of Japan's overnight call rate averages 0% in both years.

The forecasts and analysis in this *ADO* are based on information available to 9 March 2022.

ABBREVIATIONS

ADB	Asian Development Bank
ADO	*Asian Development Outlook*
COVID-19	Coronavirus Disease 2019
CPI	consumer price index
CSIs	cottage and small industries
DRM	domestic resource mobilization
ECB	European Central Bank
ETS	emission trading system or scheme
FCAS	fragile and conflict-affected situation
FDI	foreign direct investment
FOMC	Federal Open Market Committee
FSM	Federated States of Micronesia
FY	fiscal year
G20	Group of Twenty
GDP	gross domestic product
GHG	greenhouse gas
ICT	information and communication technology
Lao PDR	Lao People's Democratic Republic
LAYS	learning-adjusted years of schooling
LGU	local government unit
Libor	London interbank offered rate
LNG	liquefied natural gas
M2	broad money that includes cash and highly liquid accounts
M3	broad money that adds time accounts to M2
MSMEs	micro, small, and medium-sized enterprises
NDC	nationally determined contribution
NPL	nonperforming loan
OECD	Organisation for Economic Co-operation and Development
OPEC	Organization of the Petroleum Exporting Countries
PFM	public financial management
PMI	purchasing managers' index
PNG	Papua New Guinea
PRC	People's Republic of China
Q	quarter
ROK	Republic of Korea
SDG	Sustainable Development Goal
SMEs	small and medium-sized enterprises
SNG	subnational government
SOE	state-owned enterprise
SOFAZ	State Oil Fund of Azerbaijan
SWIFT	Society for Worldwide Interbank Financial Telecommunication
tCO_2e	ton of carbon dioxide equivalent
UHC	universal health coverage
VAT	value-added tax

ADO 2022—HIGHLIGHTS

The Russian invasion of Ukraine has heightened geopolitical uncertainty and rattled commodity and financial markets—and this amid a global pandemic. Fortunately, COVID-19's Omicron variant has had a milder impact than other variants and progress on vaccination has allowed economies across developing Asia to remain more open than in previous COVID-19 waves. Solid exports and strong domestic demand will keep the region's growth strong at 5.2% in 2022 and 5.3% in 2023. The region's inflation rate is forecast to rise to 3.7% this year and 3.1% next year as economic recovery continues and energy and commodity prices remain elevated. Monetary authorities should remain vigilant to incipient inflationary pressures.

Several downside risks cloud the region's outlook. Escalating geopolitical tensions could impede trade and production, and stoke inflationary pressures. Aggressive monetary policy tightening in the United States may lead to financial instability. And COVID-19 remains a threat: the current Omicron outbreaks in the People's Republic of China could endanger regional growth and supply chains, and more deadly variants could still emerge. Scarring from the pandemic poses significant medium-term risks, including learning losses from continued school closures that could further exacerbate economic inequality.

Tackling developing Asia's varied medium-term challenges will require substantial investments. The region's economies urgently need to mobilize fiscal resources to restore the health of public finances after COVID-19 passes and to build a more inclusive and sustainable future. While more efficient spending can free up some fiscal resources, much more is needed to be able to effectively advance inclusive development.

Opportunities to strengthen revenue will depend on economy-specific circumstances, but more efficient value-added tax and better-optimized tax incentives hold promise for many economies. Strengthening personal income and property taxes can raise additional revenue and make tax systems more progressive. Significant opportunities exist to expand the use of tax and other fiscal instruments to tackle environmental and health priorities while raising revenue. Reform to reduce developing Asia's large informal sector is another way to lift revenue. Fundamental tax reform to mobilize revenue better can be achieved, and it is best done in tandem with efforts to strengthen tax administration and improve taxpayer morale.

Albert F. Park
Chief Economist
Asian Development Bank

Recovery continues amid global headwinds

New challenges complicate the outlook

- **The Russian invasion of Ukraine has upended the global economic outlook and greatly amplified uncertainty for a world economy still contending with COVID-19.** The war's outbreak in late February severely disrupted global economic conditions. Shockwaves have been felt in financial and commodity markets, and energy and food prices have spiked sharply and threaten to remain elevated or rise further. The highly uncertain outcome of the invasion is an additional hurdle for developing Asia's economies, many of which are still grappling with COVID-19.

- **The pandemic was fueled by the highly transmissible Omicron variant at the start of 2022.** New infections spiked in developing Asia and across the world, following Omicron's emergence in late 2021. Daily new cases in the region rose sharply from 46,000 at the end of December to 448,000 in January, declined to 274,000 in February, before surging again, to over 600,000 in early March. While vaccination disparities remain, coverage in developing Asia caught up with rollouts in advanced economies. As of 9 March, 66.6% of the region's population was fully vaccinated, compared with 65.2% in the United States and 72.6% in the European Union.

- **Omicron's less severe health impact, coupled with increased immunity, allowed developing Asia to remain relatively open in early 2022.** Because of this, regional economies fared better during the Omicron wave than previous COVID-19 outbreaks. Manufacturing and services continued to expand in January and February, albeit at a slightly slower pace than in the fourth quarter of last year in some economies. A partial exception is the People's Republic of China (PRC), where factory output contracted slightly in January on stringent containment measures to curb sporadic COVID-19 outbreaks.

- **Developing Asia's economy rebounded by 6.9% in 2021, but the recovery is still largely incomplete in most of the region.** Expansion in the Caucasus and Central Asia, supported by higher commodity prices, nevertheless left gross domestic product (GDP) at 4% below its pre-pandemic trend. In South Asia, the gap remained at about 8%, despite strong growth led by a surge in consumption and investment in India. Southeast Asia's gap was 10% and the Pacific's 12%. The recovery in these subregions was delayed by severe pandemic-containment restrictions on domestic activity and international travel, which especially hampered tourism-dependent economies. East Asia bucked the trend on buoyant external demand; its gap was just 1% below the pre-pandemic trend.

- **Remittances remained resilient; tourism showed signs of incipient recovery.** Resilient remittances continued in the third quarter of last year, when they were 7% above the same quarter in 2019. Tourist arrivals remained negligible in economies still quarantining incoming travelers. But where restrictions were lifted, arrivals, particularly from Europe, have picked up.

- **Developing Asia's financial conditions have weakened slightly since late 2021.** Financial conditions have softened since November, tracking expectations of a shift in the Federal Reserve's monetary stance and then the Russian invasion of Ukraine. Most regional currencies depreciated in 2021, a trend that continued in the first 10 weeks of 2022. Risk premiums started rising since November and strong gains in regional equity markets have gradually given way to losses. Excluding the PRC, the region recorded net portfolio outflows last year, but foreign direct investment—from both within and outside the region—exceeded pre-pandemic levels on solid medium-term fundamentals.

■ **Fiscal and monetary policies in developing Asian economies remain broadly accommodative, but the region may be on the cusp of a tightening cycle.** While fiscal policy remained supportive even after substantial loosening to cushion the impact of COVID-19 in 2020 and 2021, authorities are expected to start unwinding pandemic emergency measures and gradually shift to fiscal consolidation this year and next. A few central banks started tightening their stances in the second half of 2021 and others are expected to follow in response to domestic macroeconomic conditions, including rising inflationary pressures.

■ **GDP growth in developing Asia is expected to stay strong, at 5.2% in 2022 and 5.3% in 2023.** The pace of the recovery, however, varies across subregions. But in general, regional growth is being supported by a robust recovery in domestic demand in economies that are continuing to catch up with their pre-pandemic trend, particularly in South Asia. Here growth will remain strong in 2022 at a forecast 7.0%, accelerating to 7.4% in 2023. East Asia converged to its pre-pandemic trend in 2021 and growth rates are expected to normalize to 4.7% in 2022 and 4.5% in 2023. Growth rates in the other subregions will return to their pre-pandemic averages this year or next.

■ **Inflation in developing Asia stayed below the global trend in 2021, but is expected to rise.** Because of relatively low food inflation, less severe supply disruptions, and the incomplete recovery, regional inflation remained moderate at 2.5% last year. Price pressures were less broad-based than in advanced economies, including the US where inflation averaged 4.3%, and emerging economies in Latin America and the Caribbean, and Sub-Saharan Africa, where prices increased by 9.3% and 10.7%, respectively. Inflation in developing Asia this year and next will be driven by continuing recovery and elevated energy and commodity prices. The regional inflation rate is forecast to rise to 3.7% in 2022, before dipping to 3.1% in 2023. Headline inflation is expected to accelerate in all subregions but the Caucasus and Central Asia. Monetary authorities should keep a close watch for incipient inflationary pressures.

■ **Developing Asia's current account surplus is forecast to narrow from 1.3% of GDP in 2021 to 0.9% this year and inch up to 1.0% in 2023.** Export volumes from the PRC stabilized last year, but continued to rise in the rest of the region to reach 18% above pre-pandemic levels in December. Over the forecast horizon, slower growth rates and a shift in consumption back toward services in advanced economies will temper demand for developing Asia's exports, while imports will rise as economies recover. East Asia's current account surpluses will continue to shrink, while deficits will widen in South Asia. Commodity-exporting economies, such as those in the Caucasus and Central Asia, will mostly see current accounts improving this year.

■ **Several downside risks cloud developing Asia's outlook.** Escalating global geopolitical tensions arising from the Russian invasion of Ukraine could spill over to the region, particularly via sharper-than-expected increases in commodity prices and heightened financial stability risks, as discussed in this report's *Special Topic* on the economic impact of the war. Aggressive monetary policy tightening in the US may trigger financial market volatility, rapid capital outflows, and sharp currency depreciations. COVID-19 remains a threat, as more deadly variants could still emerge, and the PRC's current Omicron outbreaks could jeopardize regional growth and supply chains. In the medium-term, scarring from the pandemic poses significant risks, including learning losses from continued school closures that could further exacerbate economic inequality, as highlighted in the *Special Topic* on the effects of COVID-19 school closures.

The economic fallout of the Russian invasion will most affect the Caucasus and Central Asia

■ **The direct fallout from the invasion will likely be limited for developing Asia, except in the Caucasus and Central Asia.** Indeed, the limited exposure will curtail the direct impact of the war in most of the region, but the effects will be large for the Caucasus and Central Asia, as well as Mongolia, which all have close trade and financial linkages with the Russian Federation. Declining remittances from Russia will weigh on the external balances of economies heavily reliant on these inflows.

■ **Indirect effects will be felt across the region, through higher energy and food prices.** Oil and natural gas prices rose sharply following the invasion, and they are expected to remain elevated this year. Energy bills will rise for energy importers, pushing inflation up and weighing on demand. Energy exporters will benefit from rising prices. Russia and Ukraine are also key producers of sunflower seed oil, wheat, barley, corn, and fertilizers. And global prices for these products and certain substitutes have surged. Limited access to Black Sea ports and a disrupted spring planting season in Ukraine will keep prices high throughout the year. International sanctions might also affect the availability of base metals, including aluminum, nickel, palladium, and titanium, from Russia, a key exporter of these metals.

■ **Further escalation or a prolonged war could have a more lasting effect on global sentiment and commodity markets.** This would further delay the recovery from the COVID-19 pandemic. Heightened risk could hit consumer, producer, and investor confidence, hurting developing Asia's exports. A flight to safety could spur capital outflows from emerging markets, compounding the tighter financial conditions from the US Federal Reserve raising its policy rate.

Falling further behind: The cost of COVID-19 school closures by gender and wealth

■ **School closures during the COVID-19 pandemic led to losses equivalent to over half a year's worth of learning.** This foregone learning will hinder students' ability to earn income in the future. Their estimated losses in lifetime earnings have reached $3.2 trillion (in constant 2020 values)—13% of developing Asia's GDP in 2020.

■ **Poor students and girls were hit harder by school closures.** Children from low-income households have less access to quality remote education, higher exposure to economic stress during the COVID-19 pandemic, and a greater tendency to drop out of school as a result of economic adversity. Because of this, foregone learning for students from the poorest quintile is 33% more than those for students from the richest quintile. This will translate into losses in expected earnings that are 47% more for the poorest students, exacerbating income inequalities. Estimated gender gaps in foregone learning are small but translate into earning losses that are 28% higher for girls than for boys because of the higher return on girls' education.

■ **Inequality in learning and earning losses will grow unless investments are made to promote equality of access.** While supply side improvements in the quality of remote education reduce aggregate losses from school closures, inequality will grow because these improvements largely benefit those who have more access to educational resources. Investments are necessary to make them beneficial for all students, including poor children and girls. These investments include ensuring the safety of holding face-to-face classes (especially for schools serving low-income populations), supporting innovative approaches to recover foregone learning, bridging the digital divide, strengthening social safety nets for low-income families, and building flexibility and emergency resilience into education systems.

Mobilizing taxes for development

Summary

❖ **Asia must mobilize taxes and expenditure for sustainable development.** *Achieving the Sustainable Development Goals (SDGs) for a greener and more inclusive future requires vast public spending. While more efficient spending can free up some fiscal resources, much greater resources are needed to promote inclusive development in earnest. Tax revenue was gradually rising in the region before the COVID-19 pandemic but was still comparatively low. Restoring fiscal sustainability after COVID-19 adds to the urgency of making all forms of fiscal resource mobilization more effective, especially taxes.*

❖ **The region needs to augment fiscal space through higher tax revenue.** *Estimates that benchmark current tax revenue against key economic characteristics suggest that economies in developing Asia could increase tax revenue from a pre-pandemic average equal to about 16% of GDP by, on average, 3–4 percentage points. Options to strengthen revenue depend on economy-specific circumstances, but two priorities with broad promise are better optimization of tax expenditures—forgone taxes—and more efficient collection of value-added tax (VAT), including appropriate taxes on the fast-growing digital economy. In addition, strengthening personal income and property taxes can raise additional revenue and make tax systems more progressive.*

❖ **Green and health taxes contribute to both revenue and development goals.** *Environmental tax instruments continue to grow and positively guide investment and consumption in developing Asia. Some regional governments have long experience in levying environmental taxes, notably on pollutants and fossil fuels. More recently, Asian economies have actively explored carbon pricing instruments to curb emissions. The region can draw valuable lessons from early adopters, especially by ensuring sufficiently high tax rates and pollution prices and effective monitoring, reporting, and verification systems. Higher corrective health taxes, primarily on alcohol and tobacco, can raise additional tax revenue by as much as 0.6% of GDP while improving health outcomes and cutting medical costs.*

❖ **Tax and other reform to lift revenue is hard but doable.** *New analysis finds that reducing business registration costs can expand the share of the formal sector in the whole economy and the taxes it pays. Tax reform to boost revenue may be politically challenging, but global experience shows that strong leadership can enable success. Effective strategies strengthen tax administration, including through better use of information and communication technology, and improve taxpayer morale by, for example, improving the quality of public spending.*

Taxes must be mobilized to support sustainable development

- **Resuming the region's stellar economic progress will entail vast expenditure.** Developing Asia's traditional fiscal prudence, characterized by small government and low debt, has well served the regional goals of poverty elimination and higher living standards. However, it is now under pressure. The COVID-19 pandemic has set back development progress and highlighted weaknesses in government finances. To ensure that inclusive and sustainable development resumes and that the SDGs are achieved, spending needs to be ramped up in the key areas of health care, education, infrastructure, and social protection, as well as in climate change adaptation and mitigation.

- **Taxes need to be mobilized to meet regional expenditure needs.** While private finance has an important role to play, much of the required spending will need to come from government. Taxes are the main government revenue source, with higher-tax economies tending to spend more on education, health care, and social protection. While gradually rising before the COVID-19 pandemic in tandem with rapid development, tax revenue in developing Asia remained low, even relative to a developing economy peer such as Latin America. Accounting for about half of all tax revenue, consumption taxes, notably VAT, are revenue mainstays in the region, supported by robust corporate tax receipts. Personal income tax revenue accounts for a small share by comparison. This tax mix is efficient but less progressive than in high-income economies and therefore less inclusive.

- **The COVID-19 pandemic hit public finances hard.** Tax stimulus was widely used to support households and businesses even as tax receipts plunged under an unprecedented economic downturn. This substantially expanded fiscal deficits and debt. While deficits are starting to narrow again, additional careful fiscal consolidation will be needed in many economies to safeguard fiscal sustainability. Given structurally low spending and continued pressure in such important areas as education and health care, governments should strive to improve spending efficiency and wind back tax and other stimulus measures in a timely way. Further, they should carefully consider options to increase tax revenue, especially in economies where it is very low.

Priorities for mobilizing tax revenue depend on economy-specific circumstances

- **Scope to increase tax revenue exists but depends on economy-specific circumstances.** Newly formulated tax capacity estimates, which benchmark revenue against key economic features, indicate that economies in developing Asia could increase tax revenue from a pre-pandemic average of about 16% of GDP by, on average, 3–4 percentage points. However, this potential varies within the region and is generally higher in Southeast Asia, where revenue is often lowest.

- **Tax expenditures providing special exemptions need to be optimized.** Tax expenditures—or tax not collected—are widely used in the region, including to support households and businesses hard hit by the pandemic. Some tax expenditures lack any clear policy justification, however, while significantly reducing revenue. Government reporting of tax expenditures is often lax, but estimates suggest that on average they curtail tax revenue in the region by about 14%. Tax incentives to lure businesses are often ineffective and can undermine healthy competition. Governments should weigh costs and benefits and consider ways to promote investment that are less expensive and more effective. Meanwhile, most governments need to improve tax expenditure transparency and regularly report costs.

■ **Taxes can be tailored to improve both revenue and social equity.** Low tax efficiency and comparatively low tax rates indicate that potential exists to increase VAT revenue in some economies. Tax authorities need to ensure appropriate taxation of imported digital products to ensure that online commerce does not erode VAT revenue. Increasing personal income tax revenue is a challenge, especially where collection capacity is weak, and it may undermine work incentives. However, personal income tax can make tax systems more progressive and thus societies more equitable. More revenue can be raised as well from property taxes, which can bolster local government finances and are readily efficient and progressive.

■ **Corporate tax revenue faces pressure from digitalization and tax competition.** The two-pillar solution developed under the Inclusive Framework on Base Erosion and Profit Shifting enables economies to share corporate income taxing rights, and it proposes a global minimum tax rate. This initiative is welcome, but few economies in developing Asia will likely see significant revenue impact in the near term. The economies that stand to benefit most from reallocated taxing rights are likely to be resource exporters and those with large domestic markets. Investment hubs may lose revenue. Similarly, the revenue impact of introducing a 15% global minimum corporate income tax rate is likely to be small in developing Asia, as most economies in the region already meet it.

Green and health taxes strengthen revenue and development

■ **Tax instruments for the environment have begun to realize their promise.** In some Asian economies, fiscal instruments such as pollutant and fossil fuel taxes, most notably on gasoline and coal, are long established and help to reduce pollution, guide energy consumption, and generate revenue. Recently, some economies in developing Asia have introduced carbon pricing instruments to combat climate change, with Kazakhstan, the People's Republic of China, and the Republic of Korea implementing national schemes for trading emissions. Singapore and Indonesia have introduced a carbon tax. As carbon prices and tax rates are low, and implementation gradual, revenue from these instruments remains modest but has potential to grow and reduce air pollution and carbon emissions.

■ **Environmental tax instruments must be well designed and implemented.** Effective carbon pricing and environmental taxes require sound instrument design and careful implementation that features reliable monitoring, reporting, and verification systems. Carbon prices and environmental taxes must be significant to be effective. Gradual implementation addresses competitiveness concerns but reduces revenue generation and alignment with environmental goals. Revenue transfers such as rebates and subsidies can encourage innovation and cushion adverse effects on vulnerable groups. Earmarking can facilitate public acceptance and implementation. Consistent application of carbon pricing across economies and regions would amplify their benefits and minimize costs.

■ **Corrective health taxes both raise revenue and improve public well-being.** Lifestyle diseases exact heavy costs on health and wealth in developing Asia. Led by tobacco, alcohol, and unhealthy diets, they cause 77% of all deaths in the region. Associated productivity loss is estimated to equal 2% of GDP. Corrective health taxes can be powerful tools to reduce harmful consumption. Tax design and implementation should consider demand responses, distributional consequences, and how to use the tax revenue thus collected, including through earmarks. Regionally, corrective health tax revenue still falls below associated costs incurred for medical treatment and from productivity lost to death and disability. Higher corrective health taxes could raise additional revenue by as much as an estimated 0.6% of GDP, while improving health outcomes and cutting medical costs.

Reform to reduce informality and lift tax revenue is hard but doable

■ **Easier business registration can reduce informality and boost revenue.** Generally relaxed regulatory barriers and low tax burdens in the region have helped keep unemployment low and growth rapid. However, the high cost of business registration is an exception, which partly explains the region's large informal sector. Policy simulations using a simple two-sector model, both formal and informal, indicate that lower registration costs are particularly effective at reducing informality and increasing tax revenue, productivity, and wages. Stronger enforcement of existing laws and regulations can also reduce informality and increase tax revenue.

■ **Tax reform to increase revenue is politically difficult but achievable.** Governments often attempt tax reform but then fail, leaving them stuck with low revenue. However, experience from around the world demonstrates that it is possible to implement policies that lift tax revenue by the equivalent of several percentage points of GDP or more. Successful tax reform requires strong leadership with clearly articulated priorities toward feasible policies. Also helpful is a reform road map supported by international cooperation and technical assistance. As major crises sometimes pave the way for tax reform, the current period of pandemic recovery may be an opportune time to embark on ambitious tax reform.

■ **Better tax collection hinges on improved tax administration and taxpayer morale.** While the impositions of tax compliance have eased across the region, they remain substantial in some economies. Tax administrators can harness technology more effectively to reduce their own administrative costs, improve access to information, and so facilitate compliance. Organizational reform to improve utilization of scarce resources, enhance administrative autonomy, and incentivize performance promises to strengthen tax administration. Tax reform is best accompanied by efforts to strengthen the social contract and tap intrinsic willingness to pay taxes, most notably by improving the quality of government spending. Empirical evidence informed by behavioral insights suggests that significant opportunities exist for governments to experimentally apply sticks as well as carrots, including deterrence messages.

GDP growth rate and inflation, % per year

	GDP growth				Inflation			
	2020	2021	2022	2023	2020	2021	2022	2023
Developing Asia	**−0.8**	**6.9**	**5.2**	**5.3**	**3.2**	**2.5**	**3.7**	**3.1**
Caucasus and Central Asia	**−2.0**	**5.6**	**3.6**	**4.0**	**7.7**	**8.9**	**8.8**	**7.1**
Armenia	−7.4	5.7	2.8	3.8	1.2	7.2	9.0	7.5
Azerbaijan	−4.3	5.6	3.7	2.8	2.8	6.7	7.0	5.3
Georgia	−6.8	10.6	3.5	5.0	5.2	9.6	7.0	4.0
Kazakhstan	−2.5	4.0	3.2	3.9	6.8	8.0	7.8	6.4
Kyrgyz Republic	−8.4	3.6	2.0	2.5	6.3	11.9	15.0	12.0
Tajikistan	4.5	9.2	2.0	3.0	9.4	8.0	15.0	10.0
Turkmenistan	...	5.0	6.0	5.8	10.0	12.5	13.0	10.0
Uzbekistan	1.9	7.4	4.0	4.5	12.9	10.7	9.0	8.0
East Asia	**1.8**	**7.6**	**4.7**	**4.5**	**2.2**	**1.1**	**2.4**	**2.0**
Hong Kong, China	−6.5	6.4	2.0	3.7	0.3	1.6	2.3	2.0
Mongolia	−4.6	1.4	2.3	5.6	3.7	7.1	12.4	9.3
People's Republic of China	2.2	8.1	5.0	4.8	2.5	0.9	2.3	2.0
Republic of Korea	−0.9	4.0	3.0	2.6	0.5	2.5	3.2	2.0
Taipei,China	3.4	6.4	3.8	3.0	−0.2	2.0	1.9	1.6
South Asia	**−5.2**	**8.3**	**7.0**	**7.4**	**6.5**	**5.7**	**6.5**	**5.5**
Afghanistan	−2.4	...	...	...	5.6	5.2	...	...
Bangladesh	3.4	6.9	6.9	7.1	5.7	5.6	6.0	5.9
Bhutan	−10.1	3.5	4.5	7.5	5.6	7.4	7.0	5.5
India	−6.6	8.9	7.5	8.0	6.2	5.4	5.8	5.0
Maldives	−33.5	31.6	11.0	12.0	−1.4	0.5	3.0	2.5
Nepal	−2.1	2.3	3.9	5.0	6.2	3.6	6.5	6.2
Pakistan	−1.0	5.6	4.0	4.5	10.7	8.9	11.0	8.5
Sri Lanka	−3.6	3.7	2.4	2.5	4.6	6.0	13.3	6.7
Southeast Asia	**−3.2**	**2.9**	**4.9**	**5.2**	**1.5**	**2.0**	**3.7**	**3.1**
Brunei Darussalam	1.1	−1.5	4.2	3.6	1.9	1.7	1.6	1.0
Cambodia	−3.1	3.0	5.3	6.5	2.9	2.9	4.7	2.2
Indonesia	−2.1	3.7	5.0	5.2	2.0	1.6	3.6	3.0
Lao People's Dem. Rep.	−0.5	2.3	3.4	3.7	5.1	3.7	5.8	5.0
Malaysia	−5.6	3.1	6.0	5.4	−1.1	2.5	3.0	2.5
Myanmar	3.2	−18.4	−0.3	2.6	5.7	3.6	8.0	8.5
Philippines	−9.6	5.6	6.0	6.3	2.4	3.9	4.2	3.5
Singapore	−4.1	7.6	4.3	3.2	−0.2	2.3	3.0	2.3
Thailand	−6.2	1.6	3.0	4.5	−0.8	1.2	3.3	2.2
Timor-Leste	−8.6	1.8	2.5	3.1	0.5	3.8	2.6	2.7
Viet Nam	2.9	2.6	6.5	6.7	3.2	1.8	3.8	4.0
The Pacific	**−6.0**	**−0.6**	**3.9**	**5.4**	**2.9**	**3.1**	**5.9**	**4.7**
Cook Islands	−5.2	−29.1	9.1	11.2	0.7	2.2	4.3	4.0
Federated States of Micronesia	−3.8	−1.2	2.2	4.2	−2.9	2.0	4.6	2.0
Fiji	−15.2	−4.1	7.1	8.5	−2.6	0.2	4.5	4.0
Kiribati	−0.5	1.5	1.8	2.3	2.3	1.0	5.0	3.7
Marshall Islands	−2.2	−3.3	1.2	2.2	−0.8	1.0	4.1	4.0
Nauru	0.8	1.5	1.0	2.4	0.9	1.2	2.3	2.2
Niue	...	...	...	...	2.7	...	...	...
Palau	−9.7	−17.1	9.4	18.3	0.7	0.5	4.3	4.2
Papua New Guinea	−3.5	1.3	3.4	4.6	4.9	4.5	6.4	5.1
Samoa	−2.6	−8.1	0.4	2.2	1.5	−3.0	8.9	3.2
Solomon Islands	−4.5	−0.5	−3.0	3.0	3.0	−0.2	5.0	4.0
Tonga	0.7	−3.0	−1.2	2.9	0.2	1.4	7.6	4.2
Tuvalu	1.0	1.5	3.0	3.0	1.6	6.7	3.8	3.3
Vanuatu	−7.5	−1.0	1.0	4.0	5.3	2.1	4.8	3.2

... = unavailable, GDP = gross domestic product.

Notes: Some historical data for Turkmenistan are not presented for lack of uniformity. A fluid situation permits no estimates or forecasts for Afghanistan in 2021–2023.

1

RECOVERY CONTINUES AMID GLOBAL HEADWINDS

RECOVERY CONTINUES AMID GLOBAL HEADWINDS

The Russian invasion of Ukraine has severely disrupted the outlook for developing Asia, which is still contending with COVID-19. The pandemic's second year ended on a mixed note. The more infectious Omicron variant has fueled fast-spreading outbreaks since late 2021, but progress on vaccinations—combined with Omicron's less serious health impact—softened the blow, allowing economies to remain more open compared with previous waves. Growth in developing Asia rebounded by 6.9% last year on rising domestic economic activity and a sustained expansion in exports. Inflation in the region decelerated to 2.5% in 2021 from 3.2% in 2020 on declining food prices for rice and pork, relatively resilient supply chains, and substantial remaining slack. Remittances to developing Asian economies continue to be strong and international tourism is showing signs of an incipient recovery in economies that are reopening. Fiscal and monetary policies are still accommodative, but the region may be on the cusp of a policy tightening cycle. Financial conditions remained robust last year but started weakening in November on expectations of monetary tightening in the United States, and weakened further early this year following the Russian invasion of Ukraine.

Against this backdrop, gross domestic product growth (GDP) in developing Asia will continue to be strong—at 5.2% in 2022 and 5.3% in 2023. But output in most economies will remain below its pre-pandemic trend this year. Inflation is expected to rise to 3.7% in 2022 and moderate to 3.1% in 2023, but price dynamics will vary across economies. Monetary authorities should remain vigilant of any emerging inflationary pressures. Current account surpluses will narrow, as the growth in exports stabilizes and imports rise on continued recovery.

Several downside risks cloud the short-term outlook for developing Asia, including the direct and indirect impacts from an escalation of the war in Ukraine, spillovers from monetary policy tightening in the US, the possible emergence of more lethal COVID-19 variants, and disruptions associated with outbreaks in the People's Republic of China (PRC). Various medium-term risks linger, including the continued accumulation of large learning losses from school closures that threaten to further exacerbate economic inequalities.

This section was written by Abdul Abiad, Shiela Camingue-Romance, David Keith De Padua, Jules Hugot, Matteo Lanzafame (lead), Nedelyn Magtibay-Ramos, Yuho Myoda, Pilipinas Quising, Irfan Qureshi (colead), Arief Ramayandi, Marcel Schroder, Dennis Sorino, Shu Tian, and Mai Lin Villaruel of the Economic Research and Regional Cooperation Department (ERCD), Asian Development Bank (ADB), Manila, and Jesson Pagaduan, Reizle Jade Platitas, and Michael Timbang, ERCD consultants.

As developing Asia reckons with Omicron and incomplete recoveries, Russia's invasion of Ukraine disrupts global conditions

The world economy has been severely disrupted by the war. Its start in late February has upended the global economic outlook. Indeed, geopolitical risks for the world economy have already spiked on a scale comparable to the Iraq war in the early 2000s (Figure 1.1.1). When tensions between the Russian Federation and Ukraine turned into a war, shockwaves were immediately felt in financial and commodity markets. Energy, food, and other commodity prices surged as the impact of the war and sanctions against Russia came into focus (Figure 1.1.2). As described in this report's *Special Topic* on the economic impact of the Russian invasion of Ukraine, the potential effects of the war—working via direct and indirect channels—are subject to a high degree of uncertainty. Even so, the war is an additional hurdle for the global and regional economies that are still grappling with the COVID-19 pandemic.

Figure 1.1.2 Commodity prices

Global energy and food prices surged since the start of the Russian invasion of Ukraine.

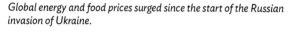

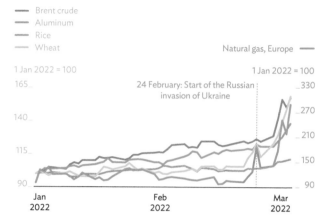

Source: Bloomberg (accessed 6 March 2022).

Figure 1.1.1 Geopolitical risk index

Geopolitical risks from the Russian invasion of Ukraine are comparable to the Iraq war peak.

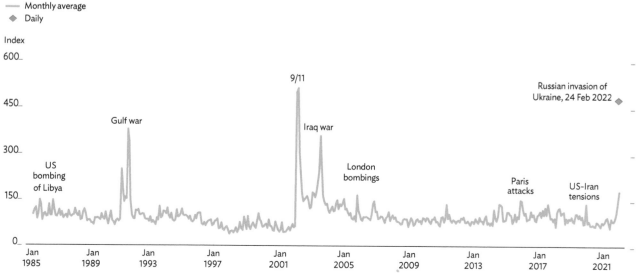

US = United States.
Source: Geopolitical Risk Index (accessed 9 March 2022).

The COVID-19 pandemic ended its second year on waves of the highly transmissible Omicron variant. New daily cases worldwide peaked at 3.4 million in January before declining to 1.5 million as of 9 March, the data cutoff date for this report (Figure 1.1.3, panel A). In developing Asia, daily cases rose from 46,000 at the end of December to over 600,000 in early March. Across subregions, daily new cases reached 342,000 in South Asia in January, but remained below the peak during the Delta-variant wave. In February, cases peaked at 38,000 in the Caucasus and Central Asia and 848 in the Pacific (Figure 1.1.3, panel B). In East Asia and Southeast Asia, new cases surged to about 300,000 in each subregion in early March, excluding the PRC, which maintained its zero-tolerance COVID-19 approach.

Vaccination coverage in developing Asia has caught up with advanced economies, although some in the region are lagging behind. As of 9 March, 66.6% of the region's population had been fully vaccinated, ahead of the US, at 65.2%, but lagging the European Union (EU), at 72.6% (Figure 1.1.4).

Several economies in the region have commenced booster campaigns, notably the Republic of Korea and Singapore, where more than 60% of the population has received a booster shot. But in several economies, particularly in the Caucasus and Central Asia and the Pacific, less than half of the population has been fully vaccinated.

Developing Asia's economies remained relatively open in early 2022, despite Omicron's spread. Adding to increasing immunity in populations, owing to higher vaccination coverage and previous infections, Omicron's less severe health impact has resulted in declining COVID-19 fatality rates—both in developing Asia and the world (Figure 1.1.5). This allowed governments in the region to react less strongly than during previous COVID-19 waves with only a mild tightening in the stringency of containment measures, despite a rapid increase in cases (Figure 1.1.6, panel A). This excludes the Pacific where several island economies had COVID-19 infections for the first time in early 2022 and imposed lockdowns (Figure 1.1.6, panel B).

Figure 1.1.3 Daily new COVID-19 cases

A. World and developing Asia

With the arrival of the Omicron variant, COVID-19 cases rose sharply in the world ...

— European Union
— US
— World
— Developing Asia

New cases, 7-day moving average, thousand

B. Developing Asia subregions

... and across developing Asia's subregions, particularly in South Asia.

— Caucasus and Central Asia
— East Asia
— South Asia
— Southeast Asia
— The Pacific

New cases, 7-day moving average, thousand

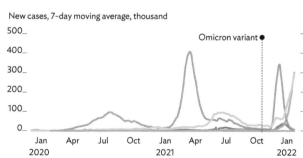

COVID-19 = Coronavirus Disease 2019, US = United States.
Note: Vertical line indicates 26 November 2021, the date the World Health Organization classified Omicron as a variant of concern.
Source: Our World in Data (accessed 7 March 2022).

Figure 1.1.4 COVID-19 vaccination coverage in developing Asian economies

Vaccination coverage has increased, but some economies are still lagging behind.

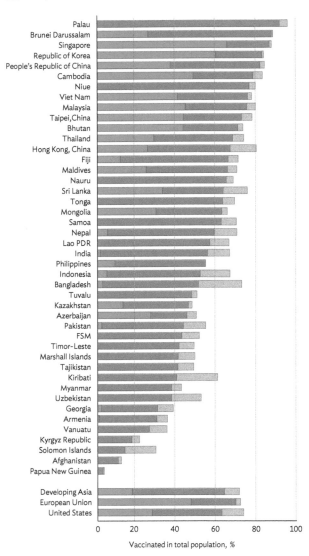

Vaccinated in total population, %

COVID-19 = Coronavirus Disease 2019, FSM = Federated States of Micronesia, Lao PDR = Lao People's Democratic Republic.

Notes: Fully vaccinated is the total number of people who received all doses prescribed by the vaccination protocol; total booster is the total number of COVID-19 vaccination booster doses administered (i.e., doses administered beyond the number prescribed by the vaccination protocol). Data as of 9 March 2022.

Source: Our World in Data (accessed 11 March 2022).

Figure 1.1.5 COVID-19 case fatality rate, 14-day moving average

With the milder Omicron variant and increased vaccination, COVID-19 gradually became less severe.

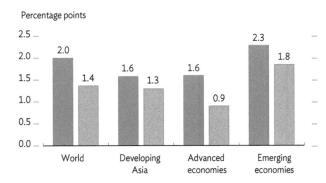

Note: The World Health Organization classified Omicron as a variant of concern on 26 November 2021.

Source: Our World in Data (accessed 7 March 2022).

Southeast Asia and some economies in East Asia have continued to relax containment measures. In the PRC, authorities imposed strict restrictions, especially during the Lunar New Year, and localized lockdowns to control sporadic virus outbreaks.

With containment measures generally less restrictive, developing Asian economies are faring better during the Omicron wave than in previous outbreaks. Following the easing of restrictions in the fourth quarter of 2021, readings of the manufacturing purchasing managers' index (PMI) in January and February remained above the 50-mark that separates improvement from deterioration in most economies (Figure 1.1.7). The index rose slightly in the Republic of Korea, Thailand, and Viet Nam, but COVID-19 outbreaks impeded manufacturing growth in Malaysia and Indonesia. In the PRC, tough containment measures led to a slowdown in factory output in January and services expanded at their slowest pace in 6 months in February. In India, the services PMI fell from 55.5 in December to 51.5 in January on the reimposition of curfews to contain the pandemic in parts of the country before improving slightly to 51.8 in February as outbreaks receded.

Figure 1.1.6 Government stringency index in developing Asia

A. Developing Asia

Despite surging COVID-19 cases, containment measures were only slightly tightened ...

B. Developing Asia subregions

... and some subregions were able to continue easing restrictions.

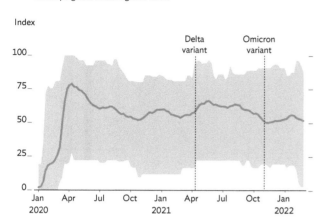

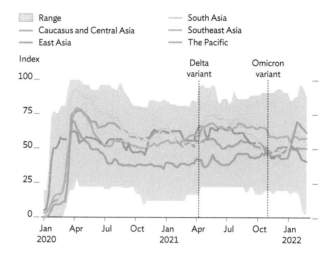

COVID-19 = Coronavirus Disease 2019.

Notes: Vertical lines indicate the dates when the World Health Organization classified Delta as a variant of interest (4 April 2021) and Omicron as a variant of concern (26 November 2021).

Source: CEIC Data Company (accessed 9 March 2022).

Figure 1.1.7 Manufacturing and services purchasing managers' index in developing Asian economies

Amid generally less restrictive containment measures, manufacturing and services continued to expand in early 2022 in most of the region.

Manufacturing purchasing managers' index, seasonally adjusted

| | 2021 | | | | | | | | | | | | 2022 | |
| | Q1 | | | Q2 | | | Q3 | | | Q4 | | | Q1 | |
Economy	Jan	Feb	Mar	Apr	May	Jun	Jul	Aug	Sep	Oct	Nov	Dec	Jan	Feb
PRC	51.5	50.9	50.6	51.9	52.0	51.3	50.3	49.2	50.0	50.6	49.9	50.9	49.1	50.4
India	57.7	57.5	55.4	55.5	50.8	48.1	55.3	52.3	53.7	55.9	57.6	55.5	54.0	54.9
Indonesia	52.2	50.9	53.2	54.6	55.3	53.5	40.1	43.7	52.2	57.2	53.9	53.5	53.7	51.2
Malaysia	51.9	50.7	52.9	56.9	54.3	42.9	43.1	46.4	51.1	55.2	55.3	55.8	50.5	50.9
Philippines	52.5	52.5	52.2	49.0	49.9	50.8	50.4	46.4	50.9	51.0	51.7	51.8	50.0	52.8
Republic of Korea	53.2	55.3	55.3	54.6	53.7	53.9	53.0	51.2	52.4	50.2	50.9	51.9	52.8	53.8
Taipei,China	60.2	60.4	60.8	62.4	62.0	57.6	59.7	58.5	54.7	55.2	54.9	55.5	55.1	54.3
Thailand	49.0	47.2	48.8	50.7	47.8	49.5	48.7	48.3	48.9	50.9	50.6	49.5	51.7	52.5
Viet Nam	51.3	51.6	53.6	54.7	53.1	44.1	45.1	40.2	40.2	52.1	52.2	52.5	53.7	54.3

Services purchasing managers' index, seasonally adjusted

PRC	52.0	51.5	54.3	56.3	55.1	50.3	54.9	46.7	53.4	53.8	52.1	53.1	51.4	50.2
India	52.8	55.3	54.6	54.0	46.4	41.2	45.4	56.7	55.2	58.4	58.1	55.5	51.5	51.8

PRC = People's Republic of China, Q = quarter.

Note: For Malaysia, the series is adjusted by adding 3 points, as historical experience suggests that an index value above 47 is consistent with improvement. Pink to red indicates deterioration (<50), and white to green indicates improvement (>50).

Source: CEIC Data Company (accessed 7 March 2022).

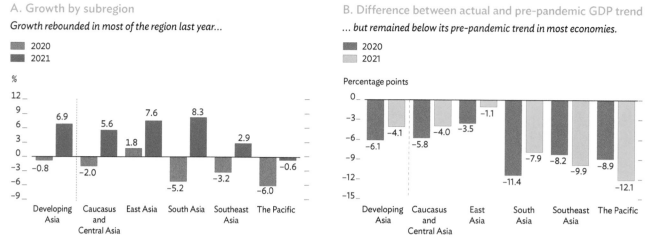

Figure 1.1.8 Economic performance by subregion in developing Asia

A. Growth by subregion

Growth rebounded in most of the region last year...

B. Difference between actual and pre-pandemic GDP trend

... but remained below its pre-pandemic trend in most economies.

COVID-19 = Coronavirus Disease 2019, GDP = gross domestic product.

Sources: *Asian Development Outlook* database; Asian Development Bank estimates.

Developing Asia's growth momentum continues apace after 2021's 6.9% rebound, but the recovery is incomplete in most economies. East Asia's GDP expanded by 7.6%, driven by strong growth in the PRC (8.1%) and Taipei,China (6.4%) (Figure 1.1.8, panel A). East Asia is just 1.1% below its GDP trend before the outbreak of COVID-19 (panel B). The 5.6% expansion in the Caucasus and Central Asia was supported by higher commodity prices, but the subregion's economy was still 4.0% below its pre-pandemic trend.

South Asia grew by 8.3%, led by India's 8.9% expansion, but GDP was 8.0% below the pre-pandemic trend. In Southeast Asia, the gap below trend widened to 10% as severe public health restrictions during the Delta wave slowed growth to 2.9%. International travel restrictions continued to keep tourists away from the Pacific for a second consecutive year. The subregion's economy contracted by 0.6% in 2021, leaving its GDP at 12.0% below its pre-pandemic trend after a 2-year recession.

Figure 1.1.9 Demand-side contributions to growth in developing Asian economies

Stronger consumption supported Q4 growth in some economies, but falling investment and net exports slowed recovery in others.

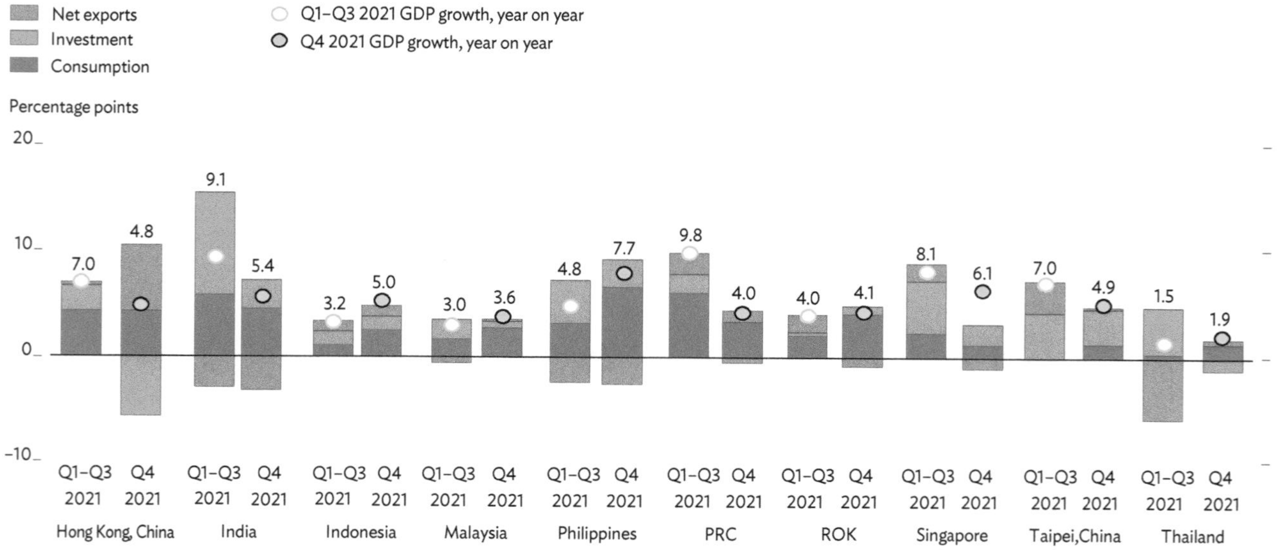

GDP = gross domestic product, PRC = People's Republic of China, Q = quarter, ROK = Republic of Korea.

Note: Chart excludes statistical discrepancies.

Source: CEIC Data Company (accessed 3 March 2022).

Figure 1.1.10 Headline inflation in developing Asia

A. Annual headline inflation

Headline inflation was lower in 2021 than in 2020 ...

B. Monthly headline inflation

... even though prices increased over most of the year.

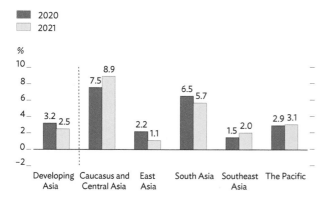

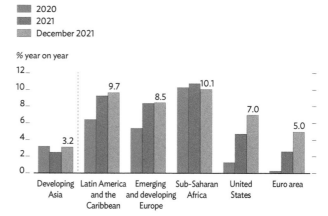

Note: The Pacific is excluded in Panel B due to data unavailability.

Sources: *Asian Development Outlook* database; CEIC Data Company (accessed 7 March 2022).

The performance of developing Asian economies was mixed in late 2021. Year-on-year growth picked up in five of the region's 10 largest economies in the fourth quarter, supported by higher consumption (Figure 1.1.9). As COVID-19 restrictions were eased and mobility improved, economic activity rebounded in Southeast Asia, with particularly large gains in the Philippines. The recovery, however, slowed elsewhere on declining investment, especially in Hong Kong, China; India; and Singapore. Lower net exports contributed to slower growth in the PRC, the Republic of Korea, Singapore, and Taipei,China.

Inflation in developing Asia was lower than in other regions in 2021, despite rising over the year. Regional headline inflation averaged 2.5%, down from 3.2% in 2020 (Figure 1.1.10, panel A). But price pressures increased over the course of the year, with the inflation rate climbing from just 1.2% in January to 3.2% in December (Figure 1.1.10, panel B). In December, the rate was highest in the Caucasus and Central Asia, at 9.6%, followed by South Asia (6.5%), Southeast Asia (2.4%), and East Asia (1.8%). But at these levels, inflation rates in the region were well below those in other parts of the world (Figure 1.1.11). The big exceptions were some economies in the Caucasus and Central Asia and South Asia that are showing signs of rising inflationary pressures, particularly Azerbaijan, Pakistan, and Sri Lanka.

Figure 1.1.11 End-of-year inflation rate, 2021

Inflation remained moderate in developing Asia unlike in other regions.

Source: CEIC Data Company (accessed 2 March 2022).

Low food prices played a key role in keeping headline inflation moderate in developing Asia, although not in the Caucasus and Central Asia. Food is a large component in the region's consumer price index (CPI) baskets, ranging from 16% in the Republic of Korea to 49% in Tajikistan (Figure 1.1.12, panel A). Regional food inflation declined from 8.3% in 2020 to 1.1% in 2021, well below the 5-year pre-pandemic average (Figure 1.1.13). This was driven by a 27% decline in global prices for rice, which takes up a significant share of the CPI's food weighting (Figure 1.1.12, panel B).

Figure 1.1.12 Food weights in the consumer price index baskets in developing Asian economies

A. Food and nonalcoholic beverages

Food is a substantial component in regional consumer price index baskets.

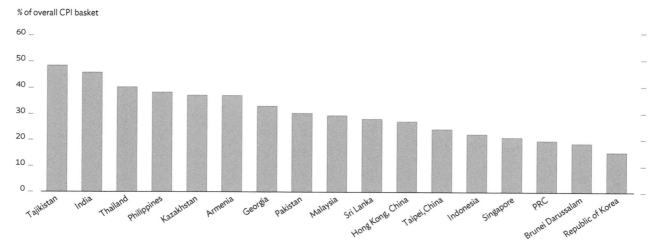

B. Cereal and related products

Rice and wheat are important staples across developing Asia.

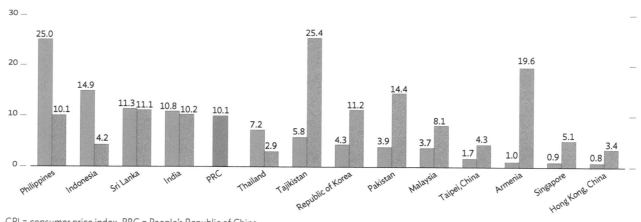

CPI = consumer price index, PRC = People's Republic of China.
Note: For the PRC, there is no breakdown of cereal and related products, but some reports use this to proxy for the share of rice.
Sources: Haver Analytics; national sources (all accessed 17 February 2022).

In the PRC, the supply of pork recovered last year after the 2019–2020 African swine fever outbreak. As a result, pork prices in the country declined by more than 50% last year, contributing to food-price deflation of 0.9% in East Asia. This contrasts to the Caucasus and Central Asia, where wheat is a more important staple than rice, as reflected in the weights of the food CPI basket. Global wheat prices soared by 19.0% in 2021—an increase that was partly passed through to local consumers, accounting to some extent for the 11.6% surge in food prices in the subregion.

An incomplete recovery, resilient supply chains, and higher energy prices also explain developing Asia's inflation dynamics in 2021.

Figure 1.1.13 Food prices in developing Asia

Food inflation declined in 2021 in developing Asia.

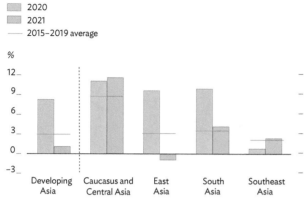

Sources: CEIC Data Company (accessed 20 January 2022); Asian Development Bank estimates.

Figure 1.1.15 Energy prices in developing Asia

Prices surged in 2021, especially in the Caucasus and Central Asia and South Asia.

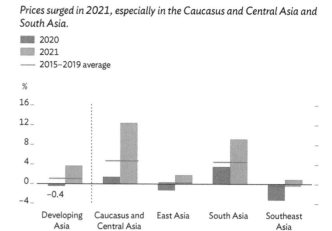

Sources: CEIC Data Company (accessed 20 January 2022); Asian Development Bank estimates.

Figure 1.1.14 Supply chains and inflation

Shorter delivery delays in developing Asian economies are linked to moderate inflation.

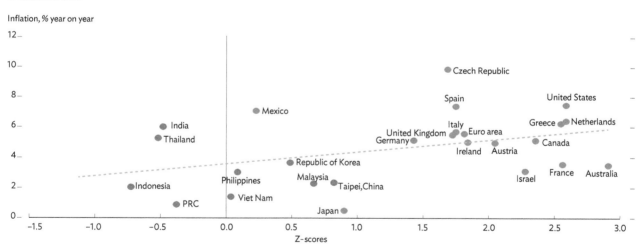

PRC = People's Republic of China.
Notes: Z-scores measure how many standard deviations the Purchasing Managers' Index suppliers' delivery times index is above or below the mean. Data points for inflation and the suppliers' delivery time indices were the latest available for each economy as of 9 March 2022.
Source: CEIC Data Company (accessed 9 March 2022).

With most economies below their pre-pandemic trend, substantial remaining slack contributed to moderate inflation rates, particularly in Southeast Asia. Another factor that mitigated inflationary pressures was the region's resilient supply chains during the pandemic. Delays in delivery times have been much more pronounced in many advanced economies, including the US, compared with developing Asian economies

(Figure 1, Box 1.1.1). Delivery delays are typically associated with inflationary pressures, a pattern that is observed for a sample of advanced and developing Asian economies (Figure 1.1.14). In contrast, energy inflation in the region, at 3.6% last year, was higher than the 5-year pre-pandemic average and a major contributing factor to headline inflation, especially in the Caucasus and Central Asia and South Asia (Figure 1.1.15).

Figure 1.1.16 Real exports in developing Asia

PRC exports stabilized in 2021, but exports in the rest of the region continued rising.

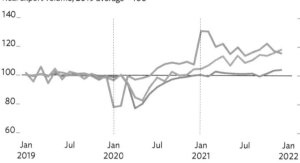

— Advanced economies
— PRC
— Developing Asia excluding PRC

PRC = People's Republic of China.
Note: In this figure, developing Asia excluding the PRC comprises Hong Kong, China; India; Indonesia; the Republic of Korea; Malaysia; Pakistan; the Philippines; Singapore; Taipei,China; Thailand; and Viet Nam.
Source: CPB World Trade Monitor (accessed 9 March 2022).

Figure 1.1.17 Nominal exports by sector in developing Asia

Exports of base metals, mineral fuels, and textiles surged in 2021 on growing global demand.

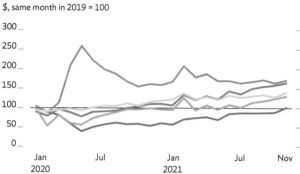

— Mineral fuels   — Textiles and footwear
— Base metals   — Electronics and machinery
— Pandemic-related goods

Sources: International Trade Centre. Trade Map; Observatory of Economic Complexity; United Nations Comtrade Database (all accessed 9 March 2022).

Exports become more broad-based

Exports from developing Asian economies in 2021 remained robust and became more broad-based across sectors. Real exports stabilized at about 16% above pre-pandemic levels last year, supported by the recovery of global demand and less hampered by supply disruptions than in other regions (Figure 1.1.16 and Box 1.1.1). Exports of pandemic-related goods remained strong even as external demand became more broad-based across products and sectors. In nominal terms, mineral fuel exports surged 66%, base metals 49%, and textiles 35%. Exports of electronics and machinery also performed strongly, increasing by 18% (Figure 1.1.17).

The PRC's export performance stabilized in 2021 while exports continued rising in the rest of the region. The PRC's real export volume declined from 31% above pre-pandemic levels in January and February to about 17% in May. Real exports from the rest of the region rose over the year, reaching 18% above pre-pandemic levels in December. This rebalancing was largely driven by South Asia, whose exports soared by 39% in nominal terms from 2020's level (Figure 1.1.18) on buoyant demand for jewelry, refined oil, base metals, and textiles (Figure 1.1.19, panel A).

Figure 1.1.18 Nominal exports by subregion in developing Asia

Exports from the Caucasus and Central Asia, and from South Asia, surged in 2021.

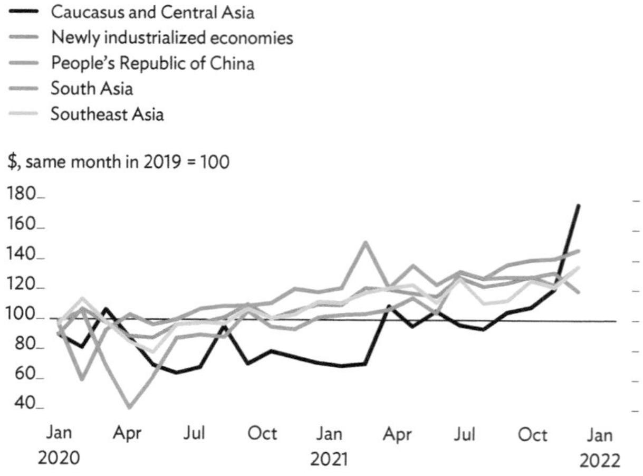

— Caucasus and Central Asia
— Newly industrialized economies
— People's Republic of China
— South Asia
— Southeast Asia

$, same month in 2019 = 100

Note: Asia's newly industrialized economies are Hong Kong, China; the Republic of Korea; Singapore; and Taipei,China. Southeast Asia in this figure excludes Singapore.

Sources: International Monetary Fund. Direction of Trade Statistics; International Trade Center. Trade Map (both accessed 9 March 2022).

Figure 1.1.19 Sector contributions to nominal export growth by subregion in developing Asia

A. South Asia[a]

Exports surged on regional demand for jewelry and refined oil, and global demand for base metals and textiles.

% change from same month in 2019

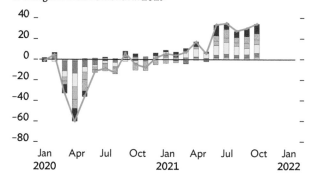

B. Caucasus and Central Asia[b]

Exports rose above pre-pandemic levels, supported by rising commodity prices.

% change from same month in 2019

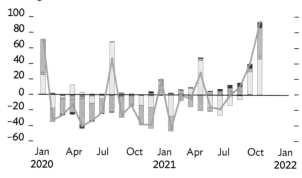

C. People's Republic of China

Electronics and mechanical machinery exports offset declining demand for pandemic-related goods.

% change from same month in 2019

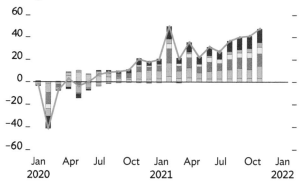

D. Southeast Asia[c]

Exports broadened to offset declining demand for pandemic-related goods.

% change from same month in 2019

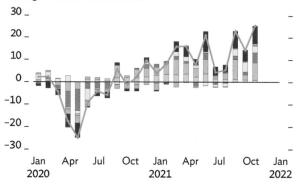

E. Newly industrialized economies[d]

Exports continued rising on robust electronics demand.

% change from same month in 2019

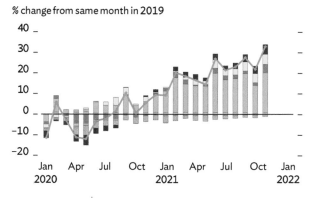

Pandemic-related goods
Textiles and footwear
Electronics
Mineral fuels
Mechanical machinery and vehicles
Metals and jewelry
Others
— Overall change

[a]India and Pakistan.[b]Armenia, Azerbaijan, Georgia, the Kyrgyz Republic, and Uzbekistan.[c]Malaysia, the Philippines, and Thailand.[d]Hong Kong, China; Republic of Korea; Taipei,China; and Singapore.

Sources: International Trade Centre. Trade Map; Observatory of Economic Complexity; United Nations Comtrade Database (all accessed 9 March 2022).

Textile exports rebounded in Bangladesh, Sri Lanka, and Pakistan, where they account for the majority of exports. Nominal exports in the Caucasus and Central Asia also rose sharply, by 33%, due to rising prices for energy and other commodities (panel B). In the PRC, declining exports of pandemic-related goods were more than offset by rising exports of electronics and mechanical machinery (panel C). In Southeast Asia and Asia's newly industrialized economies, nominal exports rose by 21% and 22%, respectively, boosted by strong global demand for electronics and lessening supply disruptions following the relaxation of COVID-19 mobility restrictions, notably in Malaysia and Viet Nam (panels D and E). Rising commodity prices also buoyed exports of oil from Indonesia, copper from the Philippines, iron from Thailand, and palm oil from Malaysia.

Data for early reporters suggest that developing Asia's exports increased sharply in February.
External demand for regional goods remained buoyant despite the global economy's slow start in 2022 on outbreaks of the Omicron COVID-19 variant. The Republic of Korea's exports rose by 19% in February, relative to the previous month, while the PRC's exports increased by 8% (Figure 1.1.20).

Figure 1.1.20 Nominal exports for developing Asia's early reporters

Exports remained strong overall in early 2022.

— Taipei,China   — People's Republic of China
— Singapore   — Republic of Korea

Index, December 2019 = 100

Source: Haver Analytics (accessed 8 March 2022).

Tourism remains depressed in most developing Asian economies, but is rebounding in some that have reopened. Foreign tourists remained virtually absent in 2021, in economies still enforcing zero COVID-19 policies; among them, Hong Kong, China; Samoa; Taipei,China; and Vanuatu (Figure 1.1.21).

Figure 1.1.21 International tourist arrivals in developing Asian economies

A. Economies where tourism has not recovered

Tourism remains depressed in most economies ...

— Cambodia   — Myanmar   — Taipei,China
— Hong Kong, China   — Republic of Korea   — Thailand
— Indonesia   — Samoa   — Vanuatu
— Japan   — Singapore   — Viet Nam
— Malaysia

% change from 2018–2019 monthly average

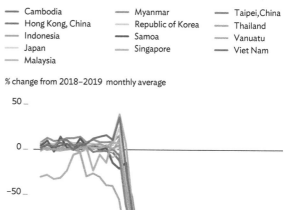

B. Economies where tourism has rebounded

... but is recovering in some.

— Cook Islands   — India   — Palau
— Fiji   — Maldives   — Sri Lanka
— Georgia   — Nepal

% change from 2018–2019 monthly average

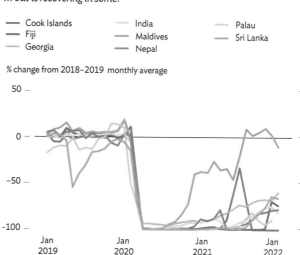

Note: Economies are included in panel B if the latest reading corresponds to at least 20% of the 2018–2019 average for the corresponding month.
Sources: CEIC Data Company; national sources (both accessed 9 March 2022).

Figure 1.1.22 Remittance growth in developing Asian economies

Remittances maintained their positive momentum in 2021.

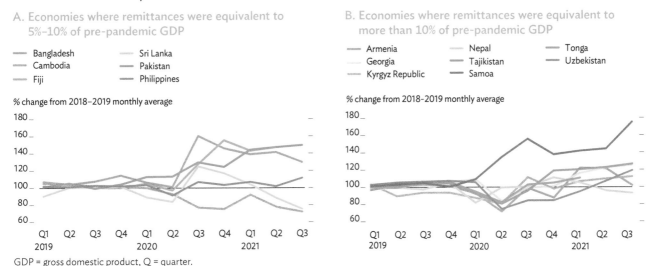

A. Economies where remittances were equivalent to 5%–10% of pre-pandemic GDP

— Bangladesh — Sri Lanka
— Cambodia — Pakistan
— Fiji — Philippines

% change from 2018–2019 monthly average

B. Economies where remittances were equivalent to more than 10% of pre-pandemic GDP

— Armenia — Nepal — Tonga
— Georgia — Tajikistan — Uzbekistan
— Kyrgyz Republic — Samoa

% change from 2018-2019 monthly average

GDP = gross domestic product, Q = quarter.
Sources: CEIC Data Company; International Monetary Fund. Balance of Payments and International Investment Position Statistics; World Bank. World Development Indicators (all accessed 9 March 2022).

Tourist arrivals remain depressed where quarantines were enforced throughout most of last year, even for vaccinated travelers, as in Cambodia, Malaysia, and Singapore. Tourism has yet to pick up pace in economies where quarantines are still to some extent being enforced, such as in Indonesia, Thailand, and Viet Nam. Tourism is rebounding in some developing Asian economies where tourists are not required to quarantine on entry. This is benefiting Georgia, Nepal, Maldives, and Sri Lanka. This recovery has been accentuated in economies with large shares of tourists from Europe and North America, where intercontinental travel has been easier (Box 1.1.2).

Remittances stayed strong in 2021. For the 22 Asian economies with data available up to the third quarter of last year, remittances grew by 7% compared with the same quarter in 2019 (Figure 1.1.22). Incoming money transfers were higher in all economies in the region for which data are available except Cambodia, Nepal, and Sri Lanka. The apparent sharp decline in Sri Lanka was associated with parallel exchange rates making it worthwhile for overseas workers to remit money through unofficial channels. In Bangladesh, Pakistan, and Samoa, remittances in the third quarter were more than 30% above their pre-pandemic levels.

Remittances were also robust in the Kyrgyz Republic and Tajikistan, two economies that rely heavily on remittances, which represent about 30% of their GDPs. As discussed in the *Special Topic* on the economic impact of the Russian invasion of Ukraine, remittances to these economies will suffer from the fallout of the war.

Financial conditions worsened slightly on anticipated monetary tightening in the US and the war

Developing Asia's regional financial conditions have weakened since late 2021 on expectations of shrinking global liquidity. The region's financial position remained sound for most of last year, supported by ample global liquidity and accommodative monetary stances—most regional central banks left policy rates unchanged. But financial conditions started deteriorating from November, tracking growing expectations of tightening in the US monetary stance, and weakened further in early 2022 after the Russian invasion of Ukraine.

Figure 1.1.23 Levels and changes in the security holdings of major central banks

Liquidity conditions to tighten on US Federal Reserve rate hikes and possible reduction of asset holdings in 2022.

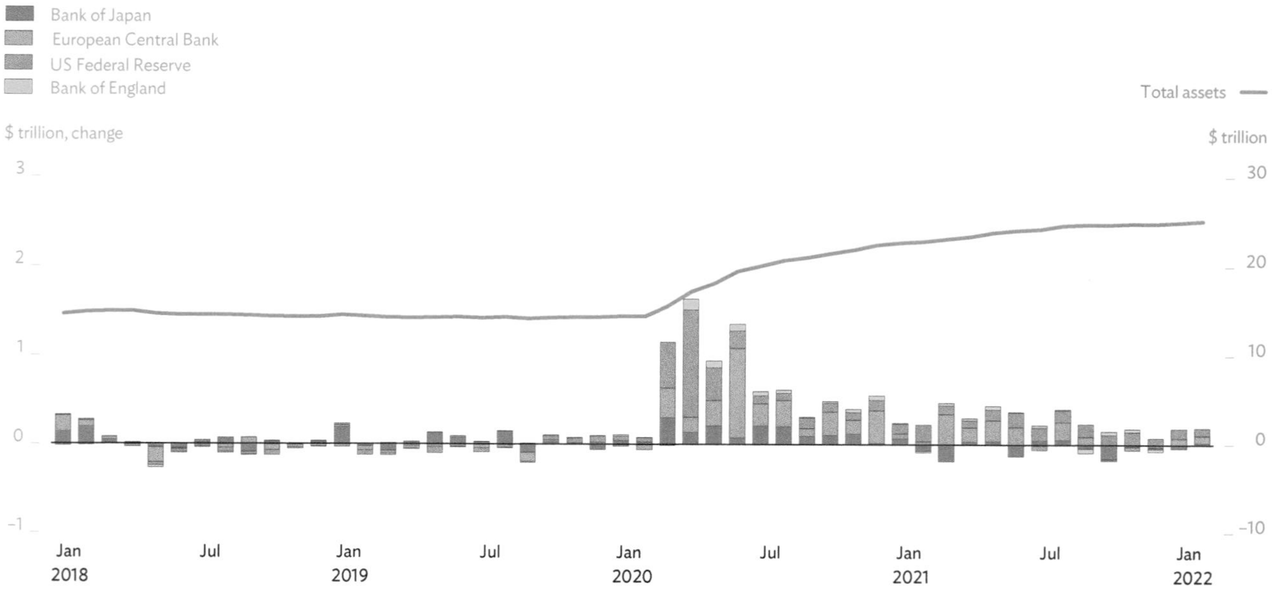

US = United States.
Source: CEIC Data Company (accessed 10 March 2022).

In November, the Federal Reserve announced that it would start tapering net asset purchases and it reduced the monthly accumulation of holdings to an average of $87.9 billion from December to February from an average of $130.6 billion during the first 11 months of last year. While these actions did not significantly change global liquidity conditions, the forward guidance in the December Federal Open Market Committee (FOMC) meeting—consistent with net zero securities purchases in March and a rate hike of 75 basis points in 2022—resulted in market expectations of declining liquidity this year (Figure 1.1.23 and Box 1.1.3). The March FOMC meeting raised the federal funds rate by 25 basis points and updated projections indicated a possible 175 basis points increase in the federal funds rate during 2022 and additional increases in 2023. The March meeting also indicated that the Federal Reserve may start to reduce its asset holdings in the near future. Since late February, investor sentiment has been further negatively affected by the fallout from the Russian invasion of Ukraine, which has created major uncertainties for the global economic outlook.

Currencies in developing Asia weakened in 2021 and continued depreciating in early 2022. Twenty-six out of 36 currencies in the region depreciated against the dollar last year, as the US currency strengthened on robust growth and expected monetary tightening by the Federal Reserve. Several economies in the region saw relatively large exchange rate depreciations, including Afghanistan and Myanmar, due to domestic tensions, and the Lao People's Democratic Republic and Sri Lanka, due to debt-related financial risks (Figure 1.1.24). This trend continued at the start of this year, with 27 currencies weakening against the dollar from 1 January to 9 March 2022. The currencies of many economies in the Caucasus and Central Asia, including those of Kazakhstan, the Kyrgyz Republic, and Georgia, recorded larger depreciations amid the Russian invasion of Ukraine.

Developing Asia's equity markets have faltered since November after a strong performance for most of 2021. Supported by accommodative liquidity conditions, regional stock markets made a value-weighted average return of 18.8% in first 10 months of 2021, outperforming average gains of 17.0% in the US and 11.2% in a group of major nonregional emerging markets, including Brazil, Russia, and South Africa.

Figure 1.1.24 Performance of currencies in developing Asian economies

The US recovery and, in early 2022, concerns on the Russian invasion of Ukraine rattled Asian currencies.

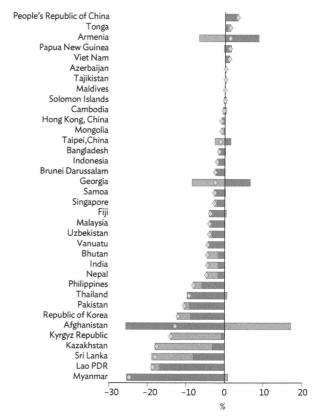

Lao PDR = Lao People's Democratic Republic, US = United States.
Source: Bloomberg (accessed 10 March 2022).

Figure 1.1.25 Equity index performance in developing Asia

Strong gains weakened from late 2021 on Federal Reserve tapering and the Russian invasion of Ukraine.

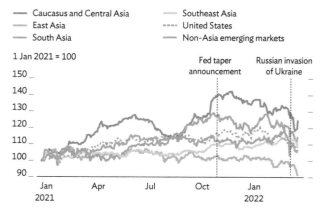

Note: Non-Asia emerging markets comprise Brazil, the Russian Federation, and South Africa.

Source: Bloomberg and CEIC Data Company (both accessed 10 March 2022).

But the strong performance of Asian markets ceased when the Federal Reserve, in November, announced tapering and hinted at raising interest rates to stem mounting inflationary pressures. The outbreak of the Russian invasion of Ukraine at the end of February further weighed on equity markets by souring risk sentiment. Regional equities posted an average loss of 7.1% from 1 November to 9 March 2022. During that period, equity markets in the Caucasus and Central Asia fell by 10.3%, followed by East Asia, down 9.7%, and South Asia, down 9.0%. Southeast Asia bucked the trend, gaining 1.6% on a strong economic performance in the fourth quarter of 2021 compared with the third quarter (Figure 1.1.25).

Risk premiums started rising in late 2021 on subdued investment sentiment. Risk premiums in most developing Asian markets declined during the first 10 months of last year, as measured by J. P. Morgan's Emerging Market Bond Index stripped spread. But the trend changed in November. Weighted average risk premiums in the region increased by 45 basis points from 1 November 2021 to 9 March 2022 and by 38 points excluding Sri Lanka and the Caucasus and Central Asia economies (Figure 1.1.26). The weighted average risk premium in markets in the Caucasus and Central Asia rose by 207 basis points on the Russian invasion of Ukraine. Increased risk premiums tracked worsened investor sentiment on an expected tightening in US monetary policy, uncertainty over the war, and market-specific factors, including rising debt burdens and inflationary pressure.

Foreign capital inflows into developing Asian economies declined in 2021 due to shrinking portfolio investment, but foreign direct investment (FDI) remained resilient. Foreign investment flows to the region declined to $150.9 billion in the third quarter of last year—a level still exceeding the average of $141.6 billion in the third and fourth quarters of 2019—from $258.6 billion in the first quarter of last year. Foreign investment flows to the region were

Figure 1.1.26 J. P. Morgan EMBI stripped spreads in developing Asian economies

Risk premiums increased since late 2021 on an array of investor concerns.

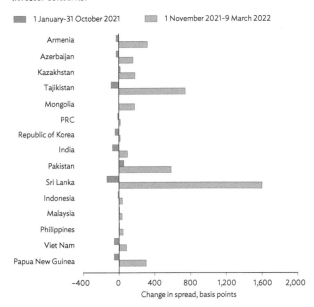

EMBI = Emerging Market Bond Index, PRC = People's Republic of China.
Source: Bloomberg (accessed 10 March 2022).

largely supported by resilient FDI from within and outside the region. FDI inflows averaged $141.4 billion in the first three quarters of last year, nearly twice the average of $76.9 billion in the same period in 2019, reflecting solid medium-term fundamentals. The share of nonregional FDI was 56.4% in the third quarter of 2021, a shade higher than the 55.4% in the same quarter in 2019 (Figure 1.1.27, Panel A). Nevertheless, foreign investment flows to the region dropped due to slumping portfolio inflows, which fell from $93.8 billion in the first quarter to $29.9 billion in the third, largely on the strong economic performance in the US (Figure 1.1.27, Panel A). Foreign portfolio investment continued to decline in the fourth quarter and the first 10 weeks of 2022, as expected US monetary tightening and the Russian invasion of Ukraine led to a rebalancing of international portfolios toward less risky assets. While developing Asia received net portfolio inflows of $29.2 billion in 2021, the inflows were not broad-based but largely concentrated in the PRC, which attracted foreign capital on a strong economic performance and relatively high real interest rates. Excluding the PRC, the region saw net portfolio capital outflows of $38.1 billion last year (Figure 1.1.27, Panel B).

Figure 1.1.27 Foreign investment flows into developing Asia

A. Investment flows

Foreign investment flows in the region remained close to pre-pandemic levels in Q3 and Q4 in 2019 on resilient FDI ...

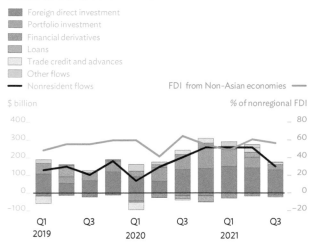

B. Portfolio flows

... but, outside the PRC, the region saw portfolio outflows.

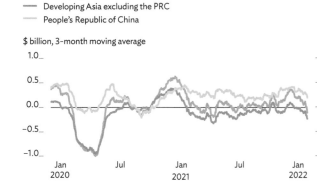

FDI = foreign direct investment, PRC = People's Republic of China, Q = quarter.
Notes: Panel A comprises Azerbaijan; Georgia; Hong Kong, China; India; Indonesia; Kazakhstan; Malaysia; the PRC; the Philippines; and Thailand. Panel B comprises India; Indonesia; Pakistan; the PRC; the Philippines; the Republic of Korea; Sri Lanka; Taipei,China; Thailand; and Viet Nam.
Sources: Panel A: Haver Analytics and CEIC Data Company (both accessed 8 February 2022); Panel B: Institute of International Finance. Capital Flow and Debt Database (10 March 2022).

Figure 1.1.28 Fiscal impulses in developing Asian economies

Policy will remain accommodative in 2022 and 2023 even as governments start tightening.

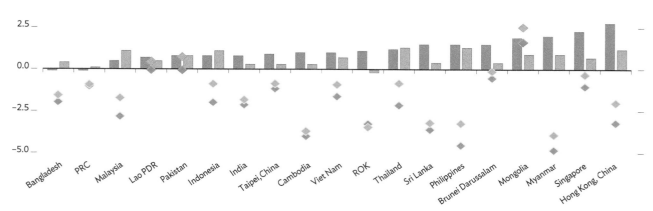

■ 2022 vs. 2021
■ 2023 vs. 2022
◆ 2022 vs. average 2015–2019
◆ 2023 vs. average 2015–2019

GDP = gross domestic product, Lao PDR = Lao People's Democratic Republic, PRC = People's Republic of China, ROK = Republic of Korea.
Note: Fiscal impulse is the change in the fiscal balance expressed as a percentage of GDP. Positive changes in the fiscal balance indicate fiscal consolidation; negative changes indicate fiscal expansion.
Sources: FocusEconomics. 2022. Consensus Forecast Reports. February; Asian Development Bank calculations.

Policy support will moderate on fiscal consolidation and monetary tightening

Fiscal deficits are expected to narrow, but will remain above pre-pandemic levels in most developing Asian economies this year and next. After providing substantial fiscal policy support to cushion the impact of the COVID-19 crisis through 2020 and 2021, most governments in the region are anticipated to start unwinding emergency measures and focus on fiscal consolidation this year (Figure 1.1.28). Increasing budget balances are also expected in 2023, although to a lesser degree than this year. Fiscal balances will still be more accommodative than they were before the pandemic to support continued recovery. The Lao People's Democratic Republic, Mongolia, and Pakistan will be the exceptions. Here, budget deficits are expected to fall below their 2015–2019 average as governments react to worsening debt and public finance conditions.

As discussed in the *Special Topic* on the economic impact of the Russian invasion of Ukraine, even as fiscal authorities turn to consolidation, adverse effects from the war may weigh on tax income and government budgets—particularly in Mongolia and economies in the Caucasus and Central Asia, which have close trade links with Russia. Improving fiscal sustainability without derailing economic recovery will be an important objective for most economies, adding to the urgency of strengthening domestic resource mobilization, as discussed in this report's theme chapter.

Monetary policy continues to be accommodative, but a tightening cycle has started in several economies. With inflation still contained and an incomplete recovery leaving substantial slack in economies, most central banks have not yet begun tightening policy. Monetary stances therefore continue to be accommodative in much of the region, with many economies recording negative real interest rates—defined as nominal rates adjusted for either actual or forecast headline inflation (Figure 1.1.29).

Figure 1.1.29 Real interest rates in developing Asian economies

Monetary stances remain expansionary, but incipient inflationary pressures require vigilance.

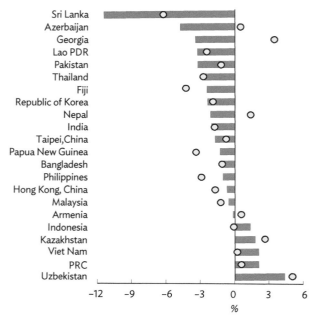

Figure 1.1.30 Change in policy rates in developing Asian economies

Most rates are still at 2020 lows, but some central banks have started hiking.

ADO = Asian Development Outlook, Lao PDR = Lao People's Democratic Republic, PRC = People's Republic of China.

Notes: Real interest rates are the difference between latest policy rates and headline inflation rates (blue bars) or the forecast inflation rates for 2022, as reported in *Asian Development Outlook 2022* (yellow dots). Latest available headline inflation refers to January 2022 for all economies except Armenia, Azerbaijan, and Nepal (December 2021) and Papua New Guinea (September 2021).

Sources: Haver Analytics (accessed 1 March 2022); ADO database.

Lao PDR = Lao People's Democratic Republic.
Source: Bloomberg (accessed 10 March 2022).

But some central banks started tightening their monetary stances in the second half of 2021. Interest rates were increased in response to rising inflationary pressures in Azerbaijan, Kazakhstan, Pakistan, and the Republic of Korea. In Sri Lanka rates were also raised in response to macroeconomic stability concerns, which contributed to spurring the central bank into tightening monetary policy (Figure 1.1.30). Other economies in the region may soon need to tighten to ward off projected increases in inflation as recovery from the COVID-19 pandemic continues.

The withdrawal of policy support in developing Asia may be hastened by external factors. As economies in the region continue to recover, accommodative policies remain necessary for a smooth return to pre-pandemic activity levels. A gradual policy normalization will facilitate this transition. The pace of withdrawing policy support may, however, change depending on developments on two external fronts. Central banks in the region may be compelled to tighten policy faster than expected in response to the actions of the Federal Reserve, as discussed in Box 1.1.3. And the spike in energy and other commodity prices due to the Russian invasion of Ukraine provides another reason for monetary authorities in the region to remain vigilant.

Developing Asia's outlook remains positive despite global tensions

The global economy faces renewed challenges, but growth is expected to remain robust over the forecast horizon. The Russian invasion of Ukraine is a serious economic destabilizer. Its effect on the global economy is being felt through several channels, particularly the significant upward pressure on energy and commodity prices. Growth in the euro area will be hardest hit because of its dependence on energy imports from Russia, but the war could also undermine global sentiment and weaken producer and consumer confidence in other advanced economies. The baseline assumes the war will be confined to just Russia and Ukraine and that sanctions on Russia will remain in place over the 2022–2023 forecast horizon. With the COVID-19 pandemic under control due to improving vaccination and the milder Omicron variant, global economic activity will resume at a faster pace as the latest COVID-19 waves dissipate. GDP growth for the major industrial economies is forecast to remain strong at 3.5% in 2022 before normalizing to 2.4% in 2023 (Table 1.1.1). With GDP levels converging to their pre-pandemic trends, the euro area and the US will complete their recoveries by the end of this year. Solid growth in major advanced economies will continue to underpin the upturn in global demand.

Spillovers from the war, strong global demand, and lingering supply disruptions will increase inflationary pressure. Global energy and food prices will remain elevated this year after near-record increases in 2021. The war will not only be the main source of price pressures but also contribute to supply-chain disruptions; these have already turned out to be more persistent than initially expected and are likely to start dissipating only in the second half of this year. The global economy's sustained progress will continue stoking inflation through several channels. Because of these dynamics, average inflation in the major industrial economies will remain at higher levels this year after accelerating in 2021.

Oil prices are expected to remain elevated over the forecast horizon after spiking on the war. Brent crude's spot price soared last year on recovering global demand before surging to over $100/barrel for the first time since September 2014 following the war's outbreak. March 8 saw $130/barrel breached as the US and other economies stepped up sanctions against Russia, and geopolitical tensions continued to rise. Oil prices are expected to average $107/barrel this year before falling to $93/barrel in 2023 (Figure 1.1.31).

Table 1.1.1 Baseline assumptions on the international economy

COVID-19 slowed recovery in major industrial economies, but growth will remain solid this year and next.

	2020	2021	2022	2023
GDP growth, %				
Major industrial economies	−4.7	5.0	3.5	2.4
United States	−3.4	5.7	3.9	2.3
Euro area	−6.5	5.2	3.3	2.6
Japan	−4.5	1.7	2.7	1.8
Prices and inflation				
Brent crude spot prices, average, $/barrel	42.35	70.44	107.00	93.00
Consumer price index inflation, major industrial economies' average, %	0.7	3.3	4.8	2.1

COVID-19 = Coronavirus Disease 2019, GDP = gross domestic product.

Note: Major industrial economies' average growth rates are weighted by GDP at purchasing power parity (current international US dollars).

Sources: Haver Analytics; World Bank. *Global Commodity Markets* (both accessed 9 February 2022); Asian Development Bank estimates.

Figure 1.1.31 Brent crude prices

Spillovers from the Russian invasion of Ukraine will keep prices elevated in 2022.

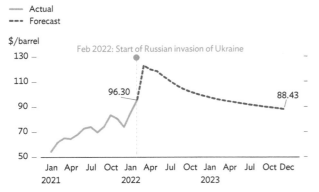

Sources: Bloomberg (accessed 10 March 2022); Asian Development Bank estimates.

Lost supply from Russia could partly be compensated by rising shale production and by Iranian oil coming back on the market if there is an Iran–US nuclear agreement. But oil prices are nevertheless expected to remain elevated due to Russia's energy supply being largely kept out of the global market. As COVID-19 waves recede, the normalization of international travel will significantly increase demand for jet fuel, adding further upward pressure on oil prices.

Monetary policy tightening in advanced economies will complicate developing Asia's economic outlook. Robust global demand will continue to support growth in the region, particularly in export-oriented economies. Stronger inflation pressures, coupled with external factors weighing on the recovery, will cause monetary policy tightening in advanced economies, especially in the US—and tightening there will in due course lead to tighter global financial conditions. The effects of rate hikes in advanced economies may be compounded by shrinking domestic liquidity in developing Asia, as some monetary authorities may follow suit and tighten their policy stance to stem capital outflows even as the recovery remains incomplete (Box 1.1.3).

Growth in developing Asia is forecast at 5.2% in 2022 and 5.3% in 2023, but progress will vary across subregions. After last year's sharp rebound, continued expansion in the region will be mainly supported by recovering domestic demand and robust exports (Table 1.1.2). However, growth dynamics will differ across the subregions.

Growth in the Caucasus and Central Asia is projected to weaken from 5.6% in 2021 to 3.6% in 2022 and recover to 4.0% in 2023. Economic sanctions imposed on Russia will weigh heavily on growth, which will decline in seven of the subregion's eight countries this year (*Special Topic* on the economic impact of the war). Armenia, Georgia, the Kyrgyz Republic, and Tajikistan in particular will experience sharp slowdowns as remittances from migrant workers in Russia contract. Only Turkmenistan, a natural gas exporter with limited ties to Russia, will see growth increase in 2022, to a projected 6.0%. The subregion's growth will pick up in 2023, but slow slightly in Turkmenistan and continue to decline in Azerbaijan, to a forecast 2.8%.

Growth in East Asia is forecast to moderate to 4.7% in 2022 and 4.5% in 2023. Growth patterns in the subregion will vary. In the PRC, growth is projected to moderate to 5.0% in 2022 due to lackluster domestic demand as the COVID-19 pandemic continues to weigh on consumer confidence. Growth in 2023 will slow further, to a forecast 4.8%, as the labor force shrinks and investment declines. Growth in Mongolia will be moderately higher this year and pick up in 2023 as closed borders reopen and COVID-19 disruptions ease. Growth will be lower in the Republic of Korea and Taipei,China this year and next. COVID-19 will dampen Hong Kong, China's economic prospects in 2022, but growth should strengthen next year.

Growth in South Asia is projected to slow to 7.0% in 2022, before picking up to 7.4% in 2023. The subregion's growth dynamics are largely driven by India and Pakistan. Growth in India is forecast at 7.5% this year and 8.0% in 2023, driven by strong investment growth over the forecast horizon. Pakistan's growth is forecast moderating to 4.0% in 2022 on weaker domestic demand from monetary tightening and fiscal consolidation before picking up to 4.5% in 2023. Other economies will see varying growth trajectories. Bangladesh's rapid growth in 2021 will continue into 2022 and 2023, and growth will accelerate in Bhutan and Nepal. After a vigorous rebound in 2021, growth in Maldives will slow but remain strong, supported by the recovery in global tourism. Weaker growth is expected in Sri Lanka as consumption and investment remain muted due to monetary policy tightening, supply shortages, and inflationary pressures.

Table 1.1.2 GDP growth rate in developing Asia, % per year

The region will continue to grow robustly, but at differing speeds across economies.

Economy	2020	2021	2022	2023
Developing Asia	**−0.8**	**6.9**	**5.2**	**5.3**
Caucasus and Central Asia	**−2.0**	**5.6**	**3.6**	**4.0**
Armenia	−7.4	5.7	2.8	3.8
Azerbaijan	−4.3	5.6	3.7	2.8
Georgia	−6.8	10.6	3.5	5.0
Kazakhstan	−2.5	4.0	3.2	3.9
Kyrgyz Republic	−8.4	3.6	2.0	2.5
Tajikistan	4.5	9.2	2.0	3.0
Turkmenistan	...	5.0	6.0	5.8
Uzbekistan	1.9	7.4	4.0	4.5
East Asia	**1.8**	**7.6**	**4.7**	**4.5**
Hong Kong, China	−6.5	6.4	2.0	3.7
Mongolia	−4.6	1.4	2.3	5.6
People's Republic of China	2.2	8.1	5.0	4.8
Republic of Korea	−0.9	4.0	3.0	2.6
Taipei,China	3.4	6.4	3.8	3.0
South Asia	**−5.2**	**8.3**	**7.0**	**7.4**
Afghanistan	−2.4	...	...	...
Bangladesh	3.4	6.9	6.9	7.1
Bhutan	−10.1	3.5	4.5	7.5
India	−6.6	8.9	7.5	8.0
Maldives	−33.5	31.6	11.0	12.0
Nepal	−2.1	2.3	3.9	5.0
Pakistan	−1.0	5.6	4.0	4.5
Sri Lanka	−3.6	3.7	2.4	2.5
Southeast Asia	**−3.2**	**2.9**	**4.9**	**5.2**
Brunei Darussalam	1.1	−1.5	4.2	3.6
Cambodia	−3.1	3.0	5.3	6.5
Indonesia	−2.1	3.7	5.0	5.2
Lao PDR	−0.5	2.3	3.4	3.7
Malaysia	−5.6	3.1	6.0	5.4
Myanmar	3.2	−18.4	−0.3	2.6
Philippines	−9.6	5.6	6.0	6.3
Singapore	−4.1	7.6	4.3	3.2
Thailand	−6.2	1.6	3.0	4.5
Timor-Leste	−8.6	1.8	2.5	3.1
Viet Nam	2.9	2.6	6.5	6.7
The Pacific	**−6.0**	**−0.6**	**3.9**	**5.4**
Cook Islands	−5.2	−29.1	9.1	11.2
Federated States of Micronesia	−3.8	−1.2	2.2	4.2
Fiji	−15.2	−4.1	7.1	8.5
Kiribati	−0.5	1.5	1.8	2.3
Marshall Islands	−2.2	−3.3	1.2	2.2
Nauru	0.8	1.5	1.0	2.4
Niue	...	...	...	...
Palau	−9.7	−17.1	9.4	18.3
Papua New Guinea	−3.5	1.3	3.4	4.6
Samoa	−2.6	−8.1	0.4	2.2
Solomon Islands	−4.5	−0.5	−3.0	3.0
Tonga	0.7	−3.0	−1.2	2.9
Tuvalu	1.0	1.5	3.0	3.0
Vanuatu	−7.5	−1.0	1.0	4.0

... = data not vailable, GDP = gross domestic product, Lao PDR = Lao People's Democratic Republic.

Notes: New weights have been used for aggregating economy-level data. This might cause growth rates reported in this table for 2020 for developing Asia and for the five subregions to slightly differ from those reported in previous editions of the *Asian Development Outlook (ADO)*. See the box in statistical appendix and notes in *ADO 2022*.

Source: *ADO database*.

Southeast Asia's recovery will gain momentum; the subregion's GDP is projected to grow by 4.9% in 2022 and 5.2% in 2023. The stronger momentum will be visible in most of the subregion's economies as COVID-19 vaccination coverage increases and mobility restrictions are eased. Growth in Indonesia, the Lao People's Democratic Republic, Malaysia, the Philippines, and Timor-Leste will be underpinned by stronger domestic consumption, investment, and consumer and business confidence. The external sector will be important growth drivers in Cambodia, Singapore, Thailand, and Viet Nam. Brunei Darussalam will see strong growth due to a significant expansion in oil and gas output. Myanmar's economy will continue contracting in 2022 on protracted political instability and a worsening security situation.

After a 2-year recession, growth in the Pacific is expected to resume, to 3.9% in 2022 and 5.4% in 2023. Rising vaccination rates should help most of the subregion recover from the effects of the pandemic. In Fiji and other tourism-dependent economies, such as Cook Islands and Palau, growth is projected to recover strongly in 2022 and 2023 as vaccination coverage increases further, borders are reopened, and tourism recovers. In Papua New Guinea, recovery in the key minerals sector will drive growth. The economy of Solomon Islands is expected to contract this year due to mobility restrictions imposed in response to COVID-19 community transmission in the first quarter. A major volcanic eruption in Tonga in January is likely to contribute to contraction of the country's economy.

Varying growth outlooks among subregions will translate into differing recovery paths. After last year's rebound, East Asia's GDP will remain close to its pre-pandemic trend over the forecast horizon, while South Asia will continue to catch up (Figure 1.1.32). GDP in the Caucasus and Central Asia, Southeast Asia, and the Pacific will see more persistent or even permanent output losses relative to their pre-pandemic trends. The recovery trajectories within subregions will also vary. In East Asia, Mongolia lags behind and Taipei,China will continue to outperform its pre-pandemic trend. In South Asia, gaps with the pre-pandemic trend are narrowing in the larger

economies, but remain wide in Sri Lanka, Maldives, and Nepal. The catch-up in the Caucasus and Central Asia will be completed in Azerbaijan, but not in the other economies because of the impact of the Russian invasion of Ukraine. Recovery gaps will remain large in most Southeast Asia economies, as well as in Fiji and Papua New Guinea, which dictate the shape of the Pacific subregion's recovery.

Regional inflation will pick up

High energy and commodity prices resulting from the Russian invasion of Ukraine will push up inflation in developing Asia this year—albeit to varying degrees. Inflation in the region is forecast to accelerate from 2.5% in 2021 to 3.7% in 2022 and slow to 3.1% in 2023. Inflation will moderate in the Caucasus and Central Asia, where it is coming down from high levels, but strengthen in the other subregions (Figure 1.1.33). Projections of lower inflation in the Caucasus and Central Asia are primarily underpinned by the impact of monetary tightening in Georgia, Kazakhstan, and Uzbekistan. Closing output gaps in most economies will contribute to inflationary pressures in East Asia, alongside higher energy and commodity prices—the main driver of inflation in the other subregions. The war will loom large on regional price dynamics. Disruptions to energy, food, and other commodity markets could leave global prices elevated. These disruptions will add upward pressure on prices in developing Asia, particularly in economies with historically higher average inflation rates. Spillovers from unsettled energy markets will be especially challenging for monetary authorities. Oil prices this year could be 50% higher or more relative to 2021 and potentially boost headline inflation by up to 2 percentage points—particularly in economies that are large energy importers and where transport has larger weight in the CPI basket. Prices of wheat, corn, vegetable oils, and other food staples are also likely to remain elevated since Russia and Ukraine are large global suppliers of these commodities. The impact of higher global food prices will vary across the region and its intensity will depend on dietary factors and the share of food imports in domestic consumption.

Figure 1.1.32 Projected GDP paths in developing Asia's subregions

Recovery trajectories differ as East Asia leads the catch-up and Southeast Asia and the Pacific lag behind.

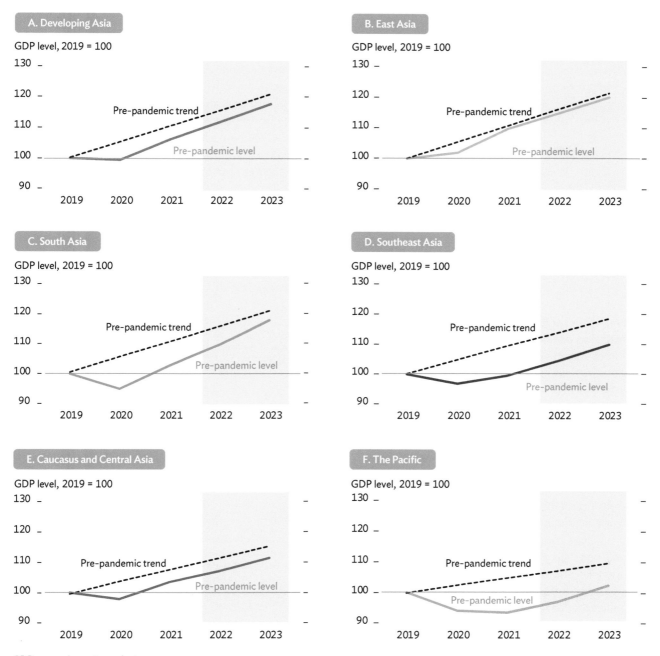

GDP = gross domestic product.

Sources: *Asian Development Outlook* database; Asian Development Bank estimates.

Figure 1.1.33 Forecast inflation in developing Asia

High energy and commodity prices will elevate regional inflation this year.

— Caucasus and Central Asia
— East Asia
— South Asia
— Southeast Asia
— The Pacific
▬ Developing Asia

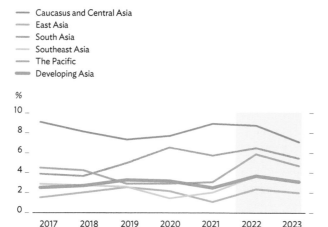

Source: *Asian Development Outlook* database.

Several other factors will contribute to shaping the inflation outlook this year and next.

The supply-chain disruptions that emerged alongside the global recovery will continue to add upward pressure on prices and—while they have so far been less severe in developing Asia than in other parts of the world—may be exacerbated by additional disruptions from Russia's invasion of Ukraine (Box 1.1.1 and the *Special Topic* on the economic impact of the war). Sanctions on Russia and raised global tensions will hamper trade and disrupt the supply of inputs including neon gas, nickel, and palladium, which are critical for the production of semiconductor chips, catalytic converters, and electric batteries. This will boost production costs in the automotive and electronics industries. Exchange rate depreciation will also boost inflationary pressures, particularly for currencies that have already depreciated substantially, and if regional currencies continue to weaken in response to monetary policy tightening in the US. Faced with this uncertain and rapidly evolving price environment, monetary authorities in the region should continue to monitor their inflation situations closely and not fall behind the curve.

Developing Asia's current account surplus will narrow as imports outperform exports

The short-term outlook for exports remains bright for most economies. Export orders remain strong after gathering pace in the last months of 2021 in Taipei,China and Southeast Asia—notably in Indonesia, Singapore, and Viet Nam (Figure 1.1.34). In the PRC, however, the new manufacturing export orders index declined to 46.5 in January, thus falling below the value of 50 separating improvement from deterioration.

Figure 1.1.34 New manufacturing export orders index in developing Asian economies

The short-term outlook for exports remains bright for most economies, but clouding for the PRC.

— India
— Republic of Korea
— Taipei,China
— People's Republic of China
— Southeast Asia

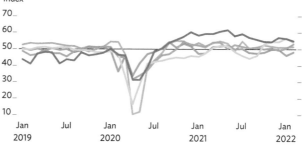

PRC= People's Republic of China.

Notes: In this figure, Southeast Asia comprises Indonesia, Malaysia, Singapore, Thailand, the Philippines, and Viet Nam.

Index over 50 indicates higher new manufacturing export orders relative to the previous month. The aggregate index for Southeast Asia is computed as an average across the six economies, weighted by manufacturing exports in 2019. For the PRC, the primary source for the index is Caixin-Markit. For Singapore, the index is for the whole economy and not just manufacturing.

Sources: CEIC Data Company; IHS Markit; Observatory of Economic Complexity (all accessed 8 February 2022).

Developing Asia's current account surplus will continue to narrow. This is forecast declining from 1.3% of GDP in 2021 to 0.9% this year before improving to 1.0% in 2023. The faster rise in regional imports than exports in 2021, driven mainly by the larger economies in East Asia and South Asia, offset the improved surpluses of commodity-exporting economies, such as those in the Caucasus and Central Asia. Moderating growth and a shift in consumption patterns back to services from goods in advanced economies will temper demand for exports, while imports will increase as regional economies continue recovering (Box 1.1.1). Current account dynamics across subregions will differ (Figure 1.1.35). East Asia's current account surplus will narrow this year, as export growth slows and imports rise in the PRC on high international commodity prices and higher imports in the Republic of Korea and Taipei,China to support investment. Current account deficits in South Asia will widen due to rising demand for imports in India and Pakistan. Current account surpluses will improve in Southeast Asia, driven by rising exports in Brunei Darussalam, Cambodia, Myanmar, Thailand, and Viet Nam. An increase in the aggregate for the Pacific primarily reflects a larger surplus in Papua New Guinea due to rising commodity prices and the reopening of a gold mine.

Figure 1.1.35 Current account balance forecasts for developing Asia's subregions

Surpluses will narrow as imports continue outpacing exports to support the recovery.

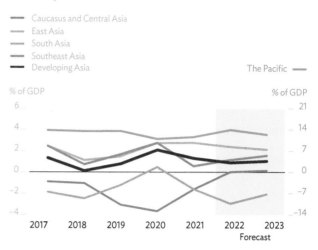

GDP = gross domestic product.
Source: *Asian Development Outlook* database.

Global turbulence and lingering COVID-19 risks

Several downside risks cloud the horizon in developing Asia. A particular worry is an escalation of the war. Protracted fighting, the involvement of other countries, and escalating sanctions could have even more severe repercussions on global energy markets. Natural gas prices could remain elevated for a long time, particularly if the standoff results in Russia curtailing supplies to European Union countries or intensified sanctions hit Russia's energy sector. Higher demand for other energy sources to substitute for natural gas could also lead to persistently higher oil prices. Rising financial stability risks could tighten global liquidity and disruptions to supply chains could affect trade linkages over the forecast horizon and beyond. The impact on developing Asia of all this will probably vary substantially across economies and work through a variety of possible channels, as discussed in the *Special Topic* on the economic impact of the war.

Spillovers from monetary policy tightening in the US remain a risk. With the global economy continuing its recovery from the COVID-19 pandemic, policy normalization around the world has gathered pace. In the US concerns that the current inflationary pressures may become entrenched have accelerated the shift toward a less-expansionary monetary stance. While the global economic impact of the Russian invasion of Ukraine may prompt a less aggressive tightening cycle, the Federal Reserve is now widely expected to raise policy rates several times this year, which will have implications for developing Asia. This tightening, particularly if faster than expected, could trigger financial market volatility, rapid capital outflows, and sharp currency depreciations in the region. This is especially so for economies with weaker macroeconomic fundamentals, which are more vulnerable to this type of external shock. Thus, a more restrictive monetary stance in the US may complicate the recovery in developing Asia, as discussed in Box 1.1.3.

The COVID-19 pandemic is a persistent threat. The progress being made on vaccination means that developing Asia will be increasingly better prepared to withstand any new COVID-19 waves. But outbreaks driven by the Omicron variant remain a challenge and could still hamper economic activity in the region. Most notably, the PRC's current outbreaks—and the lockdowns being implemented under its zero-COVID policy—pose a downside risk to growth in the region's largest economy, and could jeopardize regional and global supply chains. The appearance of more deadly or more vaccine-resistant variants cannot be ruled out. Economies where vaccine rollouts are lagging behind are particularly exposed to this threat, making the need for an equitable and timely distribution of vaccines more urgent than ever.

Scarring from the pandemic remains a significant medium-term risk. The large projected learning losses from continued school closures threaten to further exacerbate economic inequalities, as highlighted in this report's *Special Topic* on the cost of COVID-19 school closures. Students from the poorest income quintile and girls will be disproportionately affected by school closures. Persistent negative effects can also be expected in labor markets, where workers who lost their jobs during the pandemic have seen their skills deteriorate and may need time to find a new job, and even become structurally unemployed. Firms, especially smaller more entrepreneurial ones, could close permanently. All of this could dent the regional economy's productive capacity and, via this channel, reduce its potential for growth going forward. But medium-term risks are not limited to scarring from the COVID-19 crisis. Economies in developing Asia will have to grapple with the increasingly damaging effects of climate change and many are also dealing with aging populations. Addressing these medium-term challenges will require the mobilization of adequate fiscal resources, as discussed in this report's theme chapter.

Box 1.1.1 Developing Asia's resilient supply chains

Supply disruptions have emerged alongside the global recovery, but they have been less severe in developing Asia. The COVID-19 pandemic has created supply and demand mismatches, and reallocated global demand from services to goods. Both have resulted in supply bottlenecks. Developing Asia, however, has been less affected than other regions, as reflected initially by smaller increases in delivery times by suppliers in the manufacturing sector and subsequently by a slight decrease in delivery times (box figure 1, panel A). What is more, deliveries were significantly faster in February 2022 than they were on average over 2016–2021 in Indonesia, Thailand, India, and the People's Republic of China (PRC) (panel B). In Malaysia, the Republic of Korea, and Taipei,China delivery times increased, but far less than in the euro area, the United States (US), and several other advanced economies. This box assesses the demand and supply forces behind the resilience of supply chains in developing Asia.

Demand in developing Asia did not shift from services to goods as much as it did in the US. Services activity in the region continued to be hindered by COVID-19 mobility restrictions in 2021 (box figure 2). Malaysia, the Philippines, and Thailand imposed national lockdowns as the Delta variant led to a spike in cases in the second half of last year; city-level lockdowns were imposed in Indonesia and the PRC. Reduced spending on services, however, did not boost purchases of goods as much as it did in the US and in some other advanced economies. This was partly because disposable incomes recovered more slowly in developing Asia than they did in advanced economies, and because fiscal stimulus—especially direct cash transfers to households—was much larger in the US.

The upstream position of some developing Asian economies protected them from supply-chain bottlenecks. Production or shipping bottlenecks at any point along a value chain can affect downstream industries from this point. More complex value chains are more prone to disruptions because they rely on a wider variety of components. Conversely, upstream industries are somewhat more sheltered from supply-chain disruptions (box figure 3). This notably includes the manufacturing of inputs for electronics, which is the backbone of the economies of the Republic of Korea and Taipei,China, among others.

1 Purchasing managers' index of delivery times of suppliers

Supply chains in developing Asia were more resilient than globally.

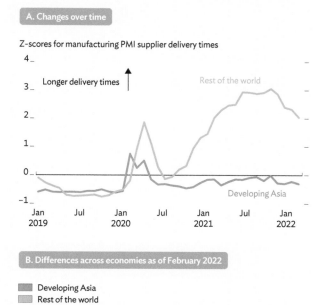

A. Changes over time

B. Differences across economies as of February 2022

PMI = purchasing managers' index, PRC = People's Republic of China.

Notes: Z-scores measure the number of standard deviations between the PMI suppliers' delivery time index and the full sample mean over 2016–2021 for all economies with data.

Developing Asia is the average of India, Indonesia, Malaysia, the People's Republic of China, the Philippines, the Republic of Korea, Taipei,China, Thailand, and Viet Nam weighted by gross domestic product based on purchasing power parity.

Sources: CEIC Data Company; International Monetary Fund. *World Economic Outlook Database: October 2021* (both accessed 9 March 2022).

continued on next page

Box 1.1.1 *Continued*

2 Goods and services consumption

Demand in developing Asia did not shift from services to goods as much as in the United States.

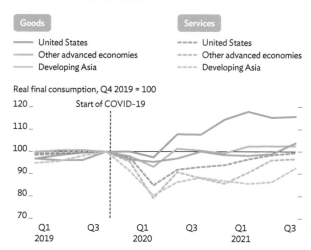

Goods		Services	
—— United States		---- United States	
—— Other advanced economies		---- Other advanced economies	
—— Developing Asia		---- Developing Asia	

Real final consumption, Q4 2019 = 100

COVID-19 = Coronavirus Disease 2019, Q = quarter.

Notes: Developing Asia in this figure comprises Hong Kong, China; Indonesia; the Philippines; the Republic of Korea; Taipei,China; and Thailand. Other advanced economies comprise Canada, Finland, France, Germany, Ireland, Italy, Japan, the Netherlands, Sweden, and the United Kingdom. The indexes for other advanced economies and developing Asia are averaged using gross domestic product based on purchasing power parity for 2020 as weights.

Sources: CEIC Data Company; Haver Analytics; Organisation for Economic Co-operation and Development; Statistics Canada; United Kingdom Office for National Statistics (all accessed 14 March 2022).

Asia has been less affected by rising shipping costs. Increased demand for shipping from the PRC to advanced economies inflated freight rates up to 15 times their pre-pandemic levels in September 2021 before they declined in the year's closing months (box figure 4). In contrast, the cost of shipping a container from Bangkok to main ports in Asia remained about 2.5 times above pre-pandemic levels for most of 2021. Intra-Asia shipping costs, however, have risen since mid-November, reaching 4.7 times pre-pandemic levels at the end of February. This increase reflects port disruptions caused by outbreaks of the Omicron variant and the reduced availability of containers and ships as resources were reallocated to other, more lucrative routes. Freight costs from the PRC to Europe and the US rose again in the second half of February on the Russian invasion of Ukraine, but intra-Asia shipping costs did not budge.

Global supply chain strains are likely to persist amid geopolitical tensions. The Russian invasion of Ukraine will add to supply-chain disruptions, as both economies are key global suppliers of certain inputs used in manufacturing industries—see the *Special Topic* on the economic impact of the war.

3 Relationship between the upstream position of economies and supply-chain disruptions

The upstream position of certain industries helped protect against the cascading effects of supply-chain disruptions.

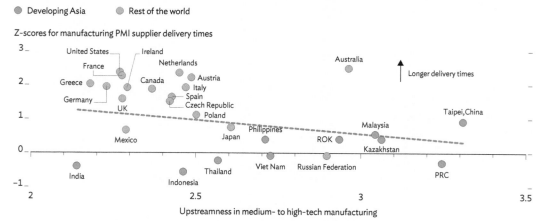

ROK = Republic of Korea, PMI = purchasing managers' index, PRC = People's Republic of China, UK = United Kingdom.

Notes: Z-scores measure the number of standard deviations between the index as of January 2022 and its mean over 2016–2021. Upstreamness is calculated based on P. Antràs and D. Chor. 2013. On the Measurement of Upstreamness and Downstreamness in Global Value Chains. *NBER Working Paper.* No. 24185. National Bureau of Economic Research.

Sources: CEIC Data Company, ADB MRIO database (both accessed 9 February 2022).

Box 1.1.1 *Continued*

4 Container freight rates

The rise in shipping costs within Asia was markedly lower than between Asia and the US, and Asia and Europe.

Same week in 2019 = 100

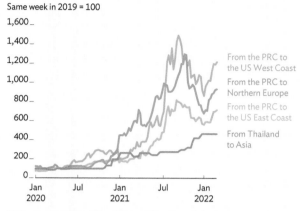

PRC = People's Republic of China, US = United States.

Note: Freight costs from Thailand to Asia are computed as the average of freight costs from Thailand to Hong Kong, China; Shanghai; and Japan for a 40-foot container.

Sources: Freightos Baltic Index; Thai National Shippers' Council (both accessed 9 March 2022).

5 Orderbooks by number of ships and 20-foot equivalent units

New cargo vessel deliveries will relieve shipping bottlenecks from 2023 if nothing else does.

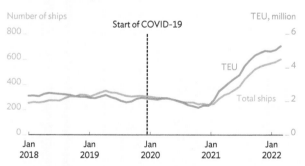

COVID-19 = Coronavirus Disease 2019, TEU = 20-foot equivalent unit.

Note: Vessels on order are those for which a confirmed contract has been reported.

Sources: CEIC Data Company (accessed 9 March 2022).

The Russian Federation notably supplies 24% of global palladium exports and 23% of nickel exports, and neon gas from Ukraine makes up 70% of global supply. These raw materials are key inputs for making catalytic converters, electric batteries, and semiconductor chips. Restrictions in their supply would put further pressure on developing Asia's automobile and electronics industries. Higher shipping costs have pushed carriers to expand rail services via Russia—a route that is now at risk given the sanctions imposed on Russian Railways. The airspace ban above Russia and the suspension of cargo bookings to and from Black Sea ports further complicate existing transport challenges.

If global demand for goods remains strong, relief to shipping will only come from 2023.
Shipping bottlenecks could be relieved by a decline in global demand for goods. This will likely happen when consumers rebalance their spending toward services as economies continue to recover from the COVID-19 pandemic. But demand for goods may decline only gradually and even then could remain higher than pre-pandemic levels. Lastly, replenishing inventories will add to the demand for final goods for some time after the consumption of goods has normalized. In anticipation of a prolonged adjustment process, shippers placed large numbers of orders for new vessels in 2021. As of February this year, about 600 new vessels were on the order books of shipyards around the world. Because building a ship takes at least 2 years, the corresponding 5.3 million 20-foot equivalent units of container capacity will only start coming into operation from 2023 (box figure 5).

This box was written by Jules Hugot, economist, and Reizle Platitas, consultant, Economic Research and Regional Cooperation Department, Asian Development Bank, Manila.

Box 1.1.2 Lessons from early revivals of tourism in developing Asia

International tourism in developing Asia remains constrained by COVID-19 pandemic restrictions, but green shoots are emerging. Still, a slow recovery in the sector may have long-term impacts on the region's tourism-dependent economies, including through business closures and delayed investment in physical infrastructure, such as hotels, restaurants, and transport. A slow recovery may also depreciate and hinder investment in human capital in the industry. As regional economies continue to recover from the pandemic, speeding up the return of international tourists is an important policy objective. This box explores the lessons that can be learned from the experience of the last 2 years, including the recent improvements in some economies.

Tourist arrivals are recovering in a handful of economies in the region that have loosened quarantine restrictions. Maldives, for example, reopened to international travel in July 2020, ahead of other Asian destinations. A rapid vaccination campaign boosted confidence in visiting Maldives as 80% of tourism-sector employees were fully vaccinated by mid-2021. As a result, tourist arrivals were back to pre-pandemic levels by the end of the year. The removal of mandatory quarantines for inbound travelers also led to increasing arrivals in Armenia, Georgia, and Sri Lanka.

Lifting quarantine restrictions upon return has enabled tourists from Europe, North America, India, and Kazakhstan to resume traveling. International flights were still down in the last quarter of 2021, but far less so from these regions and countries (box figure 1). Flights from Europe were down by 35% from the same quarter in 2019 and by 26% from North America. But flights from Australia and New Zealand, East Asia, and Southeast Asia were down by more than 70%. Travel from India and Kazakhstan also recovered somewhat earlier. The faster recoveries of air traffic were supported by eased COVID-19 restrictions for outbound travelers. Since April 2021, residents in the United States (US) only need to present a negative COVID-19 test result when returning home, and many countries in the European Union (EU) have relaxed testing requirements for vaccinated travelers. In contrast, Australia, the Republic of Korea, and the People's Republic of China (PRC), as of 9 March, still imposed mandatory quarantines on return of 7 to 21 days, even for vaccinated travelers in some cases.

Because of high vaccination rates and the use of globally recognized vaccines, visitors from Europe and North America have been able to travel to certain destinations more freely.

1 International departure flights by region of origin

International travel recovered much faster in Europe and North America than in developing Asia.

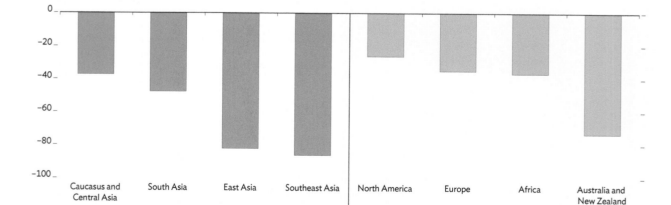

% change in Q4 2021 relative to Q4 2019

Q = quarter.

Source: International Civil Aviation Organization (accessed 9 March 2022).

continued on next page

Box 1.1.2 *Continued*

Some developing Asian economies lifted mandatory quarantines for fully vaccinated tourists in the fourth quarter of 2021, including Cambodia, Fiji, and Singapore. The rapid rollout and global recognition of the EU Digital Covid certificate also facilitated travel for tourists from the EU.

Tourism recovered faster in economies receiving travelers from regions where outward mobility was eased. Easier international mobility in origin economies contributed to the revival of tourism in Armenia, Georgia, and Maldives (box figure 2). Tourist arrivals from western Europe in particular, have been more resilient—notably in Maldives. Although their share decreased from 43% in 2019 to 37% in 2021 (box figure 3), over 200,000 more tourists visited Maldives from this region than in 2020. The share of Russian tourists increased to 17% in 2021 from 5% in 2019, but it is likely to fall this year due to the financial and economic crisis in the Russian Federation. Similarly, in Georgia the share of tourists from western Europe and former Soviet Union countries (except Russia) also increased.

And in both Maldives and Sri Lanka, the share of tourists from India increased as quarantine requirements were removed in October for vaccinated travelers returning home. In contrast, arrivals from Australia and the PRC collapsed in 2020 and remained minimal in 2021. Strict travel restrictions in the PRC have weighed on the recovery in destinations that largely rely on tourists from that country, including Cambodia, Thailand, and Viet Nam.

Relaxing restrictions for incoming tourists, while a necessary precondition, have not always translated into tourism recoveries. Destinations that are popular with tourists from East Asia, Southeast Asia, and Oceania continue to record depressed tourist flows, despite reopening efforts. For example, Thailand—where the PRC alone accounted for 28% of tourist arrivals in 2019— has not succeeded in reviving tourism, despite significant government efforts. And even the modest response to Thailand's phased reopening was led by visitors from the US, the United Kingdom, and Germany (McKinsey & Company 2021).

2 Tourist arrivals and outward mobility restrictions in origin markets

Tourism recovered faster in destinations popular among people who faced fewer travel restrictions.

% change, Q3 2021 relative to Q3 2019

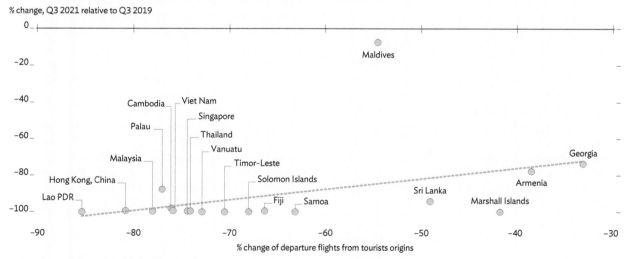

Lao PDR = Lao People's Democratic Republic.

Notes: The sample is restricted to economies where tourism accounted for more than 5% of gross domestic product in 2019. The variable "departure flights from tourist origins" is a weighted average of departure flights from all tourist origins, where the weights are the tourist-origin shares in a destination's total arrivals.

Sources: CEIC Data Company; International Civil Aviation Organization (accessed 11 February 2022); national sources; UN World Tourism Organization; World Bank. World Development Indicators database (both accessed 9 February 2022).

continued on next page

Box 1.1.2 *Continued*

3 Tourist origin markets

Tourist arrivals from western Europe, the former Soviet Union, and India have been relatively resilient.

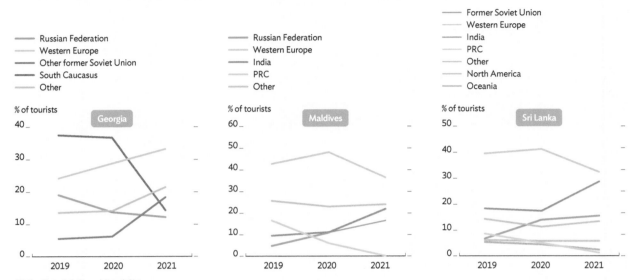

PRC = People's Republic of China.

Note: Definitions of Western Europe are as per the respective sources.

Sources: Georgian National Tourism Administration; Ministry of Tourism of the Maldives; Sri Lanka Tourism Development Authority (all accessed 9 March 2022).

The recovery of Thailand's tourism industry will heavily depend on large Asian economies relaxing the restrictions they impose on outward mobility. This will also be the case in several Pacific island countries; Cambodia; Indonesia; Malaysia; the Philippines; Singapore; Taipei,China; and Viet Nam.

Based on the experience of early reopeners, other destinations in developing Asia should also recover rapidly once travel restrictions are relaxed. As of 9 March, some destinations that have been historically popular with European tourists were still imposing various levels of restrictions on international travel, including Bhutan, Nepal, and Mongolia. Tourism prospects in these countries should brighten significantly on the full reopening of their borders (box figure 4). Destinations most attractive for tourists from India and North America are also well positioned for rapid recoveries, albeit to a lesser extent than economies favored by European tourists, who travel to developing Asia in larger numbers.

The Russian invasion of Ukraine will dent the tourism recovery in developing Asia. The war will limit European tourism in Asia as Russia's airspace can be expected to remain closed for the foreseeable future. This will result in time-consuming and costly detours for air travel between Europe and Asia, particularly as oil prices are high. Arrivals from Russia and Ukraine will collapse, cutting off a tourist flow to developing Asia that had increased rapidly in 2021. The rise in the share of Russian tourists was particularly sharp in Maldives and Sri Lanka, where Russia went from the sixth and seventh largest origin market in 2019, respectively, to the second largest last year (Ministry of Tourism of the Republic of Maldives 2022, Sri Lanka Tourism Development Authority 2022).

References:

McKinsey & Company. 2021. *Reimagining Travel: Thailand Tourism after the COVID-19 Pandemic.*

Ministry of Tourism of the Republic of Maldives. 2022. *Tourism Yearbook 2021.*

Sri Lanka Tourism Development Authority. 2022. *Monthly Tourist Arrivals Report. December 2021.*

continued on next page

Box 1.1.2 *Continued*

4 Share of tourists from Europe and North America and extent of the recovery

Tourism recovered faster in the destination markets favored by Europeans and North Americans.

- COVID-19 screening
- Quarantine arrivals from high-risk regions
- Ban on high-risk regions
- Total border closure

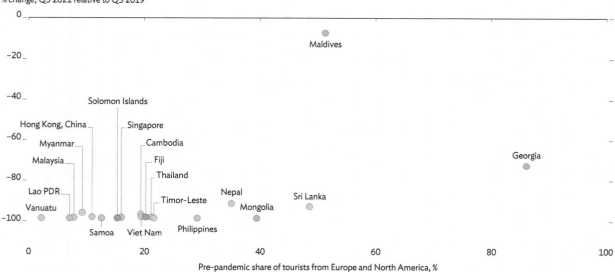

% change, Q3 2021 relative to Q3 2019

COVID-19 = Coronavirus Disease 2019, Lao PDR = Lao People's Democratic Republic, Q = quarter.

Note: The sample is restricted to economies where tourism accounted for more than 2% of gross domestic product in 2019.

Sources: CEIC Data Company; national sources; Oxford COVID-19 Government Response Tracker; UN World Tourism Organization; World Bank. World Development Indicators database (all accessed 9 February 2022).

This box was written by Jules Hugot, economist, and Reizle Platitas, consultant, Economic Research and Regional Cooperation Department, Asian Development Bank, Manila.

Box 1.1.3 The likely implications of more aggressive monetary tightening in the US

High inflation in the United States has prompted the Federal Reserve to take a more hawkish stance on monetary policy. The consumer price index (CPI) in the US increased by 7.9% in February 2021, the highest in 4 decades. The broad-based acceleration in inflation, particularly for shelter, food, and transport, has further heightened price stability concerns. With supply-chain disruptions proving more persistent than anticipated, expectations that inflation will remain elevated have been further reinforced by the Russian invasion of Ukraine, which caused a spike in international oil prices that will feed into energy inflation. In response, the Fed started its tightening cycle by raising interest rates by 25 basis points (bps) on 16 March. The baseline scenario in *Asian Development Outlook 2022*, which is based on information available up to the report's data cutoff date of 9 March, assumes the policy rate will rise gradually and end the year at 1%. But Federal Open Market Committee projections released on 16 March suggest a much more aggressive hiking cycle, with possible hikes in each committee meeting that could bring the policy rate to 1.75%–2.0% by the end of the year (Board of Governors of the Federal Reserve System 2022).

How would the more forceful monetary tightening in the US affect Asia? Faster-than-expected tightening by the Fed could complicate the global economic recovery, including in developing Asia, by slowing US growth and triggering currency depreciations, rapid capital outflows, and financial market volatility. To illustrate how gross domestic product (GDP) growth and inflation in the region may be affected, a modified version of the Global Projection Model—a multiregional general equilibrium model that features Asian economies, including India, the People's Republic of China, and other emerging economies in the region.[a] The model simulates a scenario that incorporates the Fed's latest median projected path for the federal funds rate compared with the baseline used here. It is assumed that the rise in US interest rates—and the Russian invasion of Ukraine—will not spark a global or regional financial crisis.

An aggressive monetary policy response in the US may slow the global economic recovery. A stronger-than-anticipated rise in borrowing costs in the US would dent domestic demand and slow economic growth, which in turn would have negative spillovers on the global economy. Higher interest rates would also tighten international financing conditions by raising the cost of capital. The impact of this on the simulation is a slower global economic recovery, with GDP growth in developing Asia decelerating by 0.2 percentage points from the baseline forecast in 2022 and by 0.1 points in 2023, as panel A in the box figure shows.

Policy choices will become more complex for central banks in developing Asia. The Fed tightening monetary policy creates a positive differential between interest rates in the US and regional economies, which will induce capital outflows. Central banks in developing Asia will face a trade-off. They can let exchange rates depreciate to absorb the impact, which would boost exports and so cushion part of the hit to economic growth. However, weaker currencies emanating from this may accelerate inflation even though the pace of economic activity softens (panel B in the box figure). Or regional authorities could opt to raise domestic interest rates to narrow or close the differential with US rates. This would moderate the inflationary effects associated with exchange rate depreciation, but at the cost of reducing domestic demand and likely deepening the growth decline.

The response to the Fed tightening will likely be economy-specific. If domestic inflation and capital outflows are kept under control, allowing the exchange rate to depreciate will minimize the negative impact on domestic demand. But if domestic inflation threatens to balloon, keeping it in check by raising policy rates would ensure price stability. A mixed strategy combining the two policy responses could be a viable option for many economies in developing Asia—but striking the right balance will not be straightforward. In economies operating closer to their potential, monetary authorities may opt more for interest rate hikes to control inflationary pressures.

continued on next page

Box 1.1.3 *Continued*

Impact of faster hikes in the US policy rate

Weaker recovery in the US may worsen growth prospects elsewhere.

Regional inflation may rise slightly as exchange rates depreciate following capital outflows.

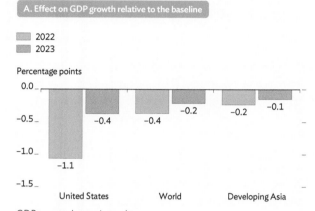

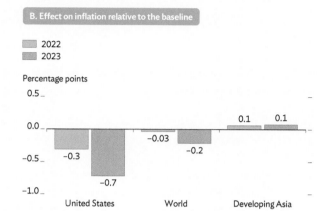

GDP = gross domestic product.

Note: Developing Asia in this figure comprises Hong Kong, China; India; Indonesia; the Republic of Korea; Malaysia; the Philippines; the People's Republic of China; Singapore; Taipei,China; and Thailand.

Source: Asian Development Bank estimates using the Global Projection Model.

However, economies characterized by larger negative output gaps may afford a more substantial currency depreciation to minimize the negative impact on growth. Other factors to consider include the extent to which exchange rate depreciations pass through to inflation and generate negative balance sheet effects (e.g., if an economy has substantial foreign currency liabilities).

An even faster pace of rate hikes in the US remains a key risk for developing Asia's outlook.
Given the record-high inflation expectations in the US, the likelihood that the Fed may pursue an even tighter monetary policy stance should not be discounted.[b] More restrictive moves to restore price stability in the US, if realized, could further complicate global economic recovery prospects, including that of developing Asia.

Clear forward guidance from the Fed would help regional policy makers better cope with any likely negative implications on their economies.

[a] For more information on the basic model, see https://igpmn.org/#/about.

[b] Inflation expectations increased to a record-high 6% median rate in February 2022, according to the Federal Reserve Bank of New York's Survey of Consumer Expectations.

Reference:

Board of Governors of the Federal Reserve System. 2022 Federal Open Market Committee. The Fed – March 16, 2022: FOMC Projections materials, accessible version.

This box was written by Arief Ramayandi and Dennis Sorino, Economic Research and Regional Cooperation Department, Asian Development Bank, Manila.

Russia's invasion of Ukraine: Implications for developing Asia

The direct fallout from the Russian invasion of Ukraine will likely be limited for developing Asia, except in the Caucasus and Central Asia. Indeed, the limited exposure will curtail the direct impact of the war in most of the region, but the effects will be large for the Caucasus and Central Asia, as well as for Mongolia, which all have close trade and financial links with the Russia. Declining remittances from Russia will also weigh on the external balances of economies heavily reliant on these inflows.

Indirect effects will be felt across the region through higher energy and food prices. Oil and natural gas prices rose sharply following the invasion, and they are expected to remain elevated this year. Energy bills will rise for oil and gas importers, pushing inflation up and weighing on demand. Energy exporters will benefit from rising prices. Russia and Ukraine are also key producers of sunflower seed oil, wheat, barley, corn, and fertilizers. And global prices for these products and certain substitutes have surged. Limited access to Black Sea ports and a disrupted spring planting season in Ukraine could keep prices high throughout the year. International sanctions might also affect the availability of base metals, including nickel and palladium, as Russia is a key exporter of these metals.

Further escalation or a prolonged war could have a lasting impact on global sentiment and commodity markets. This would further delay the recovery from the COVID-19 pandemic. Heightened risk could negatively affect consumer, producer, and investor confidence, reducing developing Asia's domestic demand, hurting exports, and delaying investment. A flight to safety could spur capital outflows from emerging markets, compounding the effect of tighter financial conditions from the US Federal Reserve raising its policy rate.

Extent of the sanctions and impact on the Russian economy

The sanctions imposed by Western countries and their partners on Russia are particularly harsh.[1] Following the invasion of Ukraine on 24 February, sanctions were imposed by the EU and the US, as well as Australia; Canada; Japan; New Zealand; the Republic of Korea; Singapore; Switzerland; Taipei,China; and the United Kingdom (UK). The sanctions vary, but they generally include travel bans and freezing the assets of individuals, as well as the following:

- **Export bans.** These not only target goods with military applications but also civilian aircraft and spare aircraft parts, semiconductors, and equipment for oil refineries and telecommunications.

The US sanctions apply to exports from any location as long as they embody certain US goods or technology.

- **Disconnection from SWIFT.** The Society for Worldwide Interbank Financial Telecommunication (SWIFT) enables exchanges of cross-border payment orders. Seven Russian banks have been disconnected from SWIFT, including state-owned VTB Bank.

- **Central bank asset freeze.** The Central Bank of the Russian Federation is banned from trading assets in euros, US dollars, pound sterling, Swiss francs, and yen, either to prop up the ruble or to settle a bilateral trade deficit.

This section was written by Jules Hugot of the Economic Research and Regional Cooperation Department, ADB, Manila.

[1] The information underlying this *Special Topic* is as of 25 March 2022.

This freezes about 60% of the central bank's $630 billion of international reserves. On 24 March, leaders of the G7 also banned gold transactions with the central bank, with gold accounting for another 22% of prewar reserves.

The UK and the US announced energy embargoes, and the US sanctioned all large Russian banks. On 8 March, the US President banned imports of Russian fossil fuels and the British Prime Minister announced an embargo on Russian oil imports by the end of the year. Together, these sanctions will reduce the potential market for Russian oil and gas by 5%. The US Treasury froze the assets of all the largest banks and disconnected them from capital markets. These sanctions apply to majority state-owned Sberbank and VTB Bank, Russia's largest and second largest bank, respectively, holding a combined 75% market share.

Sanctions induce self-sanctioning, notably in the energy sector. Although the sanctions have spared commodities, many buyers have slashed purchases from Russia for fear of future sanctions or reputational damage. Banks, insurers, and shipping companies have also become wary. This has translated into Russian oil selling at a 31% discount as of 25 March. Many foreign companies are also exiting Russia, including car manufacturers, oil majors, retailers, and service providers. This will depress foreign investment and may directly cause about a million job losses.

The ruble depreciated by 48% against the euro from 16 February to 7 March, and it was still down, by 23%, on 25 March. To curtail capital outflows and prop up the ruble, the Central Bank of the Russian Federation raised the policy rate from 9.5% to 20.0%. It also imposed capital controls: foreign currency sales are suspended, dividends and coupon payments to nonresidents are restricted, and exporters are forced to convert 80% of the foreign currency they receive to rubles. Even if the implications are unclear, the Russian President has also demanded that 48 economies deemed "hostile" pay for gas deliveries in rubles. These measures prevented bank runs and reversed the ruble's free fall, although the currency was still down by 23% as on 25 March (Figure 1.2.1). The weaker ruble has increased the cost of imports and pushed inflation from an already high 9.2% in February to 14.5% on 18 March. This will hurt living standards and dampen growth prospects.

The sanctions could trigger a financial crisis in Russia. The initial stock market crash was steeper than in all previous financial crises in Russia (Figure 1.2.2 and Box 1.2.1). The benchmark stock market index fell by 52% from 10 February—its preinvasion peak—to 24 February, when trading on the Moscow stock exchange was halted. Trading reopened on 24 March, but not all shares were allowed to trade and foreigners were not allowed to sell their shares. This makes the slight rebound difficult to interpret. Fitch Ratings, Moody's Investors Service, and S&P Global Ratings downgraded Russia's sovereign debt to "junk," and sovereign default is no longer improbable, according to the managing director of the International Monetary Fund (CBS 2022). Private sector borrowers are allowed to repay their foreign currency debt owed to lenders from "hostile" economies in rubles.

Figure 1.2.1 Euros per ruble

The ruble lost 21% of its value against the euro from 16 February to 25 March 2022.

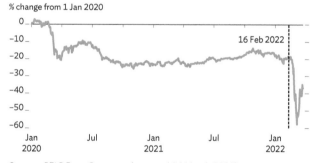

Source: CEIC Data Company (accessed 26 March 2022).

Figure 1.2.2 Russian Trading System stock market index

The initial stock market crash was steeper than in previous financial crises.

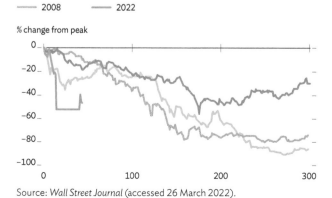

Source: *Wall Street Journal* (accessed 26 March 2022).

Contagion in global financial markets has been moderate—the Euro Stoxx 50 lost 8% of its value from 10 February to 25 March, and the S&P 500 gained 1%. Domestic consumption and investment are expected to collapse. As of mid-March, estimates by global investment banks for GDP growth in 2022 range from a 7% contraction to a 12% decline in growth. For 2023, expectations vary from 0% to a 4% decline.

Direct impacts will be large in the Caucasus and Central Asia, but limited elsewhere in developing Asia

The war will have modest effects on investment and trade in developing Asia because of the region's limited exposure to Russia and Ukraine. The two countries supplied 2.6% of developing Asia's imports in 2019 and they were the destination of only 1.6% of the region's exports. Developing Asia accounts for 5% of foreign investment in Russia, far less than the EU and even the UK (Figure 1.2.3, panel A). Singapore is the largest regional investor, with an FDI stock of $4 billion.

Sanctions and economic crisis in Russia will curtail nascent recoveries in some tourism-dependent economies in developing Asia. The recovery of tourism and GDP in Georgia, where Russians accounted for 16% of foreign tourists and tourism for 9% of GDP before the COVID-19 pandemic, are likely to be affected. Similarly, early tourism recoveries in Maldives and Sri Lanka may be reversed since they have been largely driven by tourists from Russia—and also Belarus, Kazakhstan, and Ukraine—who have to some extent offset falling arrivals from Australia, the PRC, and other traditional regional markets (Box 1.1.2).

Armenia and Tajikistan are particularly vulnerable to falling investment from Russia. Liquidity needs to support core operations in Russia may limit future investments in the Caucasus and Central Asia. This would weigh on the GDPs of economies in this subregion in the short term and on productivity in the longer term. The impact is expected to be the largest for Armenia, where Russia-based investors hold

Figure 1.2.3 Foreign direct investment stock, 2020

A. In the Russian Federation

Developing Asia accounts for 5% of FDI in the Russian Federation.

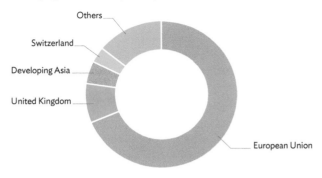

B. From the Russian Federation to the Caucasus and Central Asia

FDI from the Russian Federation is vital for Armenia and Tajikistan.

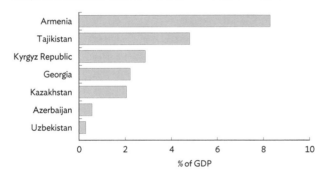

FDI = foreign direct investment, GDP = gross domestic product.
Note: Bahamas, Bermuda, and British Virgin Islands are excluded.
Source: Haver Analytics (accessed 16 March 2022).

$1 billion worth of investments, equivalent to 8.3% of GDP (Figure 1.2.3, panel B). These include investments in food production, mining, manufacturing, real estate, and railways. Tajikistan holds $400 million worth of Russian-owned assets, equivalent to 4.8% of GDP. Russia is also an important creditor to the banking sector in the Caucasus and Central Asia, particularly in Armenia, where Russia-based investors own 74% of banking sector assets (Figure 1.2.4).

Most countries in the Caucasus and Central Asia, as well as Mongolia, have close trade links with Russia. The economic downturn and the ruble's depreciation will reduce exports to Russia, which account for about 20% of total exports in Armenia and Georgia, and more than 10% in the Kyrgyz Republic and Uzbekistan (Figure 1.2.5, panel A).

Figure 1.2.4 Russian Federation asset holdings as a share of total bank liabilities

Armenia's banks are particularly exposed to financing from the Russian Federation.

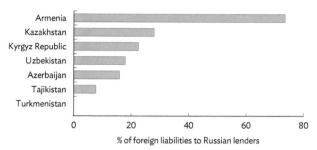

Note: Data as of 30 September 2021.
Sources: Bank for International Settlements; Central Bank of the Russian Federation (both accessed 16 March 2022).

Figure 1.2.5 Trade exposure to the Russian Federation and Ukraine

Countries in the Caucasus and Central Asia and Mongolia have close trade links with the Russian Federation.

A. Share of bilateral exports in total exports

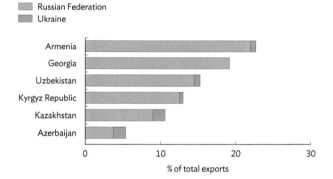

B. Share of bilateral imports in total imports

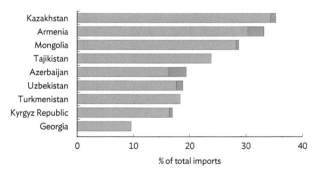

Note: The figure includes the economies for which the Russian Federation and Ukraine account for more than a combined 5% of total exports or imports.
Sources: Observatory of Economic Complexity; World Bank. World Development Indicators database (both accessed 15 March 2022).

Exposure to Russian demand is lower in Azerbaijan, Tajikistan, and Turkmenistan, which mostly export energy products and base metals to the EU, the PRC, and Turkey. The downturn in Russia may also cause supply disruptions, particularly affecting countries importing large volumes from Russia. Russia accounts for more than 15% of imports for all countries in the Caucasus and Central Asia, except Georgia (panel B). Exposure exceeds 25% for Armenia, Kazakhstan, and Mongolia. The war may also disrupt trade routes for some of these economies.

Falling remittances from Russia will also affect economies in the Caucasus and Central Asia.
The value of remittances from Russia will be slashed by the economic crisis in the country lowering migrant workers' incomes, the disconnection of key Russian banks from SWIFT complicating money transfers, and the ruble's depreciation. Coupled with rising energy prices, the drop in remittances will weaken balances of payments. The impact will be the strongest where remittances are equivalent to large shares of GDP—in the Kyrgyz Republic and Tajikistan, for example (Figure 1.2.6). By reducing consumption and investment, declining remittances will also weigh on tax income and government budgets.

Figure 1.2.6 Remittances in the Caucasus and Central Asia

Remittances from the Russian Federation exceed 15% of GDP in the Kyrgyz Republic and Tajikistan.

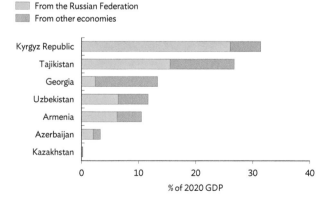

GDP = gross domestic product.
Sources: Ratha and Kim 2022; World Bank. World Development Indicators database (both accessed 9 March 2022).

Declining remittances, combined with declining receipts from exports to Russia, will also lower demand for local currencies, adding pressure on already depreciating exchange rates (Figure 1.2.7). Weaker currencies will reinforce inflationary pressures, and large depreciations may also create liquidity risks in economies with substantial foreign currency-denominated debt, such as Armenia, Georgia, and Uzbekistan.

The largest impact for developing Asia will be through energy prices

Energy prices spiked following the Russian invasion of Ukraine and are expected to remain elevated. Russia is the second largest global exporter of oil and the fourth of natural gas, with market shares of 11% and 9%, respectively. Energy prices soared on actual and potential disruptions to Russia's supplies. On 25 March, Brent crude oil traded at $121, up by 27% from 16 February, and in Asia, prices for liquefied natural gas (LNG) were up by 50% (Figure 1.2.8). These sharp increases added to preexisting price pressures. Oil prices rose by 50% in 2021, driven by the global economic recovery and the slow unwinding of output cuts agreed to by Organization of the Petroleum Exporting Countries (OPEC) Plus members. LNG prices increased by 113% in Asia last year. The US and UK embargoes on Russian mineral fuels will further strain prices, although the two countries' oil imports from Russia only account for 0.7% of global oil trade. The impact of a possible EU embargo on Russia's oil exports would be more than tenfold higher since the EU absorbs 49% of Russia's oil sales, accounting for 5% of global oil trade. Available estimates suggest that a sudden halt in Russian oil exports would boost prices to $160–$200 per barrel (Bain 2022; Thomson Reuters 2022). Elevated oil price futures indicate that markets expect a prolonged period of high prices ahead.

Rising output could curtail the increase in oil prices. Replacing lost Russian supplies would require a coordinated global effort. Increases in production from US shale operators are unlikely in the short term because this will require drilling new rigs, but supply pressures could ease if strategic reserves are released.

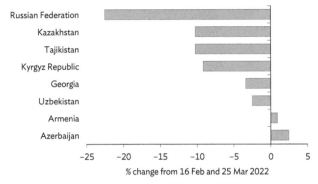

Figure 1.2.7 Euros per local currency units

Some currencies from the Caucasus and Central Asia are already sliding along with the ruble.

% change from 16 Feb and 25 Mar 2022

Source: CEIC Data Company (accessed 26 March 2022).

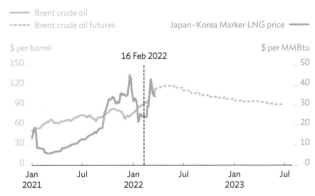

Figure 1.2.8 Oil and natural gas prices

Energy prices surged after the Russian invasion of Ukraine.

LNG = liquefied natural gas, MMBtu = million British thermal units.
Note: 7-day moving average.
Sources: CEIC Data Company; Investing.com (both accessed 26 March 2022).

Market demands for paying dividends rather than increasing production and environmental considerations are also making new investment in shale operations less attractive. OPEC members, however, have spare oil production capacity equivalent to 45% of Russia's output (Figure 1.2.9). A meaningful boost to OPEC production would require breaking the agreement made with Russia in the OPEC Plus framework to only gradually unwind the current output cuts. On 9 March, the United Arab Emirates announced its interest, but this would have to involve Saudi Arabia, which controls the largest spare capacity. The lifting of sanctions on Iran and, to some extent, Venezuela would also contribute to increasing supply.

Figure 1.2.9 Russian production and
OPEC spare capacity

OPEC's spare capacity accounts for 45% of Russian production.

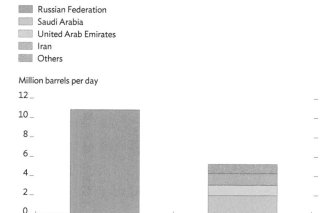

OPEC = Organization of the Petroleum Exporting Countries.
Sources: International Energy Agency. *Oil Market Report, February 2022*;
US Energy Information Administration. *Short-Term Energy Outlook,
March 2022* (both accessed 15 March 2022).

High energy prices will aggravate inflation and pose challenges for growth in developing Asia.

On average, oil prices this year could be 50%
higher or more relative to 2021. Estimates suggest
that oil prices could push up headline inflation by
2 percentage points and even more for economies
where transport looms larger in the consumer
basket (Choi et al. 2018). Economies where oil
imports are equivalent to large shares of GDP will
also be particularly affected, including Cambodia,
several Pacific island nations, Singapore, the Kyrgyz
Republic, and Tajikistan (Figure 1.2.10, panel A).
On the external front, rises in energy import bills
will have the greatest impact on energy-importing
economies that are managing balance-of-payment
strains, including Sri Lanka, whose currency
depreciated by 30% from 9 to 25 March. Rising energy
prices will also add to strains on public finance,
notably where fuel is subsidized—such as in Pakistan,
where spreads for 10-year sovereign bonds widened
by 57 basis points from 16 February to 25 March.
Higher inflation will weigh on regional growth by
squeezing consumers' disposable incomes and
may trigger policy rate hikes, which would further
dampen growth. Slower growth in Europe because of
higher energy prices may also weigh on demand for
Asian goods.

Figure 1.2.10 Oil and natural gas net trade-to-GDP
in developing Asian economies

A. Net imports-to-GDP

*Oil and gas net imports exceed 5% of GDP
in 16 developing Asian economies.*

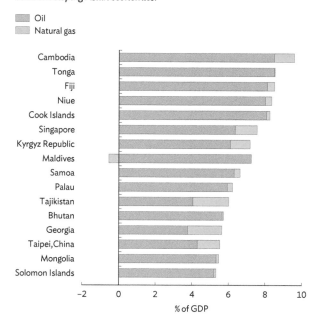

B. Net exports-to-GDP

*Oil and gas net exports exceed 5% of GDP
in six developing Asian economies.*

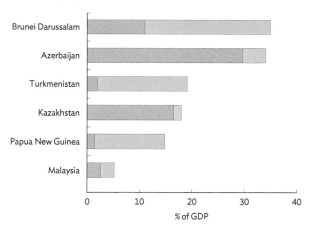

GDP = gross domestic product.
Note: The sample is restricted to economies where net oil and gas
imports or exports exceeded 5% of GDP in 2019.
Sources: Observatory of Economic Complexity; World Bank. World
Development Indicators database (both accessed 15 March 2022).

Higher energy prices will benefit oil and gas exporters. These include Azerbaijan and Brunei Darussalam, where oil and gas export account for more than one third of GDP, and also Kazakhstan, Papua New Guinea, and Turkmenistan, where the shares of energy exports in GDP range from 15% to 19% (Figure 1.2.10, panel B). Kazakhstan's ability to export oil, however, has been reduced by the war as about 60% is transported by pipeline to the Russian Black Sea port of Novorossiysk, where it is mixed with Russian oil. This and the proximity of Novorossiysk to the war zone have put off buyers and insurers. The Government of the Russian Federation announced on 22 March that loading bays at the port of Novorossiysk were damaged by a storm, forcing the pipeline to close for at least 1.5 months.

Higher prices and supply disruptions for non-energy commodities will also affect developing Asia

Food prices have increased on actual and potential supply disruptions. Ukraine and Russia account for a combined 55% of global exports of sunflower seed oil, 22% for wheat, 17% for barley, and 12% for corn (Figure 1.2.11). The geography of the war has cut production centers in central and eastern Ukraine from ports in the southwest of the country. In addition, most shipping companies cannot get insurance to approach Black Sea ports in Russia and Ukraine. While food products are not subject to sanctions, Russia's grain exports will be constrained by capital controls, lack of trade finance and insurance, and self-sanctioning. The war also threatens the harvests of winter crops already sown, notably wheat and barley, and the sowing of spring crops, including corn and sunflowers. These existing and potential disruptions to global supply have pushed prices up. As of 25 March, global wheat prices rose by 38% and 15% for corn from 20 January—the day prior to the recognition of the breakaway republics of Donetsk and Luhansk by Russia (Figure 1.2.12). Prices also increased by 9% for palm oil, which is a substitute for sunflower oil and can be processed into biofuel. This comes in addition to a 44% increase in palm oil prices from 1 January 2021 to the outbreak of the war due to adverse weather in South America and Southeast Asia. As of 25 March, rice prices remained stable in Asia.

Figure 1.2.11 Non-energy commodity export shares

Ukraine and the Russian Federation account for large shares of global grain, vegetable oil, and other commodity exports.

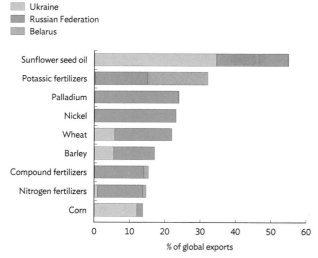

Source: Observatory of Economic Complexity (accessed 15 March 2022).

Figure 1.2.12 Prices of key agricultural exports

Grain and palm oil prices have spiked since the Russian invasion of Ukraine.

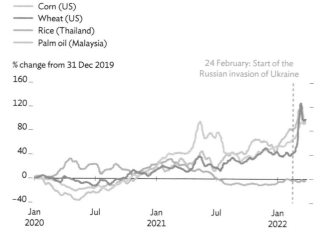

US = United States.
Source: CEIC Data Company (accessed 26 March 2022).

Fertilizer prices have increased. Natural gas is the key input in nitrogen fertilizers, with Russia accounting for 13% of global exports. Russia and Belarus also account for a combined 32% of global potassic fertilizer exports. Rising gas prices and sanctions imposed on Russia and Belarus have boosted fertilizer prices.

As of 25 March, the North America Fertilizer Price Index increased by 45% from 20 January. Increases in fertilizer prices are particularly concerning for India, which is the world's largest nitrogen fertilizer importer and where food accounts for 46% of the consumer basket. Besides fertilizers, elevated oil prices also make farming more costly, which will further kindle food inflation.

The supply of inputs into industrial value chains may be disrupted by sanctions and the war itself. Ukraine accounts for 70% of the global supply of neon, a gas critical for the lasers used to engrave semiconductor chips. Neon itself is a byproduct of Russian steel manufacturing that is refined in Ukraine. Russia provides 24% of the global supply of palladium, an input in catalytic converters that turn toxic exhaust gas into less toxic gases. Russia also supplies 23% of the global exports of nickel, which is used in stainless steel and batteries. Supply-chain disruptions may also affect products transported across Russia. This will particularly impact shipments between Central Asia and Europe, for which alternative routes are much more costly. Shipping from the PRC to Europe is also affected. Zyxel Communications—a manufacturer of information technology network equipment—notably stopped shipping from the PRC to Europe by rail. Large logistics companies also suspended rail shipping routes through Russia, including CMA CGM, Maersk, and MSC.

A further escalation or a prolonged war could have a lasting impact on global sentiment and commodity markets. In the first 2 weeks of March, geopolitical tensions surged to levels not seen since the Iraq war, as measured by reports in English-language newspapers (Figure 1.1.1). Heightened geopolitical risk may depress business and consumer sentiment, translating into delays in investment and depressed consumption. This would compound effects from the hiking cycle started by the Federal Reserve in March. Capital outflows from emerging markets may also increase as financial conditions tighten. Members of the Russia-led Eurasian Economic Union, including Armenia, Kazakhstan, and the Kyrgyz Republic, could be particularly affected.

Longer-term impacts on developing Asia

EU oil and gas diversification could be a boon for Azerbaijan, Kazakhstan, and Turkmenistan. Efforts by the EU to diversify its natural gas supply will accelerate, possibly benefiting Azerbaijan and Kazakhstan, which both have operational pipelines. Turkmenistan does not have a pipeline to Europe and would need to ship oil by tanker across the Caspian Sea until one is built. The EU's diversification efforts might also benefit LNG exporters, such as Brunei Darussalam, Indonesia, and Malaysia.

The diversification of central banks' foreign reserves may result in higher gold prices and a stronger yuan. Although magnitudes and contexts are vastly different, the freezing of the Central Bank of the Russian Federation's assets follow the US freezing of the reserves of Afghanistan's central bank last August. These precedents may push other central banks to diversify their foreign reserves, since euros and US dollars together account for 80% of global foreign reserves, but yuan assets only account for 3%. The PRC holds the largest foreign reserves globally, but India and other developing Asian economies also accumulated substantial reserves following the Asian financial crisis in 1997. The diversification of these reserves would put upward pressure on gold prices, benefiting regional gold exporters, such as the Kyrgyz Republic, the Lao People's Democratic Republic, and Mongolia. Significant increases in yuan-denominated foreign reserve holdings, however, may require deeper and more liquid markets.

The Russian invasion of Ukraine might speed up the green transition in developing Asia. High fossil fuel prices increase the attractiveness of switching to more reliable renewable energy. Initiatives to reduce dependence on Russia will also push governments to accelerate the green transition. In the short term, however, energy security concerns might boost the extraction of fossil fuels where they are available. Oil and gas supply disruptions in Europe might also boost purchases of coal. Australia and Indonesia are the world's largest coal suppliers.

Prolonged tensions between Russia and Europe could increase the number of Russian refugees in the Caucasus and Central Asia. The vast majority of Ukrainian refugees are in the EU, but many Russians have also fled Russia to countries in the Caucasus and Central Asia, where visas are not required. Exact figures are difficult to assess, but available estimates suggest that at least 200,000 Russians have, 2 weeks into the war, fled Russia.

The mayor of Tbilisi has said that 25,000 Russians have arrived in Georgia and authorities in Armenia have counted 80,000 Russians arriving in Yerevan. Other reports describe shortages of accommodation in Bishkek and Tashkent and an increasing number of bank account openings by Russians in Armenia. Many of these refugees are highly skilled, notably in the information technology sector. Although many will settle in other countries, some will stay and contribute to boosting long-term productivity.

Box 1.2.1 Impact of sanctions on the Russian Federation after the annexation of Crimea

The sanctions imposed on Russia after the annexation of Crimea in 2014 had a limited impact on economic growth, but they were milder. These sanctions triggered large capital outflows, a fall in investment, and a sharp depreciation in the ruble. The Russian economy grew more slowly than those of other oil-exporting economies during 2014–2021, as the box figure shows. The International Monetary Fund estimated that sanctions subtracted 0.2 percentage points from gross domestic product (GDP) growth over 2014–2018—against 0.9 points due to low oil prices (IMF 2019). Both factors added to systemic constraints to development, including weak governance and rule of law.

Real gross domestic product

Growth in Russia has been lower than for other oil-exporting economies since 2014.

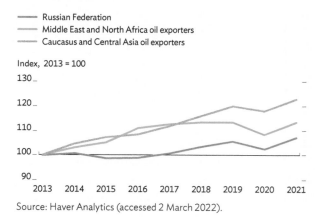

Source: Haver Analytics (accessed 2 March 2022).

The government has strengthened fiscal and external buffers since 2014. The National Wealth Fund is worth $198 billion—equivalent to 12% of GDP, largely invested domestically. Before the invasion of Ukraine, international reserves were equivalent to 2.6 years of imports at their 2019 levels. Most importantly, the share of reserves held in US dollars, euros, and pound sterling declined from more than 85% in 2014 to 55% at the end of 2021. This was compensated by rising shares of gold and yuan-denominated securities. External debt has also declined: 82% of private sector debt is now owned domestically, limiting refinancing risks.

Sovereign debt is limited, at 18% of GDP. These buffers, however, will be much less useful to withstand the crisis over the invasion of Ukraine given the freezing of most of the overseas assets of the Central Bank of the Russian Federation.

Reference:
International Monetary Fund. 2019. *Staff Report for the Article IV Consultation*. August.

References

Bain, C. 2022. The Consequences of an End to Russian Energy Trade. Capital Economics. 7 March.

CBS. 2022. Transcript: IMF Managing Director Kristalina Georgieva on "Face the Nation", 13 March 2022.

Choi, S., et al. 2018. Oil Prices and Inflation Dynamics: Evidence from Advanced and Developing Economies. *Journal of International Money and Finance* 82.

Ratha, D. and E. J. Kim. Russia–Ukraine Conflict: Implications for Remittance flows to Ukraine and Central Asia. *World Bank Blogs*. 4 March. World Bank.

Thomson Reuters. 2022. Oil Could Hit $200 a Barrel, Says Rystad Energy. 8 March.

Falling further behind: The cost of COVID-19 school closures by gender and wealth

School closures during the COVID-19 pandemic led to losses equivalent to over half a year's worth of learning. This foregone learning will hamper students' productivity and ability to earn income in the future. Children from low-income households have less access to quality remote education, more exposure to economic hardship during COVID-19, and a greater tendency to drop out of school in response to the pandemic. Because of this, learning losses for students from the poorest quintile are 33% more than those for students from the richest quintile. These will translate into losses in expected earnings that are 47% more for the poorest students, exacerbating income inequalities. Estimated gender gaps in foregone learning are small but translate into earning losses that are 28% higher for girls than for boys because of the higher return on girls' education. While supply-side improvements in the quality of remote education reduce aggregate losses from school closures, inequality will grow if improvements largely benefit those who have more access to educational resources. Investments are necessary to ensure improvements benefit all students, including poor children and girls.

COVID-19 disrupted education in most of the world

Almost all economies implemented nonpharmaceutical interventions in 2020 to curb the spread of COVID-19.[1] These included community quarantines, curfews, travel restrictions, and school closures. Most empirical evidence points to these interventions having the intended proximate effect on social contact and viral transmission (Wang et al. 2021), albeit with substantial variation between and within economies and waning effectiveness over time. Nonpharmaceutical interventions have had knock-on environmental and economic effects (Mandel and Veetil 2020), some of which will propagate long after the pandemic ends (Pujol 2020).

The height of school closures was from March to May 2020, when about 70% of economies worldwide took the emergency measure of closing all schools to prevent COVID-19 infections. Over 60% of economies had kept schools closed, whether in part or in full, by June 2020. Since then, most economies started reopening schools for in-person classes, yet all schools remained closed in as many as 21% of economies and some schools stayed closed in as many as 50% of economies from June 2020 to October 2021 (Figure 1.3.1).

Setbacks in the early stages of life can have lasting effects. Foundational skills are the building blocks of other skills that schoolchildren can acquire as they grow older. If they miss the opportunity to learn these vital skills early in life, they will have to spend precious time catching up instead of progressing to next levels. Indeed, past episodes of school closures due to war or natural disaster had long-term impacts on student learning and lifetime earnings.[2]

This section was written by Rhea Molato Gayares and Milan Thomas of the Economic Research and Regional Cooperation Department (ERCD), ADB, Manila. It benefited from comments from Abdul Abiad, Elisabetta Gentile, Ryotaro Hayashi, Sameer Khatiwada, Albert Park, Jukka Tulivuori, Jeffrey Xu, Yumiko Yamakawa, and participants at a seminar organized jointly by ADB's Education Sector Group and ERCD on 24 November 2021. The authors thank Ann Jillian Adona for excellent research assistance.

[1] Oxford COVID-19 Government Response Tracker (accessed 31 October 2021).

[2] See, for example, Ichino and Winter-Ebmer (2004).

Figure 1.3.1 Status of schools, February 2020 to October 2021

Most economies closed schools in Q2 2020 and some kept them closed through 2021.

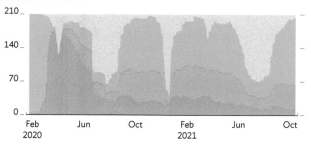

- Closed due to COVID-19
- Partly closed
- Fully open
- Academic break

Number of economies

COVID-19 = Coronavirus Disease 2019, Q = quarter.
Source: Authors based on data from *UNESCO Global Monitoring of School Closures* (accessed 17 November 2021).

The cost of school closures is borne unevenly.
Students who have better access to alternative modes of education and adult supervision are in a better position to keep learning than those who have not. A wealth of evidence already shows that students from disadvantaged backgrounds have less access to remote learning opportunities (Azubuike, Adegboye, and Quadri 2021) and worse learning outcomes during the COVID-19 pandemic.[3]

This analysis of the cost of COVID-19 school closures by gender and wealth estimates the magnitude of inequality in learning and earning losses. While it is not surprising that disadvantaged groups are expected to suffer more from school closures, quantifying the inequality highlights the need for more concerted action to support innovative solutions and extend assistance where it is needed the most.

Measuring the losses in learning and earnings

To project the foregone learning that came with school closures, this analysis applies the framework in Azevedo et al. (2021) and uses data from UNESCO's Global Monitoring of School Closures to estimate the reduction in learning-adjusted years of schooling (LAYS)—a measure of learning that accounts for both the quantity and quality of education.

School closures affect LAYS in three ways.
First, in the absence of distance learning and remedial education, every year of school closure lowers the expected years of schooling completed (quantity), which has a linear effect on learning (Filmer et al. 2020). This loss can be mitigated by continued remote education while schools remain physically closed. Second, school disruptions, together with economic shocks, lead to more students dropping out of school, thus reducing the average expected years of schooling for an economy. And third, school closures reduce the quality of learning due to the inefficacy of remote education compared with in-person classes. The following adjustments were made in estimating the losses in learning and earnings.

Learning adjustment

The effectiveness of remote education depends on two independent factors: access to remote instruction and the efficacy of remote learning. Early evidence on learning outcomes during the COVID-19 pandemic confirms that students gained less from remote education than from classroom learning. With distance learning, primary school students gained less than half of their learning from in-person classes in Switzerland (Tomasik, Helbling, and Moser 2021). Standardized test scores are lower among the cohort of students who learned remotely in several developed economies, including Belgium, Germany, and the Netherlands, where standardized exams were administered.[4] Math and reading achievement declined among students in Mexico (Hevia et al. 2021). Less engagement in education activities was documented in Ethiopia (Habtewold 2021).

---

[3] See, for example, Andrabi, Daniels, and Das (2021) and Ichino and Winter-Ebmer (2004).

[4] Belgium: Maldonado and De Witte (2021); Germany: Schult et al. (2021); the Netherlands: Engzell, Frey, and Verhagen (2021).

Evidence based on test scores in 2020 and 2021 are consistent with evidence before COVID-19's outbreak on the limited efficacy of remote education. These studies find a wide range of learning losses. After only 9 weeks of closures, average scores of primary students in the Flemish region of Belgium were 0.19 standard deviations lower in math and 0.29 standard deviations lower in Dutch compared with the previous cohort of students who were unaffected by school closures (Maldonado and De Witte 2021). Learning assessments done in 2019 and 2021 in Campeche and Yucatan, Mexico, showed reductions of 3%–23% in reading comprehension scores and 2%–70% in math scores, increasing with the subject's level of complexity (Hevia et al. 2021).

Because of the wide range of estimated learning losses following COVID-19 school closures, this analysis considers a range of possibilities and explores three scenarios—high, medium, and low—for the efficacy of remote education. These scenarios are based on evidence from the literature on efficacy of remote learning (Technical Appendix 1). These scenarios were factored into this analysis in estimating how well distance learning substitutes for in-person classes.

Dropout adjustment

To project the loss of LAYS in each economy from dropouts caused by the COVID-19 pandemic, the increase in dropout rates when income declines is measured. This is estimated by using a panel data regression of economies' out-of-school rates on GDP per capita over pre-pandemic years.[5] From this regression and the income shocks of 2020 and 2021, the change in out-of-school rates is estimated.[6] The dropout rate is approximated by dividing the change in the out-of-school rate by the ratio of pre-pandemic enrollment and out-of-school rates. The estimates show that on average 0.36% of primary students and 0.70% of secondary students dropped out due to COVID-19 income shocks in 2020 and 2021. Nationally representative data measured dropout rates of about 0.7% in Uganda (Uwezo Uganda 2021),

1.6% in Senegal (Mbaye et al. 2021), 2% in Ghana (Abreh et al. 2021), and up to 6% in Pakistan (Idara-e-Taleem-o-Aagahi 2021) and South Africa (Spaull et al. 2021). It is assumed that each new dropout loses the average years of schooling in their economy net of schooling years attained before the pandemic.[7]

This calculation understates the effect of school closures on dropping out because closures affect this through channels other than reduced household income, such as student demotivation. Studies of lower-middle income economies showing double-digit dropout rates in some contexts—for example, Dessy et al. (2021) for Nigeria—suggest that non-income channels may have been critical throughout the pandemic, but few report the dropout rate before COVID-19, making it difficult to draw firm conclusions or incorporate non-income channels into the dropout adjustment (Moscoviz and Evans 2022).

Differences by gender

The analysis considers two channels by which school closures affect boys and girls differently. First, access to remote education differs by gender, and this can be represented by the difference in internet access during the pandemic (Figure 1.3.2). This is because internet access is necessary for students to be able to participate in online learning, which is generally perceived as the most effective mode of remote education during the pandemic (UNESCO, UNICEF, and World Bank 2020). Second, girls have a higher propensity to drop out of school. A 1% drop in per capita income is associated with a 0.57% increase in the likelihood of girls being out-of-school versus 0.52% for boys of primary school age. Dropout rates for girls of secondary-school age also respond to income shocks more than boys of the same age group. It is likely that other non-income, social, and cultural factors caused more girls to drop out of school during the pandemic in some economies. Because these factors are beyond the scope of this analysis, the estimates likely understate the full extent of gender differentials in dropout rates.

---

[5]   A log-log regression is used to estimate the elasticity of out-of-school rates with respect to GDP per capita.

[6]   International Monetary Fund. *World Economic Outlook Database*. October 2021.

[7]   Because the median age of students covered in this analysis is 10 years, the median years of schooling attained before the COVID-19 pandemic is assumed to be 5 years.

Figure 1.3.2 Internet users by region and gender, %

In most regions, girls have slightly lower internet access than boys.

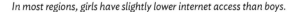

■ Female
■ All
■ Male

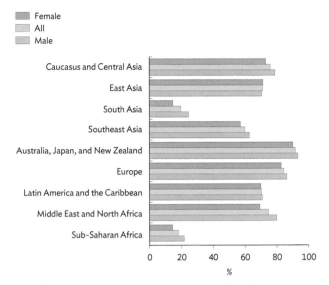

Note: Data on internet use by gender are not available for North America and the Pacific.
Source: International Telecommunications Union. *World Telecommunication/ICT Indicators Database* (accessed 22 October 2021).

Figure 1.3.3 School-age children with internet access at home, by wealth quintile

Poor children are about four times less likely than rich children to have internet access at home.

▨ Poorest 20%
▨ Average
▨ Richest 20%

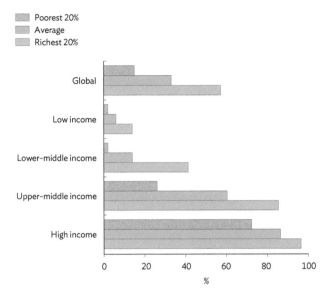

Source: UNICEF and International Telecommunication Union 2020.

Differences by wealth

Access to remote education is one channel through which school closures affect rich and poor students differently. UNICEF and International Telecommunications Union data show internet access at home is about four times higher for school-age children from the richest 20% of households than for children from the poorest 20%. The difference is most pronounced in middle-income economies (Figure 1.3.3).

While internet access at home is not the same as access to distance learning, it is a requirement for access to online learning via computer, tablet, or mobile phone. Lack of access means students need to resort to other modes of remote learning, such as paper-based modules, radio, or television. But under these alternatives, teachers cannot observe students or respond to their questions right away and students cannot immediately respond to teachers' questions or communicate their progress. Data on access to distance learning from the Asian Development Bank Institute's 2020 Households Survey are 70% correlated with internet access at home.

Poor students are also more likely to drop out during the COVID-19 pandemic because they are more sensitive to income shocks and these shocks are bigger than those affecting richer students. This higher sensitivity is accounted for by using data on out-of-school rates for the poorest and richest wealth quintiles and estimating their sensitivity to changes in GDP per capita. In addition, Furceri et al. (2021) showed that in response to previous pandemics, the richest quintile's share of income rises and the poorest quintile's share falls. Thus, poor students are much more likely to drop out in response to school closures not only because they are more sensitive to shocks but also because their shocks are bigger.

Earnings adjustment

Losses in learning can reduce future productivity and hamper the earning potential. Labor market compensation of workers typically rises with years of completed schooling. To measure the reduction in wages associated with foregone learning, economy- and gender-specific data on returns to education are applied to convert learning losses into lifetime earning losses.[8]

---

8   Data on returns to education are based on Psacharopoulos and Patrinos (2018) and Montenegro and Patrinos (2014).

Because labor market return estimates are based on years of schooling completed and not LAYS, returns to LAYS are estimated by calibrating returns to years of schooling. If the return to 1 year of schooling is X%, and it takes Z years of schooling to complete one LAYS, then the returns to one LAYS can be approximated as Z * X%. Z is computed as the ratio of average years of schooling to LAYS in each economy. Earning losses are expressed in terms of constant 2020 US dollars.

Limitations of methodology

A limitation in assessing losses in learning and earnings is that it only accounts for losses in cognitive development. Psychosocial development and the development of soft skills are also acquired in schools, but there is much less evidence on how much the shift to remote education has affected these. In this sense, the full extent of losses is underestimated in this analysis.

The assessment of inequality in losses also has limitations. Rich households can afford better internet connection, which facilitates learning, meaning that inequality in internet access is even higher after adjusting for connection quality. Internet access, however, is an incomplete measure for gauging the efficacy of remote education. Richer households (and in many settings, boys) are more likely to have access to complementary inputs to learning, such as time, space, hardware, and private tutors. Learning efficacy itself (not just access) is likely to vary with gender and household wealth. But both go in the same direction, understating expected losses and expected inequality in losses.

Because data on partial school closures do not give a comprehensive account of the extent and coverage of closures within economies, this analysis treats partial closures uniformly. Each day of a partial school closure in this analysis is assumed to be equivalent to half a day of full closure, based on media reports and government advisories (Australian Government 2020; Inquirer Net 2021; Chopra 2021; Yoon 2020; Dagur 2021). In practice, partial closures can add to the inequality in learning losses as they affect one segment more (or less) than the others. This data limitation may lead to understated estimates of inequality.

A simulation model in Kaffenberger (2021) showed that a short period of school closures can lead to losses that accumulate over time even after schools have reopened. Three months of school closures were found to cause learning losses that accumulate up to 1.5 years of learning 7 years later because children miss out on foundational and essential skills and so they fall "further and further" behind (Kaffenberger 2021). This is another reason why the estimates in this analysis may be understated.

Remedial measures to recover lost learning can attenuate the long-term losses. Economies all over the world have started to undertake or plan strategies to make up for the damage caused by school closures. This analysis so far does not account for the effects of remedial measures, which have the potential to make a huge dent (Kaffenberger 2021). Rather, these estimates of long-term losses highlight the importance of effective action to recover lost learning.

Projecting the long-term effects of school closures comes with inherent limitations in the face of uncertainty and variety across different contexts. Even so, these findings draw attention to the magnitude of learning losses and call for measures to limit them.

Learning losses are substantial and are borne unevenly

Four key findings can be drawn from this analysis:

Foregone learning due to COVID-19 school closures is estimated to have reached on average 0.57 LAYS for developing Asia and 0.52 LAYS for the world. School closures up to October 2021 are estimated to have led to foregone learning equivalent to 7% of the average LAYS before COVID-19's outbreak (Figure 1.3.4). These learning losses are expected to translate into earning losses equivalent to 6% of average pre-pandemic earnings in both developing Asia and the world (Figure 1.3.5). Expected losses in lifetime earnings reached $3.2 trillion in constant 2020 US dollars—equivalent to 13% of developing Asia's GDP in 2020. Technical Appendix 2 gives the expected losses by economy.

Figure 1.3.4 Projected foregone learning by region

A. Developing Asia and subregions

Learning losses are equivalent to 7% of expected liftetime learning for developing Asia …

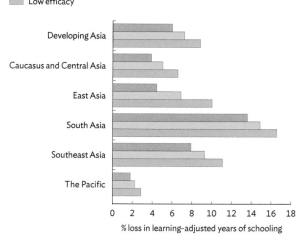

B. World

… and 7% for the world.

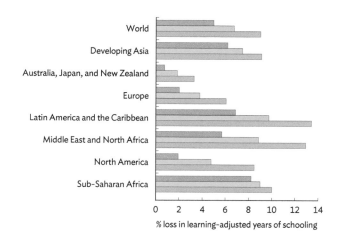

Source: Asian Development Bank estimates.

Figure 1.3.5 Projected earning losses by region

A. Developing Asia and subregions

Expected losses in future earnings are equivalent to 6% of pre-pandemic earnings for developing Asia …

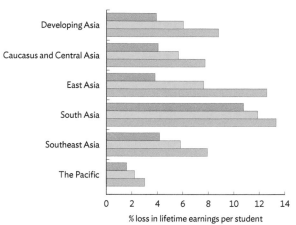

B. World

… and 6% for the world.

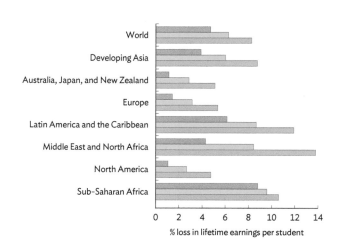

Source: Asian Development Bank estimates.

Expected learning losses are higher in areas where schools have been closed longer. School closures took the biggest toll in South Asia, where they were long and pre-pandemic LAYS were already low. Learning losses are also higher than the world average in Latin America and the Caribbean, the Middle East and North Africa, and Sub-Saharan Africa, but losses in South Asia exceeded losses in those regions (Figure 1.3.4).

In developing Asia, learning losses for the poorest quintile of students are projected to be 33% higher than for the richest quintile of students in their economy. The lower access of poor students to remote education during the pandemic is projected to have widened learning disparities between rich and poor. In developing Asia, students from the poorest quintile are expected to lose 0.65 LAYS, equivalent to an 8.4% decline in average LAYS, while students from the richest quintile within the same economy are expected to lose 0.49 LAYS, equivalent to a 6.3% decline (Figure 1.3.6).

Wealth gaps in foregone learning are higher in economies where schools have been closed for longer. This points to the double burden on poor students in economies with more instruction days closed.

Wealth gaps in foregone learning are expected to translate into wealth gaps in earning losses—the poorest quintile of students is expected to lose 47% more than the richest quintile of students within the same economy in developing Asia (Figure 1.3.7). Globally, the average wealth gap within economies is 39% in foregone learning and 37% in earning losses.

Expected earning losses for girls are projected to be 28% higher than for boys in developing Asia. Because girls and boys have similar access to online learning in many economies, as can be seen in Figure 1.3.2, and dropout contributes a small share of foregone learning, estimated gender gaps in absolute foregone learning are small. On average, girls in developing Asia are expected to lose 0.64 LAYS or 8.3% of the average pre-pandemic LAYS, while boys lose 0.62 LAYS or 8.0% of the average pre-pandemic LAYS (Figure 1.3.8). However, there are some economies, largely in South Asia, where girls' foregone learning is significantly greater than boys' in relative terms because of high preexisting gender inequality in schooling.

Figure 1.3.6 Projected foregone learning for the poorest and richest wealth quintiles by region

A. Developing Asia and subregions

In developing Asia, the poorest students incurred 33% more learning loss than the richest students in their economy ...

B. World

... and for the world at large, that wealth gap within economies is 39%.

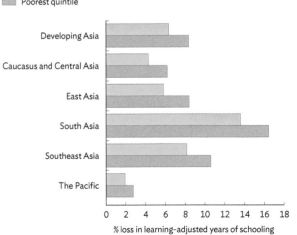

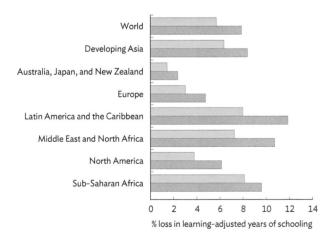

Note: This figure shows estimates in the medium-efficacy scenario of remote education.
Source: Asian Development Bank estimates.

Figure 1.3.7 Projected earning losses for the poorest and richest wealth quintiles by region

A. Developing Asia and subregions

B. World

In developing Asia, expected losses in future earnings are 47% higher for the poorest students than for the richest students in their economy ...

... and for the world at large, that wealth gap within economies is 37%.

Note: This figure shows estimates in the medium-efficacy scenario of remote education.
Source: Asian Development Bank estimates.

Figure 1.3.8 Projected foregone learning for male and female students by region

A. Developing Asia and subregions

B. World

Gender gaps in learning losses are small in much of developing Asia ...

... and in most of the world.

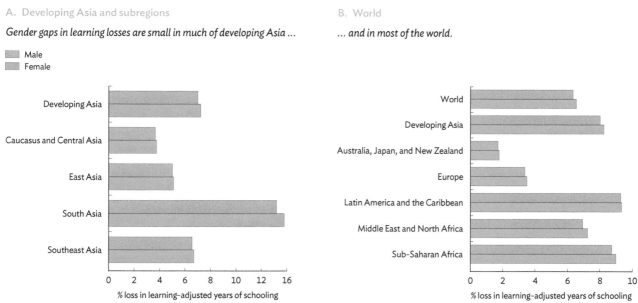

Notes: This figure shows estimates in the medium-efficacy scenario of remote education. Data on internet use by gender are not available for North America and the Pacific.
Source: Asian Development Bank estimates.

Figure 1.3.9 Projected earning losses for male and female students

A. Developing Asia and subregions

B. World

*Expected losses in girls' future earnings are 28% higher
than for boys in developing Asia ...*

... and that gender gap is 24% globally.

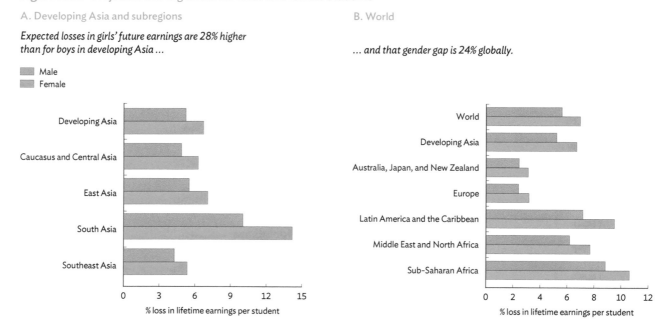

Notes: This figure shows estimates in the medium-efficacy scenario of remote education. Data on internet use by gender are not available for North America and the Pacific.
Source: Asian Development Bank estimates.

Furthermore, since labor markets place a higher premium on the education of girls than that of boys, these small learning gaps are projected to result in substantial earning gaps. The return on educating girls is about 2 percentage points higher than for boys, so that every year of schooling lost entails more foregone income for girls than for boys (Psacharopoulos and Patrinos 2018). Thus, foregone learning translates to expected earning losses for girls that are, on average, 28% higher than for boys in developing Asia (Figure 1.3.9). These projected losses likely understate the true extent to which school closures have exacerbated gender inequality. Internet access is just one input into remote learning processes, and there are complementary inputs that are likely more available to boys, notably, hardware and time. Girls have a higher burden of chores in many developing economies (Boyden, Hardgrove, and Knowles 2012; Webbink, Smits, and De Jong 2012).

As remote education methods improve, aggregate losses due to school closures will be lower, but inequality in losses will grow unless equality of access is promoted. The higher efficacy of remote education lowers average expected losses in learning, but uneven access between rich and poor means that higher efficacy also comes with a wider wealth gap in foregone learning (Table 1.3.1).

Table 1.3.1 Trade-off between remote-learning efficacy and the wealth gap in foregone learning and earning losses

Increasing the effectiveness of remote education reduces aggregate losses, but comes with wider wealth gaps.

Remote learning efficacy	Average loss in learning relative to pre-pandemic levels, %	Wealth gap in learning losses, %	Wealth gap in earning losses, %
Low	9	14	16
Medium	7	33	47
High	6	58	127

Note: Average projections for developing Asia.
Source: Asian Development Bank estimates.

Improving the efficacy of remote learning is critical for mitigating the impact of school closures, but unless there are complementary investments to promote access for poor students, any improvement in remote education technology or pedagogy will drive a bigger wedge between groups within economies.

Taken together, these key findings point to a double burden on girls from poor families. Without making up for losses, school closures will have reduced average LAYS by about 7%, but losses will be suffered unevenly within economies. Girls lose more learning and expected earnings than boys, and the poor lose about 33% more than the rich. Improvements in instruction must be accessible to all, otherwise the gap will grow as poor students gain disproportionately less from technological and pedagogical improvements.

Policies can help abate losses and growing inequalities

The larger projected learning losses shouldered by girls and lower-income students during COVID-19 will exacerbate economic inequalities that were already substantial before the pandemic. To tackle this, policy makers can pursue a range of policies. The following are six priorities.

Ensure the safety of holding classes in school, especially those serving low-income populations. Foregone learning grows with the days of closure because in most settings remote education is an imperfect substitute for classroom learning. Further losses can be prevented if classes are conducted in schools under conditions that are COVID-19 safe. Ensuring the safety of in-person classes involves both community and school actions to achieve herd immunity through the full vaccination of eligible populations and instituting school upgrades conducive to physical distancing. These upgrades include handwashing and sanitation stations, ensuring proper ventilation, expanding space to accommodate students under social distancing guidelines, scheduling mealtimes to avoid crowding, and monitoring symptoms.

Because students of similar socioeconomic backgrounds tend to cluster in schools, those serving students from low-income families can be targeted for further support for instituting upgrades. While these upgrades can be costly, providing financial assistance to schools that need them can go a long way in curbing losses for disadvantaged students.

Support innovative approaches to encourage catch-up learning. This analysis found that sizable learning losses were incurred during COVID-19 school closures and even more so for disadvantaged students. The good news is that foregone learning can be made up. Strategic efforts to recoup these losses are important to help students get back on track. This is an opportunity to rejuvenate education systems in ways that are overdue considering the learning gaps that existed even before the pandemic (Newman, Gentile, and Dela Cruz 2020). Innovative strategies that have proven effective are ripe for implementation. These include tracking students (Duflo, Dupas, and Kremer 2011) and teaching at the right level (Teaching at the Right Level 2022). These low-cost and simple approaches are now more relevant and essential given the lost learning from school closures. Rigorous experimentation is needed because taking small, calculated risks can reveal solutions that when scaled up can pay for themselves many times over from a social perspective (Kremer et al. 2021). When innovation improves learning outcomes, it generates global education public goods because the approaches can be adapted to other settings.

The simulation in Kaffenberger (2021) showed that short-term remedial action can curb long-term losses by half and that long-term remedial measures can fully offset these losses and even lead to better learning outcomes. Short-term remedial action makes up for the period of school closures immediately on reopening then resumes the business-as-usual school curriculum after 1 year. Long-term remedial measures continue perpetually and teach at the individual child's level. Implementation involves formative assessments to identify children's learning levels, training, and empowering teachers to conduct these assessments and adapt their instruction to students' levels and needs, curriculum adjustment to better match the level and pace of children's learning, and ensuring all children master foundational skills.

Even before the pandemic, programs for teaching at the students' level have significantly improved learning outcomes—for example, in India and Kenya.

Invest in bridging the digital divide through connectivity, hardware, and software.
COVID-19 made digital infrastructure essential for work, communication, and education. Disproportionate access exacerbates inequality in opportunities. Disadvantaged groups will have better chances if they have adequate access to digital connectivity, and hardware and software. Funds can be allocated to facilitate access for girls through gender-sensitive digital literacy campaigns and improve internet access for low-income households. Arrangements can be made with internet service providers to make subscription plans more affordable; for example, by offering subsidies for these plans.

Strengthen social safety nets for girls and low-income families to encourage school participation. Because girls and poor students are more likely to drop out of school, school feeding programs and cash transfers for girls and poor families can be strengthened to boost attendance and reenrollment for those who dropped out of school because of COVID-19. Cash transfers explicitly labeled for education have been found to bring huge gains in school participation (Benhassine et al. 2015). Bangladesh's Female Secondary Stipend and Assistance Program, for instance, improved girls' secondary school enrollment and completion rates in the short term and women's employment and marriage outcomes in the long term (Khandker et al. 2021).

Blend some distance learning methods into the regular curriculum. The pandemic brought about innovations in pedagogy and education technology that could be useful once COVID-19 passes. These innovations can be blended into the regular curriculum and make education more effective than before. Teacher training for digital pedagogy can be conducted on a regular basis. Students can be better equipped to optimize the use of distance learning equipment. Stimulating television education programs can be used to complement classroom instruction. Improving the efficacy of distance learning for all students and blending some of its useful methods into regular classes can make education in general more effective.

Build flexibility and emergency resilience into education systems. School disruptions will occur again in response to natural and humanitarian disasters. Now that the technology is in place, the capacity to shift to remote schooling at short notice must be built into education systems and all stakeholders—teachers, parents, students, and administrators—must be ready. This is an unprecedented opportunity to utilize the tools developed and sharpened during the pandemic, conduct simulation exercises in preparation for future disruptions, and build resilience, stress tests, and disaster-preparedness into education systems.

References

Abreh, M. K., et al. 2021. What Happened to Dropout Rates after COVID-19 School Closures in Ghana? Center for Global Development. Blog post. 6 July. Center for Global Development.

Andrabi, T., B. Daniels, and J. Das. 2021. Human Capital Accumulation and Disasters: Evidence from the Pakistan Earthquake of 2005. *Journal of Human Resources*. Online version. 9 June.

Asian Development Bank. 2021. Learning and Earning Losses from COVID-19 School Closures in Developing Asia. Special topic of *Asian Development Outlook 2021*.

Australian Government. 2020. *China's Education Arrangements during COVID-19 Pandemic Period*. 20 May.

Azevedo, J. P., et al. 2021. Simulating the Potential Impacts of COVID-19 School Closures on Schooling and Learning Outcomes: A Set of Global Estimates. *World Bank Research Observer* 36(1).

Azubuike, O. B., O. Adegboye, and H. Quadri. 2021. Who Gets to Learn in a Pandemic? Exploring the Digital Divide in Remote Learning during the COVID-19 Pandemic in Nigeria. *International Journal of Educational Research Open* 2.

Benhassine, N., et al. 2015. Turning a Shove into a Nudge? A "Labeled Cash Transfer" for Education. *American Economic Journal: Economic Policy* 7(3).

Boyden, J., A. Hardgrove, and C. Knowles. 2012. Continuity and Change in Poor Children's Lives: Evidence from Young Lives. In A. Minujin and S. Nandy, eds. *Global Child Poverty and Well-Being: Measurement, Concepts, Policy and Action*. The Policy Press.

Chopra, R. 2021. Explained: What Will Change for Students and Staff When Schools Reopen? *Indian Express*. 4 March.

Dagur, R. 2021. *Indonesia Moves to Reopen Schools amid Covid-19 Risk*. Union of Catholic Asian News. 4 January.

Dessy, S., et al. 2021. *COVID-19 and Children's School Resilience: Evidence from Nigeria*. World Bank.

Duflo, E., P. Dupas, and M. Kremer. 2011. Peer Effects, Teacher Incentives, and the Impact of Tracking: Evidence from a Randomized Evaluation in Kenya. *American Economic Review* 101(5).

Engzell, P., A. Frey, and M. D. Verhagen. 2021. Learning Loss Due to School Closures during the COVID-19 Pandemic. *National Academy of Sciences* 118(17).

Filmer, D., et al. 2020. Learning-Adjusted Years of Schooling (LAYS): Defining a New Macro Measure of Education. *Economics of Education Review* 77.

Furceri, D., et al. 2021. Will COVID-19 Affect Inequality? Evidence from Past Pandemics. *IMF Working Paper* WP/21/127. International Monetary Fund.

Habtewold, T. M. 2021. Impacts of COVID-19 on Food Security, Employment and Education: An Empirical Assessment during the Early Phase of the Pandemic. *Clinical Nutrition Open Science* 38.

Hevia, F. J., et al. 2021. Estimation of the Fundamental Learning Loss and Learning Poverty Related to COVID-19 Pandemic in Mexico. *International Journal of Educational Development* 88.

Ichino, A. and R. Winter-Ebmer. 2004. The Long-Run Educational Cost of World War II. *Journal of Labor Economics* 22(1).

Idara-e-Taleem-o-Aagahi. 2021. *Measuring the Impact of Covid-19 on Education In Pakistan*.

Inquirer Net. 2021. *South Korea to Expand In-Person Classes for Younger Students This Year*.

Kaffenberger, M. 2021. Modelling the Long-Run Learning Impact of the Covid-19 Learning Shock: Actions to (More Than) Mitigate Loss. *International Journal of Educational Development* 81.

Khandker, S. R., et al. 2021. The Female Secondary Stipend and Assistance Program in Bangladesh: What Did It Accomplish?" *ADB South Asia Working Paper Series* No. 81. Asian Development Bank.

Kremer, M., et al. 2021. Is Development Innovation a Good Investment? Which Innovations Scale? Evidence on Social Investing from USAID's Development Innovation Ventures. *Working paper*. University of Chicago.

Maldonado, J. E. and K. De Witte. 2022. The Effect of School Closures on Standardised Student Test Outcomes. *British Educational Research Journal* 48(1).

Mandel, A. and V. Veetil. 2020. The Economic Cost of COVID Lockdowns: An Out-Of-Equilibrium Analysis. *Economics of Disasters and Climate Change* 4(3).

Mbaye, S., et al. 2021. What Happened to Senegalese Students after the COVID-19 School Closure? Center for Global Development.

McKinsey & Company. 2020. *COVID-19 and Student Learning in The United States: The Hurt Could Last a Lifetime*. 1 June.

Montenegro, C. E. and H. A. Patrinos. 2014. Comparable Estimates of Returns to Schooling around the World. *Policy Research Working Paper* No. 7020. World Bank.

Moscoviz, L. and D. K. Evans. 2022. Learning Loss and Student Dropouts during the COVID-19 Pandemic: A Review of the Evidence Two Years after Schools Shut Down. *Working Paper* 609. Center for Global Development.

Newman, K., E. Gentile, and N. A. Dela Cruz. 2020. Education for Innovation: Sorting Fact from Fiction. Background Paper for *Asian Development Outlook 2020* theme chapter. Asian Development Bank.

Paul, J. and F. Jefferson. 2019. A Comparative Analysis of Student Performance in an Online vs. Face-to-Face Environmental Science Course from 2009 to 2016. *Frontiers in Computer Science* (1)7.

Psacharopoulos, G. and H. A. Patrinos. 2018. Returns to Investment in Education: A Decennial Review of the Global Literature. *Education Economics* 26(5).

Pujol, T. 2020. The Long-Term Economic Cost of Covid-19 in the Consensus Forecasts. *Covid Economics* 44.

Schult, J. N., et al. 2021. Did Students Learn Less during the COVID-19 Pandemic? Reading and Mathematics Competencies Before and After the First Pandemic Wave. Preprint.

Spaull, N., et al. 2021. National Income Dynamics Study (NIDS)—Coronavirus Rapid Mobile Survey (CRAM). 13.

Teaching at the Right Level. 2022. Focusing on the Foundations: Education in the Time of COVID-19.

Tomasik, M. J., L. A. Helbling, and U. Moser. 2021. Educational Gains of In-Person vs. Distance Learning in Primary and Secondary Schools: A Natural Experiment during the COVID-19 Pandemic School Closures in Switzerland. *International Journal of Psychology* 56(4).

UNESCO, UNICEF, and World Bank. 2020. *What Have We Learnt? Overview of Findings from a Survey of Ministries of Education on National Responses to COVID-19*.

UNICEF and International Telecommunication Union. 2020. *How Many Children and Young People Have Internet Access at Home? Estimating Digital Connectivity during the COVID-19 Pandemic*.

Uwezo Uganda. 2021. Are Our Children Learning? Illuminating the Covid-19 Learning Losses and Gains in Uganda. Uwezo National Learning Assessment Report, 2021. Kampala: Uwezo Uganda.

Wang, S., et al. 2021. Observing the Silent World under COVID-19 with a Comprehensive Impact Analysis Based on Human Mobility. *Scientific Reports* 11(1).

Webbink, E., J. Smits, and E. De Jong. 2012. Hidden Child Labor: Determinants of Housework and Family Business Work of Children in 16 Developing Countries. *World Development* 40(3).

Yoon, D. 2020. *South Korea's Coronavirus Lesson: School's Out for a While. Wall Street Journal*. 9 September.

Effectiveness of remote education versus classroom learning

Scenarios on the effectiveness of remote education compared with in-person classes build on the scenarios in Learning and Earning Losses from COVID-19 School Closures in Developing Asia, the Special Topic of *Asian Development Outlook 2021*. The table shows the effectiveness assumed in *ADO 2021* under each scenario for high-income economies.

Effectiveness of remote education relative to classroom learning

Efficacy level	Remote learning effectiveness in high-income economies, %
High	88
Medium	66
Low	37

Source: Asian Development Bank. 2021. Learning and Earning Losses from COVID-19 School Closures in Developing Asia. Special Topic of *Asian Development Outlook 2021*.

These scenarios are based on evidence of online-learning efficacy: Paul and Jefferson (2019) for the high-efficacy scenario and McKinsey & Company (2020) for the medium- and low-efficacy scenarios.[1]

The efficacy rate in each scenario is multiplied by the average internet penetration in high-income economies, representing access to remote learning during the period of school closures.

The scenarios for other economies are derived by applying an adjustment factor to Table A1. In this analysis, the adjustment factor applies economy-specific data on internet access. The following adjustment factor applies to economy c:

$$F_c = w \times (IP_c/IP_{HIC}) + (1-w) \times (TVP_k/TVP_{HIC}) \times (TVE_k/OLE_{HIC}),$$

where w is the weight of online learning relative to the television mode of instruction, IP_c is the average internet penetration in economy c, and IP_{HIC} is the average internet penetration in high-income economies. Economy c is classified into income group k, where k is either high, upper-middle, lower-middle, or low income. TVP_k is average television penetration in economy group k, TVP_{HIC} is the average television penetration in high-income economies, TVE_k is the effectiveness of television, and OLE_k the effectiveness of online learning in economy k.

---

[1]   The high-efficacy scenario is an upper-bound estimate for students at the preprimary, primary, and secondary levels covered in this analysis because remote education may be more effective for college students in the sample of Paul and Jefferson (2019).

Technical Appendix 2

Learning and earning losses in developing Asia

Table A2.1 Expected losses in learning-adjusted years of schooling in developing Asia

	Expected LAYS losses			Pre-COVID-19 LAYS	% loss in LAYS		
	High efficacy	Medium efficacy	Low efficacy		High efficacy	Medium efficacy	Low efficacy
Developing Asia	0.48	0.57	0.70	7.72	6.2	7.4	9.1
Caucasus and Central Asia							
Armenia	0.21	0.29	0.40	7.99	2.6	3.6	5.0
Azerbaijan	0.41	0.59	0.83	8.28	5.0	7.1	10.0
Georgia	0.41	0.60	0.84	8.27	5.0	7.3	10.2
Kazakhstan	0.35	0.50	0.70	9.13	3.8	5.5	7.7
Kyrgyz Republic	0.62	0.67	0.74	8.65	7.2	7.7	8.6
Tajikistan	0.00	0.00	0.00	6.79	0.0	0.0	0.0
Turkmenistan	0.34	0.37	0.41	9.13	3.7	4.1	4.5
Uzbekistan	0.18	0.20	0.24	2.23	2.24	2.64	9.13
East Asia							
Hong Kong, China	0.33	0.82	1.44	11.89	2.8	6.9	12.1
Mongolia	1.10	1.19	1.31	9.15	12.0	13.0	14.3
People's Republic of China	0.25	0.37	0.52	9.27	2.7	4.0	5.6
Republic of Korea	0.24	0.59	1.06	11.68	2.1	5.1	9.1
South Asia							
Afghanistan	0.80	0.82	0.85	5.05	15.8	16.2	16.8
Bangladesh	1.20	1.30	1.42	5.99	20.0	21.7	23.7
Bhutan	0.74	0.80	0.87	6.33	11.7	12.6	13.7
India	0.97	1.04	1.14	7.10	13.7	14.6	16.1
Nepal	1.19	1.22	1.27	7.23	16.5	16.9	17.6
Pakistan	0.85	0.92	1.01	5.08	16.7	18.1	19.9
Sri Lanka	0.56	0.81	1.13	8.46	6.6	9.6	13.4
Southeast Asia							
Brunei Darussalam	0.13	0.33	0.59	9.22	1.4	3.6	6.4
Cambodia	1.01	1.09	1.20	6.84	14.8	15.9	17.5
Indonesia	0.75	0.81	0.89	7.83	9.6	10.3	11.4
Lao PDR	0.55	0.59	0.65	6.25	8.8	9.4	10.4
Malaysia	0.87	1.24	1.72	8.89	9.8	13.9	19.3
Myanmar	1.29	1.38	1.51	6.79	19.0	20.3	22.2
Philippines	1.42	1.54	1.68	7.49	19.0	20.6	22.4
Singapore	0.06	0.16	0.29	12.81	0.5	1.2	2.3
Thailand	0.35	0.49	0.68	8.68	4.0	5.6	7.8
Timor-Leste	0.47	0.51	0.56	6.29	7.5	8.1	8.9
Viet Nam	0.57	0.61	0.68	10.68	5.3	5.7	6.4
The Pacific							
Federated States of Micronesia	0.43	0.46	0.51	7.19	6.0	6.4	7.1
Fiji	0.37	0.54	0.75	6.95	5.3	7.8	10.8
Kiribati	0.06	0.07	0.07	7.38	0.8	0.9	0.9
Marshall Islands	0.05	0.06	0.07	5.66	0.9	1.1	1.2
Nauru	0.00	0.00	0.00	6.51	0.0	0.0	0.0
Palau	0.09	0.17	0.27	8.69	1.0	2.0	3.1
Papua New Guinea	0.14	0.15	0.16	6.00	2.3	2.5	2.7
Samoa	0.05	0.07	0.10	7.25	0.7	1.0	1.4
Solomon Islands	0.09	0.10	0.11	4.68	1.9	2.1	2.4
Tonga	0.03	0.04	0.05	7.14	0.4	0.6	0.7
Tuvalu	0.08	0.12	0.17	6.00	1.3	2.0	2.8
Vanuatu	0.06	0.07	0.07	5.62	1.1	1.2	1.2

Lao PDR = Lao People's Democratic Republic, LAYS = learning-adjusted years of schooling.

Source: Asian Development Bank estimates.

Table A2.2 Expected losses in earnings per student in developing Asia

	Expected losses in per capita earnings (constant 2020 $)			Pre-COVID-19 annual earnings (constant 2020 $)	% loss in annual/lifetime earnings per capita		
	High efficacy	Medium efficacy	Low efficacy		High efficacy	Medium efficacy	Low efficacy
Developing Asia	**313**	**483**	**702**	**7,997**	**3.9**	**6.0**	**8.8**
Caucasus and Central Asia							
Armenia	67	95	131	2,863	2.3	3.3	4.6
Azerbaijan	257	371	519	4,605	5.6	8.1	11.3
Georgia	346	500	701	5,580	6.2	9.0	12.6
Kazakhstan	288	417	586	6,613	4.4	6.3	8.9
Kyrgyz Republic	20	21	23	248	8.1	8.5	9.3
Tajikistan	0	0	0	...	0.0	0.0	0.0
Uzbekistan	130	141	156	3,566	3.6	4.0	4.4
East Asia							
Hong Kong, China	891	2,217	3,925	24,870	3.6	8.9	15.8
Mongolia	761	823	904	5,252	14.5	15.7	17.2
People's Republic of China	389	565	795	11,114	3.5	5.1	7.2
Republic of Korea	989	2,482	4,416	38,512	2.6	6.4	11.5
South Asia							
Afghanistan	287	310	340	2,111	13.6	14.7	16.1
Bangladesh	246	265	291	2,596	9.5	10.2	11.2
Bhutan	368	379	394	2,360	15.6	16.1	16.7
India	247	267	292	2,303	10.7	11.6	12.7
Nepal	135	195	273	2,561	5.3	7.6	10.7
Pakistan							
Sri Lanka	345	871	1,557	19,918	1.7	4.4	7.8
Southeast Asia	**76**	**82**	**90**	**3,059**	**2.5**	**2.7**	**2.9**
Brunei Darussalam	256	276	304	1,898	13.5	14.5	16.0
Cambodia	267	289	317	3,797	7.0	7.6	8.3
Indonesia	1,069	1,529	2,121	9,136	11.7	16.7	23.2
Lao PDR	334	360	393	1,779	18.8	20.2	22.1
Malaysia	545	589	645	3,494	15.6	16.9	18.5
Myanmar	232	584	1,048	40,066	0.6	1.5	2.6
Philippines	153	216	297	5,825	2.6	3.7	5.1
Singapore	512	551	602	4,033	12.7	13.7	14.9
Thailand	246	267	294	3,540	6.9	7.5	8.3
Timor-Leste							
Viet Nam	395	570	799	6,828	5.8	8.3	11.7
The Pacific	**0**	**0**	**0**	**...**	**0.0**	**0.0**	**0.0**
Federated States of Micronesia	52	74	103	6,219	0.8	1.2	1.7
Fiji	37	53	73	8,732	0.4	0.6	0.8
Kiribati	76	82	90	6,432	1.2	1.3	1.4
Marshall Islands	0.05	0.06	0.07	5.66	0.9	1.1	1.2
Nauru	0.00	0.00	0.00	6.51	0.0	0.0	0.0
Palau	0.09	0.17	0.27	8.69	1.0	2.0	3.1
Papua New Guinea	0.14	0.15	0.16	6.00	2.3	2.5	2.7
Samoa	0.05	0.07	0.10	7.25	0.7	1.0	1.4
Solomon Islands	0.09	0.10	0.11	4.68	1.9	2.1	2.4
Tonga	0.03	0.04	0.05	7.14	0.4	0.6	0.7
Tuvalu	0.08	0.12	0.17	6.00	1.3	2.0	2.8
Vanuatu	0.06	0.07	0.07	5.62	1.1	1.2	1.2

... = not available, Lao PDR = Lao People's Democratic Republic.

Source: Asian Development Bank estimates.

Table A2.3 Expected losses in learning-adjusted years of schooling, poorest vs. richest wealth quintiles in developing Asia

| | Expected LAYS losses | | | | | | Wealth gap in expected learning losses, % | | |
| | High efficacy | | Medium efficacy | | Low efficacy | | High efficacy | Medium efficacy | Low efficacy |
	Poorest	Richest	Poorest	Richest	Poorest	Richest			
Developing Asia	**0.57**	**0.36**	**0.65**	**0.49**	**0.74**	**0.65**	**58.3**	**32.7**	**13.8**
Caucasus and Central Asia									
Armenia	0.31	0.13	0.37	0.23	0.45	0.37	138.5	60.9	21.6
Azerbaijan	0.62	0.26	0.75	0.48	0.92	0.77	138.5	56.3	19.5
Georgia	0.63	0.26	0.76	0.48	0.93	0.78	142.3	58.3	19.2
Kazakhstan	0.52	0.21	0.63	0.40	0.78	0.65	147.6	57.5	20.0
Kyrgyz Republic	0.68	0.50	0.71	0.58	0.76	0.69	36.0	22.4	10.1
Tajikistan	0.00	0.00	0.00	0.00	0.00	0.00	0.0	0.0	0.0
Uzbekistan	0.37	0.28	0.39	0.32	0.42	0.38	32.1	21.9	10.5
East Asia									
Hong Kong, China	0.65	0.10	1.05	0.65	1.57	1.35	550.0	61.5	16.3
Mongolia	1.19	0.89	1.26	1.03	1.35	1.22	33.7	22.3	10.7
People's Republic of China	0.38	0.16	0.46	0.30	0.57	0.48	137.5	53.3	18.8
Republic of Korea	0.47	0.07	0.77	0.47	1.15	0.99	571.4	63.8	16.2
South Asia									
Afghanistan	0.87	0.75	0.89	0.78	0.91	0.82	16.0	14.1	11.0
Bangladesh	1.30	0.98	1.37	1.13	1.46	1.33	32.7	21.2	9.8
Bhutan	0.80	0.60	0.84	0.69	0.90	0.82	33.3	21.7	9.8
India	1.05	0.79	1.11	0.91	1.18	1.07	32.9	22.0	10.3
Nepal	1.22	1.13	1.25	1.18	1.28	1.25	8.0	5.9	2.4
Pakistan	0.93	0.69	0.98	0.80	1.04	0.94	34.8	22.5	10.6
Sri Lanka	0.84	0.35	1.02	0.65	1.24	1.04	140.0	56.9	19.2
Southeast Asia									
Brunei Darussalam	0.26	0.04	0.43	0.26	0.64	0.55	550.0	65.4	16.4
Cambodia	1.10	0.82	1.16	0.95	1.24	1.12	34.1	22.1	10.7
Indonesia	0.81	0.61	0.86	0.70	0.92	0.83	32.8	22.9	10.8
Lao PDR	0.59	0.44	0.63	0.51	0.67	0.61	34.1	23.5	9.8
Malaysia	1.29	0.55	1.55	1.01	1.89	1.59	134.5	53.5	18.9
Myanmar	1.39	1.05	1.47	1.21	1.56	1.42	32.4	21.5	9.9
Philippines	1.54	1.16	1.63	1.34	1.73	1.58	32.8	21.6	9.5
Singapore	0.13	0.02	0.21	0.13	0.31	0.27	550.0	61.5	14.8
Thailand	0.52	0.23	0.63	0.40	0.76	0.63	126.1	57.5	20.6
Timor-Leste	0.52	0.39	0.55	0.44	0.58	0.52	33.3	25.0	11.5
Viet Nam	0.61	0.46	0.65	0.53	0.70	0.63	32.6	22.6	11.1
The Pacific									
Federated States of Micronesia	0.47	0.35	0.49	0.40	0.53	0.47	34.3	22.5	12.8
Fiji	0.56	0.23	0.68	0.43	0.83	0.69	143.5	58.1	20.3
Kiribati	0.07	0.05	0.07	0.06	0.08	0.07	40.0	16.7	14.3
Marshall Islands	0.07	0.04	0.08	0.05	0.08	0.06	75.0	60.0	33.3
Nauru	0.00	0.00	0.00	0.00	0.00	0.00	0.0	0.0	0.0
Palau	0.16	0.05	0.23	0.13	0.31	0.25	220.0	76.9	24.0
Papua New Guinea	0.16	0.11	0.17	0.13	0.18	0.15	45.5	30.8	20.0
Samoa	0.08	0.03	0.09	0.06	0.11	0.09	166.7	50.0	22.2
Solomon Islands	0.10	0.08	0.11	0.09	0.12	0.10	25.0	22.2	20.0
Tonga	0.04	0.02	0.05	0.03	0.06	0.05	100.0	66.7	20.0
Tuvalu	0.12	0.05	0.15	0.10	0.18	0.15	140.0	50.0	20.0
Vanuatu	0.07	0.05	0.07	0.06	0.08	0.07	40.0	16.7	14.3

Lao PDR = Lao People's Democratic Republic, LAYS = learning-adjusted years of schooling.

Note: The wealth gap in expected learning losses is calculated as the difference in LAYS lost by the poorest and richest quintiles, expressed as a percentage of the richest quintile's lost LAYS.

Source: Asian Development Bank estimates.

Table A2.4 Expected losses in earnings, poorest vs. richest wealth quintiles in developing Asia

| | Expected losses in per capita earnings (constant 2020 $) | | | | | | Wealth gap in expected earning losses, % | | |
| | High efficacy | | Medium efficacy | | Low efficacy | | High efficacy | Medium efficacy | Low efficacy |
	Poorest	Richest	Poorest	Richest	Poorest	Richest			
Developing Asia	450	198	584	397	759	655	127.3	47.1	15.9
Caucasus and Central Asia									
Armenia	101	43	121	77	147	121	134.9	57.1	21.5
Azerbaijan	389	160	469	299	575	479	143.1	56.9	20.0
Georgia	521	215	630	403	773	647	142.3	56.3	19.5
Kazakhstan	435	179	527	336	647	541	143.0	56.8	19.6
Kyrgyz Republic	21	16	22	18	24	22	31.3	22.2	9.1
Tajikistan	0	0	0	0	0	0	0.0	0.0	0.0
Uzbekistan	142	105	150	123	161	145	35.2	22.0	11.0
East Asia									
Hong Kong, China	1,765	262	2,861	1,756	4,279	3,674	573.7	62.9	16.5
Mongolia	826	617	871	716	932	845	33.9	21.6	10.3
People's Republic of China	588	242	714	455	878	735	143.0	56.9	19.5
Republic of Korea	1,964	287	3,203	1,964	4,812	4,133	584.3	63.1	16.4
South Asia									
Bangladesh	310	234	327	270	349	318	32.5	21.1	9.7
India	267	201	281	232	300	272	32.8	21.1	10.3
Nepal	377	351	386	367	398	387	7.4	5.2	2.8
Pakistan	268	201	283	232	302	273	33.3	22.0	10.6
Sri Lanka	203	85	245	158	300	252	138.8	55.1	19.0
Southeast Asia									
Brunei Darussalam	688	100	1,126	689	1,698	1,457	588.0	63.4	16.5
Cambodia	83	62	87	72	93	84	33.9	20.8	10.7
Indonesia	278	207	293	240	314	284	34.3	22.1	10.6
Lao PDR	290	217	306	251	327	296	33.6	21.9	10.5
Malaysia	1,595	677	1,917	1,240	2,335	1,964	135.6	54.6	18.9
Myanmar	362	274	381	315	406	368	32.1	21.0	10.3
Philippines	591	443	623	513	664	603	33.4	21.4	10.1
Singapore	462	67	756	461	1,144	979	589.6	64.0	16.9
Thailand	229	99	273	175	331	274	131.3	56.0	20.8
Timor-Leste	564	418	593	480	630	560	34.9	23.5	12.5
Viet Nam	268	199	283	232	303	275	34.7	22.0	10.2
The Pacific									
Fiji	595	246	719	460	881	738	141.9	56.3	19.4
Nauru	0	0	0	0	0	0	0.0	0.0	0.0
Samoa	79	33	94	60	115	95	139.4	56.7	21.1
Tonga	55	25	66	43	81	68	120.0	53.5	19.1
Vanuatu	87	62	91	71	97	83	40.3	28.2	16.9

Lao PDR = Lao People's Democratic Republic.

Note: The wealth gap in expected earning losses is calculated as the difference in expected earning losses of the poorest and richest quintiles, expressed as a percentage of the richest quintile's expected earning losses.

Source: Asian Development Bank estimates.

Table A2.5 Expected losses in learning-adjusted years of schooling, male versus female students in developing Asia

| | Expected LAYS losses | | | | | | Gender gap in expected learning losses, % | | |
| | High efficacy | | Medium efficacy | | Low efficacy | | High efficacy | Medium efficacy | Low efficacy |
	Male	Female	Male	Female	Male	Female			
Developing Asia	**0.46**	**0.48**	**0.62**	**0.64**	**0.82**	**0.83**	**4.3**	**3.2**	**1.2**
Caucasus and Central Asia									
Armenia	0.19	0.19	0.28	0.28	0.39	0.39	0.0	0.0	0.0
Azerbaijan	0.26	0.30	0.48	0.51	0.77	0.79	15.4	6.3	2.6
Georgia	0.33	0.34	0.54	0.54	0.81	0.81	3.0	0.0	0.0
Kazakhstan	0.20	0.22	0.40	0.40	0.65	0.65	10.0	0.0	0.0
Kyrgyz Republic	0.35	0.36	0.47	0.48	0.63	0.63	2.9	2.1	0.0
Tajikistan	0.00	0.00	0.00	0.00	0.00	0.00	0.0	0.0	0.0
Uzbekistan	0.19	0.21	0.26	0.28	0.35	0.36	10.5	7.7	2.9
East Asia									
Hong Kong, China	0.15	0.21	0.68	0.73	1.37	1.39	40.0	7.4	1.5
Mongolia	0.74	0.71	0.92	0.90	1.16	1.15	−4.1	−2.2	−0.9
People's Republic of China	0.22	0.21	0.34	0.34	0.50	0.50	−4.5	0.0	0.0
Republic of Korea	0.05	0.07	0.45	0.47	0.98	0.99	40.0	4.4	1.0
South Asia									
Afghanistan	0.73	0.78	0.77	0.80	0.82	0.84	6.8	3.9	2.4
Bangladesh	1.13	1.20	1.24	1.30	1.39	1.42	6.2	4.8	2.2
Bhutan	0.69	0.74	0.76	0.80	0.86	0.88	7.2	5.3	2.3
India	0.89	0.96	0.99	1.04	1.11	1.14	7.9	5.1	2.7
Nepal	1.07	1.13	1.14	1.18	1.22	1.25	5.6	3.5	2.5
Pakistan	0.81	0.86	0.89	0.93	0.99	1.01	6.2	4.5	2.0
Sri Lanka	0.86	0.94	1.03	1.09	1.25	1.28	9.3	5.8	2.4
Southeast Asia									
Brunei Darussalam	0.08	0.00	0.29	0.23	0.57	0.54	−100.0	−20.7	−5.3
Cambodia	0.55	0.55	0.75	0.75	1.01	1.01	0.0	0.0	0.0
Indonesia	0.52	0.56	0.64	0.67	0.80	0.81	7.7	4.7	1.3
Lao PDR	0.32	0.33	0.43	0.43	0.56	0.56	3.1	0.0	0.0
Malaysia	0.47	0.52	0.95	0.98	1.56	1.58	10.6	3.2	1.3
Myanmar	1.16	1.24	1.29	1.35	1.46	1.50	6.9	4.7	2.7
Philippines	0.85	0.87	1.11	1.13	1.45	1.46	2.4	1.8	0.7
Singapore	0.11	0.11	0.20	0.19	0.31	0.30	0.0	−5.0	−3.2
Thailand	0.26	0.27	0.43	0.44	0.64	0.65	3.8	2.3	1.6
Timor-Leste	0.29	0.30	0.38	0.38	0.48	0.49	3.4	0.0	2.1
Viet Nam	0.32	0.35	0.43	0.45	0.57	0.59	9.4	4.7	3.5

Lao PDR = Lao People's Democratic Republic, LAYS = learning-adjusted years of schooling.

Notes: Data on internet use by gender is not available for the Pacific. The gender gap in expected learning losses is calculated as the difference in LAYS lost by female and male students, expressed as a percentage of male students' lost LAYS.

Source: Asian Development Bank estimates.

Table A2.6 Expected losses in earnings, male versus female students in developing Asia

| | Expected losses in per capita earnings (constant 2020 $) | | | | | | Gender gap in expected earning losses, % | | |
| | High efficacy | | Medium efficacy | | Low efficacy | | High efficacy | Medium efficacy | Low efficacy |
	Male	Female	Male	Female	Male	Female			
Developing Asia	**211**	**282**	**418**	**537**	**685**	**867**	**33.4**	**28.4**	**26.4**
Caucasus and Central Asia									
Armenia	54	68	80	102	113	145	26.3	27.3	27.9
Azerbaijan	146	209	268	355	428	546	43.4	32.4	27.6
Georgia	248	314	402	502	602	746	26.7	24.9	23.9
Kazakhstan	150	201	290	377	474	606	34.3	29.9	28.0
Kyrgyz Republic	10	13	13	17	17	22	32.4	29.9	27.9
Uzbekistan	64	92	87	118	116	152	42.9	36.3	31.6
East Asia									
Hong Kong, China	366	618	1,669	2,181	3,344	4,189	69.0	30.6	25.3
Mongolia	455	548	567	692	714	881	20.5	22.1	23.5
People's Republic of China	298	361	468	572	692	848	21.3	22.1	22.6
Republic of Korea	174	341	1,693	2,192	3,657	4,585	96.0	29.4	25.4
South Asia									
Bangladesh	229	330	252	356	282	391	44.5	41.5	38.3
India	191	284	212	307	238	337	48.5	45.1	41.6
Nepal	289	397	307	414	330	437	37.4	35.1	32.5
Pakistan	200	286	220	308	245	336	42.6	40.0	37.2
Southeast Asia									
Brunei Darussalam	181	5	683	685	1,337	1,570	−97.2	0.4	17.4
Cambodia	18	65	25	88	33	119	257.0	257.0	256.9
Indonesia	163	206	200	247	248	301	26.6	23.7	21.3
Lao PDR	137	184	180	239	236	310	34.2	32.6	31.4
Malaysia	518	703	1,047	1,338	1,725	2,152	35.7	27.8	24.7
Myanmar	272	356	302	387	342	428	30.9	28.2	25.3
Philippines	274	387	359	501	468	648	41.2	39.6	38.3
Singapore	363	430	633	782	989	1,244	18.5	23.4	25.8
Thailand	91	142	149	227	226	339	56.1	52.2	50.2
Timor-Leste	299	350	381	441	488	560	17.2	15.8	14.7
Viet Nam	127	168	170	216	226	280	32.3	27.6	24.2

Lao PDR = Lao People's Democratic Republic.

Notes: Data on internet use by gender is not available for the Pacific. The gender gap in expected earning losses is calculated as the difference in expected earning losses of female and male students, expressed as a percentage of male students' expected earning losses.

Source: Asian Development Bank estimates.

Global growth to moderate amid threats to recovery

Growth in the major advanced economies of the United States, the euro area, and Japan is expected to moderate in 2022 and 2023. COVID-19 containment restrictions are expected to ease further now that the outbreak of the Omicron variant has peaked. But the Russian invasion of Ukraine will push oil prices and inflation up, and rising interest rates will drag on growth. In aggregate, the major advanced economies are expected to grow by 3.5% in 2022 and 2.4% in 2023 (Table A.1).

Table A.1 Baseline assumptions on the international economy

	2020	2021	2022	2023
	Actual		*ADO 2022 Forecast*	
GDP growth, %				
Major industrial economies[a]	−4.7	5.0	3.5	2.4
United States	−3.4	5.7	3.9	2.3
Euro area	−6.5	5.3	3.3	2.6
Japan	−4.5	1.7	2.7	1.8
Prices and inflation				
Brent crude spot prices, average, $/barrel	42.35	70.44	107.00	93.00
Consumer price index inflation, major industrial economies' average, %	0.7	3.3	4.8	2.1
Interest rates				
United States federal funds rate, average, %	0.4	0.1	0.5	1.3
European Central Bank refinancing rate, average, %	0.0	0.0	0.0	0.5
Bank of Japan overnight call rate, average, %	0.0	0.0	0.0	0.0
$ Libor,[b] %	0.5	0.1	0.5	1.3

ADO = *Asian Development Outlook*, GDP = gross domestic product.

[a] Average growth rates are weighted by GDP purchasing power parity.

[b] Average London Interbank Offered Rate quotations on 1–month loans.

Note: The baseline assumptions are as of 9 March 2022 .

Sources: Bloomberg; CEIC Data Company; Haver Analytics; International Monetary Fund. World Economic Outlook (all accessed 10 March 2022); Asian Development Bank estimates.

This annex was written by Jules Hugot, Matteo Lanzafame, Nedelyn Magtibay-Ramos, Yuho Myoda, Pilipinas Quising, Irfan Qureshi, Arief Ramayandi, Marcel Schroder, and Dennis Sorino of the Economic Research and Regional Cooperation Department, ADB, Manila, and Michael Timbang and Jesson Pagaduan, consultants, Economic Research and Regional Cooperation Department, ADB, Manila.

Recent developments in the major advanced economies

United States

The US economy recovered strongly in 2021 despite the disruption from the highly infectious Delta COVID-19 variant in the third quarter (Q3). Gross domestic product (GDP) expanded by 5.7% as growth rebounded to a quarter-on-quarter seasonally adjusted annualized rate (saar) of 6.9% in Q4 after a weak 2.3% in Q3 (Figure A.1). The recovery was driven mainly by strong domestic demand marked by consumption growing 7.9% and investment by 9.5%. Consumption growth was particularly strong in the first half, but dampened by COVID-19's resurgence in the second half, when investment accelerated on jumps in inventories due to large restocking in retail and wholesale trade industries. Government spending growth, at 0.5%, was muted last year, and the trade sector contributed negatively, as imports grew much faster than exports.

Figure A.1 Demand-side contributions to growth, United States

Weaker consumption in H2 2021 was compensated by stronger investment.

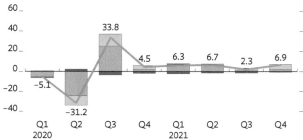

H = half, Q = quarter, qoq = quarter on quarter.
Sources: Department of Commerce. Bureau of Economic Analysis; Haver Analytics (both accessed 9 March 2022).

The outbreak of the Omicron COVID-19 variant has not significantly dented economic activity. Despite a slight decline, data suggest that consumer confidence, the purchasing managers' index (PMI), and employment remained strong when Omicron cases peaked this January, with the trend continuing into February (Figure A.2). Nonfarm employment rose by 678,000 in January, keeping the unemployment rate at 3.8%, and weekly earnings grew by 5.4% year on year. Retail sales grew by 4.4% month on month in January after falling by 2.8% in December. Industrial production expanded by 1.5% after a slight decline in December. The effects of Omicron outbreaks on economic activity are likely to be shallow and short-lived as they have not led to a large pullback in services and cases fell as quickly as they rose.

Figure A.2 Business activity, United States

Still vulnerable to COVID-19.

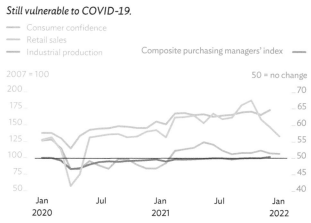

COVID-19 = Coronavirus Disease 2019.
Note: A purchasing manager's index reading < 50 signals deterioration, >50 improvement.
Source: Haver Analytics (accessed 9 March 2022).

Labor shortages, supply disruptions, and strong demand has made inflation a big concern. Headline inflation reached a 40-year high of 7.5% in January 2022 and core inflation hit 6.0%. A sharp increase in transport costs (new and used vehicles and gas prices) resulting from supply disruptions and higher energy prices was the main inflation driver early in 2021 (Figure A.3). By late 2021, it was clear that inflationary pressures were broad-based, as stronger demand was pushing up costs across a wide range of categories.

The US economy is forecast to expand by 3.9% in 2022 and 2.3% in 2023, as growth gradually returns to more normal levels. The output gap is expected to close this year. Consumption will again be the main driver of growth. Investment growth will slow somewhat in 2022 as high inventories are wound down,

Figure A.3 Inflation, United States

Transport and housing drove high inflation.

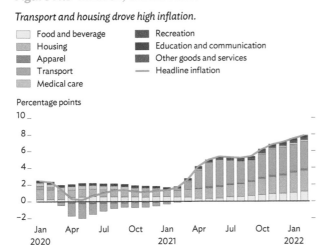

Source: CEIC Data Company (accessed 9 March 2022).

but will pick up in 2023. Exports in the forecast horizon are expected to strengthen on the global economic recovery, but this will still be outpaced by import growth.

The inflation rate is forecast to remain high at 5.6% on average in 2022 before softening to 2.5% in 2023. High inflation will ease somewhat in April as transport inflation subsides, but lingering pressures from stronger domestic demand and the closing output gap will challenge monetary policy. The baseline forecast at this report's 9 March cutoff date assumes the US Federal Reserve will end asset purchases in March and raise the policy rate steadily this year, and that it will likely start gradual quantitative tightening, which will help soften inflationary pressures.

Risks to the forecast are tilted to the downside. These are mainly associated with how inflation progresses and the Federal Reserve's response to inflation. The recovery could slow or even be derailed if persistent inflationary pressures push the Fed to more aggressive tightening. Indeed, on 16 March, the Fed indicated it would pursue a more aggressive pace of rate increases than assumed in the baseline, which will likely lower inflation but also lower growth, with implications for developing Asia (Box 1.1.3). Other risks include renewed COVID-19 outbreaks from more deadly variants and a surge in energy prices—possibly resulting from Russian invasion of Ukraine—that could further stoke inflation and depress consumer confidence.

Euro area

The euro area had record-high growth of 5.3% in 2021, despite a slowdown in Q4. Economic activity rebounded strongly last year, supported by high COVID-19 vaccination rates. But growth weakened to 1.0% saar (4.6% year on year) in Q4 as surging new cases, driven by the Omicron variant, led to the reimposition of tighter containment measures in many countries (Figure A.4). Mobility restrictions weighed on services and caused labor shortages, and both domestic and external demand softened. Soaring inflation and lingering supply bottlenecks contributed to the weak Q4 performance, felt to varying degrees across all major economies in the euro area. Germany's GDP declined by 1.4% saar (1.8% year on year). Growth dropped from double-digit rates in Q3 in France to 2.9% saar (5.4% year on year) and to 2.3% saar (6.2% year on year) in Italy, and to 8.3% (5.2% year on year) from 10.9% saar in Spain.

Figure A.4 Demand-side contributions to growth, euro area

Growth slowed in Q4 on COVID-19's Omicron wave.

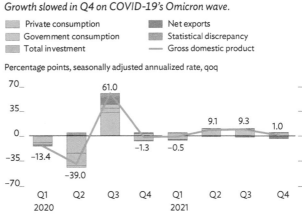

COVID-19 = Coronavirus Disease 2019, Q= quarter, qoq = quarter on quarter.
Source: Haver Analytics (accessed 9 March 2022).

Leading indicators suggest the euro area's recovery continued in early 2022, before the Russian invasion of Ukraine. After softening in January, economic activity picked up in February amid receding Omicron waves. The economic sentiment indicator inched up to 114.0 from 112.7 in January on improving confidence in services, retail trade, and construction (Figure A.5). The composite PMI increased to 55.5 in February from an 11-month low of 52.3 in January, led by significant improvement in services. Because of relaxed COVID-19 restrictions in the euro area, the services PMI rebounded to 55.5 in February, the strongest expansion in 3 months due to faster increases in new orders and employment. The manufacturing PMI fell to 58.2 in February from 58.7 in January; the slight fall was on delays in supply delivery. Nevertheless, new orders and employment growth in manufacturing remained stable and robust in that month.

Figure A.5 Economic sentiment and purchasing managers' indexes, euro area

Economic activity picked up in February 2021 after a weak January.

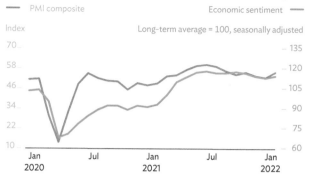

PMI = purchasing managers' index.
Source: CEIC Data Company; Haver Analytics (both accessed 9 March 2022).

Growth in the euro area is projected to moderate to 3.3% in 2022 and decelerate to 2.6% in 2023. The outlook hinges on the Russian invasion of Ukraine and is, thus, subject to a significant degree of uncertainty. Sanctions imposed on the Russian Federation are anticipated to remain in place over the forecast horizon, but energy trade with the euro area is seen continuing, albeit to an increasingly smaller extent. With soaring energy prices squeezing real incomes and high uncertainty depressing consumer confidence, domestic demand will face headwinds in the near term. Export growth will also weaken, with trade constrained by sanctions—particularly the exclusion of some Russian banks from SWIFT—and the Russian economy suffering a deep recession. Based on this, the impact of the war on the euro area economy is anticipated to be significant in the first half, but it should start waning later. The pace of growth is expected to pick from Q3, supported by still accommodative—albeit tightening—fiscal and monetary policies. Private

consumption will be the main driver of growth, spurred by rising real disposable incomes, the spending of accumulated savings, and a robust labor market marked by unemployment returning to pre-pandemic levels. Investment will also pick up, supported by national recovery plans and the European Union's recovery package. Exports are expected to gradually normalize, with the impact of the war and global supply disruptions increasingly dissipating from Q3 and fully unwinding in 2023.

Soaring energy prices stoked inflationary pressures in the euro area, lifting consumer price inflation to 2.6% in 2021. The headline inflation rate rose to 5.8% in February 2022, the highest since records began in January 1997 and well above the revised symmetric 2.0% medium-term target of the European Central Bank (ECB) (Figure A.6). The ECB is set to tighten its accommodative policy stance. On 10 March it announced that it would accelerate the tapering of net asset purchases decided last December, which is now anticipated to end in Q3. This will pave the way for a rate hike in the latter part of this year. With energy and commodity prices remaining elevated due to the Russian invasion of Ukraine, inflation will spike further in the short-term before moderating on waning base effects. The inflation rate is forecast at 4.8% for 2022 and 2.0% in 2023.

The main risks to the outlook stem from the Russian invasion of Ukraine. A prolonged war, as well as escalating sanctions from the European Union against Russia and retaliatory measures, could lead to a severe and persistent disruption of natural gas supplies

Figure A.6 Headline and core inflation, euro area

Headline inflation rose to a record high in February 2022.

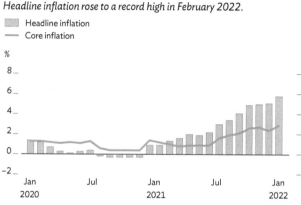

Source: Haver Analytics (accessed 9 March 2022).

to the euro area. Spillovers from the war on global energy prices and continuing supply bottlenecks could further fuel inflationary pressures, triggering more aggressive policy tightening by the ECB. This could slow the recovery and potentially reignite sovereign debt tensions in the euro area. Negative COVID-19 developments—particularly the emergence of vaccine-resistant and more deadly virus variants—remain a significant threat.

Japan

The economy recovered strongly on 4.6 % growth quarter-on-quarter saar in Q4 2021, buoyed by private consumption growth. After nationwide COVID-19 restrictions were lifted at the end of September, demand for contact-intensive services, including transport, restaurants, and accommodation recovered and private consumption reached the highest level since the start of the pandemic (Figure A.7). Exports bottomed out as automobile-related goods started recovering as supply chain disruptions, caused by the COVID-19 outbreak, abated in Southeast Asian countries. Despite a robust Q4, 2021's recovery overall was rather feeble due to repeated COVID-19 surges and renewed government mobility restrictions. The economy grew by 1.6% in 2021 after contracting 4.5% in the previous year, leaving real GDP last year almost 3% lower than in 2019. The consumer price index

(CPI), excluding fresh food, rose by 0.8% year on year in December, mainly on higher energy prices; core CPI, excluding fresh food and energy, remained below 2020's level, reflecting the negative effect of last April's reduction in mobile phone charges.

A surge in new COVID-19 cases and renewed mobility restrictions starting from January dampened economic recovery in Q1. Despite reportedly weaker toxicity, the soaring number of new cases from this highly infectious variant led to a record number of deaths and hospitalizations in Japan from January to March. Extensive new restrictions were imposed, partly because only a small share of the population had received a booster shot when Omicron emerged (less than 5% at the end of January). Operating-hour restrictions, combined with declining consumer confidence, will stall the recovery in services consumption in Q1 (Figure A.8). Exports will continue to pick up, but growth will be modest because tight global chip supply will hinder vehicle manufacturers from entirely making up production lost in the preceding quarter.

Figure A.8 Services indicators, Japan

Services leading indicators showed signs of slowing in January 2021.

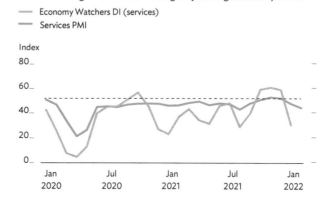

DI = diffusion index, PMI = purchasing managers' index.
Source: CEIC Data Company (accessed 9 March 2022).

Figure A.7 Demand-side contributions to growth, Japan

A strong rebound in private consumption led the recovery in Q4 2021.

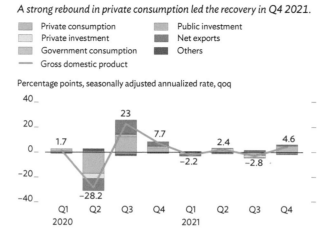

Q = quarter, qoq = quarter on quarter, saar = seasonally adjusted annualized rate.
Source: Cabinet Office (accessed 9 March 2022).

The economy is forecast to grow by 2.7% in 2022 and 1.8% in 2023. The recovery trajectory largely depends on private consumption and nonresidential investment. As the Omicron COVID-19 wave eases and mobility restrictions are lifted, private consumption will recover to its 2019 level by the end of this year, partially supported by the release of excess household savings accumulated during the pandemic. With both domestic and foreign demand recovering, private investment will pick up in the second half of 2022. In 2023, growth will moderate, as recovering domestic demand pushes up imports and net exports become balanced, and public demand gradually becomes neutral toward the end of the year.

The inflation rate is forecast at 1.3% in 2022 and 0.5% in 2023. Rising oil and energy prices, and higher commodity prices, will partially pass through to consumer prices in 2022 (Figure A.9). Once the negative effect of the mobile phone charge reduction dissipates in Q2, core CPI will likely turn positive. And as inflationary pressure from energy prices abates in 2023, core inflation will further increase on the output gap closing next year. Despite these expected developments, the Bank of Japan will likely maintain its monetary policy throughout the forecast period as inflation is not likely to exceed its target of 2% in a sustained way.

Figure A.9 Inflation by component, Japan

Transitory effect of mobile phone charge reduction masks inflation from high energy prices.

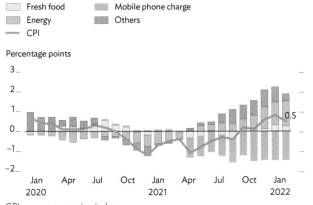

CPI = consumer price index.
Source: CEIC Data Company (accessed 9 March 2022).

Risks are tilted to the downside. The Russian invasion of Ukraine inflates the risk of further and prolonged increases in imports and energy prices, which may accelerate inflation beyond the Bank of Japan's target before the economy fully recovers. With stagnant wage growth, import-led inflation may hurt household purchasing power and delay the recovery of private consumption. The war may also slow global demand further and cause further global supply-

chain disruptions, which may slow the recovery of exports from automakers. The possible emergence of more deadly COVID-19 variants remains a risk to the economy because of the government's preference for a quasi-zero COVID-19 policy. Further delays in the normalization of border controls could lead to labor shortages in manufacturing, among other industrial sectors.

Recent developments and outlook in nearby economies

Russian Federation

Russia is facing a financial crisis following its invasion of Ukraine. International sanctions include export bans for specific technologies and freezing of overseas assets of certain individuals, companies, and commercial banks, as well as those of the central bank. Key Russian banks were disconnected from the interbank messaging service of the Society of Worldwide Interbank Financial Telecommunication (SWIFT). The US banned imports of Russian fossil fuels, and the United Kingdom declared an embargo on Russian oil that will come into effect at the end of the year. The European Union has not imposed an embargo, but it has announced deep cuts in its oil imports from Russia, which account for 52% of Russian oil sales and about 10% of GDP. These sanctions are compounded by self-sanctioning from international companies pulling out of Russia, including manufacturers, retailers, and service providers such as insurers and shippers. As a result of all this, the Russian stock market collapsed (Figure A.10) and the ruble plunged (Figure A.11). One of this report's Special Topics examines further the impact of the Russian invasion of Ukraine.

Fast-rising inflation and capital outflows pushed the Central Bank of the Russian Federation to hike its key interest rate. Inflation was already at 9.2% in February—its highest level since 2015 and far above the central bank's 4.0% target (Figure A.12). With price pressures escalating further due to currency depreciation and the unavailability of imported goods, and in an effort to curtail capital outflows, the central bank more than doubled the policy rate to 20% on 28 February.

Figure A.10 MSCI Russia stock market index

The stock market plunged by 86% from 3 January to 9 March 2022.

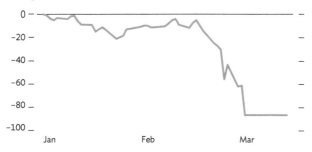

% change from 3 Jan 2022

Source: Investing.com (accessed 9 March).

Figure A.11 Euro per ruble

The ruble lost 43% against the euro from 1 January to 9 March 2022.

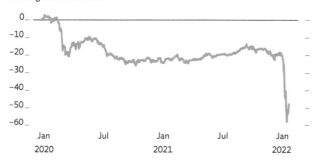

% change from 1 Jan 2020

Source: CEIC Data Company (accessed 9 March 2022).

Figure A.12 Inflation and policy rate, Russian Federation

Sharply rising inflation and capital outflows triggered drastic policy rate hike.

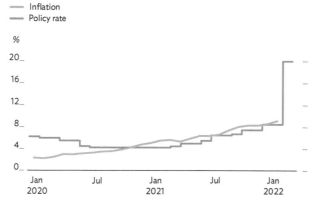

— Inflation
— Policy rate

Source: Haver Analytics (accessed 10 March 2022).

The growth outlook deteriorated dramatically due to deep financial and macroeconomic stability concerns. The outlook is highly uncertain because of the war. The international sanctions will drive foreign capital out from Russia, and soaring inflation and a credit crunch caused by the drastic interest rate hike will severely depress domestic demand. Supply-chain disruptions, cascading defaults, and escalating political and economic isolation further dampen the outlook. Available growth forecasts as of mid-March reported by Consensus Economics for 2022 vary widely, but they are generally strongly negative. ING Bank expects a 7% contraction; Barclays forecasts a 12% decline. For 2023, expectations vary from a 0% (UniCredit) to a 4% decline (Barclays).

Australia

The economy rebounded in Q4 on eased containment measures; the labor market remains resilient. After growth contracted in Q3, GDP in the following quarter expanded by 14.4% saar on surging household spending that increased consumption by 18.7% (Figure A.13). A signal of robust consumption was a 5.3% increase in seasonally adjusted retail sales. The manufacturing index moved above the 50-threshold indicating expansion, rising to 53.2 in February from 48.4 in January. The labor market continued to improve. In December, the unemployment rate dropped to 4.2%, the lowest in 13 years and stayed at that level in January. Inflation accelerated from 0.9% in 2020 to 2.9% in 2021, the highest rate in 10 years, but still within the central bank's 2%–3% target range. On the downside, lower fixed capital investment dragged growth down by 1.5 percentage points on lower private business investment. Exports were down by 6.0% and imports fell 3.5% on global supply-chain disruptions.

Robust growth is projected this year and next on strong domestic demand supported by accommodative financing conditions, accumulated savings, and easing COVID-19 restrictions. At its meeting on 1 March, the Reserve Bank Board retained the cash rate at 0.10%. The government bond purchases at a rate of A$4 billion a week continued until mid-February. As of 23 March, 95% of the population age 16 and over had been fully vaccinated and 66.8% of those eligible for booster shots had received these jabs. The level of vaccination meant the economy remained relatively open in early 2022, despite a surge in daily new COVID-19 cases. The main risks to the outlook are worse-than-expected repercussions from the Russian invasion of Ukraine, the pandemic taking a turn to the worse, and potentially rising tensions with the People's Republic of China. Consensus Forecasts, as of 7 March 2022, had GDP growing by 4.0% in 2022 and 3.1 % in 2023.

Figure A.13 Demand-side contributions to growth, Australia

Growth rebounded in Q4 2021 on surging household spending.

Percentage points, seasonally adjusted annualized rate, qoq

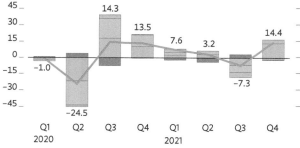

Q = quarter, qoq = quarter on quarter.
Source: CEIC Data Company (accessed 9 March 2022).

New Zealand

As containment measures gradually eased in Q4, the economy expanded on surging consumption and investment. In that quarter, GDP grew by 10.7% saar, driven by a 22.1% increase in consumption and 52.4% higher fixed capital investment. But both a lower change in inventories and exports weighed on growth (Figure A.14). And some private sector indicators sent mixed signals. The manufacturing index rose from 51.3 in November to 53.8 in December, indicating expansion. But the business confidence index declined further, to –23.2 in December from –16.4 in November, and the consumer confidence index remained below the 100-point threshold, signaling pessimism. Even so, the 3.2% decline in the seasonally adjusted unemployment rate in Q4 was the lowest in

Figure A.14 Demand-side contributions to growth, New Zealand

Growth declined in Q3 2021 mainly due to a large contraction in consumption.

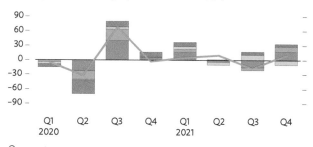

Percentage points, seasonally adjusted annualized rate, qoq

Q = quarter, qoq = quarter on quarter.
Source: CEIC Data Company (accessed 28 March 2022).

35 years. Inflation inched up to 5.9% in Q4, the highest rate in over 2 decades and exceeding the central bank's 1%–3% target range.

Solid growth this year and next will be driven by a pick-up in domestic and external demand. Although the Monetary Policy Committee raised the official cash rate to 1% in February 2022, pent-up demand amid easing COVID-19 restrictions should support domestic economic activity, while buoyant global demand for commodities will benefit the external sector. The economic fallout from renewed COVID-19 outbreaks should be limited. As of March 23, 95.1% of the population age 12 and older were fully vaccinated and 72.7% of eligible individuals had received booster jabs. The government announced a five-step border reopening plan starting in February with fully vaccinated citizens entering from Australia and concluding in October with all remaining visitors and students. The Russian invasion of Ukraine could spur inflation and hamper consumer confidence, which could derail the recovery. The emergence of more lethal COVID-19 variants and intensifying global supply-chain disruptions are other potential downside risks. Consensus Forecasts, as of 7 March 2022, had GDP growing by 3.3% in 2022 and 3.0% in 2023.

Oil prices

Oil prices rose in 2021 as the swift global economic recovery and limited oil production increases resulted in world oil demand rising faster than supply. Spot Brent crude started 2021 at $51/barrel and increased to $86/barrel in late October before declining in the year's final weeks on concerns over a global demand slowdown caused by the economic impact of the spreading Omicron COVID-19 variant (Figure A.15). Brent crude's 2021 annual average of $70/barrel is the highest since 2018.

Figure A.15 Brent crude price

Oil prices reached multiyear highs on strong demand and tight supply.

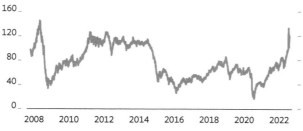

Source: Bloomberg (accessed 24 March 2022).

After a brief respite toward the end of 2021, oil prices increased throughout January and into March. The Russian invasion of Ukraine pushed oil prices to their highest levels in close to 14 years. Additional demand for oil resulted from the substitution of oil for natural gas, as gas prices increased by 187% in 2021—close to three times the rate of Brent's price increase. Although the Organization of the Petroleum Exporting Countries (OPEC) Plus agreed in February and March to continue its policy of modest monthly increases in oil production, it has been producing 2.6 million barrels a day less than just before it started cutting production in April 2020. This is because several members have been struggling to increase output. In recent years, the shale industry in the US has been consolidating with firms focusing on reducing debt and returning cash to shareholders rather than increasing production. Long-term trends toward renewable energy also restrained investment and led to fewer rig additions than was observed at similar levels of oil prices in previous years. Although the rig count has steadily increased since September 2020, it remains 22% below its level at the start of 2020.

Brent crude oil prices are expected to remain elevated, averaging $107/barrel in 2022 and $93/barrel in 2023. The Russian invasion of Ukraine and the import restrictions on Russian oil, among other supply- and demand-side factors, will drive the outlook for oil prices this year (Figure A.16). With the reduced supply of Russian oil to the international market and the expected robust demand recovery (3.3% to 100.6 million barrels per day) this year implied by February's expansionary global manufacturing and services PMI, the US Energy Information Administration estimates global oil inventory to build only in the second quarter of 2022. As the Brent crude futures curve indicates, the oil market is expected to ease from the current tightness ($121.86/barrel, as of March 23). Upward price pressures will be relieved to some extent as supply from non-OPEC countries led by the US and OPEC Plus is expected to increase, although the additional supply will not be enough to fully cover Russia's supply, at least in the short-term. On the demand-side, high oil prices could hamper growth and reduce consumption, exerting downward price pressure. Oil prices are expected to fall to $88.43/barrel by the end of 2023, which is still higher than the prewar level. A prolonged war and a complete ban on Russian energy imports pose significant upside risks. A faster-than-expected normalization of international travel will add upward pressure to oil prices. Downside risks include the conclusion of an Iran–US nuclear deal and a faster pace of production by oil producers in response to higher prices.

Figure A.16 Brent crude oil price forecast path

Oil prices are forecast to remain elevated.

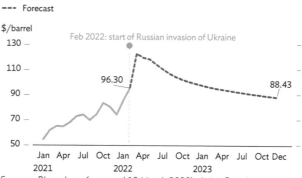

Sources: Bloomberg (accessed 10 March 2022); Asian Development Bank estimates.

2

MOBILIZING TAXES FOR DEVELOPMENT

MOBILIZING TAXES FOR DEVELOPMENT

Achieving the Sustainable Development Goals (SDGs) for a greener and more inclusive future will require vast public spending in developing Asia. What currently adds urgency to fiscal resource mobilization is the need to restore fiscal sustainability in the wake of the Coronavirus Disease 2019 (COVID-19) pandemic.

More efficient public spending can free up additional fiscal resources and promote inclusive development, but revenue mobilization remains essential to augment fiscal space across the region. Potential exists to increase tax revenue, with tax capacity estimates, which benchmark revenue against key economy characteristics, suggesting that developing Asia could increase tax revenue from a pre-pandemic average of about 16% of gross domestic product (GDP) by 3–4 percentage points.

Opportunities to strengthen revenue will depend on economy-specific circumstances including institutional capacity. However, promising options across economies include better use of value-added tax (VAT), rationalized tax exemptions, and appropriate taxation of the fast-growing digital economy. Strengthening personal income and property taxes can boost their currently low revenue yield and make taxes more progressive.

Green and health taxes can both raise revenue and contribute directly to meeting SDGs. Environmental tax instruments continue to grow and guide investment and consumption behavior in developing Asia but could be better used. Asian economies have actively explored carbon pricing to curb emissions, and the region as a whole can draw valuable lessons from early adopters. Corrective health taxes, primarily on alcohol or tobacco, could raise additional tax revenue of up to 0.6% of GDP while improving health outcomes and cutting medical costs.

Tax reform to boost revenue is politically challenging, but global experience shows that strong leadership can inspire buy-in and bring success. Strengthening tax administration can help, including through better use of information and communication technology and improved services, and taxpayer morale can be buttressed by improving the quality of public spending. New analysis finds that cutting business registration costs can reduce the share of the economy occupied by the informal sector and boost tax revenue.

This chapter was written by Sam Hill, Yothin Jinjarak, Donghyun Park, and Shu Tian, with substantive contributions from Eugenia Go, Yuho Myoda, Pilipinas Quising, and Anton Miguel P. Ragos. We gratefully acknowledge the administrative support of Heili Ann D. Bravo and Oth Marulou M. Gagni, as well as background and other material provided by Eduardo Banzon, Sandeep Bhattacharya, Arin Dutta, Maria Hanna Jaber, Go Nagata, Daisuke Miura, Ashish Narain, Marcel Schroder, and Aiko Kikkawa Takenaka, and external consultants. The chapter benefited from comments received from colleagues across ADB. Strategic advice from Albert Park, Joseph Zveglich, and Abdul Abiad is gratefully acknowledged.

Taxes must be mobilized to support sustainable development

Developing Asia has a long history of prudent fiscal policy characterized by small governments and light tax burdens. Governments have channeled modest public resources toward investment in growth-enhancing physical infrastructure, education, and other basic public services, while keeping public debt low (ADB 2014, 2020). This has supported high savings and investment while creating space for the private sector to flourish, with government playing a critical enabling role. Fiscal prudence has served the region well, promoting macroeconomic stability and stellar growth to drive down poverty and lift living standards.

However, Asia and the Pacific face significant spending pressure as the region transitions toward more sustainable and inclusive growth. Even before the COVID-19 pandemic, the United Nations Economic and Social Commission for Asia and the Pacific estimated that achieving the SDGs by 2030 required the region to spend an additional $1.5 trillion annually, equal to 5% of GDP (UNESCAP 2019). This includes substantial amounts for education, health, energy, water supply and sanitation, and combating climate change. For a sample of Asian Development Bank (ADB) developing member countries, the International Monetary Fund estimated additional annual spending needs equal to about 9% of GDP on average (Figure 2.1.1). Adding to the challenge, additional spending needs are typically larger in the poorest countries (Gaspar et al. 2019). Moreover, COVID-19 likely widens these shortfalls (Benedek et al. 2021).

Fiscal pressure on developing Asia will endure beyond 2030, the target year for the SDGs. Achieving net-zero emissions by 2050 will require massive investment in clean energy (IEA 2021). An aging population will require higher spending on pensions and health care, while rising affluence may increase demand for public goods and services (Akitoby et al. 2006).

To meet vast spending demands, economies need to draw on the full range of public and private financial resources at their disposal. Private finance has a critical role to play, notably in providing green and social finance (ADB 2021a). However, private financial flows can be unreliable, and development assistance, concentrated in very poor economies, can suffer as policy priorities shift in development partners. The ability of governments to borrow varies, and revenue from state-owned operations can be unreliable. For most governments, taxes are the primary source of revenue and stand alone as the best option to reliably expand government resources.

It is imperative for the region to mobilize tax revenue to finance the additional public spending required to meet social and other needs. Demand is especially great in the region's poorest countries, where tax revenue remains very low. A central challenge is for governments to raise additional revenue without sacrificing the economic growth vital to further reduce poverty and raise living standards. As the region emerges from the COVID-19 pandemic, now is an opportune time to take stock of tax challenges and explore options to mobilize taxes.

Taxes central to inclusive and sustainable development

Toward promoting sustainable and inclusive development, a fundamental role of government is to provide essential public goods and services and, where necessary, direct support to households to tackle poverty and meet redistribution goals. It falls to governments to provide public goods that would otherwise fall short if left to the private sector (Besley and Ghatak 2006). Social returns often exceed private returns on some necessary spending, notably on health care, education, and many types of physical infrastructure such as for water supply, sanitation, and mass transit.

Figure 2.1.1 Additional annual spending needed to achieve the SDGs

Developing Asia faces vast spending needs to achieve the SDGs.

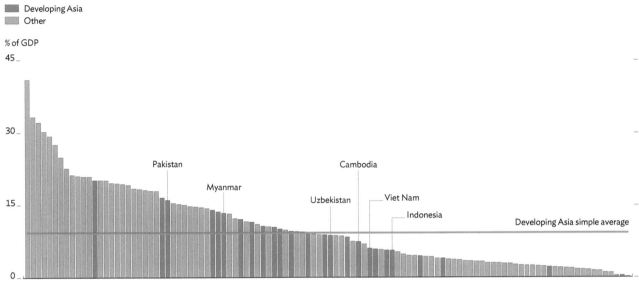

GDP = gross domestic product, SDG = Sustainable Development Goal.

Notes: Additional annual spending required to achieve the SDGs by 2030 is estimated using methodology detailed in Gaspar et al. (2019). Economies are included only if they have agreed to release their spending estimates and additional spending needs.

Sources: Gaspar et al. 2019; International Monetary Fund. IMF SDG Costing Tool (second edition) (based on Gaspar et al. 2019).

Especially in developing countries with underdeveloped and constrained credit markets, poor households rely on the government to provide such essential goods and services.

Domestic resource mobilization—fundamentally adequate tax revenue efficiently spent—is central to domestic development. It is also a focus of international development efforts (Addison, Niño-Zarazua, and Pirttila 2018). In 2015, the Third United Nations Conference on Financing for Development focused on mobilizing financial resources to meet development goals, concluding with the Addis Ababa Action Agenda. The agenda urges "the mobilization and effective use of domestic resources ... [in recognition] that domestic resources are first and foremost generated by economic growth, supported by an enabling environment at all levels" (UN 2015). Domestic resource mobilization can be conceptualized as a virtuous cycle of domestic revenue generation, its efficient and effective allocation, and the contribution this makes to sustainable economic growth and development (Figure 2.1.2). In this framework, tax revenue is a vital component of domestic resources.

Figure 2.1.2 The virtuous cycle of domestic resource mobilization

Tax revenue is a vital component of domestic resource mobilization.

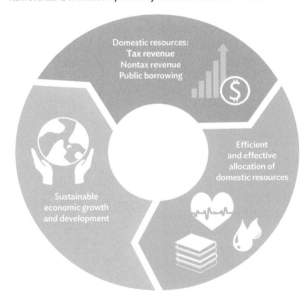

Source: *Asian Development Outlook.*

A robust tax system is important not only to raise revenue to fund public spending. It is integral to building the capacity of the state to promote broader development (Besley and Persson 2014; Keen and Slemrod 2021). The authority to raise taxes is a defining feature of the modern state that underpins the contract between government and society and enables the development of strong legal frameworks. State institutions and tax systems evolve together to be mutually reinforcing, as stronger tax systems provide states with the resources to build strong institutions able to support development, which in turn encourages willing tax compliance and simplifies tax collection. Capacity to raise adequate taxes strengthens state sovereignty by reducing dependency.

Strong tax policy can also support specific public policy objectives and macroeconomic stability. While taxes generally distort economic activity and impose welfare costs, an efficient and equitable tax mix contributes to strong and inclusive economic growth (Box 2.1.1). Taxes can address negative externalities that cause social harm, such as environmental pollution and unhealthy lifestyle habits. Equally important is ensuring that government resources are competently deployed to minimize wasteful spending and tax burdens, support tax compliance, and avoid crowding out private expenditure. Adequate and efficient tax revenue, sound spending, and prudent use of public debt promote resilient government finance and enable effective fiscal policy for macroeconomic stabilization (Delong and Summers 2012; Cottarelli, Gerson, and Senhadji 2014).

Developing Asia's tax and expenditure landscape before COVID-19

In the 2 decades before COVID-19, tax revenue across developing Asia rose on average from about 14% of GDP to 16% (Figure 2.1.3). The increase was fast in the early 2000s, then slower during and after the global financial crisis of 2008–2009. Tax revenue in developing Asia reached levels similar to sub-Saharan Africa but continued to lag Latin America, where revenue also rose. The ratio of tax to GDP in high-income members of the Organisation for Economic Co-operation and Development (OECD) stood at 26%, half again more than developing Asia collected.

Figure 2.1.3 Tax revenue in selected regions

In developing Asia, tax revenue rose before COVID-19 but remained comparatively low.

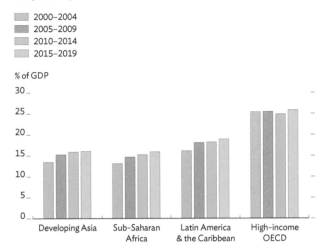

- ▮ 2000–2004
- ▮ 2005–2009
- ▮ 2010–2014
- ▮ 2015–2019

GDP = gross domestic product, OECD = Organisation for Economic Co-operation and Development.

Notes: Twenty-six economies in developing Asia, 28 in sub-Saharan Africa, 27 in Latin America and the Caribbean, and 33 among high-income OECD members. See Go et al. (2022) for details.

Sources: OECD. Global Revenue Statistics Database; International Monetary Fund. Government Finance Statistics online database (both accessed 31 January 2022); Asian Development Bank estimates.

These figures omit social security contributions, which, except most notably in the People's Republic of China (PRC) and the Republic of Korea (ROK), are not large in developing Asia, reflecting underdeveloped social protection systems or reliance on general revenue to fund social protection. However, social security contributions can be significant, particularly in OECD countries, where they often equal 10% or more of GDP. The revenue gap between developing Asia and OECD countries is even greater when taking these contributions into account.

Encouragingly, over these 2 decades, tax revenue rose in most of developing Asia. Increases were particularly large in Cambodia, Georgia, and Nepal (Figure 2.1.4). Rapid economic growth across the region has underpinned improvement in tax revenue performance. Tax buoyancy has been strong in much of the region (Box 2.1.2). Asian economies with the highest tax revenue before COVID-19, mostly in the Caucasus and Central and East Asia, collected tax revenue sometimes exceeding 20% of GDP, comparable to the United States.

Figure 2.1.4 Average tax revenue in selected Asian economies, 2000–2004 versus 2015–2019

Most economies in developing Asia boosted tax revenue before COVID-19, but in many it remained very low.

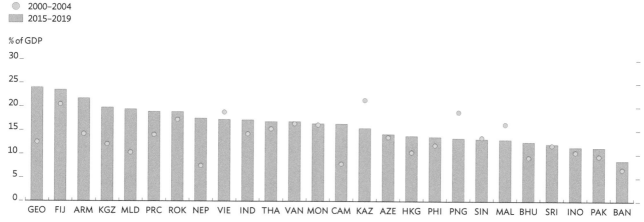

○ 2000–2004
▨ 2015–2019

ARM = Armenia, AZE = Azerbaijan, BAN = Bangladesh, BHU = Bhutan, CAM = Cambodia, FIJ = Fiji, GDP = gross domestic product, GEO = Georgia, HKG = Hong Kong, China, IND = India, INO = Indonesia, KAZ = Kazakhstan, KGZ = Kyrgyz Republic, MAL = Malaysia, MLD = Maldives, MON = Mongolia, NEP = Nepal, PAK = Pakistan, PHI = Philippines, PNG = Papua New Guinea, PRC = People's Republic of China, ROK = Republic of Korea, SIN = Singapore, SRI = Sri Lanka, THA = Thailand, VAN = Vanuatu, VIE = Viet Nam.
Note: See Go et al. (2022) for details.
Sources: OECD. Global Revenue Statistics Database; International Monetary Fund. Government Finance Statistics online database (both accessed 31 January 2022); Asian Development Bank estimates.

However, despite this progress, tax revenue in several economies in developing Asia remained very low by international standards. Indeed in some revenue was below an often-applied minimum threshold of about 15% of GDP, which is associated with improved state capacity and growth acceleration (Gaspar, Jaramillo, and Wingender 2016b). Notable among them are Bangladesh, Indonesia, Pakistan, Papua New Guinea, and Sri Lanka, showing that tax revenue is lowest in some of the poorest economies in the region.

Developing Asia relies heavily on VAT introduced widely throughout the region since the 1980s and 1990s. Other consumption taxes including excises are also important (Figure 2.1.5). Consumption taxes account for a little under half of tax revenue in regional economies, on average, of which half is from VAT, making it the single most important tax category. These shares are comparable to those in other economies. In developing Asia, corporate income taxes account for about 21% of tax revenue, a little higher than in other developing regions and double the share in OECD countries. Personal income taxes account for 13% of tax revenue in developing Asia, in line with other developing regions but much lower than in OECD countries, where they account for over a third.

Figure 2.1.5 Tax revenue share by source, average in 2015–2019

As do other developing regions, developing Asia relies heavily on consumption and corporate income tax.

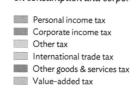

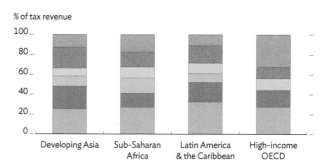

OECD = Organisation for Economic Co-operation and Development.
Note: See Go et al. (2022) for details.
Sources: OECD. Global Revenue Statistics Database; International Monetary Fund. Government Finance Statistics online database (both accessed 31 January 2022); Asian Development Bank estimates.

Finally, while lower than Sub-Saharan Africa, international trade taxes account for about 10% of tax revenue in developing Asia, in line with Latin America but much higher than in OECD countries, where such taxes are negligible.

While useful, such comparisons obscure differences in the amount of revenue generated by each tax. Despite their large share of revenue in developing Asia, VAT and other consumption taxes equal only about 8% of GDP, lower than in Latin America or OECD countries (Figure 2.1.6). Personal income tax generates revenue equal to a paltry 2% of GDP, a quarter of the yield in OECD countries. By contrast, corporate income tax generates revenue in developing Asia on a par with Latin America and OECD countries.

Reliance on VAT and other consumption taxes is especially high in a diverse group of developing economies in Asia that includes Cambodia, the PRC, Vanuatu, and Viet Nam (Figure 2.1.7). In others, tax revenue sources are generally more diverse, with a greater balance between consumption and corporate income taxes.

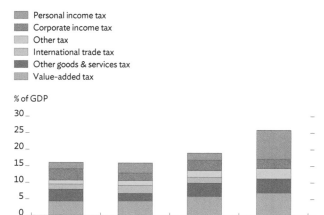

Figure 2.1.6 Tax revenue by source, average in 2015–2019

Developing Asia collects much less consumption and personal income tax than do high-income countries.

- Personal income tax
- Corporate income tax
- Other tax
- International trade tax
- Other goods & services tax
- Value-added tax

GDP = gross domestic product, OECD = Organisation for Economic Co-operation and Development.

Note: See Go et al. (2022) for details.

Sources: OECD. Global Revenue Statistics Database; International Monetary Fund. Government Finance Statistics online database (both accessed 31 January 2022); Asian Development Bank estimates.

Figure 2.1.7 Tax revenue share by source in selected economies, average in 2015–2019

Consumption taxes provide more than half of tax revenue in most economies in developing Asia.

- Personal income tax
- Corporate income tax
- Other tax
- International trade tax
- Other goods & services tax
- Value-added tax

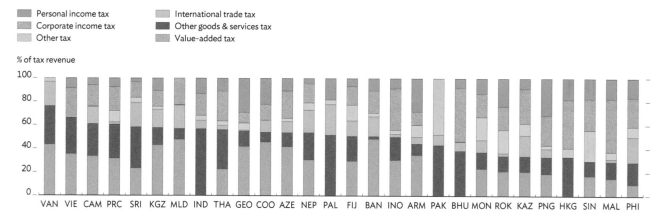

ARM = Armenia, AZE = Azerbaijan, BAN = Bangladesh, BHU = Bhutan, CAM = Cambodia, CIT = corporate income tax, COO = Cook Islands, FIJ = Fiji, GEO = Georgia, HKG = Hong Kong, China, IND = India, INO = Indonesia, KAZ = Kazakhstan, KGZ = Kyrgyz Republic, MAL = Malaysia, MLD = Maldives, MON = Mongolia, NEP = Nepal, PAK = Pakistan, PAL = Palau, PHI = Philippines, PIT = personal income tax, PNG = Papua New Guinea, PRC = People's Republic of China, ROK = Republic of Korea, SIN = Singapore, SRI = Sri Lanka, THA = Thailand, VAN = Vanuatu, VAT = value-added tax, VIE = Viet Nam.

Notes: Bhutan recently adopted goods and services tax. Hong Kong, China does not levy VAT. For India, VAT is subsumed under taxes on goods and services, which includes general taxes on goods and services, excise taxes, taxes on specific services, and taxes on the use of/permission to use goods. As no data are available on PIT in Maldives, it is subsumed into other taxes. As no data are available on VAT, CIT, or PIT in Pakistan, VAT is subsumed into other goods and services tax, and CIT and PIT are subsumed into other taxes. Palau does not levy VAT or make available data on CIT, which is subsumed into other taxes. Singapore and Viet Nam report no revenue from international trade tax. Vanuatu reports no revenue from CIT or PIT. See Go et al. (2022) for further details.

Sources: OECD. Global Revenue Statistics Database; International Monetary Fund. Government Finance Statistics online database (both accessed 31 January 2022); Asian Development Bank estimates.

Figure 2.1.8 Tax revenue by source in selected economies, average in 2015–2019

Personal income tax revenue is very small in most of developing Asia.

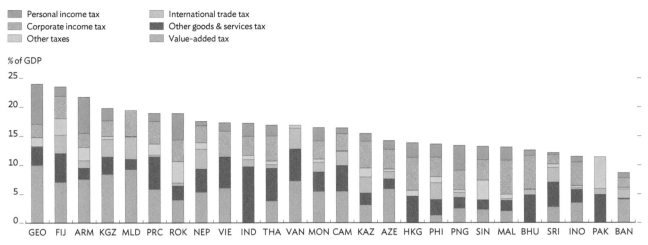

ARM = Armenia, AZE = Azerbaijan, BAN = Bangladesh, BHU = Bhutan, CAM = Cambodia, CIT = corporate income tax, FIJ = Fiji, GEO = Georgia, GDP = gross domestic product, HKG = Hong Kong, China, IND = India, INO = Indonesia, KAZ = Kazakhstan, KGZ = Kyrgyz Republic, MAL = Malaysia, MLD = Maldives, MON = Mongolia, NEP = Nepal, PAK = Pakistan, PHI = Philippines, PIT = personal income tax, PNG = Papua New Guinea, PRC = People's Republic of China, ROK = Republic of Korea, SIN = Singapore, SRI = Sri Lanka, THA = Thailand, VAN = Vanuatu, VAT = value-added tax, VIE = Viet Nam.

Notes: Bhutan recently adopted goods and services tax. Hong Kong, China does not levy VAT. For India, VAT is subsumed under taxes on goods and services, which includes general taxes on goods and services, excise taxes, taxes on specific services, and taxes on the use of/permission to use goods. As no data are available on PIT in Maldives, it is subsumed into other taxes. As no data are available on VAT, CIT, or PIT in Pakistan, VAT is subsumed into other goods and services tax, and CIT and PIT are subsumed into other taxes. Palau does not levy VAT or make available data on CIT, which is subsumed into other taxes. Singapore and Viet Nam report no revenue from international trade tax. Vanuatu reports no revenue from CIT or PIT. See Go et al. (2022) for further details.

Sources: OECD. Global Revenue Statistics Database; International Monetary Fund. Government Finance Statistics online database (both accessed 31 January 2022); Asian Development Bank estimates.

In Armenia, Georgia, and Papua New Guinea, the personal income tax share of revenue is a quarter or more, but elsewhere much lower. Despite the region's reliance on VAT and other consumption taxes, they generate revenue short of 5% of GDP in many economies (Figure 2.1.8). In several, personal income tax amounts to less than 2% of GDP. Even where personal income tax collections are highest, in Armenia and Georgia, they are below the OECD average.

In most economies, taxes are the primary source of government revenue and therefore largely define the public spending envelope over the medium and longer term. While government spending normally exceeds tax revenue, with the balance made up from borrowing and nontax revenue, spending rises with tax revenue in developing Asia and elsewhere (Figure 2.1.9). Within developing Asia, the correlation is much weaker among Pacific island economies.

This reflects the high cost of providing government services to dispersed populations and unusually high nontax revenue from—variously—fisheries, foreign fishing vessel licenses, and official development assistance (Cabezon, Tumbarello, and Wu 2015). Excluding Pacific island economies, average public spending in developing Asia equals about 27% of GDP, which is comparable to developing peer regions but far below OECD countries (Figure 2.1.10).

While education, health, and social protection spending rises with tax revenue around the world, higher education and health spending stands out in developing Asia (Figure 2.1.11). With lower tax revenue, developing Asia excluding Pacific island economies spends less on education and health than Latin America, let alone OECD members (Figure 2.1.12). Spending in developing Asia on social protection compares a little more favorably with developing region peers but is less than a third of the share in OECD countries.

Figure 2.1.9 Tax and expenditure, average in 2015–2019

Around the world, higher taxes are associated with higher government spending.

○ Developing Asia
◇ OECD
✕ Other

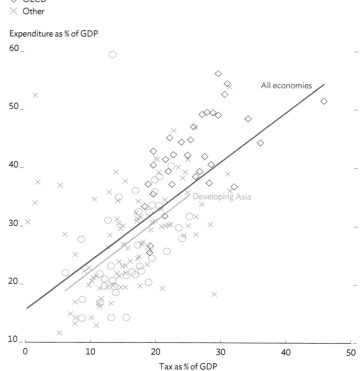

Expenditure as % of GDP

All economies

Developing Asia

Tax as % of GDP

GDP = gross domestic product, OECD = Organisation for Economic Co-operation and Development.

Notes: Excludes Timor-Leste, where tax is 24.8% and expenditure 90.3%; Nauru, where tax is 30.3% and expenditure 99.6%; Kiribati, where tax is 23.4% and expenditure 115%; and Tuvalu, where tax is 30.5% and expenditure 116.3%. See Go et al. (2022) for further details.

Sources: OECD. Global Revenue Statistics Database; International Monetary Fund. Government Finance Statistics online database; International Monetary Fund. World Economic Outlook October 2021 online database (all accessed 31 January 2022); Asian Development Bank estimates.

Figure 2.1.10 Expenditure in selected regions, average in 2015–2019

Government spending in developing Asia is comparatively low, especially excluding Pacific island economies.

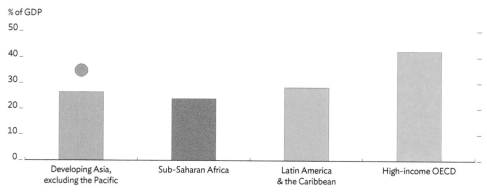

% of GDP

GDP = gross domestic product, OECD = Organisation for Economic Co-operation and Development.

Notes: ● is the unweighted average for developing Asia including the Pacific. See Go et al. (2022) for details.

Sources: International Monetary Fund. World Economic Outlook October 2021 online database (accessed 31 January 2022); Asian Development Bank estimates.

Figure 2.1.11 Tax and selected expenditure, 2015–2019

Higher taxes are associated with higher government spending on education, health, and social protection but not defense.

○ Developing Asia
◇ OECD
✕ Other

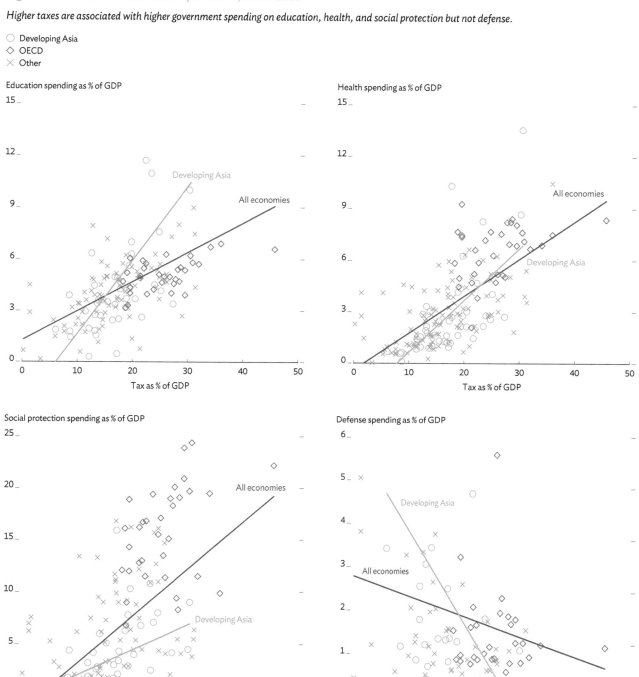

GDP = gross domestic product, OECD = Organisation for Economic Co-operation and Development.

Notes: Expenditure on education, health, and defense is the 2015–2019 average for each region, social protection 2020 or latest value. See Go et al. (2022) for details.

Sources: OECD. Global Revenue Statistics Database; International Monetary Fund. Government Finance Statistics online database; International Monetary Fund. World Economic Outlook October 2021 online database (all accessed 31 January 2022); Asian Development Bank estimates.

Figure 2.1.12 Selected expenditure by region, 2015–2019

Government spending on education, health, and social protection is comparatively low in developing Asia.

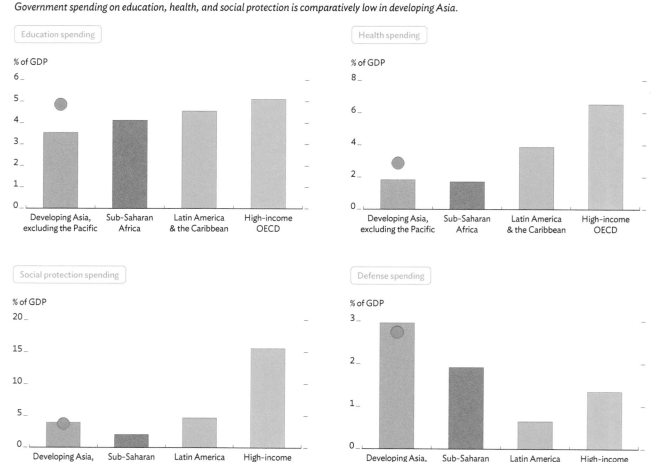

GDP = gross domestic product, OECD = Organisation for Economic Co-operation and Development.

Notes: ● is the unweighted average for developing Asia including the Pacific. Expenditure on education, health, and defense is the 2015–2019 average for each region, social protection 2020 or latest value. See Go et al. (2022) for further details.

Sources: World Bank. World Development Indicators online database; ILO. World Social Protection Report 2020–22 (both accessed 20 October 2021); Asian Development Bank estimates.

By contrast, defense spending negatively correlates with tax revenue, suggesting that it receives a disproportionately high share of government spending in many of the lowest-taxed and poorest countries. Defense spending is, on average, comparatively high in developing Asia. While correlation does not imply causation, these trends suggest that increased tax revenue is often directed toward promoting development. This claim is strengthened by more detailed empirical evidence on taxes and health spending (Carter and Cobham 2016; Hall et al. 2021).

The fiscal impact of COVID-19

The COVID-19 pandemic has had unprecedented impacts on the regional economy, setting back development progress and profoundly affecting government finances. Growth in developing Asia, though more resilient than in most regions, turned negative in 2020 for the first time since 1962. Some economies in the region—particularly those that have endured lengthy lockdowns or rely heavily on badly affected industries such as tourism—shrank by double digits. The human cost was high as developing Asia suffered large numbers of infections and deaths.

COVID-19 adversely affected employment and incomes, hitting the poor hardest and slowing poverty reduction. The share of people in developing Asia living below the extreme poverty line of $1.90 per day rose by about 2 percentage points in 2020 compared with a scenario of no COVID-19 (ADB 2021c). Aside from the direct health impact of COVID-19, the pandemic disrupted health-care systems and magnified food insecurity and malnutrition. School closures hindered learning, the future earnings losses from which are estimated to equal more than 13% of regional GDP in 2020 (see Part 1 of this report).

Across developing Asia, fiscal policy responses to COVID-19 were appropriately substantial, exceeding those to the global financial crisis of 2008–2009. In some economies fiscal policy was supported by central bank asset purchase programs (ADB 2021a; Cerutti and Helbling 2021; World Bank 2021a). Announced fiscal policy measures amounted to 5% of GDP or more in many cases (Figure 2.1.13). In almost all economies, stimulus packages comprised both spending measures and generally smaller tax measures. Spending focused on health, cash transfers, food subsidies, and child benefit payments.

Business support included loan interest repayment and wage subsidies to encourage worker retention.

Tax stimulus spanned the full range of personal income, corporate income, property, trade, and consumption taxes. Measures included tax deferrals on personal and business income taxes, reduced tax rates, tax exemptions, and waivers for late fees and interest payments for outstanding tax liabilities. Measures aimed at poorer households included VAT exemption for selected foods and income tax waivers. Some economies waived taxes and duties on health and medical equipment.

Economic collapse and large discretionary tax policy responses sharply curtailed tax receipts across developing Asia in 2020 (Figure 2.1.14). These declines generally correlated with broader economic conditions as revenue fell furthest in some small island economies including Fiji, Maldives, and Vanuatu, as well as in other hard-hit economies such as Indonesia, Malaysia, and Sri Lanka. Data on individual taxes in 2020, while limited, indicate broad revenue decline.

Figure 2.1.13 Fiscal policy responses to COVID-19, as of 15 November 2021

Across much of developing Asia, announced COVID-19 fiscal stimulus packages were very large.

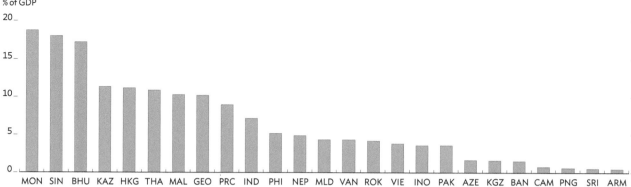

ARM = Armenia, AZE = Azerbaijan, BAN = Bangladesh, BHU = Bhutan, CAM = Cambodia, GEO = Georgia, HKG = Hong Kong, China, IND = India, INO = Indonesia, KAZ = Kazakhstan, KGZ = Kyrgyz Republic, MAL = Malaysia, MLD = Maldives, MON = Mongolia, NEP = Nepal, PAK = Pakistan, PHI = Philippines, PNG = Papua New Guinea, PRC = People's Republic of China, ROK = Republic of Korea, SIN = Singapore, SRI = Sri Lanka, THA = Thailand, VAN = Vanuatu, VIE = Viet Nam.

Notes: Figures comprise health care and public health measures and income support through forgone government revenue associated with tax deferral, policy rate reduction, and other adjustments. Excludes Fiji where stimulus package is estimated at 56.1% of GDP.

Sources: ADB. COVID-19 Policy Database (accessed 31 January 2022); Asian Development Bank estimates.

Figure 2.1.14 Change in tax revenue from 2019 to 2020

Tax revenue fell sharply in 2020 in most of developing Asia.

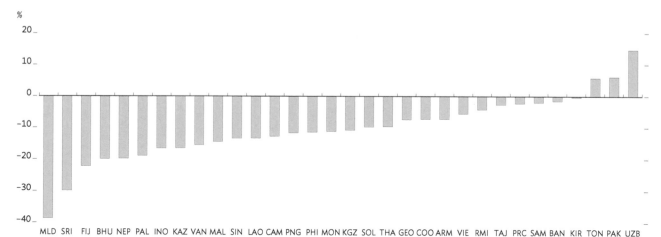

ARM = Armenia, BAN = Bangladesh, BHU = Bhutan, CAM = Cambodia, COO = Cook Islands, FIJ = Fiji, GEO = Georgia, INO = Indonesia, KAZ = Kazakhstan, KGZ = Kyrgyz Republic, KIR = Kiribati, LAO = Lao People's Democratic Republic, MAL = Malaysia, MLD = Maldives, MON = Mongolia, NEP = Nepal, PAK = Pakistan, PAL = Palau, PHI = Philippines, PNG = Papua New Guinea, PRC = People's Republic of China, RMI = Republic of the Marshall Islands, SAM = Samoa, SIN = Singapore, SOL = Solomon Islands, SRI = Sri Lanka, TAJ = Tajikistan, THA = Thailand, TON = Tonga, UZB = Uzbekistan, VAN = Vanuatu, VIE = Viet Nam.

Sources: IMF. Government Finance Statistics online database; ADB. *Asian Development Outlook 2021* (all accessed 31 January 2022); Asian Development Bank estimates.

At the same time, expenditure increased significantly in most economies (Figure 2.1.15). Consistent with government stimulus announcements, limited data suggest that health and social protection spending rose sharply.[1]

Weaker revenue and higher spending erased fiscal surpluses or expanded deficits across developing Asia. Generally, economies suffering the biggest output and revenue falls saw the largest increases in deficits. Higher deficits fueled marked increases in government debt as average public gross debt soared from 51.9% of GDP in 2019 to 65.3% in 2021.[2] While debt remains comparatively low in many regional economies, in others it has reached uncomfortable levels and is projected to rise further in the coming years, continuing an upward trend that preceded the pandemic (Ferrarini, Giugale, and Pradelli 2022).

Developing Asia thus emerges from COVID-19 with significantly weakened government finances. The region faces a difficult balancing act to maintain fiscal stimulus where necessary while safeguarding fiscal sustainability. Economic recovery will help strengthen revenue, as will the expiry of some stimulus measures. However, the pandemic may cast a long fiscal shadow. The costly challenge of managing COVID-19 may persist, particularly where vaccine rollout has been slow. Stimulus measures will continue to weigh on government finances. In the Philippines, for example, the window for carrying forward operating loss deductions has been extended to 5 years. As noted in Part 1 of this report, recovery in many economies is incomplete, leaving tax bases below pre-pandemic levels. Indeed, the pandemic risks economic scarring and revenue recovery slowed by diminished tax compliance, as can occur during crises (Brondolo 2009; Fernal and Li 2021).

[1]   International Monetary Fund. Government Finance Statistics (accessed 31 January 2022).
[2]   International Monetary Fund. World Economic Outlook October 2021 online database (accessed 22 October 2021).

Figure 2.1.15 Change in expenditure from 2019 to 2020

Government spending increased significantly in 2020 in most of developing Asia.

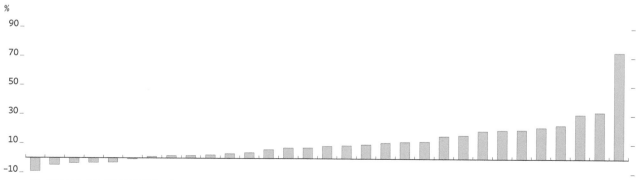

ARM = Armenia, BAN = Bangladesh, BHU = Bhutan, CAM = Cambodia, FIJ = Fiji, GEO = Georgia, INO = Indonesia, KAZ = Kazakhstan, KGZ = Kyrgyz Republic, KIR = Kiribati, LAO = Lao People's Democratic Republic, MAL = Malaysia, MLD = Maldives, MON = Mongolia, NEP = Nepal, PAK = Pakistan, PAL = Palau, PHI = Philippines, PNG = Papua New Guinea, PRC = People's Republic of China, RMI = Republic of the Marshall Islands, SAM = Samoa, SIN = Singapore, SOL = Solomon Islands, SRI = Sri Lanka, TAJ = Tajikistan, THA = Thailand, TON = Tonga, UZB = Uzbekistan, VAN = Vanuatu, VIE = Viet Nam.

Sources: IMF. World Economic Outlook October 2021 online database (accessed 31 January 2022); Asian Development Bank estimates.

While low interest rates currently underpin favorable debt dynamics, financial conditions could change abruptly. Timely fiscal consolidation will be required in many economies to ensure fiscal sustainability (Blanchard, Felman, and Subramanian 2021; Favara, Minoiu, and Perez-Orive 2021; Kose et al. 2021). Paramount needs are to support health-care systems, protect the most vulnerable, and promote green and inclusive recovery (Hepburn et al. 2020; Furceri et al. 2021). Fiscal consolidation strategies should be tailored to economy-specific circumstances and guided by key principles, with tax policy playing a vital role (Box 2.1.3).

It is abundantly clear that Asia and the Pacific must strengthen tax revenue mobilization as COVID-19 recedes, to fund vast public spending needed to achieve the SDGs. Tax mobilization can also support fiscal repair. While public expenditure is beyond the scope of the chapter, improving spending efficiency is an important additional avenue for expanding fiscal space and achieving better outcomes (Box 2.1.4).

Box 2.1.1 Tax policy principles and tradeoffs

Good tax policy follows the principles of efficiency, equity, and simplicity and ensures sufficient and stable revenue for government spending needs. By altering prices, taxes distort economic behavior, causing deadweight or welfare losses. An efficient tax system minimizes any distortion of economic behavior by taxing goods and services for which demand is less sensitive to price changes, and by taxing income with low marginal rates to avoid work disincentives and consequent income losses.

Equitable income taxes are progressive, taxing individuals who earn higher incomes more heavily but treating taxpayers with equivalent incomes equally and without gender or other biases. An important nuance in tax equity is the difference between statutory incidence, or who is legally responsible for paying a tax, and economic incidence, or who actually bears its cost. Generally, economic incidence can be shifted to those whose behavior is less responsive to the tax. For example, corporate income tax legally targets a firm's shareholders, but firms can shift the burden to consumers if higher prices do not excessively curtail demand.

continued on next page

Box 2.1.1 *Continued*

Finally, the tax system should be as simple and transparent as possible to reduce compliance costs for taxpayers. Simplicity also reduces uncertainty and—importantly where institutional capacity is weak—tax administration cost and difficulties for governments. Further, simplicity reduces the risk that taxpayers exploit complicated tax rules in ways that undermine equity.

The box table summarizes the broad pros and cons of different taxes with respect to the key principles of efficiency, equity, and simplicity. Consumption taxes applied to a broad base are typically less distortive but less equitable. By contrast, progressive personal income taxes are more equitable but more distortive. Corporate income taxes on highly mobile capital are often more distortive, while taxes on immobile property are often both efficient and equitable.

However, tax characteristics depend heavily on their specific design and implementation. For example, personal income tax at a flat rate is less equitable but more efficient. Consumption tax with exemptions for certain goods and services may be more equitable but less efficient.

Context also matters greatly. For example, property tax based on outdated property values may be less equitable. Finally, any tax can be simply designed or else made complex with multiple rates and exemptions.

In practice, the tax policy principles of efficiency, equity, and simplicity are individually desirable but difficult to satisfy simultaneously. Indeed, any tax features strengths and weaknesses in the trade-off between efficiency and equity. An efficient tax system achieves its goals with low marginal tax rates and broad tax bases, while an equitable tax typically requires higher rates on a relatively narrow base of richer taxpayers. Tax policy should consider all three principles and must be viewed through the lens of revenue needs and political and administrative feasibility. As there is no perfect tax system, policy makers must strike a balance that reflects the government's priorities, national institutional capacity, and societal expectations.

Reference:
Bhattacharya, S. and J. Stotsky. 2022. *A Tax Primer: With Applications to Asia-Pacific Countries.* Asian Development Bank.

Concise summary of the properties of major taxes

Different taxes offer pros and cons against the key principles of efficiency, equity, and simplicity

Tax	Efficiency	Equity	Simplicity
Personal income tax	Low (assuming progressive marginal tax rates)	High (assuming progressive marginal tax rates)	Low (high information needs that include third-party reporting, and withholding at source)
Corporate income tax	Low (difficult to capture economic concept of profit)	Moderate (statutory incidence falling primarily on capital income, but burden may shift to consumers and workers)	Moderate (often complex, but collection may focus on a small number of high-value taxpayers)
Value-added tax	Moderate (a uniform and moderate rate causing little consumption distortion)	Moderate (generally regressive with a uniform rate)	Moderate (invoice credit approach offering advantages but, if poorly designed, becoming difficult to administer)
Excise	Moderate (can address externalities and often levied on products with less elastic demand)	Moderate (like value-added or other general consumption taxes, depending on how applied)	Moderate (but can require accurate valuation and adjustment of rates per unit, adding complexity)
Import duty	Low (discriminatory between domestic and foreign producers and particularly inefficient if rates are high and variable)	Moderate (like general consumption taxes, depends on how applied; like corporate income taxes, burden may shift to domestic consumers)	Moderate (complicated by any variable rate structure, smuggling, or problems with valuation or determining content)
Property tax	High (not easily evaded in the short and medium term)	High (assuming valuations are based on accurate records and market transactions)	Moderate (requires up-to-date records and valuations)

Sources: Bhattacharya and Stotsky 2022; *Asian Development Outlook.*

Box 2.1.2 Tax buoyancy in developing Asia

Tax buoyancy, or how tax revenue responds to change in GDP, is crucial to understanding tax revenue performance and fiscal sustainability.
It informs how tax revenue rises and falls in economic cycles and over the longer term. It further offers insights on the stabilizing role of taxes over the business cycle.

Buoyancy greater than one means tax revenue rises more than in proportion to increased GDP.
Tax revenue thus structurally increases and is sufficient to support fiscal sustainability even with some increase in public spending. A buoyant tax system also helps stabilize output over the short run. During upturns, revenue increases more than GDP, dampening demand, and preventing overheating. During downturns, revenue decreases disproportionately, supporting economic activity. If, by contrast, tax buoyancy is less than one, tax revenue structurally decreases and threatens fiscal sustainability in the absence of spending cuts (Creedy and Gemmel 2008; Dudine and Jalles 2018; Gupta, Jalles, and Liu, forthcoming; Lagravinese, Liberati, and Sacchi 2020).

Tax buoyancy estimates therefore help assess tax revenue performance in developing Asia.
To estimate tax buoyancy in the region, an error-correction model of tax revenue and nominal GDP was estimated for a sample of 25 economies from 1998 to 2020 using both time-series and panel data approaches (Hill, Jinjarak, and Park 2022). This yielded two sets of coefficients, the instantaneous impact of changes in GDP on tax revenue, or short-run tax buoyancy, and the relationship between GDP and taxes over the long term, or long-run tax buoyancy. During a major downturn like the COVID-19 pandemic, tax buoyancy may be affected by policy change or increased tax evasion (Sancak, Xing, and Velloso 2010). To investigate the regional impact of COVID-19, analysis included a dummy variable taking the value of one for 2020 and zero otherwise.

Regression results show that short-run and long-run tax buoyancy in developing Asia are both very close to one and statistically significant.
The results also indicate that the pandemic reduced revenue growth in the region by a tenth of a percentage point in 2020 after controlling for declining GDP. To explore tax buoyancy by economy, the same model was estimated for individual economies, and long-run tax buoyancy was found to be one or higher in many of them (box figure 1).

1 Long-run tax buoyancy coefficients

Long-run tax buoyancy is estimated to be one or higher in many economies in developing Asia.

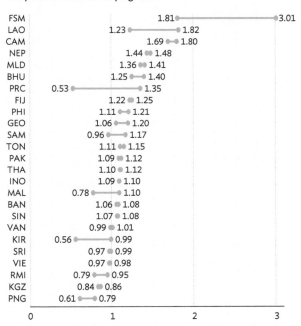

BAN = Bangladesh, BHU = Bhutan, CAM = Cambodia, FIJ = Fiji, FSM = Federated States of Micronesia, GEO = Georgia, INO = Indonesia, KGZ = Kyrgyz Republic, KIR = Kiribati, LAO = Lao People's Democratic Republic, MAL = Malaysia, MLD = Maldives, NEP = Nepal, PAK = Pakistan, PHI = Philippines, PNG = Papua New Guinea, PRC = People's Republic of China, RMI = Marshall Islands, SAM = Samoa, SIN = Singapore, SRI = Sri Lanka, THA = Thailand, TON = Tonga, VAN = Vanuatu, VIE = Viet Nam.

Note: Upper and lower bounds of estimates from time series autoregressive distributed lags and panel mean-group estimator.

Source: Hill, Jinjarak, and Park 2022.

continued on next page

Box 2.1.2 *Continued*

Analysis using the regression results further underscores adverse revenue implications of COVID-19. Using estimates from economy-specific equations, a simple counterfactual analysis was undertaken to estimate excess tax revenue lost in 2020 from the pandemic over and above what would normally be expected in the GDP downturn. Excess revenue loss was estimated by subtracting model predicted revenue for 2020 from actual tax revenue. The median estimated excess tax revenue lost because of COVID-19 equaled 0.7 percentage points of 2019 GDP, as shown in box figure 2. In summary, the results suggest that tax buoyancy in the region was generally strong before COVID-19 and that subsequently revenue declined more than expected given the GDP downturn.

References:
Creedy, J. and N. Gemmel. 2008. Corporation Tax Buoyancy and Revenue Elasticity in the UK. *Economic Modelling* 25.

Dudine, P. and J. Jalles. 2018. How Buoyant Is the Tax System? New Evidence from a Large Heterogenous Panel. *Journal of International Development* 30.

Gupta, S., J. Tovar Jalles, and J. Liu. Forthcoming. Tax Buoyancy in Sub-Saharan Africa and Its Determinants. *International Tax and Public Finance*.

Hill, S., Y. Jinjarak, and D. Park. 2022. *How Do Tax Revenues Respond to GDP Growth? Evidence from Developing Asia, 1998–2020.* Asian Development Bank.

2 Actual minus model-estimated 2020 taxes (% of 2019 GDP)

In 2020, tax revenue in developing Asia declined by more than expected from GDP change alone.

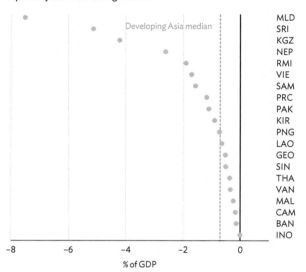

BAN = Bangladesh, CAM = Cambodia, GDP = gross domestic product, GEO = Georgia, INO = Indonesia, KGZ = Kyrgyz Republic, KIR = Kiribati, LAO = Lao People's Democratic Republic, MAL = Malaysia, MLD = Maldives, NEP = Nepal, PAK = Pakistan, PNG = Papua New Guinea, PRC = People's Republic of China, RMI = Marshall Islands, SAM = Samoa, SIN = Singapore, SRI = Sri Lanka, THA = Thailand, VAN = Vanuatu, VIE = Viet Nam.

Notes: Negative values are tax loss beyond what would normally be expected in the GDP downturn. Excludes the Federated States of Micronesia, whose revenue loss is estimated equal to 19.8% of GDP.

Source: Hill, Jinjarak, and Park 2022.

Box 2.1.3 Strategies for successful fiscal consolidation

As economies emerge from COVID-19 with weakened government finances, policy makers face substantial challenges deciding how and when it is best to pursue fiscal consolidation to narrow deficits. To put this challenge in context, deficits and debts are now higher across the region than following the global financial crisis of 2008–2009 (box figure). History tells that consolidation following a major shock can be slow and difficult. Years after the global financial crisis many developing Asian economies had yet to restore their precrisis fiscal balances.

A key parameter for informing any successful consolidation strategy is the magnitude required, guided by debt dynamics and sustainability. Economies with low debt can appropriately target debt stabilization. Others may need to target a downward debt trajectory. Timing is critical, informed by economic conditions and prospects, as well as by the path of monetary policy. Where supportive monetary policy can be maintained, fiscal consolidation may proceed more promptly.

The composition of consolidation, particularly the mix of tax and expenditure measures, can have short- and longer-term consequences including distributional impacts. The ideal package of measures can be informed by the drag associated with various tax and expenditure measures, reflected in the size of fiscal multipliers. While multiplier estimates vary, tax multipliers may be smaller than expenditure multipliers, including in developing Asia, implying less drag on recovery from tax measures (Ramey 2019; Dime, Ginting, and Zhuang 2021). Indeed, in low-income economies, growth tends to be lower following expenditure-led fiscal consolidation (Clements et al. 2021). A further reason to favor tax measures to achieve consolidation is that government spending is already low across the region.

1 Developing Asia fiscal deficits and gross debt, 2009 and 2021

In developing Asia, fiscal deficits and debt are now much higher than following the global financial crisis.

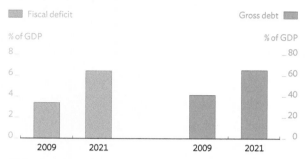

GDP = gross domestic product.
Sources: International Monetary Fund. World Economic Outlook October 2021 online database (accessed 31 January 2022); Asian Development Bank estimates.

Tax measures should be carefully sequenced to avoid overburdening taxpayers and damaging confidence (Sen 2021). First, temporary stimulus measures should be allowed to expire so they will not become permanent and erode the tax base. Next, tax deferrals should be wound back and then stimulus tax cuts gradually removed. Additional tax consolidation should focus on widening tax bases, notably by minimizing wasteful exemptions to value-added and income taxes, which may impose less drag on recovery than would higher tax rates (Dabla-Norris and Lima 2018).

On the spending side, health care needs to be prioritized to support continued COVID-19 vaccination and bolster health infrastructure. Well-targeted spending on social protection needs to be maintained to alleviate the worst suffering in poorer households and tap their higher spending propensity to spur economic recovery.

continued on next page

Box 2.1.3 *Continued*

Education spending is another priority because of long-term scarring left by school closure. Governments need to spend efficiently despite politics playing a significant part in determining the size and composition of COVID-19 fiscal programs (Aizenman et al. 2021). Recovery provides breathing space to seek savings without sacrificing service delivery or support for the poor. Pro-poor fiscal adjustments include reducing subsidies that favor more affluent households, such as on energy use. Temporarily freezing civil service salaries or new hires may yield savings without sacrificing recovery.

Consolidation options may be more constrained for economies facing acute revenue shortfalls and macroeconomic instability. Revenue can be substantially boosted by reducing wasteful exemptions and raising rates on key taxes, notably value-added tax, and some excises, especially on alcohol and tobacco. Eliminating inefficient spending is imperative. While usually difficult, such measures may be easier to justify during a crisis, when they credibly signal the government's commitment to restore stability.

References:

Aizenman, J. et al. 2021. The Political Economy of the COVID-19 Fiscal Stimulus Packages of 2020. *NBER Working Paper* No. 29360. National Bureau of Economic Research.

Clements, B. et al. 2021. Low-Income Developing Countries Will Surely Need More Debt Relief Down the Line. Center for Global Development Blog.

Dabla-Norris, E. and F. Lima. 2018. Macroeconomic Effects of Tax Rate and Base Changes: Evidence from Fiscal Consolidations. *IMF Working Paper* WP/18/220. International Monetary Fund.

Dime, R., E. Ginting, and J. Zhuang. 2021. Estimating Fiscal Multipliers in Selected Asian Economics. *ADB Economics Working Paper* No. 638. Asian Development Bank.

Ramey, V. A. 2019. Ten Years after the Financial Crisis: What Have We Learned from the Renaissance in Fiscal Research? *Journal of Economic Perspectives* 33(2).

Sen, T. 2021. Exit Strategy to Ease or Eliminate Tax Responses to the COVID-19 Pandemic. *The Governance Brief* 43. Asian Development Bank.

Box 2.1.4 Public spending efficiency for better health, education, and social outcomes

In many parts of developing Asia, government spending needs to be ramped up in areas critical for promoting inclusive growth. Low public health spending can hinder inclusive growth because good health supports educational attainment and broader development (Cole and Neumayer 2006). Low public health spending leaves households dependent on private health care with high out-of-pocket costs. If health care is unaffordable, catastrophic accidents or illness can push vulnerable households into poverty. Developing Asia exhibits strong correlation between income and educational attainment, especially if years of schooling are adjusted to accommodate learning quality (World Bank 2018). Inclusive growth therefore requires adequate education spending to ensure quality and retain poor children, who are the most likely to drop out of school and thus suffer lower lifetime earnings.

Efficient government spending maximizes benefits. Data envelopment analysis, which shows achievable outcome improvement without additional spending, found significant scope to improve education and health spending efficiency in developing Asia (Clements, Gupta, and Jalles 2022). Spending inefficiency on health care in the region is estimated to average 7%, comparable with Latin America but worse than in advanced economies (box figure 1). Improvement can come from sharper targeting of poor regions, emphasis on preventative and primary care, and coordination of services across levels of government, as well as by providing more autonomy to health-care providers.

Educational outcomes can improve with increased education spending and better spending efficiency. Education spending inefficiency averages 16% in developing Asia, about a third better than in Latin America but much worse than in advanced economies (box figure 2). Efficiency can be improved by reallocating resources to primary and secondary education, focusing spending on essential school inputs, and reducing teacher absenteeism.

COVID-19 highlights how social assistance can mitigate adverse poverty impacts from large shocks. Takenaka (2022) found cash transfer programs in Viet Nam, for example, shielded 1.2 million people from poverty during the pandemic.

1 Inefficiency in government health expenditure

Government health spending efficiency in developing Asia is comparable with Latin America but lower than in advanced economies.

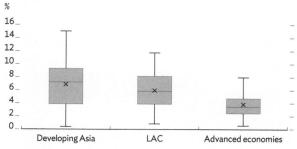

LAC = Latin America and the Caribbean.

Notes: Figures estimate inefficiency by economy using data envelopment analysis. Inefficiency is measured as the percentage increase in life expectancy that could be achieved if public per capita health spending were perfectly efficient. In each box plot, X marks the mean and the horizontal line the median. Box height accommodates half of the sample from the 75th percentile to the 25th, and extended whiskers include the whole sample. Developing Asia comprises 37 economies, LAC 30 countries, and advanced economies 35 countries.

Source: Clements, Gupta, and Jalles 2022.

2 Inefficiency in government education spending

Government education spending in developing Asia is much less efficient than in advanced economies.

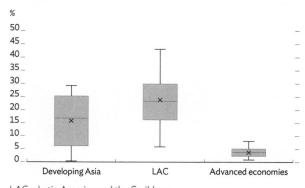

LAC = Latin America and the Caribbean.

Notes: Figures estimate inefficiency by economy using data envelopment analysis. Inefficiency is measured as the percentage increase in test scores and net enrollment rates that could be achieved if public spending per secondary school student were perfectly efficient. In each box plot, X marks the mean and the horizontal line the median. Box height accommodates half of the sample from the 75th percentile to the 25th, and extended whiskers include the whole sample. Developing Asia comprises 6 economies, LAC 13 countries, and advanced economies 28 countries.

Source: Clements, Gupta, and Jalles 2022.

continued on next page

Box 2.1.4 *Continued*

However, despite social benefit programs absorbing large government outlays in developing Asia, their effect on poverty and inequality is muted by incomplete coverage and modest individual benefits. Less than half of households in the poorest 20% of the population are covered by social protection and labor programs (box table). The average benefit paid by social protection programs is only 31% of the post-transfer income of the poorest quintile, which, as a result, receives only 10% of spending on these programs. Bad targeting is reflected as well in the low ratio of benefits accruing to the poor per dollar spent on these programs, which is only 19% in developing Asia.

References:
Clements, B., S. Gupta, and J. T. Jalles. 2022. *Fiscal Policy for Inclusive Growth in Asia.* Asian Development Bank.
Cole, M. and E. Neumayer. 2006. The Impact of Poor Health on Total Factor Productivity. *Journal of Development Studies* 42(6).
Takenaka, A. 2022. *Impact of Social Assistance on Vulnerable Vietnamese Groups during COVID-19: Evidence from Microsimulations.* Asian Development Bank.
World Bank. 2018. *Global Development Report.*

Performance of social protection and labor programs, developing Asia versus Latin America and the Caribbean

Social protection coverage is lower in developing Asia than Latin America.

	Developing Asia	Caucasus and Central Asia	Other developing Asia	LAC
Coverage (%) poorest quintile	43.40	57.60	38.90	66.30
Adequacy (%) poorest quintile	31.40	49.10	26.10	26.60
Poverty headcount reduction (%) from social protection and labor programs	18.80	36.80	13.10	14.40
Benefit incidence (%) poorest quintile	10.30	15.70	8.40	5.60
Benefit–cost ratio of social protection and labor programs	0.19	0.32	0.15	0.10

LAC = Latin America and the Caribbean.
Notes: Developing Asia comprises 26 economies and LAC 20 countries. Data are the latest available for each economy. For definitions of variables, refer to Clements, Gupta, and Jalles (2022).
Source: Clements, Gupta, and Jalles 2022.

Priorities for mobilizing tax revenue depend on economy-specific circumstances

Scope exists to mobilize tax revenue in developing Asia. It can be broadly assessed by estimating tax capacity and comparing it with current tax collection. Tax capacity is the theoretical maximum tax revenue an economy can mobilize given its characteristics, thus representing a revenue benchmark. Factors such as underdevelopment, low educational attainment, and a large agriculture sector tend to reduce tax capacity (Mawejje and Sebudde 2019). Tax effort is the ratio of actual tax revenue to tax capacity. High tax effort indicates actual tax collection close to tax capacity and thus less potential to increase revenue. Low effort indicates tax collection far short of tax capacity—possibly reflecting low tax rates, narrow tax bases, or poor compliance—and therefore strong potential for higher revenue.

Potential to increase developing Asia's tax revenue

New indicative tax capacity estimates suggest that developing Asia can increase tax revenue on average by the equivalent of 3%–4% of GDP, which is significant given current low tax collection. This benchmark tax revenue is estimated controlling for GDP per capita, the size of the agriculture sector, education spending, and trade openness (Gupta and Jalles 2022). Substantial subregional variation exists in tax capacity and tax effort. Tax effort is low and the potential to increase taxes is correspondingly great in Southeast Asia, particularly in Malaysia and Thailand. By contrast, tax effort and actual revenue are relatively high in the PRC, the ROK, and some Pacific island economies. In a few economies, notably the Lao People's Democratic Republic (Lao PDR), Papua New Guinea, and Timor-Leste, tax effort is high despite low actual tax collection (Figure 2.2.1).

Figure 2.2.1 Tax potential in Asia: tax capacity and tax revenue, latest available year

Potential to raise tax revenue is generally high in Southeast Asia.

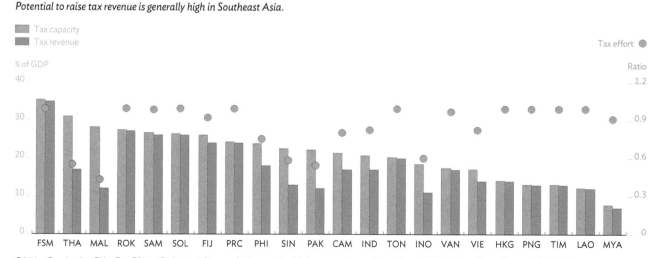

CAM = Cambodia, FIJ = Fiji, FSM = Federated States of Micronesia, GDP = gross domestic product, HKG = Hong Kong, China, IND = India, INO = Indonesia, LAO = Lao People's Democratic Republic, MAL = Malaysia, MYA = Myanmar, PAK = Pakistan, PHI = Philippines, PNG = Papua New Guinea, PRC = People's Republic of China, ROK = Republic of Korea, SAM = Samoa, SIN = Singapore, SOL = Solomon Islands, THA = Thailand, TIM = Timor-Leste, TON = Tonga, VAN = Vanuatu, VIE = Viet Nam.

Source: Gupta and Jalles 2022.

Regional variation underscores the need for economy-specific approaches to increasing revenue while avoiding excessive tax burdens that stifle economic growth.

Tax policy priorities to reflect economy-specific circumstances

Increasing tax revenue across developing Asia requires that governments make the most of key revenue sources—particularly VAT, personal and corporate income, and property taxes—in a manner consistent with local priorities and capacity. Some economies with very narrow tax bases have few options and need to carefully make the most of both tax and nontax revenue (Box 2.2.1). In many, weak enforcement capacity can be further hamstrung by scarce third-party information on taxpayers from firms (Kleven et al. 2011; Kleven, Kreiner, and Saez 2016; Pomeranz and Vila-Belda 2019). Acceleration in the digital economy under COVID-19 is creating new economic opportunities but also significant tax challenges, especially in regard to cross-border transactions.

While growth-friendly tax systems are essential, making tax progressive can be especially important in highly unequal economies with weak transfer systems. Income inequality generated by market forces before government taxes and social benefits is lower in developing Asia than in Latin American or high-income countries, as indicated by a lower Gini coefficient (Table 2.2.1). However, taxes and social benefits achieve only modest redistribution because taxes are less progressive and social benefits are modest and poorly targeted. Fiscal policies can promote economic growth without exacerbating income inequality. Empirically, inclusive growth episodes are more likely to occur in developing Asia where the population is better educated, spending on health and social benefits is higher, and tax and benefit systems are more redistributive (Clements, Gupta, and Jalles 2022).

Tax and spending policies therefore need to be considered together when weighing options to improve equity. Tax revenue typically contributes to inclusive development primarily by funding public expenditure that promotes equity. Even in OECD countries that rely heavily on progressive personal income taxes, transfers account for about three-quarters of combined reduction in income inequality achieved through transfers, personal income taxes, and social security contributions (Causa and Hermansen 2017).

A further consideration is fiscal decentralization, by which many economies in developing Asia allow subnational governments (SNGs) to generate their own revenue and take responsibility for sizeable spending. SNG proximity to residents can improve the design and implementation of public spending, facilitating efficient government. Fiscal decentralization is hindered, however, by imbalances between SNG expenditure obligations and own fiscal resources (Figure 2.2.2). The imbalance leaves SNGs vulnerable to central government decisions that make it difficult for SNGs to provide adequate public goods and services. To strengthen SNG own revenue and mitigate such risks, certain taxes are especially attractive for SNGs—notably property tax, as discussed below.

Table 2.2.1 Redistributive effects of fiscal policy, latest available data

Fiscal policy reduces inequality much less in developing Asia than in advanced economies.

	Gini coefficient, before tax and benefits	Gini coefficient, after tax and benefits
Developing Asia	42.7	38.4
Latin America and the Caribbean	48.1	45.4
Advanced economies	48.3	30.4

Notes: Calculations use the latest data available for each economy from 2010 to 2020. Developing Asia comprises 38 economies, Latin America and the Caribbean 26 countries, and advanced economies 30 countries. The redistributive effect of fiscal policy is the difference between the market income Gini coefficient and the net Gini coefficient.

Source: Clements, Gupta, and Jalles 2022.

Figure 2.2.2 Subnational government share of revenue and spending

Subnational government tax revenue in developing Asia is sometimes low compared with spending.

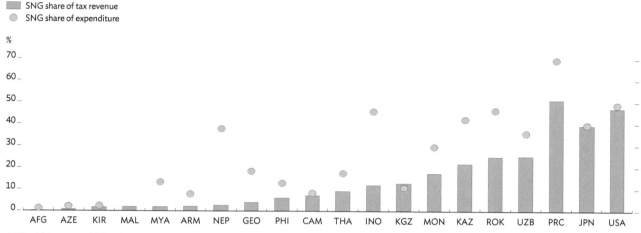

AFG = Afghanistan, ARM = Armenia, AZE = Azerbaijan, CAM = Cambodia, GEO = Georgia, INO = Indonesia, JPN = Japan, KAZ = Kazakhstan, KGZ = Kyrgyz Republic, KIR = Kiribati, MAL = Malaysia, MON = Mongolia, MYA = Myanmar, NEP = Nepal, PHI = Philippines, PRC = People's Republic of China, ROK = Republic of Korea, SNG = subnational government, THA = Thailand, USA = United States, UZB = Uzbekistan.

Notes: For Malaysia and the Philippines, the subnational figure is the difference between general and central government revenue. Subnational expenditure data is not available for Malaysia. The figure shows the most recent year with all entries for both revenue and expenditure: 2015 for the Republic of Korea; 2017 for Afghanistan and Cambodia; 2018 for Kiribati, the Philippines, Mongolia, Uzbekistan, the PRC, and the US; and 2019 for all other economies.

Sources: Asian Development Bank estimates based on IMF GFS Revenue and Expenditure by Function of Government (accessed 31 January 2022); and the Bureau of Local Government Finance for Philippine SNG expenditure data (accessed 16 February 2022).

But no one-size-fits-all and Box 2.2.2 examines the specific challenges facing the Philippines. ADB, for its part, is assisting SNGs in developing Asia to develop strategies to improve own-source revenues.

Costly tax expenditures used strategically and transparently

Optimizing taxes and ensuring tax system integrity requires careful management of special exemptions. Tax expenditures are concessions granted to specific industries, activities, or groups. They include exemptions, deductions, credits, deferrals, and lower tax rates intended to enhance social welfare, promote development, and support other policy goals (Haldenwang, Redonda, and Aliu 2021). Tax incentives, a type of tax expenditure, are designed to lure business activity, particularly foreign direct investment (FDI). Unlike direct expenditure, tax expenditures are not typically reported in a reliable, comparable, or open manner (CBO 2012; CRS 2019). Indeed, the costs and benefits of tax expenditures are assessed only infrequently and often unknown.

In a survey of 43 members of the Group of Twenty (G20) and OECD, only a small minority, including Australia and the ROK, published regular, comprehensive, and rigorous tax expenditure reports (Redonda and Neubig 2018). Thus, tax expenditures characteristically lack transparency and accountability, effectively permitting "spending" outside the budget (Burman and Phaup 2011).

Aside from costing revenue, tax expenditures render the tax system less efficient by narrowing the tax base. Concessions favoring certain taxpayers require governments to offset revenue losses by imposing higher tax burdens elsewhere (Bird 2008). Tax incentives for certain businesses can tilt the playing field and undermine competition. They may send an unwelcoming signal to some investors, potentially deterring less politically visible but beneficial investment. While it is often claimed that tax incentives create new investment that ultimately boosts revenue, they are associated with lower overall corporate tax revenue (Kronfol and Steenbergen 2020). Finally, tax expenditures likely increase enforcement costs and give rise to fraud and rent-seeking that further erode the tax base.

Tax expenditures are widely used in developing Asia and cause significant revenue loss. Surveys of regional tax authorities show tax incentives are used in almost every economy in the region, with tax holidays and tax rate reductions particularly prevalent (ADB 2022). The Global Tax Expenditure Database reveals tax expenditures in the region typically including exemptions, deductions, and reduced rates for taxes on income and consumption. While lower than the global average, possibly reflecting lower average tax rates, forgone revenue in a sample of economies in developing Asia was nevertheless substantial, equal on average to 2% of GDP or 14% of tax revenue, and particularly high in Armenia (Figure 2.2.3). These figures are conservative, as costs are unavailable for some tax expenditures (Haldenwang, Redonda, and Aliu 2021).

Figure 2.2.3 Revenue forgone to tax expenditures, selected economies

Widely used tax expenditures forego revenue equal to about 2% of GDP in developing Asia.

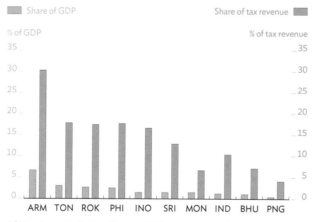

ARM = Armenia, BHU = Bhutan, GDP = gross domestic product, IND = India, INO = Indonesia, MON = Mongolia, PHI = Philippines, PNG = Papua New Guinea, ROK = Republic of Korea, SRI = Sri Lanka, TON = Tonga.
Note: Latest reference year with available data is 2019 for Armenia, the Philippines, Indonesia, the ROK, and Sri Lanka; 2018 for Bhutan, India, Mongolia, and Papua New Guinea; and 2014 for Tonga.
Sources: Global Tax Expenditure Database (accessed 1 December 2021); Asian Development Bank estimates.

Like direct expenditure, tax expenditures should have clear policy objectives and justifications and meet goals efficiently, cost effectively, and better than policy alternatives. Provided that intended beneficiaries are part of the tax system, well-designed tax expenditures can advance social policy objectives—as does, for example, a long-standing earned income tax credit in the US that supports poorer households (Hoynes and Patel 2018). Tax expenditures can similarly promote gender inclusion (Box 2.2.3). However, as discussed below, exemptions and other special arrangements for income and consumption taxes are often poorly targeted and inequitable.

While lower corporate income tax rates can attract FDI, evidence casts doubt on the effectiveness of tax incentives. This is particularly so for greenfield investment (Kinda 2014; Klemm and Van Parys 2012; Appiah-Kubi et al. 2021). Investor surveys consistently report that tax is only one of many factors that influence investment location and less important than political stability or the regulatory environment (World Bank 2018), and that many investments would proceed without tax incentives (James 2013). Incentives for FDI motivated by access to large markets or resources are likely to be particularly ineffective and wasteful (Andersen, Kett, and von Uexkull 2018). Broader, less-costly reform to improve the business environment may therefore attract FDI more effectively than tax incentives.

Stronger governance and improved reporting with cost estimates are essential to ensure that tax expenditures are optimized. Few economies in developing Asia provide regular, detailed tax expenditure assessments, though headway is being made. A tax incentive revenue impact statement is published with the Indian annual budget, and some Southeast Asian countries publish sporadic tax expenditure estimates (MOF 2022; ADB 2021d). In many economies, numerous government agencies, notably investment boards and sector ministries, can grant tax incentives, sometimes creating a proliferation of poorly designed and costly incentives (James 2016). Tax incentives should therefore be codified in tax law with only the finance minister authorized to grant discretionary incentives.

Value-added tax, a revenue mainstay to be optimized

Revenue from VAT, a relatively efficient tax, will likely remain a mainstay in developing Asia and therefore must be optimized. The self-enforcement property of VAT adds to its value. Firms pay VAT only on the value-added portion of their sales, with a tax deduction for inputs. To receive the deduction, firms require their suppliers to provide a receipt, creating an auditable paper trail and incentive for firms to report their activities correctly to tax authorities (Pomeranz 2015). Such self-enforcement can be strengthened. In the PRC, for example, a new digital invoice system narrowed scope for misreporting input costs and substantially boosted VAT revenue (Fan et al. 2021).

VAT is often considered regressive because poorer households spend more of their income. However, this depends on consumption patterns and tax design. Exemptions and lower rates often apply to food and other necessities, and evidence on equity is mixed (Alavuotunki, Haapanen, and Pirttila 2019; IMF 2019). Further, many poor households grow their own food and purchase goods and services from small vendors, leaving much of their consumption beyond the VAT net.

After accounting for consumption patterns, VAT may even be progressive in developing countries (Bachas, Gadenne, and Jensen 2021).

VAT revenue performance indicators show scope to increase VAT collection in developing Asia. C-efficiency is the ratio of actual to potential revenue, assuming a single VAT rate without exemptions that spans consumption with perfect compliance. High C-efficiency values therefore imply strong revenue performance. C-efficiency has gradually increased in developing Asia but varies across the region (Figure 2.2.4).

To increase VAT revenue, exemptions should be reviewed and tightened. This enables tax base broadening which is more conducive to economic growth than increasing tax rates (Acosta-Ormaechea and Morozumi 2021). VAT exemptions may benefit the poor, but they often benefit the wealthy even more because they consume more, making exemptions generally inefficient improvers of equity. Adverse impacts on the poor that occur as exemptions are removed can be offset by higher pro-poor spending financed by greater revenue. Simplification that removes exemptions and adopts streamlined rate structures can improve compliance. Complexity was a factor motivating Malaysia to abolish its goods and services tax in 2018 (Nutman, Isa, and Yussof 2021).

Figure 2.2.4 Value-added tax C-efficiency in developing Asia, 2000–2018

Across developing Asia, value-added tax efficiency varies but has generally improved.

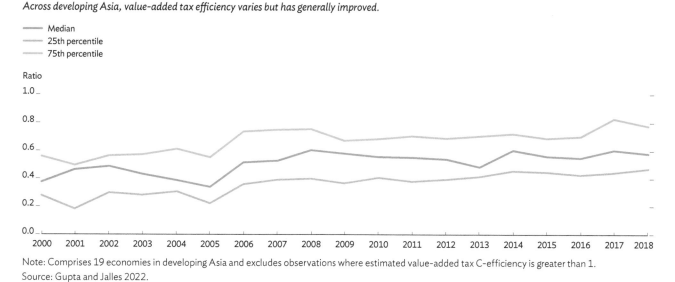

Note: Comprises 19 economies in developing Asia and excludes observations where estimated value-added tax C-efficiency is greater than 1.
Source: Gupta and Jalles 2022.

Across developing Asia, VAT rates average 11.9%, lower than 15.0% in Latin America and 19.7% in high-income OECD countries. At 10% or less, VAT rates are especially low in Maldives; Sri Lanka (lowered from 15% to 8% in 2019); Taipei,China; and Thailand (Figure 2.2.5). While less efficient than base broadening, raising VAT tax rates offers scope to lift revenue, particularly where existing rates are very low (Gunter et al. 2021). Indeed, as part of major tax reform to increase revenue, Indonesia hiked its VAT rate from 10% to 11% in 2022 and plans a further increase to 12% in 2025.

The VAT registration threshold for firms should balance revenue gains and compliance costs. A lower threshold supports revenue but increases compliance burdens for very small businesses and tax authorities, and it may encourage firms to underreport activity to stay small (Liu et al. 2021). This can have adverse consequences. In Thailand, unregistered firms had significantly lower growth rates than registered firms, especially those near registration thresholds (Muthitacharoen, Wanichthaworn, and Burong 2021).

Finally, rising digital commerce in the region needs careful management by tax authorities. VAT on imported goods can normally be collected at the border, but not for imported digital products delivered directly online to consumers. Foreign suppliers are often not required to register for or pay VAT. Further, imports may fall under VAT exemptions for low-value imports. The sharing economy, in which transactions are mostly on digital platforms, poses another risk to VAT.

VAT on digital imports bolsters revenue, ensures a level playing field for domestic suppliers, and is gradually being introduced across developing Asia. Half of Asian economies with VAT have rules that apply it to the digital economy (Mullins 2022). However, at this stage, few economies have VAT rules for goods and services supplied via domestic digital platforms. India is one, requiring suppliers and platform operators to register for the goods and services tax, with the operator collecting tax from suppliers.

Figure 2.2.5 VAT rates in developing Asia and average rate in selected regions

Across developing Asia, value-added tax rates are generally low.

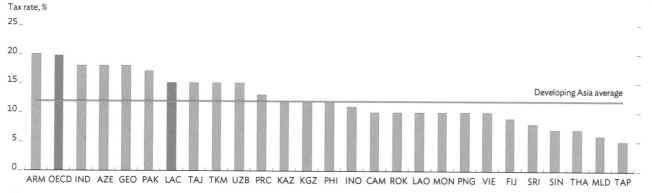

ARM = Armenia, AZE = Azerbaijan, CAM = Cambodia, FIJ = Fiji, GEO = Georgia, IND = India, INO = Indonesia, KAZ = Kazakhstan, KGZ = Kyrgyz Republic, LAC = Latin America and the Caribbean, LAO = Lao People's Democratic Republic, MLD = Maldives, MON = Mongolia, OECD = Organisation for Economic Co-operation and Development, PAK = Pakistan, PHI = Philippines, PNG = Papua New Guinea, PRC = People's Republic of China, ROK = Republic of Korea, SIN = Singapore, SRI = Sri Lanka, TAJ = Tajikistan, TAP = Taipei,China, THA = Thailand, TKM = Turkmenistan, UZB = Uzbekistan, VAT = value-added tax, VIE = Viet Nam.

Notes: General rate is shown for economies with multiple VAT rates. The Pakistan rate of 17% shown in the figure is the VAT on goods; 13% is levied on services. India has multiple VAT rates up to 28%, but the figure shows the general rate of 18%. Maldives has a general rate of 6% but imposes a higher rate of 12% on tourism goods and services.

Sources: PricewaterhouseCoopers. World Tax Summary (accessed 24 January 2022); Asian Development Bank estimates.

Personal income taxes to raise revenue and promote equity

Central to a progressive tax system is personal income tax with marginal rates that impose proportionately higher tax liability on higher earners. As noted above, they play a key role in OECD countries but are far less prominent in developing economies. In developing Asia, comparatively little revenue is generated by personal income tax, weakening its redistributive capacity (Vellutini and Benitez 2021). Across developing Asia, personal income tax revenue productivity—the amount of revenue generated by an incremental tax rate increase—is similar to other regions, but it varies enormously across the region (Gupta and Jalles 2022). In some economies, including Bangladesh, it is very low, suggesting significant shortcomings in policy design and enforcement and scope for personal income tax to generate more revenue and become more progressive.

A key challenge to increasing personal income tax revenue in developing economies is prevalent self-employment. This contributes to a dearth of third-party information on taxable income hindering enforcement and shrinking the tax base (Jensen 2022). Indeed, personal income tax is often paid only by high-income wage earners. However, a gradual transition away from self-employment readily enables governments to expand the personal income tax base. Typically, self-employment recedes as development transitions economies from agriculture to manufacturing and services (Gindling and Newhouse 2014). Developing Asia is no exception, with the average rate of self-employment falling from 56% in 2000 to 46% by 2019—still significantly higher than the OECD average but converging toward Latin America (Figure 2.2.6). However, developing Asia encompasses substantial variation, with self-employment very high in Afghanistan, India, and the Lao PDR but at less than one-quarter in Kazakhstan and the ROK (Figure 2.2.7).

While potentially making tax collection higher and more equitable, personal income tax can be economically costly. These costs can be especially high if marginal tax rates rise steeply (Heathcote, Storesletten, and Violante 2014; Blundell 2016; Keane and Wasi 2016; Wheaton 2022).

Higher tax rates reduce work incentives and can dampen labor supply, especially for highly skilled and internationally mobile workers (Akcigit, Baslandze, and Stantcheva 2016; Kleven et al. 2020). Personal income tax levied on household income can discourage female labor participation, exacerbating gender inequality (Box 2.2.3). By reducing lifetime earnings, progressive income tax weakens incentives to invest in human capital, compounding efficiency and output losses (Guvenen, Kuruscu, and Ozkan 2014).

The top marginal personal income tax rate has generally declined across developing Asia (Figure 2.2.8). The average rate of about 27% is much lower than 40% in OECD countries, but this obscures enormous variation within the region. India, Papua New Guinea, and the PRC have top marginal rates comparable to the OECD average or even higher. Meanwhile many Caucasus and Central Asian economies apply a flat tax rate of 10%–13%.

Except where rates are flat, the top marginal rate often applies to relatively high incomes. The average top marginal rate in developing Asia applies to income more than 12.3 times GDP per capita, much higher than 6.6 fold in Latin America and 4.1 fold in OECD countries (Figure 2.2.9). In economies where this threshold is high relative to average incomes, it could be lowered to boost personal income tax revenue.

Figure 2.2.6 Self-employment in selected regions, 2000–2019

Self-employment has steadily become less prevalent in developing Asia but is still higher than in OECD countries.

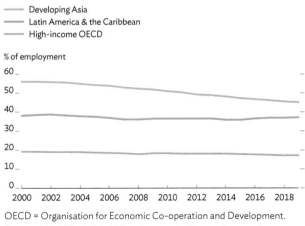

OECD = Organisation for Economic Co-operation and Development.
Sources: World Bank World Development Indicators (accessed 1 December 2021); Asian Development Bank estimates.

Figure 2.2.7 Self-employment in selected Asian economies, 2000 and 2019

The share of self-employment varies widely in developing Asia.

○ 2000
▨ 2019

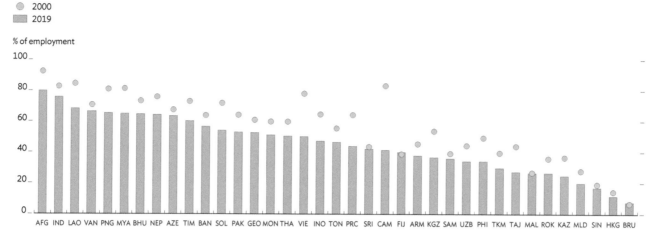

% of employment

AFG = Afghanistan, ARM = Armenia, AZE = Azerbaijan, BAN = Bangladesh, BHU = Bhutan, BRU = Brunei, CAM = Cambodia, FIJ = Fiji, GEO = Georgia, HKG = Hong Kong, China, IND = India, INO = Indonesia, KAZ = Kazakhstan, KGZ = Kyrgyz Republic, LAO = Lao People's Democratic Republic, MAL = Malaysia, MLD = Maldives, MON = Mongolia, MYA = Myanmar, NEP = Nepal, PAK = Pakistan, PHI = Philippines, PNG = Papua New Guinea, PRC = People's Republic of China, ROK = Republic of Korea, SAM = Samoa, SIN = Singapore, SOL = Solomon Islands, SRI = Sri Lanka, TAJ = Tajikistan, THA = Thailand, TIM = Timor-Leste, TKM = Turkmenistan, TON = Tonga, UZB = Uzbekistan, VAN = Vanuatu, VIE = Viet Nam.
Source: World Bank World Development Indicators (accessed 1 December 2021); Asian Development Bank estimates.

Figure 2.2.8 Personal income tax top marginal rates in developing Asia

Top marginal personal income tax rates have been trending down in developing Asia.

—— Median
—— 25th percentile
—— 75th percentile

Tax rate, %

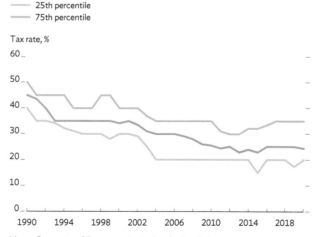

Note: Comprises 22 economies in developing Asia.
Source: Gupta and Jalles 2022.

Many economies in developing Asia apply a tax-free threshold, or zero tax bracket. By exempting the lowest earners, a threshold promotes progressivity and reduces potentially high compliance costs. In developing Asia, the threshold applies at more than the GDP per capita, lower than in Latin America but much higher than in OECD countries (Figure 2.2.9). To expand the tax base, the zero tax bracket could be lowered, particularly where it is comparatively high, enforcement capacity is strong, and third-party information on earnings is accessible. Where it is not currently applied, including in economies with flat taxes, a zero tax bracket could be added to strengthen progressivity. Some economies have potential to expand personal income tax collected through withholding arrangements (ADB 2021d).

Taxing individuals' capital income can promote progressivity, because wealthy individuals own a disproportionate share of capital, and better ensure appropriate taxing of self-employed entrepreneurs, who can shift their income from labor to capital. For this reason, similar tax rates should apply to capital and labor income. Capital income taxation is complicated in developing countries by scarce third-party information and the high mobility of capital.

Figure 2.2.9 Personal income tax maximum and minimum rate thresholds, selected regions

In developing Asia, top marginal personal income tax rates apply to income that is more than 12 times GDP per capita, higher than in other regions.

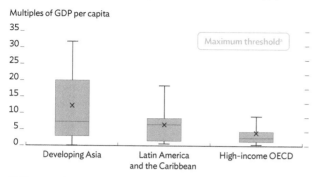

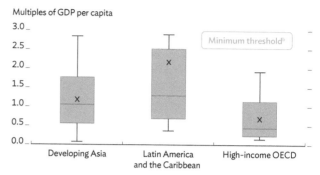

GDP = gross domestic product, OECD = Organisation for Economic Co-operation and Development.

a Comprises 23 economies in developing Asia, 18 economies in Latin America and the Caribbean, and 26 OECD countries. In each box plot, X marks the mean and the horizontal line the median. Box height accommodates half of the sample from the 75th percentile to the 25th, and extended whiskers include the whole sample, excluding as outliers Austria at 22.2 and the Philippines at 46.3.

b Comprises 24 economies in developing Asia, 16 economies in Latin America and the Caribbean, and 27 OECD countries. In each box plot, X marks the mean and the horizontal line the median. Box height accommodates half of the sample from the 75th percentile to the 25th, and extended whiskers include the whole sample, excluding as outliers the Slovak Republic at 3.0, Guatemala at 8.3, and Trinidad and Tobago at 9.2.

Source: Gupta and Jalles 2022.

The wealthy often locate their assets offshore, especially in tax havens, hindering tax enforcement. A voluntary disclosure scheme in Colombia revealed hidden wealth equal to 1.7% of GDP, of which 87% had been concealed offshore (Londoño-Vélez and Ávila-Mahecha 2021). Help could come from initiatives to improve information exchange between tax authorities, notably the Global Forum on Transparency and Exchange of Information for Tax Purposes, which includes 27 economies in developing Asia.

While many economies apply preferential tax schemes to certain types of capital income, this should be minimized. Such arrangements can distort investment, erode progressivity and the tax base, and complicate enforcement. Tax breaks to encourage retirement savings, for example, may encourage taxpayers not to save more but merely to shift their savings into tax-sheltered accounts, causing revenue losses that worsen inequity (Chetty et al. 2014).

Challenges posed by wealth taxes

Wealth inequality has worsened around the world along with income inequality. Interest in wealth taxes has intensified with public concern over wealthy individuals minimizing or avoiding tax obligations

(Piketty and Zucman 2014), as recently epitomized by the Panama Papers and Pandora Papers scandals. Comprehensive wealth taxes that feature appropriate tax-exempt thresholds can reduce inequality and make taxes more progressive (Saez and Zucman 2019). A wealth tax can be levied on transfers such as inheritance or gifts, on wealth holdings, or on wealth holdings that net the difference between assets and liabilities. In principle, all assets can be covered so that taxpayers cannot adjust their tax liability by shifting wealth from one asset class to another. Moreover, as tax is levied regardless of asset returns, individuals may be encouraged to invest in higher-yield assets, which could make asset allocation more efficient across the economy (Guvenen et al. 2019).

Notwithstanding these advantages, a wealth tax poses considerable implementation challenges in developing Asia. It requires significant administrative resources for recurrent asset evaluation, made harder by the absence of reference prices for some asset classes (IMF 2015; OECD 2018). Administrative costs are even higher for a net wealth tax, which requires valuations of both assets and liabilities. In addition, a wealth tax may entail equity concerns when two taxpayers with the same wealth, and hence the same tax liability, achieve different returns on their wealth. Taxpayers with illiquid assets may find it difficult to pay their tax liabilities.

The complexity of administering wealth taxes explains why they are used in only five countries: Colombia, France, Norway, Spain, and Switzerland. Moreover, even in these countries, which have strong administrative capacity, they generate little revenue, equal to about 0.5% of GDP in 2019 (OECD 2020). A few developing economies have experimented with wealth taxes, and their experiences cast further doubt on their potential in developing Asia (Scheuer and Slemrod 2021). India abolished its wealth tax in 2015 because of its high administrative cost and low revenue (*The Hindu* 2015). Given their low tax administration capacity, developing economies in Asia may be better off focusing on progressive taxes that are administratively simpler, particularly property taxes.

Property taxes similarly promoting equity

If well designed, property taxes are potentially progressive, efficient, and difficult to evade. Tax liability on immovable property cannot be readily shifted, making property tax less distortive than many others. The tax burden generally falls on property owners, who tend to be wealthier, though pass-through to renters may be possible depending on market dynamics. Property taxes can be levied on buildings— or on property transfers, though this is less efficient and housing price cycles can make revenue volatile.

Property taxes can bolster revenue for subnational governments in particular. Therefore property taxes can also advance fiscal decentralization, which is a challenge in some parts of developing Asia, as noted above (Bahl and Bird 2018; McCluskey, Bahl, and Franzsen 2022). Across the region, property taxes are administered by central or local authorities or both, but revenue generally accrues to localities. Rapid urbanization lifts land values, which bodes well for property tax that can help fund urban services and infrastructure. Property taxes can encourage owners to use scarce urban land efficiently, reducing sprawl and making cities more livable, sustainable, and productive.

Most economies in developing Asia levy property taxes. However, they generally raise little revenue, on average equal to a few tenths of a percentage point of GDP (McCluskey, Bahl, and Franzsen 2022).

Revenue is greater, at about 1% of GDP or more, in a handful of economies in developing Asia including the PRC, Georgia, the ROK, Singapore, and Uzbekistan, and about 2% in OECD countries. Thus, substantial scope exists to increase property tax revenue in developing Asia.

Governments must improve property valuation to capture rising value and enable growth in the tax base. The ratio of assessed value to market value is estimated at only 30%–50% in low-income countries (Kelly, White, and Anand 2020). Accurate property valuation is fair, and perceived subjectivity can subject valuation to criticism (Slack and Bird 2014). Broadly, valuation is determined by land area and the size of buildings or else uses market prices to estimate capital or rental values (Franzsen and McCluskey 2013).

Area valuation approaches are typically used where property markets are insufficiently developed to credibly determine value. While administratively simpler, they may unfairly fail to capture rising values or differences in property quality (McCluskey and Franzsen 2013; Rao 2008). Market valuation requires careful implementation, especially with frequent updating of market value, but in some economies in developing Asia several years may pass before revaluation (McCluskey, Bahl, and Franzsen 2022). Gradually shifting to more extensive use of market assessment as markets develop can strengthen property taxes, including in the Caucasus and Central Asia where, despite the rapid rise of private markets, area assessment continues to be widely used.

Technology can help keep property registers and values updated in a timely and cost-effective manner. Spatial data from remote imagery can be used to estimate building footprints and the built-up area and, combined with land prices, enable mass appraisal of property taxes (Ali, Deininger, and Wild 2018). Where price data are scarce, prices can be estimated using models that draw on spatial data.

Finally, property tax rates need to be sufficiently high and tax bases sufficiently broad. Raising low property tax rates in developing economies could yield substantial revenue gains (Kalkuhl et al. 2018). In addition to accurate registers, a strong tax base requires strictly judicious use of exemptions and preferential tax treatment. In developing Asia, property taxes generally cover both land and buildings, which broadens the tax base (McCluskey, Bahl, and Franzsen 2022). While taxing buildings may discourage property development, this can be minimized by applying a higher tax rate to land than buildings.

Multilateral initiatives to address corporate income tax challenges

While generally buoyant, corporate income tax revenue faces pressure in developing Asia. Motivated by a desire to attract internationally mobile capital and maintain competitiveness, governments have steadily reduced corporate income tax rates across the region over the past few decades, following a global trend (Figure 2.2.10). They are now typically 20% across developing Asia, down from 30% in 2000 and a little lower than Latin American and OECD averages. As noted above, tax incentives for business are widespread in developing Asia, reducing the effective tax rate.

Figure 2.2.10 Statutory corporate income tax rates in developing Asia

Following global trends, corporate income tax rates have declined in developing Asia.

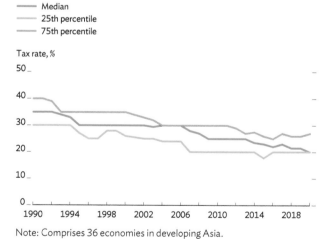

Note: Comprises 36 economies in developing Asia.
Source: Gupta and Jalles 2022.

Corporate tax revenue is also threatened by tax avoidance. A weak international tax framework and differences across economies in tax policy, especially tax rates, can be exploited by multinational enterprises (MNEs) to reduce their tax liability.

Firms can engage in transfer pricing, or mispricing transactions between their subsidiaries, and route income through economies with the most advantageous tax treaties. This enables shifting of income and profit to lower-tax jurisdictions to reduce tax liability. Global revenue losses from tax avoidance have been estimated at 4%–10% of corporate income tax revenue, with larger losses for developing economies (IMF 2014; OECD 2015; Crivelli, De Mooij, and Keen 2016). Within Asia, estimated revenue loss in South Asia equals 1.7%–1.9% of GDP, and in East Asia and the Pacific 0.6%–0.7% (Cobham and Jansky 2018). MNE tax avoidance distorts the location of FDI and mobile assets and gives MNEs unfair competitive advantage.

The rise of the digital economy in developing Asia exacerbates corporate income tax avoidance. Digitalization makes it hard to tell the economy from which profits are derived as, for example, software sold from a platform in one economy is downloaded by a user in another economy. Further, intangible assets such as licenses, trademarks, and data, which are easy to shift to lower-tax jurisdictions, are prevalent in the digital economy. The difficulty of determining arm's length prices for digital intangibles increases firms' ability to exploit transfer pricing. It is likely that digital MNEs benefit significantly from tax planning and enjoy lower effective tax rates (Mullins 2022).

Pressure from tax competition and avoidance has fueled concern that firms do not always pay their fair share of tax. The need to address international tax challenges arising from or worsened by digitalization has led a growing number of governments, including in developing Asia, to introduce discrete digital service taxes. However, they have generated little revenue and provoked retaliatory trade measures (ADB 2022; Mullins 2022), spurring efforts to secure multilateral solutions, notably the G20–OECD project on base erosion and profit shifting and subsequent work by the Inclusive Framework, which includes 20 economies in developing Asia. In 2021, the Inclusive Framework endorsed a new international tax framework featuring two pillars. Under Pillar 1, profits and taxing rights are shared by economies to include those where MNEs derive revenue. Pillar 2 proposes a global minimum corporate income tax rate of 15%. Together, the two pillars aim to be fair, mitigate a race to the bottom on corporate income tax rates, and provide more certainty to taxpayers and tax administrations.

Revenue impact on developing Asia from the reallocation of taxable profits under Pillar 1 is expected to be small. For example, estimated revenue gains or losses for most economies in the region are generally around 0.01% of GDP (IMF 2021). Resource-rich economies that host MNEs, such as Papua New Guinea, and larger economies such as the PRC and the ROK gain the most, while Singapore and Hong Kong, China lose the most in their roles as investment hubs. Additional global tax revenue from Pillar 2 is estimated at about $150 billion per year (OECD 2021a). Again, the immediate revenue impact on developing Asia will likely be modest because corporate income tax rates already exceed 15% in most regional economies. However, tax incentives that reduce the effective tax rate may be undone by the Pillar 2 minimum tax and hence should be reassessed.

Economies agreeing to the new rules will need to implement required changes to local laws. Those not agreeing have the option of waiting and ensuring that any commitment is consistent with domestic priorities and administrative capacity. Economies may retain their tax on digital services until Pillar 1 transition requirements are settled. Natural resource revenue—important in a small number of commodity-rich economies in developing Asia—faces additional unique challenges that need to be carefully managed (Box 2.2.4).

Governments in developing Asia must mobilize tax revenue to fund the vast public spending needed to achieve the SDGs. At the same time, some taxes yield double dividends by contributing directly to the SDGs and raising revenues. The next section discusses two such taxes: green taxes that promote a cleaner environment, and corrective health taxes that encourage healthier lifestyles.

Box 2.2.1 Revenue-mobilizing priorities in small Pacific island economies and fragile and conflict-affected situations

Heterogenous developing Asia needs economy-specific approaches to mobilizing tax revenue, especially in Pacific island economies (PIEs) and fragile and conflict-affected situations (FCASs). These economies suffer sometimes low and volatile tax revenue and often rely on nontax revenue (box figure). In 2020, some of the steepest declines in tax revenue across Asia and the Pacific occurred in these economies. At the same time, they require significant public expenditure for infrastructure, health and education, and combating climate change.

The small and undiversified PIEs have narrow tax bases that rely heavily on tourism and fishing. Other challenges include large informal sectors and natural hazards. FCASs face serious challenges to tax collection, especially from poor security and frequent economic shocks. Moreover, implementing complex tax reform following conflict, when the state remains weak, poses major difficulties. A further complication is that often large official development assistance can weaken incentives for governments to mobilize domestic revenue (Thornton 2014; Benedek et al. 2014).

Given difficult circumstances and low institutional capacity in PIEs and FCASs, tax policy needs to be pragmatic. Revenue mobilization may require governments to resort to less efficient taxes, such as on trade, or rely heavily on fewer taxpayers, particularly large companies. In FCASs, the authorities must prioritize viable collection points such as border checkpoints and economic activity in large cities and other areas under government control (Mansour and Schneider 2019).

Despite the challenges, before COVID-19, PIEs were generally mobilizing revenue well—better than Caribbean island economies. Average ratios of tax to GDP rose from 18.2% early in the 2010s to 21.5% later in the decade. Encouragingly, this coincided with a shift from trade taxes to more efficient indirect taxes. Impressive gains were achieved as well in nontax revenue, especially license fees from foreign fishing vessels.

continued on next page

Box 2.2.1 *Continued*

Ratio of tax to GDP in 2010–2019 and
revenue composition in 2015–2019

While tax collection in PIEs and FCASs has improved,
nontax revenues remain vital.

- 2010–2014
- 2015–2019

% of GDP

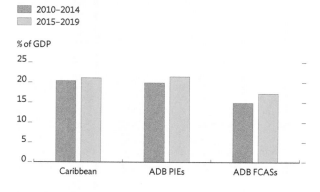

- Tax revenue
- Nontax revenue
- Grants

%

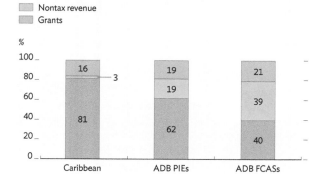

ADB = Asian Development Bank, FCAS = fragile and conflict-affected
situation, PIE = Pacific island economy.

Notes: The Caribbean is represented by nine economies. Ten countries
in the Pacific, South Asia, and Southeast Asia are counted as FCASs,
and seven countries in the Pacific as PIEs.

Sources: OECD. Global Revenue Statistics Database; IMF.
Government Finance Statistics online database (both accessed
31 January 2022); ADB staff estimates.

How was this achieved? In the 2000s, PIEs
embarked on several tax policy and administration
reforms. Some introduced value-added tax (VAT)
or adjusted VAT rates. Vanuatu, for example,
raised its VAT rate from 12.5% to 15.0% in 2018,
boosting tax collection by over 15% in 2 years.
The average VAT rate for PIEs is now about 12%,
still somewhat lower than the global average.
Many PIEs increased excise taxes on fuel, alcohol,
tobacco, and unhealthy food. Importantly, Pacific
economies strengthened their tax administration
capacity with information technology and improved
organizational capacity and planning.

FCASs similarly improved tax revenue before
COVID-19, albeit from a low starting point.
Reducing conflict intensity facilitates tax collection
(Chowdhury and Murshed 2016), as does
modernizing tax administrations. Reducing tax
exemptions, prioritizing industries with high revenue
potential, and increasing excises on alcohol, tobacco,
and fuel can also help (Akitoby et al. 2020).

References:
Akitoby, B. et al. 2020. Tax Revenue Mobilization Episodes in
Developing Countries. *Policy Design and Practice* 3(1).
Benedek, D. et al. 2014. Foreign Aid and Revenue:
Still a Crowding-Out Effect? *FinanzArchiv/Public Finance
Analysis* 70. March.
Chowdhury, A. R. and S. M. Murshed. 2016. Conflict and
Fiscal Capacity. *Defence and Peace Economics* 27.
Mansour, M., and J.-L. Schneider. 2019. How to Design Tax
Policy in Fragile States. *IMF Note* 19/04. International
Monetary Fund.
Thornton, J. 2014. Does Foreign Aid Reduce Tax Revenue?
Further Evidence. *Applied Economics* 46.

Box 2.2.2 Local fiscal revenue mobilization in the Philippines

To fund local services, subnational governments in the Philippines, called local government units (LGUs), depend heavily on intergovernmental fiscal transfers. In particular, they rely on internal revenue allotments (IRA) from the central government (box figure). Raising revenue locally is challenged by low capacity for own-sourced revenue mobilization, legal impediments, the disincentive effect of internal revenue allotments, and fiscal policy politics. The 1991 Local Government Code mandates LGUs to impose and collect various types of local taxes, but they still rely on allotments from the national government as their main income source, which inhibits fiscal responsibility and autonomy. Further, property taxes are low in most LGUs because property is undervalued, the values not updated regularly.

To strengthen the LGU framework, the President of the Philippines signed on 1 June 2021 Executive Order No. 138. This created a committee to devolve certain executive branch functions to LGUs in line with the Constitution and the 1991 Local Government Code. A Supreme Court ruling on the Mandanas–Garcia case in 2018, confirmed in 2019, mandates that the calculation of internal revenue allotment include not just taxes collected by the Bureau of Internal Revenue but all taxes and duties collected by government agencies including the Bureau of Customs. The order will (i) establish oversight and monitoring mechanisms

to resolve issues and concerns that may arise in implementing the Mandanas ruling; (ii) set up the Growth Equity Fund to address issues on marginalization, unequal development, high poverty incidence, and capacity disparity in LGUs; and (iii) adopt transition plans to ensure continuous service delivery by national government agencies and LGUs.

Various reforms aim to improve LGU resource mobilization. The government's current reform of real property valuation and assessment aims to centralize real property valuation functions in the Bureau of Local Government Finance. With ADB support, a database will be established to make real property valuation more efficient and gradually bring taxable value closer to market value. LGUs will be expected to adhere to the bureau's standardized schedule of market values to mitigate local political intervention that tends to keep taxable value artificially low. In addition, a mechanism has been developed to encourage LGUs to step up revenue performance. Under the Seal of Good Local Governance, the government has introduced minimum public financial performance standards, including own-sourced revenue performance, and an incentive fund to provide additional fiscal resources to LGUs that pass annual evaluation exercises offered by the Department of the Interior and Local Government.

Sources of revenue for local government units in the Philippines in 2020, %

Less than half of local government revenue comes from local taxes.

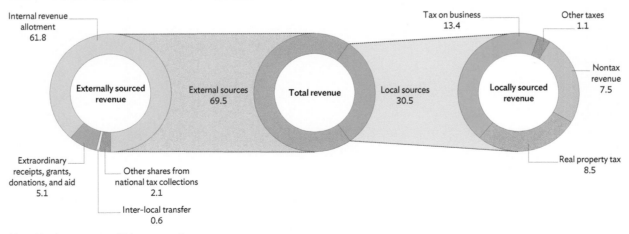

Note: Numbers may not add due to rounding.

Source: Asian Development Bank estimates using data from the Bureau of Local Government Finance (accessed 12 February 2022).

Box 2.2.3 Tax policy and gender equality

Developing Asia suffers a persistent gender gap in labor participation (box figure). Such gaps can be exacerbated by personal income taxation that effectively imposes a higher tax rate on second earners in a household because of how joint filing and various household tax credits work (OECD 2021). Evidence exists that joint taxation—with married females more likely than males to be second earners—keeps some married women out of the labor force (Bick and Fuchs-Schündeln 2017).

Tax credits encourage lower earners to work more and can therefore support female labor participation. Evidence suggests that such schemes increase the working hours of eligible mothers, though not wages over the long term (Bastian 2020). However, as tax credits are household benefits, they may discourage married women from working (Francesconi, Rainer, and Van Der Klaauw 2009). By increasing household income, tax credits reduce the need for a second earner, more likely a woman. Tax credits are also costly to administer, unlikely to benefit informal workers, and typically used in developed economies.

Other types of taxes may also have gender consequences. As women are overrepresented among the poor, they may be disproportionally affected by consumption taxes (Actionaid 2016). Exempting some necessities from value-added tax may help low-income households headed by single mothers (Bhattacharya and Stotsky 2022). While corporate income taxes are gender-neutral, offering tax incentives for hiring more female workers can promote gender equality, as can expanding tax exemptions on, for example, menstrual hygiene goods and childcare services (Stotsky, forthcoming).

Labor participation by sex, 2019

Labor participation gender gaps are especially large in South Asia.

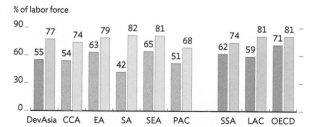

■ Female
□ Male

% of labor force

CCA = Caucasus and Central Asia, DevAsia = Developing Asia, EA = East Asia, LAC = Latin America and the Caribbean, OECD = Organisation for Economic Co-operation and Development, PAC = Pacific, SA = South Asia, SEA = Southeast Asia, SSA = Sub-Saharan Africa.

Source: World Bank World Development Indicators (accessed 22 December 2021).

References:
Actionaid. 2016. *Making Tax Work for Women's Rights.*
Bastian, J. 2020. The Rise of Working Mothers and the 1975 Earned Income Tax Credit. *American Economic Journal: Economic Policy* 12(3).
Bhattacharya, S. and J. G. Stotsky. 2022. *Tax Primer: With Applications to Asia-Pacific Countries.* Asian Development Bank.
Bick, A. and N. Fuchs-Schündeln. 2017. Quantifying the Disincentive Effects of Joint Taxation on Married Women's Labor Supply. *American Economic Review* 107(5).
Francesconi, M., H. Rainer, and W. Van Der Klaauw. 2009. The Effects of In-Work Benefit Reform in Britain on Couples: Theory and Evidence. *Economic Journal* 119(535).
OECD. 2021. *Taxing Wages.* Organisation for Economic Co-operation and Development Publishing.
Stotsky, J. Forthcoming. *Taxation and Social Protection.* Asian Development Bank.

Box 2.2.4 Raising revenue from natural resources

Natural resources provide a substantial share of government revenue in resource-rich developing economies, including some in developing Asia. This share exceeds 50% in most oil-rich economies and about 10% in mining economies (IMF 2012; Baunsgaard and Devlin 2021). Appropriate tax design for this revenue is essential to ensure that nonrenewable natural resources support sustainable development (Calder 2014). Standard tax codes may not apply to large and profitable resource projects that involve powerful multinationals, which often enjoy greater bargaining power than host governments over resource rents (McMillan and Waxman 2007; Davies and Schröder 2019). Low administrative capacity and transparency, political imperatives and corruption, and urgent needs for government revenue can weaken government bargaining positions. By contrast, stable fiscal regimes and reliable adherence to agreements are attractive to foreign investors, improving governments' bargaining power.

The "government take" from resource projects varies substantially within and between economies, reflecting bargaining power and other factors. The share of resource output accruing to the government—a crude proxy for its take—is on average higher in the region's oil-producing countries than in mining economies (box figure). It correlates positively with commodity prices as several tax instruments are based on profit, so government takes declined across economies with the end of the commodities super cycle in 2014 and the onset of COVID-19 in 2020. The take also varies over the lifecycle of resource projects, tending to be low initially as investors recover their costs, rising in the mature stage with higher profits, and falling again toward the end as marginal costs increase.

Variations in government take over time can induce macroeconomic instability. For example, a fall in government take—as several regional economies have experienced since 2014—often requires painful reduction in fiscal spending and lower incomes. Even absent fiscal adjustment, currency overvaluation in real effective terms may reduce growth and employment.

Government take in selected economies in developing Asia

Oil-rich economies have higher government takes, but they fluctuate with commodity cycles.

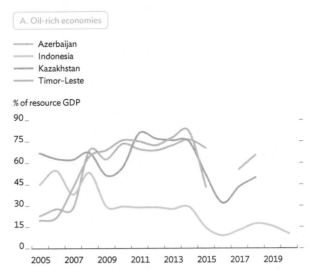

A. Oil-rich economies

— Azerbaijan
— Indonesia
— Kazakhstan
— Timor-Leste

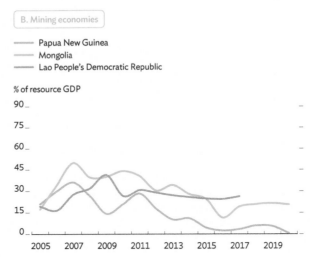

B. Mining economies

— Papua New Guinea
— Mongolia
— Lao People's Democratic Republic

GDP = gross domestic product.

Notes: No data on resource revenue are available for Azerbaijan in 2016. Papua New Guinea also produces oil and liquefied natural gas.

Sources: CEIC Data Company; Haver Analytics; Australian National University Development Policy Centre. PNG Budget Database; National Statistics Office of Mongolia. Mongolian Statistical Information Service; International Centre for Tax and Development Government Revenue Dataset (all accessed October 2021).

continued on next page

Box 2.2.4 *Continued*

Aside from capturing a reasonable share of resource rents, an important design objective is smoothing government revenue over time. While the governments of resource-rich developing economies cannot stabilize global commodity prices, they can avoid excessive backloading of revenue as is common in the life cycle of resource projects. This can be achieved by relying more on production levies or sales royalties than on profit-based taxes. Such measures provide early revenue and are relatively stable during commodity price downturns.

Governments can also secure payments up front through lump-sum bonuses tied to specific events such as reaching certain production thresholds. Although some governments favor equity participation in resource projects—often for nonfiscal considerations such as wanting a "seat at the table" (IMF 2012)—this may significantly defer revenue if debt financing is involved. Further, tax incentives such as arrangements for accelerated depreciation or loss carried forward can exacerbate the challenge of backloaded revenue. Experience in Papua New Guinea highlights the importance of these issues. Falling commodity prices, generous tax concessions, and failure to capture early revenue from a large liquefied natural gas project have combined to cause a precipitous collapse in revenue.

Finally, resource sector tax compliance risks can be large. While they can be mitigated by international initiatives such as the Group of Twenty and Organisation for Economic Co-operation and Development joint project on base erosion and profit shifting, governments need to pay careful attention to tax design strategies. Double tax treaties typically supersede domestic legislation and can feature tax concessions, creating "treaty shopping" risks.

To mitigate threats to revenue posed by transfer pricing, specific rules related to transfer pricing costs should be incorporated into tax legislation and investment agreements (Lemgruber and Shelton 2014). Appropriately designed ring-fencing regimes are crucial to limit cost deductions for tax purposes across different projects of the same tax-paying entity. Some economies ring-fence license areas while others ring-fence individual resource projects (Baunsgaard 2001; Calder 2014). In practice, administering ring-fencing rules is complex, requiring adequate capacity building.

References:
Baunsgaard, T. 2001. A Primer on Mineral Taxation. *IMF Working Paper* No. 01/139. International Monetary Fund.
Baunsgaard, T. and D. Devlin. 2021. Resource-Rich Developing Countries and International Tax Reforms. In R. de Mooij, A. Klemm, and V. Perry, eds. *Corporate Income Taxes under Pressure: Why Reform Is Needed and How It Could Be Designed.* International Monetary Fund.
Calder, J. 2014. *Administering Fiscal Regimes for Extractive Industries: A Handbook.* International Monetary Fund.
Davies, M. and M. Schröder. 2019. Does the PNG Government Get Its Fair Share from the Resource Sector? Presented at 2019 PNG Update.
IMF. 2012. *Fiscal Regimes for Extractive Industries: Design and Implementation.* International Monetary Fund.
Lemgruber, A. and S. Shelton. 2014. Revenue Administration: Administering Revenues from Natural Resources— A Short Primer. *Technical Notes and Manuals* No. 14/02. International Monetary Fund.
McMillan, M. and A. R. Waxman. 2007. Profit Sharing between Governments and Multinationals in Natural Resource Extraction: Evidence from a Firm-Level Panel. *Brookings Trade Forum Foreign Direct Investment.* Brookings Institution Press.

Green and health taxes strengthen revenue and development

Green and health taxes are levied to change behavior—discouraging bad or encouraging good—and to generate revenue. They can address negative externalities such as pollution and thus contribute to meeting the SDGs. These taxes are product-specific, levied in addition to general consumption taxes, and often labeled excise taxes. They continue to grow and guide investment and consumption in developing Asia. Some Asian economies have long histories of using specific environmental taxes, with taxes on pollutants and fossil fuels like coal and gasoline widely used. More recently, governments have explored carbon pricing instruments to help curb greenhouse gas (GHG) emissions, drawing on valuable lessons from early adopters. Many economies in developing Asia have also adopted corrective health taxes, primarily on alcohol, tobacco or sugar-sweetened beverages, that can raise additional tax revenue up to the equivalent of 0.6% of GDP while improving health outcomes and cutting medical costs.

Green taxes for clean environment and revenue generation

During its decades of rapid growth, developing Asia adopted a strategy of "pollute first and clean up later." Consequently, the region now faces significant environmental challenges, particularly severe air pollution from high industrial emissions and other causes (Arimura et al. 2022). Population-weighted exposure to the small particulate matter that is especially damaging to health, abbreviated PM2.5, is often very high in developing Asia (Figure 2.3.1). Most of the deaths from air pollution recorded annually around the world are in Asia and the Pacific (UNEP 2019). Developing Asia produces half of global GHG emissions, which are rising in many regional economies. In response, Asia is bolstering its efforts to promote sustainable development,

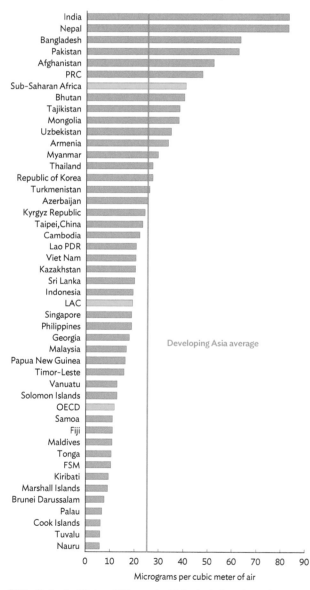

Figure 2.3.1 Average annual population-weighted air pollution exposure in 2019 in Asia

Exposure to air pollution is often high in developing Asia.

FSM = Federated States of Micronesia, LAC = Latin America and the Caribbean, Lao PDR = Lao People's Democratic Republic, OECD = Organisation for Economic Co-operation and Development, PRC = People's Republic of China.

Sources: State of Global Air (accessed 13 January 2021); Asian Development Bank estimates.

with many governments pledging to work toward net zero emissions and adopting environmental tax and carbon-pricing instruments. This section reviews Asia's experiences with these policies, broadly finding that they can use them better to raise revenue and secure environmental benefits.

Use of environment taxes in Asia

Some Asian economies have long histories of using specific environmental taxes. Studies have shown that such policies can effectively reduce emissions and pollution in the region (Wang et al. 2020). Beginning in the 1980s, for example, the PRC applied a pollutant discharge fee to a broad range of pollutants. It generated a modest but steadily rising revenue stream that reached about $2.8 billion by 2015 (Figure 2.3.2). In 2018, the fee was replaced with an environment protection tax to improve monitoring, collection, and accountability. While revenue continued to rise, reaching $3.2 billion by 2019, it remained a negligible share of all tax revenue. Similarly, India started charging a water cess—a specific tax with earmarked revenue—to curb water pollution in the late 1970s and a coal cess to reduce coal production and consumption in 2010 (Figure 2.3.3). These measures generated revenue to fund pollution reduction and clean energy development until 2017, after which a new goods and services tax took over as the funding source.

More generally, many Asian economies tax fossil fuels, notably gasoline. Often these taxes were not motivated by environmental goals but by other objectives such as energy security. Nevertheless, they yield environmental benefits by suppressing fossil fuel demand and reducing pollution and congestion, amounting in effect to a carbon tax. Many economies in the region apply complementary automobile fees and taxes to suppress private vehicle usage in favor of public transportation. Together, such taxes can yield considerable revenue. In Japan, gasoline and diesel tax revenue reached $31.8 billion in 2020, and automobile tax $84.3 billion, collectively providing 11% of tax revenue (JAMA 2020).

Despite similar supply costs for road transport fuel, retail diesel and gasoline prices vary enormously across the region because of taxes, subsidies, price regulation, and other factors.

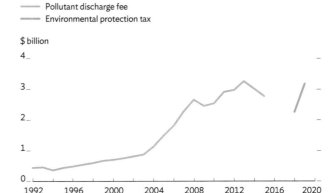

Figure 2.3.2 PRC revenue from the pollutant discharge fee and environmental protection tax, 1992–2019

Revenue from past and current PRC environmental taxes is modest but on the rise.

PRC = People's Republic of China.
Note: No data for 2016 and 2017.
Sources: Ministry of Ecology and Environment of the People's Republic of China (accessed 7 October 2021); OECD. Revenue Statistics in Asia and the Pacific (accessed 23 September 2021); CEIC Data Company (accessed 1 March 2022); Asian Development Bank estimates.

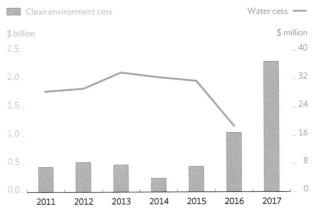

Figure 2.3.3 India revenue generated by water and clean environment cess

In India, a water cess and a clean environment cess generated revenue until they were replaced in 2017 by a goods and services tax.

Sources: Government of India, Ministry of Finance. *Union Budget Reports* (various years); IISD 2017; IISD 2020; Chandra 2021; Asian Development Bank estimates.

In Singapore and Hong Kong, China, prices are higher even than in wealthy OECD countries, which generally impose heavy taxes on gasoline (Figure 2.3.4). In Japan, for example, gasoline tax accounts for more than one-third of the pump price.

Figure 2.3.4 Retail fuel prices in Asia on 10 January 2022, $/liter

Retail gasoline and diesel prices vary greatly within the region.

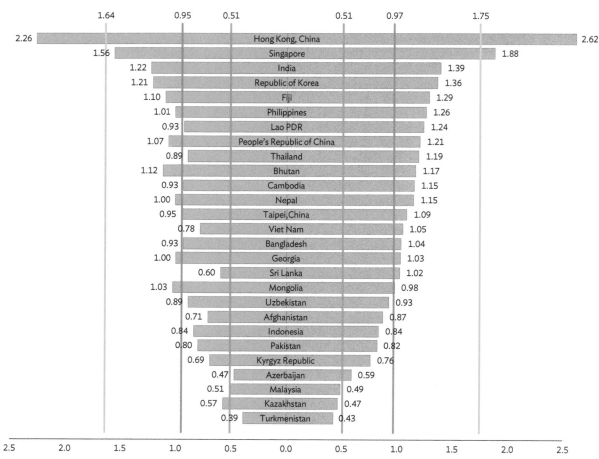

Lao PDR = Lao People's Democratic Republic, OECD = Organisation for Economic Co-operation and Development.
Sources: Global Petrol Prices; Bloomberg (both accessed 18 January 2022); Asian Development Bank estimates.

However, in many Asian economies, prices remain very low by international standards. More generally, in many economies including India, Indonesia, the PRC, the ROK, and Viet Nam, prices for diesel, gasoline, coal, and natural gas are below the estimated "efficient price," which takes in account environmental externalities (Parry, Black, and Vernon 2021). This suggests significant scope for raising fossil fuel taxes to support revenue generation and environmental goals.

Carbon pricing nascent in the region but with great promise

Governments in Asia and elsewhere implement carbon pricing by either applying a carbon tax or launching emission trading systems or schemes (ETSs) to spur low-carbon development and tackle climate change. By 2021, carbon pricing had been implemented in many regional economies, including Japan, Kazakhstan, the PRC, the ROK, and Singapore, with Indonesia planning to follow in 2022.

If well designed and implemented, carbon pricing can cost-effectively incentivize low-emitting production processes and consumption choices, as well as general economizing on carbon-emitting activities. While not a tax, ETSs closely resemble carbon taxes and similarly generate revenue.

Asian economies have adopted a gradual approach to introducing carbon-pricing instruments.
They have applied carbon tax rates generally much lower than in Canada or Europe (Table 2.3.1). Singapore's carbon tax introduced in 2019 targets around 40 large emitters, mostly petroleum-refining, chemical, and semiconductor companies, which contribute about 80% of Singapore's GHG emissions. Singapore's carbon tax rate was initially set low to allow firms time to adjust, with plans to increase rates from $3.70 per ton of carbon dioxide equivalent (tCO_2e) in 2019 to $18.60 in 2024 and $33.40 in 2026, rising further from 2028 to $37.10–$59.40 by 2030, as indicated in its 2022 budget. According to Haver Analytics, carbon tax revenue was $150.4 million in 2020 and $143.5 million in 2021, accounting for about 0.3% of $45.7 billion in tax revenue in 2020 and $54.2 billion in 2021, according to Ministry of Finance data.

Indonesia announced a carbon tax beginning in 2022 with an initial price of $2.10 per tCO_2e.

The ROK emissions trading system commenced in 2015 with phased implementation to 2024 that gradually expands coverage. All emission permits were initially distributed without charge, but by the final phase of implementation, at least 10% of permits will be auctioned to lift revenue. By August 2021, revenue from the system was $407.3 million, of which $210.4 million was collected in 2020 alone (ICAP 2021). The government has proposed options for earmarking revenue, including GHS mitigation, low-carbon innovation, and technological support (IETA 2020).

The PRC implemented a national ETS in July 2021.
It focused on carbon dioxide emission intensity, covering 2,225 electric power operators that account for about 40% of PRC energy emissions. Initially, emission allowances are free, but auctions may be introduced later. The national system follows eight subnational pilot ETSs with different designs and practices that will be integrated into the national ETS (Table 2.3.2).

Table 2.3.1 Carbon taxes in selected economies

Carbon tax rates are low in Asia compared with Canada and Europe.

Economy	Introduction year	Emissions covered, %	Fuels covered	Exempted sectors or fuels	Tax rate in 2021, $/$tCO_2e$	Revenue in 2020, $ million
Asia						
Singapore	2019	80	NA	Yes	3.7	198
Japan	2012	70	All fossil fuels	Yes	2.5[a]	2,192
Indonesia	2022	NA	NA	NA	2.1[b]	NA
Other economies						
Mexico	2014	23	All fuels except natural gas	NA	3.0	230
British Columbia (Canada)	2008	78	All fuels and tires burned	Yes	36.0	1,266
Sweden	1991	40	All fossil fuels	Yes	137.0	2,284
France	2014	35	All fossil fuels	Yes	52.0	9,632
South Africa	2019	80	NA	Yes	9.0	43
Chile	2017	39	All fossil fuels	NA	5.0	165

NA = not available, tCO_2 = ton of carbon dioxide, tCO_2e = ton of carbon dioxide equivalent.
[a] $/$tCO_2$.
[b] The price is for 2022.
Source: Arimura et al. 2022.

Table 2.3.2 Pilot emission trading systems in the People's Republic of China

Pilot emission trading systems in the People's Republic of China generated modest revenue.

City/Province	Launch	Revenue to 2020, $ million
Shenzhen	June 2013	0.4
Beijing	November 2013	NA
Shanghai	November 2013	14.8
Guangdong	December 2013	118.2
Tianjin	December 2013	50.7
Hubei	April 2014	30.7
Chongqing	June 2014	NA
Fujian	September 2016	0.2

NA = not available.

Source: ICAP 2021, various reports.

As benchmarks gradually tighten, the national ETS is expected to start cost-effectively reducing power industry carbon emissions before 2030 (IEA 2021).

Elsewhere in the region the Kazakhstan ETS, introduced in 2013, was also implemented gradually. The emissions cap increased over time as sector coverage expanded. It included during 2013–2015 the electric power, centralized heating, oil and gas mining, metallurgy, and chemical industries, adding in 2018 brick production and the processing of cement, lime, and gypsum. In Southeast Asia, Thailand's pilot Thailand Voluntary Emission Trading System focused from 2015 to 2017 on testing its monitoring, reporting, verification, and allowance allocation systems in four carbon-intensive industries, then from 2018 to 2020 on testing the registry and trading platform in nine industries. Indonesia has also outlined plans to establish an ETS by 2025 while Viet Nam enforced the Law on Environmental Protection on 1 January 2022 that mandates the creation of a pilot ETS by 2025, fully operational by 2027.

Challenges and opportunities of environmental taxes and pollution pricing

Environmental tax and pricing instruments hold great promise, and developing Asia can draw valuable lessons from early adopters to strengthen their design and implementation, amplify their benefits, and minimize their costs. Planning can also help governments anticipate changes in revenue from environmental taxes. Fossil fuel taxes effectively curb consumption and generate revenue depending on how responsive consumers are to energy price changes and the availability of alternative public transport. Fossil fuel price elasticity tends to be low in the short run but higher with time (Arimura, Duan, and Oh 2021). Higher fossil fuel taxes may thus generate significant revenue in the near term, but eventually firms and consumers will adjust and demand will weaken, lowering pollution but also revenue.

Environmental taxes can cut pollution and generate significant revenue only if set sufficiently high on a broad range of pollutants. Despite their widespread use in developing Asia, their revenue is low, likely reflecting low tax rates and patchy coverage. Revenue from energy, pollution, and transport taxes equaled 2.3% of GDP in OECD countries in 2018, for example, but only 0.8% of GDP in a sample of economies in developing Asia.[3] Globally, only one-fifth of GHG emissions are covered by pricing (World Bank 2021b), averaging a low price of $3 per ton (Parry 2021). Increasing carbon prices can support climate change targets and lift revenue in developing Asia. In a sample of economies in Asia and the Pacific, a carbon price of $25 per ton would generate additional revenue estimated to equal 0.8% of GDP (Dabla-Norris et al. 2021).

Setting environmental tax rates and pollutant prices too high, however, can inflict economic harm. It can jeopardize competitiveness, particularly if firms face higher energy and emission costs than their competitors. As noted above, many governments in Asia and elsewhere have implemented carbon pricing gradually to provide time for firms to adjust.

---

[3]   OECD. Policy Instrument for the Environment (accessed 14 January 2021); Asian Development Bank estimates.

Some have allowed exceptions. Japan, for example, exempts energy-intensive industries from carbon and energy taxes, and the European Union ETS offers those industries free allowances. Competitiveness concerns have prompted some governments to consider border adjustment mechanisms that introduce carbon tariffs or permits purchased at the border. For example, the European Union proposed in July 2021 the Carbon Border Adjustment Mechanism. While the mechanism needs further clarification under World Trade Organization rules, the need to adapt to it provides impetus for carbon pricing in developing Asia (Mehling et al. 2019). Like other charges, environmental taxes and carbon pricing have distributional effects that can hurt poorer households. In high-income economies, energy is a greater share of spending for the poor, making carbon taxes and pricing instruments likely regressive (Arimura et al. 2022). In developing economies, by contrast, the poor typically use proportionately less energy, making a moderate carbon price likely progressive in the poorest economies (Dorband et al. 2019).

Developing Asia should accelerate its use of environmental taxes and pollution-pricing instruments to address environmental challenges and lift revenue. Higher rates for fossil fuel taxes, which are often well established, easy to administer, and likely to generate more revenue in the short term than carbon pricing should be prioritized. Even in OECD and G20 countries, revenue from fossil fuel taxes is far greater than from carbon tax and ETSs (Martin and van Dender 2019). A related high priority is to phase out fossil fuel subsidies, which remain significant in some regional economies (Box 2.3.1).

Governments can tax pollutants directly, use ETSs, or both. Direct taxation offers greater price predictability and simpler administration. Carbon tax can be imposed on coal, natural gas, and liquid fuels on a relatively small number of upstream firms, either producers or at the border, to minimize compliance costs and opportunities for evasion (Stretton 2020). When implementing a carbon tax, governments need to ensure that related energy taxes are not unduly cut, which can undermine revenue, as experienced in Europe (Haites 2018). Effective implementation of an ETS requires a strong monitoring, reporting, and verification system to underpin the market for polluting permits.

Monitoring, reporting, and verification can pose challenges, as demonstrated by PRC pilot ETSs (Li et al. 2021). The private sector can play a critical role in monitoring and verifying emissions as independent third-party verifiers.

Asian governments need to carefully manage revenue generated from these instruments. Revenue can be earmarked to promote low-carbon technology, renewable energy, and energy efficiency, or to address environmental damage, as in Japan and Singapore. Japan has used a sulfur charge, for example, to compensate air pollution victims. Such approaches can build public acceptance. Where environmental taxes have adverse distributional effects, governments can implement offsetting revenue recycling transfers or rebates. These are widely used, as in Singapore, where rebates cushion price impacts from the carbon tax and gasoline duty. Where revenue is allocated to the general account, governments can lower other taxes or fund priority spending. This approach was adopted alongside the introduction of energy taxes (Goulder 1995) in Germany (Beuermann and Santarius 2006) and the United Kingdom (Agnolucci 2009). In Canadian British Columbia, carbon tax revenue recycling enabled both higher employment and lower emissions (Yamazaki 2017). No Asian economies have adopted this practice.

Finally, as pollution mitigation often entails significant investment, governments need to be clear about their policy frameworks. Where they intend to generate revenue from an ETS and initially allocate free permits, a clear transition to auctioned permits must be specified, as in the ROK. Equally, they need to review implementation to ensure consistency with policy goals and that revenue does not unintentionally erode over time. When Singapore recently reviewed its carbon tax, the government signaled that it may need to hasten tax rate adjustment to meet its commitments to tackle climate change (Tan 2021; Xu 2021).

While promising progress, environmental tax instruments, alone, cannot solve developing Asia's daunting environmental challenges. Their scope is too small and some pollutants are difficult to price. Complementary regulation is needed to clean up Asia. For example, energy efficiency and other environmental standards are important and widely used in many high-income economies. Renewable energy is promoted by feed-in tariffs in the European Union and elsewhere, and by renewable portfolio standards in the US.

Corrective taxes for addressing burdens of unhealthy consumption and lifestyles

Like environmental taxes, corrective health taxes are levied to change behavior, in their case by increasing the cost of consuming unhealthy products. Taxes on alcohol, tobacco, and unhealthy foods are widely applied in developing Asia to deter consumption that has adverse health and social outcomes. This addresses two costs. Social externalities from tobacco include illness from secondhand smoke and damage from accidental fires; from alcohol, traffic accidents, violence, and crime; and from both products health costs not borne by the consumer, such as publicly subsidized health care. Self-imposed costs from behavior that discounts future consequences of present consumption arise from either impatience or lack of information relating to health and nutrition. For tobacco use and unhealthy diets, self-imposed costs are significantly higher than uncompensated social costs. For alcohol use, the costs are more balanced but vary across economies.

Corrective taxes on alcohol, tobacco, and sugar-sweetened beverages are proven tools to reduce harmful consumption. They therefore help prevent lifestyle disease, complementing policies such as regulation and health promotion.

Public health-care spending needs have risen in developing Asia on account of COVID-19, and corrective health taxes can go a long way toward meeting them (Summan et al. 2020; Dutta 2022). The next section first briefly reviews the rising burden of lifestyle disease in developing Asia and the costs associated with unhealthy consumption before examining how corrective health taxes can mitigate them and generate revenue. It considers products on which corrective taxes have commonly been applied: tobacco, alcohol, and sugar-sweetened beverages.

The rising burden of unhealthy lifestyles in developing Asia

Lifestyle diseases pose a global emergency. In developing Asia, their share of deaths rose from 52% in 1990 to 77% in 2019, with increases in all subregions (Figure 2.3.5). In 2019, the incidence of death from them in East Asia was on a par with advanced economies and worse than Latin America. The Caucasus and Central Asia also exceeds Latin America, while lifestyle disease is rising rapidly in South and Southeast Asia. These developments broadly reflect improved health systems reducing communicable disease mortality and rising incomes supporting the consumption of tobacco, alcohol, and diets high in processed sugars and fats, all key risk factors in lifestyle disease.

Figure 2.3.5 Rising burden of lifestyle disease, 1990–2019

Lifestyle diseases account for a growing share of deaths, especially in developing economies.

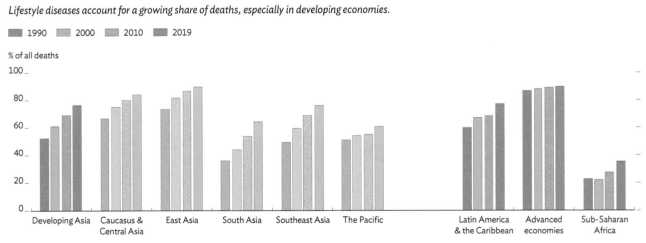

Source: Lane 2022.

Across developing Asia, alcohol, tobacco, and diet are linked, on average, to over one-third of all deaths. Tobacco and unhealthy diet account for the largest shares, each at 16%–17% of all deaths on average, with alcohol at 4%. The risk burden is particularly high in the Caucasus and Central Asia, and East Asia. Further, lifestyle diseases such as diabetes, hypertension, chronic respiratory illness, and chronic kidney and liver conditions greatly increase the risk of severe COVID-19 illness.

Alcohol, tobacco, and unhealthy diets generate economic costs when productivity is lost to premature death or disability, medical treatment costs, and other social costs. Individuals bear some of these costs as out-of-pocket medical expenses and income lost with death or disability, but other costs, such as for public health care, are socialized. In developing Asia, average productivity loss from death and disability caused by alcohol, tobacco, or a diet high in sugar-sweetened beverages was estimated equal to 2.1% of GDP in 2019.

Losses are particularly high in the Caucasus and Central Asia and Mongolia (Figure 2.3.6). To put these losses in perspective, average general government health-care spending in developing Asia is a little under 3% of GDP. Tobacco use is the largest cause of productivity loss in most economies in developing Asia where data is available, equal on average to 1.3% of GDP, with alcohol use the largest factor in some economies, particularly in the Caucasus and Central Asia, averaging 1.4% of GDP. Losses from sugar-sweetened beverages are generally small except in some Pacific island economies. Beyond productivity losses, estimates of medical and other social costs vary but can be significant. A global survey using 2012 data estimated average health expenditure in developing Asia on disease attributable to smoking equaled to 0.2% of GDP. Estimated costs are significantly higher in economies where smoking is prevalent, notably Bangladesh and Sri Lanka.

Figure 2.3.6 Productivity loss in developing Asia from death and disability caused by alcohol, tobacco, or a diet high in sugar-sweetened beverages, 2019

Unhealthy products impose a heavy productivity cost on the region.

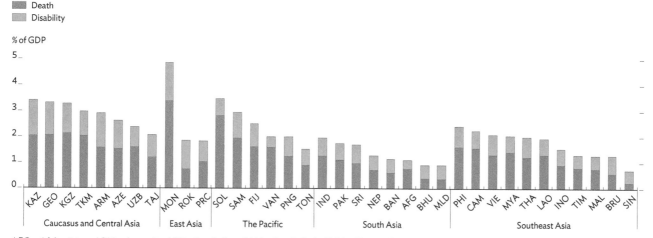

AFG = Afghanistan, ARM = Armenia, AZE = Azerbaijan, BAN = Bangladesh, BHU = Bhutan, BRU = Brunei Darussalam, CAM = Cambodia, FIJ = Fiji, GDP = gross domestic product, GEO = Georgia, IND = India, INO = Indonesia, KAZ = Kazakhstan, KGZ = Kyrgyz Republic, LAO = Lao People's Democratic Republic, MAL = Malaysia, MLD = Maldives, MON = Mongolia, MYA = Myanmar, NEP = Nepal, PAK = Pakistan, PHI = Philippines, PNG = Papua New Guinea, PRC = People's Republic of China, ROK = Republic of Korea, SAM = Samoa, SIN = Singapore, SOL = Solomon Islands, SRI = Sri Lanka, TAJ = Tajikistan, THA = Thailand, TIM = Timor-Leste, TKM = Turkmenistan, TON = Tonga, UZB = Uzbekistan, VAN = Vanuatu, VIE = Viet Nam.

Source: Lane 2022.

Health and revenue benefits from corrective health taxes

Raising corrective health taxes is a highly effective way to reduce or deter harmful consumption of alcohol, tobacco, and sugar-sweetened beverages. A substantial body of research over many decades in many countries shows that significantly increasing the tax on tobacco products and their prices is the single most effective tool for reducing tobacco use (Lane 2022). The World Health Organization (WHO) Framework Convention on Tobacco Control, ratified by 168 WHO member states, encourages tax measures to reduce demand for tobacco. For alcohol, the WHO SAFER initiative recommends raising prices on alcohol through excise taxes and other pricing policies. A review of 50 studies associated a 10% increase in alcohol tax with a 3.5% decline in all harm from disease and injury related to alcohol.

Significant scope exists to increase revenue from corrective health taxes. As a short-term benchmark in low- and middle-income economies, up to the equivalent of 0.6%–0.7% of GDP in additional revenue could be collected from alcohol, tobacco, and sugar-sweetened beverages (Lane 2022). This benchmark comprises 0.24% of GDP from tobacco, by raising excise toward 70% of pack price, and 0.35% of GDP from alcohol, by moving toward norms in economies where alcohol is heavily taxed. It includes less than 0.1% of GDP from sugar-sweetened beverages, based on recent revenue yields. Another simulation of tax increases that raised tobacco, alcohol, and sugar-sweetened beverage prices by up to 50% (or less where taxes are already high) found revenue increased by up to 0.7% of GDP in upper-middle-income economies, 1.0% in low-income economies, and 1.2% in lower-middle-income economies. Higher estimates largely reflect more ambitious alcohol tax increases. Increases of this magnitude could avert 50 million premature deaths worldwide over the next 50 years while raising over $20 trillion in additional revenue.

Tobacco tax illustrating corrective health tax in Asia

Developing Asia has made some progress in raising corrective taxes on tobacco products over the past decade. Tax rates in the region on cigarettes are now above those in Latin America and gradually approaching those in advanced economies (Figure 2.3.7). Between 2008 and 2020, taxes as a share of the retail price of the best-selling cigarette brand rose from 38% to 47% in developing Asia, with the Caucasus and Central Asia, and East Asia making the most progress. However, this still leaves significant room to reach the WHO recommendation of 75% of pack price for all taxes on tobacco.

Figure 2.3.7 Cigarette tax on the best-selling brand by subregion, 2008–2020

Tax accounts for a growing share of the retail price of cigarettes in developing Asia.

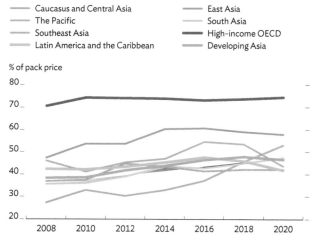

OECD = Organisation for Economic Co-operation and Development.
Source: World Health Organization. 2021. *Report of the Global Tobacco Epidemic.*

However, across developing Asia, the economic cost of tobacco consumption often exceeds corrective tax revenue. This indicates that taxes are still too low, especially as the economic cost does not include social costs. Across 34 economies in developing Asia, 30 suffer an annual economic cost from death and disability attributable to tobacco higher than corrective tax revenue (Figure 2.3.8). Among them, 22 cover less than half the cost, and 15 cover less than a quarter of it.

Figure 2.3.8 Corrective tax yield in developing Asia versus productivity loss from tobacco-induced death and disability

Corrective tax revenue falls short of the economic cost of tobacco consumption across the region.

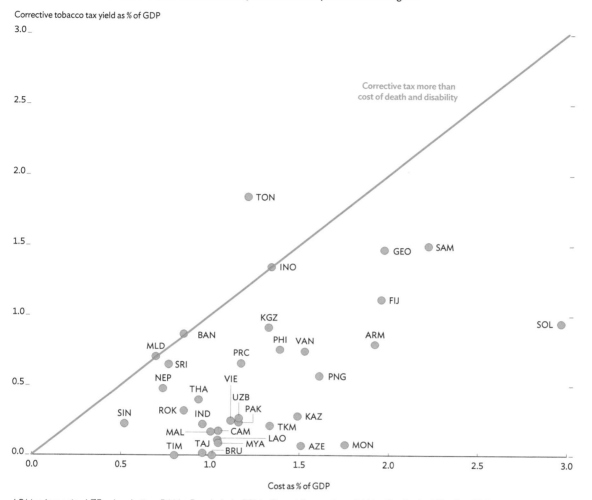

Corrective tobacco tax yield as % of GDP

ARM = Armenia, AZE = Azerbaijan, BAN = Bangladesh, BRU = Brunei Darussalam, CAM = Cambodia, FIJ = Fiji, GDP = gross domestic product, GEO = Georgia, IND = India, INO = Indonesia, KAZ = Kazakhstan, KGZ = Kyrgyz Republic, LAO = Lao People's Democratic Republic, MAL = Malaysia, MLD = Maldives, MON = Mongolia, MYA = Myanmar, NEP = Nepal, PAK = Pakistan, PHI = Philippines, PNG = Papua New Guinea, PRC = People's Republic of China, ROK = Republic of Korea, SAM = Samoa, SIN = Singapore, SOL = Solomon Islands, SRI = Sri Lanka, TAJ = Tajikistan, THA = Thailand, TIM = Timor-Leste, TON = Tonga, TKM = Turkmenistan, UZB = Uzbekistan, VAN = Vanuatu, VIE = Viet Nam.

Note: Data from 2019 or most recent year.

Sources: Institute for Health Metrics and Evaluation, World Health Organization, and World Bank literature survey of tobacco tax yields, most recent year available; Asian Development Bank estimates.

Adding in publicly financed health-care cost would likely show that all except Tonga levy corrective taxes that are insufficient to cover lost productivity and social costs. Corrective taxes are particularly low relative to costs in most of the Caucasus and Central Asia, Mongolia, Myanmar, Pakistan, Solomon Islands, and Viet Nam. Similarly, revenue from corrective taxes on alcohol and sugar-sweetened beverages are well below the economic costs from their consumption.

Strategy for successful corrective health taxes

Developing Asia should explore corrective health tax reform, which can deliver significant benefits, as in the Philippines (Box 2.3.2). Reform is often stymied by misplaced equity concerns. While the tax burden may be heavier for low-income households, especially for tobacco, this may be outweighed by long-term health benefits from reduced consumption.

Moreover, corrective tax revenue tends to come disproportionately from higher-income households, and its use can be pro-poor. Concerns about job losses in tobacco, alcohol, and sugary beverage industries must be weighed against the new jobs created by consumption shifting to healthier products, as well as jobs created by spending corrective tax revenue. Other concerns include overstated revenue and health gains, and increased illicit trade. However, experience indicates that taxes have little impact on illicit market share, which depends on other factors such as weak regulatory frameworks and social acceptance of black markets.

No single blueprint can guide the design and implementation of corrective tax reform in the region. However, a successful strategy must consider several factors, including the incidence of tax burdens and responses from firms. Implementation can be supported by marshalling best practice advice and successful international experience, and by publicizing the health and economic rationales for taxes. Another consideration is expenditure policy, as strong public health spending, especially for the poor, can secure political support for reform. Policy makers should note that, as with environmental taxes, they need to be alert to and plan for reduced revenue over the longer term as higher tax rates and prices succeed in driving down demand. As with other taxes, health tax collection can benefit from effective enforcement strategies to address noncompliance. Finally, corrective taxes and product regulation are complementary and mutually reinforcing, requiring close cooperation between finance and health ministries.

It matters how consumers react to price changes resulting from corrective taxes. Healthy substitution can support desired behavior change, and unhealthy substitution can undermine it, which may warrant uniform taxes across a broad range of products. High taxes may have only a muted impact on consumption if applied by value and tiered to protect low-cost production, inducing consumers to change to cheaper brands that pay less tax. In Tonga, for example, a nearly 50% increase in tax on imported cigarettes reduced tobacco consumption, especially in lower-income groups, but effects were muted by a shift to cheaper locally made cigarettes (ADB 2021d).

This section showed how environmental and corrective health taxes can both contribute directly to the SDGs and raise revenue. While the revenue potential from such taxes is not negligible, they can generate at best only a fraction of the vast fiscal resources that governments in developing Asia need to build a more sustainable future. The next section takes a deeper dive into reform options available to the region to secure those resources.

Box 2.3.1 Fossil fuel subsidies bad for the environment and public finances

Many Asian economies depend heavily on fossil fuels, especially coal, to satisfy rapidly rising energy demand cost-effectively. Some, particularly in the Caucasus and Central Asia, allocate significant government spending to fossil fuel subsidies. While the amount declined through the 2010s, partly due to lower fossil fuel prices (box figure), these subsidies encourage overconsumption that harms the environment and dampens investment in improved energy efficiency and developing cleaner energy sources. Negative environmental impacts are not limited to carbon emissions and climate change. Outdated fossil fuel power plants emit large amounts of nitride and sulfur compounds and particulate matter, exposing nearby residents to significant health threats and compounding urban air pollution in developing Asia (World Health Organization 2018).

Aside from damaging human health and the environment, these subsidies impose substantial fiscal and economic costs. In this way they reduce the resources available for priorities such as managing COVID-19. Indeed, East Asian and Pacific economies stand to gain the most revenue by adopting market prices for fossil fuels (Parry, Black, and Vernon 2021). Moreover, reallocating outlays for fossil fuel subsidies to health, education, and infrastructure can boost long-term growth (ADB 2016). Savings from repealed subsidies can be reallocated to cushion blows to vulnerable households and other pro-poor spending.

References:
ADB. 2016. *Fossil Fuel Subsidies in Asia: Trends, Impacts, and Reforms.* Asian Development Bank.
Parry, I., S. Black, and N. Vernon. 2021. *Still Not Getting Energy Prices Right: A Global and Country Update of Fossil Fuel Subsidies.* IMF Working Paper 2021/236. International Monetary Fund.
World Health Organization. 2018. Ambient Air Quality Database 2018: Annual Mean PM2.5 Concentration in Urban Areas.

Fossil fuel subsidies in selected Asian economies, 2010–2020

Fossil fuel subsidies have generally declined in developing Asia but still fluctuate with global fossil fuel prices and remain substantial in some economies.

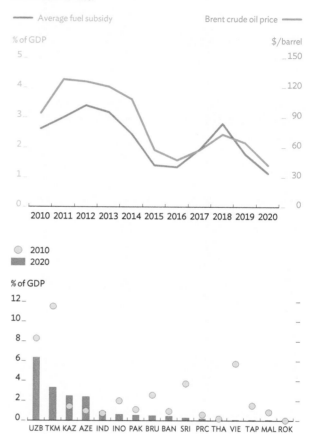

AZE = Azerbaijan, BAN = Bangladesh, BRU = Brunei Darussalam, GDP = gross domestic product, IND = India, INO = Indonesia, KAZ = Kazakhstan, MAL = Malaysia, PAK = Pakistan, PRC = People's Republic of China, ROK = Republic of Korea, SRI = Sri Lanka, TAP = Taipei,China, THA = Thailand, TKM = Turkmenistan, UZB = Uzbekistan, VIE = Viet Nam.

Source: IEA Fossil Fuel Subsidies Database (accessed 1 Dec 2021).

Box 2.3.2 Sin taxes and universal health coverage in the Philippines

In the Philippines, before reform in 2012, "sin taxes" collected on alcohol and tobacco declined as a percentage of GDP from 1.1% in 1997 to 0.5% in 2012. This reflected in part the 1996 tax provisions and price tiers for both products. The tiers provided higher tax rates for higher-priced products, incentivizing manufacturers and suppliers to manage retail prices to get products into the lower tax tiers and thus avoid higher tax rates.

The 2012 passage of the Sin Tax Law reformed these taxes and increased sin tax revenue to 1.2% of GDP in 2019 (box figure). The law simplified and raised tax rates for alcohol and tobacco, removing price and tax tiers and introducing a single tax rate for all products by 2017. The government pledged to allocate 85% of the increased revenue to health care through annual general appropriations or the national budgeting process. About 80% was used to finance membership for indigent Filipinos in the National Health Insurance Program, and the remaining 20% to fund capital investment through the Health Facility Enhancement Program.

The Comprehensive Tax Reform Program further reformed sin taxes, building upon the 2012 Sin Tax Law. The enhancement of tax revenue allocated to universal health coverage (UHC) included (i) increases in excise taxes on cigarettes and sugar-sweetened beverages in 2018, with part of increased revenue pledged for health care; (ii) the imposition in July 2019 of excise taxes on heated tobacco and vapor products, as well as higher tax rates for other tobacco, their inclusion as part of total revenue and not just incremental revenue; and (iii) a law that increased in early 2020 taxes on heated tobacco and vapor products and alcohol.

This series of sin tax reforms has helped increase central government budgetary allocation for health care. The allocation increased from $700 million in 2011 to nearly $4 billion in 2021, with revenue from sin taxes for health care increasing from $764.9 million in 2014 to $1.9 billion in 2020 (Department of Health 2021). Revenue from sin taxes helped to finance UHC in the Philippines through national health insurance subsidies, investment in national and local government hospitals and health facilities, and medical assistance programs.

Expected financing of UHC from tax collected on unhealthy consumer products improves both revenue and health outcomes. It expands the revenue base and mobilizes the finance needed for UHC and suppresses unhealthy eating, smoking, and drinking habits. The Tax Reform for Acceleration and Inclusion (TRAIN) Law, 2017 and the 2019 and 2020 sin tax reforms raised excise taxes on sweetened beverages from zero in 2017 to $653.9 million in 2020 and collected in the latter year $3.5 million in taxes on heated tobacco and vapor products.

Reference:
Department of Health. *2021 Annual Report. Sin Tax Law. Incremental Revenue for Health.*

Sin tax revenue in the Philippines, 1994–2019

Sin tax revenue in the Philippines rose markedly following a series of reforms.

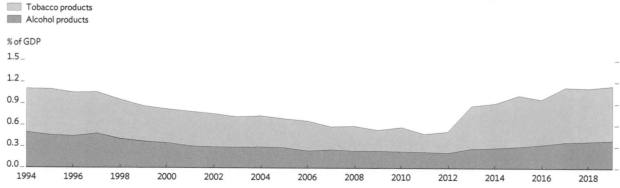

GDP = gross domestic product.
Sources: OECD. Revenue Statistics in Asia and the Pacific; World Bank World Development Indicators (both accessed 31 January 2021).

Reform to reduce informality and lift tax revenue is hard but doable

As outlined above, developing Asia has many opportunities to boost tax revenue. Seizing opportunities often requires fundamental tax policy reform that is difficult but achievable. In addition, as tax collection is heavily influenced by structural economic features, broader economic reform can indirectly play a key role in mobilizing revenue. In developing Asia, this especially includes reform to reduce informality—economic activity hidden from the authorities—and substantially expand the tax base.

Informality and taxation in developing Asia

Developing economies characteristically have a large informal sector encompassing from a third to half of economic activity. Pervasive informality presents several development challenges, notably widespread tax avoidance and weaker fiscal capacity (Auriol and Warlters 2005; Kanbur and Keen 2015).

This is particularly important in developing Asia, where tax revenue is generally low and informality widespread. Indeed, compared with Latin America, developing Asia has very high shares of informal workers and unregistered businesses (Table 2.4.1). Comparing some key drivers of informality highlights opportunities for reform to reduce informality in developing Asia. While the tax burden on business and the time taken to start a business are typically low in developing Asia, the cost of registering a formal business is very high.

Reform that reduces informality draws more activity into the tax net, supporting revenue mobilization and other improvements. Informality may, however, be a rational response to inefficient and burdensome institutions. The informal sector can absorb workers prevented from functioning in the formal sector by onerous regulations, job displacement, or labor market mismatch. Indeed, most developing economies in Asia have high informality but low unemployment. Any consideration of potential benefits from reduced informality should thus consider potential to worsen unemployment.

Table 2.4.1 Informality and regulatory costs in developing Asia versus Latin America

Informality and the costs of registering a business are higher in developing Asia than in Latin America.

	Developing Asia	Latin America
Regulatory costs:		
Taxes, % of profit	47.6	61.1
Cost of registering a business, % of income per capita	34.9	16.3
Time required to start a business, days	32.4	67.4
Informality and unemployment:		
Informal worker share, %	84.5	57.4
Share of unregistered startups, %	16.8	9.9
Unemployment rate, %	3.1	6.9

Note: Figures for developing Asia include 20 Asian Development Bank developing member economies.
Source: Ulyssea 2022.

Determinants of informality

The costs of operating formally can be broadly divided into those of entering the formal sector and those of staying there. The former stem from regulations on entry and the latter from tax burdens and the continuing costs of complying with laws and regulations (Djankov et al. 2002; Ulyssea 2020). Governments can incentivize firms to formalize by reducing either type of cost or both. Alternatively, they can increase the cost of informality with more inspections and stronger enforcement of existing laws and regulations.

Several studies have examined policies that aim to reduce the costs of formality. These often focus on business registration, which is regarded as a major constraint on firm creation and formalization (De Soto 1989; Djankov et al. 2002). Evidence on the impact of such reform on firm formalization is mixed (Bruhn and McKenzie 2014). However, much of it comes from Latin America, where regulations differ from developing Asia. Other studies, some examining the economywide impact, have shown that reducing formal sector entry costs can have substantial benefits (Ulyssea 2010a; D'Erasmo and Boedo 2012; Charlot, Malherbet, and Terra 2015; Ulyssea 2018). Other evidence suggests that formalization is triggered by stronger enforcement of existing laws and regulations, which increases informal costs (de Andrade et al. 2014).

Policy simulations framework

New analysis examines the effects of reduced business registration costs and of stiffer enforcement of existing laws and policies. It examines the impact on unemployment, informality, productivity, and tax revenue in developing Asia using counterfactual policy simulations (Ulyssea 2022). Estimates for the region are obtained by averaging results across 20 economies in developing Asia weighted by population.[4] Simulations use a simple two-sector model, formal and informal, developed in Ulyssea (2010b). It captures many of the dimensions discussed above and includes the registration cost of

entering the formal sector, the tax cost of remaining there, unemployment and other effects of transition into and out of the formal and informal sectors, differences in productivity between the two sectors, variation in enforcement intensity, and the main aggregate outcome variables mentioned above.

There are limitations to the analysis. As the model does not account for variation in firm productivity or size, it does not capture composition effects from policy changes or allow for worker reallocation from less productive to more productive firms. These effects are potentially important, especially for policies that stiffen enforcement (Dix-Carneiro et al. 2021). In practice, if firms are highly heterogeneous and the more productive formal ones have scope to expand, stricter enforcement can increase aggregate economic output and tax revenue (Ulyssea 2018). Thus, some potentially important policy effects are muted in the current analysis, so results should be interpreted as indicative.

Main findings from policy simulations

Simulation results for developing Asia suggest that reducing entry cost can significantly reduce informality prevalence and increase tax revenue while reducing unemployment. These positive effects reflect lower entry cost spurring greater firm entry and production in the formal sector, thereby lifting output. The calibrated value for the baseline economy is determined using data from the Doing Business survey (Ulyssea 2022). The average entry cost in developing Asia in this baseline is high, more than four times higher than in Brazil, which itself has high entry cost by global standards.

Results show that reducing entry cost in developing Asia by a quarter would significantly increase revenue. It would have little effect on unemployment—which is already very low in the baseline—but would reduce the informal sector share by 5 percentage points as detailed in Table 2.4.2 (Ulyssea 2022). This reduction in informality is associated with gains in average productivity and

---

[4]   Armenia, Bangladesh, Cambodia, Fiji, Georgia, India, Indonesia, the Kyrgyz Republic, the Lao People's Democratic Republic, Mongolia, Myanmar, Nepal, Pakistan, Samoa, Sri Lanka, Thailand, Timor-Leste, Tonga, Vanuatu, and Viet Nam.

wages because the share of aggregate output from the more productive formal sector rises. These changes increase tax revenue by almost 19%. This result discounts possible responses such as tax evasion and firms bunching below tax thresholds, so it should be seen as an upper bound of potential revenue gains. Additional policy simulations indicate that when strengthening the enforcement of existing laws and regulations to reduce the informal sector share by 5 percentage points, tax revenue increases by about 5%. Hence, for an equivalent reduction in the informal share as in Table 2.4.2, the increase in revenue is tangibly smaller. This is because lowering entry cost reduces economic distortion, with higher formal sector output increasing total output. With stricter enforcement only and no change in the regulatory framework, two opposite forces come into play. First, an increase in the cost of operating in the informal sector reduces the informal share and so increases tax revenue. Second, higher unemployment and reduced output lowers tax revenue. Tax revenue increases, but the gain is smaller than would be obtained by reducing entry cost.

As noted above, simulation results should be seen as indicative of policy effects, not precise estimates. The absence of firm heterogeneity in the model likely overstates tax revenue increase from lower entry cost because it precludes the possibility of less productive firms formalizing. Effects from greater enforcement are likely understated, by contrast, as the model precludes the possibility of resources being reallocated from less productive informal firms to more productive formal ones. Finally, any mismeasurement in data used to calibrate the model would distort results.

In summary, this analysis finds reducing entry cost to be an effective policy to curtail informality and thus increase tax revenue, while concomitantly improving unemployment, wages, and productivity. Stricter enforcement similarly curtails informality but with a lower tax revenue gain. While most regulatory costs are not high in developing Asia, the cost of formal sector entry is high, which helps explain high informality in the region. Reducing this cost while strengthening enforcement can start a virtuous cycle of lower informality and higher wages and tax revenue. However, it is only one dimension of a broader multidimensional process. The rest of this section delves into the other dimensions.

Table 2.4.2 Simulation of effects from reduced cost of formal sector entry

A model simulation shows reducing entry cost can reduce informality and increase revenue.

	Baseline	Scenario
Entry Cost	100	75
Unemployment	0.031	0.030
Informal sector share	0.811	0.763
Average wage	1.000	1.024
Average productivity	1.000	1.105
Tax revenue	1.000	1.185

Notes: (i) Impacts on tax revenue are in percentage change in local currency. Ulyssea (2022) presented alternative entry cost scenarios that showed further reduction in entry cost yielding greater tax revenue increase. (ii) Entry cost is calculated using formal sector entry cost reported in the World Bank's Cost of Doing Business Database, expressed as a share of an economy's income per capita. The values for developing Asia are calibrated against the cost in Brazil for comparability and model consistency with Ulyssea (2010b).
Source: Ulyssea 2022.

Fundamental tax reform certainly possible

Tax reform is one of the most technically and politically difficult policy changes governments can attempt, especially if aimed at increasing revenue. Despite offering clear benefits, individuals and businesses alike rarely want to pay higher taxes. Most tax reform creates winners and losers, and losers concentrated in smaller groups may more effectively coalesce to voice opposition, drowning out the voices of more numerous winners (Ilzetzki 2018). Not surprisingly, political resistance to tax reform is often stiff. As a result, many economies have been unable to increase tax revenue significantly, despite concerted effort, or even achieve less ambitious goals such as improving the tax mix for more efficiency or equity.

A prerequisite for successful tax reform is therefore strong leadership and political will at the highest levels of government. Influential champions must recognize the opportunity and build necessary consensus and buy-in, in part by strengthening social contracts (Bird 2004; Owens 2005; Brys 2011; Gaspar, Jaramillo, and Wingender 2016a; Akitoby et al. 2018).

Vested interests must be tackled to create conditions conducive to effective implementation. Strong leadership is especially important when change in political dynamics stokes resistance. Factionalism in political parties can weaken central authority and embolden local leaders who may prioritize local constituents over national interests (Bonvecchi 2010). Strong political leadership needs support from capable institutions that plan, analyze, and implement the reform process, as well as such constitutive institutions as the rule of law (Bird 2004; Brys 2011).

Timing can significantly affect tax reform success, especially as economies emerge from the COVID-19 pandemic. Governments often undertake reform in good economic times, when budget surpluses can be used to compensate reform losers (Brys 2011; Castanheira, Nicodeme, and Profeta 2012). Voters' recency bias ("What have you done for me lately?") induces officials to time spending cuts and tax increases early in the political cycle (Fuest et al. 2021; Strobl et al. 2021). However, fundamental tax reform may actually be easier to carry out in times of crisis. Faced with dire circumstances, the body politic may be more willing to embrace sacrifices and oppose vested interests (Olofsgard 2003; Bahl 2006; Akitoby et al. 2018). Indeed, some evidence shows past pandemics spurring tax reform in developing countries (Gupta and Jalles 2021). Now may thus be an opportune time for developing Asia to consider fundamental tax reform.

Governments should take time to garner social support for tax reform and avoid tax-boosting reform that is quick and easy to implement but ultimately poor policy. Financial transaction taxes introduced in Latin America over the last 2 decades, for example, disrupted financial services and ultimately became an unreliable revenue source (Cornia, Gomez-Sabaini, and Martorano 2011; Matheson 2011). Phased implementation allows the economy to adjust (Fairfield 2013). However, where political support is at risk of waning, it may be best to move more quickly.

Economy-specific priorities and feasibility should guide the design of tax reform in developing Asia. Changes in tax rates, bases, or compliance can all yield higher revenue, and an appropriate balance will reflect local capacity and address weaknesses

revealed by diagnostic analysis (Brockmeyer et al. 2021; Basri et al. 2021). Tax policy changes should focus on feasible policy levers, particularly indirect taxes such as excises and VAT, informed by compliance costs and the availability of third-party information (Cnossen 2020). In doing so, the authorities need to be alert to rapid structural change that can affect the tax base, especially in a dynamic region like developing Asia, such as through digitalization or labor market modernization.

While reform to make taxes fairer can be important, it can be more technically and politically difficult. An alternative is for governments to increase revenue from all sources and use the proceeds to promote inclusive development, including support for the poor and women. As noted above, earmarking revenue, especially from green or health taxes, may strengthen support for tax increases. However, the benefits of earmarking should be balanced against impeded spending flexibility and budget management. The design and collection of taxes can affect their salience or visibility to taxpayers, with more visible and direct taxes likely to face greater political resistance. Cabral and Hoxby (2012) found unpopular property tax less salient with the use of less obtrusive payment methods.

The challenging and complex nature of tax reform highlights the need for a comprehensive reform plan grounded in evidence-based policy. Framing this over a medium-term horizon helps anchor efforts that can be derailed by short-term political or economic developments, particularly sudden windfalls from resource revenue (Ross 2015). A comprehensive and transparent plan can ease taxpayer anxiety about how much they may stand to lose personally, which can erode support, and avoid the need for frequent small changes that push up administrative and compliance costs and stoke economic uncertainty (Lakin 2020). Development partners can support reform plans by providing technical advice and sharing international experiences. Ultimately, however, reform success requires government ownership. In this context, Medium-Term Revenue Strategy, a comprehensive approach for effective tax reform developed and supported by international organizations including ADB, encompasses key elements of a comprehensive reform plan. They include revenue targets consistent with expenditure needs; the formulation of a reform plan covering tax policy, administration, and legal frameworks; clear government commitment to reform; and resources and support secured for implementation (Mullins 2020).

Despite considerable challenges, the past few decades have witnessed successful tax reform in numerous economies. These reforms substantially and durably increased tax revenue, including in developing Asia (Martinez-Vasquez 2022). A comparison of some of the most successful reform episodes, where ratios of tax to GDP rose by more than a half, highlights the diverse experiences of countries at different stages of development (Box 2.4.1). While no one-size-fits-all tax reform strategy exists, reform commonly follows major political or economic upheavals and entails strengthened VATs (Akitoby, Honda, and Primus 2020). Experience also highlights the importance of reforming tax administration to boost compliance.

Modernizing and strengthening tax administrations essential

A strong tax administration is central to a sound tax system. It affects tax yield, incidence, and efficiency (Casanegra de Jantscher 1990; Bird 2014). Tax administration and tax policy reforms are therefore highly complementary and reinforce each other. For instance, recent evidence from developing countries suggests that increased tax rates yield more revenue in a strong enforcement environment (Bergeron, Tourek, and Weigel 2021). Good tax administration deters tax evasion, facilitates voluntary compliance, and instills trust. Third-party information is crucial for tax collection, but this needs to be complemented by effective compliance and strong audit capacity (Carrillo, Pomeranz, and Singhal 2017).

Tax administrations seek to raise revenue efficiently, with the lowest administrative and taxpayer compliance costs. Where costs are high relative to revenue raised, tax administration reform is particularly beneficial (Keen and Slemrod 2016). In Indonesia, for example, increasing tax administration staff oversight of selected firms, which required only a small increase in overhead, more than doubled revenue

from them—an achievement that otherwise would have required a substantial corporate tax rate hike (Basri et al. 2021). This example highlights the benefits of investing in tax administration capacity.

Across developing Asia, tax compliance burdens have eased with tax system simplification and improved tax administration capacity, but scope for improvement remains. Over the past decade, the average number of hours required for companies to comply with taxes in developing Asia declined from 236 to 196, a significant improvement and below Latin American and Sub-Saharan African averages but still higher than the OECD average of 158 (Figure 2.4.1). Developing Asia continues to lag OECD countries as well on measures of efficiency after tax return filing.

Effective tax administration requires adequate resources and use of information technology. Many tax administrations in developing Asia suffer low staffing, however, especially compared with OECD countries (Figure 2.4.2). Expanding tax administration resources may therefore significantly improve compliance and tax collection. In many developing economies, reform has prioritized strategically deploying limited resources. Special units to manage large taxpayers, for example, deploy highly skilled auditors to focus on big firms. They have been established across developing Asia, most recently in Hong Kong, China; the PRC; Solomon Islands; and Uzbekistan. However, the region has few dedicated taxpayer units for wealthy individuals (ADB 2022). Evidence is mixed on the revenue impacts of special taxpayer units (Ebeke, Mansour, and Rota-Graziosi 2016; Baum et al. 2017). In Indonesia, an experimental unit for wealthy individuals suffered serious administrative challenges and failed to meet revenue expectations, but a special unit for medium-sized taxpayers has shown far more promise (Widhartanto and Braithwaite 2016; Basri et al. 2021). How effective such units are appears to hinge on careful design and implementation. Finally, the use of information technology has expanded, digitalizing records, automating processes, and facilitating sophisticated data analytics, all of which improve taxpayer services and make better use of limited capacity. While developing Asia has embraced many digital innovations, scope exists to further expand their use (Box 2.4.2).

Figure 2.4.1 Tax compliance time for companies, 2010 and 2019

Tax compliance burdens have generally declined in developing Asia but remain higher than in OECD countries.

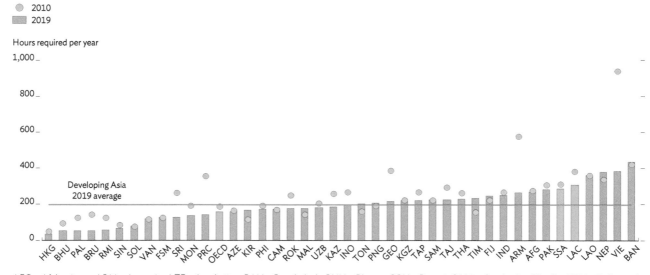

AFG = Afghanistan, ARM = Armenia, AZE = Azerbaijan, BAN = Bangladesh, BHU = Bhutan, BRU = Brunei, CAM = Cambodia, FIJ = Fiji, FSM = Federated States of Micronesia, GEO = Georgia, HKG = Hong Kong, China, IND = India, INO = Indonesia, KAZ = Kazakhstan, KGZ = Kyrgyz Republic, KIR = Kiribati, LAC = Latin America and the Caribbean, LAO = Lao People's Democratic Republic, MAL = Malaysia, MLD = Maldives, MON = Mongolia, NEP = Nepal, OECD = Organisation for Economic Co-operation and Development, PAK = Pakistan, PAL = Palau, PHI = Philippines, PNG = Papua New Guinea, PRC = People's Republic of China, RMI = Marshall Islands, ROK = Republic of Korea, SAM = Samoa, SIN = Singapore, SOL = Solomon Islands, SRI = Sri Lanka, SSA = Sub-Saharan Africa, TAJ = Tajikistan, TAP = Taipei,China, THA = Thailand, TIM = Timor-Leste, TON = Tonga, UZB = Uzbekistan, VAN = Vanuatu, VIE = Viet Nam.

Note: In the sample, economies in developing Asia number 40, OECD countries 33, SSA countries 44, and LAC countries 28.

Sources: World Bank. Doing Business data (accessed 14 December 2021); Asian Development Bank estimates.

Figure 2.4.2 Full-time equivalent tax administration staff per 100,000 population, 2019

Many tax administrations in developing Asia are less well resourced than their OECD and Latin American counterparts.

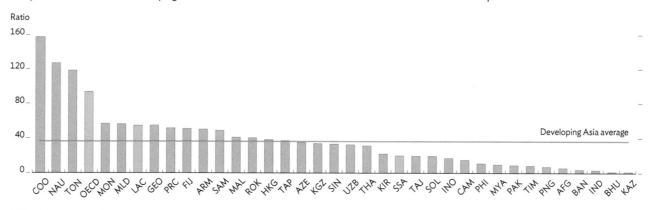

AFG = Afghanistan, ARM = Armenia, AZE = Azerbaijan, BAN = Bangladesh, BHU = Bhutan, CAM = Cambodia, COO = Cook Islands, FIJ = Fiji, GEO = Georgia, HKG = Hong Kong, China, IND = India, INO = Indonesia, KAZ = Kazakhstan, KGZ = Kyrgyz Republic, KIR = Kiribati, LAC = Latin America and the Caribbean, LAO = Lao People's Democratic Republic, MAL = Malaysia, MLD = Maldives, MON = Mongolia, MYA = Myanmar, NAU = Nauru, OECD = Organisation for Economic Co-operation and Development, PAK = Pakistan, PHI = Philippines, PNG = Papua New Guinea, PRC = People's Republic of China, ROK = Republic of Korea, SAM = Samoa, SIN = Singapore, SOL = Solomon Islands, SSA = Sub-Saharan Africa, TAJ = Tajikistan, TAP = Taipei,China, THA = Thailand, TIM = Timor-Leste, TON = Tonga, UZB = Uzbekistan, VIE = Viet Nam.

Sources: Revenue Administrations Fiscal Information Tool. 2020 International Survey of Revenue Administration (accessed 26 January 2021); Asian Development Bank estimates.

Many developing economies, including in Asia, have reconfigured governance arrangements to make tax administrations more autonomous. Semi-autonomous revenue agencies have been widely introduced in Latin America that feature more flexible employment and remuneration than elsewhere in the civil service. In principle, they also offer greater freedom from political pressure and stronger enforcement capacity able to stand up to elites (Cornia, Gomez-Sabaini, and Martorano 2011). Across developing Asia, tax administration governance arrangements are diverse, including semi-autonomous bodies and single departments within finance ministries (ADB 2022). As with special taxpayer units, evidence on the revenue impact of semi-autonomous revenue agencies in developing countries is mixed (von Haldenwang, von Schiller, and Garcia 2014; Ebeke, Mansour, and Rota-Graziosi 2016; Dom 2019). While reform creating such agencies significantly increased revenue in Peru, the impact in Africa has been less conclusive. More autonomous tax administration should therefore be considered not a panacea but part of broader organizational efforts to strengthen core governance and business processes (Junquera-Varela et al. 2019; Gbato, Lemou, and Brun 2021).

Weak tax collection has motivated authorities in developing economies to experiment with incentives for tax collectors, with promising results. One well-designed study found that performance pay substantially increased property tax collection (Khan, Khwaja, and Olken 2016). However, it also increased the frequency of bribes, indicating that incentives may spur corruption and thus require complementary monitoring. Nonfinancial incentives may help. For example, a performance system in Pakistan that took into account tax officials' preferred posting locations substantially increased tax collection (Khan, Khwaja, and Olken 2019).

Improving taxpayer morale to enhance compliance and tax collection

In addition to strengthening tax administration and enforcement, governments can increase tax collection by improving taxpayer morale, or willingness to pay taxes voluntarily.

Understanding the many factors that shape taxpayer behavior can inform better tax policy, improve government accountability and responsiveness, and feed a virtuous cycle of more effective government, stronger taxpayer morale, better compliance, and higher revenue (Torgler 2007; Luttmer and Singhal 2014; Horodnic 2018; OECD 2020). Stronger taxpayer morale also eases tax administration burdens, freeing up resources to tackle the toughest evasion challenges.

Taxpayer morale operates through several channels. Motivation to pay taxes can arise from pride, altruism, or a sense of civic duty (Luttmer and Singhal 2014; Alm 2019). Peer pressure, cultural factors, and social norms also likely play important roles. As tax compliance is higher where it is considered the norm, taxpayer morale may improve with more information about others' compliance. Further, taxpayers will be more willing to comply where they know they receive something in return from the government, most importantly high-quality public goods and services that reflect social priorities.

Trust in government and the quality of public governance and service delivery are critical for taxpayer morale. Trust encompasses the breadth of government, with trust in agencies that deliver services, such as the police and tax enforcement agencies, especially important (Horodnic 2018; Koumpias, Leonardo, and Martinez-Vazquez 2021). Surveys show willingness to pay tax is on average lower in developing Asia than in Latin America and OECD countries (Figure 2.4.3). Further, developing Asia displays a positive correlation between willingness to pay and perceived absence of corruption (Figure 2.4.4).

Tax authorities communicate with taxpayers through a variety of channels to shape perceptions of enforcement capacity, raise taxpayer morale, and influence tax compliance. Direct communication includes compliance reminders, information about tax audit policy and penalties, and equitable provision of government services funded by tax revenue (Jensen 2022; Martinez-Vasquez 2022). Communication can target certain groups of taxpayers and publicly expose tax evaders. As the cost of communicating with taxpayers is low compared with other interventions, this strategy can be highly cost-effective. Many countries have offered tax amnesties to encourage taxpayers to register and reveal their liability while they can escape penalties for past failure (Alm and Beck 1990; Hasseldine 1998;

Figure 2.4.3 Willingness to pay taxes, selected regions

Willingness to pay taxes in developing Asia lags other regions.

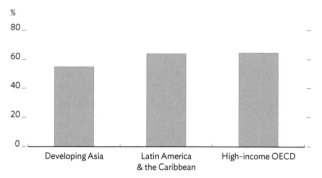

OECD = Organisation for Economic Co-operation and Development.
Note: Average percentage of survey respondents who answered that cheating on taxes is "never justifiable."
Sources: World Values Survey, 2017–2020 (accessed 15 November 2021); Asian Development Bank estimates.

Figure 2.4.4 Willingness to pay taxes and corruption perception, selected economies

Willingness to pay taxes is higher in economies with lower perceived corruption.

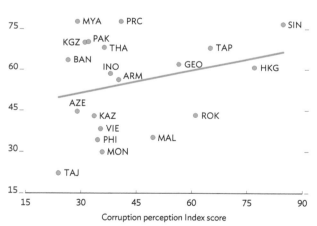

ARM = Armenia, AZE = Azerbaijan, BAN = Bangladesh, GEO = Georgia, HKG = Hong Kong, China, INO = Indonesia, KAZ = Kazakhstan, KGZ = Kyrgyz Republic, MAL = Malaysia, MON = Mongolia, MYA = Myanmar, PAK = Pakistan, PHI = Philippines, PRC = People's Republic of China, ROK = Republic of Korea, SIN = Singapore, TAJ = Tajikistan, TAP = Taipei,China, THA = Thailand, VIE = Viet Nam.
Notes: Average percentage of survey respondents who answered the World Values Survey that cheating on taxes is "never justifiable." The corruption perception index top score 100 is "very clean" and bottom score 0 is "highly corrupt," with economy average taken from 2017 to 2020 for compatibility.
Sources: World Values Survey, 2017–2020 (accessed 15 November 2021); Transparency International Corruption Perception Index (accessed 17 November 2021); Asian Development Bank estimates.

Uchitelle 1989; Bird 2014; Alm, Martinez-Vazquez, and Wallace 2009). However, amnesties have sometimes backfired, triggering discontent among compliant taxpayers who consider them unfair, and may ultimately worsen taxpayer morale.

Interest is growing about how tax administration communication can be improved by drawing on behavioral insights. Recent global evidence that behavioral nudges can motivate tax compliance has important policy implications (OECD 2021b), and highlights opportunities for policy experimentation (Box 2.4.3). First, providing taxpayers with information about the enforcement environment can cost-effectively increase tax collection but needs to be backed up by actual enforcement. Second, programs providing social rewards or punishments appear to be effective but require careful implementation to address privacy concerns (Perez-Truglia 2020). Third, tax administrations may be able to help stimulate taxpayer morale by strengthening reciprocity, or the sense that taxpayers get high-quality public services in return.

Ultimately, however, governments must play a broader lead role in improving taxpayer morale, one tailored to local circumstances and addressing taxpayer concerns. Taxpayer attitudes are likely deeply rooted and not easily shifted, particularly those that reflect cultural norms (Jensen 2022). Therefore, broader government reform to improve public goods and services may be required to alter beliefs. A stronger social contract is an important element in fundamental tax reform. In the meantime, help can come from incremental improvement in government service delivery and efforts to reduce corruption and informality—as well as from consequent enhanced perception of fairness (Joshi, Prichard, and Heady 2014).

Mobilizing taxes to support Asia's development

Developing Asia emerges from the COVID-19 pandemic with weakened public finances.
This theme chapter has discussed the fiscal challenges facing the region and argues for urgent tax revenue mobilization to support sustainable development.

While private finance has a crucial role to play, achieving the SDGs for a greener and more inclusive future requires vast public spending. More efficient public spending can free up additional fiscal resources, but the mobilization of additional revenue is essential to augment fiscal space across the region. Encouragingly, tax revenue in the region started to increase before the pandemic. The right policies can restore this trend.

Tax reform balancing efficiency, equity, and simplicity can mobilize taxes for development. Opportunities seized to mobilize tax revenue need to be tailored to economy-specific circumstances, but more efficient VAT and optimized tax incentives hold promise across the region. Many economies have scope to increase revenue from personal income and property taxes and improve progressivity.

Multilateral initiatives can reduce pressure on corporate income tax and ensure appropriate taxation of the digital economy. Significant opportunities exist to expand the use of tax and other fiscal instruments that address environmental and health priorities while raising revenue: carbon and other environmental taxes, and corrective taxes on alcohol, tobacco, and other unhealthy consumption. Finally, reform is needed to reduce Asia's large informal sector and thus increase revenue, especially by reducing the cost of business registration. Moreover, while often politically difficult, fundamental tax reform to increase revenue is achievable and best done in tandem with efforts to strengthen tax administration and improve taxpayer morale.

Box 2.4.1 Successful tax reform and revenue mobilization in developing countries

Over the past few decades, several developing countries have successfully undertaken tax reform to substantially increase low tax revenue. It is informative to examine the main features of successful reform in a diverse set of developing countries that generated some of the largest tax revenue increases anywhere over the past few decades (box figure). In these countries reforms led to tax to GDP ratios soaring by more than a half.

Colombia's tax reform during the 1990s and early 2000s illustrates the importance of a strong social contract, with reform motivated by economic, social, and political demands stemming from a new constitution. Taxes were devolved to subnational governments, social services widened, and security institutions strengthened. The corporate tax rate was cut, a lower rate was introduced for income from repatriated capital, and stock market dividends were made tax exempt. The value-added tax (VAT) base was broadened, the rate increased to 14%, and a tax surcharge was introduced to fund national security measures. Tax administration reform included computerized risk analysis to inform audit cases, stiffened penalties, and improved collection of tax arrears.

Following economic crises in Asia and the Russian Federation and consequent heightened uncertainty, the VAT base was further broadened. Compliance improved through electronic filing, supported by stronger taxpayer morale built on improved governance and service quality and curtailed corruption.

The People's Republic of China had, prior to 1994, a tax system heavily reliant on taxing state enterprises, with taxes administered and collected by provinces and a portion remitted to the central government. The ratio of tax to GDP declined as provincial governments protected local enterprises and did not consistently enforce payment. The 1994 Tax Sharing System Reform highlighted how intergovernmental fiscal reform that clearly delineates central and subnational government tax responsibilities can support comprehensive tax reform. The central government created its own revenue administration, the State Administration of Taxation, charged with collecting and enforcing all central and shared taxes. Reform simplified and standardized taxes, lowered income tax rates, and established a VAT with a general rate of 17%, later lowered to 13%.

continued on next page

Box 2.4.1 *Continued*

Index of tax revenue as a share of GDP before and after major reform

In some developing countries in Asia and Latin America tax revenue soared following reform.

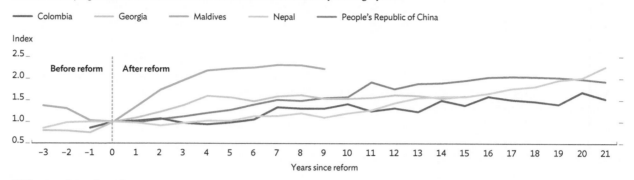

GDP = gross domestic product.

Notes: The ratio of tax to GDP is indexed to the year of reform in each country: Colombia 1991, Georgia 2004, Maldives 2010, Nepal 1997, and the People's Republic of China 1995.

Sources: IMF–Government Finance Statistics (accessed 31 January 2022); World Revenue Longitudinal Data (accessed 22 October 2021).

Georgia implemented fundamental tax reform in three waves from 2004 to 2011. Reform simplified a previously complex tax system and was complemented by provisions to improve the business environment and public service delivery. A progressive income tax was replaced with a flat tax of 20%, and tax rates on dividends and interest were cut. The VAT rate fell from 20% to 18%, while the corporate income tax rate was reduced from a maximum of 20% to a flat rate of 15%. Fifteen types of taxes were eliminated. Tax and customs agencies were consolidated into the State Revenue Service. Tax administration infrastructure was upgraded, electronic tax filing introduced, and customs checkpoints and tax service centers upgraded. Anticorruption reform greatly improved compliance.

Maldives suffered major fiscal pressures following a tsunami in 2004 and the global financial crisis of 2008–2009. They spurred tax reform aiming to broaden a narrow tax base and boost revenue. A tourist goods and services tax (GST) was introduced—later replaced by a general GST—and a business profit tax was established with a flat rate of 15% on taxable profits. GST and business registration increased significantly from 2011 to 2015, supported by extensive public awareness programs. In 2010, the first central revenue collector, the Maldives Internal Revenue Authority, was established with authority to conduct audits and investigations and to freeze the bank accounts of noncompliant taxpayers.

Nepal introduced major tax reform starting in the 1990s. In 1997, a VAT with a general rate of 10% replaced a sales tax, lifting VAT revenue to the equivalent of 2.7% of GDP by 2000. The VAT rate later rose to 13%, and revenue continued to rise as more businesses entered the formal sector. A new excise was introduced in 2002, and a new customs tax in 2007. Taxpayers were assigned a permanent account number in 2002, and revenue rose with a 35% tax bracket added to personal income tax in 2010 targeting high-income individuals. The Internal Revenue Department was established in 2001, consolidating separate tax services and expanding the use of information technology. By fiscal year 2015, 98% of tax filings and nearly all tax registrations were conducted online, improving public perception of the Internal Revenue Department.

Reference:
Martinez-Vazquez, J. 2022. *Successful Tax Reforms in the Recent International Experience: Lessons in Political Economy and the Nuts and Bolts of Increasing Country Tax Revenue Effort.* Asian Development Bank.

Box 2.4.2 Digital technology to strengthen tax administration in developing Asia

The COVID-19 pandemic is spurring governments to accelerate the adoption and use of digital technology, including in tax administration. As economies recover, tax authorities will need to rejuvenate their operations to strengthen tax collection and compliance, which declined during the pandemic. The digital transformation of tax administration is key to achieving these goals and to supporting international tax cooperation, particularly for the exchange of information. Digitalization in the region needs to shift from the basic use of taxpayer data to more advanced applications to improve compliance, policy, and efficiency. Tax administration reform using innovative digital technology—sometimes called "Tax Administration 3.0" (OECD 2020)—offers several potential advantages, most notably enhanced data security through digital platforms that drive core tax administration functions and compliance costs minimized through streamlined processes and user-friendly interfaces. Also helpful are optimized and automated administration of tax systems using data analytics (Estevão 2020).

Tax administration digitalization has come in three waves. First, basic digital technology enabled the digital storage of tax information, with e-filing as a first step in digitalizing data and moving away from paper. Second, digital technology facilitated taxpayer service innovations like prefiled tax returns and enhanced tax compliance with e-invoicing and data-matching technology. The third wave featured such innovations as artificial intelligence, machine learning, and predictive analytics. Data collection can take the form of data file transfer between government agencies or may even be embedded into systems that taxpayers use to run their businesses. Artificial intelligence and machine learning technology enable automated assessment of taxpayers' data against norms, alerting tax administrations to possible tax avoidance.

Tax authorities across developing Asia have made substantial progress in using digital innovations to reduce costs and improve service. Malaysian tax authorities, for example, strengthened tax system integration and enhanced their capacity in data analytics to reduce batch job processing costs by a target of 70% while improving compliance risk management and taxpayer service experience (OECD 2021). However, significant scope exists to adopt more digital technologies. A recent survey found the average rate of electronic filing of tax returns for three main taxes in developing Asia reached only about 60% in 2019, much lower than about 90% in Organisation for Economic Co-operation Development (OECD) countries (box figure 1). Further, while a higher share of authorities in the region reported using e-invoicing than in OECD countries (box figure 2), the region lags considerably in the use of such advanced digital technologies as artificial intelligence and data analytics (box figure 3).

1 Percentage of economies with electronic filing, 2019

The use of electronic filing in developing Asia lags OECD countries.

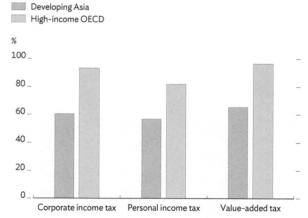

- Developing Asia
- High-income OECD

OECD = Organisation for Economic Co-operation and Development.
Note: Data for developing Asia average 21–31 economies and for OECD 32–35 economies, in both cases the least for value-added tax and the most for corporate income tax.
Sources: Revenue Administrations Fiscal Information Tool. 2020 International Survey of Revenue Administration (accessed 26 January 2021); Asian Development Bank estimates.

continued on next page

Box 2.4.2 *Continued*

2 E-invoicing and prefiling of tax return, 2019

While electronic tax invoicing is well used in developing Asia, significant scope remains to expand electronic prefiling.

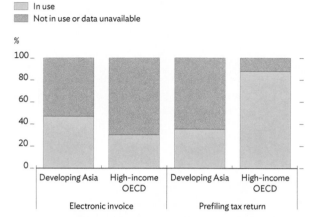

OECD = Organisation for Economic Co-operation and Development.
Note: Data include 34 economies in developing Asia and 33 high-income OECD economies.
Sources: Revenue Administrations Fiscal Information Tool. 2020 International Survey of Revenue Administration (accessed 26 January 2021); Asian Development Bank estimates.

3 Advanced digital technologies, 2019

The use of advanced data analytics can be greatly expanded to support tax administrations in developing Asia.

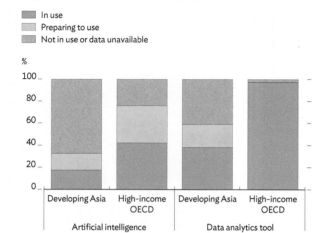

OECD = Organisation for Economic Co-operation and Development.
Note: Data include 34 economies in developing Asia and 33 high-income OECD economies.
Sources: Revenue Administrations Fiscal Information Tool. 2020 International Survey of Revenue Administration (accessed 26 January 2021); Asian Development Bank estimates.

A carefully developed and implemented digitalization strategy can help authorities fully harness the benefits of digitalization. It can also avoid incoherent strategies that produce poorly connected systems. Inadequate workforce engagement and capability can hamper implementation. Other common challenges include replacing legacy systems that contain vital data, earmarking financial resources, obtaining political buy-in, and navigating unequal digital access (ICAEW 2019). Further, developing economies face challenging technological and institutional capacity constraints.

The careful application of information technology can reduce but not eliminate tax governance deficiencies. Digitalization should be viewed as a complement to other governance-strengthening measures. The Asian Development Bank, through the newly established Asia Pacific Tax Hub, is helping regional governments develop digitalization roadmaps.

This includes analyzing the gap between the current baseline and future goals and a guidance note (ADB, forthcoming) that provides a basic assessment of existing legal, procedural, institutional, and technological capacity.

References:
ADB. Forthcoming. *Launching a Digital Tax Administration Transformation: What You Need to Know.* Asian Development Bank.
Estevão, M. 2020. Why Digital Transformation Matters for Taxation. *World Bank Blogs.* World Bank.
ICAEW. 2019. *Digitalisation of Tax: International Perspectives.* Institute of Chartered Accountants in England and Wales.
OECD. 2020. *Tax Administration 3.0: The Digital Transformation of Tax Administration.* Organisation for Economic Co-operation and Development.
———. 2021. *Tax Administration Comparative Information on OECD and other Advanced and Emerging Economies.* Organisation for Economic Co-operation and Development.

Box 2.4.3 Evidence on policy interventions to improve taxpayer morale and compliance

Recent empirical studies from around the world have used randomized control trials and other methods to test how effectively policy interventions, including letters from tax authorities, improve taxpayer morale and compliance. They found that compliance can generally be boosted through deterrence messages about tax enforcement audits and penalties (Kleven et al. 2011; Slemrod 2019; De Neve et al. 2021). Such interventions may even have spillover effects, with neighbors of households that receive letters being themselves more likely to comply (Drago, Mengel, and Traxler 2020). Messaging also appears to raise compliance by firms (Bergolo et al., forthcoming; Boning et al. 2020). However, deterrence messages sometimes have only small or even adverse effects. In Rwanda, deterrence messages backfired, while reminders that highlight the civic virtue of paying taxes helped (Mascagni and Nell 2022). Similar effects were found in the US (Slemrod, Blumenthal, and Christian 1999). Negative effects appear to concentrate among higher earners, possibly because deterrence messages counter their intrinsic motivation to pay.

Several studies have analyzed whether it works to prime taxpayers about the social norm to comply. Results are mixed. One study found that messages about how most taxpayers correctly report their income and assets induced previous evaders to report more of their income held abroad (Bott et al. 2020). Similarly, an intervention about how most citizens pay their taxes on time made timely tax payment more likely (Hallsworth et al. 2017). Most studies, however, found little good from such measures and sometimes harm (Luttmer and Singhal 2014). Programs that seek to stimulate social considerations by making taxpayer information public have proved more successful, suggesting that a threat to reputation is a powerful driver of tax compliance. In Pakistan, researchers studied an intervention where the largest 100 taxpayers were socially recognized, and another where taxpayers' names and tax payment amounts were made publicly available (Slemrod, Rehman, and Waseem 2022). Both programs significantly improved compliance, particularly among heretofore delinquent taxpayers most likely to be singled out after tax records were made public.

Studies have examined interventions that aim to improve compliance by strengthening reciprocity, again with mixed results. In Rwanda, priming taxpayers about the link between taxes paid and public goods substantially increased tax payments more than did deterrence messages (Mascagni and Nell 2022). However, another study reported that providing information on the shares of tax receipts devoted to different public goods lowered tax payment (De Neve et al. 2021). Other studies found no effect from such reciprocity letters (Luttmer and Singhal 2014).

However, more promising results emerged from studies in developing economies that examined how actual public service delivery—not just information provision—affects reciprocity. For example, tax compliance improved in Pakistan when local governments committed to spend more property tax revenue in the neighborhood from which it was collected (Khwaja et al. 2020). Compliance increased when officials allocated a portion of tax revenue to fund priorities identified by taxpayers. In general, though, tax revenue increments from such programs were low relative to their often-large cost. These interventions may thus be less cost-effective than letter interventions or social shaming and recognition programs.

References:
Bergolo, M. et al. Forthcoming. Tax Audits as Scarecrows. *American Economic Journal.*
Boning, W. et al. 2020. Heard It through the Grapevine: The Direct and Network Effects of a Tax Enforcement Field Experiment on Firms. *Journal of Public Economics* 190(1).
Bott, K. et al. 2020. You've Got Mail: A Randomized Field Experiment on Tax Evasion. *Management Science* 66(7).
De Neve, J. et al. 2021. How to Improve Tax Compliance? Evidence from Population-Wide Experiments in Belgium. *Journal of Political Economy* 129(5).
Drago, F., F. Mengel, and C. Traxler 2020. Compliance Behavior in Networks: Evidence from a Field Experiment. *American Economic Journal: Applied Economics* 12(2).
Hallsworth, M. et al. 2017. The Behavioralist as Tax Collector: Using Natural Field Experiments to Enhance Tax Compliance. *Journal of Public Economics* 148(1).
Khwaja, A. et al. 2020. Rebuilding the Social Compact: Urban Service Delivery and Property Taxes in Pakistan. *Impact Evaluation Report* 117.

continued on next page

Box 2.4.3 *Continued*

Kleven, H. et al. 2011. Unwilling or Unable to Cheat? Evidence from a Tax Audit Experiment in Denmark. *Econometrica* 79(3).

Luttmer, E. and M. Singhal. 2014. Tax Morale. *Journal of Economic Perspectives* 28(4).

Mascagni, G. and C. Nell. 2022. Tax Compliance in Rwanda: Evidence from a Message Field Experiment. *Economic Development and Cultural Change* 70(2).

Slemrod, J. 2019. Tax Compliance and Enforcement. *Journal of Economic Literature* 57(4).

Slemrod, J., M. Blumenthal, and C. Christian. 1999. Taxpayer Response to an Increased Probability of Audit: Evidence from a Controlled Experiment in Minnesota. *Journal of Public Economics* 79(1).

Slemrod, J., O. Rehman, and M. Waseem. 2022. How Do Taxpayers Respond to Public Disclosure and Social Recognition Programs? Evidence from Pakistan. *Review of Economics and Statistics* 104(1).

Background Papers

Arimura, T. H. et al. 2022. *Green Revenues for Greener Asia.* Asian Development Bank.

Clements, B., S. Gupta, and J. T. Jalles. 2022. *Fiscal Policy for Inclusive Growth in Asia.* Asian Development Bank.

Go, E., S. Hill, M. H. Jaber, Y. Jinjarak, D. Park, and A. Ragos. 2022. *Developing Asia's Fiscal Landscape and Challenges.* Asian Development Bank.

Gupta, S. and J. T. Jalles. 2022. *Priorities for Strengthening Key Revenue Sources in Asia.* Asian Development Bank.

Hill, S., Y. Jinjarak, and D. Park. 2022. *How Do Tax Revenues Respond to GDP Growth? Evidence from Developing Asia, 1998–2020.* Asian Development Bank.

Lane, C. 2022. *Meeting Health Challenges in Developing Asia with Corrective Taxes on Alcohol, Tobacco, and Unhealthy Foods.* Asian Development Bank.

Martinez-Vazquez, J. 2022. *Successful Tax Reforms in the Recent International Experience: Lessons in Political Economy and the Nuts and Bolts of Increasing Country Tax Revenue Effort.* Asian Development Bank.

Mullins, P. 2022. *Taxing Developing Asia's Digital Economy.* Asian Development Bank.

Ulyssea, G. 2022. *Informality and Taxation in Developing Asia.* Asian Development Bank.

Background Notes

Bhattacharya, S. and J. G. Stotsky. 2022. *A Tax Primer: With Applications to Asia-Pacific Countries.* Asian Development Bank.

Dutta, A. 2022. *Health Policy Decision-Making around Taxes on Alcohol, Tobacco and Unhealthy Foods in the COVID-19 Era.* Asian Development Bank.

Jensen, A. 2022. *Review Paper: Evidence-Based Insights to Build Tax Capacity in Developing Countries.* Asian Development Bank.

McCluskey, W. R. Bahl, and R. Franzsen. 2022. *Strengthening Property Taxation within Developing Asia.* Asian Development Bank.

Takenaka, A. 2022. *Impact of Social Assistance on Vulnerable Vietnamese Groups during COVID-19: Evidence from Microsimulations.* Asian Development Bank.

References

Acosta-Ormaechea, S. and A. Morozumi. 2021. The Value-Added Tax and Growth: Design Matters. *International Tax and Public Finance* 28.

ADB. 2014. *Asian Development Outlook 2014: Fiscal Policy for Inclusive Growth.* Asian Development Bank.

———. 2020. *Asia's Journey to Prosperity: Policy, Market, and Technology over 50 Years.* Asian Development Bank.

———. 2021a. *Asian Development Outlook 2021: Financing a Green and Inclusive Recovery.* Asian Development Bank.

———. 2021b. *Asian Development Outlook 2021 Update: Transforming Agriculture in Asia*. Asian Development Bank.

———. 2021c. *Asian Development Bank Key Indicators 2021*. Asian Development Bank.

———. 2021d. *A Comprehensive Assessment of Tax Capacity in Southeast Asia*. Asian Development Bank.

———. 2022. *A Comparative Analysis of Tax Administration in Asia and the Pacific* (5th edition). Asian Development Bank.

Addison, T., M. Niño-Zarazua, and J. Pirttila. 2018. Fiscal Policy, State Building and Economic Development. *Journal of International Development* 30.

Agnolucci, P. 2009. The Effect of the German and British Environmental Taxation Reforms: A Simple Assessment. *Energy Policy* 37(8).

Akcigit, U., S. Baslandze, and S. Stantcheva. 2016. Taxation and the International Mobility of Inventors. *American Economic Review* 106(10).

Akitoby, B. et al. 2018. Tax Revenue Mobilization Episodes in Emerging Markets and Low-Income Countries: Lessons from a New Dataset. *IMF Working Paper* 18/234. International Monetary Fund.

Akitoby, B., J. Honda, and K. Primus 2020. Tax Revenues in Fragile and Conflict-Affected States—Why Are They Low and How Can We Raise Them? *IMF Working Paper* No. 20/143. International Monetary Fund.

Akitoby, B. et al. 2006. Public Spending, Voracity, and Wagner's Law in Developing Countries. *European Journal of Political Economy* 22.

Alavuotunki, K., M. Haapanen, and J. Pirttila. 2019. The Effects of the Value-Added Tax on Revenue and Inequality. *The Journal of Development Studies* 55(4). DOI: 10.1080/00220388.2017.1400015.

Ali, D. A., K. Deininger, and M. Wild. 2018. Using Satellite Imagery to Revolutionize Creations of Tax Maps and Local Revenue Collection. *Policy Research Working Paper* 8437. World Bank.

Alm, J. and W. Beck. 1990. Tax Amnesties and Tax Revenues. *Public Finance Quarterly* 18(4).

Alm, J., J. Martinez-Vazquez, and S. Wallace. 2009. Do Tax Amnesties Work? The Revenue Effects of Tax Amnesties during the Transition in the Russian Federation. *Economic Analysis and Policy* 39(2).

Alm, J. 2019. What Motivates Tax Compliance? *Journal of Economic Surveys* 33(2).

Andersen, M., B. Kett, and E. von Uexkull. 2018. Corporate Tax Incentives and FDI in Developing Countries. In World Bank Group. *Global Investment Competitiveness Report 2017/2018*.

Appiah-Kubi, S. N. K. et al. 2021. Impact of Tax Incentives on Foreign Direct Investment: Evidence from Africa. *Sustainability* 13(8661).

Arimura, T. H., M. Duan, and H. Oh. 2021. EEPS Special Issue on Carbon Pricing in East Asia. *Environmental Economics and Policy Studies*.

Auriol, E. and M. Warlters. 2005. Taxation Base in Developing Countries. *Journal of Public Economics* 89(4).

Bachas, P., L. Gadenne, and A. Jensen. 2021. Informality, Consumption Taxes and Redistribution. *Faculty Research Working Paper* RWP21-026. Harvard Kennedy School.

Bahl, R. 2006. How to Approach Tax Reform: Have the Rules of the Game Changed? In Alm, J., J. Martinez-Vazquez, and M. Rider, eds. *The Challenge of Tax Reform in the Global Economy*. Springer.

Bahl, R. and R. M. Bird. 2018. *Fiscal Decentralization and Local Finance in Developing Countries*. Edward Elgar Publishing.

Basri, M. C. et al. 2021. Tax Administration versus Tax Rates: Evidence from Corporate Taxation in Indonesia. *American Economic Review* 111(12).

Baum, A. et al. 2017. Corruption, Taxes and Compliance. *Working Paper* 17/255. International Monetary Fund.

Benedek, D. et al. 2021. A Post-Pandemic Assessment of the Sustainable Development Goals. *IMF Staff Discussion Note* SDN/2021/003. International Monetary Fund.

Bergeron, A., G. Tourek, and J. Weigel. 2021. The State Capacity Ceiling on Tax Rates: Evidence from Randomized Tax Abatements in the DRC. *CEPR Working Paper* No. 16116.

Besley, T. and M. Ghatak. 2006. Public Goods and Economic Development. In Banerjee, A. V., R. Benabou, and D. Mookherjee, eds. *Understanding Poverty*. Oxford University Press.

Besley, T. and T. Persson. 2014. Public Goods and Economic Development. Why Do Developing Countries Tax so Little? *Journal of Economic Perspectives* 28(4).

Beuermann, C. and T. Santarius. 2006. Ecological Tax Reform in Germany: Handling Two Hot Potatoes at the Same Time. *Energy Policy* 34(8).

Bird, R. M. 2004. Managing Tax Reform. *Bulletin for International Fiscal Documentation* 58.

———. 2008. *Tax Challenges Facing Developing Countries.* Inaugural Lecture of the Annual Public Lecture Series of the National Institute of Public Finance and Policy.

———. 2014. Administrative Dimensions of Tax Reform. *Annals of Economics and Finance* 15(2).

Blanchard, O., J. Felman, and A. Subramanian. 2021. Does the New Fiscal Consensus in Advanced Economies Travel to Emerging Markets? *PIIE Policy Brief* 21-7. Peterson Institute for International Economics.

Blundell, R. 2016. *Labor Supply and Taxation.* Oxford University Press.

Bonvecchi, A. 2010. The Political Economy of Fiscal Reform in Latin America: The Case of Argentina. *IDB Working Paper Series* No. IDB-WP-175. Inter-American Development Bank.

Brockmeyer, A. et al. 2021. *NBER Working Paper* 28637. National Bureau of Economic Research.

Brondolo, J. 2009. Collecting Taxes during an Economic Crisis: Challenges and Policy Options. *IMF Staff Position Note* SPN/09/17. International Monetary Fund.

Bruhn, M. and D. McKenzie. 2014. Entry Regulation and the Formalization of Microenterprises in Developing Countries. *World Bank Research Observer* 29(2).

Brys, B. 2011. Making Fundamental Tax Reform Happen. *OECD Taxation Working Papers* No. 3.

Burman, L. and M. Phaup. 2011. *Tax Expenditures: The Big Government Behind the Curtain.* VoxEU.org.

Cabezon, E., P. Tumbarello, and Y. Wu. 2015. Strengthening Fiscal Frameworks and Improving the Spending Mix in Small States. *IMF Working Paper* No. 124. International Monetary Fund.

Cabral, M. and C. Hoxby. 2012. The Hated Property Tax: Salience, Tax Rates and Tax Revolts. *NBER Working Paper* 18515. National Bureau of Economic Research.

Carrillo, P., D. Pomeranz, and M. Singhal. 2017. Dodging the Taxman: Firm Misreporting and Limits to Tax Enforcement. *American Economic Journal: Applied Economics* 9(2).

Carter, P. and A. Cobham. 2016. Are Taxes Good for Your Health? *WIDER Working Paper* 2016/171. World Institute for Development Economics Research.

Casanegra de Jantscher, M. 1990. Administering a VAT. In Gillis, M., C. Shoup, and G. Sicat, eds. *Value Added Taxation in Developing Countries.* World Bank.

Castanheira, M., G. Nicodeme, and P. Profeta. 2012. On the Political Economics of Tax Reforms: Survey and Empirical Assessment. *International Tax and Public Finance* 19.

Causa, O. and M. Hermansen. 2017. Income Redistribution through Taxes and Transfers across OCED Countries. *OECD Economics Department Working Papers* No. 1453. Organisation for Economic Co-operation and Development.

CBO. 2012. *Tax Expenditures Have a Major Impact on the Federal Budget.* Web Blog Post, Congressional Budget Office.

Cerutti, E. and T. Helbling. 2021. Unconventional Monetary Policies in Emerging Asia during the COVID-19 Crisis: Why Now? Will They Work? In Rhee, C. and K. Svirydzenka, eds. *Policy Advice to Asia in the COVID-19 Era.* International Monetary Fund.

Chandra, T. 2021. Pricing Carbon: Trade-offs and Opportunities for India. In Mitra, A., ed. *Reconciling India's Climate and Industrial Targets: A Policy Roadmap.* Observer Research Foundation.

Charlot, O., F. Malherbet, and C. Terra. 2015. Informality in Developing Economies: Regulation and Fiscal Policies. *Journal of Economic Dynamics and Control* 51.

Chetty, R. et al. 2014. Active vs. Passive Decisions and Crowd-Out in Retirement Savings Accounts: Evidence from Denmark. *The Quarterly Journal of Economics* 129.

Cnossen, S. 2020. Excise Taxation for Domestic Resource Mobilization. *CESinfo Working Paper* No. 8442.

Cobham, A. and P. Jansky. 2018. Global Distribution of Revenue Loss from Corporate Tax Avoidance: Re-estimation and Country Results. *Journal of International Development* 30.

Cornia, G., J. Gomez-Sabaini, and B. Martorano. 2011. A New Fiscal Pact, Tax Policy Changes and Income Inequality. *UNU-WIDER Working Paper* No. 2011/70.

Cottarelli, C., P. Gerson, and A. Senhadji. 2014. Policy Lessons from the Crisis and the Way Forward. In Cottarelli, C., P. Gerson, and A. Senhadji, eds. *Post-Crisis Fiscal Policy*. MIT Press.

Crivelli, E., R. De Mooij, and M. Keen. 2016. Base Erosion, Profit Shifting and Developing Countries. *FinanzArchiv* 72.

CRS. 2019. *Spending and Tax Expenditures: Distinctions and Major Programs*. Congressional Research Service.

Dabla-Norris, E. et al. 2021. Digitalization and Taxation in Asia. *IMF Discussion Paper* DP/2021/017. International Monetary Fund.

de Andrade, G. H., M. Bruhn, and D. McKenzie. 2014. A Helping Hand or the Long Arm of the Law? Experimental Evidence on What Governments Can Do to Formalize Firms. *Policy Research Working Paper* No. 6435. World Bank.

Delong, J. B. and L. Summers. 2012. Fiscal Policy in a Depressed Economy. *Brookings Papers on Economic Activity* 1.

D'Erasmo, P. and H. Boedo. 2012. Financial Structure, Informality and Development. *Journal of Monetary Economics* 59(3).

De Soto, H. 1989. *The Other Path*. Harper & Row.

Dix-Carneiro, R. et al. 2021. Trade and Informality in the Presence of Labor Market Frictions and Regulations. *Working Paper Series* No. w28391. National Bureau of Economic Research.

Djankov, S. et al. 2002. The Regulation of Entry. *The Quarterly Journal of Economics* 117(1).

Dom, R. 2019. Semi-Autonomous Revenue Authorities in Sub-Saharan Africa: Silver Bullet or White Elephant. *Journal of Development Studies* 55(7).

Dorband, I. I. et al. 2019. Poverty and Distributional Effects of Carbon Pricing in Low- and Middle-Income Countries—A Global Comparative Analysis. *World Development* 115.

Ebeke, C., M. Mansour, and G. Rota-Graziosi. 2016. The Power to Tax in Sub-Saharan Africa: LTUs, VATs, and SARAs. *Development Policies Working Paper* 154. Fondation pour les études et recherches sur le développement international.

Fairfield, T. 2013. Going Where the Money Is: Strategies for Taxing Economic Elites in Unequal Democracies. *World Development* 57.

Fan, H. et al. 2021. The Dynamic Effects of Computerized Invoices on Chinese Manufacturing Firms. *NBER Working Paper* No. 24414. National Bureau of Economic Research.

Favara, G., C. Minoiu, and A. Perez-Orive. 2021. *U.S. Zombie Firms: How Many and How Consequential? FEDS Notes*. Board of Governors of the Federal Reserve System.

Fernald, J. and H. Li. 2021. *The Impact of COVID on Potential Output. Federal Reserve Bank of San Francisco Working Paper Series* 2021-09.

Ferrarini, B., M. Giugale, and J. Pradelli, eds. 2022. *The Sustainability of Asia's Debt: Problems, Policies, and Practices*. Asian Development Bank and Edward Elgar Publishing.

Franzsen, R. and W. J. McCluskey. 2013. Value-Based Approaches to Property Taxation. In McCluskey, W. J., G. C. Cornia, and L. C. Walters, eds. *A Primer on Property Tax: Administration and Policy*. Wiley-Blackwell.

Fuest, C. et al. 2021. Read My Lips? Taxes and Elections. *EconPol Working Paper* 5(71). Ifo Institute, University of Munich.

Furceri, D. et al. 2021. The Rise in Inequality after Pandemics: Can Fiscal Support Play a Mitigating Role? *Industrial and Corporate Change* 30.

Gaspar, V., L. Jaramillo, and P. Wingender. 2016a. Political Institutions, State Building, and Tax Capacity: Crossing the Tipping Point. *IMF Working Papers* WP/16/233. International Monetary Fund.

———. 2016b. Tax Capacity and Growth: Is There a Tipping Point? *IMF Working Paper* WP/16/234. International Monetary Fund.

Gaspar, V. et al. 2019. Fiscal Policy and Development: Human, Social, and Physical Investment for the SDGs. *IMF Staff Discussion Note* SDN/19/03. International Monetary Fund.

Gbato, A., F. Lemou, and J. F. Brun. 2021. Effectiveness of SARA Reform in Sub-Saharan Africa. *HAL Working Papers* ffhal-03119001. HAL Open Science.

Gindling, T. H. and D. Newhouse. 2014. Self-Employment in the Developing World. *World Development* 56.

Goulder, J. H. 1995. Environmental Taxation and the Double Dividend: A Reader's Guide. *International Tax and Public Finance* 2(2).

Gunter, S. et al. 2021. Non-Linear Effects of Tax Changes on Output: The Role of the Initial Level of Taxation. *Journal of International Economics* 131.

Gupta, S. and J. Jalles. 2021. Can COVID-19 Induce Governments to Implement Tax Reforms in

Developing Countries? *Working Papers* REM 2021/0168. Lisbon School of Economics and Management.

Guvenen, F., B. Kuruscu, and S. Ozkan. 2014. Taxation of Human Capital and Wage Inequality: A Cross-Country Analysis. *Review of Economic Studies* 81.

Guvenen, F. et al. 2019. *Use It or Lose It: Efficiency Gains from Wealth Taxation* No. w26284. National Bureau of Economic Research.

Haites, E. 2018. Carbon Taxes and Greenhouse Gas Emissions Trading Systems: What Have We Learned? *Climate Policy* 18(8).

Haldenwang, C. V., A. Redonda, and F. Aliu. 2021. *Shedding Light on Worldwide Tax Expenditures: GTED Flagship Report 2021*. German Development Institute.

Hall, S. et al. 2021. Government Revenue and Child and Maternal Mortality. *Open Economic Review* 32.

Hasseldine, J. 1998. Tax Amnesties: An International Review. *Bulletin for International Fiscal Documentation* 52.

Heathcote, J., K. Storesletten, and G. Violante. 2014. Optimal Tax Progressivity: An Analytical Framework. *NBER Working Paper* No. 19899. National Bureau of Economic Research.

Hepburn, C. et al. 2020. Will COVID-19 Fiscal Recovery Packages Accelerate or Retard Progress on Climate Change? *Oxford Review of Economic Policy* 36.

Horodnic, I. 2018. Tax Morale and Institutional Theory: A Systematic Review. *International Journal of Sociology and Social Policy* 38(9/10).

Hoynes, H. and A. Patel. 2018. Effective Policy for Reducing Poverty and Inequality? The Earned Income Tax Credit and Distribution of Income. *Journal of Human Resources* 53(4).

ICAP. 2021. *Korea Emissions Trading Scheme*. International Carbon Action Partnership (accessed 9 August 2021).

IEA. 2021. *Net Zero by 2050: A Roadmap for the Global Energy Sector*. International Energy Agency.

IETA. 2020. *Carbon Market Business Brief: Korea*. International Emissions Trading Association.

IISD. 2017. *India's Energy Transition: Mapping Subsidies to Fossil Fuels and Clean Energy in India*. International Institute for Sustainable Development.

———. 2020. *Mapping India's Energy Subsidies 2020: Fossil Fuels, Renewables, and Electric Vehicles: 2020 Annex Update*. International Institute for Sustainable Development.

Ilzetzki, E. 2018. Tax Reform and the Political Economy of the Tax Base. *Journal of Public Economics* 164.

IMF. 2014. Spillovers in International Corporate Taxation. *IMF Policy Paper Volume 2014: Issue 071*. International Monetary Fund.

———. 2015. Fiscal Policy and Long-Term Growth. *IMF Policy Paper* 2015(023). International Monetary Fund.

———. 2019. Macroeconomic Developments and Prospects in Low-Income Developing Countries—2019. *IMF Policy Paper*. International Monetary Fund.

———. 2021. *Fiscal Monitor: A Fair Shot*. International Monetary Fund.

James, S. 2013. *Tax and Non-tax Incentives and Investments: Evidence and Policy Implications*. World Bank.

———. 2016. Tax Incentives around the World. In Lehman, A., P. Toledano, L. Johnson, and L. Sachs, eds. *Rethinking Investment Incentives: Trends and Policy Options*. Columbia University Press.

JAMA. 2020. *Automobile Industry in Japan 2020*. Japan Automobile Manufacturers Association.

Jensen, A. 2022. Employment Structure and the Rise of Modern Tax System. *CID Faculty Working Paper* 371. Center for International Development at Harvard University.

Joshi, A., W. Prichard, and C. Heady. 2014. Taxing the Informal Economy: The Current State of Knowledge and Agendas for Future Research. *Journal of Development Studies* 50(10).

Junquera-Varela, R. F. et al. 2019. Thinking Strategically about Revenue Administration Reform: The Creation of Integrated, Autonomous Revenue Bodies. *World Bank Governance Discussion Paper* No. 4. World Bank.

Kalkuhl, M. et al. 2018. Can Land Taxes Foster Sustainable Development? An Assessment of Fiscal, Distributional and Implementation Issues. *Land Use Policy* 78.

Kanbur, R. and M. Keen. 2015. Reducing Informality. *Finance and Development* 52(1).

Keane, M. P. and N. Wasi. 2016. Labour Supply: The Roles of Human Capital and the Extensive Margin. *Economic Journal* 126.

Keen, M. and J. Slemrod. 2016. Optimal Tax Administration. *NBER Working Paper* 22408. National Bureau of Economic Research.

———. 2021. *Rebellion, Rascals and Revenue: Tax Follies and Wisdom through the Ages.* Princeton University Press.

Kelly, R., R. White, and A. Anand, eds. 2020. *Property Tax Diagnostic Manual.* World Bank.

Khan, A., A. Khwaja, and B. Olken. 2016. Tax Farming Redux: Experimental Evidence on Performance Pay for Tax Collector. *Quarterly Journal of Economics* 131(1).

———. 2019. Making Moves Matter: Experimental Evidence on Incentivizing Bureaucrats through Performance-Based Postings. *American Economic Review* 109(1).

Kinda, T. 2014. The Question for Non-Resource-Based FDI: Do Taxes Matter? *IMF Working Paper* WP/14/15. International Monetary Fund.

Klemm, A. and S. Van Parys. 2012. Empirical Evidence on the Effects of Tax Incentives. *International Tax and Public Finance* 19.

Kleven, H. et al. 2011. Unwilling or Unable to Cheat? Evidence from a Tax Audit Experiment in Denmark. *Econometrica* 79(3).

Kleven, H., C. Kreiner, and E. Saez. 2016. Why Can Modern Governments Tax So Much? An Agency Model of Firms as Fiscal Intermediaries. *Economica* 83(1).

Kleven, H. et al. 2020. Taxation and Migration: Evidence and Policy Implications. *Journal of Economic Perspectives* 34.

Kose, A. et al. 2021. *The Aftermath of Debt Surges. Policy Research Working Paper* No. WPS 9771. World Bank.

Koumpias, A., G. Leonardo, and J. Martinez-Vazquez. 2021. Trust in Government Institutions and Tax Morale. *FinanzArchiv/Public Finance Analysis* 77(2).

Kronfol, H. and V. Steenbergen. 2020. *Evaluating the Costs and Benefits of Corporate Tax Incentives: Methodological Approaches and Policy Considerations.* World Bank.

Lakin, J. 2020. The Politics of Tax Reform in Low- and Middle-Income Countries: A Literature Review. *International Budget Partnership Research Paper.*

Li, D. et al. 2021. Assessment of the Performance of Pilot Carbon Emissions Trading Systems in China. *Environmental Economics and Policy Studies* 23.

Liu, L. et al. 2021. VAT Notches, Voluntary Registration, and Bunching: Theory and UK Evidence. *Review of Economics and Statistics* 103(1).

Londoño-Vélez, J. and J. Ávila-Mahecha. 2021. Enforcing Wealth Taxes in the Developing World: Quasi-Experimental Evidence from Colombia. *American Economic Review: Insights* 3.

Luttmer, E. and M. Singhal. 2014. Tax Morale. *Journal of Economic Perspectives* 28(4).

Martin, M. and K. van Dender. 2019. The Use of Revenues from Carbon Pricing. *OECD Taxation Working Papers* No. 43.

Matheson, T. 2011. Taxing Financial Transactions: Issues and Evidence. *IMF Working Paper* No. 11/54. International Monetary Fund.

Mawejje, J. and R. K. Sebudde. 2019. Tax Revenue Potential and Effort: Worldwide Estimates Using a New Dataset. *Economic Analysis and Policy* 63.

McCluskey, W. J. and R. Franzsen. 2013. Non-Market Value and Hybrid Approaches to Property Taxation. In McCluskey, W. J., G. C. Cornia, and L. C. Walters, eds. *A Primer on Property Tax: Administration and Policy.* Wiley-Blackwell.

Mehling, M. A. et al. 2019. Designing Border Carbon Adjustments for Enhanced Climate Action. *American Journal of International Law* 113(3).

MOF. 2022. *Receipt Budget, 2022–2023 Appendix 7: Statement of Revenue Impact of Tax Incentives under the Central Tax System: Financial Years 2019–2020 and 2020–2021.* Ministry of Finance, Government of India.

Mullins, P. 2020. Medium-Term Revenue Strategies: Are They Realistic for Developing Countries? *CGD Policy Paper* 180. Center for Global Development.

Muthitacharoen, A., W. Wanichthaworn, and T. Burong. 2021. VAT Threshold and Small Business Behavior: Evidence from Thai Tax Returns. *International Tax and Public Finance* 28.

Nutman, N., K. Isa, and S. H. Yussof. 2021. GST Complexities in Malaysia: Views from Tax Experts. *International Journal of Law and Management* 64(2).

OECD. 2015. Examples of Successful DRM Reforms and the Role of International Co-operation. *OECD Discussion Paper.* Organisation for Economic Co-operation and Development.

———. 2018. The Role and Design of Net Wealth Taxes in the OECD. *Tax Policy Studies* No. 26.

Organisation for Economic Co-operation and Development.

———. 2020. *Global Outlook on Financing for Sustainable Development 2021: New Way for People and Planet.* Organisation for Economic Co-operation and Development.

———. 2021a. *Two-Pillar Solution to Address the Tax Challenges Arising from the Digitalisation of the Economy.* Organisation for Economic Co-operation and Development.

———. 2021b. *Behavioural Insights for Better Tax Administration: A Brief Guide.* Organisation for Economic Co-operation and Development.

Olofsgård, A. 2003. The Political Economy of Reform: Institutional Change as a Tool for Political Credibility. Background paper for the *World Development Report 2005.* World Bank.

Owens, J. 2005. Fundamental Tax Reform: The Experience of OECD Countries. *Tax Foundation* 47.

Parry, I. 2021. Five Things to Know about Carbon Pricing. *Finance & Development* 0058(003). International Monetary Fund.

Parry, I., S. Black, and N. Vernon. 2021. Still Not Getting Energy Prices Right: A Global and Country Update of Fossil Fuel Subsidies. *IMF Working Paper* 2021/236. International Monetary Fund.

Perez-Truglia, R. 2020. The Effects of Income Transparency on Well-Being: Evidence from a Natural Experiment. *American Economic Review* 110(4).

Piketty, T. and G. Zucman. 2014. Capital Is Back: Wealth–Income Ratios in Rich Countries, 1700–2010. *Quarterly Journal of Economics* 129(3).

Pomeranz, D. 2015. No Taxation without Information: Deterrence and Self-Enforcement in the Value-Added Tax. *American Economic Review* 105(8).

Pomeranz, D. and J. Vila-Belda. 2019. Taking State-Capacity Research to the Field: Insights from Collaborations with Tax Authorities. *Annual Review of Economics* 11.

Rao, V. U. A. 2008. Is Area-Based Assessment on Alternative, an Intermediate Step, or an Impediment to Value-Based Taxation. In Bahl, R., J. Martinez-Vazquez, and J. Youngman, eds. *Making the Property Tax Work: Experiences in Developing and Transitional Countries.* Lincoln Institute of Land Policy.

Redonda, A. and T. Neubig. 2018. Assessing Tax Expenditure Reporting in G20 and OECD Economies. *Discussion Note* 2018/3. Council on Economic Policies.

Ross, M. 2015. What Have We Learned about the Resource Curse? *Annual Review of Political Science* 18.

Saez, E. and G. Zucman. 2019. Progressive Wealth Taxation. *Brookings Papers on Economic Activity.* Brookings Institution.

Scheuer, F. and J. Slemrod. 2021. Taxing Our Wealth. *Journal of Economic Perspectives* 35.

Slack, E. and R. Bird. 2014. The Political Economy of Property Tax Reform. *OECD Working Papers on Fiscal Federalism* No. 18. Organisation for Economic Co-operation and Development.

Stretton, S. 2020. A Simple Methodology for Calculating the Impact of a Carbon Tax. *MTI Global Practice Discussion Paper* No. 23. World Bank Group.

Strobl, D. et al. 2021. Electoral Cycles in Government Policy Making: Strategic Timing of Austerity Reform Measures in Western Europe. *British Journal of Political Science* 51.

Summan, A. et al. 2020. The Potential Global Gains in Health and Revenue from Increased Taxation of Tobacco, Alcohol and Sugar-Sweetened Beverages: A Modelling Analysis. *BMJ Global Health* 5:e002143.

Tan, A. 2021. Budget 2021: Govt Will Review Carbon Tax Rate, which Will Remain at $5 per Tonne until 2023. *Straits Times.* 16 February.

The Hindu. 2015. Budget Punished Rich, Rescued Middle Class. 11 March.

Torgler, B. 2007. *Tax Compliance and Tax Morale.* Edward Elgar Publishing.

Uchitelle, E. 1989. The Effectiveness of Tax Amnesty Programs in Selected Countries. *Federal Reserve Bank of New York Quarterly Review* 14(3).

Ulyssea, G. 2010a. The Formal–Informal Labor Market Segmentation Hypothesis Revisited. *Brazilian Review of Econometrics* 30(2).

———. 2010b. Regulation of Entry, Labor Market Institutions and the Informal Sector. *Journal of Development Economics* 91.

———. 2018. Firms, Informality, and Development: Theory and Evidence from Brazil. *American Economic Review* 108(8).

UN. 2015. *Addis Ababa Action Agenda of the Third International Conference on Financing for Development.* United Nations.

UNEP. 2019. *Air Pollution in Asia and the Pacific: Science-Based Solutions.* United Nations Environment Programme.

UNESCAP. 2019. *Economic and Social Survey of Asia and the Pacific: Ambitions beyond Growth.* United Nations Economic and Social Commission for Asia and the Pacific.

Vellutini, C. and J. C. Benitez. 2021. Measuring the Redistributive Capacity of Tax Policies. *IMF Working Paper* WP/21/252. International Monetary Fund.

von Haldenwang, C., A. von Schiller, and M. Garcia. 2014. Tax Collection in Developing Countries— New Evidence on Semi-Autonomous Revenue Agencies (SARAs). *The Journal of Development Studies* 50(4).

Wang, K., J. Wang, K. Hubacek, Z. Mi, and Y. M. Wei. 2020. A Cost–Benefit Analysis of the Environmental Taxation Policy in China: A Frontier Analysis-Based Environmentally Extended Input–Output Optimization Method. *Journal of Industrial Ecology* 24(3).

Wheaton, B. 2022. *The Macroeconomic Effects of Flat Taxation: Evidence from a Panel of Transition Economies.*

Widhartanto, S. and V. Braithwaite. 2016. Hunting Animals in a Zoo? Regulating Indonesia's High Wealth Individual Taxpayers. *RegNet Research Paper* No. 101. Regulatory Institutions Network Australian National University.

World Bank. 2018. *Global Development Report.*

———. 2021a. *Global Economic Prospects.*

———. 2021b. *State and Trends of Carbon Pricing 2021.*

Xu, S. 2021. Singapore Says S$5 Carbon Tax 'A Start' as It Eyes Higher Levy. *Bloomberg Green.* 16 July.

Yamazaki, A. 2017. Jobs and Climate Policy: Evidence from British Columbia's Revenue-Neutral Carbon Tax. *Journal of Environmental Economics and Management* 83.

3

ECONOMIC TRENDS
AND PROSPECTS
IN DEVELOPING ASIA

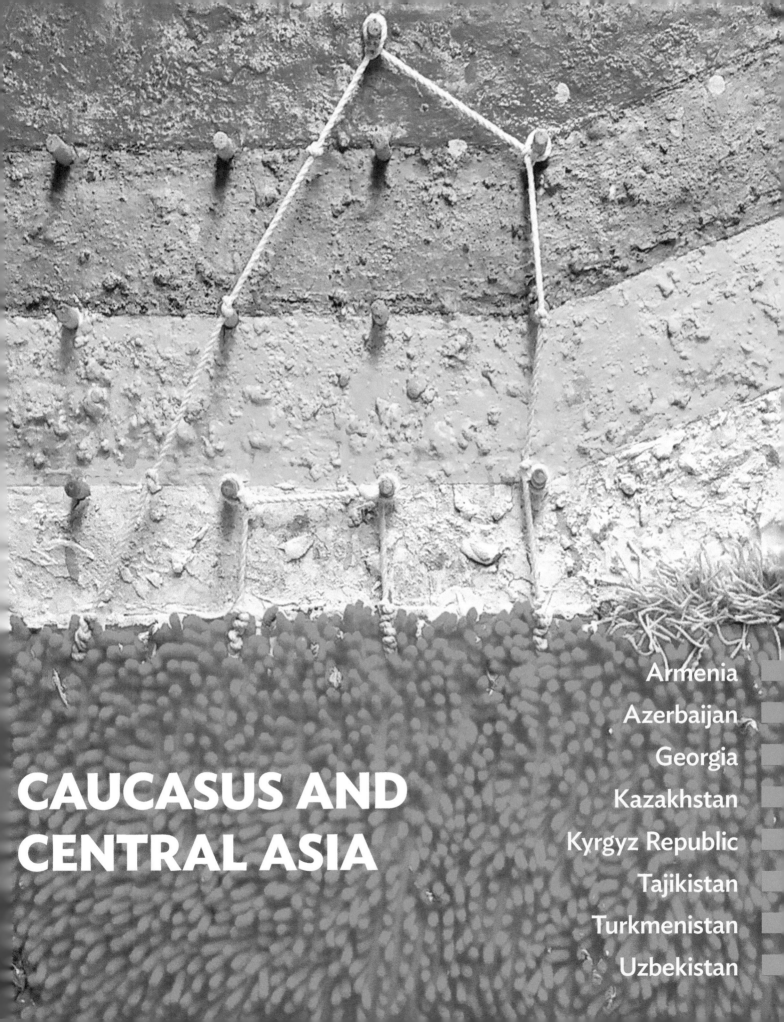

CAUCASUS AND CENTRAL ASIA

Armenia

Azerbaijan

Georgia

Kazakhstan

Kyrgyz Republic

Tajikistan

Turkmenistan

Uzbekistan

ARMENIA

The economy returned to growth in 2021 as external and domestic demand recovered. Higher commodity prices and currency depreciation sharply accelerated inflation. With external developments, growth will slow in 2022 and revive somewhat in 2023. Inflation will accelerate further in 2022 from higher global prices and utility tariffs, then ease in 2023. The current account deficit narrowed in 2021, but lower remittances and higher import costs will widen it this year and next. Higher productivity in agriculture is critical for inclusive growth.

Economic performance

Despite heightened political uncertainty in the first half of 2021, before snap elections in June, and two waves of COVID-19 in April and November, the economy reversed 7.4% contraction in 2020 to grow by 5.7%. Growth in 2021 came mainly from recovery in services, increased investment, and strong remittances that boosted private consumption.

On the supply side, services reversed 8.8% contraction in 2020 to expand by 6.8%, generating the bulk of growth (Figure 3.1.1). Expansion reflected double-digit growth in food, recreation, health, real estate, business services, and information and communication. Industry reversed 2.9% decline in 2020 with gains in manufacturing, mining and quarrying, utilities, and construction that brought 3.8% growth. Agriculture slipped by 1.4% in 2021, the sixth consecutive year of decrease.

On the demand side, private consumption followed 13.9% contraction in 2020 with 3.4% expansion fueled mainly by higher remittances. Growth in public consumption moderated from 15.2% in 2020 to 5.0% as fiscal stimulus to address the pandemic wound down. Investment reversed 6.6% contraction in 2020 to rise by 9.1% as higher private investment more than offset a slowdown in public investment. The deficit in net exports widened as imports grew more than exports.

Figure 3.1.1 Supply-side contributions to growth

Growth returned in 2021, with expansion in services, industry, and construction.

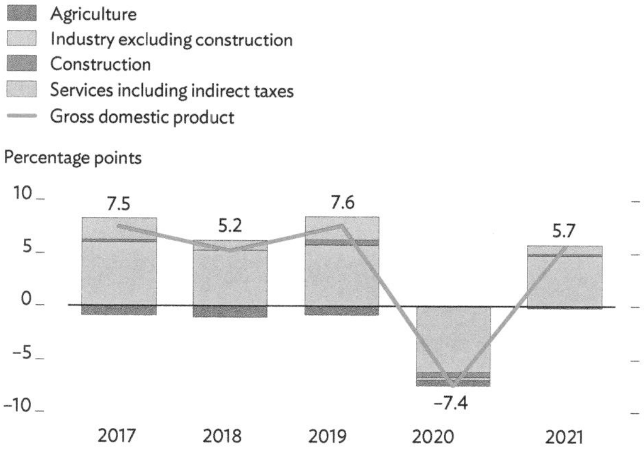

- Agriculture
- Industry excluding construction
- Construction
- Services including indirect taxes
— Gross domestic product

Source: Statistical Committee of Armenia (accessed 9 March 2022).

Average annual inflation accelerated from 1.2% in 2020 to 7.2%, reflecting supply-side shocks, cumulative 7.3% currency depreciation from October 2020 to April 2021, and rising prices for imported oil and other commodities partly caused by higher tariffs under a customs code the Eurasian Economic Union promulgated in January 2021 (Figure 3.1.2). Prices rose by 11.0% for food, 8.7% for other goods, and 1.9%

This chapter was written by Grigor Gyurjyan of the Armenia Resident Mission, ADB, Yerevan.

Figure 3.1.2 Annual inflation

Inflation accelerated in 2021 as supply side shocks boosted prices for food and other goods.

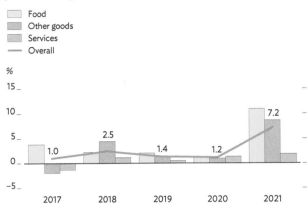

Source: Statistical Committee of Armenia (accessed 9 March 2022).

for services. Inflation in the year to December 2021 was 7.7%, well above the target range of 2.5%–5.5% set by the Central Bank of Armenia. To counter inflation, the central bank gradually tightened monetary policy, raising the policy rate by a cumulative 250 basis points in six steps to 7.75% at the end of 2021 and another 25 basis points to 8.0% in February 2022.

Broad money growth accelerated from 9.0% in 2020 to 13.1% in 2021 on a marked rise in net foreign assets and some increase in net domestic assets (Figure 3.1.3). Higher net foreign assets reflected an 11.5% rise in those of the central bank and a 14.1%

Figure 3.1.3 Contributions to broad money growth

A marked rise in net foreign assets boosted broad money growth in 2021.

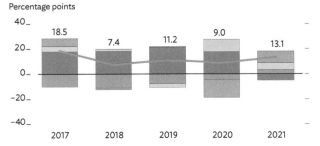

Source: Central Bank of Armenia (accessed 9 March 2022).

decline in depository organizations' foreign liabilities in excess of foreign assets. Growth in net domestic assets plunged from 22.5% in 2020 to 3.1% as monetary tightening cut credit to the economy by 3.9%, the first decline in 6 years. With increased remittances, higher deposit rates, and deposit insurance coverage limits raised from December 2020, growth in local currency deposits doubled from 4.4% in 2020 to 8.7% and foreign currency deposits rose by 4.8%.

Following stimulus implemented in 2020, the government tightened fiscal policy in 2021, narrowing the budget deficit from the equivalent of 5.4% of GDP to 4.4% (Figure 3.1.4). Economic growth and improved tax administration raised government revenue by 7.9% to equal 24.1% of GDP. Budget expenditure grew by 4.9% to equal 28.5% of GDP but fell below the budget target for capital outlays. Revenue and expenditure were both lower as a percentage of GDP than in 2020 but higher than in 2019.

Figure 3.1.4 Fiscal indicators

The budget deficit narrowed in 2021 as fiscal stimulus wound down.

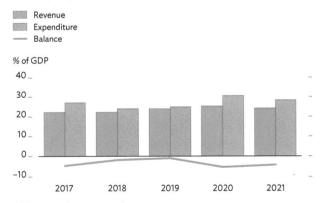

GDP = gross domestic product.
Sources: Ministry of Finance of Armenia; Statistical Committee of Armenia (both accessed 9 March 2022).

Economic growth, revenue collection above target, and prudent spending reduced public debt from the equivalent of 67.4% of GDP in 2020 to 63.4% (Figure 3.1.5). External public debt declined by about 10.8% to equal 45.7% of GDP. Domestic public debt increased by 24.3% to equal 17.7% of GDP and, in line with government efforts to gradually increase the domestic share, 28.0% of all public debt.

Figure 3.1.5 Public debt

Fiscal consolidation and faster growth trimmed the ratio of public debt to GDP in 2021.

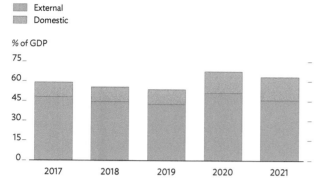

GDP = gross domestic product.
Sources: Ministry of Finance of Armenia; Statistical Committee of Armenia (both accessed 9 March 2022).

The current account deficit narrowed further from the equivalent of 3.8% of GDP in 2020 to an estimated 2.7% in 2021, reflecting a narrower trade deficit, higher personal transfers, and a larger surplus in services (Figure 3.1.6). The merchandise trade deficit narrowed from 10.7% of GDP in 2020 to 9.5% as exports expanded more than imports, reversing 19.2% contraction in 2020 to expand by an estimated 10.5%, mainly on gains in agricultural products, processed foods, other manufactures, and minerals. Imports meanwhile reversed 20.0% contraction in 2020 to

Figure 3.1.6 Current account components

The current account deficit narrowed in 2021 as the external environment improved.

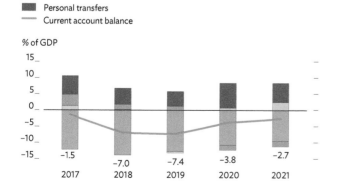

GDP = gross domestic product.
Sources: Central Bank of Armenia; Statistical Committee of Armenia (both accessed 9 March 2022).

grow by 6.0% as domestic demand recovered. The surplus in services expanded significantly from gains in finance, travel, and tourism services with the gradual lifting of COVID-19 restrictions on movement. Gross international reserves rose by 22.9% to $3.2 billion at the end of 2021, providing cover for 7.0 months of imports of goods and services (Figure 3.1.7).

Figure 3.1.7 Reserves and average exchange rates

Reserves grew significantly despite depreciation of the Armenian dram.

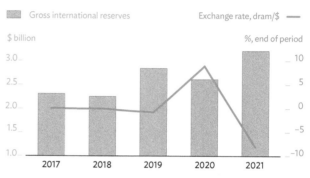

Source: Central Bank of Armenia (accessed 9 March 2022).

Economic prospects

Geopolitical developments leave the economic outlook highly uncertain and poses serious downside risks to growth, primarily because of Armenia's economic exposure to the Russian Federation, which provides about one-third of its trade, half of its remittances, and 40% of its foreign direct investment. Barring additional spillover from sanctions on Russia and their significant downside risks to baseline projections, growth is projected slowing to 2.8% in 2022 and then, assuming the impact of economic shocks wanes, revive to 3.8% in 2023 (Figure 3.1.8 and Table 3.1.1). Domestic factors supporting growth are a planned 50% increase in capital outlays in the 2022 budget, accelerating vaccination coverage, and economic and structural reform outlined in the government's program for 2021–2026 that aims to develop a more knowledge-based, export-oriented, and investment-driven economy.

On the supply side, all major sectors are expected to expand moderately. Industry excluding construction is projected to grow by 0.5% in 2022 and 2.5% in 2023 as utilities and manufacturing expand further. Agriculture is projected to grow by 2.5% in 2022 and

Figure 3.1.8 GDP growth

Growth will slow in 2022 before accelerating in 2023.

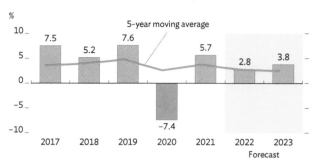

GDP = gross domestic product.
Sources: Statistical Committee of Armenia (accessed 9 March 2022); Asian Development Bank estimates.

Table 3.1.1 Selected economic indicators, %

Projections are for slowing growth, higher inflation, and persistent current account deficit.

	2020	2021	2022	2023
GDP growth	-7.4	5.7	2.8	3.8
Inflation	1.2	7.2	9.0	7.5
CAB/GDP	-3.8	-2.7	-4.5	-4.7

CAB = current account balance, GDP = gross domestic product.
Sources: Statistical Committee of Armenia; Central Bank of Armenia; Asian Development Bank estimates.

3.5% in 2023, assuming normal weather and higher spending on government programs offering subsidies for smart livestock buildings, intensive orchards, hail nets to protect crops, and drip irrigation, along with efforts to increase productivity and commercialization. Construction is expected to rise by 9.4% in 2022 and 10.0% in 2023, primarily as the North–South Road Corridor investment program receives planned public investment in its southern portion. Even assuming no severe waves of COVID-19 infections, sanctions are expected to moderate growth in services to 3.3% in 2022, before it revives to 3.7% in 2023 with gains in recreation, accommodation, and food services and lesser expansion in other services.

On the demand side, private consumption and public investment will be the main growth drivers. Although the economy is less dependent on remittances than in earlier years, lower remittance inflow from Russia and higher inflation are expected to constrain private

consumption growth further to 2.5% in 2022 before it accelerates to 3.8% in 2023 as inflation moderates slightly. Growth in public consumption is projected to slow to 3.2% in 2022 from fiscal consolidation before rising to 3.6% in 2023 as consolidation eases. Growth in investment should benefit from a planned 50% rise in government capital outlays in 2022. Net exports will likely constrain growth as import costs rise and exports fall.

With soaring international commodity prices, higher prices for imported consumer goods, currency depreciation, and higher electricity tariffs from February 2022 and natural gas prices from April 2022, average annual inflation is projected to accelerate further to at least 9.0% in 2022 before decelerating to 7.5% in 2023, assuming there are no more such domestic price hikes and that international inflationary pressure wanes. Further monetary tightening to curb inflation is expected in 2022, with policy shifting to support growth in 2023 if inflation moderates.

Fiscal policy will adhere to the budget framework for 2022–2024, which envisages continued fiscal consolidation over the medium term and gradual increase in the share of capital expenditure to support growth while reducing the ratio of public debt to GDP below the 60% ceiling in Armenia's fiscal rule. Assuming no budget revision to address the impact of external shocks, the 2022 budget projects a deficit equal to 3.1% of GDP as revenue increases to 24.7% of GDP and expenditure declines to 27.8%. With a gradual shift in spending away from current expenditure, capital outlays are planned to reach 4.4% of projected 2022 GDP, about 1 percentage point above their share in 2021. In line with the government's debt reduction program for 2021–2026, government debt is expected to decline gradually to equal 60.1% of GDP in 2022 and 58.2% in 2023, reaching 53.8% by 2026.

Considering Armenia's high vulnerability to external shocks and lost trade concessions with its graduation from the European Union's Generalized Scheme of Preferences Plus (GSP+) regime in January 2022, the current account deficit is forecast to widen to equal 4.5% of GDP in 2022 and 4.7% in 2023, as a larger merchandise trade deficit and narrower surplus in the income account offset surpluses in services (Figure 3.1.9). The merchandise trade deficit is forecast to widen to 10.1% of GDP in 2022 and 10.9% in 2023.

Figure 3.1.9 Current account balance

The current account deficit is forecast to widen over the next 2 years.

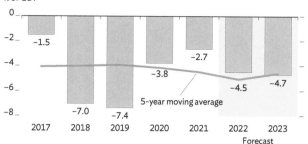

% of GDP

GDP = gross domestic product.

Sources: Central Bank of Armenia;Statistical Committee of Armenia (both accessed 9 March 2022); Asian Development Bank estimates.

Growth in merchandise exports is projected moderating to 3.5% in 2022 and, assuming the external environment becomes more favorable, accelerating again to 6.0% in 2023 on higher exports of agricultural products, nonferrous metals, machinery, and equipment. Imports are seen rising by 6.5% in 2022 and 8.0% in 2023, reflecting higher prices for commodity imports and substantial imports of goods for public investment. The service balance will likely remain in surplus, supported by further expansion of business, financial, and information technology services and a smaller deficit in tourism and travel services. Despite a smaller investment income deficit, surpluses in the income and current transfer accounts should decline as remittances fall.

Policy challenge—improving agricultural productivity

Despite significant agricultural reform in recent decades, low productivity, limited connectivity, and deficient market linkages remain major binding constraints to sector development. Agriculture's share of GDP declined from about 20% in 2011 to 11% in 2021, with persistent contraction in the past 6 years. Agriculture nevertheless remains a significant employer, absorbing about 22% of the labor force in 2020. With farms averaging only 1.5 hectares and about one-third of cultivable land unused, achieving inclusive growth requires higher efficiency all along the agriculture value chain through market-based diversification, especially into high-value crops, and increased productivity.

Many factors have constrained agricultural performance: inadequate infrastructure, insufficient irrigation, limited access to productive land, a lack of appropriate inputs and modern technology, limited access to commercial finance, vulnerability to natural hazards, and underdeveloped market mechanisms, especially for agribusiness. To ensure a transition from traditional smallholder production to a more modern, technology-based, market-driven, and value-enhancing sector, the government has approved a strategy for agriculture that defines seven key priorities with specific actions for 2020–2030 to improve competitiveness, food safety and security, export promotion, institutional and human capacity, and technological innovation.

Current government programs subsidize the production mostly of grain and legumes and support the creation of intensive orchards provided with hail nets, the adoption of drip irrigation, more extensive land leasing, and a pilot insurance program for selected crops. Besides existing state programs, new and targeted financial measures are needed to boost the adoption of selected products with high value added, develop areas for their production, and generally spur productivity. Along with traditional advisory services, more modern services using high technology can effectively disseminate knowledge and enhance the practical skills of farmers.

An integrated approach is needed to address deficiencies in sector infrastructure and investment. Only about half of arable land is irrigated, leaving high demand for investment in irrigation systems—and for investment in farm service roads. The government plans gradual increases in outlays from the state budget to 2023 for building reservoirs and constructing or renovating irrigation networks. It also plans further efforts to promote water-saving irrigation methods.

Sector development should prioritize the following: (i) adopting a medium-term approach with greater appreciation of the complexity of sector reform and the capacity of sector institutions to implement them; (ii) more consistent support for capacity building; (iii) developing modern production, postharvest, and marketing systems; (iv) integrating value chains to maximize productivity and efficiency gains; and (v) promoting collaboration between key value chain actors led by the private sector to facilitate horizontal and vertical integration while reducing the fiscal burden on the government.

AZERBAIJAN

Growth rebounded in 2021 on strong services and manufacturing. Rising utility tariffs and domestic demand boosted inflation. Higher prices for petroleum exports lifted the current account from a small deficit to a large surplus. Growth will moderate in 2022 and 2023 as private consumption and hydrocarbon gains weaken. Inflation will rise and the current account surplus widen as supply chains are disrupted and petroleum prices skyrocket. Improved governance at state-owned enterprises is key to making them more efficient.

Economic performance

The economy reversed 4.3% contraction in 2020 with a rebound by 5.6% in 2021 reflecting growth outside of the large petroleum industry, as well as robust private consumption.

On the supply side, industry replaced 5.0% decline in 2020 with 5.2% growth on strong expansion in manufacturing (Figure 3.2.1). Industry aside from petroleum grew by 7.2% with higher production of construction materials, pharmaceuticals, furniture, and machinery. Mining meanwhile expanded by only 0.4% as oil production stagnated, and subdued investment shrank construction by 2.0%. A credit support program and fuel subsidies boosted growth in agriculture from 1.9% in 2020 to 3.4%. Services, providing nearly 40% of GDP, reversed 3.5% decline in 2020 to grow by 7.8% with gains of 34.2% in tourism, 16.0% in transport and warehousing, and 5.3% in wholesale and retail trade. Tourism benefited as Azerbaijan opened its borders to visitors from more than 60 countries who complied with COVID-19 mitigation measures. Since April 2021, public gatherings and mass events have been allowed with the lifting of a ban on access to such large public facilities as trade centers, concert halls, and malls. Almost half of the population is fully vaccinated, and a quarter have received a booster dose.

On the demand side, private consumption boosted growth as it reversed 8.1% decline in 2020 with 3.7%

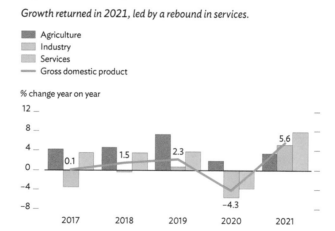

Figure 3.2.1 GDP growth

Growth returned in 2021, led by a rebound in services.

- Agriculture
- Industry
- Services
- Gross domestic product

% change year on year

Sources: State Statistics Committee; National Bank of Azerbaijan; Asian Development Bank estimates.

growth enabled by easing quarantine restrictions, higher consumer lending, and government stimulus programs. Investment declined by 8.2% in 2021, much as it had in 2020, because cuts to public spending curtailed the half of investment it provides. Oil and gas export volume soared by an estimated 58%, while import volume fell, making net exports the largest demand-side contributor to growth.

Average annual inflation accelerated from 2.8% in 2020 to 6.7% on higher energy prices, increased utility

This chapter was written Nail Valiyev of the Azerbaijan Resident Mission, ADB, Baku.

tariffs, and rising consumption (Figure 3.2.2). Prices rose by 8.1% for food, 5.1% for other goods, and 5.8% for services. Inflationary pressure persisted despite a stable exchange rate and fuel subsidies to farmers that shielded food prices to some extent from higher fuel prices.

Figure 3.2.2 Monthly inflation

Inflation spiked as food prices rose.

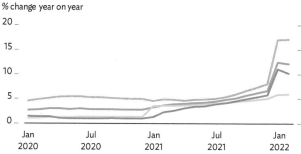

Sources: State Statistical Committee of the Republic of Azerbaijan; Haver Analytics.

Fiscal policy became less expansionary during 2021 as the budget deficit was halved from the equivalent of 2.3% of GDP in 2020 to 1.1%. Growth in revenue rose from 2.0% in 2020 to 7.0% despite reduced transfers from the State Oil Fund of Azerbaijan (SOFAZ), the sovereign wealth fund, which still provided 43% of revenue. As a share of GDP, revenue fell from 34.1% in 2020 to 28.4% because of rapid growth in nominal GDP. Tax revenue rose by 15.5% as the government successfully implemented its cashless payment program that featured refunds of value-added tax, "cash back" refunds on the amounts users paid with bank cards, and tax incentives for entrepreneurs to adopt cashless payments to reduce untraceable cash transactions to a bare minimum (Figure 3.2.3). Expenditure as a share of GDP declined to 29.5% despite rising by 3.7% in nominal terms. Public and publicly guaranteed debt, external and domestic, declined from 23.4% of GDP in December 2020 to 18.2% a year later as the government sustained its conservative policy on borrowing under its medium-term debt-management strategy. Now being updated, the strategy aims to reduce the ratio of debt to GDP to 10% by 2030.

Figure 3.2.3 Developments in budget revenue

Revenue increased as reform boosted tax revenue.

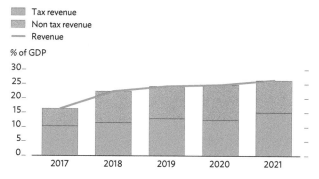

GDP = gross domestic product.
Source: Ministry of Finance of the Republic of Azerbaijan.

Monetary policy aimed for price stability. The exchange rate remained fixed at AZN1.7 per US dollar, with SOFAZ a major supplier of foreign currency in the market. The Central Bank of Azerbaijan sustained its policy rate until the third quarter of 2021, when it raised the rate from 6.25% to 7.50% in response to inflation rising above the target ceiling of 6.0%. Nevertheless, broad money growth jumped from 1.1% in 2020 to 18.7% in 2021, reflecting much higher lending (Figure 3.2.4).

Figure 3.2.4 Contributions to money supply growth

Higher lending spurred broad money growth in 2021.

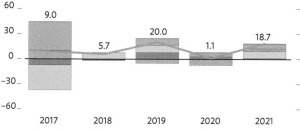

Source: Central Bank of the Republic of Azerbaijan.

Banks performed well throughout 2021 as lending rose by 17.8% with the reopening of businesses and growth in private consumption. Net bank profits rose by 7.2%, and the share of nonperforming loans fell from 6.1% in 2020 to 4.2% (Figure 3.2.5).

Figure 3.2.5 Bank lending performance

Lending rose as the percentage of nonperforming loans declined.

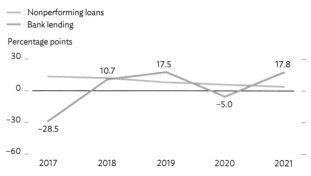

Source: Central Bank of the Republic of Azerbaijan.

The current account moved from a deficit equal to 0.5% of GDP in 2020 to an estimated surplus of 12.9% as export earnings jumped by 17.0% on higher hydrocarbon prices, with earnings from gas exports almost doubling. The trade surplus quadrupled from $2.5 billion in 2020 to an estimated $10.2 billion on higher earnings from hydrocarbon exports and tourism. Hydrocarbons accounted for 90% of all merchandise exports in 2021 as Azeri Light oil traded at $71.60 per barrel. Higher domestic demand boosted merchandise imports by 16.1%. Economic recovery in major trade partners boosted remittances by 13.3% year on year in the first 9 months of 2021. Central bank foreign exchange reserves rose by 11.0% to a record high of $7.1 billion. Including SOFAZ assets, Azerbaijan's gross international reserves rose from $50 billion at the end of 2020 to $52.1 billion, equal to 95.4% of GDP (Figure 3.2.6).

Figure 3.2.6 State oil fund assets and central bank reserves

International reserves rose further in 2021.

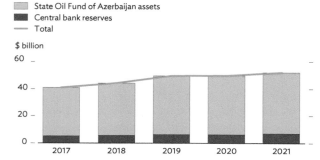

Sources: Central Bank of the Republic of Azerbaijan; State Oil Fund of Azerbaijan.

Economic prospects

Growth is projected to slow to 3.7% in 2022 and 2.8% in 2023 (Figure 3.2.7 and Table 3.2.1). In particular, hydrocarbon gains will be modest due to slower growth in oil output in 2022 and a decline in 2023, despite higher gas production including at the Shah Deniz Stage 2 gas field. Growth in industry including manufacturing is projected to decelerate to 2.5% in 2022 and 2.7% in 2023, while strong investment to reconstruct infrastructure in the Karabakh region will help construction expand by 2.7% in 2022 and 2.5% in 2023. Services growth, which depends heavily on retail trade and tourism, is also projected to slow down to 5.2% in 2022 and 3.0% in 2023. Yet, agriculture is expected to grow by 6.0% in 2022, before easing back to 5.5% expansion in 2023. The government's fuel subsidies and the leasing program are expected to boost domestic agricultural production against the background of cuts in food supply from Russia and Ukraine.

Figure 3.2.7 Gross domestic product growth

Economic growth will slow in 2022 and 2023.

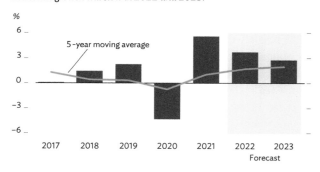

Sources: Central Bank of the Republic of Azerbaijan; Asian Development Bank estimates.

Table 3.2.1 Selected economic indicators, %

Growth will slow in 2022 and 2023, with higher inflation in 2022 and larger current account surpluses in both years.

	2020	2021	2022	2023
GDP growth	−4.3	5.6	3.7	2.8
Inflation	2.8	6.7	7.0	5.3
CAB/GDP	−0.5	12.9	20.2	16.9

CAB = current account balance, GDP = gross domestic product.
Source: Asian Development Bank estimates.

Despite higher civil service wages that will boost public consumption, real growth in private consumption is expected to moderate because of high inflation and low bank credit. Investment is projected to expand by 2.0% in 2022 and 3.5% in 2023 as the government develops green energy and invests in core infrastructure in Karabakh, and as private investment also expands. Net exports are forecast to rise, but more slowly than in 2021, on higher petroleum export volume and slowing consumption.

Despite slowing private consumption growth, inflation is projected to accelerate to 7.0% in 2022 as food imports from Russia and Ukraine, both major suppliers, are disrupted, then subside to 5.3% in 2023 (Figure 3.2.8). Increases in social expenditure, civil service wages, and the minimum wage will spur inflation. The exchange rate is projected to remain stable with higher petroleum prices. The central bank is expected to maintain the policy rate until the middle of 2022 or else raise it as inflationary pressures increase, though monetary policy could be relaxed if inflation slows to within the target band of 2%–6%. The central bank will continue to intervene in the money market, sterilizing excess Azerbaijan manat liquidity with deposit auctions and note issues, controlling the amount of currency in circulation, and offsetting downward pressure on the Azerbaijan manat.

Figure 3.2.8 Inflation

Inflation will accelerate in 2022 before slowing in 2023.

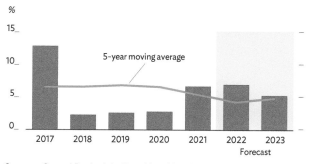

Sources: Central Bank of the Republic of Azerbaijan; ADB estimates.

Fiscal policy is expected to remain expansionary in 2022 but less so in 2023. The central government deficit is projected to widen to equal 3.1% of GDP in 2022 before narrowing to 1.5% in 2023, with revenue rising slightly in nominal terms but falling to 28.1%

of GDP in 2022 and 27.6% in 2023 as nominal GDP growth again outpaces revenue. Transfers from SOFAZ are expected to rise by 12.0% in 2022 to compensate for lower tax revenue, providing half of all revenue, and decline by 9.5% in 2023 following the adoption of new fiscal rules. Expenditure is forecast rising to equal 31.3% of GDP in 2022 as the government introduces a $3.0 billion package to support economic activity, including investment plans to reconstruct Karabakh, then decline to 29.2% of GDP in 2023. The authorities may revisit the budget in mid-2022 to increase outlays for investment. Public and publicly guaranteed debt should increase to 19.3% of GDP in 2022, largely from the domestic market to finance budget deficit and decline to 18.8% in 2023 in line with the government's debt management strategy, with external borrowing and sovereign guarantees held to $800 million in 2022.

The current account surplus is projected to widen to 20.2% of GDP on higher export volume and prices and then decline to 16.9% in 2023 as moderating oil prices and a small decline in oil export volume trim earnings—the merchandise trade surplus expanding by 48.5% in 2022, reflecting a 14.0% rise in export earnings, then falling by 10.1% in 2023 (Figure 3.2.9). Imports are projected to decline by 10.3% in 2022 and 4.8% in 2023 with supply shortfalls from Russia and Ukraine, as well as higher excise taxes on selected goods. The deficit in services is expected to narrow with rising tourism, mainly from Gulf countries, and the completion of major construction services in the oil industry. Gross international reserves including SOFAZ assets are projected to increase by 1.8% in 2022 to $53.0 billion and 2.5% in 2023 to $54.3

Figure 3.2.9 Current account balance

The current account surplus will widen in 2022 before narrowing in 2023.

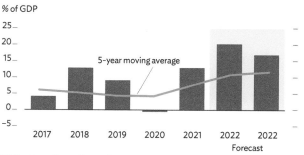

GDP = gross domestic product.
Sources: Central Bank of the Republic of Azerbaijan; ADB estimates.

billion, reflecting both higher oil prices and plans for smaller transfers from SOFAZ to the government budget (Figure 3.2.10).

Figure 3.2.10 International reserves

Reserves are projected to keep increasing in 2022 and 2023.

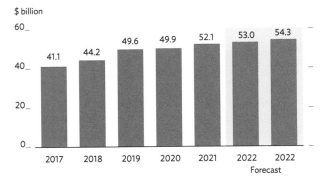

Sources: State Oil Fund of Azerbaijan, The Central Bank of the Republic of Azerbaijan.

Policy challenge—strengthening corporate governance in state-owned enterprises

State-owned enterprises (SOEs) play vital roles in Azerbaijan's economy, monopolizing oil and gas, transportation, and public utilities, including electric power and water supply. Among the 6.4% of all registered enterprises that are SOEs, 14 large ones contribute a quarter of all tax revenue, the state oil company being the largest taxpayer. Most SOEs are inefficient and pose risks to the central government budget from high debt, the need to cover recurring losses, and potential insolvency. The role of many SOEs in providing schools, hospitals, and other essential services is the main reason for operating losses, and their systemic importance means that SOE inefficiency and underperformance have deleterious effects across the whole economy.

One reason for inefficiency is SOEs being integral to government employment and social policy implementation. Their financial positions have weakened with past currency devaluation, their quasi-fiscal activity, and poor governance, such that most SOEs require fiscal support. When oil prices plunged in 2014–2015, the government provided budgetary support to keep SOEs operating but without requiring reform that might have contained losses. During the current pandemic, it created 38,000 jobs in SOEs and covered their cost with additional financial support. It sets all utility tariffs at somewhat subsidized rates below what utilities need to recover costs.

In June 2019, the government initiated an SOE reform program. It endorsed corporate governance rules and standards, including rules to assess SOE efficiency, and established a performance-based remuneration system. In August 2020, it created Azerbaijan Investment Holding to consolidate and control the functions of SOEs transferred to its administration—many of which incur significant losses—with the mandate to make them more efficient. Following the adoption of corporate governance standards, the government created supervisory boards for all large SOEs.

Further reform should be considered. Reform could develop and apply performance indicators for SOEs, improve SOE procurement processes and procedures, design a sound dividend policy framework, and implement merit-based selection of senior SOE managers and performance-based remuneration and management contracts with an eye toward bring in new management. Transparency should be strengthened through greater disclosure of external audit reports, quarterly financial data, SOE strategies and objectives, and other performance measures. Finally, more attention should be paid to the financial health of SOEs that are candidates for privatization.

GEORGIA

Broad recovery propelled the economy from contraction in 2020 to double-digit growth in 2021, and inflation neared double digits. Fallout from the Russian invasion of Ukraine will slow growth in 2022 before it rises somewhat in 2023 with recovering demand. Monetary tightening and fiscal contraction are projected to slow inflation in both years. The current account deficit, having narrowed in 2021, should widen in 2022 before narrowing again in 2023. Fiscal decentralization would improve service delivery and support growth.

Economic performance

Growth rebounded strongly from 6.8% contraction in 2020 to estimated 10.6% growth in 2021 with recovery in all major areas except construction and agriculture (Figure 3.3.1). On the supply side, services reversed 8.1% contraction in 2020 to grow by 14.5% with strong expansion in wholesale and retail trade, accommodation and food services, finance and insurance, and transportation. Industry reversed a 6.6% drop in 2020 to expand by 6.2% as recovery in manufacturing and mining offset decline in construction. After robust growth by 7.6% in 2020, agriculture shrank by 2.5% as pests and adverse weather diminished the quality of the hazelnut harvest, a key agricultural export.

Figure 3.3.1 Gross domestic product growth by sector

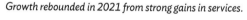

Growth rebounded in 2021 from strong gains in services.

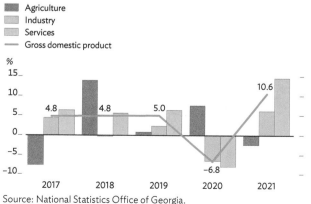

Source: National Statistics Office of Georgia.

On the demand side, growth in consumption nearly doubled from 5.4% in 2020 to 9.0% as pandemic restrictions were lifted in the second half of 2021. Growth in private consumption accelerated from 5.3% in 2020 to 9.4% as consumer spending intensified, and in public consumption from 5.6% to 7.4% as spending on health care rose. Investment reversed 3.1% contraction in 2020 to expand by 3.5% as fiscal stimulus buoyed business confidence and consequently private investment. Exports of goods and services reversed 37.9% contraction in 2020 with 32.6% growth in 2021 that featured some recovery in tourism to boost services. Despite a concomitant increase in imports, net exports turned positive. The bad news was the unemployment rate, which rose by about 2 percentage points to 20.6% as services suffered further job cuts.

Inflation accelerated from 5.2% in 2020 to 9.6%, its highest since October 2011, on rising global food and oil prices (Figure 3.3.2). Prices increased by 10.9% for food and nonalcoholic beverages, 7.1% for other goods, and 6.9% for services, notably higher transport costs. Core inflation—which excludes food and nonalcoholic beverages, energy, regulated tariffs, and transportation—was 6.3%. With higher import prices raising inflationary expectations and applying downward pressure on the local currency, the National Bank of Georgia, the central bank, raised the policy rate in 2021 by a cumulative 250 basis points in four steps to 10.5%.

This chapter was written by George Luarsabishvili of the Georgia Resident Mission, ADB, Tbilisi.

Figure 3.3.2 Monthly inflation

Inflation soared from record high global commodity prices.

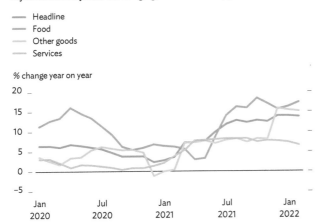

Source: National Statistics Office of Georgia.

Fiscal policy remained expansionary, though less so than in 2020. The consolidated budget deficit narrowed from the equivalent of 9.3% of GDP in 2020 to 6.4% as government revenue reversed a 3.9% decline in 2020 to increase by 22.0% in 2021 (Figure 3.3.3). Higher company sales and imports raised tax revenue, particularly value-added tax and customs duty. Moderation in social spending halved growth in total outlays from 21.6% in 2020 to 11.4%, reducing total expenditure from the equivalent of 34.5% of GDP in 2020 to 32.2%, though infrastructure spending remained equal to 8.0% of GDP. Public debt declined from 60.2% of GDP in 2020 to 52.5% as growth accelerated and external borrowing declined.

Figure 3.3.3 Fiscal indicators

Higher revenue and moderating expenditure cut the fiscal deficit.

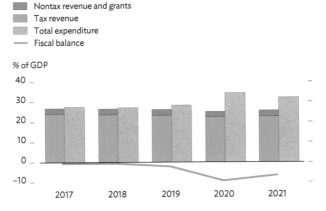

Sources: International Monetary Fund; Ministry of Finance of Georgia.

Monetary policy focused on combating inflation. Broad money growth was halved from 23.3% in 2020 to 11.3%, or slightly less than credit growth at 12.2%, which was constrained by a drawdown of bank deposits (Figure 3.3.4). Foreign currency deposits decreased from a 62.7% share of all deposits in 2020 to 58.5% (Figure 3.3.5). This occurred as interest rates on these deposits fell from 2.0% in 2020 to near zero and interest on Georgian lari deposits rose from 8.3% in 2020 to 11.2% (Figure 3.3.6). The share of loans in foreign currency also declined, from 55.1% to 50.3%, as the central bank imposed further restrictions on unhedged borrowers. The share of lari loans increased from 14.4% to 15.8% with hikes in the policy rate. Nonperforming loans decreased from 8.2% of all loans at the end of 2020 to 5.2%, which boosted bank profitability.

Figure 3.3.4 Contributions to broad money growth

Broad money growth was halved as credit growth declined.

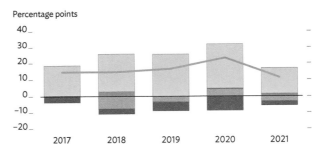

Source: National Bank of Georgia.

Figure 3.3.5 Loan and deposit dollarization rates

Dollarization in both lending and deposits declined in 2021.

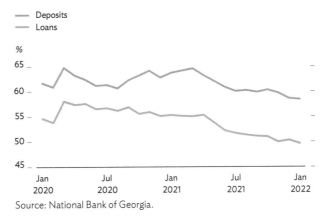

Source: National Bank of Georgia.

Figure 3.3.6 Interest rates

Lari lending and deposit rates increased in line with policy rate hikes.

— Policy rate
— Average lending rate in FX
— Average deposit rate in FX
— Average lending rate in lari
— Average deposit rate in lari

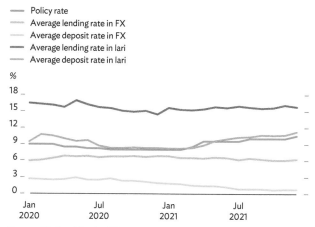

Source: National Bank of Georgia.

Lari depreciation against the US dollar slowed from 10.3% in 2020 to 3.6%, and against the euro from 12.6% by 7.5% (Figure 3.3.7). The Georgian currency appreciated by 15.6% against the Turkish lira, limiting inflationary impact from higher prices for Turkish imports.

Figure 3.3.7 Exchange rate

In 2021 the lari strengthened significantly against the Turkish lira and depreciated less against the U.S. dollar and euro.

— GEL/$
— GEL/EUR   Turkish Lira —

Monthly average   Monthly average

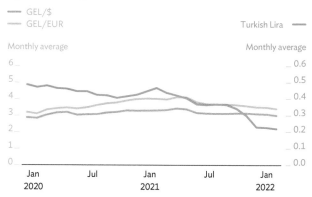

Source: National Bank of Georgia.

The current account deficit narrowed from the equivalent of 12.4% of GDP in 2020 to 9.5% as merchandise exports reversed 12.4% contraction in 2020 to grow by 25.2% on higher metal exports to the People's Republic of China and reexports of second-hand vehicles to Azerbaijan and Ukraine. GDP growth prompted merchandise imports to reverse 13.5% contraction in 2020 with 26.7% growth. The surplus in

services expanded as receipts from tourism more than doubled, though they reached only a third of record receipts in 2019. Surpluses in income and current transfers both increased, with remittances rising by 24.6% to $2.3 billion because of higher inflow from Russia, Italy, and the US. Gross foreign currency reserves excluding holdings of International Monetary Fund special drawing rights increased slightly from $3.7 billion at the end of 2020 to $3.8 billion, or cover for 4.5 months of imports. The inflow of foreign direct investment doubled from a pandemic-induced low in 2020.

Economic prospects

Growth is forecast to decline to 3.5% as the Russian invasion of Ukraine slows trade and remittances, then recover somewhat to 5.0% in 2023 with some recovery in demand—both domestic, fueled by faster credit growth, and external, with exports facilitated by structural reform to trade and connectivity (Figure 3.3.8 and Table 3.3.1).

Figure 3.3.8 Gross domestic product growth

Growth will slow in 2022 before rising in 2023 with some recovery in demand.

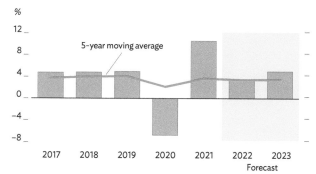

Sources: National Statistics Office of Georgia; Asian Development Bank estimates.

Table 3.3.1 Selected economic indicators, %

Projections show growth and inflation slowing, with a wider current account deficit in 2022.

	2020	2021	2022	2023
GDP growth	−6.8	10.6	3.5	5.0
Inflation	5.2	9.6	7.0	4.0
CAB/GDP	−12.4	−9.5	−10.0	−7.5

CAB = current account balance, GDP = gross domestic product.
Source: Asian Development Bank estimates.

On the supply side, growth in services is projected to slow to 3.6% in 2022 alongside decline in trade turnover and remittances, before recovery in tourism and steady improvement in financial sector performance raise it to 6.0% in 2023. Expansion in industry will similarly slow to 2.7% in 2022 and increase to 4.0% in 2023 as higher demand and phased economic reopening enable expansion in manufacturing and construction. Increased investment in agriculture is expected to raise production in the sector by 1.0% in 2022 and 1.2% in 2023.

On the demand side, private consumption is projected to expand by at least 3.0% in 2022 and 3.5% in 2023 as economic reopening raises formal employment. Investment is projected to expand by at least 4.0% in each year, led by the private sector. Net exports are forecast to rise by 6.8% in 2022 and 12.4% in 2023 as service exports expand further.

Inflation is projected to slow to 7.0% in 2022 on the expectation of further monetary policy tightening, though it will remain elevated because of electric utility hikes at the start of the year and, more importantly, higher global oil prices (Figure 3.3.9). Inflation is expected to slow further to 4.0% in 2023 with the expected waning of the pandemic and unwinding of fiscal stimulus, improved supplies of essential goods and services, and somewhat moderating global commodity prices. Broad money growth is projected to rise to 16.5% in 2022, reflecting higher international reserves and increased private sector credit, before slowing marginally to 16.0% in 2023. Less foreign currency lending by the private sector should dampen market volatility and inflationary expectations.

The staged withdrawal of fiscal stimulus, coupled with careful use of tax and savings incentives, is expected to trim the budget deficit to the equivalent of 4.5% of GDP in 2022 and 3.0% in 2023. The authorities intend to strengthen revenue administration and reduce current spending despite a recent increase in old age pensions. Continued economic growth and streamlined tax administration are expected to increase revenue to 26.0% of GDP in 2022 and 26.5% in 2023. The government will likely maintain prudent spending policies in both years while safeguarding health-care outlays needed to address the pandemic. Total expenditure is forecast to equal 30.5% of GDP in 2022 and 29.5% in 2023, with room to decrease infrastructure spending if unforeseen developments such as a protracted Russian invasion of Ukraine or a new round of COVID-19 adversely affect the economy, requiring higher current spending.

Smaller deficits and stronger growth are projected to reduce total public and publicly guaranteed debt to 51.5% of GDP in 2022 and 50.0% in 2023, though the high 80% share of debt in foreign currency risks fiscal sustainability (Figure 3.3.10). The government has thus made priorities of improving governance, strengthening the public investment management framework, and streamlining central and local government budget systems.

Figure 3.3.10 Government gross debt and gross external debt

The public debt ratio should decline with less foreign borrowing.

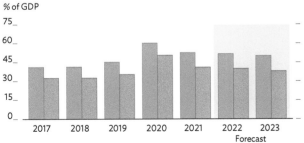

GDP = gross domestic product.
Sources: International Monetary Fund; Ministry of Finance of Georgia.

The current account deficit is projected to widen to equal 10.0% of GDP in 2022 with a forecast rise in oil prices before narrowing to 7.5% in 2023 (Figure 3.3.11). Exports are projected to increase by 12.1% in 2022

Figure 3.3.9 Inflation

Inflation should slow with tight monetary policy.

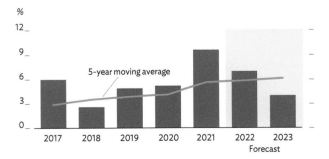

Sources: National Statistics Office of Georgia; Asian Development Bank estimates.

Figure 3.3.11 Current account balance

The current account deficit will widen in 2022 before narrowing in 2023.

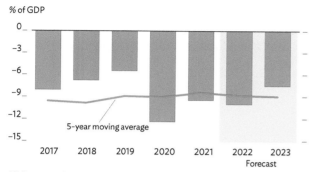

GDP = gross domestic product.

Sources: National Bank of Georgia; Asian Development Bank estimates.

and 14.9% in 2023. Domestic growth is expected to expand imports by 8.0% in 2022 and 9.6% in 2023. As economic sanctions cut growth in Russia, remittances are forecast to decrease to $1.8 billion in 2022 and $1.7 billion in 2023 (Figure 3.3.12). With foreign direct investment sustained, gross reserves are projected to reach $3.9 billion in 2022 and $4.0 billion in 2023. Public external debt is forecast to fall to the equivalent of 40.0% of GDP at the end of 2022 and 38.0% a year later as external borrowing declines.

Figure 3.3.12 Gross international reserves

Reserves should continue to rise in 2022 and 2023 as foreign direct investment revives.

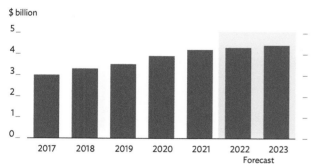

Sources: International Monetary Fund; Ministry of Finance of Georgia.

Downside risks to the forecast include the possibility of more COVID-19 cases because of slow vaccination progress and lower exports of goods and services if the Russian invasion of Ukraine is prolonged. However, any rebound in external demand that surprises on the upside or a quick end to the acute phase of the pandemic could accelerate growth.

Policy challenge—transforming municipal finances

Georgia maintains highly centralized public finances and intergovernmental fiscal arrangements despite subscribing to the European Charter of Local Self-Government, which states that tax and spending decisions should be made at the lowest practical level of government. Despite recent progress, subnational revenue remained relatively flat in the decade to 2020 at the equivalent of 5.1%–6.0% of GDP. However, the share of local government tax revenue in general government revenue rose from 5.7% in 2010 to 15.3% in 2019 as value-added tax was shared and reliance on transfers decreased. Local expenditure, mirroring revenue performance, averaged 5.7% of GDP in the same decade, below the Organisation for Economic Co-operation and Development average of 7.6%, with municipalities running small deficits equal to about 1% of GDP or occasionally a small surplus.

Municipalities lack ownership rights to land, water, forest, mineral, or other resources within their boundaries. Municipal investment is also low, reflecting local governments' underdeveloped borrowing capacity. Most road and other infrastructure projects are implemented and funded by the central government, as are most social programs. The tight financial envelope within which municipalities operate constrains regional economic development, inhibiting inclusive growth.

In 2019, the government approved the Decentralization Strategy, 2020–2025, which aims to empower local governments, strengthen their finances, and promote decentralization for efficient service provision, reliability, accountability, transparency, and a focus on results. The strategy aims for municipalities commanding resources equal to at least 7.0% of GDP by 2025 as selected activities are transferred down from the central government, with further increases in line with GDP growth. Municipalities will be allowed by the end of 2025 to borrow prudently and own unregistered property within their territory. In addition, municipalities will assume increased powers in service delivery, education, culture, local economic development, environmental policy, and some other areas.

By empowering municipalities, fiscal decentralization will rationalize fiscal policy, strengthen economic growth, promote entrepreneurship, and improve service provision and social policy. Local governments are expected to provide a broad range of infrastructure and services to their residents and support social spending. Strengthening subnational public finances will thus enable more efficient and equitable provision of services, including the complex services critical for large population centers, water supply and sanitation systems in secondary cities and towns, and for disadvantaged populations health care, education, and social protection.

To fund these services, subnational governments will need to mobilize local revenue consistent with their revenue bases and supplemented by transfers from the central government and prudent borrowing. As municipalities gain access to local revenue-generating assets and resources with property title transfer, their finances will strengthen, and additional collateral will make them more creditworthy. Legislation is thus essential to establish municipal property rights and procedures for borrowing and bankruptcy.

Georgia can benefit significantly by building capacity in municipalities. The success of fiscal decentralization will depend on developing financial management capacity in local governments and training local officials in policy development and implementation skills, such as health and education budgeting and social service delivery.

KAZAKHSTAN

Growth returned in 2021 with quarantine loosening. Drought and higher global energy prices boosted inflation, while the current account deficit narrowed. Growth will slow in 2022 because of monetary tightening and adverse consequences from the Russian invasion of Ukraine but reaccelerate in 2023 as reform takes effect. Inflation will ease with tight monetary policy, currency interventions, price controls, and higher oil production and prices yield a 2023 current account surplus. Achieving carbon neutrality requires bold action, including better targeted fuel subsidies and lower emission caps.

Economic performance

The economy reversed 2.5% contraction in 2020 to grow by 4.0% in 2021 as measures to control COVID-19 were gradually lifted and vaccination rollout accelerated (Figure 3.4.1). On the supply side, industry expanded by 3.8%, reflecting a 5.5% rise in manufacturing spurred by continued government support for light industry and machine building. Mining increased by 1.7%, with gains of 2.1% in metal ore and 4.6% in nonmetallic mineral production, while oil and gas production remained flat. Services rebounded by 3.9%, reflecting increases of 12.9% in communications, 9.2% in trade, and 3.6% in transport and warehousing. Growth in construction remained strong at 7.6% as some pension funds were used to finance housing. Agriculture contracted by 2.4% as a 6.7% decline in crop production under severe drought outweighed 3.6% expansion in livestock.

Data on the demand side, available for the first 9 months of 2021, show economic activity reviving and raising private consumption by 5.0% from the comparable period of 2020. Public consumption grew by only 1.2% as economic support measures were phased out. Growth in investment stagnated as a 3.4% decline in inventories offset a 2.0% rise in gross fixed capital formation. Net exports rose notably as import volume fell by 5.1%, outpacing 1.6% decline in export volume.

Figure 3.4.1 Supply-side contributions to growth

Growth returned in 2021, led by a rebound in services.

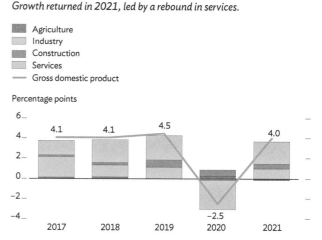

Source: Republic of Kazakhstan. Agency for Strategic Planning and Reforms. Bureau of National Statistics (accessed 14 March 2022).

Average annual inflation accelerated from 6.8% in 2020 to 8.0%, reflecting double-digit food price increases and higher production and transportation costs from rising fuel prices (Figure 3.4.2). Severe drought increased food price inflation from 10.4% in 2020 to 10.8%, with many staple food prices rising by double digits. Higher fuel costs and utility tariffs raised inflation for other goods from 5.5% in 2020 to 6.9% and for services from 3.3% to 5.5%.

This chapter was written by Genadiy Rau of the Kazakhstan Resident Mission, ADB, Nur-Sultan. Adil Sultangazy, intern and Nazarbayev University student, assisted with data collection and analysis for the policy challenge section.

Figure 3.4.2 Average inflation

Inflation accelerated, reflecting higher prices for all components.

— All goods and services
--- Food, beverages, and tobacco
--- Nonfood goods
--- Services

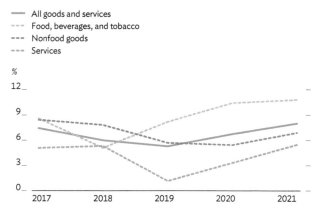

Source: Republic of Kazakhstan. Agency for Strategic Planning and Reforms. Bureau of National Statistics (accessed 14 March 2022).

In April 2021, the government revised the state budget with additional allocations equal to 1.6% of GDP for pandemic relief and economic support. Total 2021 outlays nevertheless subsided from the equivalent of 24.7% of GDP in 2020 to 22.6%, despite rising by 6.1% in nominal terms on increases of 17.2% for education and 15.5% for health care (Figure 3.4.3). State budget revenue declined from 20.7% of GDP to 19.5%, despite a 9.1% nominal increase reflecting gains of 38.4% in corporate income tax and 22.0% in personal income tax. Transfers from the National Fund of the Republic of Kazakhstan, the sovereign wealth fund, declined to 5.5% of GDP. Borrowing declined as the state budget deficit

Figure 3.4.3 Fiscal indicators

The fiscal deficit narrowed as expenditure slowed more than revenue in percent of GDP.

▮ Revenue
▮ Expenditure
— Fiscal balance

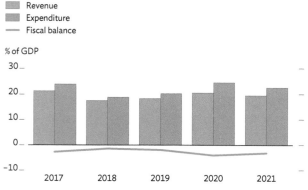

GDP = gross domestic product.
Source: Republic of Kazakhstan. Agency for Strategic Planning and Reforms. Bureau of National Statistics (accessed 14 March 2022).

shrank from the equivalent of 4.0% of GDP in 2020 to 3.1%, and the non-oil deficit shrank from 11.5% to 9.9%. Government and government-guaranteed debt declined from 30.5% of GDP at the end of 2020 to 28.5% a year later despite a 7.5% increase in nominal terms.

With inflation above the 4%–6% target range, the central bank raised the key policy rate by 25 basis points in July 2021 and twice again in September and October to 9.75% to contain inflationary expectations. Growth in broad money (M3) accelerated from 16.9% in 2020 to 20.8% as deposits grew by 22.7% and credit to the economy by 26.5% (Figure 3.4.4). However, the volume of central bank short-term securities fell by 28.2%, in part to offset a 16.2% rise in government securities issued to help finance the budget deficit. Credit growth accelerated, with growth in mortgage lending rising from 34.3% in 2020 to 40.0%—the same growth rate to which consumer lending soared from only 4.0% in 2020. Subsidized state lending programs and use of pension funds boosted homebuying. Lending to firms rebounded by 9.3% in 2021 after years of contraction, with loans to small and medium-sized enterprises rising by 29.2%. High loan volume halved the share of nonperforming loans from 6.9% at the end of 2020 to 3.3% a year later. Foreign currency deposits declined from 37.3% of all deposits at the end of 2020 to 36.0%, and foreign currency loans decreased from 13.0% of all loans to 10.3%.

Preliminary estimates show the current account deficit narrowing from 3.8% of GDP in 2020 to 3.0% as the merchandise trade surplus doubled, with higher oil and gas prices raising merchandise exports by more than a quarter while merchandise imports grew by only 6.6%.

Figure 3.4.4 Broad money growth

Money growth accelerated in 2021, contributing to inflation.

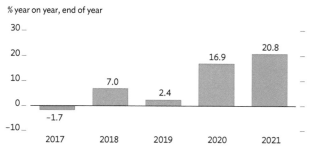

Source: Republic of Kazakhstan. Agency for Strategic Planning and Reforms. Bureau of National Statistics (accessed 14 March 2022).

The deficit in services fell by 43.1% as global pandemic restrictions constrained outbound travel, while income from cargo transit services expanded. Profit repatriation rose by 56.4%, widening the deficit in primary income, while higher outward money transfers pushed the secondary income account into deficit. Net inflow of foreign direct and portfolio investment declined.

With the central bank selling $491 million in reserves to support the currency, gross international reserves declined by 3.5% to $34.4 billion at the end of 2021, cover for 8.8 months of imports, with more than two-thirds of reserves held in gold. Sovereign wealth fund assets declined by 5.8% to $55.3 billion as transfers to the state budget exceeded earnings by 72.2% (Figure 3.4.5). External debt, 58.8% of which is private intercompany debt, declined gradually to equal an estimated 90.8% of GDP, reflecting debt repayment by foreign subsidiaries. In June, the government issued for the second time 40 billion rubles worth of ruble-denominated bonds in Russia, Kazakhstan's largest trade partner, to finance the budget deficit.

Figure 3.4.5 Foreign currency reserves and sovereign wealth fund

Reserves and assets of the sovereign wealth fund remained high.

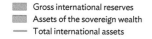

- Gross international reserves
- Assets of the sovereign wealth
- Total international assets

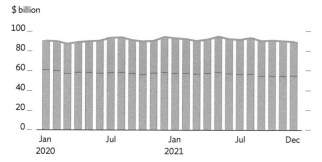

Source: Republic of Kazakhstan. Agency for Strategic Planning and Reforms. Bureau of National Statistics (accessed 14 March 2022).

Economic prospects

The Russian invasion of Ukraine undermined business confidence, which was already strained after domestic protests in January 2022. Spillover from economic sanctions imposed on Russia will, on top of tight monetary policy, slow growth in 2022. However, an economic reform program that aims to raise household incomes and support economic activity will limit spillover impact and reaccelerate growth in 2023. On these assumptions, growth is projected slowing to 3.2% in 2022 before accelerating again in 2023 to 3.9% (Table 3.4.1).

Table 3.4.1 Selected economic indicators, %

Macroeconomic indicators are gradually improving.

	2020	2021	2022	2023
GDP growth	–2.5	4.0	3.2	3.9
Inflation	6.8	8.0	7.8	6.4
CAB/GDP	–3.8	–3.0	–0.1	0.5

CAB = current account balance, GDP = gross domestic product.
Sources: Bureau of National Statistics; National Bank of Kazakhstan; Asian Development Bank estimates.

On the supply side, growth in services is forecast to slow to 3.5% in 2022 and then reaccelerate to 4.9% in 2023 as transport, trade, and catering benefit from the removal of COVID-19 restrictions with more than half of the population already fully vaccinated (Figure 3.4.6). Growth in industry is similarly forecast to slow to 3.0% in 2022 and reaccelerate to 3.7% in 2023 as rising external demand for commodities boosts mining by 1.9% in 2022 and 2.7% in 2023. Continued government support for import substitution will expand manufacturing by a somewhat slower 4.4% in 2022 and then 4.8% in 2023. As pension fund withdrawal to pay for homebuilding declines, growth in construction is forecast to moderate to 4.3% in 2022 and 3.8% in 2023, buoyed by ongoing state housing and infrastructure programs. Agriculture will rebound by 3.4% in 2022 from a low base and grow by 3.6% in 2023 as reform benefits crop and livestock production.

On the demand side, growth in consumption is projected to decelerate to 3.3% in 2022 as currency depreciation and tight monetary policy limit expansion in household incomes and consumer credit, stabilizing in 2023 at 3.5%. Investment is forecast to stagnate in 2022 as business confidence recedes and then rise by 4.9% in 2023, with gross fixed capital formation benefiting from reform and government-supported housing and infrastructure programs. Net exports will increase gradually in both years as rising commodity export volume outpaces consumption-driven imports.

Figure 3.4.6 GDP growth

Economic growth will slow in 2022 before recovering in 2023.

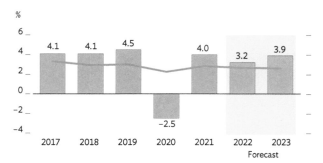

GDP = gross domestic product.
Source: *Asian Development Outlook* database.

Figure 3.4.8 Fiscal balance

The fiscal deficit will continue narrowing in 2022 and 2023.

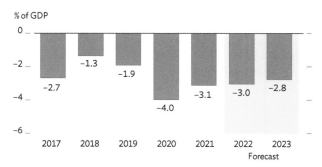

GDP = gross domestic product.
Source: *Asian Development Outlook* database.

Inflation is projected to slow to 7.8% in 2022 and 6.4% in 2023, reflecting joint central bank and government efforts to contain price increases (Figure 3.4.7). Following protests in January 2022, the government introduced a half-year moratorium on increases in gasoline, staple food, and utility prices. Together, price controls and export restrictions are projected to slow food price increases to 10.2% in 2022 and 8.4% in 2023. Tight monetary policy and central bank interventions supporting exchange rate stability will hold inflation for other goods to 6.8% in 2022 and 5.8% in 2023. Utility price regulation and intensifying competition in the service sector are expected to limit inflation in services to 5.4% in 2022 and 4.4% in 2023.

The budget deficit is projected to continue to subside, but more gradually, to the equivalent of 3.0% of GDP in 2022 and 2.8% in 2023, with the non-oil deficit declining to 8.6% and then 8.0% (Figure 3.4.8). Despite a gradual rise in tax revenue, total revenue is projected

to slide to 18.7% of GDP in 2022 and 17.8% in 2023 as transfers from the sovereign wealth fund are curtailed. Expenditure is forecast to drop further to 21.7% of GDP in 2022 and 20.6% in 2023 as extensive economic support programs are phased out, though partly offset by higher social outlays. Government and government-guaranteed debt are projected to remain at 28.5% of GDP at the end of 2022 and slip to 28.0% a year later.

Monetary policy over the next 2 years is expected to focus on bringing inflation toward the target range. As the Russian invasion of Ukraine escalated, the central bank raised its key policy rate by 325 basis points to 13.5% on 24 February 2022 and pledged a 10% premium for local currency deposits not converted or withdrawn for a year (Figure 3.4.9). Containing inflation will require further tightening of liquidity and phasing out subsidized lending programs, with broad money growth forecast to slow to 9.1% in 2022 and 6.4% in 2023.

Figure 3.4.7 Inflation

Inflation will slow in 2022 and 2023 but remain above the target range.

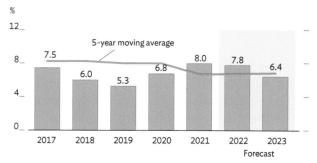

Source: *Asian Development Outlook* database.

Figure 3.4.9 Central bank policy rate

The key policy rate was raised sharply in early 2022 in response to external shocks.

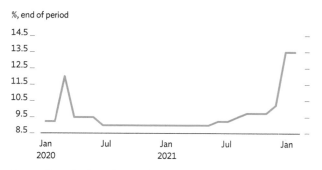

Source: Haver Analytics (accessed 14 March 2022).

The current account deficit will shrink to marginal in 2022 and turn to 0.5% surplus in 2023 (Figure 3.4.10). Record-setting commodity prices will generate merchandise export earnings last seen a decade ago expanding by 38.2% in 2022 and, as the situation stabilizes, 0.7% in 2023. Imports are projected to grow by 8.4% in 2022, driven by higher prices and volumes for consumer goods, and by 2.4% in 2023. With the resumption of international travel, the prepandemic service deficit is forecast restored by 2023. As commodity investors enjoy windfall profits, the primary income account deficit will surge by 57.6% in 2022, then narrow by 9.4% in 2023 as profits fall along with projected oil prices. Outward transfers are expected to grow by a further 26.5% in 2022, widening the secondary income deficit, but pause notably in 2023, turning that balance positive.

Figure 3.4.10 Current account balance

Sharp increases in exports will move the current account into surplus by 2023.

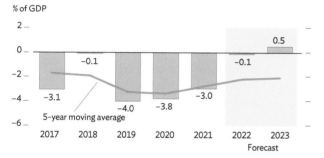

GDP = gross domestic product.
Source: *Asian Development Outlook* database.

Gross international reserves are projected to fall by the end of 2022 to $31.5 billion, or cover for 7.4 months of imports, as the central bank sells reserves to smooth exchange rate fluctuations. They should recover to $33.8 billion at the end of 2023. Sovereign wealth fund assets are forecast to expand to $58 billion in 2022 and to more than $60 billion in 2023 as budget transfers fall below inflows. External debt is expected to decline further to equal about 87% of GDP at the end of 2022 and 85% a year later as state-owned enterprises continue repaying foreign debt and foreign-owned subsidiaries repay intercompany debt (Figure 3.4.11).

Figure 3.4.11 External debt

Debt repayment will reduce the ratio of external debt to GDP.

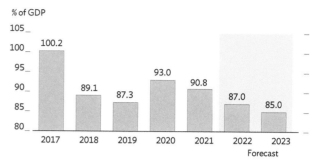

GDP = gross domestic product.
Source: *Asian Development Outlook* database.

Policy challenge—achieving carbon neutrality

Kazakhstan's economy remains carbon intensive, running on fossil fuels that leave a substantial carbon footprint. Over the past decade, greenhouse gas emissions increased by a third, exceeding 360 million tons of carbon dioxide in 2019 (Figure 3.4.12). Kazakhstan has the 12th highest global energy intensity relative to GDP, according to Enerdata's 2021 World Climate and Energy Data Yearbook. This stems primarily from its dependence on coal to generate electricity, 69.7% of which comes from coal-fired power plants (Figure 3.4.13). Households pay among the lowest electricity prices in the world.

Figure 3.4.12 Greenhouse gas emissions

Greenhouse gas emissions increased by a third over the past decade.

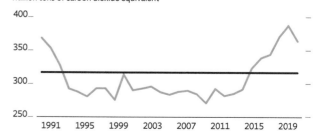

Source: Ministry of Ecology, Geology and Natural Resources. 2021. *National Report of the Republic of Kazakhstan on the Inventory of Anthropogenic Emissions from Sources and Removals by Sinks of Greenhouse Gases Not Regulated by the Montreal Protocol for 1990–2019.*

Figure 3.4.13 Electricity production by source, 2020

Coal supplies over two-thirds of electricity.

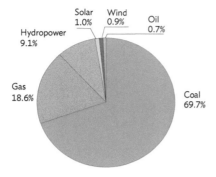

Source: Our World in Data (accessed 14 March 2022).

At only $0.042 per kilowatt-hour, they are less than a third of the global average of $0.138. Low gasoline prices at $0.47 per liter—again about a third of the world average—add to the problem, discouraging conversion to fuel-efficient cars as the average age of domestic automobiles approaches 20 years.

In 2021, oil production reached 85.7 million tons, 78.9% of which is exported. The European Union, which imports over half of Kazakhstan's oil production, is phasing in a carbon tax on imports and restricting the sale of cars with internal combustion engines, posing a major challenge to Kazakhstan and other economies dependent on crude oil exports.

In 2016, Kazakhstan signed the Paris Agreement, pledging to reduce greenhouse gas emissions in 2030 by 15% from 1990 levels. Recent government data acknowledged that emissions in 2019 were down by just 2.4% from 1990, and the Climate Action Tracker website has rated Kazakhstan's climate targets and policies highly insufficient, raising emissions, not reducing them. A case in point is the country's emissions trading system, which has since 2013 increased emission allowances. Heavy fossil fuel use also affects the quality of life, as residents, especially in the country's western and central regions, consistently voice dissatisfaction with high pollution and poor air quality.

In 2020, Kazakhstan pledged at the World Climate Ambition Summit to achieve carbon neutrality by 2060. The government is developing plans to attain this goal, including changes in legislation. Achieving carbon neutrality is a challenge because eliminating carbon

subsidies requires careful planning, a clear communication strategy, thorough implementation, and support for the vulnerable groups least able to bear the immediate costs. This may require reform in several areas.

The government's antimonopoly agency sets prices for electricity and district heating to cover only current operating expenses, without room for investment or modernization. Moreover, exports of gasoline are banned, and energy prices have been frozen to contain inflation following local protests. Indirect subsidies by which oil is supplied to domestic refineries at artificially low prices are estimated to have cost $2 billion in 2021. Tight state control of energy and fuel prices distorts the market, hampers competition, and is economically unsustainable. Yet removing controls raises energy and fuel prices and is thus politically unpopular. The government can mitigate the damage from higher prices through targeted support to low-income and vulnerable groups by subsidizing part of their utility and fuel bills. This need not raise budget outlays if the fiscal space is generated by removing more general fuel subsidies.

Careful management of inflation expectations must be included because higher energy and fuel prices may raise production and transportation costs. Thus, the government should encourage greater energy efficiency. This can involve offering firms and households matching funds, tax credits, and other incentives to undertake energy-efficient modernization of production, transport, and homes. In addition, stringent emission allowances and a robust carbon price would encourage large emitters to introduce carbon-capture technology.

Finally, global and private green investment is needed to cover some of the estimated $650 billion cost of achieving carbon neutrality by 2060. Kazakhstan has successfully stimulated renewable energy sources through auctions since 2017. In a relatively short time, $1.8 billion has been invested in 124 renewable energy projects that now generate 3.6% of electricity in Kazakhstan. However, planned new auctions are being postponed, sowing uncertainty. A multiyear auction timetable would help promote climate-related investment. Moreover, approving the earlier announced plan for achieving carbon neutrality and other legislative initiatives would improve the business climate by providing greater legal certainty, lowering costs and risks for investors.

KYRGYZ REPUBLIC

Growth returned in 2021, reflecting strong expansion in mining, trade, and transportation, along with higher consumption and public investment. Inflation jumped as continued disruption to supply chains boosted prices for food and other goods, while lower exports brought the sizable current account deficit. Growth is projected to slow in 2022 and recover slightly in 2023, with significant downside risks. Inflation will remain high, and the current account deficit will widen. Developing a greener economy will mitigate risks to sustainable development.

Economic performance

The economy reversed contraction by 8.4% in 2020 to grow by 3.6% in 2021 (Figure 3.5.1). Despite a 4.8% decline in construction, industry replaced 9.9% decline in 2020 with 3.1% growth as mining expanded by 21.2% and the processing of gold and other metals by 7.0%. Agriculture contracted by 5.0% as drought cut farm output by 11.6%. Services recovered by 6.5%, with increases of 11.4% in trade, 15.6% in transportation, and 14.3% in hospitality.

Figure 3.5.1 GDP growth by sector

Growth recovered in 2021, led by gains in services and industry.

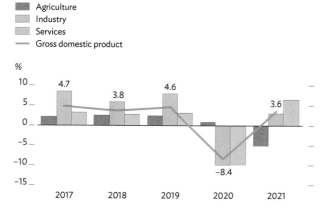

Source: National Statistics Committee of the Kyrgyz Republic (accessed 9 March 2022).

On the demand side, public consumption grew to cover COVID-19 vaccination costs and higher spending on health-care facilities. Private consumption is also thought to have risen with remittances 16% higher in 2021. However, investment fell by 5.9% despite the resumption of delayed infrastructure projects.

Average annual inflation nearly doubled from 6.3% in 2020 to 11.9% (Figure 3.5.2). Large price increases persisted for food, at 18.4%, with smaller increases of 7.1% for other goods and 4.2% for services, as supply chains were slow to recover and inflation was further boosted by Kyrgyz som depreciation against the US dollar by 18.9% in 2020 and a further 1.5% in 2021 (Figure 3.5.3).

The fiscal deficit narrowed from the equivalent of 3.3% of GDP in 2020 to 0.3% in 2021 as revenue and expenditure both rose (Figure 3.5.4). Current spending expanded to address hardship from COVID-19, raising total expenditure from 28.6% of GDP in 2020 to 29.3%. Revenue rose even more, from 25.3% of GDP to 29.0%, with improved tax administration following the 1 July 2021 introduction of digitalized tax filing and compulsory use of cash registers in most small retail businesses. Public debt fell from 57.9% of GDP at the end of 2020 to 51.8% a year later in line with a fiscal rule approved by Parliament in 2020 to cap government debt at 70% of GDP and the budget deficit at 3%.

This chapter was written by Gulkayr Tentieva of the Kyrgyz Resident Mission, ADB, Bishkek.

Figure 3.5.2 Monthly inflation

Inflation accelerated in 2021 as food prices surged.

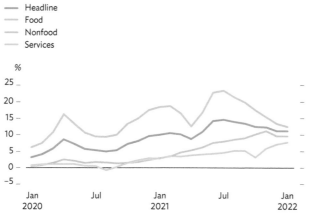

Source: National Bank of the Kyrgyz Republic (accessed 9 March 2022).

Figure 3.5.3 Exchange rate

The Kyrgyz som depreciated against the US dollar as inflation accelerated.

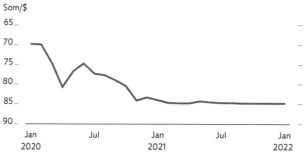

Source: National Bank of the Kyrgyz Republic (accessed 9 March 2022).

Figure 3.5.4 Fiscal indicators

The fiscal deficit narrowed in 2021 as tax administration reform boosted revenue.

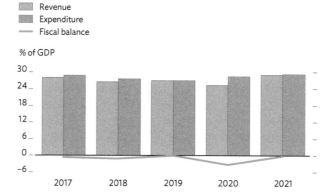

GDP = gross domestic product.
Source: Ministry of Finance of the Kyrgyz Republic
(accessed 9 March 2022).

To curb inflation from currency depreciation and manage a floating exchange rate, the National Bank of the Kyrgyz Republic, the central bank, raised its policy rate by 3.0 percentage points to 8.0% in November 2021. The average deposit rate nevertheless fell by 0.05 points in 2021, and the average lending rate by 0.92 points. Growth in broad money slowed from 23.9% in 2020 to 19.1% in 2021, with credit rising by 11.8% and deposits by 34.3%. The share of nonperforming loans worsened from 10.5% of all loans at the end of 2020 to 11.6% a year later as weak business activity raised payment arrears. Dollarization remains extensive, but the foreign currency share of loans fell from 33.0% in 2020 to 28.0%, and of deposits from 43.4% to 42.2%. To support the currency, the central bank sold $689 million in foreign exchange reserves in 2021, up from $466 million in 2020.

Falling exports and rising imports yielded a current account deficit equal to 7.0% of GDP in 2021, reversing a 4.8% surplus a year earlier. Exports declined by 15.9%, mainly because of a 68% fall in gold exports from an ongoing dispute and litigation embroiling the country's largest goldmine, Kumtor, and the introduction of external management in May 2021 (box). Higher imports of machinery and equipment, apparel, and sugar boosted total imports by 49.8%, supported by a 16.0% rise in remittances to $2.7 billion, 97% from Russia, as the number of migrant workers rose with the reopening of Russian borders (Figure 3.5.5).

Box 3.5.1 Kumtor goldmine dispute

In February 2021, a government commission investigated Kumtor Gold Company's operations and concluded that Centerra Gold Inc., the operator of the Kumtor goldmine, had caused environmental degradation at the mine. Following the May 2021 appointment of external management at Kumtor, Centerra filed cases against the Government of the Kyrgyz Republic, in the Arbitration Court in Sweden in that month and in the US Bankruptcy Court of the Southern District of New York in the following month. However, a settlement out of court is expected by the end of March 2022, with the government swapping its 26.1% stake in Centerra for full ownership of the Kumtor goldmine.

Figure 3.5.5 Remittances

Remittances rebounded in 2021 as the number of migrant workers rose.

$ billion

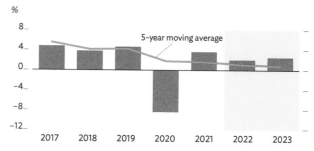

Source: National Bank of the Kyrgyz Republic (accessed 9 March 2022).

International reserves increased from $2.6 billion at the end of 2020 to $2.9 billion a year later, cover for 5.6 months of imports. External debt, including government-guaranteed and private debt, is estimated to have fallen from the equivalent of 101.2% of GDP at the end of 2020 to 90.7% at the end of September 2021 (Figure 3.5.6).

Figure 3.5.6 External debt

Public debt fell as share of GDP in 2021, but some risk of debt distress remains.

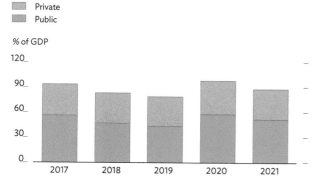

GDP = gross domestic product.
Note: Public debt includes government-guaranteed debt.
Sources: Ministry of Finance of the Kyrgyz Republic; National Statistics Committee; National Bank of the Kyrgyz Republic (all accessed 9 March 2022).

Economic prospects

With economic sanctions imposed on Russia, the Kyrgyz Republic's main trade partner, growth is projected to slow to 2.0% in 2022 and recover to 2.5% in 2023, with significant downside risks if external uncertainties are prolonged (Table 3.5.1 and Figure 3.5.7).

Table 3.5.1 Selected economic indicators, %

Growth is projected to slow in 2022 and recover slightly in 2023, with significant downside risks, while inflation increases and the current account deficit widens.

	2020	2021	2022	2023
GDP growth	–8.4	3.6	2.0	2.5
Inflation	6.3	11.9	15.0	12.0
CAB/GDP	4.8	–7.0	–10.0	–10.0

CAB = current account balance, GDP = gross domestic product.
Source: Asian Development Bank estimates.

Figure 3.5.7 GDP growth

Growth is projected to slow in 2022 and recover slightly in 2023, with significant downside risks.

%

GDP = gross domestic product.
Sources: National Statistics Committee of the Kyrgyz Republic (accessed 9 March 2022); Asian Development Bank estimates.

The government is developing an anti-crisis plan to limit currency depreciation, contain inflation, and maintain economic growth in the short term. The plan will include stimulus for the private sector and measures to diversify imports of essential goods including fuel and natural gas, equipment and machinery, grain and other food products, medicine, construction materials, and raw materials for manufacturing.

On the supply side, gold production is expected to rebound by about 10%, aided by higher prices. Industry will benefit from the resumption of infrastructure projects in energy and transport. Services are projected to grow by about 3%, reflecting gains in trade, hospitality, and transport from economic recovery and reopening borders and other transport links as COVID-19 wanes. Agriculture is forecast to expand by about 2% in 2022 and again in 2023, mainly from better livestock performance, as crop production is expected to continue suffering over the next few years from drought and lack of water for irrigation.

On the demand side, private consumption is expected to decline as economic sanctions on Russia reduce demand for migrant workers, and thus remittances, while infrastructure projects will somewhat augment public investment. Public consumption will show little change, as will net exports, with exports and imports alike declining.

Average annual inflation is expected to remain high at about 15% in 2022 and 12% in 2023, mainly from a sharp surge in fuel and gas prices by more than 20%, which may push up prices for food and other items (Figure 3.5.8). The central bank is expected to maintain its focus on attaining price stability. In March 2022, when sharp depreciation of the Russian ruble prompted a nearly 23.8% plunge in the som against the US dollar, the central bank raised the policy rate by 4.0 percentage points to 14.0% and undertook currency interventions to support the exchange rate.

The fiscal deficit is projected to expand to the equivalent of 3%–5% of GDP in 2022–2023 as higher spending resumes on infrastructure projects. However, slowing economic activity could leave a larger deficit. Revenue is projected equal to about 31% of GDP, and expenditure no less than 34%. Public debt is forecast to exceed 60% of GDP in 2022 and 2023, approaching the limit set by the recently enacted fiscal rule. The International Monetary Fund assesses that the country is still at moderate risk of debt distress.

The current account deficit is expected to widen to about 10% of GDP in both 2022 and 2023 (Figure 3.5.9). Increased gold exports should boost export growth to 5% in both years, and the resumption of delayed infrastructure projects should similarly boost imports. However, as Russia is the country's largest trade partner, with almost 32% of all external trade, economic sanctions on it may slash both exports and imports. Remittances are likely to fall in US dollar terms by at least 30%–50% from 2021 in 2022–2023, reflecting lower demand for migrant workers and a weakened ruble against the US dollar. Gross international reserves are projected in the range of $2.2 billion–$2.3 billion in 2022–2023, or cover for about 4.5 months of imports, while shrinking external debt is projected to equal 60% of GDP at the end of 2023.

Figure 3.5.8 Inflation

Inflation is expected to remain high in both 2022 and 2023.

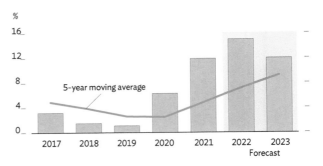

Sources: National Bank of the Kyrgyz Republic (accessed 9 March 2022); Asian Development Bank estimates.

Figure 3.5.9 Current account balance

The current account deficit is expected to widen with the resumption of infrastructure projects.

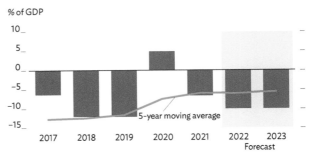

GDP = gross domestic product.
Sources: National Bank of the Kyrgyz Republic (accessed 9 March 2022); Asian Development Bank estimates.

Policy challenge—developing a green economy

In October 2021, the government adopted a new medium-term development program for 2021–2026 that is an integral part of the country's long-term development strategy to 2040. The program aims to improve public well-being by achieving key Sustainable Development Goals (SDGs) through ambitious objectives for structural reform to strengthen governance and the rule of law, develop key infrastructure to advance digitalization and improve the business environment for private sector growth, and promote a green economy.

A green economy will significantly reduce risks to the environment, preserve and enhance natural capital, promote efficient resource use, and conserve natural ecosystems. The government expressed its commitment to sustainable development through green economy priorities at the United Nations Conference on Sustainable Development in 2012. The country's Nationally Determined Contribution calls for reducing greenhouse gas emissions 16.63% by 2025 and 15.97% by 2030 under the baseline scenario; or 36.61% by 2025 and 43.62% by 2030 with international support. The estimated cost of implementing measures to adapt to climate change while mitigating it through reduced greenhouse gas emissions, as stated in the Kyrgyz Republic's updated nationally determined contribution, is about $10 billion, of which 37% will come from domestic resources and the rest from development partners.

The country faces environmental problems that threaten sustainable development, including land degradation and increased air pollution. Land degradation stems largely from unsustainable land use in agriculture, notably overgrazing and inefficient irrigation and water-management systems. Together, these factors risk people suffering greater difficulty in obtaining food and clean water, particularly as water is scarce, especially in the southern part of the country.

Worsening air pollution harms human health and the stability of ecosystems while hastening the corrosion of infrastructure. Air pollution is especially serious in cities. Experts estimate that more than 87% of the main pollutants enter the atmosphere from motor vehicles, their numbers increasing every year, as well as from burning coal in winter. Rising air pollution induces higher costs for health care and public infrastructure maintenance and endangers natural ecosystems.

Worsening natural resource depletion and environmental pollution and the risks they pose demonstrate the country's need to become a green economy. Doing so will require government policy to stimulate efforts toward energy efficiency and conservation, renewable resource use, and more efficient water and land management in urban and rural areas alike.

The government has already taken some steps in this direction. It has introduced a new national designated authority for green economy efforts and developed a standalone green economy development program for 2019–2023. Its goal is to create a framework for a green economy that involves energy, agriculture, and industry; switching to low-carbon and environmentally friendly transportation; and developing sustainable tourism and green cities.

In addition, the government has begun implementing projects for drip irrigation, organic agriculture, small hydropower plant construction, renewable energy, and water conservation. It has established a climate finance center to attract financial resources and investment from the United Nation's Green Climate Fund and other international financiers of climate change programs. The government will procure electric buses and related infrastructure for the capital city.

The recently adopted tax code provides incentives for developing a green economy and using green technologies. These include value-added tax (VAT) exemptions for technology, equipment, and components that meet criteria for energy and resource efficiency, and a 50% property tax cut for buildings and other structures that are certifiably energy and resource efficient. Besides these measures, the government has doubled the property tax for vehicles with an engine capacity of 3,000–4,500 cubic centimeters in use for up to 5 years, and tripled the tax for those with engine capacity of 4,500 cubic centimeters in use for more than 5 years. In addition, VAT-free customs and tax regimes were introduced at the beginning of 2022 for imported vehicles with electric and hybrid engines to cut pollution, especially in urban areas.

Introducing green technology into production and other economic activity requires sizable financial resources including private sector investment. To promote investment in green technologies, the government should cooperate with private firms to provide incentives for attracting foreign direct investment in this area. It should also encourage firms to produce greener products while stimulating consumer demand for local, organic, and environmentally friendly products.

TAJIKISTAN

After slowing in 2020 because of COVID-19, growth more than doubled in 2021 as trade partners reopened, industrialization accelerated, remittances rose marginally, and vaccines were successfully rolled out. Inflation slowed, but a wider trade deficit narrowed the current account surplus. Severe spillover from the expected economic downturn in Russia will slow growth significantly in 2022 and 2023, bring double-digit inflation, and cause current account deficits in both years as remittances plunge. Maintaining debt sustainability is important for macroeconomic stability.

Economic performance

The government reported growth rebounding from 4.5% in 2020 to 9.2% in 2021 on gains in industry, exports, remittances, and private lending. More than two-thirds of all adults were vaccinated against COVID-19 by the end of 2021.

On the supply side, growth in industry jumped from 9.7% in 2020 to 22.0% in 2021 with gains of 50.0% in mining, 16.3% in manufacturing, and 12.5% in electricity generation (Figure 3.6.1). Natural disasters and less favorable weather trimmed expansion in

agriculture from 8.8% in 2020 to 6.6% despite gains in fruit and vegetables, poultry, and fishing. Services reversed a 2.6% contraction to grow by 7.9%, reflecting higher remittances and a sharp boost in private lending that expanded retail trade by 12.7% (Figure 3.6.2). After declining by 4.6% in 2020, construction rose by 23.3% as investment increased, in part to celebrate the 30th anniversary of Tajikistan's independence.

On the demand side, higher growth and remittances, 95% of which come from Russia, helped boost

Figure 3.6.1 Gross domestic product growth by sector

Growth doubled in 2021, led by industry and construction.

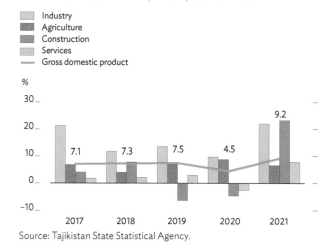

Source: Tajikistan State Statistical Agency.

Figure 3.6.2 Supply-side sources of gross domestic product

The pandemic expanded the role of industry in the economy, shrinking that of services.

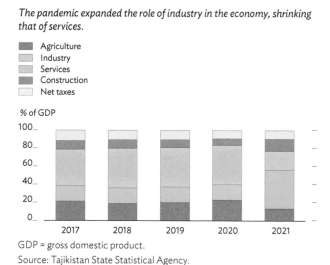

GDP = gross domestic product.
Source: Tajikistan State Statistical Agency.

This chapter was written by Muhammadi Boboev of the Tajikistan Resident Mission, ADB, Dushanbe.

consumption. Investment rose by 23.3%, mainly into mineral extraction and processing, as private and foreign investment increased but public investment slowed. The deficit in net exports deepened as restored trade links boosted imports by 33.6% and despite higher exports of gold, minerals, and textiles.

Inflation slowed from 9.4% in 2020 to 8.0%, within the 4%–8% target range of the National Bank of Tajikistan, the central bank. Prices rose by 7.3% for food, 7.5% for other goods, and 11.3% for services (Figure 3.6.3). Higher prices reflected global increases in food and fuel prices, pandemic-related supply shocks, and a 37% rise in lending.

Figure 3.6.3 Sources of inflation

Inflation slowed in 2021 with smaller increases in food prices.

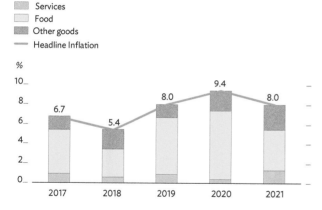

Source: Tajikistan State Statistical Agency.

Fiscal policy was less expansionary, with the deficit more than halved from the equivalent of 4.4% of GDP in 2020 to an estimated 2.0%, despite spending to maintain social protection, tighten border security, mitigate natural disaster risk, and continue building the Rogun hydropower project (Figure 3.6.4). Revenue rose from 27.2% of GDP in 2020 to 28.5% as improved tax administration, e-filing, tightened control over smuggling, and better valuation of imports boosted domestic tax collection by 9.6% and customs duties by 23.6%. Expenditure declined from 31.6% of GDP in 2020 to 30.5% with some fiscal consolidation, despite higher spending on border protection, health, and social programs. With a commitment to avoid non-concessional borrowing, public and publicly guaranteed external debt remained flat in absolute terms but fell from 40.6% of GDP in 2020 to 37.2% a

year later with rising GDP. Total public debt fell from 47.3% of GDP at the end of 2020 to 43.8% a year later (Figure 3.6.5). Nevertheless, Tajikistan's risk of debt distress remains high, according to the International Monetary Fund.

Figure 3.6.4 Fiscal indicators

The fiscal deficit was halved in 2021 as revenue rose and expenditure decreased in percent of GDP.

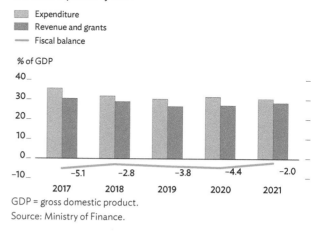

GDP = gross domestic product.
Source: Ministry of Finance.

Figure 3.6.5 Public debt

Public debt declined as a share of GDP as external public debt fell.

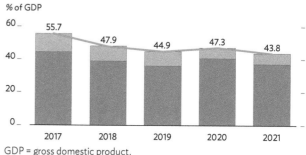

GDP = gross domestic product.
Source: Ministry of Finance.

The central bank tightened monetary policy to mitigate inflationary pressures by increasing sales of Treasury bills and central bank securities to restrain liquidity and by raising the policy interest rate in four steps from 11.00% in February 2021 to 13.25% in October. In addition, it reversed temporary easing of reserve requirements in 2020, raising reserve requirements in January–March 2021 from 5% to 9% on US dollar accounts and from 1% to 3% on Tajikistan somoni accounts. Broad money growth decelerated from 18.8%

in 2020 to 12.3% in 2021 as the central bank actively sold its deposit certificates to sterilize excess liquidity caused by its purchases of domestically produced gold and by expansion in private lending, which jumped from 4.7% in 2020 to 37.0% (Figure 3.6.6).

Figure 3.6.6 Monetary indicators

Broad money growth rose marginally with higher growth in credit to the private sector.

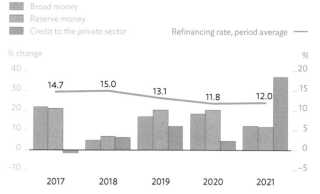

Source: National Bank of Tajikistan.

A stable local currency, along with efforts to combat dollarization and tighten foreign exchange controls, trimmed the share of foreign currency deposits from 48.2% at the end of 2020 to 44.5% a year later, and of foreign currency loans from 43.2% to 34.0%. Improved bank supervision and the liquidation of two troubled banks almost halved the share of nonperforming loans from 23.8% in 2020 to 13.7% in 2021. However, the return on bank assets fell from 2.5% in 2020 to 1.1%, and on bank equity from 9.1% to 4.8% (Figure 3.6.7).

Figure 3.6.7 Banking system soundness indicators

The percentage of nonperforming loans declined in 2021.

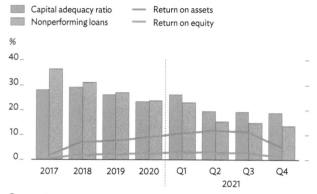

Q = quarter.
Source: National Bank of Tajikistan.

The current account surplus narrowed from the equivalent of 4.3% of GDP in 2020 to an estimated 2.6% as the trade deficit widened from $1.7 billion to $2.1 billion. Stronger demand and trade partner normalization raised imports by 33.6%, reversing 5.9% decline in 2020, while export growth jumped from 19.8% in 2020 to 52.8%, largely on record gold sales. Data from Russia, the destination for 95% of Tajikistan's migrant workers, showed remittances from this source rising by 3.1% year on year in 2021 to $1.8 billion, an amount equal to 20.5% of Tajikistan's GDP. The September 2021 resumption of regular flights to Russia likely contributed to this increase. Gross international reserves reached $2.2 billion at the end of December 2021, cover for 8.5 months of imports (Figure 3.6.8).

Figure 3.6.8 Gross international reserves

Gross international reserves were little changed in the first 3 quarters of 2021.

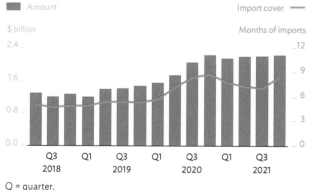

Q = quarter.
Source: National Bank of Tajikistan.

Economic prospects

Growth is forecast to decelerate to 2.0% in 2022 (Figure 3.6.9 and Table 3.6.1). The growth rate will depend, however, on impact from the economic downturn in Russia and adverse external environment, that will likely force migrant workers to return home, reducing remittances and investment, disrupting trade, creating shortages of dollars in the banks, worsening fiscal and external debt positions, and raising global oil and food prices. Gains in industry and emergency assistance from development partners to support consumption should, however, keep growth positive in 2022, rising to 3.0% in 2023.

Figure 3.6.9 Gross domestic product growth

Growth is projected to be significantly slower in 2022 and 2023.

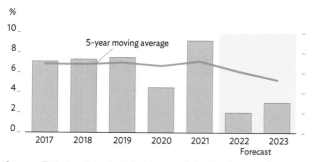

Sources: Tajikistan State Statistical Agency; Asian Development Bank estimates.

Table 3.6.1 Selected economic indicators, %

Projections show slower growth, higher inflation, and a wider current account deficit during 2022-2023.

	2020	2021	2022	2023
GDP growth	4.5	9.2	2.0	3.0
Inflation	9.4	8.0	15.0	10.0
CAB/GDP	4.3	2.6	−1.5	−2.5

CAB = current account balance, GDP = gross domestic product.
Sources: TAJSTAT; National Bank of Tajikistan; Asian Development Bank estimates.

On the supply side, industry is forecast to expand by 10% in both 2022 and 2023 as efforts continue to boost electricity generation, mining, and manufacturing. A new tax code in January 2022 reduced tax rates, created new tax incentives, and is expected to support entrepreneurship and growth. Agriculture should rise modestly by 5% each year as planted area expands. Services are projected to contract by 20% in 2022 and a further 10% in 2023 as remittances drop by at least half in 2022.

On the demand side, public investment will remain the main growth driver, though at a slower pace, as continued weakness in the business climate suppresses private investment despite the new tax code. Private consumption will drop significantly as remittances diminish. The deficit in net exports should widen in 2022 as gold sales normalize, and despite imports for the Rogun project moderating ahead of Tajikistan's likely reconnection in 2022 to the Central Asia Power System. Reconnection promises to boost electricity exports and enable higher production of import substitutes.

Inflation is projected to reach 15% in 2022, reflecting higher prices for fuel and imported food, more consumer lending, pressure on the somoni from a plummeting Russian ruble, public salaries and pensions by 20% in July 2022, higher electricity tariffs planned for November 2022, and increases for law enforcement authorities salaries up to 25% in January 2022 (Figure 3.6.10). Inflation should decline to 10% in 2023 with moderating global food and fuel prices, but it could go still higher if currency depreciation accelerates in tandem with a depreciating ruble or if needs for budget financing from domestic sources exceed expectations, boosting money growth.

Figure 3.6.10 Inflation

Inflation is projected to reach double digits in both 2022 and 2023.

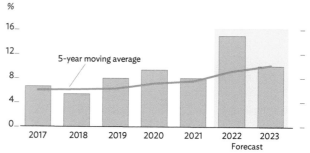

Sources: Tajikistan State Statistical Agency; Asian Development Bank estimates.

Fiscal policy will remain expansionary, with the budget deficit widening to equal 3.5% of GDP in 2022, despite outlays for the Rogun project being restricted to domestic budget resources and concessional borrowing. Achieving the deficit target will require expenditure restraint and administrative reform as cuts in revenue under the 2021 tax code and falling remittances and imports cap revenue at 25.7% of GDP in 2022 and 27.2% in 2023, when the fiscal deficit is forecast to narrow to 2.5% of GDP. Fiscal consolidation nevertheless has expenditure forecast to reach 29.2% of GDP in 2022 and 29.7% in 2023, but it could be higher with any clearing of arrears at state-owned enterprises (SOEs), faster currency depreciation, or support paid to returning migrants.

Foreign assistance is now entirely through grants, but the authorities anticipate covering any financing shortfall for infrastructure through concessional external borrowing, raising external debt—all of it public—to 42.5% of GDP by the end of 2023.

Continued fiscal deficits from high investment spending could make an already heavy debt burden unsustainable while weakening Tajikistan's external position through higher imports. Somoni depreciation threatens further debt increases in local currency terms.

Monetary policy will aim to combat inflationary pressures from currency depreciation linked to the plunge in the ruble, the currency of remittances, which equaled 20.5% of GDP in 2021. The central bank will try to contain inflation and limit currency depreciation by tightening liquidity, but tightening may be constrained by demand for budget financing. Lending to private firms may increase further with a recent decline in nonperforming loans. Given pressure from the plummeting ruble and depreciation of other trade partners' currencies, the central bank may intervene to support the local currency.

The current account is forecast to revert to deficits, equal to 1.5% of GDP in 2022 and 2.5% in 2023 (Figure 3.6.11), because of lower remittances, despite cuts in consumer imports by 15% in 2022 and 25% in 2023, as imports of capital goods for infrastructure projects will continue. Exports are projected to rise by 15% in 2022 despite lower gold sales and a further 10% in 2023 with higher electricity generation, including substantial exports of electricity to Afghanistan and Uzbekistan. Total imports are expected to drop by a third in 2022 as disposable income plunges, and by a further 20% in 2023 as a lagged effect of lower remittances. Remittances are projected to diminish in US dollar terms by 50% in 2022 as economic sanctions on Russia reduce employment for migrant workers,

Figure 3.6.11 Current account balance

The current account is projected to fall into deficit in 2022 and 2023.

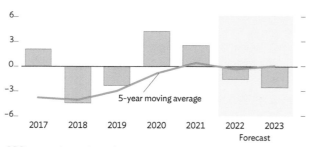

GDP = gross domestic product.
Sources: National Bank of Tajikistan; Asian Development Bank estimates.

causing many to return home, and as ruble depreciation slashes the US dollar value of most remittances received. Remittances may recover by 10% in 2023 if the international situation revives the demand for migrant workers (Figure 3.6.12). Despite central bank purchases of domestically produced gold, foreign reserves may fall below $2.0 billion to pay for currency interventions to support the somoni.

Figure 3.6.12 Remittances and GDP growth

Tajikistan's growth reflects remittance inflows and growth in Russia

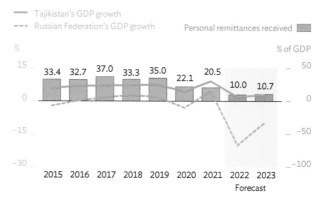

GDP = gross domestic product.
Sources: World Bank, World Development Indicators online database; National Bank of Tajikistan; Asian Development Bank estimates for Tajikistan GDP growth and remittance inflow.

Policy challenge—maintaining debt sustainability

Tajikistan's national development strategy to 2030 is estimated to cost $118.1 billion, of which 47.5% is to be financed by the state budget, 45.3% by the private sector, and the remaining 6.2% by external development partners. A midterm assessment covering 2016–2020 revealed, however, that a financing gap remains.

The latest joint debt sustainability analysis by the World Bank and the International Monetary Fund assessed in February 2022 Tajikistan's debt-carrying capacity as medium and determined that it is at high risk of debt distress for both external and public debt. At the end of 2021, Tajikistan's public debt reached the equivalent of 43.8% of GDP, of which nearly 87%

was external. External debt service equaled 15.9% of export value in 2021, somewhat above the 15.0% threshold for countries with medium debt-carrying capacity. However, this ratio is expected to stabilize after Tajikistan's eurobond is repaid in 2027 and fall below 15.0% by 2028. In 2022, the government plans $453 million in concessional borrowing from external sources. In 2020, the Debt Service Suspension Initiative of the Group of Twenty postponed more than $43 million in debt service owed by Tajikistan.

Tajikistan's high risk of debt distress reflects several factors: chronic fiscal deficits that, if measured by international standards, would count loans as financing rather than revenue; past heavy use of non-concessional borrowing, including $500 million in eurobonds with a 7.125% interest rate; failure to conduct economic assessments when selecting investment projects; and the decision to undertake the Rogun hydroelectric project, whose initial cost of $3.9 billion has risen thus far to $4.8 billion and required considerable external financing. Losses from natural disasters and the cost of pandemic response have added to the debt burden.

Various initiatives can strengthen debt sustainability. These include maintaining the prohibition on non-concessional external borrowing; using cost–benefit analysis when selecting public investment projects and limiting the size of the investment budget; improving the performance of loss-making SOEs; promoting private sector growth through measures to improve the investment climate; taking steps to rely less on external borrowing by developing the domestic capital market, including a secondary market in government securities to encourage commercial banks and other parties to buy and hold government debt; and regularly publishing Ministry of Finance reports on public debt, including the audited annual statements of the 15 largest SOEs.

The government may also consider limiting fiscal deficits to 2.5% of GDP by cutting low-priority capital expenditure, phasing out tax exemptions, prioritizing spending better, assessing public investment management and evaluating fiscal transparency toward addressing any shortcomings revealed, and enhancing debt statistics by broadening coverage to include SOE debt.

TURKMENISTAN

Higher hydrocarbon production and exports propelled recovery in 2021 and lifted the current account into surplus. Rising food import prices boosted inflation. Growth is projected to remain robust in 2022 and 2023 as hydrocarbon exports sustain momentum and pandemic restrictions ease. Higher global commodity prices are expected to keep inflation elevated, while the current account surplus should expand as exports outpace imports. Higher spending on social programs is needed for sustainable and inclusive growth.

Economic performance

The government continued strict lockdown and containment measures in 2021 to protect public health while pursuing the phased vaccination of the population against COVID-19.

Preliminary ADB estimates show growth at 5.0% in 2021, driven by higher gas production and exports. Natural gas output is estimated to have risen by 42% (Figure 3.7.1). Growth in the economy aside from hydrocarbons was limited by continuing constraints under a lockdown.

Figure 3.7.1 Natural gas production

Natural gas output jumped in 2021.

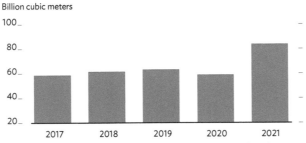

Billion cubic meters

Sources: BP Statistical Review of World Energy 2021; Asian Development Bank estimates.

On the supply side, growth came from industry, particularly oil and gas expansion but also gains in construction and, mostly under import-substitution programs, manufacturing, food processing, and textiles. Low precipitation constrained agriculture, which nevertheless managed moderate increases in cotton and wheat production. Sluggish growth in services reflected border closures, bans on external and domestic transportation, and restrictions that reduced tourism, recreation and catering, and other activities throughout the year, sometimes with the closure of shops, restaurants, and sports and entertainment venues.

On the demand side, the main contribution to growth came from gains in net exports as gas exports rose. Investment remained substantial but off earlier highs, with gross investment down by half from the equivalent of 39% of GDP in 2017 to an estimated 19% in 2021 (Figure 3.7.2). Rising prices and lower incomes attributable to a drop in employment decreased private consumption.

Preliminary ADB estimates show average annual inflation accelerating from 10.0% in 2020 to 12.5% in 2021, mainly from higher prices for imported food (Figure 3.7.3). Constraint on foreign exchange convertibility and food supply under disrupted trade raised prices for imports and domestically produced goods that require imported inputs. To maintain food security, state shops rationed food packages distributed to households at subsidized prices that contained such essentials as cooking oil, chicken, flour, eggs, and sugar.

This chapter was written by Jennet Hojanazarova of the Turkmenistan Resident Mission, ADB, Ashgabat.

Figure 3.7.2 Gross investment including foreign direct investment

Gross investment was substantial but remained below previous highs as a percentage of GDP.

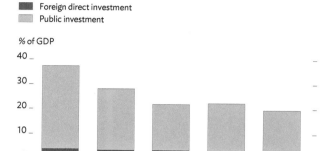

GDP = gross domestic product.
Sources: International Monetary Fund; Asian Development Bank estimates.

Figure 3.7.3 Inflation

Inflation accelerated in 2021.

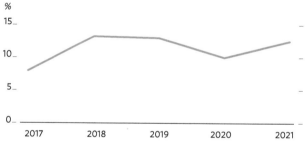

Sources: International Monetary Fund. 2021. *Regional Economic Outlook, Middle East and Central Asia*. October; Asian Development Bank estimates.

The Central Bank of Turkmenistan kept the fixed exchange rate unchanged. Growth in broad money is estimated to have accelerated from 11.8% in 2020 to 15.6% in 2021, with credit to the economy growing by an estimated 16.0% in 2021. Most lending was subsidized credit to state-owned enterprises in government-priority sectors, with some credit provided to private manufacturers engaged in import substitution.

The state budget incurred a small deficit equal to 0.3% of GDP, with the non-hydrocarbon deficit estimated at 3.7% of non-hydrocarbon GDP (Figure 3.7.4). The International Monetary Fund estimated expenditure to be a lower share of GDP in 2021 than in 2020 despite announced support for the health-care system during the pandemic (Figure 3.7.5). At the same

time, off-budget spending continued for government projects and various ad hoc needs. Public sector debt is estimated to have declined from the equivalent of 32.2% of GDP at the end of 2020 to 27.0% a year later.

Figure 3.7.4 Fiscal balances

The budget incurred a small overall deficit.

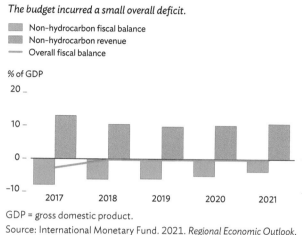

GDP = gross domestic product.
Source: International Monetary Fund. 2021. *Regional Economic Outlook, Middle East and Central Asia*.

Figure 3.7.5 Government revenue and expenditure

Both revenue and expenditure declined as a percentage of GDP.

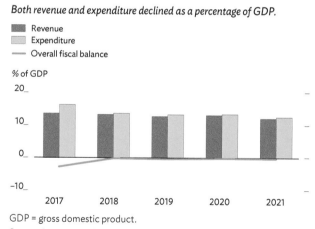

GDP = gross domestic product.
Source: International Monetary Fund. 2021. *Regional Economic Outlook, Middle East and Central Asia*.

The current account achieved a small surplus in 2021 equal to 0.6% of GDP, reflecting higher exports and efforts to limit imports through import substitution and foreign exchange controls. Export revenue is estimated to have risen by 25.6%, mainly on an estimated 35% rise in gas export earnings. Imports are estimated to have risen by only 2.4% because of continued restrictions on imports. Following substantial external loan repayment, external debt declined from an estimated 28.5% of GDP at the end of 2020 to 24.0% a year later (Figure 3.7.6).

Figure 3.7.6 External debt

Substantial loan repayment reduced external debt in 2021.

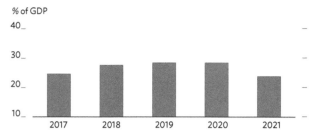

GDP = gross domestic product.
Source: International Monetary Fund. 2021. *Regional Economic Outlook, Middle East and Central Asia.*

Economic prospects

Continued economic recovery is expected with further price increases for oil and gas and with government policies to support domestic production and exports. Progress in COVID-19 vaccination is expected to bring gradual relaxation of restrictions on trade and mobility.

Following presidential elections on 12 March 2022, the new government will release details of a 30-year socioeconomic program that will guide activities until 2052. The program will contain plans and reforms to achieve inclusive, diversified, and green growth. Greater investment is expected toward meeting infrastructure and human development needs, entailing more efforts to attract foreign direct investment.

Growth is projected at 6.0% in 2022 and 5.8% in 2023 (Table 3.7.1). Hydrocarbon production and exports will continue to sustain growth in 2022 and 2023, with the expectation of higher prices and export volumes, while activities in the non-hydrocarbon economy will continue to depend on government programs for import substitution and export promotion.

Table 3.7.1 Selected economic indicators, %

Projections show growth accelerating and a larger current account surplus, with higher inflation in 2022.

	2021	2022	2023
GDP growth	5.0	6.0	5.8
Inflation	12.5	13.0	10.0
CAB/GDP	0.6	1.2	2.4

CAB = current account balance, GDP = gross domestic product.
Source: Asian Development Bank estimates.

With higher export earnings projected and bans on external transportation revoked, relaxation of import constraints should improve supplies of food and other consumer goods for the domestic market. However, inflation is projected to remain elevated at 13.0% in 2022 and 10.0% in 2023, on assumption of higher global commodity prices.

Fiscal tightening will keep the state budget nearly balanced in both years. However, off-budget spending for government projects is expected to remain substantial, obscuring the overall fiscal position.

Higher gas shipments are projected to maintain export growth in the coming years. Higher exports will outpace higher imports expected as import constraints are slowly relaxed. The current account surplus is expected to reach the equivalent of 1.2% of GDP in 2022 and 2.4% in 2023 (Figure 3.7.7). External debt is projected to decline further under scheduled debt amortization to equal 24.0% of GDP at the end of 2022 and 22.0% a year later. In February 2022, Fitch Ratings rated Turkmenistan B+, stable outlook, on the strength of its broadly balanced fiscal and external accounts, underpinned as they are by high energy prices, and willingness to service and repay debts. Among the factors with potential to earn a rating upgrade are improvements to governance standards, the business environment, and statistical reporting.

Figure 3.7.7 Current account balance

High gas and oil prices are projected to lift the current account surplus in 2022 and 2023.

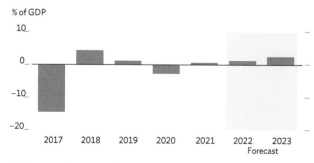

GDP = gross domestic product.
Sources: International Monetary Fund. 2021. *Regional Economic Outlook, Middle East and Central Asia;* Asian Development Bank estimates.

Policy challenge—fiscal policy to promote sustainable and inclusive growth

The pandemic has affected every dimension of country's human development, including health care, employment, incomes, nutrition, and the quality of education. Addressing adverse impacts requires urgent and sustained policy action. Fiscal policy should be at the core of the response and will determine in large part how inclusive and strong recovery will be.

Public expenditure, including off budget sources, has traditionally been skewed toward large investments in physical infrastructure, with the value of investment nearing in years past half of GDP. At the same time, spending has lagged for programs such as social protection, health care, education, and other aspects of human development.

To foster recovery from the pandemic and achieve inclusive and sustainable growth over the longer term, fiscal policy must be recalibrated. It should drive productive transformation to strengthen human capital, generate employment, and make existing public investments more efficient. This calls for greater and more efficient spending in social programs, particularly for health care, education, and social protection. State budget expenditure currently falls as a share of GDP below the average among members of the Organisation for Economic Co-operation and Development (Figure 3.7.8).

A United Nations (UN) 2021 report on the Sustainable Development Goals (SGDs) emphasized the need for greater investment to improve social outcomes. The UN SDGs dashboard for Turkmenistan identifies major challenges to addressing SDGs regarding poverty (SDG1), undernourishment (SDG2), life expectancy (SDG3), decent jobs and access to bank finance (SDG8), and access to the internet and scientific and technical skills (SDG9), as well as other dimensions of human development. Along with the need for higher spending on health and education (SDG17), the report cites the need to improve fiscal transparency, statistical performance,

Figure 3.7.8 Public spending, 2021

Social spending in Turkmenistan is below the OECD average.

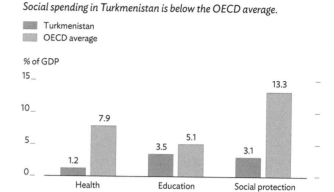

GDP = gross domestic product, OECD = Organisation for Economic Co-operation and Development.
Sources: OECD. 2021. *Government at a Glance 2021*; Asian Development Bank estimates.

and institutional strengthening. The International Monetary Fund estimates that spending an additional amount equal to 8.3% of GDP annually is needed to achieve the SDGs by 2030.

Accumulated fiscal savings provide considerable fiscal space for increased spending on health care, education, social protection, and other dimensions of human development. Greater spending can mitigate social losses during the pandemic, achieve better social outcomes, and contribute to building a more inclusive economy. This should be accompanied by reform to the system of public financial management to ensure that public funds are spent economically, efficiently, and effectively.

Participation in the Public Investment Management Assessment framework of the International Monetary Fund could inform efforts to enhance governance standards and make expenditure more efficient. The timely implementation of a new budget code elaborated with the help of international financial institutions in accordance with international best practice could increase fiscal transparency by subsuming extrabudgetary spending into the state budget, creating a medium-term budget framework, and enforcing fiscal sustainability. This would ensure the effective implementation of the government programs consistent with the SDGs and lift up human development outcomes.

UZBEKISTAN

Strong recovery in industry and services boosted growth in 2021. Inflation slowed, and the current account deficit widened. In 2022 and 2023, lower investment and remittances from Russia will likely curtail private consumption and trim expansion in industry and services. Unchanged utility tariffs in 2022 and monetary tightening should reduce inflation, with lower remittances widening the current account deficit. Uzbekistan needs to mobilize green financing and engage the private sector as it transitions into a green economy.

Economic performance

The government reported growth reviving from 1.9% in 2020 to 7.4% in 2021. On the supply side, expansion in industry rebounded strongly from a modest 0.9% in 2020 to 8.7% in 2021 on gains of 8.2% in manufacturing, with sound recovery in textiles, and 10.7% in mining and quarrying as hydrocarbons and metals recovered. Growth in services jumped from 0.7% to 9.2% on 13.0% expansion in trade, accommodation, and food services, as well as on even higher 17.2% growth in transportation and storage as recovering demand boosted business activity and enterprise production. Expansion in agriculture improved from 2.9% in 2020 to 4.0% in 2021 as 4.1% higher livestock production offset a modest slowdown in crop production from 3.2% to 3.1% caused by shortages of water for cotton and wheat. Growth in construction dropped from 9.5% in 2020 to 6.8% in 2021 as homebuilding reversed 13.5% expansion a year earlier with a marginal 0.1% decline (Figure 3.8.1).

On the demand side, growth in consumption rebounded from 0.3% in 2020 to an estimated 8.5%. Business recovery and an easing of foreign travel restrictions on Uzbek seasonal migrant workers boosted wages and remittances, accelerating expansion in private consumption from 0.4% to an estimated 8.4%. Government spending on social protection, health care, and education doubled growth in public consumption

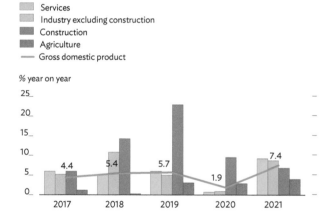

Figure 3.8.1 GDP growth

Growth rebounded in 2021, led by gains in services and industry.

- Services
- Industry excluding construction
- Construction
- Agriculture
- Gross domestic product

% year on year

Source: State Statistics Committee (accessed 11 March 2022).

from 1.4% to an estimated 2.8%. Investment recovered strongly from the pandemic, reversing 4.4% decline in fixed capital formation in 2020 to increase by 5.2% in 2021 on higher public investment in transport and urban infrastructure, while foreign direct investment rose by 18.4%. The deficit in net exports widened by 43.5% for goods and by 33.3% for services.

Inflation slowed from 12.9% in 2020 to 10.7% as electricity and natural gas tariffs remained unchanged

---

This chapter was written by Begzod M. Djalilov of the Uzbekistan Resident Mission, ADB, Tashkent.

in 2021. Food inflation decelerated from 17.3% to 14.4% as edible oil and other essential foods were exempted from import duties and as domestic food production rose by 16.9%. Inflation for goods other than food decelerated from 9.0% to 8.3% and for services from 10.6% to 8.2%.

The fiscal deficit widened from the equivalent of 4.3% of GDP in 2020 to 5.8% in 2021. Higher spending lifted outlays from 31.2% of GDP to 33.5% as those for health care and education rose by a quarter to equal 8.4% of GDP, and as expenditure increased as well for social protection, public investment, and initiatives to spur economic recovery. Revival in business activity raised revenue slightly, from 26.9% of GDP in 2020 to 27.7%. Most of the deficit was financed externally.

The central bank kept its policy rate at 14.0% as inflation remained high and growth rebounded. Credit to the economy reversed contraction by 9.6% in 2020 to grow by 30.7% in 2021 as recovering service and industrial enterprises demanded more capital. Growth in broad money jumped from 17.9% in 2020 to 30.3% as expansion in the money supply in local currency accelerated from 16.4% in 2020 to 29.7% while growth in foreign currency deposits rose from 21.2% to 31.5% (Figure 3.8.2). The Uzbek sum depreciated by a modest 3.4% against the US dollar in 2021, with steady inflow of remittances limiting the extent of depreciation.

Figure 3.8.2 Growth in broad money and key components

Broad money growth accelerated in 2021, with faster growth in net domestic assets.

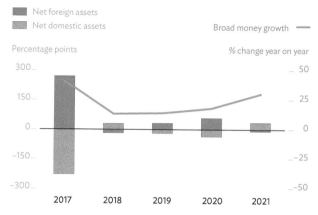

Sources: The Central Bank of the Republic of Uzbekistan (accessed 11 March 2022); Asian Development Bank estimates.

The current account deficit widened from the equivalent of 5.0% of GDP in 2020 to 6.6% in 2021, with the deficit in goods and services expanding from $8.0 billion to $11.3 billion. Exports of goods and services reversed a 15.5% drop in 2020 to grow by 13.1% as strong external demand and prices boosted exports of copper, petrochemicals, natural gas, food, machinery, and equipment, and as demand for transport services rebounded. Imports of goods and services reversed 12.8% decline in 2020 to jump by 23.7% with higher imports of hydrocarbons, petrochemicals, food, and travel services. Net inflows of primary and secondary income rose from $5.0 billion in 2020 to $6.7 billion as pandemic-induced travel restrictions for migrant workers eased (Figure 3.8.3). While net foreign direct investment edged up from the equivalent of 2.8% of GDP to an estimated 3.0%, borrowing financed most of the current account deficit as higher private sector borrowing raised external debt from the equivalent of 60.8% of GDP at the end of 2020 to an estimated 62.0% a year later.

Figure 3.8.3 Current account balance and key components

The current account deficit widened in 2021 as imports rebounded.

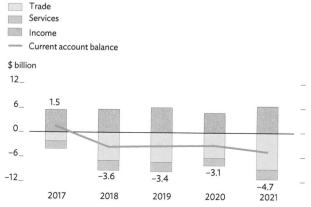

Source: The Central Bank of Uzbekistan (accessed 11 March 2022); Asian Development Bank estimates.

Even as external financing covered most of the budget deficit, public external debt edged down from 35.2% of GDP in 2020 to 35.1%. In 2021, Uzbekistan issued $635 million in 10-year eurobonds and $235 million worth of 3-year eurobonds denominated in Uzbek sum. Gross foreign reserves edged up from $34.9 billion at the end of 2020 to $35.1 billion a year later, providing cover for 15 months of imports. A 3.6% rise in gold reserves offset an 8.6% decline in foreign currency reserves (Figure 3.8.4).

Figure 3.8.4 Gross international reserves

Gross international reserves edged up in 2021 as reserves in gold rose.

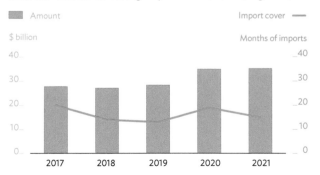

Sources: State Statistics Committee (accessed 11 March 2022); Asian Development Bank estimates.

Table 3.8.1 Selected economic indicators, %

Growth will slow with weaker remittances as tight monetary policy and other measures reduce inflation.

	2020	2021	2022	2023
GDP growth	1.9	7.4	4.0	4.5
Inflation	12.9	10.7	9.0	8.0
CAB/GDP	-5.0	-6.6	-7.0	-6.5

CAB = current account balance, GDP = gross domestic product.
Source: Asian Development Bank estimates.

Economic prospects

Growth is projected to slow to 4.0% in 2022 as moderating private consumption curbs expansion in industry and services, recovering somewhat to 4.5% in 2023 (Figure 3.8.5 and Table 3.8.1). Risks to growth stem from a tense external environment and the possible emergence of new COVID-19 variants. Economic sanctions on Russia are expected to trigger ruble depreciation and layoffs in construction and services, which are projected to cut the number of migrant workers by at least a quarter and sharply curtail remittances. The government is preparing an action plan to cushion the resulting shock, prioritizing social protection, employment generation, and price stability. The aim is to ensure stability in the financial system and company operations, the timely implementation of investment projects, and the reliability of transport and logistics networks by diversifying export destinations.

Figure 3.8.5 Growth forecast

Growth is forecast to slow in 2022 and recover slightly in 2023, led by industry and services.

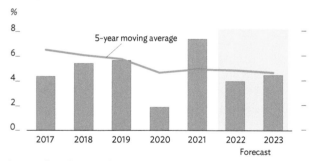

Sources: State Statistics Committee (accessed 11 March 2022); Asian Development Bank estimates.

Vaccine rollout and measures to contain emerging strains of COVID-19 will affect growth. The government retains rules on social distancing, mask wearing, and quarantine measures for travelers from countries with emerging COVID-19 variants.

On the supply side, growth in services is forecast to slow by two-thirds to 3.0% this year with stabilizing turnover in food services, accommodation, storage, and transportation, and then rise to 3.5% in 2023. Similarly, expansion in industry is expected to slow to 5.0% in 2022 after strong recovery in 2021 in textiles, food, and mining and quarrying, rising to 5.5% in 2023. Industry, by contrast, is expected to find support for growth in high domestic consumption of hydrocarbons and growing external need for metals and petrochemicals. Expansion in agriculture is projected at 4.0% in both years as ample water for irrigating cotton and wheat boosts crop production. Growth in construction is forecast to plateau at 8.0% in 2022 and 2023, sustained by planned government programs for housing and local infrastructure and by manufacturing firm expansion.

On the demand side, growth in private consumption is expected to slow to 4.5% in 2022 with cooling post-pandemic demand and the anticipated drop in remittance inflow, which will curtail household income growth, and then edge up to 5.0% in 2023. With government plans to raise wages and spending on the operation and maintenance of public schools and primary health-care facilities in 2022–2024, growth in public consumption is forecast to more than double to 6.5% this year and 7.0% in 2023. An expected drop in foreign direct investment from Russia will slow growth in investment sharply to 4.0% in 2022, recovering to 4.5% in 2023, with spending focused on urban infrastructure, particularly for education and health care, and on upgrading facilities in manufacturing, mining and quarrying, and petrochemicals. The deficit in net exports is anticipated to narrow slightly with lower demand for services and for imports of capital and intermediate goods.

Inflation is anticipated to decelerate to 9.0% in 2022 and 8.0% in 2023 (Figure 3.8.6). The central bank raised its policy rate from 14.0% to 17.0% at its March meeting and is expected to keep it there for the time being. Natural gas and electricity tariffs are forecast to remain unchanged in 2022 as lower remittances and higher unemployment slow growth in household income. The government has retained import duty exemptions for essential foods such as edible oils, poultry, wheat flour, and rice to the end of 2022 to hold down food prices. As of February 2022, annual inflation had slowed from 11.4% a year earlier to 9.7%. Broad money is projected to increase by 20.0% in both 2022 and 2023.

Figure 3.8.6 Inflation

Inflation will decelerate in 2022 and 2023 with smaller price increases for food and services.

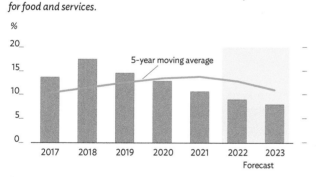

Sources: State Statistics Committee (accessed 11 March 2022); Asian Development Bank estimates.

The fiscal deficit is forecast to narrow to equal 5.0% of GDP in 2022 and 4.0% in 2023 (Figure 3.8.7). To sustain post-pandemic growth, the government adopted a national development strategy for 2022–2026 and a public investment program for 2022–2024 featuring plans to raise outlays for social protection, education, health care, and capital projects. Expenditure is forecast to grow by 9.0% in 2022 to reach 35.0% of GDP before slower growth in outlays moderates expenditure growth to 8.0% in 2023 and, with higher nominal economic growth, reduce it to 33.0% of GDP. Revenue is also projected to rise by 9.0%

in 2022 and 8.0% in 2023 with further improvement in tax collection. To stimulate consumption and expansion in services, the government plans to cut the value-added tax rate to 12.0% and the corporate income tax rate in finance and telecommunications to 15.0% in 2023. Revenue is projected to equal 30.0% of GDP in 2022 and 29.0% in 2023.

Figure 3.8.7 Fiscal balance

The fiscal deficit will narrow in 2022-2023 as pandemic-related expenditure is scaled back.

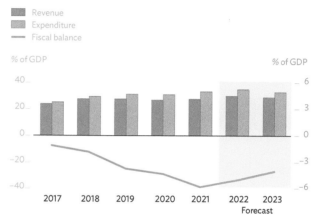

GDP = gross domestic product.
Sources: International Monetary Fund; Asian Development Bank estimates.

The current account deficit is expected to widen further to equal 7.0% of GDP in 2022 as remittances drop to about $3 billion, narrowing slightly to 6.5% in 2023 because of higher GDP as remittances stagnate at $3 billion (Figure 3.8.8). Exports of goods and services—notably of copper, gold, agricultural products, and petrochemicals—are projected to grow by 9.0% in both 2022 and 2023. Growth in imports of goods and services is forecast to plunge by almost half to 12% in both years as demand cools for transport services and for imported capital and intermediate goods. Gross foreign reserves are projected to decline to $34 billion in 2022 and 2023, cover for 11 months of imports, albeit with a modest rise in gold reserves. The authorities aim to keep public debt below 60% of GDP in 2022–2023 by setting a $4.5 billion ceiling on external borrowing in 2022, with public external debt forecast equal to 36% of GDP at the end of both years (Figure 3.8.9).

Figure 3.8.8 Current account balance

The current account deficit will widen in 2022 with declining remittances and narrow marginally in 2023 as growth accelerates.

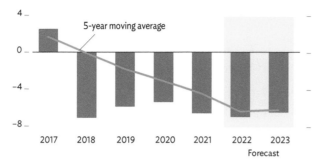

GDP = gross domestic product.
Sources: The Central Bank of the Republic of Uzbekistan (accessed 11 March 2022); Asian Development Bank estimates.

Figure 3.8.9 External debt

The ratio of external public debt to GDP will be marginally higher in 2022 and 2023.

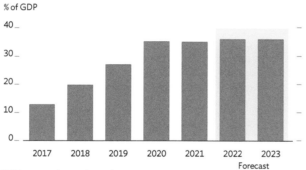

GDP = gross domestic product.
Sources: The Central Bank of the Republic of Uzbekistan (accessed 11 March 2022); Asian Development Bank estimates.

Policy challenge—enabling Uzbekistan's transition toward a green economy

Uzbekistan is extremely vulnerable to climate change. Average temperatures have risen by 0.27°C in each decade from 1950 to 2013 and are projected to be 4.8°C higher by the end of this century. Pressure on urban infrastructure and power supply is expected to intensify as climate change doubles the average number of days with temperatures above 35°C, from about 50 per year during 1986–2005 to over 100 in 2080–2099.

Agriculture, which employs 27% of the workforce, faces challenges from higher temperatures, greater fluctuations in precipitation, and further water shortages. High temperatures induce drought every 5 years, with major economic and social consequences. In 2021, Uzbekistan suffered a 25% shortfall in water resources needed for irrigation, more frequent and severe dust storms, and in some areas shortages even of drinking water. Warming is expected to melt at least one-third of the glacial mass that feeds Uzbekistan's three main rivers, leaving water shortfalls of at least 28% in each river basin by the 2040s. By the 2050s, winter wheat output is projected to drop by 43%, and cotton by 49%, threatening the food security and livelihoods of the half of Uzbekistan's population who live in rural areas.

Uzbekistan generates 90% of its electricity from fossil fuels: 82% from natural gas, 8% from coal, and only 10% from hydropower. Its greenhouse gas (GHG) emissions increased by 6.7% from 1990 to 2017, reaching 5.8 tons of carbon dioxide equivalent per capita and 2.55 kilograms per dollar of GDP. Unless Uzbekistan transforms into a green economy by raising climate awareness, strengthening institutional coordination to plan green public investment, and creating an enabling environment to develop green financing, its GHG emissions will keep rising to meet higher energy demand across the economy, not least in agriculture to power the water pumps that enable 85% of cropland to be irrigated and feed an urban population expanding by 2% annually.

Uzbekistan ratified the Paris Agreement in 2018 and submitted its updated nationally determined contribution in 2021. It aims for a 35% reduction in GHG emissions per unit of GDP from 2010 to 2030 and, toward achieving carbon neutrality in the electric power industry by 2050, expansion in the share of renewable energy sources in electric power generation from 10% in 2019 to 25% by 2030. In 2019, the government adopted its strategy for transition into a green economy during 2019–2030 and is expected to approve the carbon-neutrality action plan for electricity. In transitioning to a green economy, the authorities have prioritized improving energy efficiency, diversifying energy consumption and developing renewable energy sources, adapting to and mitigating climate change, and providing green financing and establishing a supportive regulatory framework.

To support the transition and achieve the nationally determined contribution, as well as other national targets under Sustainable Development Goal 13 on climate action, the government is developing, with external support, its capacity to address climate action in public investment planning.

Transforming into a green economy involves meeting the cost of phasing out or reducing fossil fuel subsidies to state-owned enterprises (SOEs), mobilizing public and private investment in green technologies, and institutionalizing green finance by adopting in the banking system environmental, social, and corporate governance principles when assessing climate risk. Liberalizing hydrocarbon prices and cutting subsidies to SOEs may exacerbate inflation as higher costs are passed through to households, requiring increased social protection and thus a larger fiscal deficit. It is therefore important to ensure policy consistency in the carbon-neutral electricity strategy, the energy tariff policy, SOE reform, and social protection.

As the government aims to hold the fiscal deficit to 3.0% of GDP over the medium term, it must create an enabling environment for private sector involvement in financing climate change mitigation and adaptation in industry and agriculture through green technologies. Expanding public–private partnership and credit guarantees would help mobilize private investment in renewable electric power generation and other essential infrastructure. The banking system, in which state-owned banks hold nearly 85% of assets, is just beginning to adopt green financing. Uzbekistan's transition into a green economy depends on boosting the capacity of bank staff to identify bankable projects for green financing; to introduce environmental, social, and corporate governance principles; and to adopt climate-aware risk assessment.

EAST ASIA

Hong Kong, China

Mongolia

People's Republic of China

Republic of Korea

Taipei,China

HONG KONG, CHINA

Buoyant domestic and external demand buttressed a growth rebound in 2021. Inflation picked up, and the current account surplus widened. Economic recovery will continue this year and next, albeit at a slower pace, given the lingering impact of the pandemic and a global growth slowdown. Inflation will rise in 2022 on continuing economic recovery, and the current account surplus will likely narrow this year and in 2023. Policy should aim to avert long-term economic scarring from recession in 2019–2020.

Economic performance

Following a 2-year recession, the economy in Hong Kong, China expanded by 6.4% in 2021, an 11-year high (Figure 3.9.1). With rapid vaccination progress and the COVID-19 pandemic largely contained last year, economic activity rebounded sharply to grow by 7.8% in the first half (H1) and by 5.1% in H2, supported by buoyant domestic and external demand.

Spearheading the recovery, private consumption expenditure rebounded strongly from an all-time record decline by 10.5% in 2020 to rise by 5.6% in real terms, contributing 3.7 percentage points to growth. The volume of retail sales and the value of restaurant receipts rose, supported by the distribution of consumption vouchers in H2 and easing containment measures (Figure 3.9.2). Labor market conditions also improved, with the seasonally adjusted unemployment rate falling to an average of 3.9% in the fourth quarter (Q4) of 2021, the lowest rate since December 2019.

Figure 3.9.1 Demand-side contributions to growth

GDP rebounded strongly in 2021 to reverse a 2-year contraction.

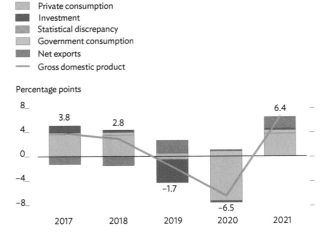

Source: Census and Statistics Department (accessed 08 March 2022).

Figure 3.9.2 Retail sales

Retail sales recovered as containment measures eased.

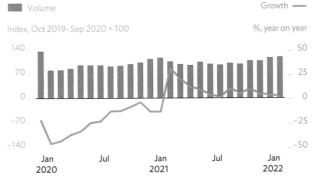

Source: Census and Statistics Department (accessed 08 March 2022).

This chapter was written by Matteo Lanzafame of the Economic Research and Regional Cooperation Department, ADB, Manila, and Michael Timbang, consultant, Economic Research and Regional Cooperation Department, ADB, Manila.

Fixed investment recovered from double-digit contraction in the previous 2 years to expand by 10.1% and add 1.7 percentage points to growth. Machinery, equipment acquisition, and intellectual property licensing rose by 16.7% on an improved investment outlook, while expenditure on buildings and construction rose by 0.3%. Meanwhile, growth in government consumption expenditure moderated only slightly to 4.6% and contributed 0.6 points to growth.

External demand surged in 2021 alongside a recovering global economy. Goods exports reversed 1.4% decline in 2020 to soar by 19.0%, underpinned by import demand from the People's Republic of China (PRC) picking up and rebound in exports to the US and the European Union as demand in these trade partners shifted from services to consumption goods (Figure 3.9.3). After the biggest annual decline on record in 2020, service exports also increased last year, by 1.1%, despite continuing collapse in tourist arrivals and receipts from travel services (Figure 3.9.4). Exports of financial services grew as cross-border financial activities gained momentum in line with buoyant global trade. Meanwhile, imports of goods reversed a 3.2% fall in 2020 to expand by 17.6% last year. Service imports also increased, replacing double-digit decline in 2020 with growth by 1.7%. On balance, net exports contributed 1.9 percentage points to growth.

Figure 3.9.3 Export and import growth

Goods exports surged on recovery in external demand.

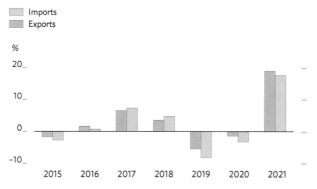

Source: Census and Statistics Department (accessed 08 March 2022).

On the supply side, most industries saw business pick up in 2021. The rebound in global trade provided a boost to the service sector, which reversed 6.7% decline in 2020 to expand by 5.7% last year, with all service industries showing robust growth (Figure

Figure 3.9.4 Tourist arrivals

Continuing travel restrictions flatlined the tourism industry.

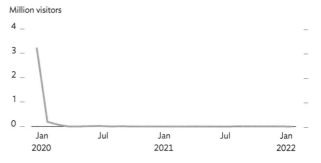

Source: CEIC Data Company (accessed 08 March 2022).

3.9.5). Manufacturing output recovered in tandem with export demand, flipping 5.8% decline in 2020 to 5.5% growth in 2021, in response to the improving external environment. Construction also bounced back, growing by 0.7% last year on an improved investment outlook.

Figure 3.9.5 Supply-side contributions to growth

Services rebounded sharply last year on increasing global trade.

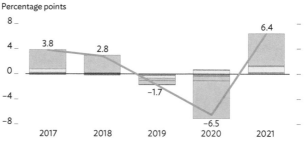

Source: Census and Statistics Department (accessed 08 March 2022).

Headline consumer price inflation accelerated from an average of 0.3% in 2020 to 1.6% in 2021 on base effects and rising commodity and energy prices. On the other hand, after netting out the effects of all government one-off relief measures, the underlying inflation rate fell from an average of 1.3% in 2020 to 0.6% last year. Meanwhile, housing prices continued to be resilient during the pandemic as average residential property prices rose by 3.0% last year, peaking in September at 4.8% higher than in December.

The current account surplus widened from the equivalent of 7.0% of GDP in 2020 to 11.2% in 2021 on positive changes in merchandise trade balance, net inflow of primary income, and services surplus. The overall balance of payments reversed a surplus equal to 9.8% of GDP in 2020 with a 0.3% deficit last year. Gross official reserves stood at $496.9 billion at the end of December 2021, or cover for 8.1 months of imports. Net external financial assets amounted to 5.8 times GDP at the end of 2021, providing this open economy with a thick cushion against sudden external shocks.

The government revised its estimated budget balance for fiscal year 2021 (FY2021, ended 31 March 2022) from a deficit equal to 3.6% of GDP to a surplus of 0.7%. Government revenue was 15.5% higher than the original estimate owing to higher receipts from the land premium and profit taxes. Meanwhile, lower operating expenditure dragged all expenditure down 4.0% from the projection.

Monetary policy remained broadly accommodative in 2021, and financial conditions were robust. The Hong Kong Monetary Authority maintained its base rate at 0.5%, while broad money (M3) supply increased by 4.3%, and domestic credit grew by 4.9% (Figure 3.9.6). Hong Kong, China ranked fourth globally last year among stock exchanges in terms of funds raised through initial public offerings. However, starting late in the year, market sentiment was dampened by expected tightening in US Federal Reserve monetary policy, and the Hang Seng Index plunged by 14.1% year on year in December and by 15.8% in January as stringent

regulatory requirements in the PRC and the rapid spread of the Omicron variant of COVID-19 took their toll on economic activity (Figure 3.9.7).

Figure 3.9.7 Hang Seng Index

Stocks are subdued in anticipation of tightening by the US Federal Reserve.

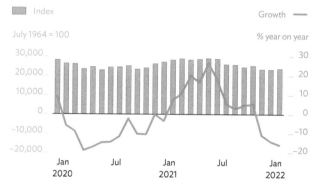

Source: CEIC Data Company (accessed 08 March 2022).

Economic prospects

After the strong rebound last year, growth is forecast to moderate to 2.0% in 2022 (Table 3.9.1). The Omicron wave is putting to the test the zero-COVID containment strategy pursued by Hong Kong, China. The baseline forecast assumes most of the impact on economic activity will be limited to Q1 2022, with the outbreak gradually coming under control and containment measures progressively eased in the latter part of Q2 and more markedly from Q3. Given the local currency's peg to the US dollar, headwinds to growth will come as well from forthcoming Fed tightening, particularly through rising mortgage rates and their depressive effect on the housing market.

Figure 3.9.6 Domestic credit and money supply growth

Growth in domestic credit and broad money supply moderated.

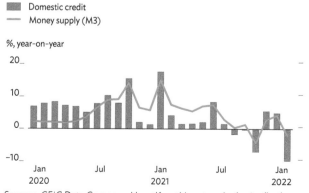

Sources: CEIC Data Company, Hong Kong Monetary Authority (both accessed 08 March 2022).

Table 3.9.1 Selected economic indicators, %

Growth will moderate, with inflation remaining low and the current account surplus narrowing.

	2020	2021	2022	2023
GDP growth	–6.5	6.4	2.0	3.7
Inflation	0.3	1.6	2.3	2.0
CAB/GDP	7.0	11.2	6.0	5.5

CAB = current account balance, GDP = gross domestic product.
Source: Asian Development Bank estimates.

As such, growth forecasts see the economy recovering its pre-pandemic GDP, as it was at the end of 2019, only in Q3 2022, and taking another year to regain GDP at the end of 2018, before violent civil disturbances over several months in 2019. With activity continuing to normalize, growth is seen to accelerate to 3.7% in 2023 (Figure 3.9.8).

Figure 3.9.8 Gross domestic product growth

Growth will moderate this year but pick up in 2023.

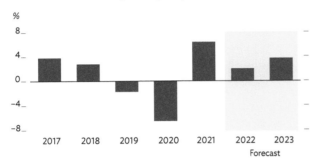

Source: *Asian Development Outlook* database.

While growing at a more moderate pace, domestic demand will remain robust in 2022, supported by a tighter labor market. Private consumption will again be the main driver of growth, benefiting from rising employment and incomes as recovery proceeds and from another round of consumption vouchers. Investment is seen to pick up this year and next, fostered by government support for infrastructure investment projects and innovative technology. Net exports will contribute less to growth with export performance weakening as growth slows in the PRC and the global economy, while imports will continue to strengthen alongside rising domestic output and consumption.

On the supply side, leading indicators suggest that the recent spike in COVID-19 cases is already weighing on business sentiment, pointing to short-term weakness. After 11 consecutive months on the expansive side of 50, the composite purchasing managers' index slipped steadily from 52.6 in November 2021 to 42.9 in February 2022, signaling coming contraction in private sector activity (Figure 3.9.9). Assuming that pandemic disruption is contained from Q2 2022, however, robust resumption in economic recovery is anticipated with services—in particular trade, financial, and professional services—leading the way.

Figure 3.9.9 Purchasing managers' index

A deepening slide in the composite index signals contraction in the coming months.

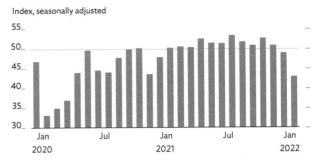

Note: A purchasing managers' index reading <50 signals deterioration, >50 improvement.
Source: CEIC Data Company (accessed 08 March 2022).

Headline inflation is forecast to edge up slightly to average 2.3% in 2022 and 2.0% in 2023, driven by economic recovery and an improving labor market (Figure 3.9.10). Price pressures will remain mild as the economy continues to operate below capacity and spillover from external price pressures remains largely contained. The rise in prices is expected to be gradual and broad based, with most consumer price index components picking up in tandem with the projected growth path.

Figure 3.9.10 Inflation

Inflation is forecast to pick up in tandem with economic recovery.

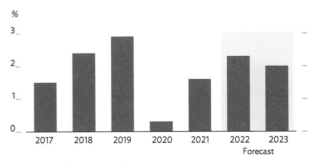

Source: *Asian Development Outlook* database.

Fiiscal policy will remain supportive in 2022, particularly in the short run, with another HK$27 billion fiscal package for the Anti-epidemic Fund set to be rolled out this year. Total government expenditure is projected to increase by 15.5%. Spending on education, social welfare, and health care will account for 60.0% of recurrent expenditure, with health care spending in FY2022 more than twice that of FY2017. Revenue from the land premium is estimated to fall by 15.0%, partly offset by a 3.3% increase in earnings and profits tax and 11.9% higher revenue from stamp duties. The FY2022 fiscal deficit is therefore expected to widen to equal 1.9% of GDP. Once the crisis is over, fiscal consolidation will resume in line with a policy objective for lower budget deficits in the medium term. However, the government forecasts that public expenditure will continue to amount to 24.9% of GDP in the medium-term and that fiscal reserves will increase to 28.9% of GDP by the end of FY2026, or coverage for 16 months of government expenditure.

The outlook for the external sector remains positive. Sustained economic recovery in major trade partners will continue to buoy exports of goods this year despite a highly uncertain global environment. Imports of goods will also rise as domestic demand continues to recover. Net service receipts, on the other hand, will depend on regional trade flows and developments regarding restrictions on the border with the PRC, which are expected to be relaxed in H2 of this year. Net income and service receipts are thus expected to rise alongside increased trade. On balance, the current account surplus is forecast to narrow to equal 6.0% of GDP this year and 5.5% in 2023 (Figure 3.9.11).

Figure 3.9.11 Current account balance

The current account surplus is projected to narrow as imports increase.

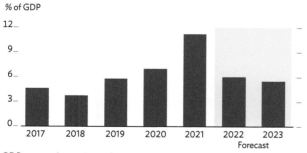

GDP = gross domestic product.
Source: Asian Development Outlook database.

The primary downside risk to the outlook remains the evolution of the pandemic. In an effort to stem rapidly spreading Omicron infections in early February, the government tightened social distancing restrictions to their strictest so far and introduced a mandatory

vaccine pass for access to many services. If the outbreak is not contained, associated disruption to economic activity may persist well beyond Q1, undermine the recovery in private consumption and gross fixed investment expected later this year, and further postpone a pickup in tourism and related activities. External sector developments are hostage to significant uncertainty as well, as the local economy's prospects could be dimmed by unexpectedly severe tightening by the US Fed, worsening PRC–US tussles over trade and technology, or a deeper slowdown in the PRC.

On the upside, early border reopening, especially with the PRC, would support stronger rebounds in household spending and service receipts and payments. In any event, the local economy is well positioned to counter any unexpected challenges to the forecast horizon as it is buffered by ample fiscal reserves, a resilient financial system, and its status as a global trade and finance hub.

Policy challenge—averting long-term economic scarring from recession in 2019–2020

The relative success of Hong Kong, China in the fight against COVID-19—with only slightly more than 200 deaths and 15,000 infections before early February 2022—has not spared its economy from significant damage. Its zero-COVID strategy (dynamic zero-COVID since the arrival of Omicron) has entailed relatively stringent containment restrictions since H2 2020. Associated disruption to economic activity compounded the effects of the global recession to bring about in 2020 a second consecutive year of contraction.

Significant historical evidence, supported by economic analysis, suggests that downturns that are deep, prolonged, or both can leave through several channels persistent scars on an economy—a business cycle feature known as "hysteresis." Indeed, along with a number of Asian economies—notably Indonesia, the Republic of Korea, the Philippines, Malaysia, and Singapore—Hong Kong, China suffered permanent output losses following the Asian financial crisis of 1997 and 1998 despite a rapid return to growth. In light of this, the 2019–2020 recession could have lasting consequences for Hong Kong, China. The challenge for policy makers is to anticipate the medium- and long-term fallout from the crisis and address it.

The labor market is one area where a temporary but deep decline in economic activity can cause persistent damage to an economy. During a downturn, rising unemployment depreciates human capital as fewer new hires have the opportunity to learn by doing and some workers' skills begin to atrophy. As a result, some workers may become structurally unemployed and others reallocated to less productive jobs, both of which lower an economy's productive capacity.

The unemployment rate increased markedly during the 2-year recession from 2.8% at the end of 2018 to a peak of 7.2% in the 3-month period ending in February 2021. It subsequently declined to 3.9% at the end of 2021, but this largely reflected shrinkage in the labor force since mid-2019 (Figure 3.9.12). Underemployment rates followed the same pattern during this period.

Figure 3.9.12 Labor market indicators

The unemployment rate fell as the labor force shrank.

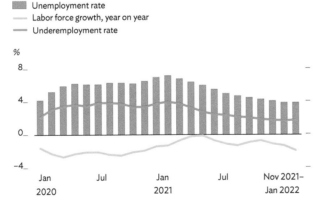

Source: Census and Statistics Department (accessed 08 March 2022).

Active labor market policies are needed to address this issue: notably boosting current education and job-training programs that aim to upgrade workers' human capital and, in particular, digital skills; enhancing job-matching measures to help businesses recruit and retain staff; and providing comprehensive support to more vulnerable workers to alleviate detachment from the labor market.

In line with its unique nature, the COVID-19 crisis may be more damaging than a more typical recession. In particular, school closures necessitated by pandemic containment may cause substantial and persistent learning losses and lower the productivity of future generations of workers. Based on intermediate assumptions regarding the effectiveness of remote learning, analysis published in Asian Development Outlook 2021 showed that in 2020 students in Hong Kong, China lost 43% of a learning-adjusted year of schooling, or school time tweaked to account for the quality of learning. Such losses continued to accumulate last year along with the day count of school closures. Closures resumed again in January 2022 in response to the recent Omicron outbreak.

Mitigating learning losses remains crucial for as long as school closures are necessary. Information and communication technology infrastructure should be strengthened, as should the provision of systematic training to improve digital literacy in students, instructors, and parents. Policy should aim to address as well accumulated learning gaps through, for example, remedial education programs and revised school curricula that allow students to pick up where they left off and are flexible enough to adjust in response to student progress as measured by regular tracking procedures.

School closures and the heavy toll the pandemic took on the labor market likely contributed to increased net migration outflow. The latest government figures show a net outflow of 89,200 residents of Hong Kong, China from mid-2020 to mid-2021. While the current outflow may be partly temporary and related to the pandemic, it nonetheless raises policy-relevant questions. Migration is a selective process, typically involving higher-skilled and better-educated workers and is thus labeled brain drain. As such, continued migration outflow may harm future economic prospects. To the extent that the current trend proves persistent, policies to attract and retain international talent will need to be reinforced.

MONGOLIA

Economic recovery was subdued in 2021 under the continued impact of COVID-19 and border closures. Inflation accelerated, and the current account deficit widened. Growth will rise slightly in 2022 and accelerate in 2023 as the impact of the pandemic wanes. Inflation will rise and the current account deficit will widen in 2022 with the hike in import prices triggered by the Russian invasion of Ukraine and the continued border closure with the People's Republic of China (PRC). Mongolia needs to strengthen its management of mounting contingent liabilities to reduce risk to debt sustainability.

Economic performance

After contracting by 4.6% in 2020, GDP expanded by an anemic 1.4% in 2021. Growth was stymied by unprecedented trade disruption caused by the closure of the main trade portal with the People's Republic of China (PRC) in October 2021, quotas set by the PRC for coal imports from Mongolia, and protracted impacts from COVID-19. Growth reflected substantial private investment and rebound from deep contraction in 2020 that saw 5.2% growth in services enabled by easier COVID-19 restrictions since May and 3.0% growth in mining encouraged by high commodity prices. By contrast, construction, having contracted by 3.8% in 2020, plunged by 31.8% to below its 2016 value, constrained by strict lockdowns in the first 5 months of the year and supply chain disruption caused by border closure. Industry other than mining contracted by 5.8%, and agriculture by 4.3% (Figure 3.10.1).

On the demand side, investment contributed 18.3 percentage points to growth as a substantial increase in private outlays was supported by stimulus measures implemented through banks and a 19.7% increase in net foreign direct investment, mainly into mining (Figure 3.10.2). Government consumption increased by 5.7% on higher social spending, contributing 1.0 point to growth. However, private consumption

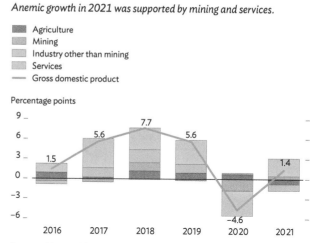

Figure 3.10.1 Supply-side contributions to growth

Anemic growth in 2021 was supported by mining and services.

- Agriculture
- Mining
- Industry other than mining
- Services
- Gross domestic product

Percentage points

Sources: National Statistics Office of Mongolia. Statistical Information Services (accessed 25 February 2022); Asian Development Bank estimates.

shrank by 6.6% and subtracted 4.5 points from growth, constrained by the lowest labor force participation rate since 1994 and high inflation—and despite significant social protection measures in response to COVID-19. The contribution of net exports turned negative, dragging growth down by 13.4 points as exports of goods and services fell by 14.5% while imports increased by 9.6%.

This chapter was written by Declan Magee and Bold Sandagdorj of the Mongolia Resident Mission, ADB, Ulaanbaatar.

Figure 3.10.2 Demand-side contributions to growth

Investment was a major driver of growth, but private consumption contracted.

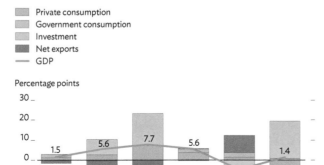

Sources: National Statistics Office of Mongolia. Statistical Information Services (accessed 25 February 2022); Asian Development Bank estimates.

Business costs and consumer price inflation rose on disrupted supply of important consumer goods and industrial inputs under COVID-19 restrictions and the closure of the main trade portal with the PRC. The average consumer price index rose from 3.7% in 2020 to 7.1% in 2021, with prices 13.4% higher in December 2021 than a year earlier. Food price inflation soared from 8.5% in 2020 to 20.4%, and prices for transportation services and hotel, dining, and catering services also rose substantially more quickly than in 2020 (Figure 3.10.3).

Figure 3.10.3 Inflation

Consumer price inflation exceeded the central bank target.

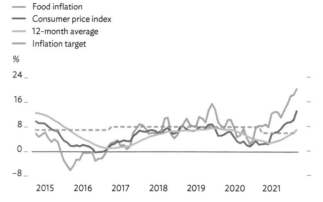

Sources: National Statistics Office of Mongolia. Statistical Information Services (accessed 25 February 2022); Parliament resolutions on monetary policy guidelines, 2014–2021 (accessed 24 January 2022); Asian Development Bank estimates.

The Mongolian togrog remained largely stable against the US dollar as the central bank frequently intervened in the foreign exchange market and pursued measures against dollarization. The togrog appreciated in real effective terms by 12.3% (Figure 3.10.4).

Figure 3.10.4 Exchange rate

High inflation caused togrog appreciation in real effective terms.

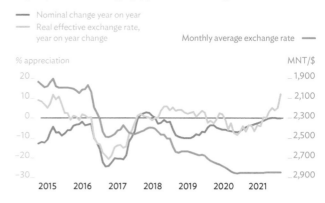

Sources: Bank of Mongolia. *Monthly Statistical Bulletin* (accessed 28 February 2022); Asian Development Bank estimates.

The fiscal balance improved to a deficit equal to 3.1% of GDP, narrower by 6.4 percentage points as revenue increased by 37.0%, outpacing 11.7% expenditure growth. However, the primary fiscal balance remained negative and the structural fiscal deficit remained high at 6.8% of GDP, albeit narrower than in 2020 and 2.0 points less than its legal ceiling (Figure 3.10.5). Public debt, including central bank external liabilities, decreased by 11.4 percentage points to equal 80.0% of GDP, the difference reflecting a 2.8% decline in government debt and 14.9% growth in nominal GDP.

The Bank of Mongolia, the central bank, maintained an accommodative monetary policy to support economic recovery, keeping the policy rate unchanged at 6.0% in 2021 and conducting repo operations to alleviate a credit crunch. It continued to defer consumer and mortgage loan repayment to ease pressure on retail borrowers, and it extended regulatory forbearance to corporate borrowers. With this support, bank credit growth recovered from 4.1% contraction in 2020 to grow by 20.0% in 2021, and broad money supply grew by 15.0% (Figure 3.10.6). The value of nonperforming loans increased by 3.5%, but their ratio to all loans shrank by 1.6 percentage points to 9.8%.

Figure 3.10.5 Government budget

The fiscal deficit narrowed in 2021 despite delayed budget consolidation.

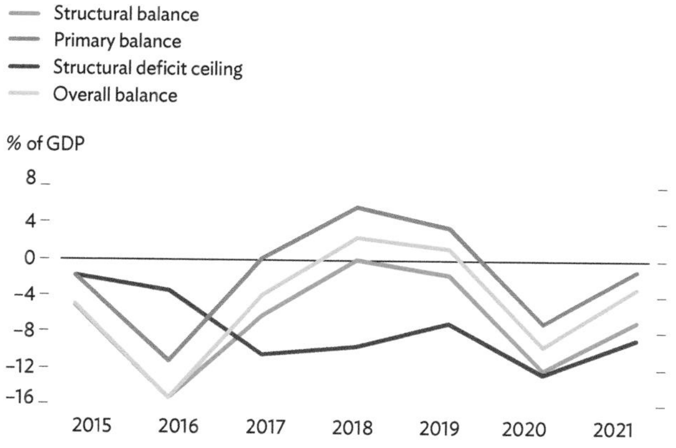

— Structural balance
— Primary balance
— Structural deficit ceiling
— Overall balance

% of GDP

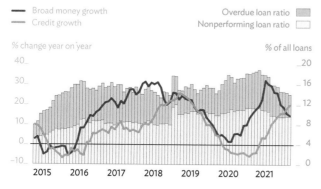

GDP = gross domestic product.

Note: The primary balance is the gap between revenue and expenditure, adjusted by interest expenditure. The structural balance is the gap between expenditure and the revenue trend over the longer term, the ceiling for which is set by the Fiscal Stability Law but subject to parliamentary amendment.

Sources: National Statistics Office of Mongolia. Statistical Information Services (accessed 25 February 2022); Parliament resolutions on government budget, 2015–2021 (accessed 25 February 2022); Asian Development Bank estimates.

Figure 3.10.6 Money and credit

Stimulus measures for smaller enterprises allowed significant recovery in loan growth.

— Broad money growth   Overdue loan ratio
— Credit growth   Nonperforming loan ratio

% change year on year   % of all loans

Sources: Bank of Mongolia. Monthly Statistical Bulletin and Banking Sector Consolidated Balance Sheet (accessed 14 February 2022); Asian Development Bank estimates.

The current account deficit expanded sharply to equal 13.0% of GDP. This partly reflected a 25.8% decline in the merchandise trade surplus as imports of goods increased by 32.7%, outpacing 18.0% growth in exports. The service deficit narrowed to equal 9.1% of GDP. However, the primary income deficit almost doubled, driven largely by a 61.7% increase

in investment income expatriation (Figure 3.10.7). Despite a 22.0% increase in the financial account surplus, the overall balance of payments recorded a deficit of $222 million. Foreign exchange reserves decreased by 3.7% to $4.37 billion, or cover for 5.8 months of imports of goods and services, 1.6 months less than in 2020 (Figure 3.10.8).

Figure 3.10.7 Current account balance

Balance of payment pressures increased as the current account deficit widened sharply.

▨ Trade balance in goods
▨ Trade balance in services
▨ Primary income balance
■ Secondary income balance
— CAB   CAB as % of GDP —

$ billion   %

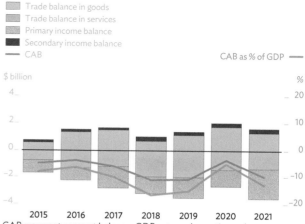

CAB = current account balance, GDP = gross domestic product.

Sources: Bank of Mongolia. *Balance of payments statistics* (accessed 14 February 2022); Asian Development Bank estimates.

Figure 3.10.8 Gross international reserves

Foreign exchange reserves remained stable, but cover for imports decreased.

▨ Gross international reserves   Months of import cover —

$ billion   Months

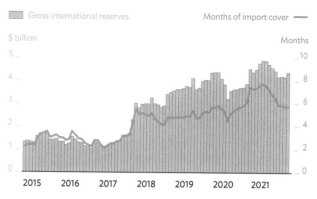

Sources: Bank of Mongolia. *External sector statistics* (accessed 14 February 2022); Asian Development Bank estimates.

Economic prospects

Recovery will be more gradual in 2022 and 2023 than anticipated in 2021 by either the authorities or international financial institutions, constrained by persistent trade disruption and its spillover into industrial output, a cautious business outlook because of high inflation, tighter external financing conditions, and complex geopolitical risks that elevate uncertainty. Agriculture is expected to rebound, however, and services will continue to contribute to growth in both years.

Driven by investment and a positive outlook for coking coal and metal prices, GDP growth is forecast to rise to 2.3% in 2022. Mutual understanding recently reached between the government and the major investors in the Oyu Tolgoi project ensures continued development of the underground mine and secures important investment funds. This will drive investment growth in Mongolia alongside a planned 54.5% increase in government capital expenditure and expected moderate growth in credit to the private sector. Fiscal policy will remain expansionary with planned expenditure growth of 15.3%. This is primarily in response to prolonged impacts from COVID-19, but spillover from Russian invasion of Ukraine is likely to exert continued pressure on spending. While private consumption will return to growth in 2022, it will continue to be constrained by low employment, real income losses to high inflation, and the phasing out of some household support measures. Net exports will drag on growth as rising imports of goods and services to supply the investment boom outpace export growth.

In 2023, business sentiment and economic prospects will improve as COVID-19 concerns and trade disruption ease. Growth will climb to 5.6%, boosted by domestic demand, investment, and stronger recovery in agriculture, industry, and services (Figure 3.10.9 and Table 3.10.1). Unlike in 2020 and the first half of 2021, Mongolia's policy to live with COVID-19 will be well founded on a successful vaccination rollout and sustained to the forecast horizon, and this will buoy domestic demand. The authorities have announced that credit-support operations to smaller enterprises will continue in 2022, but this measure is expected to be phased out in 2023. The contribution of consumption to growth is expected to increase, but that of investment will decline as mining investment winds down, and net exports will start to contribute to growth as exports rise.

Figure 3.10.9 Gross domestic product growth

Recovery will be more gradual than expected because of persistent uncertainty.

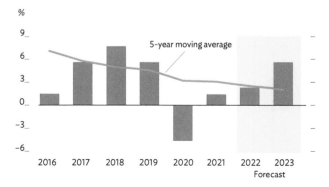

Source: *Asian Development Outlook* database.

Table 3.10.1 Selected economic indicators, %

Growth will accelerate, but inflation and the current account deficit will remain high.

	2020	2021	2022	2023
GDP growth	−4.6	1.4	2.3	5.6
Inflation	3.7	7.1	12.4	9.3
CAB/GDP	−5.1	−13.0	−16.3	−12.7

CAB = current account balance, GDP = gross domestic product.
Source: Asian Development Bank estimates.

Average inflation will accelerate further to 12.4% in 2022 as supply shocks and trade disruption continue. Significantly higher fuel prices will translate into higher business costs, and togrog depreciation will pass through to prices for imported goods. Inflation is expected to moderate to 9.3% in 2023 as these factors ease but will still exceed the central bank target of 4%–8% (Figure 3.10.10).

The current account deficit is projected to widen in 2022, mainly on an expected increase in imports of goods and services, higher international oil prices, and investment income outflow. It will narrow in 2023 as COVID-19 and its impact on trade and supply chains fades, allowing exports to increase.

Growth prospects in 2022 and 2023 will depend heavily on when the major trade portals with the PRC reopen, whether COVID-19 stages a return, and how Mongolia responds to economic and fiscal pressures

Figure 3.10.10 Average inflation

High inflation remains a major macroeconomic risk and monetary policy challenge.

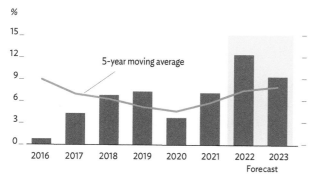

Source: *Asian Development Outlook* database.

from the Russian invasion of Ukraine. The major downside risks to the outlook stem from prolonged closures and restrictions at the main trade portals with the PRC. New waves of COVID-19 variants in either Mongolia or the PRC would delay recovery from the pandemic. Meanwhile, the Russian invasion of Ukraine may disrupt trade with the Russian Federation and exchanges between Mongolia and Europe that transit it, stoking inflation, incurring higher financing needs, and possibly causing fuel shortages. Should the situation in Ukraine continue, this will deepen impacts on the balance of payments and the government budget and would result in lower GDP growth. Domestically, possible worsening of nonperforming loans and consequent balance sheet distress in financial institutions and corporations weigh on the growth outlook over the medium term.

Policy challenge—managing risk from contingent liabilities

Mongolia faces increased contingent liabilities and associated risks because of its plan to increase financing for capital projects under the New Revival Policy, combined with large and persistent existing financing needs and its underlying economic vulnerability. These risks arise from sovereign guarantees, public–private partnership contracts, concession agreements, and the debt owed by state-owned enterprises (SOEs), notably the 100%

government-owned Development Bank of Mongolia (DBM). Further, past experience shows risk arising from disputes between the government and international investors that require international arbitration. Historically, weak monitoring and oversight, political interference, and consequent mismanagement of government assets and liabilities, including contingent liabilities, have placed large burdens on the government budget and foreign exchange reserves, as well as raised reputational risks.

As of January 2022, the DBM loan portfolio accounted for 15.4% of all bank loans. Only 16.8% of DBM loans were classified as performing, while 57.8% were nonperforming. More than two-thirds recorded insufficient collateral, indicating high risk of insolvency. DBM is now seriously challenged to repay or refinance external obligations maturing in 2023 that equal 23% of current Mongolian gross international reserves and include some bonds with sovereign guarantees. Lost confidence may render DBM unable to roll over its external obligations to international lenders and bond holders, posing contingency risks for the government budget.

The government and the Rio Tinto mining company recently agreed to write off the entire $2.3 billion loan owed by the SOE Erdenes Mongol for its ownership of the government's 34% stake in the Oyu Tolgoi project. This large stake in one of the world's most important copper projects can easily be leveraged to raise funds for other priority investments. It presents a huge opportunity but only if governance of the use of such funds is significantly strengthened. As such, the government should prioritize legal reform to better regulate SOE operations and its own contingent liabilities. The legal and regulatory framework should align with international standards and best practices through appropriate legislation and strong enforcement. Laws should aim to professionalize boards of directors and management teams, require high corporate governance and transparency and disclosure standards for all SOEs, prohibit political influence in business processes and decision making, ensure a level playing field between SOEs and private entities, and enhance state responsibility for ethical corporate strategy and performance.

PEOPLE'S REPUBLIC OF CHINA

Despite continued export strength and increased fiscal support, economic growth will likely moderate in 2022 under lackluster domestic demand. Following modest food price deflation in 2021, inflation is projected to pick up in line with higher nonfood prices before easing marginally in 2023. The current account surplus is forecast to moderate. Reform to fiscal relations between the central government and local governments is key to narrowing the local government fiscal gap and equalizing the delivery of basic public services across regions.

Economic performance

Economic growth in the People's Republic of China (PRC) recovered to 8.1% in 2021. Though growth was up from 2.2% in 2020, the economy showed signs of slowing in the second half (H2) of 2021, with GDP growth in the fourth quarter (Q4) at 4.0% (Figure 3.11.1).

Figure 3.11.1 Economic growth

The economy recovered in the first half of 2021, but retail sales slowed sharply in the second half.

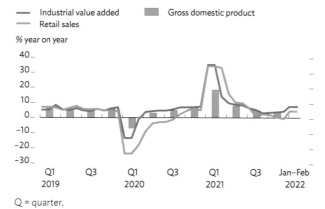

Q = quarter.
Sources: CEIC Data Company (accessed 15 March 2022); Asian Development Bank estimates.

On the demand side, consumption surged to become the main driver of growth in 2021. After subtracting 0.2 percentage points in 2020, it contributed 5.3 points in 2021 (Figure 3.11.2).

Figure 3.11.2 Demand-side contributions to growth

Consumption restored its usual strong contribution to growth in 2021.

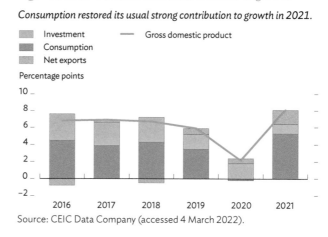

Source: CEIC Data Company (accessed 4 March 2022).

Retail sales, household income, and household consumption experienced rapid growth in H1 2021 before momentum slowed in H2. In 2021 as a whole, retail sales reversed decline by 5.3% in 2020 to grow by an estimated 10.7% in real terms, despite decelerating over the course of 2021. In December 2021, real retail sales even contracted by an estimated 0.5% year on year, reflecting new COVID-19 outbreaks and tightening restrictions to contain them. Growth in real household income accelerated from 2.1% in 2020 to 8.1% in 2021 (Figure 3.11.3). Household consumption turned around decline by 4.0% in real terms in 2020 to accelerate by 12.6% in 2021.

This chapter was written by Dominik Peschel of the People's Republic of China Resident Mission, ADB, Beijing and Wenyu Liu, consultant.

Figure 3.11.3 Growth in income and consumption expenditure per capita

Income and consumption growth were subdued in Q4 2021.

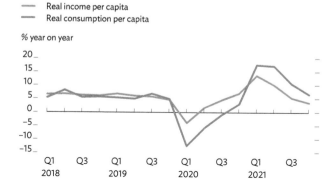

— Real income per capita
— Real consumption per capita

% year on year

Q = quarter.
Sources: CEIC Data Company (accessed 4 March 2022); Asian Development Bank estimates.

A slowdown in infrastructure and real estate investment dragged down the contribution of investment to growth. At 1.1 percentage points in 2021, the contribution was down from 1.8 percentage points in 2020. Growth in fixed asset investment surged to 12.6% in H1 2021, slowed in H2, and settled at 4.9% for the full year, which was still above 2.9% in 2020 (Figure 3.11.4).

Figure 3.11.4 Growth in fixed asset investment

Manufacturing investment grew strongly in 2021, while infrastructure investment remained virtually unchanged.

— All fixed assets   — Infrastructure
— Manufacturing   — Real estate

% year on year, year to date

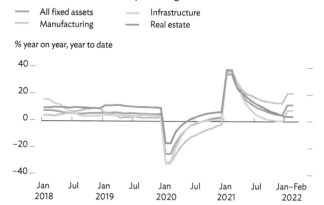

Source: CEIC Data Company (accessed 15 March 2022).

Driven by strong growth in high-tech manufacturing, manufacturing investment recovered from contraction by 2.2% in 2020 to grow by 13.5% in 2021. Infrastructure investment edged down from 0.9% in 2020 to 0.4% as new special bond issuance by local

governments to finance infrastructure investment was slow in H1 2021. Real estate investment contracted in H2 2021 as tightening measures affected the real estate market, slowing growth from 7.0% in 2020 to 4.4% in 2021. Strong exports increased the contribution of net exports to growth in 2021 from 0.6 percentage points a year earlier to 1.7 points.

On the supply side, services were the main contributor to growth, their contribution increasing from 1.0 percentage point in 2020 to 4.4 points in 2021 (Figure 3.11.5).

Figure 3.11.5 Supply-side contributions to growth

Services contributed more than industry to growth in 2021.

▨ Services   — Gross domestic product
■ Industry
■ Agriculture

Percentage points

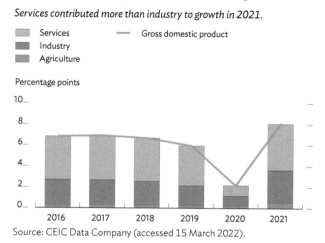

Source: CEIC Data Company (accessed 15 March 2022).

Within services, transportation and information technology grew rapidly, while accommodation and catering recovered from a low base, as did wholesale and retail trade. Industry's contribution to growth in 2021 expanded from 1.0 percentage point a year earlier to 3.1 points. Growth in the secondary sector accelerated from 2.5% in 2020 to 8.2%. Within this sector, value added in industry expanded by 9.6% in 2021, while construction grew by only 2.1%, held down by contraction in H2 2021. Growth in agriculture swelled from 3.1% in 2020 to 7.1% in 2021 on record-high grain output and recovery in pork production, improving its contribution to GDP growth from 0.2 percentage points in 2020 to 0.5 points.

The labor market recovered only gradually in 2021. The surveyed urban unemployment rate edged down by 0.5 percentage points to 5.1% in 2021. New urban jobs increased by 830,000 to 12.69 million in 2021, exceeding the annual goal of 11 million. However, the surveyed unemployment rate for workers aged 16–24 stood at 14.3% in 2021, more than triple the 4.4% for workers aged 25–59, showing pressure on the youth labor market. The number of rural labor migrants working in urban areas edged up by 2.1 million to 171.7 million at the end of 2021, reflecting gradual improvement in urban labor market conditions. However, the figure was still 2.5 million lower than before the pandemic.

Despite much higher producer prices, consumer price inflation slowed from an average of 2.5% in 2020 to 0.9% in 2021 (Figure 3.11.6). Food prices retreated sharply from 10.9% inflation in 2020 to 1.4% deflation in 2021 as pork prices normalized. Nonfood inflation picked up over the course of the year from an average of 0.4% in 2020 to 1.4%. At the same time, pass-through from higher producer prices to consumer prices was moderate in 2021. Producer prices surged by 8.1% on average in 2021, having declined by 1.8% a year earlier. Reflecting government moves to stabilize rising raw material prices and ease an energy shortage, producer price inflation moderated from a peak in October 2021 that was the highest in decades.

Figure 3.11.6 Monthly inflation

Producer prices rose sharply in 2021, while consumer price inflation remained moderate.

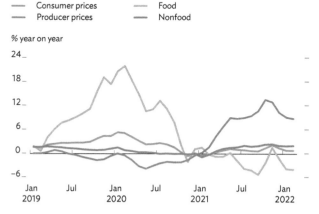

Source: CEIC Data Company (accessed 15 March 2022).

Government measures to cool the real estate market brought temporary market turmoil in H2 2021, slowing price increases for newly constructed homes in the top 70 cities from an average of 4.9% in 2020 to 3.6% in 2021 (Figure 3.11.7). Price increases in tier 1 cities

nevertheless accelerated by 1.7 percentage points in 2021 to an average of 5.3%, while increases slowed in tier 2 and tier 3 cities.

Figure 3.11.7 Price increase for newly constructed homes

Price rises in first tier cities outpaced the overall trend in 2021.

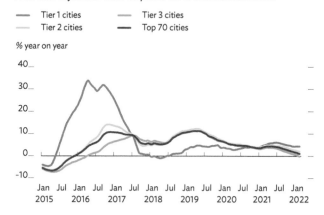

Note: Tier 1 cities are Beijing, Guangzhou, Shanghai, and Shenzhen; tier 2 has 31 provincial capitals and larger municipalities; and tier 3 has 35 other cities.
Sources: CEIC Data Company (accessed 16 March 2022); Asian Development Bank estimates.

Monetary policy remained largely unchanged in 2021. The 1-year loan prime rate edged down from 3.85% to 3.80% in December 2021 to have only marginal impact on the financing costs of corporations and households, then it declined further after a cut by 10 basis points in the 1-year medium-term lending facility to 2.85% in mid-January 2022 (Figure 3.11.8).

Figure 3.11.8 Bank lending and policy rates

No changes were made to policy rates in 2021.

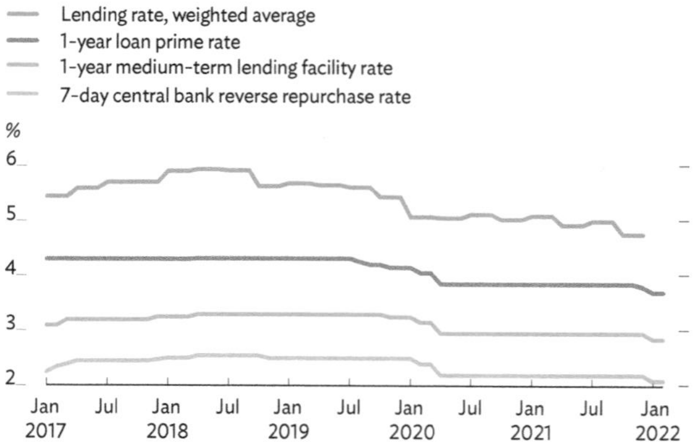

Source: CEIC Data Company (accessed 4 March 2022).

The People's Bank of China, the central bank, also cut the 7-day reverse repurchase rate by 10 basis points to keep it aligned. Furthermore, it lowered the required reserve ratio for banks twice in 2021, by 50 basis points in July and the same in December 2021 (Figure 3.11.9).

Figure 3.11.9 Reserve requirement ratios for financial institutions

The ratio has been cut twice since mid-2021.

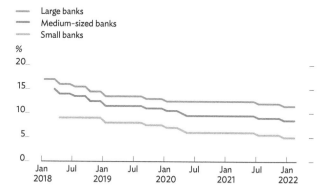

Source: CEIC Data Company (accessed 15 March 2022).

Credit growth moderated in 2021. Total social financing—a broad credit aggregate that includes bank loans, government and corporate bonds, and shadow bank and equity financing—was up by 10.3% at the end of 2021 from a year earlier (Figure 3.11.10).

Figure 3.11.10 Growth in broad money, credit outstanding, and government bonds outstanding

Stricter reining in of shadow bank financing resumed in 2021.

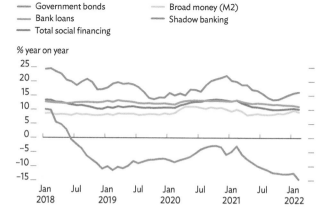

Note: Shadow banking comprises entrust loans, trust loans, and banks' acceptance bills.
Source: Asian Development Bank calculations using data from CEIC Data Company (accessed 15 March 2022).

Bank loans outstanding had increased by 11.6% by the end of 2021, growth slowing from 13.0% at the end of the previous year. Government bonds outstanding rose by 15.2%, while shadow bank financing declined by 12.8% with the resumption of government efforts to rein it in. Growth in broad money (M2) moderated from 10.1% in 2020 to 9.0%.

The annual budget deficit improved in 2021 as fiscal expenditure grew only marginally. The deficit narrowed from the equivalent of 6.2% of GDP in 2020 to 3.8% in 2021 (Figure 3.11.11).

Figure 3.11.11 General government fiscal revenue and expenditure

A high fiscal deficit in Q4 2021 partly undid earlier fiscal consolidation efforts in 2021.

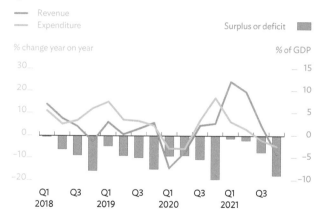

GDP = gross domestic product, Q = quarter.
Note: Public finance budget only.
Source: Asian Development Bank calculations using data from CEIC Data Company (accessed 4 March 2022).

After declining by 3.9% in 2020, fiscal revenue expanded by 10.7% in 2021, with value-added tax revenue recovering by 11.8% in line with general tax revenue higher by 11.9%. Fiscal expenditure grew marginally by 0.3% in 2021 with expenditure cuts for environmental protection, agriculture, and transportation creating space for increases in science, education, and social security and employment. New local government special bond issues—not included in the general budget—amounted to CNY3.58 trillion in 2021, slightly lower than the annual quota of CNY3.65 trillion (Figure 3.11.12).

Figure 3.11.12 Local government special bond issues

Special bond issues picked up in the second half of 2021.

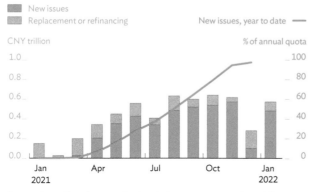

Source: Asian Development Bank calculations using data from CEIC Data Company (accessed 16 March 2022).

The current account surplus edged down from the equivalent of 1.9% of GDP in 2020 to 1.8% in 2021, the merchandise trade surplus down from 3.5% of GDP to 3.1% (Figure 3.11.13).

Figure 3.11.13 Current account balance and merchandise trade

Export performance remained strong in 2021.

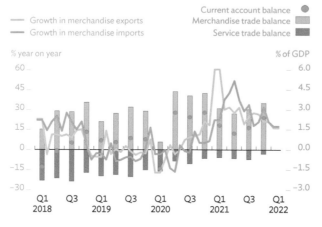

GDP = gross domestic product, Q = quarter.
Note: January–February data are combined to exclude the Lunar New Year effect.
Source: Asian Development Bank calculations using data from CEIC Data Company (accessed 18 March 2022).

Outperforming expectations during the global pandemic, growth in merchandise exports surged from 4.6% in 2020 to 29.0% in 2021, while imports reversed 0.6% decline to increase by 34.6%, driven

by higher commodity prices. Acceleration in exports was broad, extending from mechanical and electrical products to base metals and such consumer goods as furniture, toys, and apparel. Geographically, exports to the European Union increased by 32.2%, to the US by 27.5%, to Southeast Asia by 25.6%, and to Japan by 16.2%. The service deficit is estimated to have narrowed further with a smaller deficit in tourism.

Net foreign direct investment increased from the equivalent of 0.7% of GDP in 2020 to 1.2% in 2021 (Figure 3.11.14). Inflow expanded in line with a recovering economy, while outflow stayed broadly stable. Meanwhile, net capital outflow from the PRC in the form of loans to foreign entities and deposits abroad fell sharply from a high in Q1 2021 alongside a cooling domestic economy, with loans even reversing direction in Q3 2021. Yield on the 10-year PRC government bond moderated from 3.15% at the end of 2020 to 2.78% a year later. Reserve assets edged up to $3.43 trillion at the end of 2021, adding $70.4 billion from a year earlier.

Figure 3.11.14 Balance of payments

The current account surplus was solid in 2021, and net FDI improved.

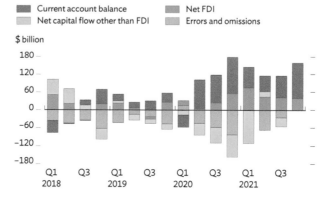

FDI = foreign direct investment, Q = quarter.
Note: For Q4 2021, only data on the current account and FDI is available.
Source: Asian Development Bank calculations using data from CEIC Data Company (accessed 4 March 2022).

The renminbi appreciated by 2.3% in nominal terms against the US dollar in 2021 to CNY6.38 at year-end (Figure 3.11.15). The currency appreciated by 8.0% in nominal effective terms and—taking inflation into account—by 4.4% in the real effective terms.

Figure 3.11.15 Renminbi exchange rates

The renminbi appreciated in 2021.

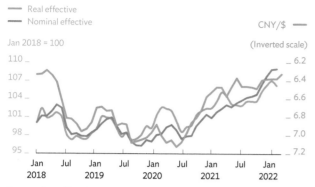

Source: Asian Development Bank calculations using data from CEIC Data Company (accessed 4 March 2022).

Economic prospects

Economic growth is expected to remain moderate in early 2022 before picking up slightly in the middle of the year. Despite some slowing, merchandise export growth should continue to contribute to growth in industry in 2022 while services gradually recover further in line with improving household consumption. Fine-tuning of housing market restrictions promises to stabilize the housing market and enable construction to pick up. Monetary policy will likely ease in 2022 to support higher fiscal expenditure—including infrastructure investment—and shore up economic growth. On balance, GDP is expected to grow by 5.0% in 2022, slowing to 4.8% in 2023 in line with moderating potential growth as the labor force shrinks and return to investment declines (Figure 3.11.16 and Table 3.11.1).

Figure 3.11.16 GDP growth forecast

GDP growth has been on a declining trend.

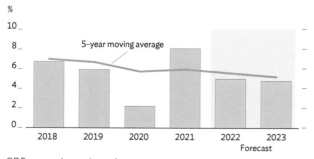

GDP = gross domestic product.
Source: *Asian Development Outlook* database.

Table 3.11.1 Selected economic indicators, %

After recovery in 2021, economic growth is forecast to slow this year and next.

	2020	2021	2022	2023
GDP growth	2.2	8.1	5.0	4.8
Inflation	2.5	0.9	2.3	2.0
CAB/GDP	1.9	1.8	1.5	1.2

CAB = current account balance, GDP = gross domestic product.
Source: Asian Development Bank estimates.

Domestic demand is expected to improve gradually in 2022. COVID-19 persistence (Figure 3.11.17) continues to weigh on consumer confidence and thus dampen growth in household demand. Investment looks set to improve in 2022. Real estate investment will likely pick up in 2022 with borrowing curbs on the sector sustained but adjusted to facilitate market stabilization and gradual recovery. Growth in manufacturing investment should hold up, and infrastructure investment will accelerate, reflecting carryover from new local government special bonds issued in Q4 2021 and government plans to increase infrastructure investment. Improving real estate and infrastructure investment should help stabilize economic growth this year.

Figure 3.11.17 Weekly new confirmed COVID-19 cases

In the fourth quarter of 2021, new COVID-19 cases increased but from a very low base.

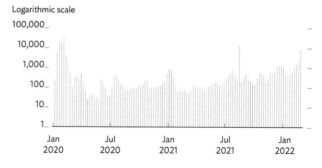

COVID-19 = coronavirus disease 2019.
Source: Asian Development Bank calculations using data from CEIC Data Company (accessed 15 March 2022).

The weak contribution of investment to growth in 2021 should thus revert in line with higher infrastructure investment, while that of net exports will ease in 2022 as export growth slows. Consumption should keep its position as the primary contributor to growth in 2022 and again in 2023, followed by investment and net exports.

On the supply side, services are expected to outpace industry, supported by gradual recovery in household consumption. At the same time, hospitality, recreation, and tourism will remain hampered by the zero-tolerance COVID-19 policy and consequent lockdowns and travel restrictions. In line with continued export growth, manufacturing will continue to support growth in industry, while restrictions on the housing market are expected to remain and, notwithstanding their fine-tuning, dampen recovery in construction and related industries. In addition, supply chain disruption, rising input costs, and moderating growth in external demand may weigh on growth in manufacturing, though high-tech and innovative industries will continue to benefit from government support. Agriculture should expand steadily but less than in 2021, a particularly strong year.

The labor market outlook is mixed. It is expected to profit from increased government fiscal spending and from higher infrastructure and real estate investment. However, COVID-19 continues to weigh on consumer spending, capping improvement potential in the labor market for services. Also, the government expects 10.76 million new college and university graduates to enter the labor force in 2022, an all-time high that will apply further pressure on the youth labor market.

Consumer price inflation is forecast at 2.3% in 2022, notably higher than in 2021 (Figure 3.11.18). Food price deflation should fade and nonfood inflation rise as some producers pass on higher input prices, a step that many have avoided so far given lackluster domestic demand. As commodity price pressures are unlikely to subside in 2022, and global energy prices are forecast to rise sharply, producer price inflation is expected to stay elevated, which may force producers to pass on higher input prices. However, only moderate transmission from higher producer prices to consumer prices is expected as higher input prices can be passed on to end consumers only gradually because household demand is still recovering and downstream competition is stiff, constraining room for markups. In 2023, inflation is expected to moderate to 2.0% in line with lower GDP growth.

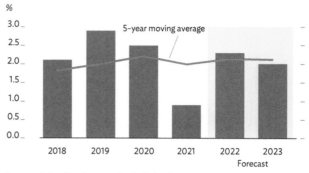

Figure 3.11.18 Inflation forecast

Inflation is forecast to pick up but stay within its previous range.

Source: Asian *Development Outlook* database.

Monetary policy will likely ease in 2022. The central bank faces two major policy challenges. The first pertains to credit allocation, the second to setting interest rates in a global environment that features the central banks of most major economies preparing to tighten monetary policy while economic conditions in the PRC call for monetary loosening.

Credit to the real estate sector will remain regulated. However, a cap on such loans in 2021 caused friction that the country can hardly afford with a weaker growth outlook for 2022. Borrowing restrictions will therefore need to be adjusted to allow gradual recovery in the housing market, and bad loans to real estate developers must be addressed. Further, credit to micro and small firms will likely suffer given their weaker collateral in an environment of declining economic growth, and nonperforming loans are expected to increase after a loan repayment moratorium for such firms expired at the end of 2021. This could make banks even less willing to lend to micro and small firms, which are often riskier loans. Aside from tighter credit, continuing measures to rein in shadow bank financing will curtail companies' financing options aside from banks. Under these circumstances, frequent regulatory fine-tuning is expected from the central bank to guide bank lending in 2022. A reduction in the required reserve ratio for commercial banks is likely this year to support credit growth.

A further small reduction in short-term policy rates is likely. The cut in the 1-year medium-term lending facility in mid-January 2022 was followed by a cut by 5 basis points to 4.60% in the 5-year medium-term lending facility rate, which affects mortgage pricing. Further reductions in short-term policy rates are expected in 2022 to lighten the interest burden on the real economy. At the same time, rate reductions cannot do more than supplement the increases in fiscal spending needed to stimulate lackluster domestic demand. Cutting policy rates without providing fiscal support to stimulate growth courts the danger of pushing up asset prices, especially housing prices in major cities, where prices are already high. Further, given the tendency toward monetary policy tightening in major economies, pronounced policy rate cuts in the PRC could weaken the renminbi, which could spur a pick-up in hot money outflows, necessitating tighter capital controls.

Fiscal policy is expected to be more supportive on the spending side in 2022. The government targets 8.4% higher on-budget fiscal expenditure in 2022, versus 0.3% actual growth in 2021. Though the government's fiscal deficit target in 2022 at about 2.8% of GDP is on paper lower than the deficit target of about 3.2% in 2021, fiscal policy may still be more expansionary than last year because the fiscal deficit and the general public budget deficit differ in scope. The fiscal deficit is determined after taking into account funding from several non-debt sources, such as carryover funds, transfers from the central budget stabilization fund, and in 2022 a special profit submission from designated state-owned enterprises and a special transfer from the central bank of foreign exchange reserve operating income in recent years. All of this will help achieve this year's fiscal deficit target. However, the general public budget deficit— the unadjusted gap between fiscal revenue and expenditure—will likely be nearly 1 percentage point higher in 2022 than last year's deficit at 3.8% of GDP. In addition, part of the special receipts mentioned above will be used for additional infrastructure financing, while, to contain new public debt, the 2022 annual quota for new local government special bond issues remains unchanged from 2021 at CNY3.65 trillion.

General government debt may rise slightly in 2022. Though general government debt equal to 67.6% of GDP at the end of Q3 2021 reflected fiscal consolidation efforts (Figure 3.11.19), it may increase

in 2022 in line with stronger fiscal support and slower GDP growth. A rising concern is a substantial local government fiscal gap, which is discussed in the policy challenge section below. Fiscally weaker local governments tend to have higher public debt. In addition, local banks with weak balance sheets are often located in those regions. Enabling them to cope with their nonperforming loans effectively and avoid the need for recapitalization from local governments remains a challenge, as outlined in Asian Development Outlook 2021.

Figure 3.11.19 Debt structure

Debt declined slightly in the first three quarters of 2021.

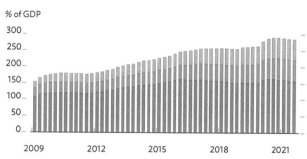

GDP = gross domestic product.
Source: Bank for International Settlements (accessed 4 March 2022).

External trade should continue to perform well overall. This is despite moderating export growth in 2022 caused by base effects and slowing growth in external demand from advanced economies. The ongoing COVID-19 pandemic prolongs global demand for consumer goods, many of them produced in the PRC. Import growth will reflect higher commodity prices as domestic demand recovers only gradually. With the service deficit expected to remain broadly unchanged in 2022 before widening in 2023 as international travel picks up, the current account surplus is forecast to retreat to the equivalent of 1.5% of GDP in 2022 and narrow further to 1.2% in 2023.

A narrowing interest rate spread could burden the renminbi. Capital flows to and from the PRC may continue to follow their 2021 path, with credit to foreign entities and deposits abroad playing a smaller role while hot money outflow picks up in response to a narrower interest rate spread over the advanced economies. Though the 10-year US Treasury note yield has increased recently, the PRC government bond yield stayed above the US benchmark (Figure 3.11.20).

Figure 3.11.20 Difference in government bond yields

The spread over US yields narrowed in 2021.

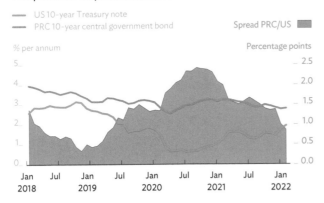

PRC = People's Republic of China, US = United States.
Note: Yields are monthly averages.
Source: Asian Development Bank calculations using data from CEIC Data Company (accessed 15 March 2022).

Risks to the outlook are both domestic and external. Domestic risks include, first and foremost, the unpredictability of COVID-19 outbreaks and virus mutations, which could endanger the recovery in domestic consumer demand. Another domestic risk to the outlook is mounting credit risk in the financial system, especially at smaller banks, that could trigger a need for policy responses that induce temporary tensions in the financial market. External risks are the impact of spillovers from the Russian invasion of Ukraine and frictions in global value chains from temporary supply shortages or transport bottlenecks.

Policy challenge—addressing the local government fiscal gap

Fiscal expenditure is highly decentralized in the PRC. Comprehensive fiscal reform in 1994 launched a redistribution of fiscal revenue from provinces to the central government, while the bulk of fiscal responsibilities stayed with local governments (Figures 3.11.21 and 3.11.22).

Figure 3.11.21 Government fiscal expenditure

The local government share of fiscal expenditure reached about 85% several years ago...

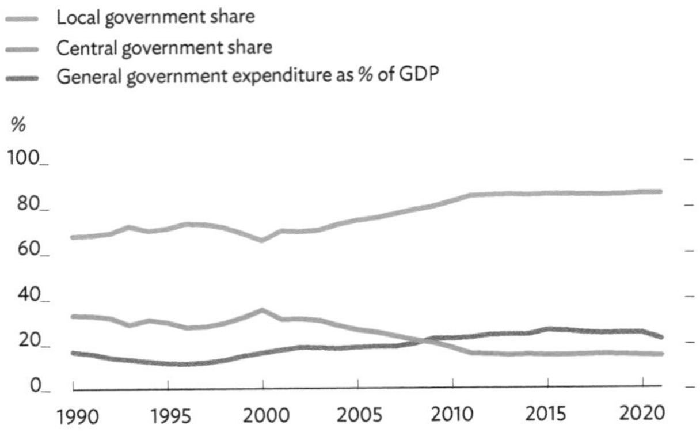

— Local government share
— Central government share
— General government expenditure as % of GDP

GDP = gross domestic product.
Note: Public finance budget only.
Source: Asian Development Bank calculations using data from CEIC Data Company (accessed 15 March 2022).

Figure 3.11.22 Government fiscal revenue

...but the local government share of fiscal revenue has languished at only about half since reform in 1994.

— Local government share
— Central government share
— General government revenue as % of GDP

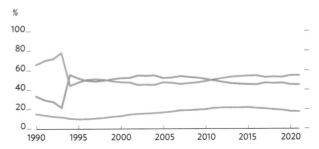

GDP = gross domestic product.
Note: Public finance budget only, before fiscal transfers and tax rebates.
Source: Asian Development Bank calculations using data from CEIC Data Company (accessed 15 March 2022).

While a formal intergovernmental fiscal transfer system was established with the intention to ameliorate regional fiscal disparity, it could not prevent an increase in the local government fiscal gap over time (Figure 3.11.23).

Pronounced regional differences persist in basic public services and social security benefits. This is a result of local governments providing the vast bulk of basic public services, such as health care and education, and administering social security including pensions. The upshot is unequal public service delivery, with wealthier provinces spending more per capita. The local government fiscal gap must be addressed to narrow disparities. This can be done by centralizing some fiscal expenditure responsibilities, raising fiscal transfers to poorer provinces, or increasing local government fiscal revenue, or combining such responses.

Figure 3.11.23 Local government fiscal imbalance

The fiscal gap has increased over time.

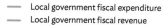

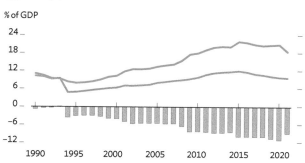

GDP = gross domestic product.
Notes: Public finance budget only, before fiscal transfers and tax rebates.
Source: Asian Development Bank calculations using data from CEIC Data Company (accessed 15 March 2022).

In 2016, the State Council announced fiscal reform aiming to minimize fiscal responsibilities held jointly between the central government and local governments, centralize key functions at the central government level, and consolidate and enhance the fiscal transfer system to strengthen the financial resources of less-developed regions.

Many public service categories remain classified as joint expenditure. As for the delineation of joint responsibilities, 18 public service categories, many of them critical to people's well-being, remain classified as joint fiscal expenditure, including compulsory education, student subsidies, employment services, pensions, basic medical insurance, health and family planning, living assistance, and affordable housing. Central government fiscal expenditure excluding transfers was in 2021 equal to 3.1% of GDP. Expenditure by local governments equaled 18.5% of GDP. Hence, the central government accounted for less than 15% of general government expenditure. Central government expenditure on health

has remained negligible and on education very low compared with that of local governments.

Unemployment insurance has not been centralized, and national pooling of basic pensions started only in 2022. With respect to centralizing key functions, the government should—in line with international best practice—centralize unemployment insurance and unify pension policies. However, this would not address the unequal provisioning of public health and education services, nor the dependence of these basic public services on local government financing.

Transfer classifications were changed in 2019. A new type of shared-function transfer was introduced that gave poorer provinces a higher share of the amount paid by the central government. This progress notwithstanding, fiscal transfers to poorer provinces still need to be increased. Fiscal transfers in aggregate from the central government to local governments have not increased in recent years when measured as a percentage of GDP—though 2020, under COVID-19, was an exception (Figure 3.11.24). An aging population and higher GDP per capita will increase demand for basic public services, fueling higher fiscal expenditure. Fiscal transfers to poorer regions must therefore be increased to avoid further widening of the gap in basic public service delivery between richer and poorer regions.

Figure 3.11.24 Central government fiscal transfers to local government

Measured as a percentage of GDP, fiscal transfers to local governments have stagnated.

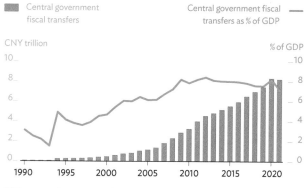

GDP = gross domestic product.
Notes: Includes only public finance budget. Transfers comprise special and general transfers, and tax rebates.
Source: Asian Development Bank calculations using data from CEIC Data Company (accessed 15 March 2022).

How to increase fiscal transfers to poorer regions remains a challenge. As the redistribution of transfers from richer to poorer provinces will likely face opposition from richer provinces and therefore can be achieved only gradually, if at all, tax revenue must be increased to finance higher fiscal transfers to poorer regions. In the years before the COVID-19 crisis, the central government already transferred roughly 80% of its fiscal revenue—in 2020 it transferred slightly more than it took in, followed by nearly 90% of fiscal revenue in 2021. Higher tax revenue would benefit local governments as well through the existing tax-sharing system for major taxes, particularly value-added tax and corporate income tax. Tax collection in the PRC is weaker than in members of the Organisation for Economic Co-operation and Development (OECD). In 2019, tax revenue in OECD countries, including social security contributions, equaled on average 33.8% of GDP. In the PRC, it was 22.1%, of which 16.0 percentage points was tax and 6.1 points social security contributions. Cuts to value-added tax and, to a lesser extent, personal income tax have lowered tax revenue in recent years (Figure 3.11.25).

There is room to increase personal income tax collection, and recurrent property tax has yet to be rolled out nationwide. In 2021, personal income tax equaled only 1.2% of GDP in the PRC. It averaged 8.0% of GDP across OECD countries in 2019, the latest year for which data are available. Important steps would be to broaden the tax base and make personal income tax more progressive, in part by correcting recent reforms. Special deductions on top of high general deductions have substantially narrowed the share of the population that pays personal income tax. Further, personal income tax in the PRC does not cover all forms of personal income, as capital income, for example, is generally taxed at a flat rate. Including more forms of income would make income tax more progressive and thereby improve its equity and revenue potential.

Another good step would be a nationwide rollout of locally collected recurrent property tax. This would provide local governments with additional revenue. And it could open a window of opportunity to shift more fiscal transfers to poorer provinces because richer ones would profit disproportionally from property tax revenue.

Figure 3.11.25 General government fiscal and tax revenue versus fiscal expenditure

Fiscal consolidation efforts sharply reduced 2021 expenditure as a percentage of GDP.

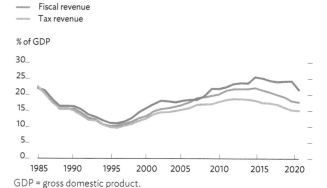

GDP = gross domestic product.

Note: Public finance budget only.

Source: Asian Development Bank calculations using data from CEIC Data Company (accessed 4 March 2022).

REPUBLIC OF KOREA

Growth rebounded in 2021, propelled by domestic demand and exports. Inflation rose on higher prices for food and services, and the current account surplus widened as exports surged. Growth will decelerate this year and the next but remain robust, underpinned by expansion in exports and private spending. Inflation will accelerate slightly in 2022 on higher energy costs before easing in 2023, and the current account surplus will narrow relative to GDP as prices rise for imported energy products.

Economic performance

The economy recovered from a slump in 2020 to grow by 4.0% in 2021, the highest rate in a decade. After declining in 2020, private consumption grew by 3.6% and contributed 1.7 percentage points to GDP growth (Figure 3.12.1). It was supported by successful COVID-19 containment, mass vaccination, an easing of movement restrictions, and recovery in the labor market from a downturn in 2020 as employment growth reached a 7-year high and the unemployment rate fell from 4.0% in 2020 to 3.6%. Growth in government consumption accelerated from 5.0% in 2020 to 5.5%, adding 1.0 point to GDP growth. Gross capital formation increased by 1.5%, adding 0.5 points to growth, as lower government investment was offset by higher private investment in export-oriented industries responding to recovery in the global demand for their products.

As exports of goods and services grew by a robust 9.7%, outpacing 8.4% growth in imports, net exports contributed 0.8 points to GDP growth. Information technology products performed particularly well, notably microchip packages, organic light-emitting diodes, semiconductors, and solid-state disks. Also growing briskly were exports of petroleum products, petrochemicals, and steel products. Exports to all major partner economies expanded, most rapidly to Mexico, Singapore and Taipei,China.

Figure 3.12.1 Demand-side contributions to growth

Private consumption and investment led recovery.

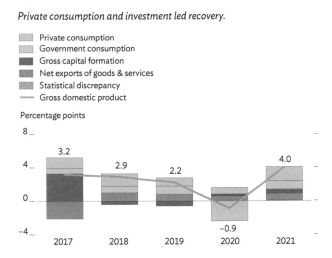

Note: Statistical discrepancy arises as contributions to the growth exclude net indirect taxes.
Source: CEIC Data Company (accessed 10 March 2022).

On the supply side, services contributed the most to GDP growth with recovery in wholesale and retail trade, accommodation and food, transportation and storage, education, and cultural and other services. After contracting by 0.9% in 2020, manufacturing output increased by 6.6%, fueled by strong export demand, and capacity utilization in manufacturing rose from an average of 71.3% in 2020 to 74.3% in 2021. By contrast,

---

This chapter was written by Yothin Jinjarak and Pilipinas Quising of the Economic Research and Regional Cooperation Department, ADB, Manila.

construction declined for a fourth consecutive year as slowdowns affected civil engineering works and specialized construction.

Propelled by higher input costs and demand, producer and consumer prices rose throughout 2021, with a 6.4% producer price index increase greatly outpacing 2.5% for the consumer price index (Figure 3.12.2). The prime drivers of producer price inflation were metals, chemicals, and coal and petroleum products, while the main contributors to consumer price inflation were food, transport, restaurants and hotels, and housing and utilities. Core inflation, which excludes food and energy, rose to 1.4%, the highest since 2017. Housing prices were 9.9% higher year on year at the end of 2021. Against this backdrop of inflationary pressure, the Bank of Korea, the central bank, raised its policy rate by 25 basis points in August and another 25 basis points in November.

Figure 3.12.2 Monthly inflation

Inflation is on the rise.

— Consumer price index
— Producer price index
— Core consumer price index

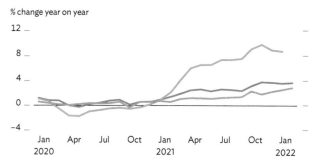

Source: CEIC Data Company (accessed 10 March 2022).

Responding to measures to improve access to credit for small and medium-sized enterprises and self-employed individuals, lending to the private sector increased by 11.3%, raising growth in domestic liquidity from 9.8% in 2020 to 12.9% in 2021. Household debt, more than half of it mortgages, climbed further by 7.8% year on year to equal 90.5% of GDP at the end of 2021, which was higher than before the pandemic (3.12.3).

The current account surplus widened from the equivalent of 4.6% of GDP in 2020 to 4.9% in 2021 as the trade surplus grew by 11.0%, and net primary

Figure 3.12.3 Credit to households and house price

Household debt increased in lockstep with housing price appreciation.

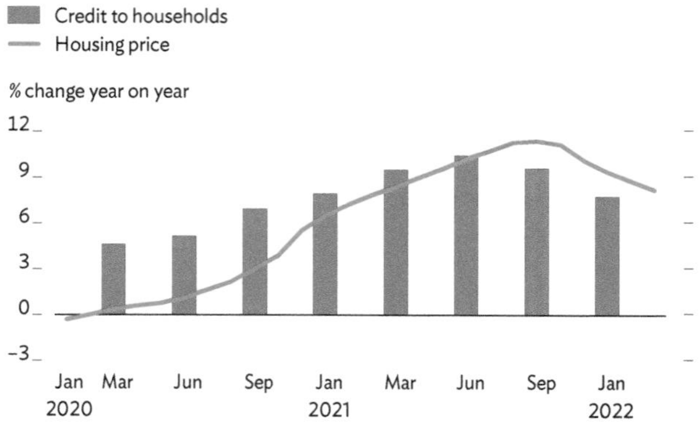

■ Credit to households
— Housing price

% change year on year

Note: The housing price is the deposit for a 2-year lease on an apartment under the jeonse system.
Source: CEIC Data Company (accessed 10 March 2022.).

income receipts by 43.0%, while the net service deficit shrank (Figure 3.12.4). After falling substantially in 2020, net foreign direct investment recovered quickly in 2021, and net portfolio investment flows surged (Figure 3.12.5), pushing the overall balance of payments surplus to the equivalent of 0.8% of GDP. Official foreign reserves rose to $463.1 billion, sufficient to cover 10 months of merchandise imports. The Republic of Korea (ROK) won nevertheless depreciated by 8.2% against the dollar and by 4.7% in real effective terms on worries over new COVID-19 variants and expected monetary tightening in the US as the Federal Reserve tapers it stock holdings.

Figure 3.12.4 Current account balance

Surpluses in goods and primary income improved the external balance.

■ Goods
■ Services
■ Net income   Current account balance —

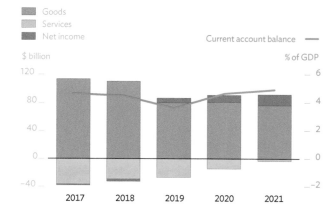

GDP = gross domestic product.
Source: CEIC Data Company (accessed 10 March 2022).

Figure 3.12.5 Inward investment

Foreign direct investment recovered, and portfolio investment surged.

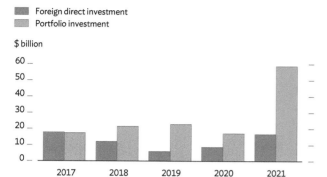

Source: CEIC Data Company (accessed 10 March 2022).

Fiscal policy remained supportive of growth in 2021 with the passage of two supplementary budgets, in March and July 2021, that allocated an additional $42.4 billion to support 8.2 million people unemployed or otherwise affected by prolonged disease-prevention measures, and to facilitate recovery from the crisis, particularly by smaller businesses. Expenditure increased by 9.7% from 2020, but revenue improvement spurred by unexpectedly rapid economic recovery narrowed the 2021 budget deficit to an estimated 5.3% (or 1.5% including Social Security Contributions) of GDP. Government debt was estimated equal to 47.0% of GDP.

Economic prospects

After exceptionally high growth in 2021 from a low base in 2020, the economy is expected to settle into more sustainable growth at 3.0% in 2022 and 2.6% in 2023 (Table 3.12.1 and Figure 3.12.6). Higher domestic consumption and a sustained global appetite for exports will support robust expansion in private investment.

Table 3.12.1 Selected economic indicators, %

Growth will accelerate, but inflation and the current account deficit will remain high.

	2020	2021	2022	2023
GDP growth	−0.9	4.0	3.0	2.6
Inflation	0.5	2.5	3.2	2.0
CAB/GDP	4.6	4.9	3.8	3.5

CAB = current account balance, GDP = gross domestic product.
Source: Asian Development Bank estimates.

Figure 3.12.6 Gross domestic product

GDP growth will settle down to a more sustainable rate.

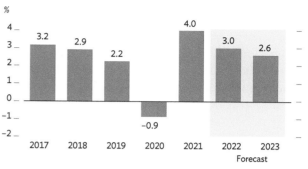

GDP = gross domestic product.
Sources: *Asian Development Outlook* database; Asian Development Bank estimates.

Continued recovery in private consumption will be driven by an improved job market. As the economy reopens, the unemployment rate should continue its decline in the coming quarters. Impact from a recent resurgence of COVID-19 infections is expected to be muted by a high vaccination rate and a resulting low mortality rate, and therefore unlikely to require tighter restrictions. Consumer sentiment remained above the 100-point threshold in the first 2 months of the year, signaling optimism (Figure 3.12.7). To boost consumption, the government has extended for 1 year a special tax deduction on additional consumption.

Figure 3.12.7 Consumer confidence

Consumers remain optimistic.

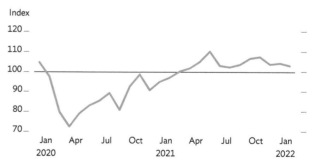

Note: A consumer confidence reading >100 indicates optimism.
Source: CEIC Data Company (accessed 10 March 2022).

Business conditions are improving. The manufacturing business confidence index inched up to 92 in February and 93 in March, signaling improving sentiment. Likewise, the Markit manufacturing purchasing managers' index rose in February to an 8-month high of 53.8, signaling accelerating improvement in business conditions (Figure 3.12.8). Supply chain bottlenecks still bedevil business but somewhat less so, as indicated by a slight decline in delivery times. Manufacturing is expected to drive investment as export growth continues and domestic demand revives. Capacity utilization increased from 104.9 points in December to 105.3 points in January, inducing companies to invest in plant and equipment. However, as investment that was postponed at the height of the pandemic was largely resumed in 2021, investment growth will likely moderate in 2022.

Figure 3.12.8 Manufacturing indicators

Supply chain bottlenecks appear to be clearing.

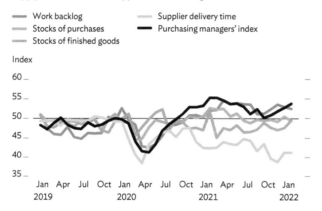

Note: A purchasing managers' index reading <50 signals deterioration, >50 improvement.
Source: CEIC Data Company (accessed 10 March 2022).

Growth in services will likely continue to recover despite uncertainty surrounding the pandemic. Hospitality, recreation, and tourism will profit from vaccination progress. As of late February, 87% of the population had been fully vaccinated.

Merchandise exports are expected to grow as persistent restrictions on movement in many parts of the world fuel demand for consumer goods to use at home. Demand for heavy industrial products, semiconductors, and metal goods in the largest export destinations—the People's Republic of China (PRC), the US, and Viet Nam—is expected to expand steadily as those economies recover. In line with this positive outlook, merchandise exports jumped by 18% year on year in the first 2 months of 2022.

As domestic demand recovers, imports should pick up—especially of commodities, capital goods, and oil products, which amount to 11% of all imports—and pick up all the more given current upward trends for energy and other commodity prices. The trade surplus is thus forecast to shrink, narrowing the current account surplus to the equivalent of 3.8% of GDP in 2022 and to 3.5% in 2023. Foreign direct investment inflow is expected to increase, in particular with an eye toward solid growth prospects for the PRC export market.

Inflation is forecast higher at 3.2% in 2022, standing for a second year above the 2% central bank inflation target (Figure 3.12.9). Headline inflation has continued to edge up, from 3.6% year on year in January 2022 to 3.7% the following month. Temporary factors such as higher global oil and food prices may explain recent acceleration, but core inflation has also been on the rise since September 2021, with rising demand a contributing factor. The central bank raised the policy interest rate by another 25 basis points in January but paused in February. More interest rate hikes are anticipated in 2022, however, to rein inflation back to within the central bank target. As global price increases for oil and food moderate in 2023, inflation is forecast to subside to 2.0%.

Figure 3.12.9 Inflation

Inflation will accelerate in its second year above the central bank target of 2.0%.

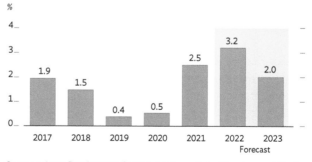

Sources: *Asian Development Outlook* database; Asian Development Bank estimates.

Fiscal support is likely to moderate as the government reprioritizes reining in the budget deficit and reducing to a more sustainable level infrastructure spending financed by new local government special bond issues. Nevertheless, expenditure is expected to rise by 8.9% in 2022 on continued tax relief for small taxpayers, but revenue looks set to improve in line with higher economic growth, which should create fiscal space and lower the fiscal deficit to 2.5% GDP. National debt is projected to increase in 2022 to the equivalent of 50.0% of GDP, or 2.7% points higher than the planned national debt ratio in 2021.

Risks to the outlook arise from a range of uncertainties, notably developments in the Russian invasion of Ukraine, the COVID-19 pandemic, monetary tightening in the US, and ROK macroeconomic policy. While neither the Russian Federation nor Ukraine is major trade partner of the ROK, prolonged conflict could have wider effects on its external trade. Alternatively, a new and deadly virus variant could stymie the economic recovery now under way. Widely expected tightening by the US Federal Reserve may induce financial volatility in the ROK in light of its highly open capital account.

Some tightening of ROK policy is expected, as the central bank has made clear that its main priority is to control financial risk posed by surging home prices and household debt. The growth outlook will thus depend in part on how the central bank resolves the trade-off between growth and inflation. Further, public and private investment outlays will be influenced by the direction of government policy and fiscal incentives under a new administration to be installed on 10 May 2022.

Policy challenge—promoting entrepreneurship in the digitalized ecosystem

The ROK is about to begin investment to develop 6G telecommunication technology. The country is already at the frontier of 5G network technology and a major player—along with the PRC, the US, and Europe—in global research on this technology. With the implementation of the Digital New Deal, a policy initiative funded by public and private investment, improved digital infrastructure should place the ROK at the forefront of digital service providers, both at home and abroad.

Meanwhile, the global environment for 6G technology is becoming more competitive. Global internet companies plan to roll out digital service taxes on income from the ROK, which has significant implications for prices and

the profits of market participants in the ROK, given its large market, which is still growing briskly despite already high penetration. The streaming market is one area of intense competition between local and foreign providers, and realignment in the domestic digital services industry is creating another.

The fast-changing digital landscape provides opportunities but also poses challenges to local entrepreneurs and startups. The ROK is well placed to face these challenges in light of its high rate of urbanization, high income per capita, large market, dynamic private sector, technologically complex market economy, and strong corporate governance and financial auditing and reporting standards. Entrepreneurship is further enhanced by ample human capital generated by high-quality education and entrepreneurship ecosystems.

Scope still exists, however, for policies designed to make markets more competitive and equitable. The foremost prerequisite is transparency in the national regulatory framework and appropriate mechanisms to prevent anticompetitive practices. These prerequisites are particularly critical for growing online businesses and platforms in the domestic market. Further, the collection of user data—a key feature of global digital markets—poses a challenge to regulators, who must balance the protection of consumer rights with legitimate corporate interests.

The government recognizes these needs. In 2021, it stopped regulating youngsters' participation in online gaming at night, which was pursued under a youth protection law promulgated in 2012. The Korea Fair Trade Commission recently extended its enforcement of laws to ensure competition among digital platforms and fair online transactions. A 2021 bill amending the Telecommunication Business Act improved how Google and Apple do business with application developers, and the Digital Signature Act, 2020 allows public and private actors to select their authentication protocols for internet access. These policies have brought improvement but, as underscored by a global study of digitalization and the entrepreneurship ecosystem conducted by ADB, the government must ensure that such fiscal measures as subsidies and tax breaks promote rather than distort competition. Further, scope exists to improve procedures for the resolution of private sector legal challenges to government actions and regulations.

TAIPEI,CHINA

With COVID-19 largely contained, economic growth accelerated in 2021, driven mainly by surges in exports and investment. Inflation rose, and the current account surplus widened relative to GDP. In 2022 and 2023, growth will moderate as the surge in investment abates, inflation will slow as supply bottlenecks are resolved and economic activity moderates, and the current account surplus will widen further. Policy action is needed to address climate change effectively and minimize damage to the economy.

Economic performance

Recovery accelerated to boost economic growth to 6.4% in 2021 as global demand bolstered exports and private investment surged. Exports grew by 17.0%, and imports by 17.9% but from a lower base, such that net exports still contributed 1.9 percentage points to GDP growth. Investment expanded by 17.3% to contribute 4.2 points to growth, largely riding a wave of investment in machinery, transportation, and construction equipment in the second half of the year spurred at least in part by government investment assistance programs. Weighed down by pandemic restrictions, private consumption contracted by 0.4%, shaving 0.2 percentage points from growth. Meanwhile, government consumption expanded by 3.8% and contributed 0.5 points to growth as pandemic-related support continued (Figure 3.13.1).

On the supply side, industry posted strong expansion at 12.8%, contributing 4.8 points to growth as the production of electronic parts continued to pick up. Services grew by 3.0% and contributed 1.8 points to growth, driven by the tech and finance industries. Agriculture, on the other hand, contracted by 4.2% as the sector was hit by the worst drought in over 5 decades in June and by Typhoon Chanthu in September.

Figure 3.13.1 Demand-side contributions to growth

Growth accelerated last year but will moderate in the coming years.

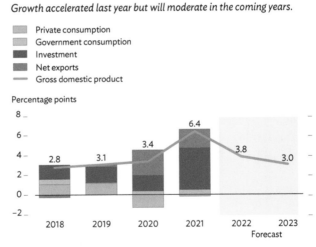

Source: CEIC Data Company (accessed 28 February 2022).

The unemployment rate rose to 4.8% in June, during a spike in COVID-19 cases, but fell gradually to reach in December the pre-pandemic rate of 3.6%. Inflation returned at 2.0% in 2021 as food, transportation, and crude oil prices rose, but core inflation, which excludes food and energy prices, remained fairly stable at 1.3% (Figure 3.13.2).

This chapter was written by Irfan Qureshi and David Keith De Padua of the Economic Research and Regional Cooperation Department, ADB, Manila.

Figure 3.13.2 Inflation

Inflation is expected to moderate as pressure from rising global oil prices will likely be contained

— Core
— Overall

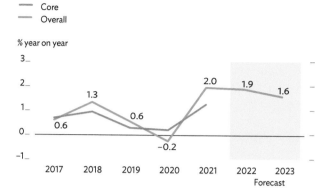

Sources: CEIC Data Company (accessed 25 February 2022); Asian Development Bank estimates.

Figure 3.13.3 Growth in exports to the People's Republic of China and the United States

Exports to these two large markets grew strongly in 2021.

— United States
— People's Republic of China

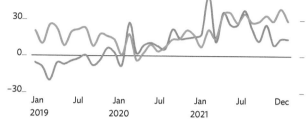

Source: CEIC Data Company (accesed 28 February 2022).

The continuing surge in merchandise exports in 2021 was driven by strong export demand in two of this economy's largest trade partners. Exports to the People's Republic of China (PRC) grew by 23.0% and those to the US by 29.7% (Figure 3.13.3). By category, exports of electronics swelled by 26.9%, and of information and communication technology products by 24.8%, reflecting robust demand for technology goods, while other categories also posted robust growth (Figure 3.13.4). Imports of petroleum products and thermionic, cold, and photo-cathode valves—inputs for electronic products—grew broadly in pace with exports. Net service exports increased from the equivalent of 0.6% of GDP in 2020 to 1.6% in 2021, while net income components declined from 2.4% of GDP to 1.8%. In sum, the current account surplus widened to equal 15.0% of GDP (Figure 3.13.5). Gross foreign exchange reserves grew by 3.5% in the year to December and were sufficient to cover 15.7 months of imports. The domestic currency meanwhile appreciated by 1.6% against the US dollar and by 7.4% in real effective terms.

Monetary and fiscal policies remained broadly accommodative in 2021. The central bank has kept its policy rate unchanged at 1.125% since March 2020. In June 2021, following a spike in COVID-19 cases, the government increased its pandemic relief budget to $30.0 billion to provide more cash relief, loans, and pandemic subsidies to families with children, bringing

Figure 3.13.4 Growth and value of exports by category, $ million

Exports of electronics and related products were strongest, but those of other goods were also robust.

% change year on year

```
90_

                                                    Refined petroleum
                                                    products,
                                   Iron & steel      9,693
                                   products,
           Plastics &             22,030
60_        rubber,
  Electronic 29,868
  parts,                                            Electrical
  171,994                         Chemicals,         machinery,
                                  23,407            14,355
30_                                                              Textiles
                         Machinery,                              9,028
            ICT           27,831           Optical
            products,                      instruments or parts,
            61,325                         20,097
 0_ _____
              size of bubble: value of export, million USD
```

ICT = information and communication technology.

Notes: Export categories are arranged left to right by export value, graphically indicated by circle size.

Source: Ministry of Finance (accessed 8 March 2022).

the cost of all fiscal measures related to COVID-19 to a value estimated to equal 3.9% of GDP. Budgetary revenue remained stable at 11.0% of GDP for both 2020 and 2021. Meanwhile expenditure climbed from 12.4% of GDP in 2020 to 12.5%, widening the budget deficit slightly from 1.4% of GDP to 1.5%.

Figure 3.13.5 Balance of payments

The current account surplus widened on strong export performance.

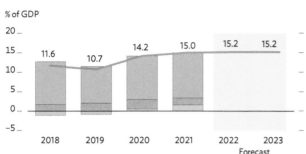

GDP = gross domestic product.
Source: CEIC Data Company (accessed 2 March 2022).

Economic prospects

Growth will moderate to 3.8% in 2022 as export growth softens somewhat and imports rise to supply domestic investment, together paring back the external sector's contribution to growth (Table 3.13.1). Growth will then recede further to 3.0% as the investment surge wanes. Growth will still be driven by robust investment as companies expand manufacturing capacity to meet foreign demand for technology products and continue to re-shore their operations, mainly from the PRC. Private consumption will also drive growth as upbeat consumer confidence and robust retail trade indicators bode well for higher consumer spending in the coming year.

Table 3.13.1 Selected economic indicators, %

Growth and inflation will moderate and current account surplus widen.

	2020	2021	2022	2023
GDP growth	3.4	6.4	3.8	3.0
Inflation	-0.2	2.0	1.9	1.6
CAB/GDP	14.2	15.0	15.2	15.2

CAB = current account balance, GDP = gross domestic product.
Source: Asian Development Bank estimates.

With robust economic activity in the key export markets of the PRC and the US, exports are expected to be a key contributor to growth, albeit not as strongly as in 2021. This is evidenced by continued growth in export orders, a leading indicator of future shipments, which grew by 20% in 2021, bolstered by strong demand for electronic parts and rising demand for new technological applications, such as 5G and high-performance computing. Import growth will likewise continue in line with ongoing investment by domestic firms.

Inflation is expected to moderate slightly to 1.9% in 2022 and recede further to 1.6% in 2023 (Figure 3.13.2). Upward pressure from global oil prices in 2022 looks likely to be contained within transportation and, in any case, will be moderated by the government's oil price stabilization mechanism. The current account surplus will widen slightly to equal 15.2% of GDP in 2022 and 2023 as the merchandise trade surplus and service exports grow slightly, and as income from abroad remains flat.

Monetary policy is expected to remain accommodative, but the policy rate could be raised if inflation accelerates, pandemic-hit sectors start to rebound more than anticipated, or more major economies abroad start raising their policy rates. Fiscal policy, too, will support growth with social welfare, education and science, and defense outlays accounting for the bulk of government expenditure. However with the COVID-19 Special Budget expected to be phased out gradually this year, expenditures will decline by 6.4%. With budgetary revenues forecast to decline by 5%, the budget deficit is expected to narrow to the equivalent of 1.2% of GDP.

Risks to the outlook include further COVID-19 outbreaks delaying recovery in private consumption, as the zero-COVID policy pursued by Taipei,China would likely trigger new rounds of harsh restrictions. Unexpectedly fast tightening by the US Federal Reserve could roil financial markets and hamper growth. Finally, unexpectedly slow growth in key trade partners could weaken exports and thus dampen growth prospects. Risks to the outlook for inflation include higher global prices for food and raw materials and, especially in view of the conflict in Ukraine, a sustained increase in global oil prices that could translate into broader inflation.

Policy challenge—adapting to climate change while reaching net-zero emissions

Climate change will have a significant impact on the local economy if adaptation and mitigation measures are not aggressively implemented in a timely way. Current forecasts predict more extreme weather by the end of the century if global warming continues at its current pace. These extreme events could include more intense tropical storms but, perversely, less rain in the spring. This could cause a substantial decline in already stretched water supplies, starving agriculture and industry of this key input. Through its impact on human health, climate change threatens to undermine worker productivity and potential output. More uncertainty about the cost of inputs, energy, transportation, and insurance caused by climate change will likely raise production costs and erode investor sentiment.

The authorities have focused environmental policy on cleaning up pollution and achieving net-zero emissions by 2050—a substantial bolstering of a previous commitment to halve emissions over the same period (Figure 3.13.6). In line with this, the Environmental Protection Administration announced policies such as collecting carbon fees from emitters and using the revenue to subsidize carbon mitigation technology. A plan outlining a path to net-zero is expected to be announced this year. Authorities need to implement a plan quickly and take the steps necessary to reduce

risk from extreme climate events such as Typhoon Chanthu last September. Finally, Taipei,China needs to have a more comprehensive climate strategy.

There will be challenges ahead. The economy's steel, cement, petrochemical, and heavy transport industries account for 40% of carbon dioxide emissions—but their emissions are considered especially hard to abate. Some analyses suggest that energy intensity in these industries must be cut by 30% to achieve net-zero emissions by 2050, with at least 60% of freight trucks electrified.

To enhance the likelihood of achieving net zero by 2050, other steps should include the following. Incentives such as tax rebates for research and development should be provided to encourage companies to adopt and advance decarbonization technologies that are available but not yet commercially viable, such as electric cement kilns and furnaces. To enable the electrification of heavy transport, investment in electric vehicle charging infrastructure is needed along key roadways. In addition, current efforts should be accelerated, notably to install 20 gigawatts of solar energy by 2025, of which only 7.8 gigawatts had been installed by January of this year.

The blueprint for achieving net zero should be complemented with a plan to adapt to unavoidable impact from climate change, in particular to insulate those most vulnerable to climate-related risk. Policy makers need to follow through on the Disaster Prevention and Protection Act, as amended in 2019, to ensure the implementation of mandated measures to enhance disaster prevention and response. Meanwhile, farmers should be encouraged to adopt precision irrigation systems and less water-intensive crops, and desalination technology should be explored to augment limited water reserves as this technology becomes more cost-effective.

More broadly, policy makers should allocate adequate resources to invest in climate technologies and partner with civil society and the private sector to champion change. Putting Taipei,China on the path to decarbonization while insulating it from climate-related risks will take concerted efforts toward transformative policy making, innovation and compliance from business, and buy-in from everyone.

Figure 3.13.6 Net-zero emissions target

The authorities set an ambitious goal of net-zero emissions by 2050.

— Net zero emissions by 2050
- - Previous emissions goals

Tons of carbon dioxide emissions annually per capita

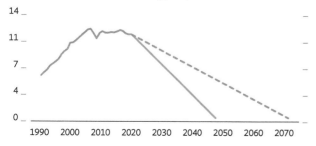

Source: Our World in Data (accessed 21 February 2022).

SOUTH ASIA

Afghanistan
Bangladesh
Bhutan
India
Maldives
Nepal
Pakistan
Sri Lanka

AFGHANISTAN

The economy faced many challenges in 2021. After a short recovery in the first quarter, aided by a pickup in services, it suffered drought, a sharp rise in COVID-19 cases, and regime change that led to international isolation. These shocks may cut real GDP by as much as 30% over the medium term. Reducing dollarization is a major policy challenge.

Economic performance

Drought, increased violence, a huge jump in COVID-19 cases, and subsequent containment measures took a heavy toll on the Afghan economy in the first half of 2021. Adding to these problems was a regime change on 15 August that triggered a sudden suspension of international assistance and other financial inflows, including remittances and export revenue. These shocks severely depressed economic activity and stifled domestic demand. Investor confidence was undermined, leading to severe disruptions in the country's financial markets. All sectors of the economy were affected. Services, the biggest contributor to GDP, suffered the most, with wholesale and retail trade, insurance, transport, hospitality, and education declining substantially.

Severe cash shortages and a widespread liquidity shock followed the suspension of international transfers, the freezing of international reserves and the foreign exchange reserves of commercial banks held at the central bank, and interruptions in printing afghani (national currency) notes. The regime limited withdrawals of bank deposits, estimated to have plunged by 40% in 2021, after a run on commercial banks caused liquidity shortages. These events accompanied massive layoffs and business closures in the months following the regime change.

Border closures and the suspension of international payments critically disrupted industrial activity, choking off supplies of raw materials and components and

blocking the access of firms to the international market. Depressed domestic demand and Afghanistan's poorly functioning financial markets seriously weakened the business climate, causing many businesses to close. A severe drought hit 25 of the country's 34 provinces, contributing to a poor harvest that saw wheat production falling an estimated 40%. This and the loss of food imports caused food insecurity to reach crisis levels in much of the country.

The economic downturn propelled unemployment to levels not seen in over 20 years. Real wages of skilled workers fell by 24% last year and 11% for unskilled workers. The International Labour Organization estimates Afghanistan has lost more than half a million jobs since the regime change. In the third quarter of 2021 alone, unemployment rose by 8% and the unemployment of women by 16%, reflecting workers pushed out of jobs amid the economic uncertainty enveloping the country.

Headline inflation averaged 5.15% year on year in 2021, accelerating from 2.50% in the first half to 10.40% in the fourth quarter (Figure 3.14.1). The Afghani's depreciation, border closures, drought, and domestic and international supply chain disruptions led to sharp price rises for food and essential goods and services. Depressed domestic demand only partially offset these effects. The biggest contributors to inflation were rising cooking oil prices, up 63.4% year on year in December, followed by increases in

This chapter was written by Abdul Hares Halimi and Ahmad K. Miraj of the Afghanistan Resident Mission, ADB, Kabul. ADB placed on hold its assistance in Afghanistan effective 15 August 2021. ADB Statement on Afghanistan.

Figure 3.14.1 Inflation

Inflation has risen with the acceleration of food prices.

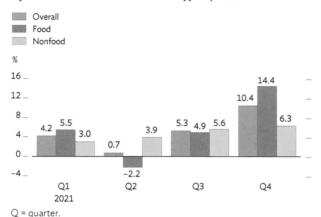

Q = quarter.
Sources: Official statistics from national and international sources.

Figure 3.14.3 Inflation by type

Oils and fats, sugar, bread, and cereals were the biggest contributors to inflation in Q3 and Q4 2021.

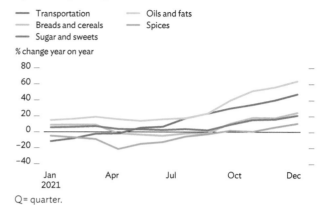

Q= quarter.
Sources: Official statistics from national and international sources.

transportation (47.2%), sugar (24.6%), and bread and cereal (24.0%) (Figures 3.14.2 and 3.14.3).

The regime change curtailed the financing of the current account deficit, shrinking imports and putting pressure on the afghani. From July to November 2021, imports from Pakistan, one of Afghanistan's biggest trading partners, plunged by 37% from the same period in 2020, even though exports to Pakistan rose by 14%. Over 2021, the afghani depreciated by 34.4% against the US dollar, and it also depreciated markedly against the currencies of the country's main trading partners (Figure 3.14.4).

Figure 3.14.4 Exchange rate index

The afghani fell sharply against the US dollar after the regime change in August 2021.

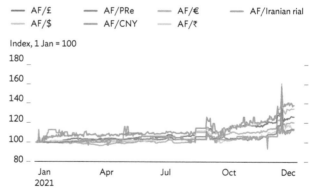

Note: Higher means a depreciation on the exchange rate index.
Sources: Official data from national and international sources.

Economic prospects

The Asian Development Bank has analyzed the prospects for Afghanistan's economy using several scenarios with different underlying assumptions. In the baseline scenario, which assumes a continuation of current political policies, a continued freeze of international development assistance significantly weakens economic activity in 2022. Real GDP is simulated to contract by 30% over the medium term. Reduced fiscal space and lower domestic revenue collection limit the regime's ability to provide basic services and finance development projects. Services and industry are projected to remain subdued. Some

Figure 3.14.2 Monthly inflation

Food price inflation surged in Q3 and Q4 2021 on the afghani's depreciation and other pressures.

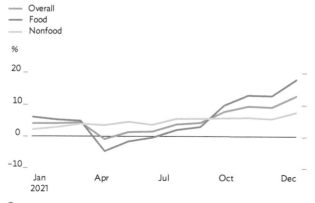

Q = quarter.
Sources: Official statistics from national and international sources.

recovery in agriculture could occur due to reportedly high levels of rainfall, which could contribute to a strong harvest in 2022. But worsening economic conditions would raise unemployment, causing a further drop in household consumption.

Recognizing the severity of the situation, the international community and UN agencies have pledged to deliver strong humanitarian support to Afghanistan to respond to the enormous humanitarian crisis. On 11 January 2022, UN agencies reported that $4.4 billion in aid is needed to alleviate the crisis in 2022.

Under the baseline scenario, Afghanistan's international reserves and assets are expected to remain frozen. International settlement and payment systems would remain suspended, further hampering trade in 2022. Trade with Iran and Pakistan could mitigate the decline in earnings from exports. But investment from domestic and overseas sources would continue to be subdued. Continued uncertainty, low domestic demand, cross-border trade disruptions, and a negative economic outlook could cause a balance of payments crisis that in turn could trigger a substantial depreciation in the afghani, already at its lowest level in 2 decades. Given the significant pass-through of the exchange rate into inflation, supply shortages, and escalated inflationary expectations, a significant further rise in the prices of food and essential goods and services is expected in 2022, adding to inflation.

In the alternative scenario, the regime establishes an inclusive government that shows a strong commitment to basic human rights, pursues policies acceptable to the international community, and receives some international recognition. Doing this could lead to the limited resumption of international development assistance and unlock frozen assets. Together with improvements in the security situation and an increase in trade, the economic contraction in 2022 could be reduced, with the possibility of a small rebound in growth following 2021's large contraction. A resumption of international development assistance would help narrow the fiscal gap, and domestic revenue mobilization would improve with the implementation of value-added tax. Greater economic activity and higher revenue collection would strengthen the budget, allowing more spending on basic services. In the longer term, foreign direct investment inflows would increase, leading to a further rise in economic activity.

Policy challenge— tackling dollarization

Afghanistan's dollarization dates from the civil war in the 1970s. Recurring episodes of sharp depreciation and hyperinflation severely undermined confidence in the afghani. Substantial inflows of international assistance from 2001 exacerbated currency substitution, leading to the widespread use of US dollars in business transactions. Afghanistan's financial sector is also highly dollarized. As of 2020, 70% of deposits and half of loans were in foreign currency, mainly US dollars (Figures 3.14.5 and 3.14.6).

Figure 3.14.5 Deposits in afghanis

Nearly 70% of all deposits were in foreign currency in July 2021.

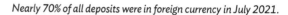

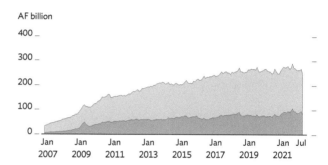

Source: Official statistics published before regime change on 15 August 2021.

Figure 3.14.6 Loans in Afghanis

Half of all credit was in foreign currency in July 2021.

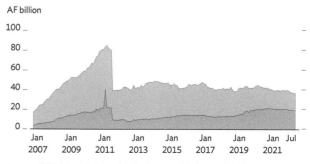

Source: Official statistics published before 15 August 2021.

Dollarization has affected the design and effectiveness of monetary policy. Before the regime change last August, the central bank targeted reserve money growth, which excluded foreign currency, to achieve price stability. This made it impossible to tackle the influence of foreign currency in circulation, whether from frequent moves between domestic and foreign currency holdings by firms and households or uncontrolled flows of foreign currency in and out of the country. With widespread currency substitution limiting monetary control, the central bank's exchange rate policy involved regular and unsustainable interventions in the foreign currency market in an effort to maintain the afghani's purchasing power.

High dollarization has exacerbated the risk of a crisis in Afghanistan's financial and foreign exchange markets. Currency mismatch between the assets and liabilities of banks has made the financial sector vulnerable to liquidity and solvency risks. In the absence of large international banks and with limited interbank lending, dollarization has weakened the central bank's ability to serve as a lender of last resort, forcing it to use international reserves for foreign exchange market interventions to satisfy the financial sector's liquidity needs. The freezing of Afghanistan's international

reserves and the foreign exchange reserves of commercial banks, as well as disruptions in printing afghanis, has led to severe shortages of US dollars, causing a widespread liquidity shock and worsening the banking sector's health.

Macroeconomic stability and prudent financial market regulation will be vital for successfully de-dollarizing the economy. Low inflation, a sustainable current account, and fiscal consolidation are especially important. Low inflation reduces the need to hold foreign currency to preserve purchasing power. Fiscal consolidation and a sustainable current account can reduce foreign currency borrowing, thereby helping to stabilize the exchange rate. A higher reserve requirement on foreign currency deposits raises the cost of foreign currency liabilities, reducing the incentives for dollarization. This can mitigate the liquidity risk of dollarization by enhancing the central bank's capacity as lender of last resort and provide incentives for financial institutions to operate in the domestic currency. Dollarization in cash transactions can be discouraged by regulations requiring market prices, accounting, and financial reporting to be denominated in afghanis and providing convenient and discounted payment services in that currency.

BANGLADESH

Growth revived in fiscal 2021 on a rebound in global trade and stimulus measures—and notwithstanding the impact of COVID-19 containment measures. Inflation remained moderate and the current account deficit narrowed. Growth will continue to be strong in the current and following fiscal year, but below pre-pandemic levels because growth in industrialized economies is expected to slow on disruptions from the Russian invasion of Ukraine. A major policy challenge is managing climate change for ensuring inclusive and environmentally sustainable growth.

Economic performance

GDP grew by 6.9% in fiscal year 2021 (FY2021, ended 30 June 2021), up from 3.4% in FY2020 (Figure 3.15.1). The rise in external trade and the swift implementation of supportive fiscal and monetary stimulus measures to tackle the impact of the COVID-19 pandemic helped to foster a solid expansion in FY2021. The recovery was largely driven by rising industrial activity, up 10.3% from 3.6% in FY2020, on impressive manufacturing growth of 11.6%, reflecting stronger exports bolstered by garment orders from key export markets. Services grew by 5.7%, up from 3.9%, on a recovery mainly in wholesale and retail trade, but also stronger demand for accommodation and food services. The growth in agriculture output, however, slowed to 3.2% from 3.4% due to a cyclone and prolonged flooding early in the fiscal year.

Private consumption was a major contributor to growth in FY2021 as a sharp increase in worker remittances boosted domestic income. The rise in private consumption was achieved despite restrictions imposed in the final quarter to contain a second COVID-19 wave. Public investment increased due to higher annual development expenditure though there was no additional financing for development spending in the last quarter of FY2021. Growth in private investment still remained below the pre-pandemic level due to the cautious approach adopted by investors. Although

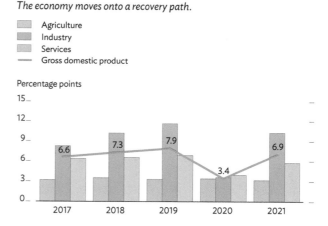

Figure 3.15.1 GDP growth by sector

The economy moves onto a recovery path.

- Agriculture
- Industry
- Services
- Gross domestic product

Percentage points

Note: Years are fiscal years ending on 30 June of that year.
Source: Bangladesh Bureau of Statistics (accessed 18 March 2022).

exports rebounded on the recovery in global trade after a sharp fall in FY2020, net exports remained a drag on growth due to a marked rise in imports.

Inflation averaged 5.6% in FY2021, a tad lower than in FY2020. Nonfood inflation slowed in the first half of FY2021 on tepid domestic demand, but accelerated in the second half as higher domestic incomes and remittances took hold (Figure 3.15.2). Food inflation,

This chapter was written by Soon Chan Hong, Barun K. Dey, and Mahbub Rabbani of the Bangladesh Resident Mission, ADB, Dhaka.

conversely, accelerated rapidly in the first half due to the floods, but moderated toward the end of the fiscal year on a good winter crop harvest and increased rice imports.

Figure 3.15.2 Monthly inflation

Price pressures eased in FY2021.

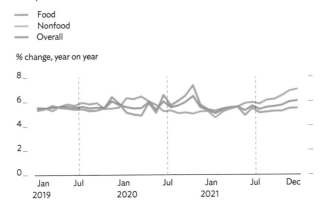

Note: Dotted lines denote ends of fiscal years.
Source: Bangladesh Bank. *Monthly Economic Trends. January 2022.*

Broad money growth edged up to 13.6% in FY2021 from 12.6% in FY2020 and was below its 15.0% monetary program target (Figure 3.15.3). Private sector credit growth, at 8.3%, was below the 14.8% target; both investors and banks were cautious in making new investments amid continuing uncertainty. Growth in net credit to the public sector was 19.0%, well below

Figure 3.15.3 Growth of monetary indicators

Private sector credit moderated in FY2021.

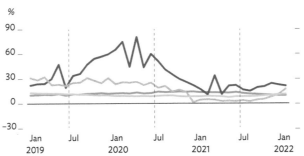

Note: Dotted lines denote ends of fiscal years.
Source: Bangladesh Bank. *Major Economic Indicators: Monthly Update. February 2022.*

the 31.7% target, as budget financing responded to strong demand for government-issued national savings certificates, driven by attractive interest rates. Market interest rates declined substantially on a build-up of commercial bank reserves and as part of its accommodative monetary policy, Bangladesh Bank, the central bank, cut policy rates to a 4.00%–4.75% corridor in July 2020 (Figure 3.15.4).

Figure 3.15.4 Interest rates

Policy rates cut to revive the economy.

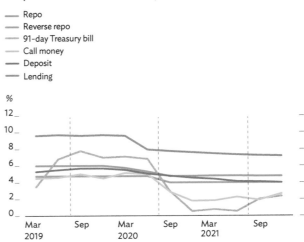

Note: Dotted lines denote ends of fiscal years.
Source: Bangladesh Bank. *Monthly Economic Trends. January 2022.*

Fiscal policy remained expansionary in FY2021 to support the economic recovery and mitigate the impact of COVID-19 on the poor and vulnerable. Government spending rose by 9.1% to 13.0% of GDP on an 11.4% rise in current expenditure to accommodate pandemic-related spending on health care and the stimulus measures. Development spending rose moderately by 6.1%. Revenue rose by 23.6% to Tk3.3 trillion, equivalent to 9.3% of GDP due to a rise in both direct and indirect taxes. The budget deficit, at 3.7% of GDP, was below the customary policy ceiling of 5.0%. Public sector external debt remained low, indicating a low risk of debt distress.

Exports rose by 15.4% to $37.9 billion in FY2021 after contracting 17.1% in the previous fiscal year. The rebound reflects economic recovery and greater demand from major export markets. Garment exports, accounting for 80% of total exports, grew by 12.5%, bolstered by the reinstatement of previously cancelled or delayed orders. Exports of jute goods, agricultural commodities, leather and leather products, and engineering goods increased sharply to lift other exports by 27.5%.

Imports increased by 19.7% to $60.7 billion after contracting by 8.6% in FY2020. A third of the increase came from higher petroleum and petroleum products, partly due to sharply higher prices. Imports of garment industry intermediates rose by 8.0%, reflecting the recovery in and stronger demand from export destinations. And there was double-digit import growth for other intermediates, consumer products, and capital goods. Rice imports increased sharply in FY2021 as government stocks were replenished and to contain pressure on rice prices.

With growth in imports ($10.0 billion) exceeding growth in exports ($5 billion), the trade deficit widened to $22.8 billion or 5.5% of GDP in FY2021. Remittances grew by 36.1% to $24.8 billion, underpinned by the 2% cash incentive given for transfers through official channels and relaxed documentation requirements. Remittances helped the current account deficit to narrow to $3.8 billion or 0.9% of GDP (Figure 3.15.5). The financial account surplus increased by $5.3 billion to $13.1 billion, mainly due to the increased use of trade credit to finance the surge in imports. With net financial

inflows significantly exceeding the current account deficit, gross foreign exchange reserves increased to $46.4 billion, cover for 7.8 months of imports of goods and services (Figure 3.15.6).

Figure 3.15.6 Gross foreign exchange reserves

Central bank builds up reserve buffer.

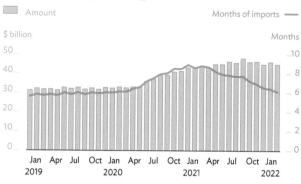

Source: Bangladesh Bank. *Economic data* (accessed 23 February 2022).

The taka, the local currency, remained stable against the US dollar in FY2021 as Bangladesh Bank continued its managed float policy. Reflecting a reduced current account deficit and much larger net financial account inflows, Bangladesh Bank bought $7.9 billion from the interbank foreign exchange market and sold $235 million to commercial banks to contain pressures for appreciation. Accounting for inflation differentials, the real effective exchange rate index depreciated by 2.1% in FY2021, suggesting improved export competitiveness (Figure 3.15.7).

Figure 3.15.5 Current account components

Narrowing deficit reflected robust remittances.

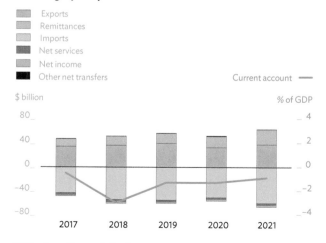

GDP = Gross Domestic Product.
Note: Years are fiscal years ending on 30 June of that year.
Source: Bangladesh Bank. 2021. *Annual Report 2020-2021.*

Figure 3.15.7 Exchange rates

Taka remained stable against the US dollar.

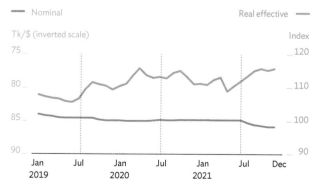

Note: Dotted lines denote ends of fiscal years.
Source: Bangladesh Bank. *Monthly Economic Trends. January 2022.*

Economic prospects

GDP is projected to continue to grow strongly at 6.9% in FY2022 on stepped-up budget spending, a strong expansion in exports and a slight improvement in agricultural output (Figure 3.15.8 and Table 3.15.1). With large available funding, public investment will increase to support the implementation of priority large infrastructure projects. Private investment will get stronger, reflecting solid growth in private sector credit and imports of industrial raw materials and capital goods. Growth in private consumption, however, may be affected by a decline in remittances through official channels.

Figure 3.15.8 Demand-side contributions to growth

Robust consumption supports the recovery.

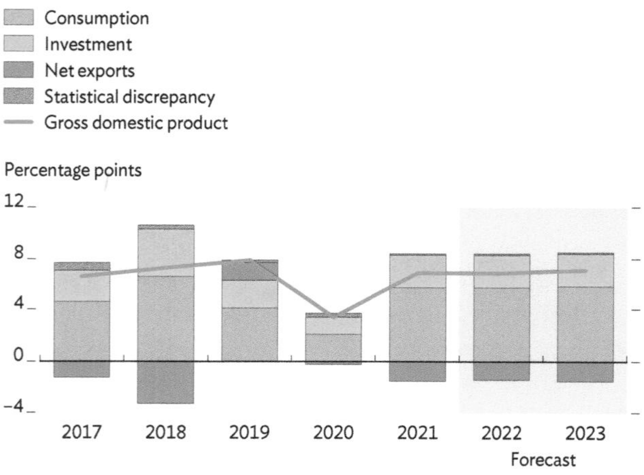

■ Consumption
■ Investment
■ Net exports
■ Statistical discrepancy
— Gross domestic product

Note: Years are fiscal years ending on 30 June of that year.
Sources: Bangladesh Bureau of Statistics; Asian Development Bank estimates.

Table 3.15.1 Selected economic indicators, %

Economy on the recovery path.

	2020	2021	2022	2023
GDP growth	3.4	6.9	6.9	7.1
Inflation	5.7	5.6	6.0	5.9
CAB/GDP	–1.3	–0.9	–2.7	–1.8

CAB = current account balance, GDP = gross domestic product.
Note: Years are fiscal years ending on 30 June of that year.
Sources: Bangladesh Bureau of Statistics; ADB estimates.

Growth in agriculture output is forecast at 3.4%, a tad higher than in FY2021, lifted by an increase in the targeted planted acreage of the monsoon rice crop (*aman*) on better weather, favorable rice prices, and policy support, including the timely provision of sufficient low-cost credit. Industry is expected to grow by 10.2% on still buoyant exports. The quantum index of medium and large-scale manufacturing production grew by 17.0% in the first quarter of FY2022, and small-scale manufacturing by 26.3%. Services are forecast to grow by 5.6% in FY2022.

GDP growth in FY2023 is expected to edge up to 7.1%. Private consumption will continue to be the main contributor to growth, buoyed by a modest increase in remittances. Private investment is expected to rise on a further improvement in investor confidence. Rising public investment in large infrastructure projects will also contribute to growth in FY2023. If normal weather prevails, agriculture growth is forecast at 3.6%. Industry output is projected to rise by 10.4% due to rising earnings from apparel exports on government policy support and demand for Bangladesh's garment products. Services growth, forecast at 5.8%, will be slightly higher, following the trend in agriculture and industry.

The headline inflation rate steadily increased from 5.4% in July 2021, the first month of the current fiscal year, to 6.1% in December 2021, lifted by rising global prices for food and commodities, especially for oil. The headline inflation rate rose to 6.1% in December 2021 from 5.3% in December 2020, food inflation increased to 5.5% from 5.3%, and nonfood inflation to 7.0% from 5.2%. Inflation will edge up in FY2022 to a forecast average of 6.0% due to rising global food and fuel prices. In November 2021, domestic diesel and kerosene prices rose by 23.1%. Further upward pressure on inflation will come from increased fiscal and monetary stimulus measures totaling $22.1 billion (5.4% of GDP). The inflation rate in FY2023 is forecast dipping to 5.9% on softer global food and fuel prices.

Monetary policy is expected to continue to be accommodative and expansionary in FY2022, while containing inflation and maintaining financial stability. To prevent the economy from slowing, Bangladesh Bank is implementing numerous monetary stimulus programs and will facilitate the flow of the funds to the production sector, especially for agriculture; cottage, small, and medium-sized enterprises; export-oriented industries; and for informal sector activity.

Broad money grew by 9.6% year on year in January 2022, but underperformed its annual monetary program target of 15.0%. Credit to the public sector increased by 20.7%, below the target of 32.5%, and net credit to the private sector, at 11.1%, improved on rising business optimism. The level was marginally higher than the target. With accelerating credit to the private sector and fiscal stimulus, broad money growth will likely reach its 15.0% annual growth target by the end of FY2022.

Exports grew by 30.3% in the first 7 months of FY2022 after a 1.1% contraction in the same period in FY2021 (Figure 3.15.9). There were sharp increases in most export products, with garment exports rising by 30.3%, while other exports grew at same pace on significant expansions in agricultural, leather, and engineering products. With economic growth in Bangladesh's major markets expected to be buoyant, the country's momentum of export growth is expected to continue over the rest of the current fiscal year. But because of the higher export base in the year earlier period and a slight decrease in exports due to the Russian invasion of Ukraine, overall export growth in FY2022 is projected at 26.2%. The government's draft export policy 2021-2024 proposes to extend policy benefits provided to the garment industry to other industries to enhance their export competitiveness. Nevertheless, export growth in FY2023 is forecast to decline to 8.1% on slower global growth and demand, as well as the high export base.

Rebounding on the normalization of economic activity, imports rose by 46.2% in the first 7 months of FY2022 after contracting 0.2% in the same period in FY2021. A 50.1% increase in imports of intermediates accounted for 64.0% of the increase in total imports. Half of imports of intermediates went to the garment industry and half to other manufacturing. Imports of food grains and other basic consumer goods increased by a combined 55.3%; imports of capital goods expanded by 46.0%, reflecting improving business confidence. With inventories replenished, imports are expected to level off in second half. Import growth for the whole of FY2022 is forecast at 24.3%. Import growth in FY2023 is expected to slow on a higher base, easing global oil and other commodity prices, and lower food imports on an uptick in agriculture.

Remittances fell by 19.9% in the first 7 months of FY2022, reflecting an unusually large 34.9% increase in the same period a year earlier. This is mainly due to the increased use of unofficial channels for transfers with resumption of international travel despite the 2% cash incentive offered by the government since FY2020 (Figure 3.15.10). Remittances are forecast falling to $21.8 billion in FY2022, down 12.0% on FY2021, reflecting a high base and greater use of unofficial channels by remittance senders. Despite expectations of lower remittances in the current fiscal year, the forecast level is nevertheless well above pre-pandemic FY2019's $16.4 billion. Remittances in FY2023 are projected to rebound to $23.3 billion, up 6.8%, on an additional 0.5% increase in the cash incentive and increased government efforts to curb the use of unofficial channels take hold.

Figure 3.15.9 Exports growth

Merchandise exports rebound on the global recovery.

Note: Years are fiscal years ending on 30 June of that year.
Source: Export Promotion Bureau.

Figure 3.15.10 Remittance growth

Remittances through official channels increase strongly in 2021.

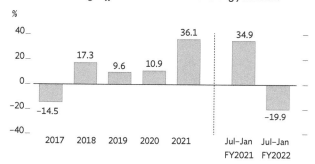

Note: Years are fiscal years ending on 30 June of that year.
Source: Bangladesh Bank. *Economic data* (accessed 23 February 2022).

Lower remittances in FY2022 will affect the current account deficit, which is expected to widen to 2.7% of GDP from 0.9% of GDP in FY2021 (Figure 3.15.11). The deficit in FY2023 is forecast narrowing to 1.8% of GDP on rebounding remittances and slower import growth.

Figure 3.15.11 Current account balance

Deficit will widen in 2022 on robust imports and lower remittances.

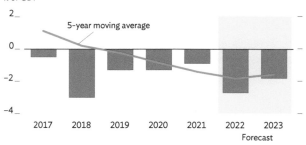

Note: Years are fiscal years ending on 30 June of that year.
Sources: Bangladesh Bank. *Annual Report 2020–2021*; Asian Development Bank estimates.

The FY2022 budget targets 10.7% growth in revenue to 9.8% of GDP and a 12.0% increase in expenditure (15.3% of GDP) compared with the revised FY2021 budget. Current spending is targeted increasing by 8.7% due mainly to continued high health care and welfare spending. The annual development program is budgeted to expand by 14.0%, mainly for infrastructure projects. The fiscal deficit will increase to 5.5% of GDP, above the 5.0% customary policy limit (Figure 3.15.12). Tax revenue collected by the National Board of Revenue grew by 16.8% to Tk1.3 trillion during the first half FY2022, about a third of the overall revenue target for the fiscal year, but only 24.1% of annual development program was implemented. Even with current expenditure broadly on target, the full implementation of government budget targets will not be realized, as has been the case in previous years.

The taka depreciated by 1.1% in nominal terms against the US dollar at the end of December 2021 from June even though Bangladesh Bank sold about $3.2 billion and purchased only $210 million in this period to contain market volatility on strong import demand. In real effective terms the currency appreciated by 4.2% over this period.

The outlook is subject to downside risks. The main uncertainty is the fallout on the global economy from the Russian invasion of Ukraine. Higher prices for oil and imports, and the loss of export sales beyond those built in the present forecasts, are the key risks to the outlook. And as ever, extreme weather events are always a possibility.

Figure 3.15.12 Fiscal indicators

Fiscal deficit widens, reflecting higher expenditure for recovery.

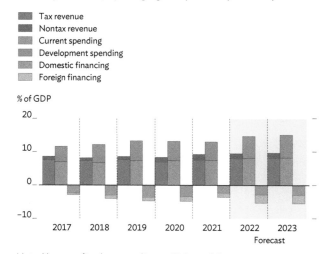

Note: Years are fiscal years ending on 30 June of that year.
Source: *Asian Development Outlook* database.

Policy challenge—managing climate change for inclusive and sustainable green growth

Bangladesh is one of the world's most vulnerable countries to climate change. With a deltaic topography going into the Bay of Bengal, the country is severely affected by floods, droughts, salinity intrusion, sea-level rise, erratic monsoon precipitation and runoff, tropical cyclones and tidal waves, riverbank erosion, and heat and cold waves. The Global Climate Risk Index ranked Bangladesh the 7th most-affected country by natural disasters during 2000–2019. Combating climate impacts and achieving environmentally sustainable growth for poverty reduction and other Sustainable Development Goals are key challenges for the country. The Eighth Five Year Plan, 2021–2025 estimates the effects of climate change could cause an average annual GDP loss of 1.3% up to 2041—a loss that would greatly hinder the country's long-term development.

Agriculture, which contributes 12% of GDP and employs 40% of the labor force, is the most vulnerable sector. The variability of precipitation and extreme weather events has already resulted in a decline of arable land and major crop losses. Salinity intrusion in arable land threatens food production in coastal areas, which disproportionately affects the poor. Climate change affects water resources as the increased incidence of drought depletes surface water availability and quality. Extreme flooding is a key threat. Studies estimate a potential increase of 6 million–12 million people being affected by extreme flooding during 2035–2044. The textile industry, agro-processing, and light-engineering, among other manufacturing sectors, will be affected by lower availability of raw materials, a shrinking water supply, and reduced storage facilities. Inundation can badly disrupt infrastructure facilities, such as transport, power, and communications, curtailing economic activities. The increased incidence of drought, extreme rainfall, and floods, as well as higher temperatures, are drivers of waterborne diseases.

Bangladesh has been proactive in tackling the severe climate challenges that it faces, developing a wide range of mitigation and adaptation options, strategies, and action plans. The 2005 National Adaptation Program of Action identified adaptation needs and developed strategies to deal with them. In 2008, the government adopted the Bangladesh Climate Change Strategy and Action Plan, which was revised and updated in 2009, and set up the publicly funded Climate Change Trust Fund to implement the strategy and action plan.

In 2018, it formulated Bangladesh Delta Plan 2100 to integrate the country's development goals with the long-term challenge of sustainably managing water, ecology and environment, and land resources. To further this effort, the government developed the Mujib Climate Prosperity Plan to mobilize financing to implement climate resilience initiatives by establishing a carbon market, issued Bangladesh Delta Plan 2100 resilience bonds for developing climate-resilient agriculture and fisheries, and accelerated digital support, training, and skills development.

The government is developing a national adaptation plan that is expected to be completed in 2022. As part of this effort, a climate risk–informed master plan should be drawn up for each sector and development unit. Climate resilient infrastructure and services should be a key imperative. Capacity for better accessing and utilizing climate risk analysis should be mainstreamed in public financial management decisions across government. A carbon tax on fossil fuels needs to be introduced and environmentally harmful subsidies to fossil fuels phased out. Financial policies should be designed to incentivize the private sector to create products or services that facilitate climate mitigation or adaptation actions. Fiscal incentives should be provided for green investments, the development and adoption of green technologies, and for greening existing industries. Programs in the social sector need to adapt to the effects of climate change on health by targeting social protection programs, including for waterborne diseases.

BHUTAN

Growth rebounded moderately in 2021 as economic activity picked up on the government's stimulus measures and steps to ease supply chain disruptions caused by COVID-19 restrictions following a sharp economic contraction in 2020. The progressive relaxation of containment measures, including opening the country to tourism, and continued robust policy measures will enable the economy to grow faster in 2022 and 2023. Creating a conducive environment for private sector development is a major policy challenge.

Economic performance

Bhutan's GDP growth expanded by an estimated 3.5% in 2021, reversing a deep 10.1% contraction in 2020. Growth was buoyed by fiscal and monetary stimulus measures and the easing of supply-chain problems caused by pandemic containment measures (Figure 3.16.1).

Figure 3.16.1 Supply-side contributions to growth

All sectors registered moderate growth in 2021 led by industry.

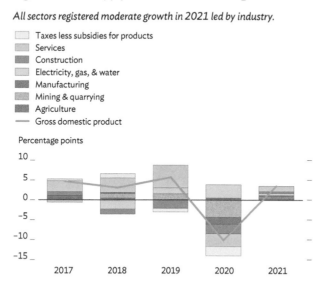

Sources: Haver Analytics; National Statistics Bureau (both accessed 4 February 2022); Asian Development Bank estimates.

All sectors are estimated to have grown in 2021 on strong domestic demand supported by the government's counter-cyclical programs and monetary relief measures. Industry output is estimated to have increased by 4.7%, accounting for nearly half of GDP growth. The construction and export-oriented electricity subsectors accounted for two-thirds of industry growth, and manufacturing, mining, and quarrying for the rest. Agriculture growth slowed to an estimated 3.6% from 4.6% in 2020 because of an unfavorable monsoon. Services continued to be affected by the closure of international tourism, but nevertheless grew by 2.8%, reversing the 6.9% contraction in 2020. The services sector, which accounts for 40% of GDP growth, was buoyed by a revival in retail trade and other domestic businesses.

Total consumption expenditure, comprising 82% of GDP, is estimated to have grown by 5.4% in 2021 (Figure 3.16.2). Government current expenditure increased by 22.5% in fiscal year 2021 (FY2021, ended 30 June 2021) to fund higher spending to mitigate the impact of COVID-19, including on social relief, economic support, and wages and salaries. This spending helped support private consumption. Gross fixed investment is estimated to have contracted by 6.9% due to labor shortages, as many expatriate workers left the country at the onset of the COVID-19

This chapter was written by Shamit Chakravarti of the Bhutan Resident Mission (BHRM), ADB, Thimphu, Phuntsho Choden, consultant, BHRM, and Rana Hasan of the India Resident Mission, ADB, New Delhi.

Figure 3.16.2 Demand-side contributions to growth

Government spending supported private consumption, but investment contracted in 2021.

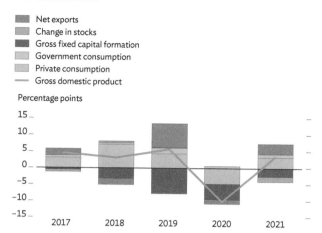

Sources: Haver Analytics; National Statistics Bureau (both accessed 4 February 2022); Asian Development Bank estimates.

Figure 3.16.3 Inflation

Inflation edged up in 2021 due to supply chain disruptions.

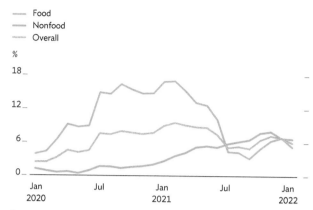

Sources: Haver Analytics; National Statistics Bureau (both accessed 4 February 2022).

pandemic, and a lack of material supplies because of border closures and mobility restrictions within Bhutan. These factors markedly lowered the utilization of the government's large capital budget allocation (Figure 3.16.2).

The contraction in economic activity in 2020 resulted in the loss of many jobs. Some 50,000 people were laid off from tourism and allied sectors alone. Bhutan's unemployment rate is estimated at 4.7% in 2021 after hitting an all-time high of 5.0% in 2020. The government's stimulus packages to revive the economy, the Build Bhutan Project, and job creation schemes helped reduce the unemployment rate in 2021.

Average inflation accelerated to 7.4% in 2021 from 5.6% in the previous year. Food inflation averaged 9.9%, but declined from high year-on-year inflation at the start of year at 14.8%. The inflation rate fell to 6.9% in December as the constraints eased. The nonfood inflation rate averaged 5.6%, but followed the opposite trajectory to food inflation by starting the year on low year-on-year inflation of 2.0% and rising to 6.8% in December as consumer demand quickened on the economic recovery and rising income. (Figure 3.16.3).

Fiscal policy in FY2021 was expansive to counter the socioeconomic impact of the pandemic. Fiscal spending focused on health care, social protection, and other countercyclical measures (Figure 3.16.4). Total current expenditure increased by 22% to reach 24% of GDP, the increase largely reflected pandemic-related spending, including social relief and funding for economic support measures. Although a generous capital expenditure allocation was made in FY2021, utilization capacity was limited by constraints caused by a severe shortage of skilled labor due to the departure of expatriate workers, supply chain disruptions, and escalating costs. The budget deficit widened to 6.1% of GDP in FY2021 from 1.9% in the previous fiscal year.

Monetary policy remained accommodative to help revive the economy. The waiver of interest payments, deferments of loan repayments, and concessional credit to productive sectors will continue until June 2022. A reduction in the cash reserve ratio from 10% to 7% increased bank liquidity and complemented other accommodative monetary policy measures. Broad money is estimated to have increased by 17% in 2021 (through November), reflecting a large increase in net foreign assets. Growth in private credit accelerated from 7.1% in 2020 to 9.5% in 2021 (Figure 3.16.5). The ngultrum, the local currency, which is pegged to the Indian rupee, depreciated by 3% in 2021.

Figure 3.16.4 Fiscal indicators

Expansive fiscal policy deployed to counter COVID-19 pandemic.

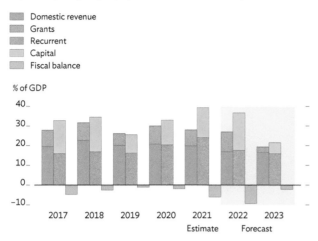

COVID-19 = Coronavirus Disease 2019, GDP = gross domestic product.
Note: Years are fiscal years ending on 30 June of that year.
Source: Ministry of Finance (accessed 4 February 2022).

Figure 3.16.5 Monetary indicators

Accommodative monetary policy to stimulate economic growth.

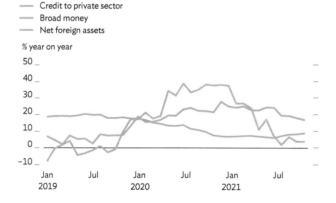

Source: Royal Monetary Authority (accessed 4 February 2022).

The current account deficit—estimated at 11.0% of GDP as compared to 13.8% in 2020—narrowed due to a decline in the trade deficit, driven by a 30.0% increase in exports, mainly electricity and minerals (Figure 3.16.6). Imports grew by 18.0%, reflecting the strong economy and offsetting the 12.6% contraction in 2020. Increased capital and financial account inflows exceeded the current account deficit, resulting in an overall balance estimated at $214 million.

Figure 3.16.6 Components of the current account

Current account deficit narrowed on strong growth in exports.

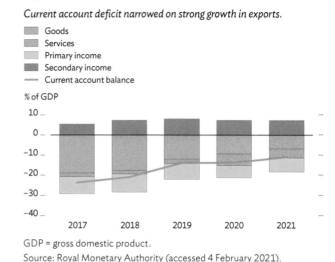

GDP = gross domestic product.
Source: Royal Monetary Authority (accessed 4 February 2021).

Gross international reserves increased by $147 million to $1.7 billion in 2021, cover for 22.5 months of imports (Figure 3.16.7). External public debt increased marginally to $3 billion (118% of GDP) (Figure 3.16.8). External debt is largely concentrated in hydropower, which accounts for 73% of external debt and is mostly denominated in Indian rupees. Since hydropower loans are linked with power purchasing agreements, they are not considered high risk. Even so, the government has initiated measures to strengthen debt management, including raising transparency and reporting standards.

Figure 3.16.7 External reserves

Gross international reserves increased.

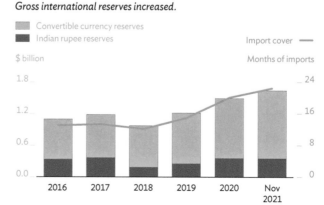

Source: Royal Monetary Authority (accessed 4 February 2022).

Figure 3.16.8 External public external debt

Moderate increase in borrowing as investment declines.

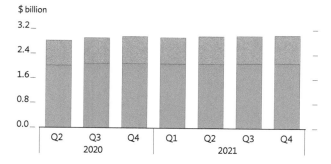

GDP = gross domestic product, Q = quarter.
Source: Ministry of Finance (accessed 18 March 2022).

Economic prospects

Two prolonged lookdowns from mid-January to March to contain the spread of the COVID-19 Omicron variant have clouded the outlook for 2022. The roll out of booster shots and the vaccination of children ages 5–11 is in progress. The government is expected to implement a new COVID-19 management strategy from April that will progressively relax restrictions and avoid future lockdowns unless hospitalization rates go up beyond certain levels. Economic activities are expected to resume. Tourism levels should gradually increase. GDP growth is forecast at 4.5% in 2022. A new hydropower plant will become operational next year. The decision to reopen the country to international tourism will lift growth further in 2023, to a forecast 7.5%.

Table 3.16.1 Selected economic indicators, %

Growth to recover, inflation to remain high in 2022 and 2023.

	2020	2021	2022	2023
GDP growth	–10.1	3.5	4.5	7.5
Inflation	5.6	7.4	7.0	5.5
CAB/GDP	–13.8	–11.0	–10.6	–10.5

CAB = current account balance, GDP = gross domestic product.
Sources: Ministry of Finance; National Statistics Bureau; Asian Development Bank estimates.

The services sector is projected to grow by 5.0% this year as COVID-19 mobility restrictions are expected to be removed during the second half, which would boost consumer demand. Industry is forecast to grow by 4.0% on stronger construction activity, estimated to rise 5.2% on a surge in budgeted capital spending as supply chain disruptions subside and labor shortages lessen. Slightly slower electricity production growth is expected due to the closure of the large Tala hydropower plant for maintenance from January to March. Agriculture growth will also slow down to a projected 2.6% due to unfavorable weather. On the demand side, private consumption expenditure is forecast to grow by 6.0 % in 2022 and 6.5% in 2023 as consumer confidence revives on a rebounding economy and the further lifting of COVID-19 restrictions. Fixed investment is expected to grow by 6.5% and grow further in 2023.

The 39% increase in the budget allocation for capital spending in FY2022 is the highest during the 12th Five Year Plan period of 2018-2023. While there may be shortfalls in implementation, capital spending is expected to support the expansion in fixed investment. Because of the constitutional requirement that current expenditure should always be funded by domestic revenue, current expenditure is budgeted to fall by 18.1% in the current fiscal year. On balance, the budget deficit is projected to widen to 9.4% of GDP in the current fiscal year from 6.3% in FY2021. The monetary policy measures to stimulate the economy during the COVID-19 pandemic will continue up to mid-year, and then give way to targeted and selective monetary measures.

Average inflation in 2022 is projected at 7.0% amid persistent upward pressure on food and nonfood prices. A normally functioning supply chain should stave off the price spikes that were a feature of last year's inflation. However, inflation will remain elevated this year due to the spillover effects of inflationary pressure from India and high global oil and commodities prices. Inflation is expected to decelerate in 2023 due to easing global oil and commodity prices; the rate is forecast at 5.5%.

The current account deficit is projected to narrow to 10.6% of GDP in 2022 owing to a slight reduction in the trade deficit from a projected 16.5% increase in exports and a 14.8% rise in imports. The deficit is projected at 10.5% of GDP next year. Substantially increased hydropower exports as a result of new capacity being added and a moderate increase in international tourism receipts are projected to slightly offset the higher import bill resulting from faster growth.

The main risks to the outlook over the forecast horizon are a new wave of COVID-19 outbreaks and the emergence of new variants, rising public debt, and a slower-than-expected recovery in the private sector.

Policy challenge—a conducive environment for private sector development

Bhutan's focus on hydropower as the main source of growth, exports, and foreign exchange earnings has come at the cost of a vibrant and competitive private sector. Net foreign direct investment inflows totaled just 0.5% of GDP in FY2019—very low compared to other economies with similar per capita incomes, such as Viet Nam at 6.2% of GDP, the Philippines at 2.3%, and South Asia's 1.6% average.

It is vital that the government does more to attract the private sector as a partner and investor in economic development, diversify the economy beyond hydropower, and reduce the oversized role played by the public sector. Public investment in commercially-oriented government-linked companies has been instrumental in developing Bhutan's energy, finance, manufacturing, and agribusiness sectors— but it has also constrained the growth of the private sector in areas where there is overlap. This is because relatively easy and affordable access to finance and preferential treatment by the government to state-owned enterprises have crowded out cottage and small-scale industries (CSIs), which account for 95% of all industries and employ over 90,000 people. Since a conducive business environment is lacking and the market size is small, private firms struggle to grow and exploit economies of scale. Less than 5.0% of registered manufacturing firms are categorized as large.

Over the years, the government has undertaken policy reforms, simplified licensing requirements, and provided incentives for the private sector. The results, however, have not been encouraging. Businesses continue to identify tight access to finance, high rents, erratic electricity supply, multiple licensing requirements, delays in getting clearances, and high-interest loans as the main obstacles affecting their operations. These obstacles raise the compliance and transaction costs for firms and are especially burdensome for CSIs. According to the Economic Census 2018, over 56% of firms are owned by women. COVID-19's impact on the economy, which has included the virtual collapse of tourism, has further added to the challenges faced by Bhutan's private sector.

To jump-start the economy and put it on a sustainable and broader-based growth path, Bhutan needs to create a conducive business environment for the private sector. An ambitious 21st Century Economic Roadmap, which is at the draft stage, is being prepared by the Gross National Happiness Commission with the participation of a group of eminent persons and private sector representatives. The draft urges the government to shift to an "allow first and regulate later" approach to make it easier for businesses to respond to market opportunities, access raw materials, and import productivity-enhancing technologies. The government needs to further review and simplify industrial licensing policies, rules and implementing guidelines for public–private partnerships and foreign direct investment, and rationalize tax rates so that there are no disincentives for CSIs to scale up.

Bhutan's commercial law, especially provisions on insolvency and bankruptcy laws for CSIs, should be updated and made more transparent. Insolvency laws need to be tailored in line with the specific needs of CSIs, which are very different compared with those of large businesses. CSIs require fewer complex procedures for restructuring and more support. Effective out-of-court negotiated settlements that save on time and cost and a modern insolvency law calibrated to the needs of CSIs would help Bhutan immensely.

A hybrid insolvency regime that offers timely and cost-effective solutions for CSIs and small firms in financial distress should be considered. The regime should include a process for liquidating assets and discharging the debt of individual entrepreneurs that is unserviceable and can be mediated or out-of-court negotiated workouts with creditor-led, simplified procedures for restructuring as an alternative to liquidation.

INDIA

The economy rebounded strongly in fiscal 2021 following a contraction in fiscal 2020. Easing supply chain disruptions softened inflation, despite rising global oil prices, and rising domestic demand turned the current account surplus into a deficit. Growth will moderate in fiscal 2022, but remain strong, buoyed by investment. Inflation will accelerate and the current account deficit widen due to the surge in global oil prices. Improving the domestic resource mobilization of the states is a key policy challenge for sustained and inclusive growth.

Economic performance

The Indian economy recovered in fiscal year 2021 (FY2021, ended 31 March 2022) after a severe contraction in FY2020. The recovery was despite two waves of COVID-19, especially of the Delta variant, which severely strained the country's health infrastructure. GDP is forecast to grow by 8.9% in FY2021 based on available data up to the third quarter (Q3, October–December) and in some instances beyond.

In seasonally adjusted terms, the economy contracted by 12.1% in the first quarter (Q1), but growth revived in Q2 and Q3, buoyed by private consumption. Investment also contributed to growth, especially in Q2 (Figure 3.17.1). Growth in domestic demand resulted in imports outpacing exports.

The economic impact of the Delta variant hit services hard in Q1, but the sector rebounded in Q2 and Q3 as COVID-19 subsided (Figure 3.17.2). Trade, hotels, and transport services were the initial drivers of services growth in Q2 and financial, real estate, and professional services picked up strongly in Q3. In these quarters, industry growth was supported mainly by construction, the country's largest employer after agriculture, and manufacturing. Agricultural production was stable.

With the spread of Omicron variant, new COVID-19 cases started surging in the first week of January 2022,

Figure 3.17.1 Demand-side contributions to growth

Private consumption has been an important contributor to growth since Q2 2021.

Percentage points quarter on quarter, seasonally adjusted

Q = quarter.
Note: Years are fiscal years ending on 31 March of the next year.
Sources: Ministry of Statistics and Programme Implementation; Haver Analytics (accessed 18 March 2022).

peaking at some 500,000 cases by the 14th. Cases have since declined. No nationwide lockdown was imposed in FY2021, although several states imposed weekend and night curfews, and closed restaurants and bars. The impact of these restrictions, coupled with the geopolitical fallout from the Russian invasion of Ukraine, may marginally lower growth in the last quarter (January–March) of the current fiscal year.

This chapter was written by Shalini Mittal and Rana Hasan of the India Resident Mission, ADB, New Delhi.

Figure 3.17.2 Supply-side contributions to growth

Services have strongly supported growth since the Delta COVID-19 variant wave subsided.

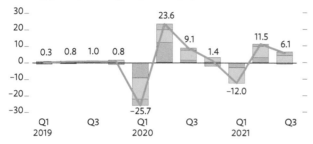

COVID-19 = Coronavirus Disease 2019, Q = quarter.
Notes: Years are fiscal years ending on 31 March of the next year.
Net taxes on products are tax receipts minus subsidies.
Sources: *Ministry of Statistics and Programme Implementation*; Haver Analytics (accessed 18 March 2022).

Headline inflation decelerated from 6.2% in FY2020 to 5.4% for most of FY2021, despite rising fuel prices and global chip shortages, as supply chain disruptions caused by local COVID-19 restrictions eased and food prices moderated (Figure 3.17.3). The inflation rate for food nearly halved to 3.8% in the first 10 months of FY2021 from 7.8% in the same period in FY2020. Prices of cereals, a staple, contracted marginally by 0.2%; vegetable prices fell by double digits. Fuel prices soared to 11.9% from 2.4%. Core inflation, which excludes food and fuel prices, inched up and remained marginally higher than 6.0% for most of FY2021, averaging 5.9% in

the first 10 months of FY2021, compared with 5.5% in the same period of FY2020.

With inflation remaining within the 2%–6% target of the Reserve Bank of India (RBI) due to easing supply-side factors and a weaker-than-expected recovery in private consumption and investment, the policy rate (repurchase rate) remained unchanged in FY2021—contrary to market expectations. The RBI, however, injected ample surplus liquidity into the banking system to nurture nascent growth impulses and support a durable recovery (Figure 3.17.4). This facilitated a more orderly conduct of the government's market borrowing program. Despite ample liquidity, the interest rate spread widened amid rising global oil prices and the anticipated hike in the United States federal funds rate. The spread between the 10-year government benchmark bond and the 91-day Treasury bill was 294 basis points at the end of January, indicating rising inflationary expectations. The geopolitical uncertainty over the Russian invasion of Ukraine caused the spread to widen further, to 307 basis points in early March (Figure 3.17.5). This may put further pressure on the central bank to increase its policy rate.

Nonfood bank credit, which excludes public sector loans for buying crops from farmers, rebounded, growing by 9.6% year on year in January 2022 from 5.5% in March 2020 (Figure 3.17.6). Credit growth remained strong across agriculture and industry, despite a contraction in loans to large firms due to a double-digit increase in loans to micro, small, and medium-sized enterprises. Growth in personal loans

Figure 3.17.3 Inflation

Headline inflation moderated while core remained elevated.

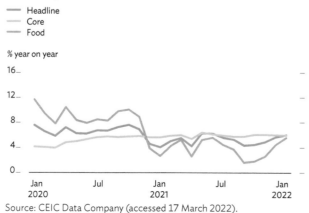

Source: CEIC Data Company (accessed 17 March 2022).

Figure 3.17.4 Interest rates

Policy rate was not raised in FY2021 as monetary policy remained accommodative.

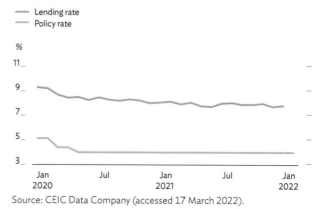

Source: CEIC Data Company (accessed 17 March 2022).

Figure 3.17.5 Bond yield spread

Bond yields continue to rise in light of global uncertainty.

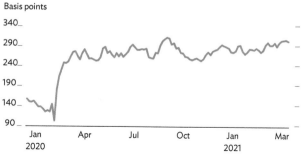

Source: CEIC Data Analytics (accessed 16 March 2022)

Figure 3.17.7 Nonperforming loans

Declining NPLs should set the stage for increased bank lending.

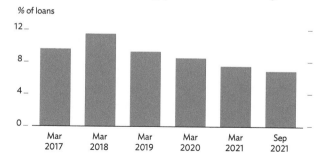

NPL = nonperforming loan.
Source: Reserve Bank of India (accessed 2 March 2022).

Figure 3.17.6 Bank credit

Bank credit remained strong supported by loans to MSMEs and a pickup in industry.

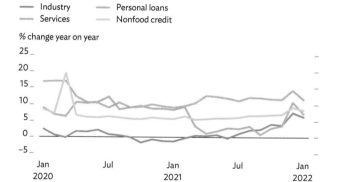

MSMEs = micro, small, and medium-sized enterprises.
Note: Nonfood credit excludes public sector loans for buying crops from farmers.
Source: *Centre for Monitoring Indian Economy Outlook Database* (accessed 11 March 2022).

almost doubled even though loans against gold jewelry moderated. Loans for consumer durables rebounded after contracting in the last fiscal year, indicating strengthening consumer purchasing power. Credit to the services sector remained strong, growing an average of 4.0% from April 2021 to January 2022, up from 2.7% for FY2020.

The nonperforming loan (NPL) ratio declined from 8.2% of total loans at the end of March 2020 to 7.3% at end-March 2021 and further to 6.9% at end-September 2021 (Figure 3.17.7). Macro-stress tests by the central bank for credit risk show the NPL ratio may increase to 8.1% by this September under the baseline scenario and to 9.5% under a severe-stress scenario. However,

the tests also show that all banks will be able to comply with the minimum capital requirements even under the severe-stress scenario.

With the rebound in economic activity resulting in a 28.8% increase in budget revenue and a reduction in pandemic-related expenditure, the fiscal deficit for FY2021 moderated to 6.9% of GDP, marginally higher than the 6.8% originally budgeted (Figure 3.17.8). Gross tax revenue rebounded by 24.1% (10.8% of nominal GDP), higher than nominal GDP growth of 17.2%. Corporate tax revenue grew by 38.7% and goods and service tax rose by 23.0%. Nontax revenue from the dividends and profits of state-owned firms increased by nearly 50.0%.

Figure 3.17.8 Federal budget indicators

Capital spending is expected to increase further and sustain the economic recovery.

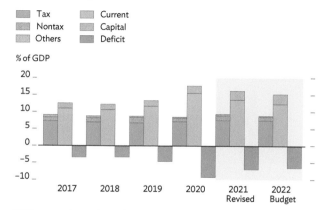

GDP = gross domestic product.
Note: Years are fiscal years ending on 31 March of the next year.
Source: *Ministry of Finance. Union Budget.*

Budget expenditure rose by ₹2.6 trillion (16.2% of GDP) in FY2021. Spending increased on the government shifting from providing subsidies to increased capital spending and higher allocations to the Mahatma Gandhi National Rural Employment Guarantee Scheme, as localized COVID-19 lockdowns made it difficult for low-income workers to find jobs in urban areas. Food subsidies contracted by 47.1% and petroleum subsidies by 83.1%. Fertilizer subsidies increased by 9.5% due to rising fertilizer prices. Interest payments rose to 3.5% of GDP, the highest since FY2005, as the government borrowed more to finance pandemic-related expenditure.

Imports and exports grew rapidly, reversing FY2020's contraction and showing clear signs of recovery (Figure 3.17.9). Merchandise imports rose by 68.1% year on year in the first 10 months of FY2021 after contracting 13.4% in FY2020. Oil imports grew by 96.5%, mainly due to rising oil prices (the volume of imports increased by only 5.4%). Non-oil imports, including gold and silver, grew by 50.3%. Merchandise exports rose by 46.5%. Exports of petroleum products increased by 151.0% as global demand for India's exports recovered, albeit more softly than anticipated. The trade deficit widened on the surge in imports.

The services trade surplus increased by 16.3% in the first 10 months of FY2021, up from 11.8% in the same period in FY2020 on services exports picking up in the later part of the fiscal year. Remittances grew by 4.7% in the first 6 months of FY2021 (April–September) following a contraction in the same period of FY2020. On balance, the current account balance, which recorded a surplus in FY2020 due to declining imports, turned a deficit of 1.6% of GDP in FY2021.

Foreign direct investment (FDI) declined to $37.8 billion in the first 9 months of FY2021 from $49.2 billion during the same period of FY2020. This was largely due to 2020's large merger and acquisition deals not being repeated. According to an UNCTAD 2021 World Investment Report, FDI in India in 2020 was pushed up by acquisitions in the information and communication technology industry, making India the fifth largest recipient of this FDI in the world. Rising concerns over an increase in US interest rates and the geopolitical fallout of the Russian invasion of Ukraine saw foreign portfolio net outflows of $15.7 billion in FY2021. But the Bombay stock exchange index rose by 12.0% as markets continue to be flush with liquidity (Figure 3.17.10). Foreign currency reserves grew by $55.8 billion to $630.0 billion in the first 10 months of FY2021, cover for 13 months of imports (Figure 3.17.11).

The Indian rupee depreciated by 3.5% against the US dollar in FY2021, falling significantly in the last 2 months of the fiscal year after the Russian invasion of Ukraine (Figure 3.17.12). It appreciated in real effective terms by 0.6% in first 10 months as domestic prices increased more than those of trade partners.

Figure 3.17.9 Trade indicators

Exports and import shares surpassed levels before the COVID-19 pandemic.

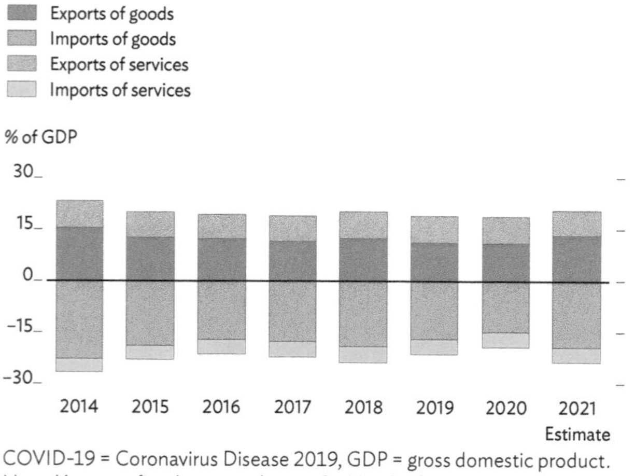

- Exports of goods
- Imports of goods
- Exports of services
- Imports of services

% of GDP

COVID-19 = Coronavirus Disease 2019, GDP = gross domestic product.
Note: Years are fiscal years ending on 31 March of the next year.
Source: CEIC Data Company (accessed 17 March 2022).

Figure 3.17.10 Stock prices

Stock prices continued to rise relative to other parts of the region.

- Emerging markets excluding Asia
- Bombay Stock Exchange Sensex Index
- MSCI AC AP excluding Japan

Percentage points

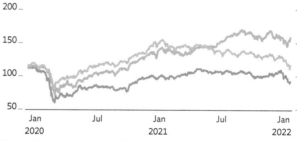

Source: Bloomberg (accessed 17 March 2022).

Figure 3.17.11 Gross international reserves

Reserves grew while import cover declined but remained healthy.

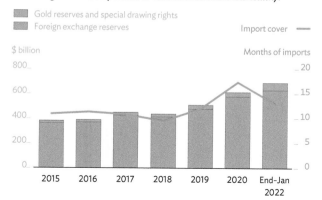

- Gold reserves and special drawing rights
- Foreign exchange reserves

Import cover ——

Note: Years are fiscal years ending on 31 March of the next year.
Source: CEIC Data Company (accessed 17 March 2022).

Figure 3.17.12 Exchange rate

The rupee has been depreciating since January 2021.

Source: Bloomberg (accessed 17 March 2022).

Economic prospects

GDP is forecast to grow by 7.5% in FY2022 and 8.0% in FY2023, driven by strong investment growth, with public investment helping crowd-in private investment (Table 3.17.1). This forecast assumes the severity of the COVID-19 pandemic subsiding and vaccination rates rising. The vaccination rate is already high, exceeding 90% of the eligible population (with at least one dose). Booster doses have been distributed for health care and frontline workers, and for those older than 60 years with comorbidities. The vaccination of those ages 15 to 18 commenced in January. Two new vaccines have been approved, taking the number of vaccines given restricted use in emergency situations in India to eight. The forecast also factors in the impact of Russian invasion of Ukraine, which will be largely felt indirectly through higher oil prices.

Table 3.17.1 Selected economic indicators, %

Growth will moderate in 2022 and pick up in 2023.

	2020	2021	2022	2023
GDP growth	−6.6	8.9	7.5	8.0
Inflation	6.2	5.4	5.8	5.0
CAB/GDP	0.9	−1.6	−2.8	−1.9

CAB = current account balance, GDP = gross domestic product.
Note: Years are fiscal years ending on 31 March of the next year.
Sources: Ministry of Statistics and Programme Implementation; Asian Development Bank estimates.

Fiscal policy is expected to be supportive of growth. The fiscal deficit for FY2022 is budgeted at 6.4% of GDP, supported by increased capital spending. Capital expenditure in FY2022's budget of ₹7.5 trillion (2.9% of GDP) is up 24.5% from the previous fiscal year; this works out as an increase of 0.3 percentage points of GDP. The higher capital spending is expected to improve the efficiency of India's logistics infrastructure, among others, crowd-in private investment, generate jobs in construction, and sustain growth. Economic activity in FY2022 will be driven by investment, with public investment playing a catalytic role. In particular, to facilitate investment projects, the government plans to improve logistics infrastructure and reduce logistics costs through its PM Gati Shakti initiative, a national master plan that brings together 16 ministries, including railways and roads, for the integrated planning and coordination of infrastructure connectivity projects. Financial and technical assistance to states will also be increased to facilitate investment projects.

To help states raise investment, the government increased FY2022's budget allocation to the Scheme of Financial Assistance to States for Capital Investment to ₹1 trillion from ₹150 billion in FY2021. The scheme provides 50-year interest-free loans over and above the normal borrowing allowed to states. States are allowed to increase their fiscal deficits to 4.0% of their GDP, of which 0.5% should be linked to their undertaking power sector reforms. The government plans to provide capacity building support to state governments to better manage infrastructure projects.

Private investment is expected to get a push in FY2022 and especially FY2023 from improvements in the ease of doing business, bank deleveraging, and cleaning up of banks' balance sheets, and improvements in logistics and further reforms planned to reduce logistics costs. Overall, the business expectations index remains high and 67.6% of the respondents of an RBI survey in December expecting next quarter's business situation to improve. Capacity utilization rates are expected to improve in first half of FY2022, indicating room for future investments (Figure 3.17.13).

Figure 3.17.13 Industry outlook

Rising capacity utilization rates since mid-2020 indicate room for future investments.

— Overall business situation
— Capacity utilization

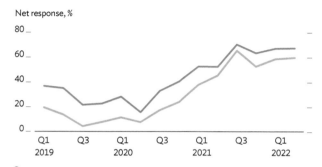

Q = quarter.
Source: CEIC Data Company (accessed 1 March 2022).

Private consumption is expected to pick up over the forecast horizon on pent-up demand for consumption goods as the severity of the COVID-19 pandemic decreases and disruptions to mobility lessen. The RBI survey, however, shows consumer confidence in November was still below pre-pandemic levels, but one-year-ahead expectations continued to improve, buoyed by optimism for higher household income and employment (Figure 3.17.14).

Agriculture output is expected to remain robust despite the government withdrawing market-oriented farm bills in light of a prolonged farmer protest. A bumper harvest, a normal monsoon, and the area sown for summer crops reaching 111.8% of the normal area by February 2022 will result in high agriculture output. Rising commodity prices in the international market, will boost wheat exports (wheat prices have risen noticeably) and improve farmers' incomes.

Figure 3.17.14 Consumer confidence

One-year-ahead expectations are improving.

— Current situation
— Future expectations

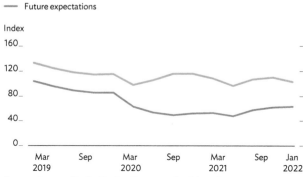

Source: Reserve Bank of India. *Consumer Confidence Survey* (accessed 2 March 2022).

The manufacturing purchasing manager's index softened in January 2022, but was above 50, indicating expansion (Figure 3.17.15). Government policies are expected to facilitate industrial production over the forecast horizon. In particular, with production-linked incentive schemes, the government aims to boost domestic production where domestic capabilities are believed to exist. Tariffs on certain products have been raised to encourage production. But it will be important to ensure that tariff increases do not become entrenched as this would raise the overall cost structure of production and discourage the greater integration of firms into global value chains.

Figure 3.17.15 Purchasing managers' index

PMI remains above 50, indicating expansion.

— Manufacturing
— Services

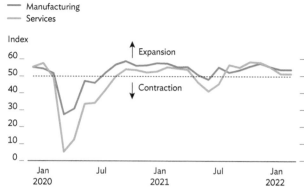

PMI = purchasing managers' index.
Note: PMI indexes are based on Nikkei, Markit.
Source: Bloomberg (accessed 4 March 2022).

Oil price increases will exert upward pressure on prices, but the impact on inflation will be moderated by fuel subsidies and oil refineries stocking up on cheap crude from the Russian Federation. With oil prices expected to average over $100/barrel in 2022, firms may readjust their prices as profitability falls, which will create further upward pressure on consumer prices. Food prices are expected to rise in tandem with increasing commodity prices. On balance, the inflation rate is forecast to average 5.8% in FY2022 and 5.0% in FY2023, within RBI's target range.

Monetary policy is expected to remain accommodative given the global uncertainties. The central bank will strive to keep the policy rate unchanged to sustain economic growth, but a tightening in the federal funds rate and rising oil prices may put pressure on it to increase policy rates in the later part of the current fiscal year.

The growth of exports and imports of goods and services will moderate in FY2022 and FY2023 in line with the slower growth of global demand. Rising oil prices are likely to increase the import bill, widening the trade deficit. But rising oil and commodity prices, as well as a depreciating Indian rupee, may provide an impetus to exports, especially petroleum products and food products. Remittances are expected to strengthen as India attracts inflows largely from Gulf countries, where economic activity should pick up on the strength of oil prices. The current account deficit is expected to widen to 2.8% of GDP in FY2022 (Figure 3.17.16). Export growth will remain strong in FY2023 as some reform initiatives take effect, including production-linked incentive schemes and investments to improve logistics infrastructure. Import growth will ease on softer oil prices. The current account deficit will shrink to a forecast 1.9% of GDP in FY2023.

FDI inflows are projected to decline over the forecast horizon amid rising global uncertainty and a tightening in global economic and financial conditions. Foreign portfolio inflows will be affected by adverse global conditions and expected increases in the US federal funds rate, making it less attractive for foreign investors to invest abroad due to a rising interest-rate differential (Figure 3.17.17).

Figure 3.17.16 Current account balance

The current account deficit will widen in 2022 due to rising oil prices.

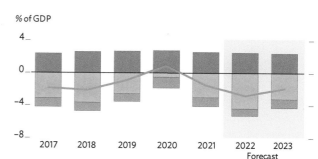

GDP = gross domestic product.
Note: Years are fiscal years ending on 31 March of the next year.
Sources: CEIC Data Company; Asian Development Bank estimates.

Figure 3.17.17 Portfolio flows

Portfolio flows turned negative due to rising global uncertainty.

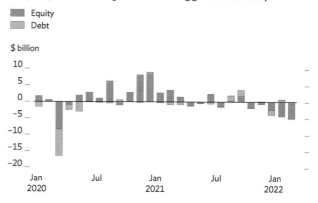

Source: Security and Exchange Board of India (accessed 3 March 2022).

Risks to the outlook are tilted to the downside. The main risks are the uncertain global economic conditions, renewed COVID-19 outbreaks and new variants, monetary policy tightening in the US, and unexpected and sharp rises in commodity prices. The Russian invasion of Ukraine could lead to even higher oil prices and supply disruptions, pushing up prices of commodities and further raising the inflation rate.

Policy challenge—improving domestic resource mobilization by the states

Mobilizing domestic resources remains a key challenge at all levels of the government given a largely unchanged tax-to-GDP ratio of 17% since the early 1990s. As highlighted by the most recent Finance Commission, a constitutional quasi-judicial body that is reconstituted every 5 years and provides recommendations on the distribution of taxes and grants between the central government and states, this ratio must be raised by mobilizing resources at both the central and especially state government levels in order to meet rising developmental needs.

This is especially important because of rising state fiscal deficits since FY2011 and higher ratios of state debt to GDP since FY2015. Worsening state finances have macroeconomic implications, especially on general government finances. India's general government debt—about a third of which is state debt—reached nearly 90% of national GDP in FY2020 and is expected to remain elevated in the medium term. Higher debt levels constrain the government's ability to undertake future development activities because the interest burden rises and further contributes to the fiscal deficit.

Fiscal rules for state governments are set out in the Fiscal Responsibility and Budget Management Act, 2003. This limits each state's fiscal deficit to 3% of its GDP; public debt is capped at 20% of state GDP. The Constitution stipulates that states may not borrow directly from external sources or raise borrowing without the consent of the central government. Thus, states have been constrained in how much and from where they can borrow. Further, the implementation of a goods and service tax in 2017 has reduced the autonomy of states to raise revenue from their own sales taxes. The economic impact of the COVID-19 pandemic has further affected the revenue of states and put a higher burden on them for financing pandemic-related expenditure. As a result, the budget deficits of states in FY2020 and FY2021 surpassed the mandated 3% limit, with the deficit going as high as 7% (Figure 3.17.18).

Figure 3.17.18 Fiscal deficits of selected states, 2020–2021

Many states have exceeded their deficit ceiling.

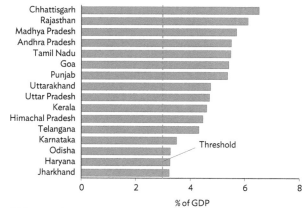

GDP = gross domestic product.

Notes: Year is fiscal year ending on 31 March 2021. The data are revised estimates for fiscal year 2020. The analysis focuses on states that have own sources of revenue of more than 30%.

Source: *Centre for Monitoring Indian Economy States of India Database* (accessed 10 March 2022).

A reason that capping the fiscal deficits of states has not been effective is that the mechanism for enforcing these limits is not well established. The 13th Finance Commission (2007–2012) tried to introduce discipline by including the fiscal performance of states as a criterion for distributing tax receipts across states, but this was abolished by the following commission. The current 15th commission assigns only a small weight to tax and fiscal efforts in recommending the devolution of tax and grant receipts to states. Market-based discipline also appears to be lacking, as reflected by the absence of a relationship between the spread on state government bonds and their debt or deficit positions. A reason may be that state debt is perceived to be backed by the central government. Because of this, states with higher debt are not obliged to pay higher interest rates to make their bonds attractive.

Recent fiscal federalism literature emphasizes the role that institutional factors play in creating adverse incentives for responsible subnational behavior. A dilemma is created when central governments are involved in financing subnational governments. Any assistance from this quarter undermines hard budget constraints, which, in turn, undermines the incentive for subnational governments to control their fiscal deficits. Moral hazard arises because subnational governments, on the basis of their past experience, might believe that higher levels of government will continue to bail out their excesses.

Empirical evidence shows that states with increasing debt-to-GDP ratios also run large primary deficits, which raises concerns over the sustainability of their debt in the medium term. Elevated public debt levels add stress to public finances, making it even more important to ensure that new debt is used to finance investments with adequate returns. Higher debt pushes up interest rates, crowds out private investment, and results in a low-growth and less sustainable debt path. Higher state debt also adds to overall general government debt and puts further pressure on overall debt sustainability.

The 15th Finance Commission has outlined an approach for containing the stress in state finances. Analyzing the major direct and indirect taxes with untapped revenue potential, the commission concluded that with appropriate corrective measures in tax administration and policy, the tax-to-GDP ratio could be raised by 5 percentage points over time. The commission recommended actions to be taken by states, which will play an important role in this process, including stepping up efforts to widen their tax base, ensuring compliance with general sales tax, and strengthening the infrastructure for collecting these taxes. The commission has also called for streamlining the collection of stamp duty by integrating computerized property records with the registration of transactions and imposing a professional tax. It also recommends performance-linked grants to state governments. This includes setting up state finance commissions for better budget management and power sector reforms—vital given the role that power subsidies have played in adding to the fiscal stress of states. The commission has provided grants to urban local governments, tying them to parameters including better air quality, improved service delivery and solid waste management in urban areas, online audits of accounts, and setting up floor rates for property taxes to improve tax collection. Implementing the recommendations of the 15th Finance Commission will be important for putting state finances on a sound footing.

MALDIVES

Growth rebounded in 2021 on soaring tourism arrivals that reversed the country's largest ever economic contraction in 2020. The current account deficit markedly improved last year. Tourist arrivals are expected to fall in 2022 from last year's high because of geopolitical events, but are expected to strengthen next year. The strong economic recovery will be sustained by still substantial tourism activity and the start of construction on large public infrastructure projects. Diversifying sources of economic growth beyond tourism is a major policy challenge.

Economic performance

GDP growth in Maldives surged by 31.6% in 2021 on a recovery in tourism after the economy contracted by 33.5% in 2020 (Figure 3.18.1). Sectors that benefit from tourism also grew strongly, reversing their 2020 contractions, including transportation and communication, financial services, and retail trade. Construction activity last year remained weak, shrinking 7.4% largely on supply-chain constraints, and that weakness was also manifested in stagnant bank financing for the construction industry and weaker real estate activity.

Tourist arrivals rose to 1.3 million in 2021 from 555,494 in 2020, up 138%. Despite the surge, arrivals were 22.4% lower than in pre-pandemic 2019. Tourism's recovery reflects the country's prudent and proactive policies to revive the industry by adopting comprehensive COVID-19 health safeguards for visitors and a campaign to promote tourism. Arrivals from Europe rose 121.7% last year, accounting for 55.3% of the growth in arrivals. With a 58.4% share of total arrivals, Europe was the largest regional market. Arrivals from Asia rose by 150.6% after a 79.7% decline in 2020; India led this market (up 363.4%). Asia accounted for the second-biggest share, at 25.5%.

Figure 3.18.1 Supply-side contributions to growth

Tourism dramatically revived in 2021 driving a rebound in growth.

- Construction
- Transport and communication
- Taxes less subsidies
- Tourism
- Other sectors
- —— Gross domestic product

Percentage points

Sources: Maldives Monetary Authority. Monthly Statistics. February 2022 (accessed 12 March 2022); Asian Development Bank.

Arrivals from the People's Republic of China—which led arrivals from Asia before COVID-19—fell to negligible levels last year because of strict travel policies to contain the pandemic. Arrivals from all other regions rose by 192.2%, attaining a 16.1% share in total arrivals.

This chapter was written by Jyotsana Varma of the South Asia Department, ADB, Manila, and Abdulla Ali and Macrina Mallari, consultants, South Asia Department, ADB, Manila.

Marked shifts were evident in the country composition of tourists last year. India and the Russian Federation accounted for 50.9% of 2021's growth in arrivals and for 38.9% of total arrivals, up from 14.6% of total arrivals in 2019 (Table 3.18.1).

Bed-night stays, a proxy for tourism earnings, totaled 9.9 million last year, up 149.1% from 2020. Preliminary estimates indicate travel receipts rose by 148.5% after falling 55.7% in 2020 (Figure 3.18.2).

Average inflation remained low at 0.5% in 2021 due to the government's administrative price controls on basic food and other essentials, one-off discounts on electricity and water bills for households and businesses in May, and controlled prices for some internet packages (Figure 3.18.3).

To mitigate the economic impact of COVID-19, the Maldives Monetary Authority, in 2021, lowered minimum deposit reserve requirements to provide

Figure 3.18.2 Tourism indicators

Strong revival in tourist arrivals in 2021 caused a sharp rebound in travel receipts.

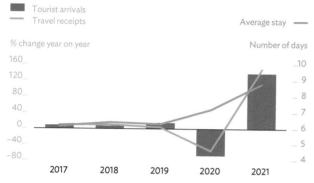

Source: Maldives Monetary Authority. Monthly Statistics. February 2022 (accessed 12 March 2022).

Figure 3.18.3 Inflation

Inflation average remained low in 2021.

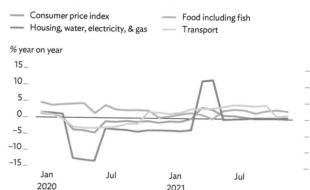

Source: Maldives Monetary Authority. Monthly Statistics. February 2022 (accessed 12 March 2022).

Table 3.18.1 Changes in top 10 source markets

India and the Russian Federation were the two largest country sources of tourists in 2021.

Rank	2019			2020			2021		
	Country	Market share, %	Contrib. to growth, %	Country	Market share, %	Contrib. to growth, %	Country	Market share, %	Contrib. to growth, %
1	PRC	16.7	0.4	India	11.3	9.0	India	22.1	29.9
2	India	9.7	34.6	Russian Federation	11.1	1.9	Russian Federation	16.8	21.0
3	Italy	8.0	14.2	United Kingdom	9.5	6.4	Germany	7.2	7.7
4	Germany	7.7	6.4	Italy	8.4	7.8	United Kingdom	4.7	1.3
5	United Kingdom	7.4	5.3	Germany	6.6	8.3	US	4.2	4.7
6	Russian Federation	4.9	5.7	PRC	6.2	21.8	Saudi Arabia	3.0	4.2
7	France	3.5	4.2	France	5.0	2.8	Spain	2.8	4.0
8	US	3.2	5.3	US	3.6	3.0	Ukraine	2.7	3.2
9	Japan	2.6	0.9	Switzerland	2.3	1.9	France	2.3	0.3
10	ROK	2.2	1.2	Ukraine	1.9	0.3	Italy	2.1	-2.5

PRC = People's Republic of China, ROK = Republic of Korea, US = United States.
Ministry of Tourism. *Monthly Publications* (accessed 12 March 2022).

banks with ample loanable funds. Despite this, credit to the private sector grew by only 4.9%, well below 2020's 8.9% growth. This was because credit demand from the tourism industry fell as business rebounded from FY2020's large contraction and cash flow turned positive. Moreover, lending to the depressed construction and real estate sectors all but dried up. Interest rates to the private sector eased by 50 basis points to 8.0% over 2021.

Tourism's rebound produced a surge in revenue that lowered the budget deficit from the equivalent of 23.5% of GDP in 2020 to 16.6% in 2021. Despite the recovery in tourism, the deficit was still higher than 2019's 6.7% (Figure 3.18.4).

Figure 3.18.4 Fiscal indicators

Fiscal deficits to narrow in 2022 and 2023, but will remain elevated.

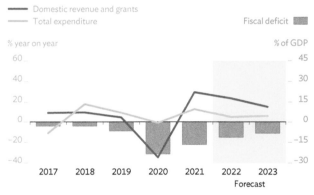

GDP = gross domestic product.
Note: Figures for 2022 and 2023 are government forecasts based on the approved 2022 budget.
Sources: Ministry of Finance. Budget 2022 (accessed 12 March 2022); Monetary Authority. Monthly Statistics. February 2022 (accessed 12 March 2022).

Government expenditure in 2021 grew by 13.0% to 42.2% of GDP due to a 16.9% increase in recurrent spending, mainly for grants, subsidies, and health insurance. Capital expenditure fell by 2.8%, largely on supply chain disruptions and COVID-19 containment measures. Total revenue rebounded by 29.3% to 25.6% of GDP on a significant increase in goods and services taxes from tourism and resort rents. Even so, revenue was 15.0% below 2019's level.

About half of the budget deficit was funded domestically by government securities and the extension of a Parliament-approved overdraft facility from the Maldives Monetary Authority. External financing was bolstered by $500 million raised through three *sukuk* issuances, with the government making its first use of the Islamic finance space in international capital markets. This funding largely offset repayments of a $400 million swap with the Reserve Bank of India and a $192 million Eurobond issue, thereby limiting the need to draw down official reserves. Under the G20 Debt Service Suspension Initiative, $69.5 million was deferred from debt service payments in 2021.

At the end of 2021, public debt, including state-guaranteed debt, increased by 8.7% to Rf94.1 billion, equal to 122.2% of GDP (Figure 3.18.5). External debt rose by 2.2% to Rf45.5 billion (58.4% of GDP), mainly due to the *sukuk* issuances. Domestic debt expanded by 15.5% to Rf49.1 billion (63.8% of GDP). An assessment in 2021 by the International Monetary Fund rated Maldives at a high risk of both external and overall debt distress. Because of a deteriorating fiscal and debt situation, Moody's Investors Service downgraded Maldives' sovereign rating to Caa1 from B3 in August. But in October, Fitch Ratings upgraded Maldives to B– from CCC on the strong recovery in tourism.

Figure 3.18.5 Public debt including guarantees

Public debt was higher in 2021, but fell as share of GDP on an economic rebound.

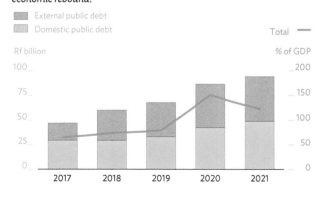

GDP = gross domestic product.
Sources: Ministry of Finance. 2022. Disbursed Outstanding Debt of Public and Publicly Guaranteed Debt of Government of Maldives as of 31 December 2021.

The current account deficit narrowed to $0.9 billion (18.0% of GDP) from $1.3 billion (35.6% of GDP) in 2020, mainly due to increased travel receipts. Services exports grew by 106.3%, according to official estimates, and payments for imports rose by 42.2%. The volume of fish exports grew by 12.9%, but fish export earnings fell by 9.8% on lower prices in international markets (Figure 3.18.6). The current account deficit was financed by net financial account inflows, including *sukuk* proceeds and the use of official reserves.

Gross international reserves in 2021 fell by $193.7 million to $791.2 million, cover for 2.8 months of imports (Figure 3.18.7).

Figure 3.18.7 Gross international reserves

International reserves declined in 2021, despite improvement in the current account.

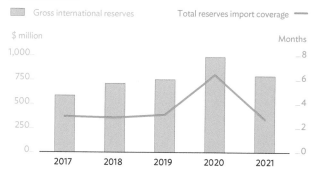

Source: Monetary Authority. *Monthly Statistics. February 2022* (accessed 12 March 2022).

Figure 3.18.6 Balance of payments

The current account deficit improved in 2021, but remained large.

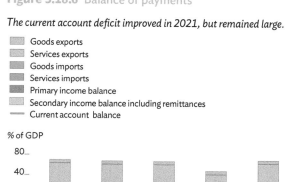

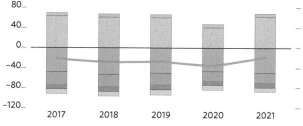

GDP = Gross domestic product.
Source: Monetary Authority. Monthly Statistics. *February 2022* (accessed 12 March 2022).

Economic prospects

Tourist arrivals in the first 2 months of 2022 rose 48.6% from the same period last year, but were still 12.3% below 2019's level. The industry has greatly benefited from the country's image as a safe destination for tourists in its one-island, one-resort model and the high COVID-19 vaccination rate. About 90.0% of the eligible population was fully vaccinated as of March.

The Russian invasion of Ukraine created uncertainty over the economic prospects of countries that are important for Maldives' tourism industry. Because of sanctions against the Russian Federation, tourist arrivals from that country, which had the second largest market share of 16.8% in 2021, are expected to fall sharply this year. Total arrivals are forecast to fall by 10.0% in 2022 from the previous year's level, but rebound next year, when arrivals are projected to grow by 26.0% on reduced geopolitical tensions.

Maldives should continue to attract visitors from beyond its core markets now that COVID-19 containment measures are in the process of being relaxed and because of pent-up demand for tourism. A promotional tourism campaign to mark the country's Tourism Golden Jubilee this year and Maldives being voted the world's leading tourism destination in the World Travel Award 2021 should attract more visitors. The introduction of homestay tourism opens a new market segment for visitors wanting to experience Maldivian life.

Construction is poised to recover this year on increased government spending on the sector. The 2022 budget allocated higher resources for capital spending. More than half of the capital expenditure will be for the Public Sector Investment Program, which will be spent mainly on transport, water and sewerage, land reclamation and roads, and health and social development projects. In 2023, the program's

Table 3.18.2 Selected economic indicators, %

Economic growth sharply rebounded in 2021 on robust tourism recovery.

	2020	2021	2022	2023
GDP growth	–33.5	31.6	11.0	12.0
Inflation	–1.4	0.5	3.0	2.5
CAB/GDP	–35.6	–18.0	–19.5	–17.5

CAB = current account balance, GDP = gross domestic product.
Note: 2021 data are government estimates.
Sources: Maldives Monetary Authority. *Monthly Statistics. February 2022* (accessed 12 March 2022); Asian Development Bank estimates.

allocation is set to increase by 21.2% to Rf6.3 billion (7.2% of GDP) and rise by 23.0% to Rf7.8 billion (8.0%). The program includes major capital projects, including the Greater Malé Connectivity Bridge and the Gulhifalhu International Port, scheduled to start this year.

With still substantial tourism activity and a revival in construction, GDP is projected to grow by 11.0% in 2022 and 12.0% in 2023, which would bring GDP to 8.8% above the 2019's level (Table 3.18.2). The main downside risks to the forecasts are a new global wave of COVID-19 outbreaks and the possible emergence of more virulent variants, and geopolitical fallout from Russian invasion of Ukraine. Both would weigh heavily on tourism growth, reduce government revenue, and threaten fiscal and debt sustainability.

Inflation is forecast to rise to 3.0% in 2022, mainly on expected higher prices for imported oil products and expansionary economic policies, including a minimum wage from January 2022. Inflation is expected to slow to 2.5% in 2023 on moderating global prices of energy and non-energy commodities.

The current account deficit is expected to edge up to 19.5% of GDP in 2022 on a decline in tourism income and a wider trade deficit on higher-priced oil imports and increased imports of construction materials, mainly for public infrastructure projects. Increased income from higher tourism in 2023 will reduce the current account deficit to a projected 17.5% of GDP.

Policy challenge—advancing economic diversification

Maldives has a narrow economic base, as do most small-island developing economies. The Maldives' dependence on tourism—which directly and indirectly accounts for 75.0% of GDP—makes the economy highly vulnerable to external shocks. When COVID-19 shut down global travel and tourism, Maldives was one of the hardest-hit countries, as its GDP contracted by a third. This experience reinforces the need for the economy to diversify into areas with potential for local production and exports.

Increasing private sector participation, which will be essential for expanding growth sources beyond tourism, needs to be tackled by strengthening the business environment; improving access to cheaper long-term credit, especially for small and medium-sized enterprises; and adopting policies that reduce the dominance of state-owned enterprises in the economy.

One promising industry where Maldives has an obvious competitive advantage is fisheries. The Maldives' fishing industry practices the traditional pole-and-line method; here fish are caught one by one, lessening unwanted bycatch and harm to other marine life. This sustainable practice has earned the country's pole-and-line skipjack fishing industry a Marine Stewardship Council certification to use an ecolabel guaranteeing consumers that its fish brands are sustainably sourced. This branding creates a market advantage and price premium for the country's skipjack products in the global market, especially in countries where environmentally sustainable fishing is highly valued.

There is potential for substantially expanding fishing within Maldives' exclusive economic zone of 900,000 square kilometers to significantly boost production, employment, and foreign exchange earnings. Fish production totaled 149,000 metric tons in 2020 and the industry employed about 18,000 fishers at the last count. Fish exports comprise 96.0% of total exports and garments and scrap iron largely account for the rest, but these segments have limited potential to be developed as growth drivers.

Despite the sizable share of fish exports, growth in export volumes has been relatively unstable, declining by 8.6% in 2018 and 14.3% in 2019. Because processed fish products account for just 21% of fish exports (the majority is fresh, chilled, and frozen fish), an opportunity exists to expand fish exports by investing in higher value-added products (Figure 3.18.8). Maldives should take advantage of the increasing demand for smoked-dried tuna in Sri Lanka and dried and smoked skipjack tuna in Japan, which fetch higher prices per unit of fish input. The scope for expanding export earnings by investing in fish storage and canning facilities is substantial, as only about 20% of fish purchases are processed in the country. The balance is sold to buyers, mainly Thai canneries, at low prices.

Figure 3.18.8 Fish exports by value, category, and share in total exports

Processed fish exports remain low, crimping export earnings.

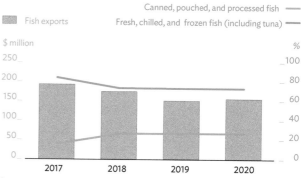

Sources: Monetary Authority. 2021. Monthly Statistics. *February 2022* (accessed 12 March 2022); Asian Development Bank estimates.

NEPAL

Fiscal and monetary stimulus and eased COVID-19 lockdowns enabled the economy to rebound in fiscal 2021. Inflation declined and the current account deficit markedly widened on rising imports. Growth will recover further in fiscal 2022 and 2023, underpinned by continued fiscal stimulus and wider vaccination coverage. Inflation will rise on high global oil prices and the current account deficit will widen further on rebounding investment. A major policy challenge is increasing exports from their low and stagnant base.

Economic performance

Nepal's GDP growth is estimated to have expanded by 2.3% in fiscal year 2021 (FY2021, ended 15 July 2021) after contracting by 2.1% in FY2020. The recovery was underpinned by continued monetary and fiscal stimulus, the global economic recovery, and nationwide lockdowns being lifted early in the year as COVID-19 infections ebbed. However, a second wave of infections in the fourth quarter dampened economic activity (Figure 3.19.1).

Agriculture, contributing a quarter of GDP, rose by an estimated 2.4% in FY2021, up from 2.2% in FY2020, on a good monsoon and increased acreage under cultivation. Industry rose by 1.7% on stronger domestic demand and a surge in exports after output contracted by 3.7% in FY2020. Services, about 60% of GDP, expanded by 2.5%, reversing a 4.0% contraction on increased mobility for shopping and work as wholesale and retail trade firms resumed operations after containment measures were eased. Tourism remained depressed. The sector, a major foreign exchange earner, collapsed in March 2020, with arrivals in 2021 at just 12.5% of 2019's level.

Preliminary estimates indicate private consumption grew by 4.6% in FY2021, lifted by the resumption of strong growth in workers' remittances (Figure 3.19.2). Fixed investment rose by an estimated 3.8%, reversing

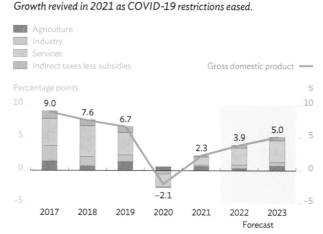

Figure 3.19.1 Supply-side contributions to growth

Growth revived in 2021 as COVID-19 restrictions eased.

Agriculture
Industry
Services
Indirect taxes less subsidies
Gross domestic product —

COVID-19 = Coronavirus Disease 2019.
Note: Years are fiscal years ending in mid-July of that year.
Sources: Central Bureau of Statistics. *National Accounts of Nepal 2020/2021*; Asian Development Bank estimates.

a 12.4% contraction, on the implementation of public projects and stronger private investment. Stocks rose markedly as inventories were rebuilt. But net exports were a drag on growth, reflecting a large increase in imports despite strong exports.

This chapter was written by Manbar Singh Khadka and Neelina Nakarmi of the Nepal Resident Mission, ADB, Kathmandu.

Average inflation decelerated significantly to 3.6% in FY2021 from 6.2% in the previous fiscal year (Figure 3.19.3). Food inflation slowed to 5.0% from 8.1% on higher production and smoother supply-chain distribution on eased COVID-19 mobility restrictions. Muted increases in housing and utility prices, which grew by 1.1%, lowered nonfood inflation, which averaged 2.5%.

Figure 3.19.2 Share of GDP by expenditure

Economic growth was supported by high private consumption.

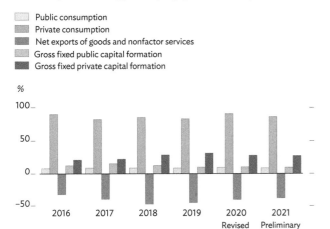

GDP = gross domestic product.

Note: Years are fiscal years ending in mid-July of that year.

Sources: Central Bureau of Statistics. *National Accounts of Nepal 2020/2021*; Asian Development Bank estimates.

Figure 3.19.3 Monthly inflation

Food inflation moderated on higher production and smoother supply-chain distribution.

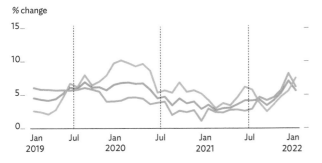

Sources: Nepal Rastra Bank. 2022. *Current Macro-Economic and Financial Situation*; Asian Development Bank estimates.

The budget deficit narrowed to the equivalent of 4.2% of GDP in FY2021 from 5.3% in FY2020. A 16.8% increase in revenue from large customs-related duties and deferred tax receipts shrank the deficit and raised total revenue to 24.2% of GDP (Figure 3.19.4). Total expenditure increased by 10.4% to 28.4% of GDP, mostly reflecting an 8.3% rise in current expenditure on substantial health care spending, social benefits, and transfers that continued in FY2021. Capital expenditure increased by 21.0%, largely offsetting FY2020's decline.

Figure 3.19.4 Fiscal indicators

The deficit narrowed on higher revenue from customs-related duties.

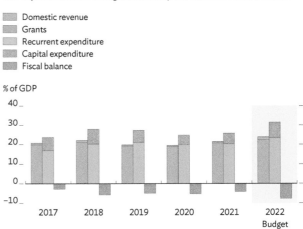

GDP = gross domestic product.

Note: Years are fiscal years ending in mid-July of that year.

Source: Ministry of Finance. Budget Speech of Fiscal Year 2021/22.

Government debt increased to 41.4% of GDP in FY2021 from an average of 25.1% during FY2016–FY2019 on higher fiscal and current account deficits stemming from increased spending to tackle COVID-19 (Figure 3.19.5). Despite the rise, Nepal's risk of debt distress is low given the high level of official concessional borrowing at long maturities.

The central bank's monetary policy remained accommodative in FY2021, with broad money growth accelerating 21.8%. A 26.3% rise in credit growth reflected the gradual normalization of economic activity on easing COVID-19 containment measures. Many businesses continued to tap the special $1.7 billion refinancing fund for pandemic-hit firms, which lifted credit growth (Figure 3.19.6).

Figure 3.19.5 Public debt

Public debt rose sharply in 2021 on increased borrowing to mitigate COVID-19 effects.

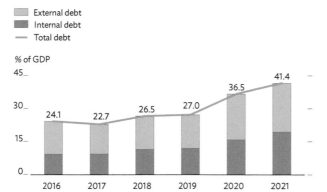

COVID-19 = Coronavirus Disease 2019, GDP = gross domestic product.
Note: Years are fiscal years ending in mid-July of that year.
Source: Central Bureau of Statistics; Financial Comptroller General Office; Public Debt Management Office.

Figure 3.19.6 Credit to the private sector and broad money

Rapid credit growth helped spur 2021's economic rebound.

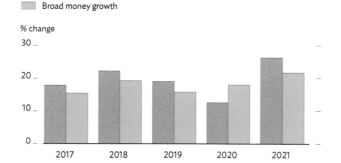

Note: Years are fiscal years ending in mid-July of that year.
Source: Nepal Rastra Bank. 2022. *Current Macro-Economic and Financial Situation.*

The current account deficit in FY2021 substantially widened to $2.8 billion—8.0% of GDP, up from 0.9% in FY2020—on a 26.5% increase in imports that increased the trade deficit to $11.5 billion. Import growth, particularly of transport equipment and manufacturing raw materials, surged in the latter half of FY2021, mainly reflecting pent-up demand following the easing of COVID-19 restrictions. Exports grew by 31.0%, but the increase had a minimal impact on the trade deficit as it was relatively small, at about 10%

of imports (Figure 3.19.7). Remittances rose by 8.4% to $8.1 billion, but this gain was offset by a decline in net services on lower tourism income. Travel receipts decreased by 88.4% in FY2021 because of pandemic-related restrictions. Primary income fell by about $200 million. The availability of financing was sufficient to meet the large current account deficit. Gross foreign exchange reserves increased marginally to $11.7 billion, cover for 10.2 months of current imports of goods and services (Figure 3.19.8).

Figure 3.19.7 Current account indicators

The deficit substantially widened in 2021 on the increased trade deficit.

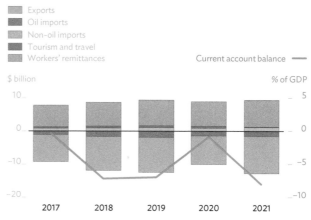

GDP = gross domestic product.
Note: Years are fiscal years ending in mid-July of that year.
Source: Nepal Rastra Bank. 2022. *Current Macro-Economic and Financial Situation.*

Figure 3.19.8 Gross international reserves and foreign exchange adequacy

Rapid growth in imports lowered import cover.

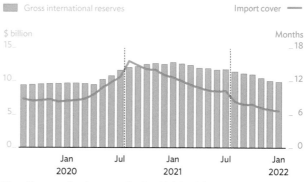

Note: Years are fiscal years ending in mid-July of that year.
Source: Nepal Rastra Bank. 2022. *Current Macro-Economic and Financial Situation.*

Economic prospects

GDP growth is forecast to increase to 3.9% in FY2022 as the economy further normalizes on increasing COVID-19 vaccine coverage setting a path to steadily higher growth (Table 3.19.1). Growth over the forecast horizon will be supported by accommodative macroeconomic policies even though the recovery in tourism will be delayed by slowing growth in advanced economies.

Table 3.19.1 Selected economic indicators, %

Growth steadily rebounds and high current account deficits start narrowing in 2023.

	2020	2021	2022	2023
GDP growth	–2.1	2.3	3.9	5.0
Inflation	6.2	3.6	6.5	6.2
CAB/GDP	–0.9	–8.0	–9.7	–6.1

CAB = current account balance, GDP = gross domestic product.
Note: Years are fiscal years ending in mid-July of that year.
Source: Asian Development Bank estimates.

To underpin durable economic growth, the government, in January 2022, entered into an International Monetary Fund support program that is aligned to its relief, restructuring, and resilience plan. The program has three main objectives: creating the financial room for increased expenditure on health, social assistance, and job growth to mitigate the economic impact of the COVID-19 pandemic; preserving macroeconomic and financial stability; and supporting a reform agenda for sustained growth and reducing poverty over the medium term.

Agriculture growth is forecast at 1.3% in the current fiscal year, down from 2.4% in FY2021. Despite abundant rainfall during the summer monsoon, unexpected rainfall and flooding in mid-October damaged ready-to-harvest crops, cutting paddy output by about 9.0%. Industry is expected to grow by 4.1% on increased consumer and investment demand, and full output from a large hydropower project. Services are projected to grow by 5.2%. Stronger services growth will be achieved by normalized activity in wholesale and retail trade, transport, and financial services made possible by increased COVID-19 vaccine coverage. International tourist arrivals will remain depressed, although the industry is already benefiting from the reopening of

trekking routes and expeditions (Figure 3.19.9). Private consumption will continue to be underpinned by sizable remittances. Fixed investment is forecast to grow by 7.5% on large budgeted capital allocations and strengthened business confidence.

Figure 3.19.9 Monthly tourist arrival

Nascent signs of a recovery in tourist arrivals, but still way below pre-pandemic levels.

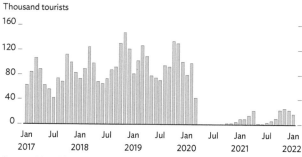

Source: Nepal Rastra Bank. 2022. *Current Macro-Economic and Financial Situation.*

Fiscal policy in FY2022 will be expansionary and continue to focus on strengthening health care and providing economic relief measures. Total expenditure is budgeted to rise by 28.9 %—with large increases in current and capital spending—to reach 35.7% of GDP from 30.3% in FY2021. Revenue is estimated to increase by 23% to 25.8% of GDP. The budget deficit is forecast at 7.3% of GDP, significantly higher than 4.2% in FY2021. Fiscal policy will provide a major stimulus for growth, although there may be implementation shortfalls.

Although monetary policy in FY2022 is intended to be accommodative, the midyear policy review announced tightening measures to restrain credit growth and inflation after private sector credit surged by 27.4% year on year in mid-January. To restrain credit growth, the floor rate was raised by 300 basis points to 4.0%, the repo-policy rate by 250 basis points to 5.5%, and the interest rate applicable under the refinancing facility by 200 basis points to 7.0%. The goal is to restrict private sector credit growth to 19.0% by the end of the current fiscal year.

Average inflation accelerated to 5.0% in the first 6 months of FY2022 from 3.7% in the same period in the previous fiscal year. Food inflation was 4.9% and nonfood inflation 6.2%. The inflation rate is forecast to average 6.5% in FY2022. The higher rate compared with FY2021's mainly reflects increased global oil prices and subsequently higher transportation costs. The rise in international oil prices because of the Russian invasion of Ukraine has contributed to inflationary pressure. A gradual recovery in domestic demand and a rise in inflation in India, a major trading partner, have also intensified inflationary pressure.

A marked expansion in oil and non-oil imports is expected in FY2022 on higher oil prices and intensifying investment activity. Imports surged by 48.9% in the first half of the fiscal year, reversing a contraction of 8.9% in the same period in the previous fiscal year. Exports rose by 95.0% after contracting by 8.4%. Remittances contracted by 6.2% after expanding by 6.7% (Figure 3.19.10). The current account deficit consequently rose, to $3 billion, in the first half of FY2022. Import growth in the second half, however, will be reduced by the higher import base in the second half of FY2021. Moreover, the government has taken measures to curtail the imports of nonessential and luxury goods, including raising margin requirements from 50% to 100% when opening letters of credit at commercial banks. Nonetheless, elevated oil prices due to the Russian invasion of Ukraine will push up the import bills and likely lead to a worsening of the trade balance. Based on these developments, the current account deficit is forecast to widen to 9.7% of GDP in FY2022 from 8.0% in FY2021.

GDP growth is forecast at 5% in FY2023 on expectations that the entire eligible population is vaccinated, the growth momentum holds, and the economic efficiency reforms planned under the International Monetary Fund's support program and aligned with the government's relief, restructuring, and resilience plan take hold. Inflation is forecast to slow to 6.2%; this assumes a normal harvest, somewhat subdued oil prices, and a decline in Indian inflation. The current account deficit is expected to moderate to 6.1% of GDP as health-related imports slow and hydroelectricity generation reduces fossil fuel consumption.

Downside risks to the outlook center on exogenous shocks, such as a new wave of COVID-19 outbreaks or the emergence of new variants, intensified geopolitical turmoil, and natural disasters, which have devastated lives and livelihoods in the past.

Policy challenge—increasing exports and reducing the trade deficit

The government's Trade Policy 2015 was formulated to reduce the country's persistently large trade deficit (Figure 3.19.11). Under the policy, the government is striving to support private export industries by stepping up export promotion, reducing transaction costs through trade facilitation, and strengthening institutional mechanisms to promote exports. The government is also striving to expand foreign markets through trade diplomacy and bilateral, regional, and multilateral trade agreements.

Figure 3.19.10 Migrant workers and remittances

A decline in outmigration limited remittance growth.

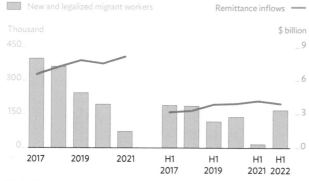

H = half.
Note: Years are fiscal years ending in mid-July of that year.
Source: Nepal Rastra Bank. 2022. *Current Macro-Economic and Financial Situation.*

Figure 3.19.11 Merchandise trade deficit

Exports contribute little to GDP due to weak competitive capacity.

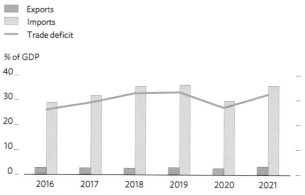

GDP = gross domestic product.
Note: Years are fiscal years ending in mid-July of that year.
Source: Nepal Rastra Bank. 2022. *Current Macro-Economic and Financial Situation.*

Nepal's exports of potentially competitive agro-products—that is, fresh agriculture products and processed food—have been dismal. Limited connectivity and market inaccessibility, further compounded by sanitary and phytosanitary issues, have held back the export potential of these products. Efficient sanitary and phytosanitary administration and technical barriers to trade standards are crucial for trade facilitation. But Nepal lacks adequate infrastructure for both; this includes sufficient testing laboratories, internationally recognized accreditation of certification, and inspection facilities. Processed ginger is an example of a missed opportunity for a competitive high-value-added export product. Nepal is the world's fourth largest ginger producer with a 9.0% share of global production. Despite high international demand for processed ginger, Nepal largely exports raw ginger. This is because traditional farming practices, small-scale farming, and the lack of a cost-effective transportation system have impeded the development of an efficient ginger processing industry.

In the aftermath of the 2015 earthquake, the United States granted Nepal preferential trade benefits for certain products, including carpets and pashmina, until 2025. Nepal still has not been able to benefit from this preferential facility. Quality, product standard issues, and limited production have held back exports of products covered by this and other preferential trade agreements. Similarly, a bilateral trade treaty with India grants most-favored-nation access to Indian markets for Nepalese products. And Nepal, as one the world's least developed economies, could benefit from special World Trade Organization provisions, concessions, and facilities. In both these cases, quality issues, lack of product standardization, and limited negotiation capabilities, including on nontariff measures, have hindered Nepal's ability to meaningfully increase exports.

Trade Policy 2015 committed to establishing ancillary industries to supply raw and semi-processed inputs to industries operating in special economic zones. The policy also envisaged setting up industrial zones for export promotion and for these zones to be expanded across the country. But the special economic zones have not been effective in attracting much private sector and foreign investment because of poor infrastructure, weak coordination among government

agencies, and the full benefits provided in the Special Economic Zone Act, 2016 not being implemented.

To enhance exports, it will be vital to strengthen the capacity of subnational government authorities in planning, developing, and promoting export-oriented industries. Trade policy authorities should explore ways of promoting interprovincial trade to gain scale for new processing industries. Plans and provisions set out in trade policies should be well aligned with other policies that could affect exports, including ways to incentivize export-oriented industries and integrate these plans and provisions with other relevant policies, such as the Special Economic Zone Act. Getting internationally recognized certification is crucial for export promotion. Trade facilitation agreements, bilateral trade agreements, and business connections need to be expanded to link the business sector in Nepal with foreign markets. Stringent requirements, such as rules of origin and negative lists, have limited Nepal's ability to utilize World Trade Organization provisions for special and differential treatment for low-income countries. Here, the government should actively lobby for more liberal implementation of these barriers.

The services sector also holds potential for expanding its exports. Travel and tourism, a traditional source of foreign exchange earnings, has considerable scope to expand. Receipts from international travelers accounted for a mere 2% of GDP annually on average during FY2017–FY2019. Poor infrastructure, especially transport infrastructure, is the main constraint to expanding and developing Nepal's tourism industry. Other factors hindering tourism are a lack of development and expansion of tourist destinations. Information technology (IT) is another sector with potential. To promote IT-related services trade, risk capital and support for accelerators and incubators are needed.

Foreign direct investment will be crucial for enhancing Nepal's export potential in manufacturing. To this end, Nepal has amended legislation, such as the Foreign Investment and Technology Transfer Act, and promulgated new acts, such as the Public–Private Partnership and Investment Act, 2019 and the Special Economic Zone Act, 2016. These reforms have the potential to attract more foreign investment. But a crucial challenge will be to ensure they are implemented in a consistent manner.

PAKISTAN

Growth rebounded in fiscal 2021, reflecting a substantial recovery in industry and services from well-coordinated fiscal and monetary responses to COVID-19. Improved food supply and lower domestic fuel prices trimmed inflation; strong remittances and higher exports narrowed the current account deficit. Growth is expected to slow in fiscal 2022 on tighter fiscal and monetary policy, but strengthen in fiscal 2023 as consumption and investment accelerate. Inflation will rise in the current fiscal year, driven by higher fuel prices, before receding in fiscal 2023, with the current account deficit widening in fiscal 2022 and narrowing in fiscal 2023.

Economic performance

Pakistan's economy grew by 5.6% in fiscal year 2021 (FY2021, ended 30 June 2021), reversing a 1.0% contraction in FY2020 (Figure 3.20.1). Industrial output expanded by 7.8% after shrinking 5.8% in FY2020, supported by fiscal incentives to key export industries and construction. Both manufacturing and construction, up 10.5% and 5.3%, respectively, reversed previous contractions. In manufacturing, textiles, food, automobiles, chemicals, and nonmetallic mineral products performed strongly. Services also rebounded, reversing a 1.3% contraction in FY2020 to expand by 5.7% in FY2021, reflecting strong gains in wholesale and retail trade, and transport and storage, after COVID-19 mobility restrictions were lifted. Growth in agriculture slid to 3.5% from 3.9% in the review period on slower livestock growth and a drop in cotton production to its lowest level in 3 decades due to excessive monsoon rains and a sharp reduction in the cotton-growing area, despite record-high output for other major crops.

Private consumption led the economic recovery, reflecting higher employment, a record increase in remittances, and cash transfers to the poor through the government's Ehsaas Emergency Cash Programme. Investment also revived, helped by higher government development expenditure, accommodative monetary conditions, including the central bank's subsidized

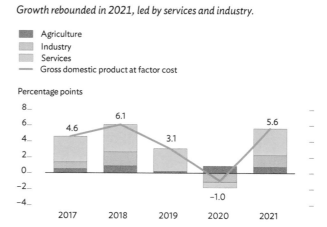

Figure 3.20.1 Supply-side contributions to growth

Growth rebounded in 2021, led by services and industry.

- Agriculture
- Industry
- Services
- Gross domestic product at factor cost

Percentage points

Notes: Years are fiscal years ending on 30 June of that year. Gross domestic product at factor cost excludes indirect taxes less subsidies.
Source: Pakistan Bureau of Statistics. *National Accounts Tables Base 2015-16* (accessed 30 January 2022).

credit facility for investment, and improved business confidence.

Headline inflation slowed from 10.7% in FY2020 to 8.9% in FY2021, largely reflecting the improved supply of perishable food, lower domestic fuel prices, and local currency appreciation (Figure 3.20.2). Food price inflation, although less than in FY2020,

---

This chapter was written by Khadija Ali, Farzana Noshab, and Maleeha Rizwan of the Pakistan Resident Mission, ADB, Islamabad.

Figure 3.20.2 Monthly inflation

Food and energy prices kept inflation elevated in 2021.

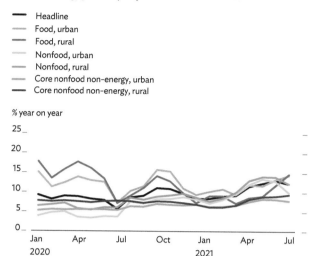

—— Headline
—— Food, urban
—— Food, rural
　Nonfood, urban
—— Nonfood, rural
—— Core nonfood non-energy, urban
—— Core nonfood non-energy, rural

Source: State Bank of Pakistan. *Economic Data* (accessed 1 March 2022).

Figure 3.20.3 Government budget indicators

The fiscal deficit narrowed slightly from 2019 to 2021.

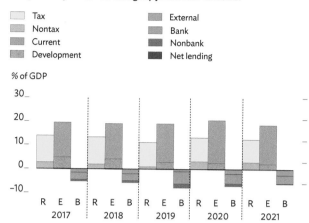

　Tax　　　　　　　External
　Nontax　　　　　Bank
　Current　　　　　Nonbank
　Development　　　Net lending

B = budget financing, E = expenditure, GDP = gross domestic product,
R = revenue.
Note: Years are fiscal years ending on 30 June of that year.
Source: Ministry of Finance. *Pakistan Summary of Consolidated Federal and Provincial Budgetary Operations, July–December 2021* (accessed 3 March 2022).

remained high at 12.5% in urban and 13.2% in rural areas. This reflected higher international food prices and increased minimum domestic support prices for wheat and sugarcane. Energy inflation accelerated in the second half of FY2021 on higher international oil prices and planned adjustments to electricity tariffs. Core inflation, excluding food and energy, moderated from 7.5% to 6.0% in urban areas and from 8.7% to 7.6% in rural areas.

The consolidated federal and provincial fiscal deficit narrowed from the equivalent of 7.1% of GDP in FY2020 to 6.1% in FY2021 (Figure 3.20.3), and the primary deficit from 1.6% to 1.2%, as expenditure moderated. The combined provincial surplus expanded to 0.6% of GDP from 0.2%. Total revenue decreased to 12.4% of GDP from 13.2% on a sizeable decline in nontax revenue after exceptionally large central bank profits and telecom license renewal fees received in FY2020. Both current and development spending fell as a share of GDP because of cost-cutting measures and smaller interest payments reflecting lower interest rates and the G-20's Debt Service Suspension Initiative. The smaller fiscal deficit trimmed gross public debt from 76.6% of GDP in FY2020 to 71.8% in FY2021 (Figure 3.20.4), still well above the 60.0% limit set by the Fiscal Responsibility and Debt Limitation Act.

Figure 3.20.4 Government domestic and external debt

Government debt declined as a percent of GDP in 2021, although external debt in US dollars rose.

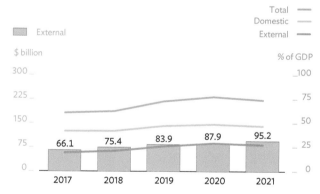

Total ——
Domestic ——
External ——

　External

GDP = gross domestic product.
Notes: Years are fiscal years ending on 30 June of that year. External debt includes government and other external liabilities and public corporations.
Source: State Bank of Pakistan. *Economic Data* (accessed 25 February 2022).

With subdued core inflation and well-anchored inflation expectations amid smaller fiscal and current account deficits, the central bank kept the policy rate unchanged at 7.0% in FY2021, but raised it starting September 2021 (Figure 3.20.5). As demand recovered, private sector credit expanded by 10.5%, led by higher lending for manufacturing, consumer finance, telecommunication, construction, and electricity generation.

Figure 3.20.5 Interest rates and inflation

The central bank raised its policy rate to 9.75% in December 2021 to combat inflation.

— Weighted average lending
— Inflation
— Policy rate

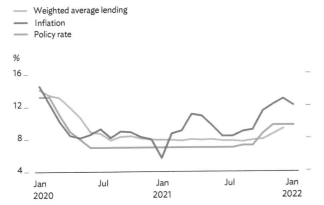

Note: The policy rate is the central bank's target rate.
Source: State Bank of Pakistan. *Economic Data* (accessed 1 March 2022).

The current account deficit narrowed from 1.5% of GDP in FY2020 to a 10-year low of 0.6% in FY2021 (Figure 3.20.6). This reflected a robust 27% rise in remittances that offset a wider deficit in goods and services, savings from deferred interest payments under the Debt Service Suspension Initiative, and lower global interest rates.

Merchandise exports reversed a 7.1% contraction in FY2020 to grow by 13.7%, helped by COVID-19 pandemic response measures and the strong economic

Figure 3.20.6 Current account components

The current account deficit narrowed in 2021, but has since widened on surging imports.

■ Current transfers, including remittances
■ Income
■ Services
■ Exports
■ Imports

Current account balance —

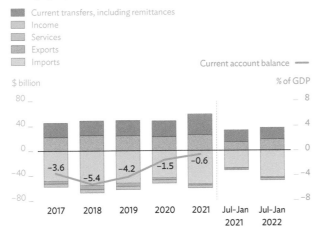

GDP = gross domestic product.
Note: Years are fiscal years ending on 30 June of that year.
Source: State Bank of Pakistan. *Economic Data* (accessed 1 March 2022).

recovery in key export markets. Merchandise imports surged in the wake of rising demand for intermediate goods and key agricultural commodities, particularly wheat, sugar, and cotton, which offset domestic supply disruptions. This surge and investment in machinery, which rose in response to a central bank concessionary lending scheme, widened the merchandise trade deficit to 8.1% of GDP from 7.0% (Figure 3.20.7). The continued shift of payment inflows from informal to formal channels supported the strong growth in remittances, as did the government's Roshan Digital Account initiative to integrate the Pakistani diaspora with the domestic banking system and facilitate household consumption and investment (Figure 3.20.8).

Figure 3.20.7 Trade balance

The trade deficit widened as imports grew faster than exports.

■ Merchandise exports
■ Merchandise imports

Trade balance —

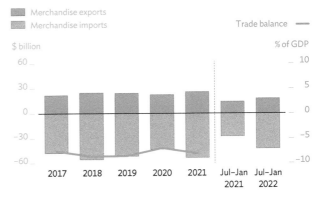

GDP = gross domestic product.
Note: Years are fiscal years ending on 30 June of that year.
Source: State Bank of Pakistan. *Economic Data* (accessed 1 March 2022).

Figure 3.20.8 Remittances

Remittances grew exceptionally fast in 2021 and extended gains in early 2022.

■ Remittances

Remittances growth —

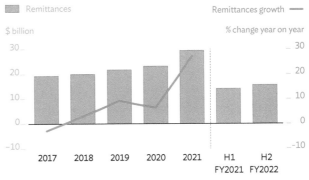

H = half.
Note: Years are fiscal years ending on 30 June of that year.
Source: State Bank of Pakistan. *Economic Data. External Sector. Balance of Payments. Worker's Remittances* (accessed 1 March 2022).

Economic prospects

GDP growth is projected to moderate to 4.0% in FY2022 and to 4.5% in FY2023 (Table 3.20.1). Slower growth in the current fiscal year reflects the government reactivating its stabilization program under the International Monetary Fund Extended Fund Facility to narrow the current account deficit, raise international reserves, and cut inflation. Domestic demand is expected to slow from monetary tightening, restrictions on automobile financing, and additional fiscal consolidation measures enacted in January 2022. The forecast for accelerated growth in FY2023 reflects stronger private consumption and investment, as key structural reforms and greater macroeconomic stability boost household and business confidence (Figure 3.20.9).

Table 3.20.1 Selected economic indicators, %

Growth will moderate in 2022, but pick up in 2023, with a lower current account deficit and inflation.

	2020	2021	2022	2023
GDP growth	–1.0	5.6	4.0	4.5
Inflation	10.7	8.9	11.0	8.5
CAB/GDP	–1.5	–0.6	–3.5	–3.0

CAB = current account balance, GDP = gross domestic product.
Note: Years are fiscal years ending on 30 June of that year.
Sources: Pakistan Bureau of Statistics. *National Accounts Tables Base 2015-16*; State Bank of Pakistan. *Economic Data: Inflation Snapshot, External Sector, Balance of Payments*; Asian Development Bank estimates.

Figure 3.20.9 GDP growth

Growth is projected to slow in 2022 before recovering in 2023.

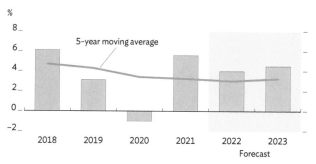

GDP = gross domestic product.
Note: Years are fiscal years ending on 30 June of that year.
Sources: Pakistan Bureau of Statistics. *National Accounts Tables Base 2015-16* (accessed 30 January 2022); Asian Development Bank estimates.

The government's package of subsidized inputs and increased support prices of wheat and sugarcane will continue to benefit agriculture in the current fiscal year. But industry growth will decelerate, reflecting fiscal and monetary tightening, a significant depreciation of the local currency resulting in costlier imports of raw materials and capital goods, and upward adjustments to domestic oil and electricity prices. Large manufacturing, which accounts for over half of industry, has weakened since September 2021, with growth slowing to 3.5% in the first 5 months of FY2022 from 6.9% in the same period of FY2021. Construction, however, is expected to support industry, helped by robust public investment spending and fiscal incentives, and subsidized credit under the government's Naya Pakistan Housing Programme. Growth in services is expected to be trimmed by a slowdown in manufacturing and the implementation of the government's stabilization program, weakening this sector's contribution to growth in FY2022.

Inflation is expected to pick up in FY2022, averaging 11.0% (Figure 3.20.10). Headline inflation accelerated to 10.5% in the first 8 months, reflecting higher international energy prices, significant currency depreciation, and elevated global food prices from supply disruptions. Core inflation in rural areas rose to 9.4% and 7.8% in urban areas in February 2022, levels that reflect the ongoing economic recovery. Because Pakistan is a net importer of oil and natural gas, with both comprising almost 20% of total imports, the country will continue experiencing strong inflationary pressure for the rest of the current fiscal year from the jump in global fuel prices related to the Russian invasion of Ukraine. A prolonged conflict could raise wheat prices and stoke higher food inflation since Ukraine is an important source of Pakistan's wheat imports. Additional tax measures in January 2022 will cause a one-time rise in prices. Inflationary pressures are likely to be less pronounced in FY2023 as fiscal consolidation progresses and oil and commodity prices stabilize, allowing inflation to moderate to a forecast 8.5%. The central bank tightened monetary policy in response to rising inflation and fast-growing external imbalances, especially during the second quarter of FY2022, raising the policy interest rate by a cumulative 275 basis points. The State Bank of Pakistan Act was amended in January 2022 to strengthen the central bank's autonomy; the act mandates price stability as the monetary authority's primary objective. The act prohibits the government

Figure 3.20.10 Inflation

Inflation will surge in 2022 before slowing in 2023 as commodity prices moderate.

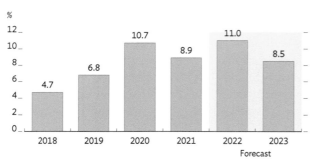

Note: Years are fiscal years ending on 30 June of that year.
Sources: State Bank of Pakistan. *Economic Data. Inflation Snapshot (2015–16)* (accessed 28 January 2022); Asian Development Bank estimates.

from borrowing directly from the central bank, which should help anchor lower inflation expectations in FY2023.

The government plans to continue its medium-term fiscal consolidation, rationalizing less essential current spending and expanding tax and nontax revenue. These reforms are projected to trim the fiscal deficit to 5.7% of GDP in FY2022 and 5.5% in FY2023, return the public debt to more sustainable levels, and reduce the crowding out of private sector borrowing. Sustained recovery boosted Federal Board of Revenue (FBR) tax collection by 30.4% in the first 7 months of FY2022, equal to 6.2% of GDP, surpassing the 5.7% target for the period. For the first half of FY2022, total fiscal revenue rose from 6.0% to 6.2% of GDP, reflecting a higher contribution from sales and income tax that offset a shortfall in the petroleum levy.

The renewed buoyancy of fiscal revenue is expected to strengthen further on the tax measures enacted in January 2022, planned further increases in petroleum levy rates, and additional policy and administrative measures to broaden the tax base. These measures include launching a track-and-trace system, the continued rollout of the point-of-sale system in the retail sector and its integration with the FBR, introducing a single sales tax portal for the FBR and provincial revenue authorities, and reviewing property valuations to bring them closer to market rates. Total government expenditure rose to 8.3% of GDP in the first half of FY2022, due to higher subsidies, from 8.1% in

the same period of FY2021, bringing the first half fiscal deficit to 2.1% of GDP.

The current account deficit is projected to widen to 3.5% of GDP in the current fiscal year as strengthening domestic demand and rising international energy and commodity prices propel import costs, outpacing export growth (Figure 3.20.11). The 55.1% surge in merchandise imports in the first 7 months of FY2022, which exceeded export growth of 27.4%, reflects rising global commodity (especially energy) prices, COVID-19 vaccine procurement, and greater demand for intermediate goods due to the domestic economic recovery. Services imports rebounded by almost 40.0%, reversing a 24.0% contraction in the first 7 months of FY2021. Services imports were underpinned by easing global travel restrictions and higher payments for transport and financial services linked to the surge in merchandise imports. Consequently, the deficit in goods and services widened from 4.0% of GDP in the first 7 months of FY2021 to 6.7% in the same period in FY2022, turning a current account surplus equivalent to 0.3% of GDP in the first 7 months of FY2021 to a deficit of 3.1% of GDP a year later.

Figure 3.20.11 Current account balance

The current account deficit will widen in 2022 on higher import prices before moderating in 2023.

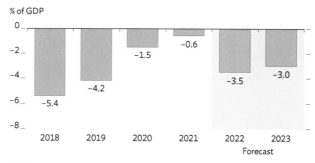

GDP = gross domestic product.
Note: Years are fiscal years ending on 30 June of that year.
Sources: State Bank of Pakistan. *Economic Data* (accessed 28 January 2022); Asian Development Bank estimates.

Rising global prices of energy, food, and other commodities due to the Russian invasion of Ukraine will continue to make imports costlier. But monetary tightening and the additional fiscal consolidation measures are expected to cool domestic demand, slowing import growth. Remittances are projected to remain buoyant, supported by the Roshan Digital Account initiative and the recovery in the global economy, providing a major source of foreign currency inflows ($15.8 billion in the first 6 months of FY2022) (Figure 3.20.12). The current account deficit is projected to narrow to 3.0% of GDP in FY2023 as stabilizing commodity prices and continued fiscal consolidation slow import growth.

Figure 3.20.12 Gross official reserves and exchange rate

Reserves increased in 2021 but have since declined as the exchange rate depreciated.

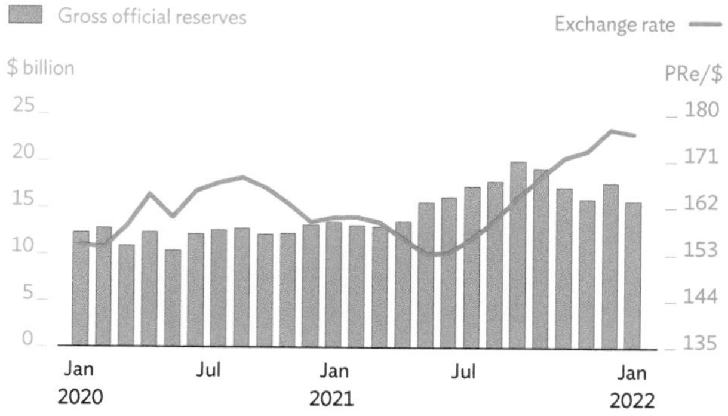

Source: State Bank of Pakistan. *Economic Data. External Sector. Balance of Payments. Foreign Exchange Reserves* (accessed 1 March 2022).

The major risks to the economic outlook emerge from higher-than-expected inflation due to a prolonged conflict following the Russian invasion of Ukraine. If global food and energy prices remain elevated longer than anticipated due to supply disruptions, heightened inflationary pressures could undermine growth prospects in the current and next fiscal year. High prices of imported food and energy products will widen the trade deficit, worsening external imbalances and exerting pressure on the local currency. A larger than projected current account deficit and a weaker Pakistan rupee will undermine fiscal consolidation. The International Monetary Fund Extended Fund Facility is scheduled for conclusion in September 2022; the possible end to reform efforts may affect the fiscal and debt outlook in the medium term.

Policy challenge—mobilizing domestic tax revenue

Pakistan has a low tax-to-GDP ratio compared to other emerging economies, averaging only 11% from FY2010 to FY2021. Low tax revenue contributes to high fiscal deficits and constrains fiscal space for infrastructure and social spending. The continued structural weaknesses of the tax system are reflected in a narrow tax base and poor taxpayer compliance due to the large informal economy, tax avoidance in the formal sector, and under-taxation in certain sectors.

Pakistan's tax regime is complex and unpredictable, marred by excessive exemptions and preferential treatment, multiple rate structures, frequent ad hoc changes in tax policy, and fragmented tax administration. Revenue from direct taxation is low compared with indirect taxes (Figure 3.20.13) and remains concentrated among salaried workers and large industries. Indirect taxes comprised two-thirds of the total tax revenue in FY2021. The extensive use of withholding and sales taxes collected by third-party agents has become a preferred mode of revenue collection. Provincial tax collection, compared to the share of federal tax revenue, remains miniscule (Figure 3.20.14), averaging 8.9% of total tax revenue over the last 5 years.

Figure 3.20.13 Direct and indirect taxes

The shares of tax revenue in GDP and direct taxes in total tax revenue have declined.

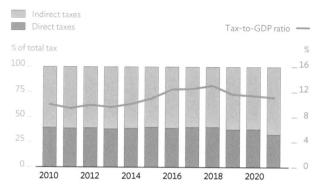

GDP = gross domestic product.

Notes: Years are fiscal years ending on 30 June of that year. Tax-to-GDP ratio computed using national accounts data with 2006 as the base year.

Source: Federal Board of Revenue, Strategic Planning Reforms and Statistics Wing.

Figure 3.20.14 Federal and provincial taxes

Provincial taxes remain less than 10% of total government tax revenue.

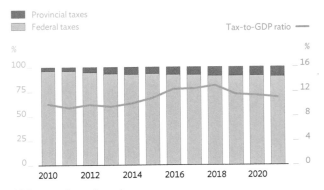

GDP = gross domestic product.
Notes: Years are fiscal years ending on 30 June of that year. Tax-to-GDP ratio computed using national accounts data with 2006 as the base year.
Source: Ministry of Finance. *Pakistan Fiscal Operations* (accessed 3 March 2022).

Recent studies by the International Monetary Fund and the World Bank on Pakistan's tax gap estimate that tax revenue could potentially reach 22.3% to 26.0% of GDP. The challenge is to tap this potential through well-defined and comprehensive reforms in tax policy and administration. A simplified and easy to understand tax system that makes it easy to file tax returns would encourage voluntary compliance and reduce tax evasion. The effective enforcement of tax laws can be achieved by improving governance, continued investment in information technology infrastructure, and more and better-trained staff. Modernizing tax administration by integrating internal database and information systems, and improved training in data management, can enhance efficiency, improve compliance risk management and audit capability, and reduce the cost of paying taxes. Gains from

recent administrative and technological improvements facilitating smoother digital filing can be increased by improving taxpayer education and facilitation services. Developing and strengthening technical capacity in data analysis can facilitate evidence-based policy making and support better compliance by identifying tax gaps and facilitating systematic monitoring and evaluation. These measures, complemented with broader efforts to improve the business climate and measures to address the trust deficit in the delivery of public services, can encourage informal businesses to enter the formal sector.

Improving the ability of provincial governments to raise revenue is critical for the success of tax reforms. Expanding the provincial tax net, particularly in services like retail trade; boosting the capacity of provincial tax collection; improving the efficiency of collecting vehicle tax; and optimizing the urban property tax would substantially increase the generation of provincial revenue. Stronger institutional arrangements are needed to improve the coordination of tax policies and administrative laws among the federal and provincial governments.

Pakistan's Medium Term Budget Strategy FY2021–FY2024 outlines directions for tax reforms, focusing on broadening the tax base and widening the tax net, removing exemptions, simplifying procedures, and digitalizing tax administration. The FBR is preparing a strategic reform plan that delineates similar reform interventions with specific and measurable outcomes over the next 5 years. If implemented in a sustained manner, tax reforms can pave the way for realizing Pakistan's tax potential, providing greater fiscal space to fund critical public services.

SRI LANKA

Growth picked up in 2021 after contracting in the previous year. The economic performance, however, was mixed. While rising domestic demand supported the economy, growth was held back by COVID-19 outbreaks and mobility restrictions, and mounting fiscal, foreign exchange, and inflation pressures. The current account deficit widened last year. A reviving tourism industry and the global economic recovery will support activity in 2022 and 2023. But macroeconomic weaknesses will continue to keep growth muted. Preparing for population aging is a major policy challenge.

Economic performance

Sri Lanka's economy grew 3.7% in 2021 after it shrank 3.6% in 2020. Growth was underpinned by domestic demand and exports. But a stronger recovery was held back by COVID-19's impact on economic activity—especially in the third quarter, when mobility restrictions caused growth to contract 1.5%—and a still weak tourism industry, albeit one showing signs of revival. Services drove a 1.4% growth in the fourth quarter. Declining government revenue, significant external debt servicing, low foreign exchange reserves, and downgrades to the country's sovereign credit ratings further weighed on growth, as did severe shortages of essentials and inflationary pressures.

Industry output grew by 5.3% in 2021 after a 6.9% contraction in the previous year (Figure 3.21.1). Manufacturing, up 7.2%, was supported by a gradual pickup in economic activity in domestic and global markets. Cement shortages and shutdowns caused by a surge in COVID-19 cases hit construction, up a muted 1.9%, and mining and quarrying, up 2.8% from double-digit contractions in 2020. Agriculture grew by 2.0% on higher production of cereals (except rice), export crops, animal production, and forestry. Services grew by 3.0%, but accommodation, restaurants, transportation, and wholesale and retail trade, suffered from the reimposition of COVID-19 restrictions.

Figure 3.21.1 GDP growth by sector

Growth improved across sectors in 2021 although from a low base.

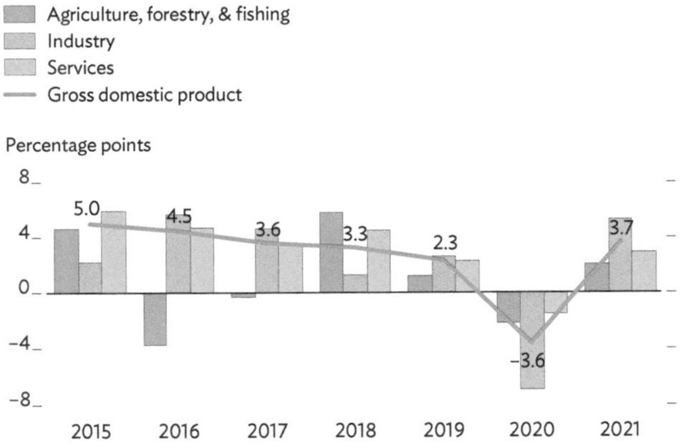

- Agriculture, forestry, & fishing
- Industry
- Services
- — Gross domestic product

Source: Department of Census and Statistics (accessed 30 March 2022).

Private consumption rose by 7.5% in the first 9 months of last year from a low base in the same period in 2020, while government consumption increased by 2.2% on COVID-19 spending. Net exports were mildly positive, as a recovery in imports was more than offset by a surge in exports, particularly for agricultural produce, apparel, rubber products, and machinery and equipment (Figure 3.21.2). Investment growth was subdued, amid macroeconomic uncertainties.

This chapter was written by Madhavi Pundit, Savindi Jayakody, and Nirukthi P. Kariyawasam of the Sri Lanka Resident Mission, ADB, Colombo.

Figure 3.21.2 Demand-side contributions to growth

Consumption and investment growth remained subdued in 2021.

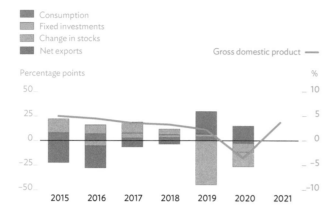

GDP = gross domestic product.
Source: Department of Census and Statistics (accessed 15 February 2022).

Inflation as measured by the Colombo consumer price index averaged 6.0% last year, up from 4.6% in 2020, on an array of factors, including higher commodity and fuel prices, the removal of price controls, supply chain disruptions caused by the spread of the Delta COVID-19 variant, a shortage of foreign exchange, and import controls (Figure 3.21.3). A chemical fertilizer ban imposed in May to promote organic cultivation also put upward pressure on inflation; the ban was lifted in November. Stronger demand fueled by accommodative monetary and fiscal policies and a depreciating currency also contributed. Inflation accelerated to 15.1% year on year in February 2022 on a 25.7% surge in food inflation, and core inflation, which excludes food and energy prices, was 10.9%.

To curb inflationary pressures and address imbalances in the external sector, Central Bank of Sri Lanka, in August 2021, raised the standing deposit and lending facility rates each by 50 basis points and the standard reserve ratio by 200 basis points. This reversed the accommodative monetary policy stance that had prevailed since the start of the COVID-19 pandemic. Credit to the private sector slowed following this tightening, although credit growth remained strong, at 13.1% in 2021. Central bank net lending to the government more than doubled to 12.5% of GDP by the end of 2021, reflecting accelerated deficit monetization. Broad money supply growth declined from 21.5% in June year on year to 11.9% at the end of January 2022

as monetary aggregates responded to the dual effects of monetary policy actions and overall weaker credit demand (Figure 3.21.4). Amid building inflationary pressures, deposit and lending rates were raised again, by 50 basis points in January 2022 and 100 basis points in March 2022. The banking sector remained resilient: capital adequacy ratios were above required levels and the ratio of nonperforming loans to total loans eased to 4.8% in the third quarter from 5.3% in the same period in 2020.

Figure 3.21.3 Monthly inflation

Headline and core inflation at double-digit levels in February 2022.

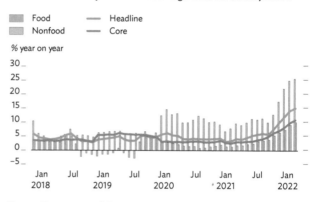

Source: Department of Census and Statistics. *Monthly CCPI* (accessed 20 March 2022).

Figure 3.21.4 Contributions to broad money growth

Monetary conditions tightened since August 2021, reversing the accommodative stance since the COVID-19 outbreak.

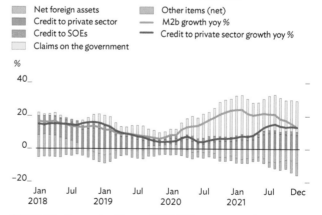

COVID-19 = Coronavirus Disease 2019, SOE = state-owned enterprise, yoy = year on year.
Note: M2b includes currency held with the public; demand, time and savings deposits of the public; and a part of foreign currency deposits held with the commercial banks.
Source: Central Bank of Sri Lanka. *Monetary sector statistics* (accessed 20 March 2022).

Government expenditure rose by 8.9% year on year in the first 9 months of 2021 to the equivalent of 19.5% of GDP. Controls on recurrent spending helped reduce overall expenditure by 0.5% of GDP, despite a 0.1% of GDP rise in capital expenditure. The ratio of revenue to GDP fell by 0.8 percentage points to 8.6% of GDP on weaker growth in tax and nontax revenue. In 2021, the fiscal deficit is expected to have narrowed to 11.1% of GDP, down from 12.7% in 2020, mainly due to lower expenditure (Figure 3.21.5). The deficit was mainly financed through domestic sources as access to international capital markets has become increasingly restricted due to rising debt and low external reserves. Central government debt at the end of 2021 was at an estimated 107.1% of GDP, raising concerns over the sustainability of public debt (Figure 3.21.6).

Figure 3.21.6 Central government debt

The pandemic triggered a steep increase in debt.

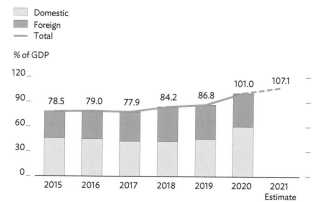

GDP = gross domestic product.

Sources: Central Bank of Sri Lanka annual reports, various years; Asian Development Bank estimates.

Figure 3.21.5 Central government finance

Lower revenue during the pandemic drove higher fiscal deficits.

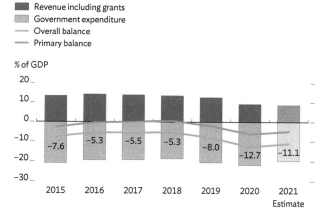

GDP = gross domestic product, IMF = International Monetary Fund.

Notes: Figures exclude revenue and expenditure transfers to provincial councils. 2019 and 2020 figures are from the IMF.

Sources: Central Bank of Sri Lanka; IMF. *World Economic Outlook Database. October 2021*; Ministry of Finance; Asian Development Bank estimates.

Figure 3.21.7 Current account balance

The current account deficit widened in 2021 amid growing trade imbalances.

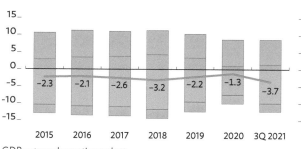

GDP = gross domestic product.

Source: Central Bank of Sri Lanka. *External sector statistics* (accessed 20 March 2022).

The current account deficit widened to an estimated 4.2% of GDP in 2021 from 1.3% in 2020 (Figure 3.21.7). Although merchandise exports rose 24.4% last year, imports grew by 28.5%, mainly reflecting higher prices (Figure 3.21.8). Thus, the trade deficit widened last year, by 35.4% year on year to 9.6% of GDP.

Remittances fell by $1.6 billion in 2021, a decline of 27.7% year on year, and dipped by another $791 million

in the first 2 months of 2022 (Figure 3.21.9). The drop may be partly due to a shift in inflows from official to informal channels given the higher US dollar exchange rate in the parallel market. To promote inflows of remittances from migrant workers through formal channels, the central bank introduced incentives, including bearing the transaction cost of inward remittances up to a certain limit. But despite these measures, remittances continued to contract.

Figure 3.21.8 Trade indices of imports

The higher import bill in 2021 partly reflected higher price of imports compared with the pre-pandemic average as volumes remain subdued.

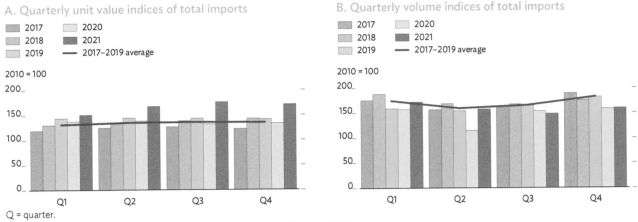

A. Quarterly unit value indices of total imports

■ 2017	□ 2020
■ 2018	■ 2021
□ 2019	— 2017–2019 average

B. Quarterly volume indices of total imports

■ 2017	□ 2020
■ 2018	■ 2021
□ 2019	— 2017–2019 average

Q = quarter.
Source: Central Bank of Sri Lanka. *External sector statistics* (accessed 9 February 2022).

Figure 3.21.9 Remittances

Significant contraction of official inflows from June 2021.

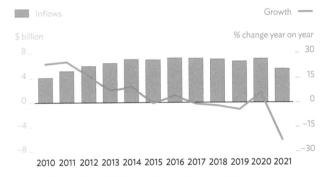

Source: Central Bank of Sri Lanka. *External sector statistics* (accessed 20 March 2022).

Figure 3.21.10 Tourist arrivals

Gradual pick up in arrivals on eased COVID-19 travel restrictions.

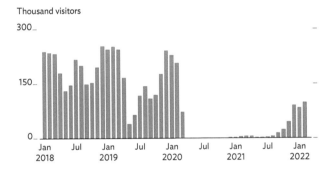

COVID-19 = Coronavirus Disease 2019.
Source: Sri Lanka Tourist Development Authority. *Monthly Tourist Arrivals Reports* (accessed 20 March 2022).

For most of 2021, Sri Lanka's tourism industry, usually a major foreign exchange earner, remained sluggish because of the COVID-19 pandemic. But tourism picked up as COVID-19 restrictions were eased, with 89,506 tourist arrivals in December compared with zero in the same month in 2020—and twice the arrivals in November. Cumulative tourist arrivals in 2021 was 194,495, which was of course a fraction of average annual arrivals over the past decade (Figure 3.21.10).

Foreign direct investment totaled $438 million in the first 9 months of 2021, just 55% of average 2017–2019 levels. Net capital outflows from the government securities market totaled $27 million and $238 million from private portfolio flows.

Foreign exchange reserves fell sharply last year amid sizable external debt servicing and the loss of access to international markets as the major credit rating agencies downgraded Sri Lanka's rating (Figure 3.21.11). Despite a $780 million special drawing rights allocation from the International Monetary Fund, reserves declined from $5.7 billion at the end of 2020 to $3.1 billion (including a currency swap equivalent to $1.5 billion with People's Bank of China) by the end of 2021, cover for less than 2 months of goods imports and well below Sri Lanka's predetermined foreign currency outflows of $6.9 billion in 2022 (Figure 3.21.12). Foreign reserves dipped further in February 2022 to $2.31 billion, estimated cover for 1.3 months of imports.

Figure 3.21.11 S&P sovereign credit rating

Downgrades in 2020 and early 2021 on challenging fiscal and debt situation and sharp decline in reserves.

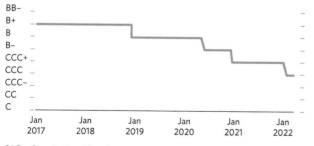

S&P = Standard and Poor's.

Source: Trading Economics. *Sri Lanka Credit Ratings* (accessed 20 March 2022).

Figure 3.21.12 Reserves and predetermined outflows

Reserves declined steadily, falling to an estimated 1.3 months of import cover in February 2022.

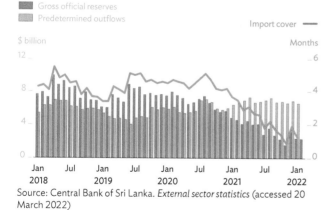

Source: Central Bank of Sri Lanka. *External sector statistics* (accessed 20 March 2022)

The average exchange rate depreciated by 7.5% against the US dollar in 2021, mainly in the first 4 months. The central bank held the exchange rate at about $1 = SLRs201 from April 2021 to February 2022. The real effective exchange rate appreciated by an average 2.8% in 2021 (Figure 3.21.13).

In October 2021, the central bank announced a 6-month roadmap to boost foreign exchange reserves, attract foreign exchange inflows into the banking system, and manage external debt service. In March 2022, the central bank allowed greater flexibility for determining exchange rates. At end March, the Sri Lanka rupee was at SLRs299 = $1, a year-on-year depreciation of 49.2% and 48.0% since greater flexibility was announced in early March. The government

Figure 3.21.13 Official and real effective exchange rates

Official rate held at about $1 = SLRs201 in 2021 followed by a sharp depreciation in early 2022.

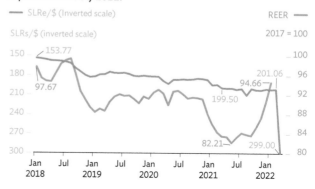

REER = real effective exchange rate.

Source: Central Bank of Sri Lanka. *Exchange rates* accessed 31 March 2022).

imposed limits on imports of some nonessential consumer goods to dampen demand for US dollars.

Economic prospects

Growth is expected to slow to 2.4% in 2022 and pick up slightly to 2.5% in 2023 (Table 3.21.1). The outlook is clouded by Sri Lanka's debt overhang and large fiscal and external financing needs. GDP growth will be constrained by low foreign exchange reserves and macroeconomic imbalances, including double-digit inflation. The forecast assumes that hesitancy in the population over receiving a COVID-19 booster will be largely overcome and there is no further surge in COVID-19 cases (Box 3.21.1). It also assumes the government will be able to meet its external financing

Table 3.21.1 Selected economic indicators, %

Growth will decelerate, inflation rise sharply, and the current account balance remain high in 2022.

	2020	2021	2022	2023
GDP growth	–3.6	3.7	2.4	2.5
Inflation	4.6	6.0	13.3	6.7
CAB/GDP	–1.3	–4.2	–4.3	–2.8

CAB = current account balance, GDP = gross domestic product.

Sources: Central Bank of Sri Lanka; Asian Development Bank estimates.

requirements—and here uncertainty remains over the sources of this financing. All in all, risks to the outlook are tilted to the downside.

Economic activity likely slowed in the first quarter of 2022 amid new COVID-19 waves and an energy shortage. Monetary policy tightening, supply shortages, and heavy inflationary pressure will weigh on domestic demand this year. Private consumption growth will moderate due to strained incomes, shortages of basic goods, and macroeconomic challenges constraining investment. Rising interest rates will further discourage domestic demand, and increasing reliance on domestic financing of the fiscal deficit will crowd out private investment. Exports will continue to grow on supportive policies and a recovering external environment. But faster growth in imports, aided by rising commodity prices, will lower growth in net exports in 2022. Crucially, economic activity will be impaired by acute fuel shortages and rising commodity prices.

Multiple pressures building across sectors will slow output this year. The fertilizer ban will likely result in a lower harvest and tighter food supply, as paddy production in the *maha* season (September to March in the following year) is expected to be smaller compared with 2021. This will lower agriculture production this year. Industry output will grow at a slower pace than in 2021 because of supply constraints faced by construction and manufacturing, fuel shortages, and load shedding. Tourism will continue to pick up, and the relaxation of COVID-19 mobility restrictions will drive services growth. An escalation of the geopolitical fallout from the Russian invasion of Ukraine will add to external pressure on Sri Lanka through reduced exports to these countries and higher oil prices.

Sri Lanka continues to face trade-offs in fiscal policy between moving toward fiscal and debt sustainability on the one hand and providing support to the economy on the other. Budget proposals for 2022 envisaged reducing the fiscal deficit to 8.8% of GDP in 2022 from a projected 11.1% in 2021 and increasing revenue by 46.0% through improvements in tax buoyancy and administration, and a few one-time tax increases, and capping expenditure growth at 15%. In early 2022, the government announced a post-budget relief package and other concessions totaling 1.3% of GDP. The package includes an SLRs5,000 monthly wage increase for public sector workers, compensation for farmers for

lost production caused by the fertilizer ban and other financial incentives for boosting cultivation.

Rising headline and core inflation suggest that underlying inflationary pressures remain strong. Inflation is forecast to accelerate to 13.3% in 2022, more than double the 2021 inflation, on higher food prices from low harvests, higher import prices, particularly higher fuel costs, supply chain disruptions, shortages stemming from the foreign exchange squeeze, and exchange rate depreciation. Inflation is projected to fall to 6.7% in 2023 on moderating global prices and easing supply constraints.

The current account deficit is expected to remain high, at 4.3% in 2022. Surging oil import prices will offset gains from pent-up demand in major export markets. Tourist arrivals this year are expected to return to near 50% of their 2018 level (pre-pandemic and pre-terrorist attacks). Remittances will get a boost from the more flexible exchange rate. The current account deficit is forecast to narrow to 2.8% of GDP in 2023 on the fading effects of COVID-19, the continued recovery in tourism, improvements in the trade balance due to strong exports, and a recovery in remittances.

In the absence of substantial foreign exchange inflows, external sector vulnerabilities are likely to persist this year amid significant external debt servicing, low reserves, and limited access to international capital markets. The economic outlook is clouded by significant downside risks from the underlying macroeconomic weaknesses, severe fuel shortages, the pandemic's lingering impacts, and external events. Efforts to restore macroeconomic stability and reduce debt through greater exchange rate flexibility, monetary policy independence, revenue-based fiscal consolidation and structural reforms in taxation, public sector management, and state-owned enterprises will be critical to restore debt sustainability and for recovery to gain traction. Further downside risks include rising global commodity and oil prices, which will add to domestic inflationary pressures, and spillovers from tightening global financial conditions. The Russian invasion of Ukraine could also adversely affect the tourist industry. The Russian Federation and Ukraine are a significant source markets for Sri Lanka's tourism industry, accounting for 12.3% of total tourist arrivals in 2021. The two countries are also important sources of wheat, soybean, and sunflower oil imports and key buyers of Sri Lankan tea.

Policy challenge—preparing for an aging society

Sri Lanka has the highest proportion of older persons (ages 65 and above) in its population of any country in South Asia (Figure 3.21.14). While the pattern of aging in Sri Lanka's population is similar to that in East Asian and Southeast Asian economies, the country's demographic transition is unfolding at a lower level of per capita income compared with economies in these subregions. In other words, Sri Lanka is growing old before becoming rich.

The working-age population is forecast to contract from 2030 and the population of older persons is expected to triple by 2038 relative to 2005 (Figure 3.21.15). Sri Lanka reached this advanced stage of demographic transition because of low fertility rates (2.2 per 1,000 women) and rising life expectancy (77 years) relative to some other Asian countries and also to those at a similar stage of economic development (Figures 3.21.16 and 3.21.17).

A declining working-age population will constrain economic growth. Aging populations will require greater outlays for pensions, health care, and the provision of long-term care, and this will add to fiscal pressures. Providing these services, however, will contribute to promoting investments and generating employment in the long term.

Sri Lanka's response to population aging should be focused on improving productivity; raising labor force participation, particularly for women to enter work; increasing the retirement age; and promoting healthy aging. To improve productivity, education and training systems should allow for learning beyond the usual academic training and facilitate skills upgrading throughout working careers. Advanced technologies can be used to create a more flexible workplace through telecommuting and improving health. These technologies can also extend working-life spans and longevity by helping older people overcome impairments and facilitate their social connectivity.

Encouraging more women to participate in the labor force can alleviate labor shortages and raise productivity. The participation rates of Sri Lankan women in the labor force remain well below those

Figure 3.21.14 Older (aged 65 and above) population in South Asia, 2020

Sri Lanka has the highest proportion of the region's older persons in its population.

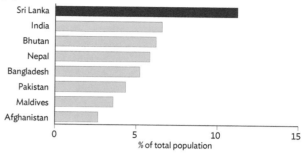

Source: United Nations Department of Economic and Social Affairs. *World Population Prospects 2019* (accessed 10 February 2022).

Figure 3.21.15 Population 1960–2100

Working-age population to slowly decline from 2030.

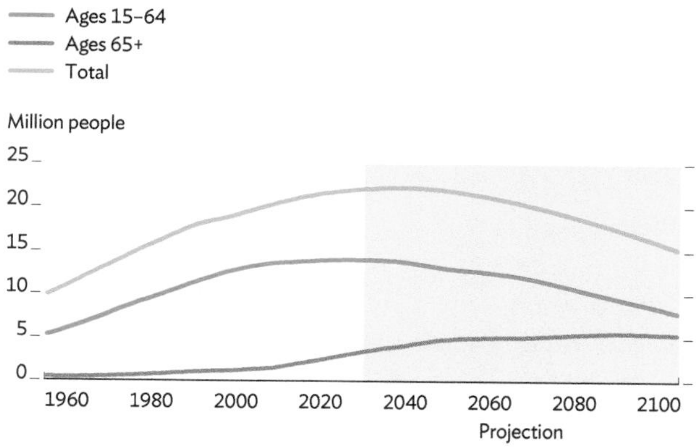

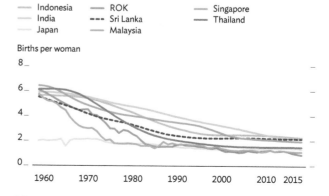

Source: United Nations Department of Economic and Social Affairs. *World Population Prospects 2019* (accessed 10 February 2022).

Figure 3.21.16 Total fertility rate in Sri Lanka and selected Asian economies, 1960–2019

Fertility rates in Sri Lanka continue their decreasing trend.

ROK = Republic of Korea.
Source: World Bank. World Development Indicators database (accessed 10 February 2022).

Figure 3.21.17 Life expectancy of income groups in Sri Lanka and selected Asian economies, 1960 and 2019

Sri Lanka's life expectancy increased at a pace higher than high-income countries during 1960–2019.

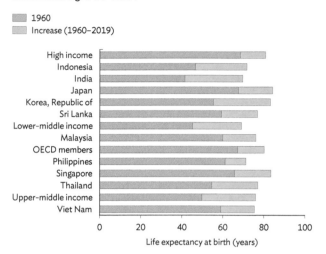

OECD = Organisation for Economic Co-operation and Development.
Source: World Bank. *World Development Indicators database* (accessed 10 February 2022).

Figure 3.21.18 Labor force participation rate

The participation rate of women has remained stagnant at about 30% since the 2000s.

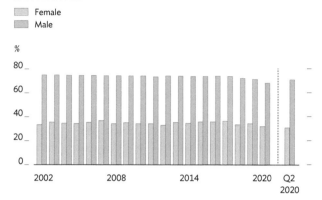

Source: Department of Census and Statistics. *Sri Lanka Labour Force Survey Annual Report* (accessed 10 February 2022); World Bank. World Development Indicators database (accessed 10 February 2022).

community-based social care, enhancing home-based care services and the psychological well-being of older persons, and strengthening training in geriatric medicine and long-term care are equally important.

of men (Figure 3.21.18). Policies to improve the participation of women in the labor force include parental leave, raising awareness on sharing household responsibilities, flexible hours, work from home, and access to affordable care services, such as childcare, and care and support services for persons with disabilities, including older persons. Policy initiatives to promote the entrepreneurship of women are also critical for closing Sri Lanka's prevalent gender gap.

Sri Lanka's retirement age was recently raised from 60 to 65 for state workers and from 55 to 60 for workers in the private sector. This initiative should be complemented not only by training programs but also by improving the primary and secondary preventive care for older persons. Developing a system for

To defray the costs of these initiatives, the contributory pension scheme for older persons announced in the Budget Speech 2022 is a step in the right direction. This will allow the responsibility of paying for retirement to be shared. Here, employees and employers both contribute to a defined percentage based on monthly earnings toward retirement. The extended retirement age would also help raise contribution rates in the medium term, with workers saving more before retirement and starting to draw down pensions at a later age. Considering the sizeable informal economy, it is important to encourage savings and expand access to adequate pensions for the informal sector, which accounts for 70% of total employment, and to take steps to formalize the sector through regulatory reforms.

Box 3.21.1 Sri Lanka's COVID-19 situation

COVID-19 vaccination in Sri Lanka accelerated in 2021 to fight off fresh waves and new variants. COVID-19 cases surged from a 7-day moving average of 580 per day at the beginning of the year to peak at 5,000 in August amid the spread of the Delta variant (Figure 1). Travel restrictions were gradually lifted toward the end of the year as COVID-19 cases declined to 646. But the Omicron variant triggered another surge in February 2022 which peaked in early-March. As of 15 March 2022, 77.5% of the population had received a first shot, 65.5% were fully jabbed, and 34.8% of the population received a booster shot.

The pandemic has disproportionately affected Sri Lanka's older population, which account for 76.8% of COVID-19 deaths (Figure 2). For Sri Lanka,

this unprecedented global health crisis has both underscored the importance of having effective systems in place to deal with public health emergencies and increasing preparedness to care for the older population.

The lockdowns and travel restrictions affected access to routine and preventive care, which resulted in an increased risk of morbidity and mortality among the older population. In particular, the loss of and breakdown in social networks associated with COVID-19 have affected mental health and psychosocial well-being in the older population. The digital divide has also impeded the access of Sri Lanka's older population to essential information on the pandemic and related health and socioeconomic measures.

1 COVID-19 cumulative daily cases and vaccination progress

Omicron wave peaked in early March 2022 amid strong vaccination drive.

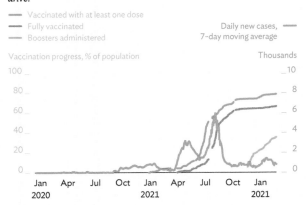

Source: Ministry of Health, Epidemiology Unit. *Corona Virus 2020–2022* (accessed on 18 March 2022).

2 COVID-19 deaths by age group

COVID-19 disproportionally affected the older population.

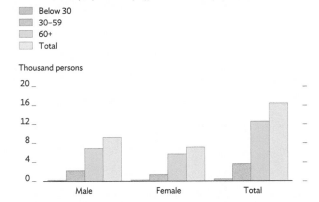

Source: Ministry of Health, Epidemiology Unit. *COVID-19 Confirmed Death* (accessed on 18 March 2022).

SOUTHEAST ASIA

Brunei Darussalam
Cambodia
Indonesia
Lao PDR
Malaysia
Myanmar
Philippines
Singapore
Thailand
Timor-Leste
Viet Nam

BRUNEI DARUSSALAM

The economy contracted in 2021 largely on the reimposition of COVID-19 mobility restrictions starting in August. Unexpected supply disruptions to the oil and gas industry and delays to foreign direct investment projects cramped the economy. Growth is expected to rebound in 2022 and 2023, led by a sharp increase in oil and gas output. A key policy challenge is the diversification of fiscal revenue away from oil and gas to enhance long-term fiscal sustainability.

Economic performance

Brunei Darussalam's economy is estimated to have contracted by 1.5% in 2021. Economic activity was disrupted by weaker oil and gas production, delays in the implementation of foreign direct investment projects, and a surge in COVID-19 cases from the third quarter (Figure 3.22.1). In that quarter, GDP contracted by 2.2% after shrinking 2.1% in the previous quarter (Figure 3.22.2). By sector, disruptions in the oil and gas industry accounted for a 2.7 percentage points decline in GDP. Output from oil and gas mining declined last year by 3.9% and 7.6% for manufacture of liquefied natural gas and other petroleum and chemical products.

Figure 3.22.2 Supply-side contributions to growth

Falling oil and gas production dragged growth down in 2021.

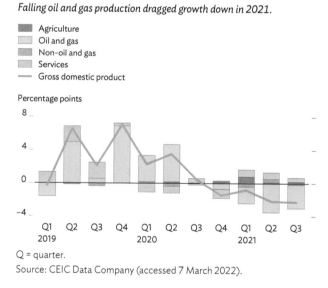

Q = quarter.
Source: CEIC Data Company (accessed 7 March 2022).

Mobility restrictions dampened services output in 2021, although the sector still grew. A significant recovery in fruit and vegetable production, and an expansion in fisheries, partially offset the oil industry's contraction.

Labor shortages and aging oil and gas fields constrained oil and gas production. The construction of the second phase of Hengyi Industries' oil refinery

Figure 3.22.1 Daily new COVID-19 cases, 7-day average

Cases started spiking in February 2022.

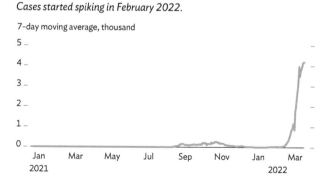

COVID-19 = Coronavirus Disease 2019.
Source: CEIC Data Company (accessed 7 March 2022).

This chapter was written by Marcel Schroder and Nedelyn Magtibay-Ramos of the Economic Research and Regional Cooperation Department, ADB, Manila.

and petrochemical plant has been postponed to 2023. Commercial production of urea fertilizers was supposed to have started in May 2021, but has now been delayed until 2022.

Net export earnings improved on rising oil and petrochemical prices, boosting GDP growth by 7.5 percentage points (Figure 3.22.3). Despite the reimposition of COVID-19 mobility restrictions, household consumption added 3.1 percentage points to growth. Government consumption decreased marginally by 0.5%, erasing 0.1 percentage points from growth. Investment plummeted by 28%, dragging growth down by 13.8 percentage points.

Figure 3.22.3 Demand-side contributions to growth

Plummeting investment extended the contraction in Q3 2021.

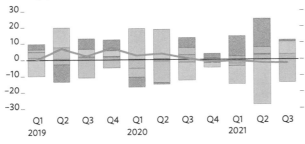

Q = quarter.
Source: CEIC Data Company (accessed 7 March 2022).

Inflation averaged 1.7% in the first 11 months of 2021, little changed from 1.9% in the same period in 2020 (Figure 3.22.4). Inflation in November 2021 was mainly driven by higher transport costs, which rose by 5.3% and contributed 1.0 percentage point to headline inflation. Higher prices for food and nonalcoholic beverages, and clothing and footwear, contributed 0.5 percentage points and 0.3 points, respectively, to headline inflation. The cost of housing and utilities remained subdued.

Merchandise exports started to recover in March 2021 and rose by 144.0% in November on higher mineral

Figure 3.22.4 Sources of inflation

Inflation remained elevated in 2021.

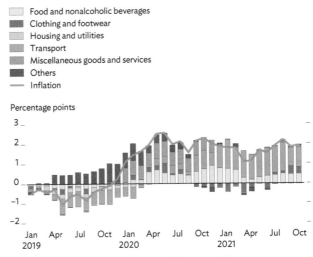

Source: CEIC Data Company (accessed 7 March 2022).

fuels exports. Imports rose by 42.2% on a 127.0% growth in mineral fuels shipments, resulting in a wider current account surplus, equal to 12.5% of 2021's GDP, up from 4.5% in 2020.

Economic prospects

Growth is expected to rebound in 2022 and 2023, led by a significant expansion of oil and gas output and improved domestic activity on a further easing in COVID-19 restrictions and high vaccination coverage. Oil and gas output is expected to surge by 30% this year after a 6.3% contraction in 2021. Both the domestic and external environment is expected to be brighter.

As of 13 March 2022, more than 94% of the population had been fully vaccinated against COVID-19 and 58.6% had received booster shots. Mobility restrictions started to be eased in November, boding well for the economy. Despite the spike in daily new COVID-19 cases in February and March, private consumption and services output are expected to pick up significantly. The resumption of construction of the second phase of Hengyi's plant next year will bolster construction investment. GDP growth is forecast at 4.2% this year and 3.6% next year (Table 3.22.1).

Table 3.22.1 Selected economic indicators, %

In 2022, growth will rebound while inflation is expected to remain elevated and the current account surplus ample.

	2020	2021	2022	2023
GDP growth	1.1	−1.5	4.2	3.6
Inflation	1.9	1.7	1.6	1.0
CAB/GDP	4.5	12.5	16.0	12.0

CAB = current account balance, GDP = gross domestic product.
Sources: CEIC Data Company (accessed 7 March 2022); Centre for Strategic and Policy Studies. 2022. *Brunei Economic Outlook 2022.* *Bandar Seri Begawan*; Asian Development Bank estimates.

Headline inflation has been high by historical standards since 2020, but it is expected to subside this year and come closer to pre-pandemic ranges on easing global supply chain pressures, although repercussions from the Russian invasion of Ukraine will counterbalance this somewhat. The Brunei dollar's parity with the Singapore dollar, coupled with domestic price controls, will also help keep inflation in check. Inflation is forecast at 1.6% this year, decelerating to 1.0% in 2023.

Rising oil and gas output, buoyed by exports and higher prices of crude oil, liquefied natural gas, refined petroleum, and petrochemical products will widen the current account surplus, forecast at 16% of GDP this year (Figure 3.22.5). Increased imports of construction material, machinery, and equipment for Hengyi's plant

expansion will narrow the surplus next year, forecast at 12% of GDP.

Unanticipated disruptions to domestic oil and gas output, and a slower-than-expected easing of global supply chain pressures, are the main downside risks to the outlook. Renewed outbreaks of COVID-19 and associated containment measures could also derail the recovery.

Policy challenge—increasing and diversifying public revenue

Increasing revenue from sources other than oil and gas is a major policy challenge to the country's efforts to achieve long-term fiscal sustainability. The government's budget is highly dependent on this revenue, accounting for 70% of total revenue in pre-pandemic years (Figure 3.22.6). The economic impact of COVID-19 has put the country's fiscal vulnerabilities in the spotlight, as lower global energy prices and domestic oil production reduced oil and gas revenue from 19.8% of GDP in fiscal year 2020 (FY2020, ended 31 March 2020) to 7.7% in FY2021. This resulted in the fiscal deficit widening from 5.6% of GDP in FY2020 to 20.0% in FY2021. Increasing the non-oil and gas component of fiscal revenue is therefore an important policy challenge for maintaining fiscal sustainability over the long term.

Figure 3.22.5 Balance of payments

The surplus is expected to widen in 2022 before narrowing again in 2023.

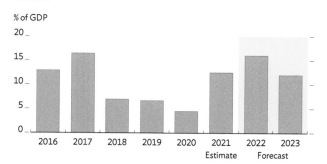

GDP = gross domestic product.
Sources: CEIC Data Company (accessed 7 March 2022); Centre for Strategic and Policy Studies. 2022. *Brunei Economic Outlook 2022.* *Bandar Seri Begawan*; Asian Development Bank estimates.

Figure 3.22.6 Fiscal revenue by sector

Oil and gas fiscal revenue dropped sharply in 2021.

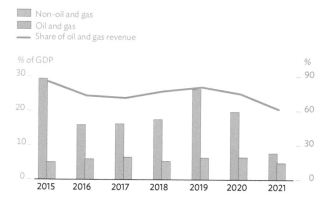

GDP = gross domestic product.
Note: Years are fiscal years ending on 31 March of that year.
Source: International Monetary Fund. Article IV Staff Reports 2019 and 2021.

Brunei Darussalam does not levy personal income tax or value-added tax (VAT), and its corporate tax rate, at 18.5%, is one of the lowest among countries in the Association of Southeast Asian Nations. Oil and gas companies, however, fall under a different tax regime as their profits are taxed at 55%. Introducing broad-based VAT would diversify the government's sources of fiscal revenue and delink fiscal policy from volatility in global oil prices.

Many developing economies in Asia rely fairly heavily on VAT and to a lesser extent on personal income tax. VAT has a self-enforcement property in that firms must receive receipts from their suppliers to qualify for tax deductions on inputs, thereby creating an auditable tax trail. But VAT as a flat tax on consumption may disproportionately affect poorer households. The effect of this can be mitigated through higher pro-poor public spending programs; for example, the Skim Kebajikan Negara welfare program that was introduced in July 2020. Financing can come either from VAT or the country's zakat system—funds from obligatory payments of rich households. Oil-rich states levy VAT, including the Kingdom of Saudi Arabia and United Arab Emirates. To manage a revenue shortfall during the COVID-19 pandemic, the Kingdom of Saudi Arabia increased its VAT rate from 5% to 15% in July 2020.

CAMBODIA

The economy rebounded faster than expected in 2021 due mainly to a strong recovery in light manufacturing. The current account deficit widened as the imbalance in goods trade rose, but the deficit is expected to narrow this year and next. Growth will accelerate in 2022 and 2023 as economic activity continues to pick up and return to normal. The main policy challenge is sustaining the rapid increase in light manufacturing in areas other than garments for a more resilient and diversified economy.

Economic performance

Growth in Cambodia rebounded to an estimated 3.0% in 2021 after a contraction of 3.1% in 2020 (Figure 3.23.1). In the second half, a robust recovery in external demand for the country's manufactured products drove the faster-than-expected rebound. Industrial output grew by 7.4% in 2021. Exports of garments, footwear, and travel goods recovered exceptionally well last year, particularly in the second half. Nongarment manufactured products continued their robust expansion, with exports rising by 30.7%.

Agriculture exports rose by 19.0% in 2021 on solid growth in cassava, banana, and rubber exports. Restrictions in pig imports to prevent outbreaks of African swine fever and better domestic prices supported the local pig industry. Fisheries performed worse than expected due to low water levels. Agriculture output expanded by 1.1%.

Services contracted by 0.4% on a continued steep decline in demand for food, accommodation, transportation, and other in-person services due to the prolonged COVID-19 outbreak and lockdowns. The poor performance of these services was partially offset by stronger growth in communication services and a gradual recovery in wholesale and retail trade and real estate. Restrictions on international travel, which were in place for most of 2021, caused an 85% drop in international tourist arrivals (Figure 3.23.2).

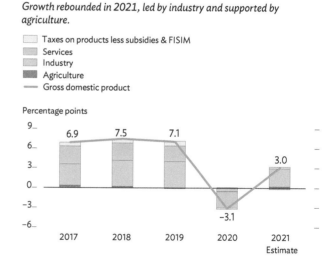

Figure 3.23.1 Supply-side contributions to growth

Growth rebounded in 2021, led by industry and supported by agriculture.

- Taxes on products less subsidies & FISIM
- Services
- Industry
- Agriculture
- Gross domestic product

FISIM = financial intermediation services indirectly measured.
Sources: Ministry of Economy and Finance; National Institute of Statistics; Asian Development Bank estimates.

Inflation was stable, edging up to 3.7% year on year at the end of 2021, mainly due to rising energy prices. Inflation averaged 2.9%, the same as in 2020. While high dollarization levels constrained monetary policy, the National Bank of Cambodia adopted measures to maintain liquidity in the banking system and facilitate loan restructuring to soften the impact of the pandemic and lockdowns on lenders and borrowers and to

This chapter was written by Poullang Doung of the Cambodia Resident Mission, ADB, Phnom Penh.

Figure 3.23.2 Tourist arrivals

Arrivals plummeted on COVID-19 international travel restrictions.

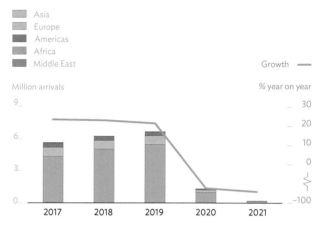

COVID-19 = Coronavirus Disease 2019.
Sources: CEIC Data Company (accessed 15 March 2022); Ministry of Tourism; Asian Development Bank estimates.

Figure 3.23.3 Fiscal indicators

The deficit widened in 2021 on declining revenue and rising expenditure.

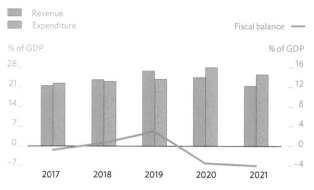

GDP = gross domestic product.
Source: Ministry of Economy and Finance.

Figure 3.23.4 Current account balance

The deficit widened sharply on weak tourism receipts and a goods-trade imbalance.

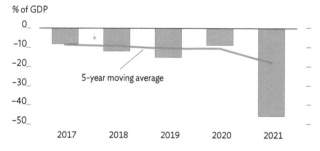

GDP = gross domestic product.
Source: *Asian Development Outlook* database.

support economic activity. Growth in money supply accelerated to 16.3% from 15.3% in 2020, mainly reflecting increases in foreign currency deposits. Private sector credit growth accelerated to 24.1% from 17.7%.

Fiscal policy was expansionary to support public health, social interventions, and firms hit by COVID-19 (Figure 3.23.3). Public spending focused on health care, cash transfers to vulnerable households, tax relief, wage subsidies and support for firms retaining workers, and loans and guarantees to pandemic-hit small businesses. These policy responses contributed to public spending at a preliminary estimate of 25.5% of GDP in 2021. Slow economic activity contributed to an estimated 7.1% decline in domestic revenue in 2021, equal to 21.4% of GDP. Because of these measures, the general government budget deficit widened to an estimated 4.0% of GDP in 2021 from 3.5% in 2020. And as a result, public external debt rose to 35.2% of GDP from 34.7%.

While 2021 saw continuing inflows of foreign direct investment and other capital, the slump in tourism receipts and lower private gold sales, exacerbated by a surge in temporary gold imports, caused the current account deficit to widen significantly (Figure 3.23.4). This led to a modest decline in international reserves to $20.2 billion, cover for 7.4 months of imports. The current account deficit for the full year widened sharply to an estimated 45.7% of GDP.

Economic prospects

The economy is forecast to grow by 5.3% in 2022 and 6.5% in 2023 (Figure 3.23.5 and Table 3.23.1). Growth in the economies of major trading partners will continue to support the strong momentum of Cambodia's merchandise exports and inflows of foreign direct investment. Industry output is expected to grow by 8.1% in 2022 and 9.1% in 2023. Growth in the garments, travel goods, and footwear segment will be driven by strong external demand supported by a relocation of orders from the People's Republic of China and neighboring countries. This growth will also be buoyed by the implementation of the Garments, Footwear and Travel Goods Development Strategy to raise competitiveness in this segment. Growth of nongarment manufacturing should reflect expected strong external demand supported by recent free trade agreements with the People's Republic of China and the Republic of Korea and a new investment law. Agriculture output is expected to grow at 1.2% over the forecast horizon.

Figure 3.23.5 GDP growth

Growth will rise above the 5-year moving average in 2022 and 2023.

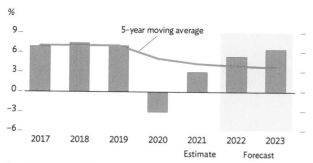

GDP = gross domestic product.
Source: *Asian Development Outlook* database.

Table 3.23.1 Selected economic indicators, %

Recovery to gather further strength in 2022 and 2023.

	2020	2021	2022	2023
GDP growth	−3.1	3.0ª	5.3	6.5
Inflation	2.9	2.9	4.7	2.2
CAB/GDP	−8.7	−45.7ª	−21.5	−16.1

ª Estimate.
CAB = current account balance, GDP = gross domestic product.
Source: Asian Development Bank estimates.

The services sector is projected to rebound to 4.8% this year and accelerate to 6.8% in 2023. This forecast, however, assumes that renewed COVID-19 infections driven by new variants will only have a mild impact on mobility. The recovery in 2022 will reflect a rebound in hotels and restaurants from the contraction of the last 2 years and continued growth in wholesale and retail trade, transport and communications, and real estate. Reopening the economy and the already remarkably high level of vaccination coverage will allow for a gradual recovery in tourism, which, in turn, will support demand for accommodation, food, transportation, and other

in-person services. The growth in services next year will build on the momentum in 2022, especially in the hospitality sector, and will likely be supported by Cambodia hosting the 2023 Southeast Asian Games and the 2023 national election.

Inflation is projected to accelerate this year, averaging 4.7% on surging energy prices caused by the Russian invasion of Ukraine and broader domestic demand. Pressure on consumer prices is expected to moderate in 2023, when the inflation rate is forecast to average 2.2%, a level in line with expectations of lower energy prices (Figure 3.23.6). Monetary policy will continue to target price stability, with the implicit goal of encouraging greater use of the riel, the local currency, and keeping the exchange rate stable against the US dollar.

Figure 3.23.6 Inflation

Inflation will rise in 2022 before slowing in 2023 on lower energy prices.

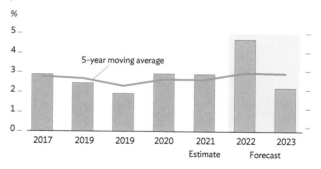

Source: *Asian Development Outlook* database.

Cambodia's authorities continue to implement policies to mitigate the impact of COVID-19 on business revenue and people's incomes and to support economic growth. The loan restructuring program has been extended to the end of June, and other regulatory forbearance measures to enable banks and microfinance institutions to continue lending are being kept in place. The finance sector remains stable and well-capitalized, but potential rises in nonperforming loans and loan impairments could put pressure on some banks and microfinance institutions. Achieving a well-managed phase-out of the loan restructuring program and other regulatory forbearance measures will be vital for the stability of the finance sector.

Fiscal policy will remain expansionary this year and next and see a gradual reduction in pandemic-related intervention. Socioeconomic intervention, however, remains a priority to support the implementation of the Strategic Framework and Programs for Economic Recovery in the Context of Living with COVID-19 in the New Normal, 2021–2023, launched in December. The fiscal budget for general government operations has a planned deficit of 5.6% of GDP in 2022. Revenue is budgeted at 20.4% of GDP and expenditure at 25.9%. A gradual drawdown in government deposits from 24.2% of GDP in 2020 is expected to meet the financing gap in the medium term. Despite the high deficit, Cambodia remains at a low risk of debt distress, as total public external debt is projected to rise to a manageable level of 36.2% of GDP in 2022 and 37.1% in 2023. The government plans to issue bonds in 2022 to help diversify its financing sources.

The current account deficit is projected to narrow to 21.5% of GDP and 16.1% in 2023, but this is contingent on unbalanced gold trade ceasing and a gradual improvement in tourism. The projected narrowing of the current account deficit reflects a smaller trade deficit. Goods and services exports are forecast to grow by 17.8% in 2022 and 18.5% in 2023 on strong external demand for Cambodian products supported by a recovery in tourism, albeit a slow one. Imports are expected to fall by 7.7% in 2022 on high base effects from 2021 before growing by 10.3% in 2023. The narrower current account deficit is expected to be offset by capital inflows, enabling an increase in gross international reserves, forecast at $24.9 billion by the end of 2023.

Downside risks to the outlook include renewed COVID-19 infections driven by new variants, a rapid increase in nonperforming loans undermining the performance of banking institutions as the loan restructuring program is phased out, weakened growth of major trading partners, global supply chain disruptions, and a worse-than-expected surge in energy and commodity prices.

Policy challenge—diversifying manufacturing

Widespread vaccination against COVID-19 has enabled Cambodia to reopen its borders, but increasing trade and tourism alone will not be enough to achieve sustained economic growth. For this, manufacturing needs to be more diverse. Although the COVID-19 pandemic severely affected large areas of the economy, light manufacturing, such as bicycles, electronic components, and wiring products, has grown dramatically, including over the pandemic (Figure 3.23.7). This growth shows that Cambodia can diversify from its traditional focus on producing and exporting garments, travel goods, and footwear. Being able to sustain this trend will go a long way toward helping the government achieve its vision of a more resilient and diversified economy.

Figure 3.23.7 Growth trend of garments, textiles, and footwear and other manufacturing

Other manufacturing continued its rapid expansion despite COVID-19.

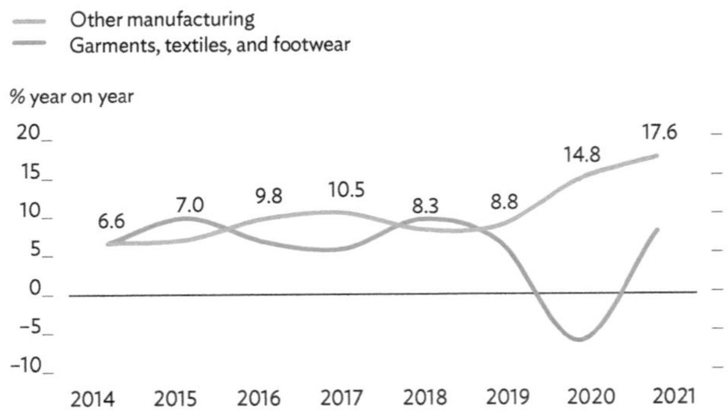

Source: Asian Development Outlook database.

The Law on Investment, adopted in October 2021, will help attract more domestic and foreign direct investment into manufacturing. The law provides a more comprehensive, transparent, and predictable legal framework to make Cambodia a more attractive investment destination. Specific incentives are provided under the law for investing in industries that support regional and global supply chains, and for the production of electronics, spare parts, mechanical and machinery equipment, and agro-processing, among other areas. In addition to incentives, the government has launched a strategic framework and programs for economic recovery that build on existing and ongoing reforms to enhance diversification and improve competitiveness in manufacturing.

Cambodia has an opportunity to develop new manufactured products for export that can sustain productivity growth to help support continued improvements in living standards. But to make the most of this opportunity, it is essential that a wider range of manufactured goods can be developed and produced.

To this end, the government should create a priority set of reforms that can be implemented as part of the strategic framework and programs for economic recovery. Ways of doing this could include using the investment law as a catalyst for a broader effort to strengthen investment promotion and facilitation; working with the operators and key tenants of special economic zones to identify opportunities to streamline regulatory processes and upgrade supporting infrastructure; developing a more comprehensive and clearer vision to leverage environmental sustainability as a source of future competitive advantage; and working with industry stakeholders to develop and implement transformation plans for manufacturing, including skills development and upgrading technology and production processes and product quality.

INDONESIA

The economy fully recovered in 2021, despite a temporary slowdown due to a COVID-19 outbreak in the third quarter. Investment picked up, exports boomed, inflation was low, and the budget deficit was lower than programmed. Key reforms were implemented last year. Stronger growth is expected this year. The downside risks—the economic impact of the Russian invasion of Ukraine and potential COVID-19 outbreaks—are significant. The medium-term policy challenge is harnessing digitalization to raise productivity and growth.

Economic performance

Real GDP grew by 3.7% in 2021, despite growth temporarily stalling in the third quarter when mobility was restricted to quell a COVID-19 Delta-variant outbreak (Figure 3.24.1). The economy has now fully recovered. Output was 1.6% higher last year than in pre-pandemic 2019 and real per capita GDP was about the same level. Growth in 2021 was broad-based (Figure 3.24.2). Private consumption, investment, and net exports each accounted for a third of growth.

Figure 3.24.1 Quarterly GDP growth

The economy briskly rebounded from the downturn in Q3 2021.

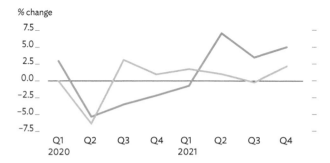

Q = quarter.
Source: Statistics Indonesia (accessed 4 March 2022).

Figure 3.24.2 Demand-side contributions to growth

Growth in 2021 was broad-based.

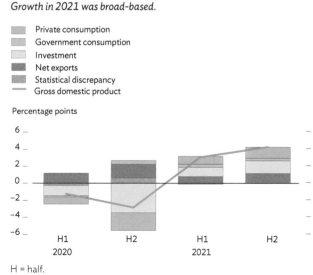

H = half.
Source: Statistics Indonesia (accessed 4 March 2022).

Private consumption, which accounts for 54% of GDP, grew by 2%, half its pre-pandemic pace. But it surged in the second quarter as mobility, incomes, jobs, and confidence improved and regained momentum after a COVID-19 lockdown. Because of base-year effects, the fastest growth was in spending on transportation,

---

This chapter was written by Priasto Aji and Henry Ma of the Indonesia Resident Mission, ADB, Jakarta.

restaurants, and hotels, which had contracted the most in 2020 (Figure 3.24.3). Government consumption grew by 4.2%, up from 1.9% in 2020, reflecting the full implementation of the fiscal stimulus that started midyear.

Figure 3.24.3 Contribution of consumption components to growth

Consumption recovered as mobility, incomes, and confidence improved.

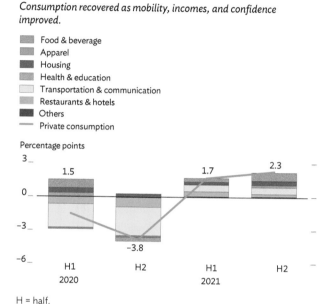

H = half.
Source: Statistics Indonesia (accessed 4 March 2022).

Investment grew by 4.1% and was robust in the second quarter—and staying so throughout the lockdown. Its drivers were recovering consumption, strong exports, and supportive monetary conditions. The strongest spending was for machinery, equipment, and vehicles. Inventory buildup continued to be small last year (Figure 3.24.4).

Net exports contributed substantially to 2021's growth. The economic recovery stimulated imports, which grew by 21% in national income account terms. Exports grew even faster, by 24%, as surging global demand for goods required inputs of Indonesia's primary commodities, including coal, palm oil, and nickel. Services exports contracted, as they did in 2020, as travel to Bali remained extremely limited.

All three main productive sectors grew last year (Figure 3.24.5). Services contributed almost half of total growth, led by health, information and communication, and vehicle sales.

Figure 3.24.4 Contribution of investment components to growth

Recovering demand and strong exports perked up all investment categories.

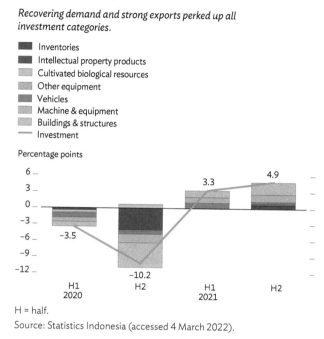

H = half.
Source: Statistics Indonesia (accessed 4 March 2022).

Figure 3.24.5 Supply-side contributions to growth

Services recovered in 2021 and contributed the most to growth.

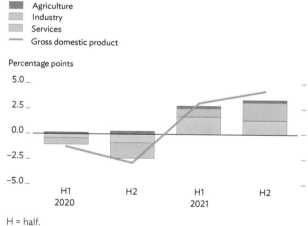

H = half.
Source: Statistics Indonesia (accessed 4 March 2022).

Industry grew by 3% and agriculture by 2%. In both sectors, the best performers were commodity-exporting segments, including plantations, metal ores, and basic metal products.

Inflation was low for most of last year (Figure 3.23.6). Headline inflation averaged 1.6% and core inflation 1.4%, lower than in 2020 and below the central bank's 2%–4% target. Inflation was subdued because the recovery was modest, inflation expectations were well-anchored, food and other basic items were ample, and the exchange rate was broadly stable. Still, inflation crept up from 1.4% in the first quarter to 1.8% in the fourth due to recovering consumption and rising food prices.

Figure 3.24.6 Inflation

Consumer price inflation was low, but broader indicators point to some pressure.

— Headline
— Core
— Producer prices
— GDP deflator

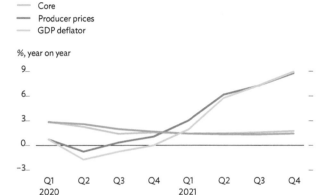

GDP = gross domestic product, Q = quarter.
Source: Statistics Indonesia (accessed 4 March 2022).

Booming commodity exports led to a record trade surplus of $44 billion last year (Figure 3.24.7). Exports of goods in US dollar terms grew by 42% to an all-time high of $233 billion. Demand was strong across the board for primary commodities, whose prices surged (Figure 3.24.8). Coal prices spiked over September–October when the People's Republic of China temporarily curbed its domestic coal output. Imports of goods rose by 40% to $189 billion last year, in line with the pickup in domestic demand. All import categories showed strong growth. The large merchandise trade surplus more than offset the persistent deficits in services and primary incomes and produced a current account surplus equivalent to 0.3% of GDP (Figure 3.24.9). Pre-pandemic deficits averaged 2.5% of GDP.

The financial account surplus grew to $11.7 billion from $7.9 billion in 2020 (Figure 3.24.10). Net portfolio debt flows turned negative in October and were in deficit for the full year due to attractive bond yields in advanced economies and the repayment of external debt by the government and by exporters with strong cash flow.

Figure 3.24.7 Merchandise trade

Export prices were high, imports recovered, and the trade surplus was at a record high.

— Import growth
— Export growth
Trade balance ▉

Source: Statistics Indonesia (accessed 4 March 2022).

Figure 3.24.8 Commodity prices

Commodity prices have been exceptionally high.

— Prospera commodity index   — 2020 average
— Coal price index   — 2021 average

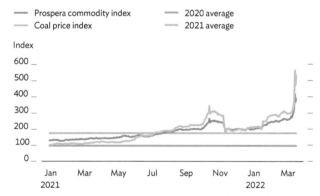

Note: Prospera commodity price index comprises palm oil, coal, nickel, rubber, and copper, weighted by export shares of these commodities in 2019.
Source: Prospera (accessed 7 March 2022).

Figure 3.24.9 Current account balance

The trade surplus led to a current account surplus.

▉ Merchandise trade   ▉ Secondary income
▉ Services trade   — Current account
▉ Primary income

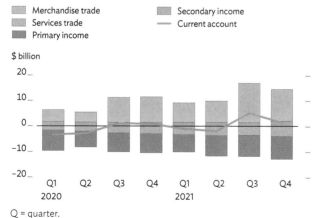

Q = quarter.
Source: Bank Indonesia (accessed 4 March 2022).

Figure 3.24.10 Balance of payments

Financial inflows, especially FDI, were healthy.

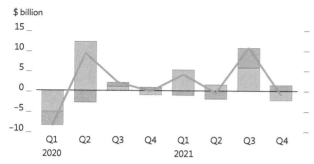

FDI = foreign direct investment, Q = quarter.
Note: Financial and capital accounts include errors and omissions.
Source: Bank Indonesia (accessed 4 March 2022).

But these outflows were more than offset by inflows of equity capital and foreign direct investment.

The current account surplus, private financial inflows, and Indonesia's share of the allocation by the International Monetary Fund of special drawing rights boosted international reserves from $136 billion at the end of 2020 to $145 billion at end-2021, cover for 7.8 months of imports and government debt payments (Figure 3.24.11). External debt was 35% of GDP in 2021 after 39% in 2020. The rupiah was broadly stable, depreciating by 1.9% against the US dollar last year.

Figure 3.24.11 Reserves and exchange rate

Reserves grew in 2021 and supported a stable exchange rate

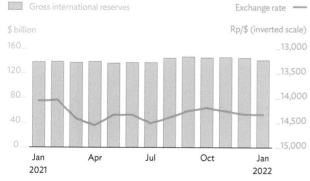

Source: CEIC Data Company (accessed 7 March 2022).

Fiscal stimulus continued, but buoyant revenue led to a lower-than-programmed budget deficit. Total spending was 7.4% higher than in 2021. Fiscal stimulus outlays totaled Rp659 trillion (3.9% of GDP) compared with Rp576 trillion in 2020. Revenue was 15% higher than projected because the recovery generated extra tax revenue and commodity exports yielded higher royalties. Because of this, the fiscal deficit narrowed to an estimated 4.6% of GDP from 6.1% in 2020 and was below the 5.7% target. Public debt was 41% of GDP in 2021 after 39% in 2020, but still below the 60% statutory ceiling.

Monetary and financial policy continued to be supportive. The central bank has kept the policy rate (the 7-day reverse repo rate) at 3.5% since February 2021. It bought Rp358 trillion in government bonds (2.1% of GDP) under the "burden sharing" agreement with the government, following purchases of Rp473 trillion (3.1% of GDP) in 2020. The financial regulator extended to March 2023 the provision passed in 2020 that gives banks breathing room by allowing them not to classify loans restructured during the COVID-19 pandemic as nonperforming.

Credit recovered last year, expanding by 5%, and financial indicators were stable. Lending to households recovered in April and to businesses in August (Figure 3.24.12). Since mid-2020, the nonperforming loan ratio has averaged 3.2% and the capital adequacy ratio 25.0%, comfortably above the regulatory minimum. Restructured loans edged down from 20% of total credit in December 2020 to 19% in June 2021.

Figure 3.24.12 Loans and deposits

Lending to businesses caught up with lending to households.

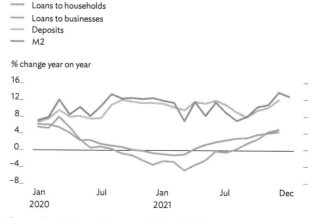

Source: Bank Indonesia (accessed 7 March 2022).

Key reforms were initiated last year that complemented the Omnibus Job Creation Law, 2020. Tax reforms passed in October will broaden the value-added-tax base, raising the rate from 10% to 11% in April 2022 and to 12% by 2025; provide a tax amnesty in return for back taxes; and introduce a small carbon tax. These measures are projected to raise tax revenue by 0.8%–1.0% of GDP by 2024. Reforms to the public finances of regions will strengthen the management of these finances and give the regions more leeway to generate revenue. These reforms will expand fiscal space, including for investments in infrastructure. The full implementation of the Omnibus Job Creation Law has, however, been stalled by a judicial ruling requiring legislative remedies for procedural flaws in the law's enactment.

Social indicators improved last year. Unemployment fell from 7.1% of the labor force in August 2020 to 6.5% in August 2021. But informality remained high, at 59.4% of all workers. People living below the poverty line fell from 27.5 million (10.2% of the population) in 2020 to 26.5 million (9.7%) in 2021. The Gini coefficient of inequality fell from 0.384 to 0.381. The World Bank reclassified Indonesia as a lower-middle-income country in July 2021, but there is a good chance it will be reclassified as upper-middle-income in 2022.

Indonesia made progress in containing COVID-19 last year. At the end of December, 114 million people, or 55% of the targeted population, were fully vaccinated, and the daily number of new cases was below 200.

Economic prospects

The economy entered 2022 with good prospects after COVID-19 mobility restrictions were eased in August. The manufacturing purchasing managers' index has been above the expansion threshold since September (Figure 3.24.13); and the consumer confidence since October (Figure 3.24.14). Retail sales were strong, and the Bank Mandiri spending index in February was 25% above the level at the start of the pandemic. Although growth projections were cut in January for Indonesia's two main trading partners, the People's Republic of China and the United States, private consumption and investment look likely to have enough momentum to replace exports as the main driver of growth.

Figure 3.24.13 Purchasing managers' index and capacity utilization

Manufacturing activity briskly recovered from the Q3 2021 lockdown.

— Capacity utilization
— Manufacturing purchasing managers' index

Source: CEIC Data Company (accessed 4 March 2022).

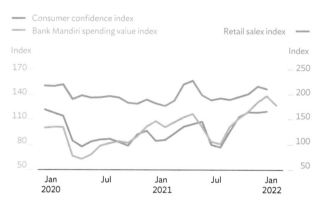

Figure 3.24.14 Consumer confidence

Rebounding consumer demand drove Q4 2021 growth.

— Consumer confidence index
— Bank Mandiri spending value index   Retail salex index —

Sources: Bank Mandiri; CEIC Data Company (accessed 4 March 2022).

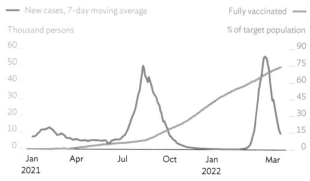

Figure 3.24.15 COVID-19 indicators

The third wave is abating.

— New cases, 7-day moving average   Fully vaccinated —

Thousand persons   % of target population

COVID-19 = Coronavirus Disease 2019.
Source: Our World in Data (accessed 24 March 2022).

Two threats to growth emerged: one internal, the other external. In January, the Omicron variant set off a third wave of COVID-19 infections (Figure 3.24.15). In February, the Russian invasion of Ukraine started.

The third COVID-19 wave should have minimal impact on growth. The daily number of new cases rose from below 200 in January, peaked at 57,491 in late February, and was at 7,951 in late March. Because Omicron symptoms have been mild and the health services coped, mobility restrictions were not strict and economic activity did not suffer significantly. As of 22 March, 74% of the targeted population had been fully vaccinated. Business and work practices have adjusted to COVID-19. Since January, more international flights land in Bali.

For now, the Russian invasion of Ukraine should have a limited impact on Indonesia's growth prospects, but risks could be significant if the war is prolonged. If that happens, the war will further constrain global demand, cut export growth, and raise inflation. With export growth halved from 2021 and cautious growth projections for private consumption and investment, GDP growth should be about 5% (Table 3.24.1).

Table 3.24.1 Selected economic indicators, %

Economic recovery will pick up further in 2022 and 2023.

	2020	2021	2022	2023
GDP growth	−2.1	3.7	5.0	5.2
Inflation	2.0	1.6	3.6	3.0
CAB/GDP	−0.4	0.3	0.0	−0.5

CAB = current account balance, GDP = gross domestic product.
Sources: Central Bureau of Statistics; Asian Development Bank estimates.

Private consumption should return to its pre-pandemic trend growth of 5% in 2022; this conservatively assumes that consumers do not fully make up for lost spending in 2020 and 2021. Consumer demand will be stimulated by the further normalization of economic activity, improvements in jobs and incomes, and the trickle-down from 2020's commodity boom. Demand will also benefit from tax breaks being extended to June, albeit at less generous rates, for buying cars and houses. The digitalization of services, particularly in commerce and finance, will support consumption through any further COVID-19 outbreaks.

Investment is forecast to grow by about 6% this year. Businesses will rebuild productive capacity and restock inventories in response to recovering demand and improvements in the business and investment climate. The legislature is moving forward with enacting remedies to enable the full implementation of the omnibus law, whose already implemented provisions remain in effect.

Higher commodity prices, including oil and wheat, and faster domestic growth will jack up inflation, which is forecast to average 3.6% this year, still within the central bank's target. Headline inflation averaged 2.1% in the first quarter. Inflation pressure could build further this year on a prolonged war. Inflation is projected to moderate to 3.0% next year on commodity price increases abating.

Fiscal policy is programmed to be contractionary, with the fiscal deficit heading for 3% of GDP in 2023. Spending on salaries, goods and services, and transfers to the regions will be cut by 9.7% in nominal terms. Spending on the national economic recovery program will be cut from Rp659 trillion in 2021 to Rp456 trillion in 2022. The central government's budget for 2022 projects Rp1,846 trillion in revenue, but tax reforms and higher growth could raise this to almost Rp2,000 trillion. So, if spending comes in as programmed, the budget deficit could be as low as 4.00% of GDP, compared with 4.85% in the budget. Higher commodity prices in 2022 will increase revenue from fuel sales and commodity exports. But this will also put pressure on electricity and energy subsidies if high oil prices persist. The net impact of all this on the fiscal balance should be negative but modest.

Monetary policy will also be less supportive this year. The central bank has announced that it will hold the policy rate at 3.5% until the end of June. But it will raise the rupiah reserve requirement for banks to 6.0% in September from 3.5%. It will also end the monetary financing of the budget deficit, the so-called burden-sharing, at the end of 2022. Although inflation is within the target, the central bank will need to be alert to pressures that could de-anchor inflation expectations.

Higher commodity prices will offset lower export volume growth and keep the current account in balance in 2022. Export volume growth will fall, albeit remaining positive, but the impact of the decline will be offset by higher commodity prices, including nickel and coal. Service exports will grow modestly because of the still-slow recovery in international tourism. Further government export bans to protect the home market could also reduce trade. In January, coal exports were banned for several weeks until domestic demand could be met. In February, palm oil exports were restricted to alleviate cooking oil shortages. Imports in US dollar terms will remain high due to higher import prices and stronger domestic demand.

The financial account should remain positive despite global financial volatility. Tightening by the US Federal Reserve and global uncertainty have in the past spurred outflows from Indonesia and other emerging markets into safe-haven US dollars and financial assets. That said, Indonesia these days is more resilient than it was during 2013's taper tantrum. International reserves are ample, about 85% of external debt is long term, and the proportion of government bonds held by nonresidents has halved since 2020 to about 20%. Modest net inflows of portfolio capital and foreign direct investment should continue, producing a financial account surplus of 0.5% of GDP. International reserves are projected to increase to $150 billion in 2022.

Economic activity is expected to continue normalizing in 2023, although this assumes the global economic fallout from the Russian invasion of Ukraine will not be severe. Private consumption growth is forecast at 5% next year and investment growth at 7%. The budget deficit is expected to return to the statutory ceiling of 3% of GDP. Inflation is forecast to ease to about 3.0% in 2023. Export and import growth will slide further, to a projected 6%–8%. Tourism next year will likely be at about 70% of its pre-pandemic level. The current account is projected to be a modest deficit.

For 2022, the risks are on the downside due to the war and concerns over new COVID-19 variants and outbreaks. For 2023, the risks are on the upside as the benefits of reforms start being felt in the economy through a better business and investment climate, increased public infrastructure, and improved private physical and human capital.

Policy challenge—advancing digitalization and technological transformation

Indonesia needs much higher growth than the average 5% it achieved from 2015 to 2019 to become a high-income economy by 2045. *Innovate Indonesia*, a joint 2020 study by the Ministry of Finance and Asian Development Bank, estimates that adopting Industry 4.0 new technologies could increase per capita GDP to the high-income level of $14,747 by 2045. Digital transformation, in particular, can boost productivity. New technologies provide opportunities for improving growth and social development, but also challenges.

Electric motorcycles and microgeneration would raise GDP as well as improve air quality. Financial technology, such as peer-to-peer lending and payments and equity crowdfunding, would improve the access to finance for micro, small, and medium-sized enterprises. Online platforms would improve market access of sellers and their profitability. Successfully exploiting Industry 4.0's opportunities requires that firms tackle the challenges of the high financial costs of adoption, lack of skilled workers, technical uncertainty, resistance to change, and digital infrastructure gaps (Figure 3.24.16). Firms need to raise their awareness of the business value of new technologies. But they will also need help in accessing technology transfer and technical support, low-cost plug-and-play solutions, and a tech-savvy workforce.

Figure 3.24.16 Barriers to technology adoption

Firms face many hurdles to adopting new technologies.

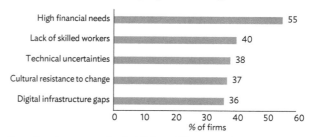

Note: Based on a survey by the Ministry of Finance and Asian Development Bank of 502 Indonesian firms exploring how artificial intelligence, robotics and automation, 3D printing, cloud computing, and big data are affecting the textiles and clothing, electronics, footwear, automotive, food and beverage, and rubber and plastics sectors.
Source: Asian Development Bank. 2020. *Innovate Indonesia: Unlocking Growth through Technological Transformation*.

The government has launched initiatives to strengthen the national innovation system through fiscal incentives, large investments in digital infrastructure, and new funding mechanisms to support public research. Despite these initiatives, Indonesia's innovation system is still in its early stages. Public and private research and development and scientific outputs are comparatively low (Figure 3.24.17). Digital infrastructure gaps persist, especially outside Java. Private investors are also frustrated by regulatory barriers. It will be critical to address gaps in both hard and soft infrastructure and to develop a national digital infrastructure and long-term research and development investment plans.

Figure 3.24.17 Research and development expenditure in selected ASEAN countries

Indonesia's R&D expenditure is lower than other ASEAN countries

% of GDP

Singapore	1.9
Malaysia	1.0
Thailand	1.0
Viet Nam	0.5
Brunei Darussalam	0.3
Indonesia	0.2

ASEAN = Association of Southeast Asian Nations, GDP = gross domestic product, R&D = research and development.

Note: 2018 or latest available year.

Source: World Bank. World Development Indicators database (accessed 9 March 2022)

Company managers are often not fully aware of the potentially high returns from new technologies. Ways to increase their awareness include developing industrial networks and business associations to promote linkages and knowledge exchange between firms in Indonesia and abroad; and creating sector and cross-sector technology forums among universities, research centers, and technology vendors.

Because Indonesian firms are at different stages in their technology transformation, customized support mechanisms will be needed (Figure 3.24.18). For the

Figure 3.24.18 Level of technology adoption of firms

Indonesian firms are at different stages in their technology transformation journey.

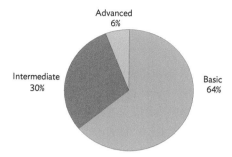

Based on a survey by the Ministry of Finance and Asian Development Bank that consulted 502 local firms to explore how artificial intelligence, robotics and automation, 3D printing, cloud computing, and big data are affecting the textiles and clothing, electronics, footwear, automotive, food and beverage, and rubber and plastic sectors. Advanced: using emerging digitally-enabled tools; intermediate: using some advanced technologies in specific operations, such as enterprise resource planning and customer relationship management systems, computer-aided manufacturing, and collaborative supply chain management (e.g., Oracle, SAP); basic: performing many activities with basic tools, such as spreadsheets and e-mail.

Source: Asian Development Bank. 2020. *Innovate Indonesia: Unlocking Growth through Technological Transformation.*

country's small group of leading firms, this will entail emphasizing support for building capacity to invent and generate new technology. For the large group of intermediate followers, this will require emphasizing support that further develops absorptive capacity and the ability to innovate. For the largest group, firms that have adopted only basic technology, this means emphasizing support to improve basic management and technology practices.

Because adopting new technology remains beyond the means of many Indonesian firms, policy makers could identify technology solutions that address common issues faced by these firms through, for example, industrial working groups and developing affordable plug-and-play technological solutions.

A lack of tech-savvy workers is also preventing Indonesia from taking advantage of the new technological opportunities. Solutions include investing in upgrading training centers to expand courses and modules in new technologies and broadening workers' access to advanced technical training.

LAO PEOPLE'S DEMOCRATIC REPUBLIC

The economy gradually recovered in 2021 from its worst contraction in decades. Growth was supported by high COVID-19 vaccination coverage. Growth in 2022 and 2023 will be underpinned by rising agriculture output, higher electricity generation, infrastructure projects, and a resumption in domestic tourism. Downside risks to the outlook are the possibility of new COVID-19 variants and inflationary pressures exacerbating an already high level of debt distress. A key policy challenge is staying on track for decarbonization commitments.

Economic performance

The economy commenced a slow recovery last year. Real GDP in the Lao People's Democratic Republic (Lao PDR) expanded by 2.3% in 2021 after shrinking 0.5% in 2020, the Lao PDR's worst contraction in decades (Figure 3.25.1). A second COVID-19 wave in April 2021 forced the government to impose a series of lockdowns, which disrupted economic activity in domestic services, including hotels, restaurants, and transportation. But by the end of 2021, half the population had been vaccinated from 18 million doses donated by the COVID-19 Vaccines Global Access program, Malaysia, the People's Republic of China (PRC), the Russian Federation, and Viet Nam.

Exporting sectors in industry and agriculture contributed to the recovery. Industry output expanded by 4% last year, supported by increased electricity and mining production, and rising construction activity. Favorable weather allowed some hydropower plants to reach their full capacity, increasing total electricity output from 39,497 gigawatt-hours in 2020 to 41,916 in 2021; most of this was exported (Figure 3.25.2). Mining grew by 2% as new and refurbished mines increased output of iron ore and gold. Construction growth was supported by the December 2021 completion of the Lao PDR–PRC rail link and ongoing urban real estate projects in special and specific economic zones.

Figure 3.25.1 Supply-side contributions to growth

The economy gradually recovered in 2021 from its worst contraction in decades.

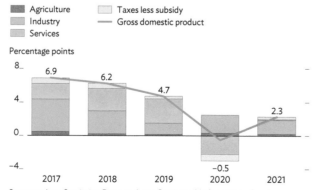

Sources: Lao Statistics Bureau. Laos Statistical Information Service. (accessed 24 February 2022); Asian Development Bank estimates.

Figure 3.25.2 Power generation capacity and production

Favorable weather bolstered electricity output.

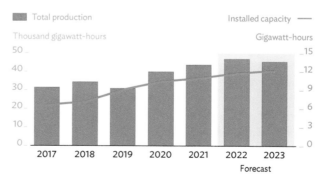

Sources: Lao Statistics Bureau. Laos Statistical Information Service. (accessed 16 March 2022); Ministry of Energy and Mines.

This chapter was written by Emma Allen and Soulinthone Leuangkhamsing of the Lao Resident Mission, ADB, Vientiane.

Agriculture exports rose in 2021 across most sector categories and output was up by 1.1.% (Figure 3.25.3). Increased crop production partially offset animal diseases that affected cattle exports in the second half. Rice production increased last year by 3.3% from 3.5 million tons to 3.7 million tons. Banana output increased by 24.6%, cassava by 12.1%, and sugar by 10.0%—the three are key agricultural exports. Last year's higher production was absorbed by robust demand from the PRC.

Figure 3.25.3 Agriculture exports

All three major products expanded in 2021.

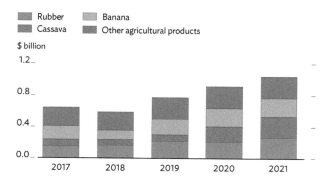

Source: Ministry of Industry and Commerce.

Services remained subdued, expanding by 0.4% in 2021. Mobility gradually recovered from the COVID-19 restrictions imposed in April and October, but remained below normal levels of mobility (Figure 3.25.4). Services sectors that were beneficial in a pandemic, such as telecommunications, saw continued high growth.

Figure 3.25.4 Mobility

Mobility gradually recovered on easing COVID-19 restrictions.

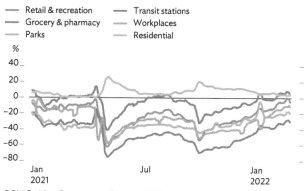

COVID-19 = Coronavirus Disease 2019.
Sources: Google COVID-19 Community Mobility Trends; CEIC Data Company (both accessed 24 February 2022).

COVID-19 spurred technology adoption, with internet users increasing by 15% last year and one in two people now using social media and other digital services.

Average inflation decelerated to 3.7% in 2021 from 5.1% in 2020 (Figure 3.25.5). But rising oil prices and the depreciation of the kip, the local currency, pushed the inflation rate to 5.3% by the end of the year. The kip depreciated by an annual average of 7.6% against the US dollar in the official market last year and by 12.1% in the parallel market on international bond maturities coming due and foreign exchange shortages (Figure 3.25.6). The central bank allowed the official exchange rate to depreciate, causing prices of imported goods to rise, especially petroleum products and construction material. The authorities increased oil prices about 13 times in 2021.

Figure 3.25.5 Monthly inflation

Inflation moderated in 2021, but rising oil prices and the kip's depreciation pushed up year-end inflation.

Sources: Lao Statistics Bureau. Laos Statistical Information Service. (accessed 24 February 2022); Asian Development Bank estimates.

Figure 3.25.6 Exchange rate

The kip fell on international bond maturities coming due and foreign exchange shortages.

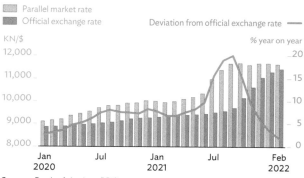

Source: Bank of the Lao PDR.

The current account balance narrowed from a deficit of the equivalent of 5.4% of GDP in 2020 to 5.0% in 2021 on robust demand for mining, electricity, and agriculture exports (Figure 3.25.7). Goods trade reached a record surplus of $353 million after a deficit of $151 million in 2020. The key contribution was exports of electricity and minerals, especially gold, copper, and iron ore, which benefitted from rising prices. Net inflows of foreign direct investment, totaling $1 billion, played a major role in lifting the performance of exporting sectors.

Figure 3.25.7 Current account balance

The deficit narrowed as demand for commodity exports remained robust.

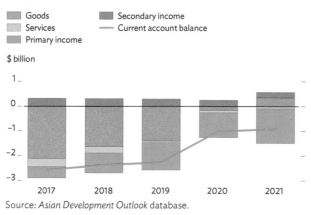

Source: *Asian Development Outlook* database.

In August 2021, the National Assembly approved an agenda to tackle the country's economic and financial difficulties, including plans to cut spending and boost revenue collection. The ongoing modernization of tax and customs administration resulted in increased tax and nontax revenue last year. Double-digit growth in value-added tax and excise duties contributed to a better revenue performance. Public expenditure was reported lower compared with 2020. But it should be noted that expenditure performance is linked to the deferred payment for capital spending, with the government settling debts to contractors implementing public investment projects by issuing a new round of arrears clearance bonds late in 2021. The bonds are provided via commercial banks and used to resolve contractors' nonperforming loans. Arrears clearance bonds have been a recurrent public finance practice, signaling a need for progress on issues related to cash flow management, contract management, and procurement.

Public and publicly guaranteed debt was last reported at 78.8% of GDP in 2021. Domestic expenditure arrears, lower economic growth, and the weakening kip in 2021 contributed to increasing the level of debt (Figure 3.25.8). The Lao PDR's external public debt servicing requirements are sizable, and are expected to average $1.3 billion annually over the next 5 years, equivalent to 7% of GDP. An attempt to issue international bonds in 2021 to refinance maturing external debt was unsuccessful.

The external position remains fragile. Gross official reserves totaled $1.3 billion at the end of 2021, cover for only 2.1 months of goods imports.

Figure 3.25.8 Fiscal indicators

Public debt rose sharply in 2021 and will remain elevated.

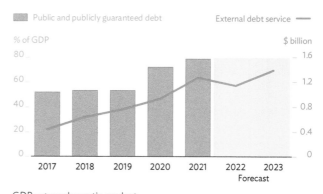

GDP = gross domestic product.
Sources: Ministry of Finance; Asian Development Bank estimates.

Economic prospects

Real GDP growth this year is forecast at 3.4% and 3.7% in 2023 (Table 3.25.1). Growth will be underpinned by recovering investment and rising output in capital intensive industries, including electricity and mining; gradually recovering tourism; and agriculture's continued steady performance.

Following resolutions at the COP26 United Nations climate change conference, strong foreign private investment inflows are expected to support the development and supply of low-carbon electricity, storage, and grid connectivity in the Lao PDR for export markets. Wind farm investments of 1.6 gigawatts are planned, including a 600-megawatt (MW) Monsoon Wind project in Xekong and Attapeu

Table 3.25.1 Selected economic indicators, %

Recovery to continue in 2022 and 2023, inflation will remain high.

	2020	2021	2022	2023
GDP growth	−0.5	2.3	3.4	3.7
Inflation	5.1	3.7	5.8	5.0
CAB/GDP	−5.4	−5.0	−6.0	−6.5

CAB = current account balance, GDP = gross domestic product.
Sources: Bank of the Lao PDR; Lao Statistics Bureau. Laos Statistical
Information Service; Asian Development Bank estimates.

provinces that will export energy to Viet Nam. These
investments are expected to result in one of the world's
largest wind farms and provide over 90 million tons
of carbon saving over their life. The Lao PDR plans to
increase the share of solar power in its energy mix to
almost 25% by 2025 from under 1% currently. To help
achieve this, an investment for a 240 MW floating
solar project at the Nam Theun 2 hydroelectric plant
has been proposed. Keppel Electric and Électricité
du Laos are putting together a joint venture to import
renewable hydropower from the Lao PDR as part of
Singapore's Green Plan 2030. Completing 11 additional
hydropower projects of state-owned enterprises in
2022 and 2023, with a total installed capacity of
1,820 MW, will help meet the demand for Lao PDR's
renewable energy in the Southeast Asia region.

To increase mineral exploration and output, the
government, in June 2021, started a 3-year pilot to
fast-track licenses for mining concessions by reducing
procedures. The government has received 201
proposals for mining operations, including 167 for iron
ore and 27 for gold, and 16 projects are expected to
start this year.

These energy and mining investments combined will
provide a stable source of foreign exchange revenue
earnings for the government. Strong and growing
demand for the Lao PDR's electricity and mining
exports will help to mitigate the risks to the country's
sovereign debt sustainability.

To spur recovery in domestic markets, including
tourism, the government, in January 2022, relaxed
its COVID-19 control measures and sped up its
vaccination program. It aims to have 80% of the
population fully vaccinated by the end of this year and
have booster and treatment programs in place over

the course of the year. Quarantine requirements are
expected to be removed by mid-year to support the
tourism industry's recovery.

Technology adoption by firms in the tourism industry
has been increasing, with the sector's recovery driven
by enhanced online and technology usage in everyday
business transactions. The Bank of the Lao PDR and
the Micro and Small Medium Enterprises Development
Fund provided more than KN2 trillion last year to
domestic businesses, including those in trade and
tourism, affected by COVID-19. China Development
Bank is expected to provide a further $100 million to
support low-interest working capital and investment
loans for these enterprises. Credit growth is therefore
expected to continue its steady recovery after
expanding by 11.5% in 2021 after 4.3% growth in 2020
(Figure 3.25.9).

Figure 3.25.9 Money supply and credit growth

Credit growth started a steady recovery in the last quarter of 2021.

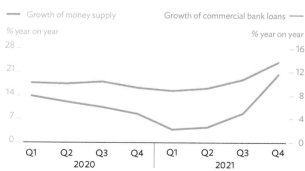

Q = quarter.
Sources: Bank of the Lao PDR; Haver Analytics (accessed 24 February
2022).

The Lao PDR–PRC rail link will help the economy
reopen further. In its first 2 months of operation, the
railway transported 101,940 passengers and 124,860
tons of cross-border goods. Transportation and
storage are set to be key drivers of services growth in
the Lao PDR.

Agriculture is projected to continue its gradual
expansion this year and next, benefiting from
favorable government credit policies and a large
export quota from the PRC for livestock, cassava,
banana, and corn.

Higher oil prices, rising domestic demand, and a weaker kip will increase inflation, with the rate's annual average forecast at 5.8% in 2022 and moderating to 5.0% in 2023. An adequate food supply will help reduce rice, vegetable, and poultry prices. But rising global inflation and geopolitical tensions, along with a depreciation in the local currency, will increase pressure on prices for imported goods. Proposed revisions to the Law on Foreign Exchange Management will tighten requirements for using the kip in trade and investor transactions via commercial banks rather than exchange bureaus. This may help to stabilize the kip and reduce differentials between official and parallel foreign exchange markets.

The current account deficit is projected at 6.0% of GDP in 2022 and 6.5% in 2023 due to higher imports of oil, construction material, and machinery and equipment needed for infrastructure projects. Growing import demand will be partially offset by strong exports of electricity, minerals, and agriculture products.

Downside risks to the outlook include the emergence of new COVID-19 variants. With inflationary pressures adding to the country's already high risk of debt distress, transparent management of external public debt is needed to restore market confidence and open opportunities for access to sustainable development finance. An additional risk is from the possible spillovers on the economy from the Russian invasion of Ukraine.

Policy challenge—staying on track for net zero emissions

The Lao PDR's greenhouse gas emissions are estimated to have grown by 0.3% a year since 2000, but GDP per capita grew by about 5% a year in this period—pointing to a relative decoupling of growth in emissions and the economy. Although the Lao PDR's emissions are low compared with other Southeast Asian economies, industrial development and increasing consumption are nevertheless contributing to growing emissions. Other indicators showing rising energy consumption are the household electrification rate, which rose to 94.3% in 2020 from 42.5% in 2000; hydropower's increased installed electricity capacity, which rose to 39,967 gigawatts from 3,438

gigawatts; and registered vehicles, which rose to 2.3 million units from 200,000, with transport fuel consumption increasing in line with this.

The Lao PDR has committed to carbon neutrality by 2050. The government announced in 2021 that it was making progress on its nationally determined contributions (NDCs) under the 2015 Paris climate change agreement, and, in a major step to achieving carbon neutrality by 2050, committed to unconditionally reduce 60% of its greenhouse emissions by 2030 compared with a 2000 business-as-usual scenario. The NDCs cover six areas, with substantial progress observed in hydropower development and the expansion of household electrification (Table 3.25.2). These efforts supported emission reductions estimated at 34% in 2020 compared with the 2000 baseline scenario.

However, policy commitments on forestry, transportation, and renewable energy were reported as "not on track." To address this, in its recent NDC revision required by all parties to the Paris Agreement, the government announced plans to implement course-correcting measures to tackle the limited progress with international support. Contingent on investment finance, the government has announced that it will increase forest cover to 70% of the total land area and deliver faster on its renewable energy commitments, particularly on wind and solar. These commitments are aligned with the long-term goals in the draft National Strategy for Climate Change and will contribute to the goal of decarbonizing the economy by 2050.

Adjusting policy targets and opening new opportunities for investments in low-carbon sectors are big opportunities for the Lao PDR to achieve net zero emissions. Demonstrating progress and increasing project preparedness will be essential for attracting new investments in projects to achieve this goal. Removing barriers to finance and addressing gaps in climate policy and institutional frameworks will be critical for ensuring a positive response from the market. Interventions for this will need to include building the capacity of line ministries. Robust quality assurance mechanisms for ensuring social and environmental safeguards compliance, as well as monitoring and verification systems for implementing the NDCs, are needed to stay on track.

Table 3.25.2 Status of the implementation of 2015 nationally determined contributions on climate action

Course-correcting measures are needed to address limited progress in some areas.

	Sector program	2015 NDC measure	Horizon	Progress
M1	Forestry strategy	Increase forest cover to 70% of land area	2020	Not achieved
M2	Renewable energy development strategy	30% renewable energy, excluding large hydropower	2025	Not on track
		Biofuel to account for 10% of transport fuel	2025	Not on track
M3	Rural electrification program	90% of households electrified	2020	Achieved
M4	Transport and urban development	Transport National Appropriate Mitigation Action	2025	Not started
M5	Expanding large hydropower	5,500 MW	2020	Achieved
		20,000 MW	2030	On track
M6	Climate change action plans	Implementing action plans	Not available	On track

M = mitigation, MW = megawatt, NDC = nationally determined contribution.
Note: This table refers to the 2015 Paris agreement NDCs.
Source: United Nations Framework Convention on Climate Change. Nationally Determined Contribution.

MALAYSIA

Growth recovered in 2021, supported by rising global demand for manufactured exports and terms-of-trade gains from exports of natural resources, and strong domestic demand. A robust health system and high vaccination rates against COVID-19 further supported the recovery. Rising imports from a pickup in domestic investment trimmed the current account surplus. Inflationary pressure is building on rising energy prices, the phasing out of an electricity subsidy, and continuing supply disruptions. Assisting poor households to return to the pre-pandemic norm is the major policy challenge.

Economic performance

Malaysia's economy rebounded in the fourth quarter (Q4) of 2021 on the relaxation of COVID-19 containment measures under the National Recovery Plan, bringing full-year growth to 3.1% after a 5.6% contraction in 2020 (Figure 3.26.1). The manufacturing purchasing managers' index returned to the 50-threshold, indicating expansion, in October. The consumer sentiment and business conditions indexes rose last year (Figure 3.26.2). Since the outbreak of the pandemic, the government has rolled out eight stimulus-cum-assistance packages totaling about $129 billion. Swift and targeted relief measures provided under a COVID-19 fund supported household incomes.

Concern over the spread of the Delta COVID-19 variant and rising goods prices caused retail sales to fall in Q3 2021. But private consumption, which accounts for close to 60% of GDP, gained momentum in Q4, resulting in a 1.9% increase in 2021 after a 4.3% contraction in 2020. Indexes for wholesale and retail trade, and motor vehicle sales, started to trend upward from Q4. Growth in public consumption, at 6.6%, remained strong last year, buoyed by public spending to tackle the pandemic.

Private investment increased by 2.6% after a double-digit contraction of nearly 12% in 2020. A surge in

Figure 3.26.1 Demand-side contributions to growth

GDP rebounded in 2021.

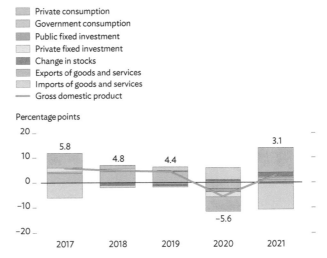

GDP = gross domestic product.
Sources: Bank Negara Malaysia. 2022. *Monthly Highlights and Statistics in January 2022*; Haver Analytics (both accessed 7 March 2022).

Delta-variant COVID-19 cases in the middle of last year stalled growth from this quarter over the first half. Housing demand improved on an increase in the number of housing units approved for construction. Investments in machinery and industrial equipment, including information and communication technology

This chapter was written by James Villafuerte and Maria Theresa Bugayong of the Southeast Asia Department, ADB, Manila.

Figure 3.26.2 Leading indicators

Business conditions improved significantly.

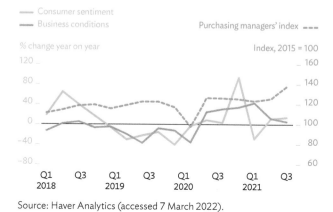

Source: Haver Analytics (accessed 7 March 2022).

Figure 3.26.3 Supply-side contributions to growth

Impressive industry and services growth in 2021, but still less than the pre-pandemic level.

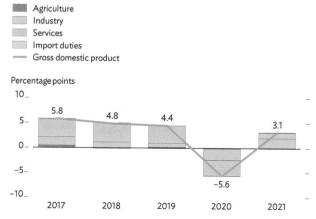

GDP = gross domestic product.
Sources: Bank Negara Malaysia. 2022. *Monthly Highlights and Statistics in January 2022*; Haver Analytics (both accessed 7 March 2022).

equipment, picked up, an indication that firms have started to expand production capacity. But public investments remained depressed, contracting 11.4%.

Exports of goods and services increased by 15.9% year on year, lifted by a strong rise in shipments of electronics and electrical products and more favorable oil prices. Imports grew 18.5% and outpaced exports. Imports of investment and intermediate goods recorded double digit growth. In October 2021, Malaysia's Prime Minister launched the National Trade Blueprint to enhance export competitiveness, increase market access, and boost exports over 2021–2025 to support the 12th Malaysia Plan.

Economic growth last year was broad-based (Figure 3.26.3). Agriculture did better than expected despite the floods in late 2021 that caused RM91 million in damage. Malaysia's production of palm oil continued to weaken, mainly due to the shortage in foreign workers. Many of these workers were unable to return to Malaysia after COVID-19 lockdowns were imposed. At present, foreigners are still not allowed to enter Malaysia except through Langkawi. External demand for palm oil appears to have slowed due to its higher price compared with close substitutes.

Manufacturing gathered pace at the start of 2021, growing an impressive 9.5% in the full year after contracting 2.6% in 2020. Manufacturing growth was solid over all quarters except for a short disruption in Q3 on an increase in COVID-19 Delta cases. The strong growth of export-oriented industries producing

electronics and electrical products continued (Figure 3.26.4). Relaxed COVID-19 containment measures and a high vaccination rate of 79% helped in the recovery of firms in consumer products, such as food, clothing, and vehicles. The improvement in the manufacturing production index growth from –3.4% in 2020 to 12.9% in 2021 was further evidence of a much healthier industrial sector.

Figure 3.26.4 Exports

Exports recovered on improving global trade.

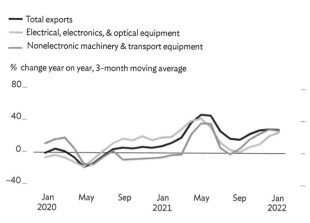

Note: Electrical, electronics, and optical equipment covers Standard International Trade Classification Revision 3 Division codes 75, 76, 77 and 87, and nonelectronic machinery and transportation covers codes 71 to 74 and 78 to 79.
Sources: Asian Development Bank estimates using data from CEIC Data Company and Haver Analytics (both accessed 12 March 2022).

Services rebounded in 2021, led by insurance, which grew by 12.3%, finance (9.5%), and information and communication (6.3%). Wholesale and retail trade and transport services also grew significantly despite Q3's surge in COVID-19. Tourism, however, remained subdued.

Inflation accelerated in February 2021 and remained elevated over the year, averaging 2.5% after deflation of 1.1% in 2020 (Figure 3.26.5). The rise in the inflation rate came mostly from the transport sector (11.0%). Three month-discounts as high as 40% on the electricity bills of domestic users ended in September; the discounts were part of the People's Well-Being and Economic Recovery Assistance package. Prices of fresh food increased sharply from September due to adverse weather, a cost push from supply disruptions, and higher feed and fertilizer costs.

Figure 3.26.5 Monthly inflation

Inflation building up, mostly from the food sector.

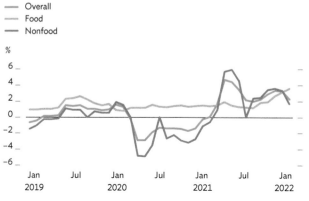

Sources: Bank Negara Malaysia. 2022. *Monthly Highlights and Statistics in January 2022*; Haver Analytics (both accessed 7 March 2022).

The labor market improved last year on the recovery in manufacturing and services from the resumption of business and social activities. The unemployment rate declined gradually from a high of 4.9% in January to 4.2% in December (Figure 3.26.6).

The US dollar value of exports rose by 27.5% in 2021 on the recovery in global trade. Electronics and electrical products were the key drivers. By destination, export growth was strong to the People's Republic of China (15.5%), Singapore (14.0%), and the United States (11.5%). Imports rose by 28.2% last year. The surplus

Figure 3.26.6 Labor indicators

Unemployment worsened for most of 2021, but improved at year-end.

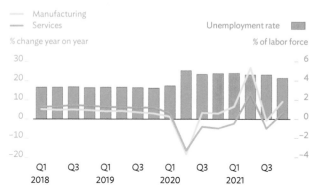

Source: Haver Analytics (accessed 3 March 2022).

in the current account in the balance of payments widened in Q4, but declined overall in 2021 to the equivalent of 3.5% of GDP from 4.2% in 2020 (Figure 3.26.7). International reserves totaled $115.8 billion as of 28 February 2022, cover for 6.1 months of imports. Malaysia's external debt totaled $257 billion, equal to 69.3% of GDP. The ringgit was only mildly affected by global trade disruptions, political instability, uncertainty over COVID-19, and rising debt, depreciating by just 1.4% against the US dollar last year.

Government revenue benefitted from higher crude and palm oil prices. Total revenue increased by 3.5% and

Figure 3.26.7 Current account balance and components

The surplus dipped in 2021, but remains high.

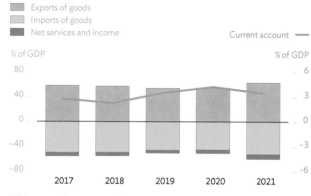

GDP = gross domestic product.
Sources: Bank Negara Malaysia. 2022. *Monthly Highlights and Statistics in January 2022*; Haver Analytics (both accessed 7 March 2022).

expenditure by 4.7%. Some RM39 billion of the total budget was set aside for health care and additional assistance to mitigate the pandemic's economic impact. The government's fiscal deficit remained elevated in 2021, at 6.1% of GDP.

Monetary policy remains accommodative. From November 2021 to January 2022, Bank Negara Malaysia, the central bank, kept the overnight policy rate at 1.75%. The banking system remains healthy with plenty of liquidity buffers, and fiscal and financial measures will continue to support economic activity. The central bank, in December, created the Disaster Relief Facility 2022 and increased the allocation by RM300 million in January, bringing the total to RM500 million, to assist the cash flow needs of micro, small, and medium-sized enterprises affected by widespread flooding. The central bank also introduced two new facilities for small and medium-sized enterprises. The Five-Year Financial Sector Blueprint was launched in January 2021 focusing on strategic support for the country's economic transformation in assistance to households and businesses, among other areas, that have been the most affected by COVID-19.

Economic prospects

Improving consumer and business confidence, bullish external demand from industrialized economies, and strong commodity prices brighten Malaysia's near-term economic prospects, although the lingering effects of COVID-19, particularly the wave of Omicron cases, could still weigh on the economy. For 2022, GDP growth is expected to accelerate to 6.0% before moderating to a more sustainable 5.4% in 2023 (Table 3.26.1 and Figure 3.26.8).

Table 3.26.1 Selected economic indicators, %

Growth to improve in 2022 and 2023, inflation to remain elevated.

	2020	2021	2022	2023
GDP growth	−5.6	3.1	6.0	5.4
Inflation	−1.1	2.5	3.0	2.5
CAB/GDP	4.2	3.5	3.3	3.0

CAB = current account balance, GDP = gross domestic product.
Source: Asian Development Bank estimates.

Figure 3.26.8 GDP growth

Growth to accelerate in 2022, but moderate in 2023.

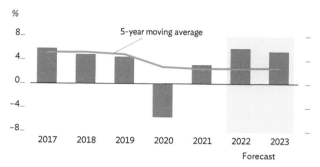

GDP = gross domestic product.
Source: *Asian Development Outlook* database.

On the demand side, private consumption is forecast to grow at an average rate of 5.3% in both 2022 and 2023, supported by strong consumer sentiment, brisk wholesale and retail trade activity, solid income growth, and government transfers to households in the lowest 40% income bracket.

Business conditions are improving significantly. In the last quarter of 2021, the business conditions index reached 122 points, double the level when the pandemic started in early 2020. Business tendency statistics showed that business performance improved from October 2021 to March 2022.

In step with the better business environment, private investment will grow strongly, led by large investments in information and communication technology, telecommunications, export-oriented manufacturing, and oil and gas. Banks will see a moderate increase in loan growth this year, fueled by robust growth in corporate and consumer loans. Growth in public investment will be underpinned by the 12th Malaysia Plan's focus on building infrastructure, the development of a gig economy, and support for strategic and high-impact industries, such as electronics and electrical products, global aerospace services, tourism, and smart agriculture.

By sector, the prospects for production are varied. Services will remain the main growth driver, as the sector benefits directly from rising private consumption. Industrial growth will be moderate, as manufacturing continues to be lifted by recovering exports. Agriculture will grow modestly on a recovery in palm oil production and production increases in other products. Construction and real estate will remain fragile, still clouded by risk aversion and uncertainty.

The inflation rate will rise on the recovery in domestic demand, rising goods and commodity prices, the end of electricity subsidies, lingering supply chain difficulties, and a tightening labor market. Inflation is forecast to accelerate to 3.0% in 2022 and slow to 2.5% in 2023.

Fiscal policy is expected to tighten this year and the federal budget deficit programmed to contract to 6.0% from the revised estimate of 6.5% in 2021. Despite the upside risk to inflation, the chance of a policy rate hike seems unlikely this year as monetary policy is expected to continue to support growth and a stable ringgit.

External demand will continue to contribute to near-term growth. Stronger growth in industrial economies will drive the growth of Malaysia's electrical and electronic products, and other manufactured exports. Exports of palm oil and liquified natural gas should pick up on higher commodity prices and strong growth in India and the People's Republic of China. Overall, the size of the current account surplus will dwindle but remain substantial, as import growth recovers.

Risks to the outlook could arise from weaker-than-expected global growth, worsening global and regional supply-chain disruptions, the emergence of severe and vaccine-resistant COVID-19 variants, and rising global geopolitical tension.

Policy challenge—regaining human development

The COVID-19 pandemic brought substantial changes to every aspect of people's lives. Setbacks have already been observed in some dimensions of human development. The most strongly affected areas are income, health, and education. In Malaysia, 41 out of the 146 indicators (28%) in the Sustainable Development Goals decreased in 2020; among them, absolute poverty and employment. The number of poor households increased from 405,400 in 2019 to 639,800 in 2020, and the incidence of absolute poverty rose from 5.6% to 8.4%. Working hours lost due to

COVID-19 in 2020 are estimated at 1.4 million to 1.6 million full-time equivalent jobs. Because of job losses and reduced working hours, the average household monthly income in 2020 decreased by 10.3% from RM7,901 in 2019 to RM7,089 (Figure 3.26.9).

Figure 3.26.9 Percentage of households with declining income since the start of COVID-19

Average monthly incomes shrank in 2020 from job losses.

- Latin America & Caribbean
- Middle East & North Africa
- Sub-Saharan Africa
- Europe & Caucasus and Central Asia
- East Asia & Pacific
- Malaysia

COVID-19 = Coronavirus Disease 2019.
Source: World Bank. COVID-19 Household Monitoring Dashboard (accessed 17 February 2022).

The 2020 *Families on Edge* study by the United Nations Population Fund and the United Nations Children's Fund observed fairly early in the COVID-19 pandemic that low-income households were being severely affected and that the effects were disproportionately large on these households. Food insecurity among low-income households increased, resulting in unhealthy diets that can worsen child malnutrition. Even with the reopening of schools, 7% of upper-secondary-age children have not returned to school, 1 in 5 have lost interest in school, and the incidence is higher among children from female-headed households. Female-headed households are especially vulnerable, as they are more likely to be unemployed and their access to social protection is lower than for men. Children in female-headed households also face greater challenges in accessing e-learning during intense periods of the pandemic.

The theme of Budget 2022 is a Prosperous Malaysian Family, and the RM332.1 billion budget is the highest budget ever. A strategy under the budget called Restoring Lives and Livelihoods has initiatives to support the welfare of households, public health care, education, employment, and social protection. The allocation for direct cash assistance to households is RM8.2 billion; it aims to reach nearly 10 million people, mostly in the lowest income bracket. Improving access to public health care is a strategic priority. One of Budget 2022's largest beneficiaries is the Ministry of Health, which has an allocation of RM32.4 billion. The ministry also has a RM2 billion allocation to manage COVID-19; this includes health kits for 3.6 million so-called B40 families in the lowest 40% income bracket. Under the education budget, the Peranti Siswa Keluarga Malaysia initiative allocated RM450 million to support access to e-learning for B40 families. Jamin Kerja Keluarga Malaysia, with an allocation of RM4.8 billion, is expected to create 600,000 jobs through its employment incentives, the MySTEP short-term employment program, and upskilling and reskilling programs. To strengthen social protection, the job-search allowance is continued with a budget allocation of RM300 million. Budget support of RM80 million to the Kasih Suri Keluarga Malaysia Programme will extend income support to housewives and widows in the event of illness and disability, as well as providing income security in old age.

Concern is growing over the shrinking fiscal space and the ability to sustain fiscal stability due to the country's COVID-19 economic recovery plans and the need for continued assistance in the coming years. Largely because of the pandemic, the statutory debt ceiling was increased from 60% to 65% of GDP. The government's ratio of debt to GDP, at 63.5% at the end of 2021, was only slightly below the new debt ceiling. And as priority expenditure on social assistance, education, and health increases, the budget deficit is expected to rise in the near term from its 2021 level of 6.1% of GDP.

In step with fiscal consolidation, it is important that the government strengthens the budget. Measures are needed to do this not only to fund programs for human development but also to build the fiscal space that can support the attainment of Malaysia's social development goals. To help achieve these goals, the government has raised taxes on foreign income, and sales and services in the digital economy, to ensure the fiscal position improves within the envisaged targets. A plan to tax remittances was reversed after much protest. On the expenditure side, the government plans a public expenditure review with the World Bank to improve the efficiency and effectiveness of public spending. Improving the targeting of cash assistance to low-income families could help programs for human development reach targeted households. These are small steps, but together they can prepare the country to respond to future shocks.

MYANMAR

Political uncertainty and the emergence of COVID-19 variants caused a broad-based contraction of the economy in fiscal 2021. The contraction is expected to continue in fiscal 2022, albeit a far less severe one. Easing political tensions and the lifting of pandemic restrictions should pave the way for a mild recovery in fiscal 2023. The current account deficit will narrow in this fiscal year on slowing imports. Achieving strong and sustained growth in agricultural production is the key policy challenge over the medium term.

Economic performance

Myanmar's GDP is estimated to have contracted by 18.4% in fiscal year 2021 (FY2021, ended 30 September 2021) after shrinking to 3.2% in FY2020 (Figure 3.27.1). All major sectors led to the decline in GDP except agriculture. But growth in this sector slowed from 1.7% in FY2020 to an estimated 0.8% in FY2021 on weaker external demand and higher prices of farm inputs (Figure 3.27.2). Political instability weighed heavily on business sentiment, and the COVID-19 pandemic created both demand and supply shocks in the economy. Industrial output shrank by an estimated 20.9% in FY2021. Services output contracted by an estimated 26.4%, reflecting significant declines in transportation, financial, trade, and social services.

The kyat, the local currency, depreciated by 32.6% against the US dollar over FY2021 on declining export earnings and lower capital inflows (Figure 3.27.3). Consumer prices, including food and beverage, started to increase sharply in the third quarter of FY2021, mainly due to the highly volatile kyat and logistics disruptions. Inflationary pressure from higher prices of fuel and other commodities, combined with the weaker kyat, were countered by lower consumer confidence and huge income losses. An estimate of 1.6 million jobs were lost in 2021 on the dual shocks of the COVID-19 pandemic and political tensions. Employment losses in the construction, garment, and tourism and

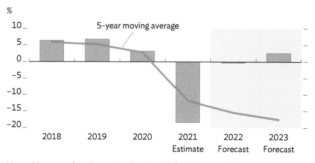

Figure 3.27.1 GDP growth

Growth will contract in the near term on continued political uncertainty and COVID-19 impacts.

Note: Years are fiscal years ending on 30 September of that year.
Sources: Central Bank of Myanmar. 2021. *Quarterly Statistics Bulletin.* Volume I; Asian Development Bank estimates.

hospitality sectors, among other sectors, were about 30%. Consequently, inflation decelerated from 5.7% in FY2020 to 3.6% in FY2021.

External trade was hit hard by mobility restrictions to contain the spread of COVID-19 and quell domestic political tensions. The US dollar value of merchandise exports declined by 13% in FY2021 on weaker earnings from most major export categories. Import growth fell by 23%, mostly on lower demand for capital and investment goods. Because of these factors, the current

---

This chapter was written by Joel Mangahas and Eve Cherry Lynn of the Myanmar Resident Mission, ADB, Nay Pyi Taw.

Figure 3.27.2 Supply-side contributions to growth

Industry and services growth will make a modest recovery in 2023.

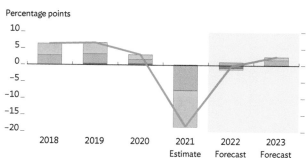

Note: Years are fiscal years ending on 30 September of that year.
Sources: Central Bank of Myanmar. 2021. *Quarterly Statistics Bulletin.*
Volume I; Asian Development Bank estimates.

Figure 3.27.3 Reference exchange rate

The kyat has depreciated sharply.

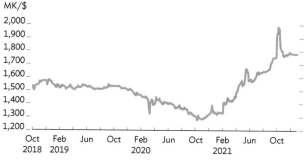

Source: Central Bank of Myanmar. *Daily Activities of Foreign Exchange Market.*

Figure 3.27.4 Current account balance

Low import growth will narrow 2022's current account deficit.

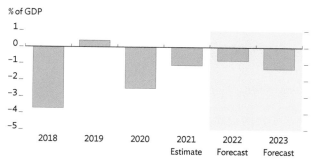

GDP = gross domestic product.
Note: Years are fiscal years ending 30 September of that year.
Sources: Central Bank of Myanmar. *Balance of Payment Statistics*
(accessed 31 January 2022); Asian Development Bank estimates.

Figure 3.27.5 FDI approvals and company registrations

Foreign investment fell sharply in Q4 2021 as uncertainties increased.

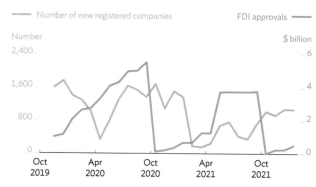

FDI = foreign direct investment, Q = quarter.
Source: Directorate of Investment and Company Administration.
Data and Statistics.

account deficit, as a percentage of GDP, narrowed from 2.5% in FY2020 to 1.1% in FY2021 (Figure 3.27.4).

Foreign direct investment commitments fell by 31.4% in FY2021 on the ongoing political uncertainty. The deteriorating business environment affected new company registrations, which dropped by 42.8% in FY2021 (Figure 3.27.5).

The fiscal deficit widened to 6% of GDP in FY2021 from 5% in FY2020. Declining revenue widened the deficit despite lower public expenditure. Tax revenue slumped 36.7%.

Economic prospects

Myanmar's economy is projected to contract by 0.3% in FY2022 on continued political instability and the worsening security situation dampening economic activity (Table 3.27.1). The emergence of the Omicron COVID-19 variant, an increasingly difficult security situation, and heavy restrictions on telecommunications will depress the services sector. Here, output is expected to shrink by 1.2% in FY2022. Agriculture output is forecast to contract by 2.9%, with production constrained by inadequate access to capital for farmers and higher input prices.

Table 3.27.1 Selected economic indicators, %

Prolonged impacts of dual shocks will undermine growth outlook in the near and medium term.

	2020	2021	2022	2023
GDP growth	3.2	–18.4	–0.3	2.6
Inflation	5.7	3.6	8.0	8.5
CAB/GDP	–2.5	–1.1	–0.8	–1.3

CAB = current account balance, GDP = gross domestic product.
Note: Years are fiscal years ending on 30 September of that year.
Sources: Central Bank of Myanmar; Central Statistical Organization; Asian Development Bank estimates.

Supply chain disruptions, worsening power shortages, and higher fuel and other input prices are expected to raise production costs, resulting in sluggish industrial growth. The outlook for industry remains weak, with output forecast to grow just 2.7% in FY2022. As of February 2022, 25 foreign firms had announced their withdrawal from Myanmar and the termination of planned and existing investments, including in electricity and telecommunication. Domestic and foreign investment is expected to slow on a weak business climate. In the first quarter of FY2022, foreign direct investment commitments fell to $2.5 billion from $3.5 billion in the first quarter of FY2021.

Inflation is forecast to accelerate to 8.0% in FY2022 and 8.5% in FY2023. In October 2021, food prices increased by 8.8% and nonfood prices by 12.0% compared with the same period in the previous fiscal year. Domestic fuel prices rose by 20.3% in January 2022, mainly on an unfavorable exchange rate and trade disruptions. The weak kyat, rising fuel prices, higher costs of imported goods, and supply-chain disruptions are likely to keep upward pressure on inflation in the near term. Exports are expected to grow by 4.2% in FY2022 on slightly better external demand. Import growth of 1.0% is projected on expectations of a gradual recovery in manufacturing. But the slow progress in planned investment projects and the weak kyat will keep import growth low, narrowing the current account deficit.

The fiscal deficit is forecast to equal 6.5% of GDP in FY2022, mainly on lower tax receipts (Figure 3.27.6). The sluggish performance of state-owned enterprises will lead to lower fiscal revenue, creating additional

pressure on the deficit to widen despite lower spending on public services and projects.

Protracted political tensions are the major downside risk to the near-term economic outlook. The continued contraction in investment raises concerns that production capacity is being eroded, undermining growth prospects for the near and medium term. The weaker-than-expected recovery among trading partners will reduce exports and challenges from rising global headwinds are additional downside risks for Myanmar.

Figure 3.27.6 Fiscal balance

Lower tax receipts will widen the fiscal deficit.

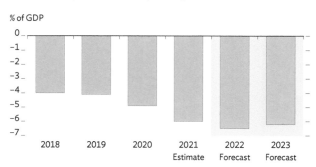

GDP = gross domestic product.
Note: Years are fiscal years ending on 30 September of that year.
Sources: Central Bank of Myanmar. 2021. *Quarterly Statistics Bulletin.* Volume I; Asian Development Bank estimates.

Policy challenge—improving access to food

Food insecurity is a growing concern in Myanmar, particularly for women and children, as household access to food has declined across the country in recent years. According to the Myanmar Humanitarian Needs Overview report based on a joint survey by the Food and Agriculture Organization, the United Nations Children's Education Fund, and the World Food Programme, an estimated 13.2 million people, 24% of the population, were food-insecure in 2021. About 52% were women and 35% children (Figure 3.27.7).

Tackling the production and marketing challenges facing farmers will be vital for ensuring food availability. Food security is being affected by

Figure 3.27.7 Food insecurity by cluster, 2021

Falling food production and rising commodity prices have stoked food insecurity.

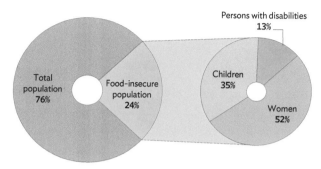

Source: United Nations Office for the Coordination of Humanitarian Affairs. 2021. *Humanitarian Needs Overview: Myanmar—Humanitarian Programme Cycle 2022.*

vulnerabilities in agriculture to supply chain disruptions, natural disasters, and climate change—and these vulnerabilities have been exacerbated by the COVID-19 pandemic and political instability.

Agriculture's growth potential is being held back by political tensions, farmers' lack of access to markets and inputs, such as fertilizer and seeds; inadequate rural infrastructure; and rising input costs. Because

the sector relies heavily on imported inputs, the cost of food production has been affected by the kyat's depreciation—and opportunities for higher output prices have not offset higher input costs. Farm income is being suppressed by expenses (plus depreciation) increasing faster than revenue for market-traded products, lower productivity and scale, and lack of access to financing. And because of climate change, extreme weather events, especially floods and drought, are becoming more frequent and severe, with the damage done to agricultural assets causing lower crop and livestock production. Gender inequalities in the sector also put women farmers at greater risk and result in heavier workloads.

Increasing agricultural production will be critically important for stabilizing food prices and improving access to food, especially for the poorer sections of the population. Increased public investment in rural infrastructure is needed to increase productivity. Putting small-scale farmers at the center of a climate-resilient agriculture system and empowering them to be able to work effectively in the system will reduce the adverse impact of the dual shocks of political uncertainties and the COVID-19 pandemic. Doing this would also strengthen the sector's resilience and promote gender parity in access to food.

PHILIPPINES

The economy rebounded in 2021 on eased COVID-19 mobility restrictions and widespread vaccination coverage. Inflation accelerated and the current account turned a deficit on brisk imports. Higher growth is expected this year and next on strengthening domestic demand and reforms supporting investment. The inflation rate will rise on higher global commodity prices. A major policy challenge is expanding support to micro, small, and medium-sized enterprises (MSMEs), which are playing a vital role in the economic recovery.

Economic performance

GDP in the Philippines grew by 5.6% last year after the economy contracted 9.6% in 2020. The second half saw growth up by 7.3% year on year as COVID-19 containment measures affecting businesses were eased and pandemic alert levels lowered in several regions, including Metro Manila. Progress in increasing vaccination coverage helped restore consumer and business confidence.

Investment and household consumption were the major growth drivers last year (Figure 3.28.1). Investment rebounded by 19.0% on rising private and public investment, reversing 2020's 34.4% contraction. Private construction picked up from the second quarter, although it still contracted by 2.0% over the full year. Public construction grew by 37.4% as the government accelerated large infrastructure projects, including railways, ports, and expressways. Outlays for machinery and transport equipment rose by 11.9%.

Household consumption, accounting for three-fourths of GDP, rose by 7.3% year on year in the second half and by 4.2% for the whole year. The unemployment rate eased; it peaked at 17.6% in April 2020 but had fallen to 6.6% in December 2021, still above the pre-pandemic level of 5.1% in 2019. Remittances from Filipinos working overseas—up by 5.1% year on year to $34.9 billion in 2021, equivalent to 8.9% of GDP—continued to support household consumption.

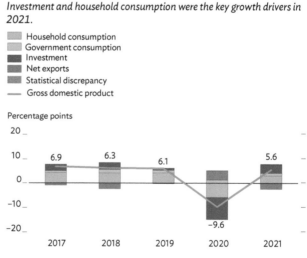

Figure 3.28.1 Demand-side contributions to growth

Investment and household consumption were the key growth drivers in 2021.

- Household consumption
- Government consumption
- Investment
- Net exports
- Statistical discrepancy
- Gross domestic product

Percentage points

Source: Philippine Statistics Authority.

The deployment of overseas workers gathered pace as major host countries reopened their economies to foreign workers. Remittances from workers excluding seafarers with contracts of 1 year or longer rose by 5.6% last year. Government consumption rose by 7% on sustained spending on social services and economic recovery programs, including vaccine procurement and support to MSMEs.

This chapter was written by Cristina Lozano and Teresa Mendoza of the Philippines Country Office, ADB, Manila

Net exports of goods and services dampened GDP growth. Although exports rebounded in 2021, they were outpaced by imports on rising domestic demand as households and businesses adjusted to easing COVID-19 restrictions. Merchandise exports rose by 11.6% in real terms and imports by 17.9%. Electronic products, comprising 62% of total exports, reversed 2020's contraction. Exports of other commodities, including machinery and transport equipment, chemicals, and processed food also rebounded. Services exports grew by 2.1% as travel and transport slowly picked up, and on gains in business process outsourcing. Imports of capital goods rose sharply in line with the recovery in investment.

All major sectors contributed to growth in 2021 except agriculture, which marginally contracted on lower pork production (Figure 3.28.2). Services were the main contributor to the rebound in growth, with the sector expanding by 5.3%, reversing 2020's 9.2% contraction. Trade, finance, information and communication, and business services were the main contributors. Industry, accounting for 30% of GDP, also rebounded, on 8.2% growth. Manufacturing, comprising two-thirds of industry, grew by 8.6%, lifted by stronger domestic demand and the recovery in exports. Growth was largely driven by food processing, which accounts for nearly half of total manufacturing output, and construction materials, computers, and electronic products. Construction grew 9.8% on relaxed mobility restrictions.

Figure 3.28.2 Supply-side contributions to growth

The services sector was the biggest contributor to growth in 2021.

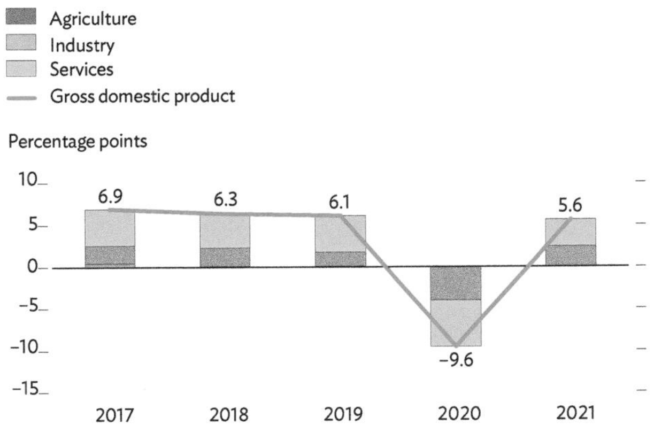

Source: Philippine Statistics Authority.

The inflation rate rose to 3.9% in 2021 from 2.4% in 2020, although it edged lower toward the end of the year. Supply-side pressures from adverse weather and African swine fever pushed food prices higher. Domestic petroleum prices rose in line with global oil price trends. The government took temporary measures last year to augment food supplies, including reducing rice and meat import tariffs and allowing more pork imports.

The key policy interest rate was maintained last year at a record low of 2% for the overnight reverse repurchase rate to stimulate faster economic growth. Liquidity growth (M3) expanded by 7.3% year on year in December 2021. Private sector credit grew by 2.8% in December after contracting in the first half.

The fiscal stance remained expansionary, with the fiscal deficit widening to 8.6% of GDP from 7.6% in 2020. Revenue rose by 5.2% year on year. Tax collection increased by 9.5%, but dividend remittances from corporations owned or controlled by the government were lower compared with 2020's sharp increase to support fiscal stimulus measures. Expenditure growth of 10.6% last year covered increases in funding for infrastructure, social services, livelihood assistance, and targeted cash transfers to help mitigate the effects of COVID-19 on the poor and vulnerable. The pandemic has reversed gains in poverty alleviation. Poverty incidence declined from 23.5% of the population in 2015 to 16.7% in 2018. But it was at 23.7% in the first semester of 2021, when 26.1 million people were below the poverty line, an increase of 3.9 million from the same period in 2018.

The current account turned a deficit of 1.8% of GDP in 2021 on rising imports after a 3.2% surplus in 2020 (Figure 3.28.3). Imports of industrial machinery and transport equipment increased sharply due to rebounding domestic investment. Imports rose by 31.7% in US dollar terms; exports rose by 12.4%. This widened the merchandise trade deficit to 13.7% of GDP from 9.3% in 2020. Rising remittances and earnings from services exports partly cushioned the merchandise trade deficit. In the financial account, foreign direct investment net inflows rose. These were partly offset by portfolio investment net outflows. The overall balance of payments surplus narrowed to 0.3% of GDP from 4.4% in 2020.

Figure 3.28.3 Current account components

The current account turned a deficit in 2021 as the economic rebound revived imports.

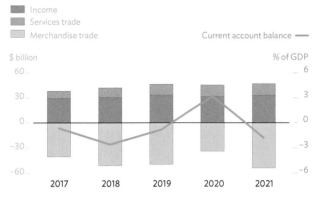

GDP = gross domestic product.
Source: CEIC Data Company (accessed 8 March 2022).

Foreign exchange reserves totaled $108.8 billion at the end of 2021, cover for 9.6 months of imports of goods and services and income payments. The ratio of external debt to GDP was 27.0% at the end of 2021, barely changed from 27.2% at the end of 2020. The peso depreciated 4.5% against the US dollar in 2021.

Economic prospects

The economic recovery is expected to gain traction this year and next, underpinned by strengthening domestic investment and consumption. GDP growth is forecast at 6.0% in 2022 and 6.3% in 2023.

Metro Manila and more areas shifted in March to alert level 1, the lowest level of COVID-19 restrictions as the surge in infections in mid-January subsided. New

Table 3.28.1 Selected economic indicators, %

Economic growth will pick up in 2022 and 2023 on strengthening domestic demand.

	2020	2021	2022	2023
GDP growth	−9.6	5.6	6.0	6.3
Inflation	2.4	3.9	4.2	3.5
CAB/GDP	3.2	−1.8	−3.2	−3.1

CAB = current account balance, GDP = gross domestic product.
Source: Asian Development Bank estimates.

daily cases averaged below 1,000 in March. Businesses and public transport are now allowed to operate at full capacity. The government issued an executive order on 21 March setting out measures to help sustain the recovery that include a further reopening of the economy, strengthening health care capacity and accelerating vaccination, returning to classroom learning, and relaxing international travel requirements. This will greatly benefit the services sector, which accounts for 60% of GDP. The further lifting of COVID-19 mobility restrictions will boost consumer sentiment and facilitate investment.

The unemployment rate in January eased further to 6.4% and should continue declining as more businesses resume operations or increase capacity (Figure 3.28.4). An additional 1.8 million jobs were generated from the start of 2021 to this January. These were largely jobs in services, but manufacturing and construction jobs also rose. Formal employment increased, especially wage and salaried jobs in private firms. Since February, the government has allowed fully vaccinated international travelers to enter the Philippines, which should boost tourism and employment in services sectors. Tourism's share of GDP fell to 5.4% in 2020 from 12.8% in pre-pandemic 2019. Tourism is a key source of jobs, accounting for 13.6% of total employment in 2019.

Figure 3.28.4 Unemployment rate

The rate has eased but it is still higher than the pre-pandemic level in 2019.

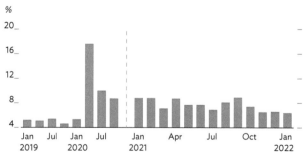

Source: Philippine Statistics Authority.

Public expenditure will continue to expand; the 2022 budget is 11.5% higher than 2021's. Increased public investment in large projects will continue to boost growth, with the government aiming to sustain infrastructure spending at over 5.0% of GDP in 2022 after 5.8% in 2021. Election-related spending ahead of national elections in May will provide a modest lift to aggregate demand.

The fiscal-deficit ceiling is programmed at 7.7% of GDP this year to accommodate continuing support to economic recovery programs before declining to 6.1% of GDP in 2023 and 5.1% in 2024 as the government undertakes fiscal consolidation (Figure 3.28.5). Boosting revenue growth will be important to narrow the deficit while at the same time meeting vital development expenditure needs. Tax revenue, which accounts for 90% of total revenue, has benefitted from reforms taken since 2018, including broadening the value-added tax base, increasing excise taxes on petroleum products, and levying excise taxes on certain products, including sugar sweetened drinks. Excise taxes on cigarettes and alcohol have also been raised. Tax revenue increased to 14.5% of GDP in 2019, the highest in over a decade, but declined to 14.0% in 2020 and 14.1% in 2021 as COVID-19 restrictions dampened economic activity (Figure 3.28.6).

Figure 3.28.5 Fiscal balance

The fiscal deficit is programmed to narrow further in 2023 and 2024.

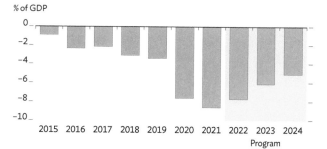

GDP = gross domestic product.
Sources: Bureau of the Treasury; National Economic and Development Authority.

Figure 3.28.6 Tax revenue

Reforms drove improvements in mobilizing tax revenue.

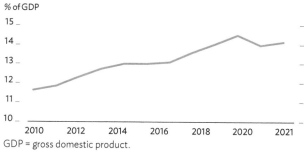

GDP = gross domestic product.
Sources: Bureau of the Treasury; CEIC Data Company (accessed 8 March 2022).

As economic recovery accelerates, revenue will continue to pick up. The government's decision to maintain excise taxes on petroleum products, despite calls to suspend them to temper spikes in pump prices, will help sustain revenue. Ongoing digitalization programs are improving tax administration and taxpayer compliance. A fuel-marking program to curb oil smuggling has improved the collection of excise tax on fuel. Additional tax reforms are pending in Congress, including reforms to real-property taxes to promote an efficient valuation system for real property and broaden the tax base for property-related taxes of the national and local governments.

The government's debt-to-GDP ratio widened to 60.5% in 2021 from 54.6% in 2020 on higher borrowing to fund programs to tackle COVID-19 (the ratio fell to a record low of 39.6% in 2019) (Figure 3.28.7). Domestic debt accounts for two-thirds of total debt, and the higher share of domestic borrowing helps alleviate vulnerability to foreign exchange shocks. Debt is largely long-term at two-thirds of the total. Under the government's fiscal consolidation plan, the debt ratio is programmed to start declining in 2023 in tandem with a narrowing fiscal deficit. The country's investment-grade sovereign credit ratings were affirmed in 2021 and 2022 by the major credit rating agencies.

Private investment indicators are favorable. Imports of capital goods have risen at double-digit levels, and the manufacturing purchasing managers' index increased to 52.8 in February 2022 (50.0 indicating expansion) (Figure 3.28.8). Bank lending to businesses rose by

Figure 3.28.7 National government debt

Debt rose from a record low in 2019 to support COVID-19 programs.

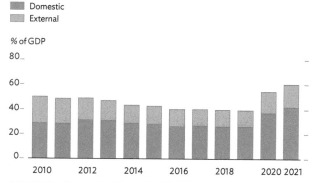

COVID-19 = Coronavirus Disease 2019, GDP = gross domestic product.
Sources: Bureau of the Treasury; CEIC Data Company (accessed 8 March 2022).

9.5% year on year in January 2022, the fastest in nearly 2 years (Figure 3.28.9). Lending growth was brisk to the information and communication, manufacturing, and real estate sectors. Foreign direct investment net inflows rebounded by 54.2% year on year in 2021, channeled mostly into manufacturing and utilities.

Figure 3.28.8 Manufacturing purchasing managers' index

The index signaled a pickup in manufacturing in early 2022.

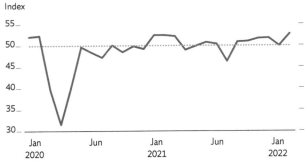

Note: A purchasing managers' index reading <50 signals deterioration, >50 improvement.
Source: Bangko Sentral ng Pilipinas.

Figure 3.28.9 Bank lending

Lending growth continued to accelerate after pulling out of a slump in mid-2021.

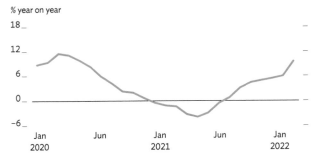

Source: Bangko Sentral ng Pilipinas.

Major investment climate reforms have been approved. In March 2022, restrictions on foreign participation in key sectors were eased by amendments to the Foreign Investment Act and the Public Service Act, allowing full foreign ownership in telecommunications, airlines, shipping, railways, and expressways and tollways. The Retail Trade Liberalization Act was amended to ease capitalization requirements for foreign investors in the retail trade sector. The Corporate Recovery and Tax

Incentives for Enterprises Law, approved in March 2021, included a reduction in corporate tax rates from 30% to 25% (20% for MSMEs) and enhanced fiscal incentives to investors by making them time-bound and performance-based. The government, through the Anti-Red Tape Authority, has reduced regulatory compliance costs for businesses by launching the Central Business Portal, a one-stop online site for business-related information and transactions, such as securing business permits, licenses, and clearances.

The rollout of the Philippine Identification System for a national ID is being fast-tracked. An executive order in February 2022 institutionalized the acceptance of a national ID as sufficient proof of identity in all government and private transactions. The ID will also improve the targeting and delivery of public services.

The inflation rate is forecast to rise to 4.2% in 2022 mainly on pressure from higher global oil and commodity prices. Inflation was a modest 3.0% in both January and February due to slower rises in food prices. But March saw increases in domestic oil prices on rising global oil prices. As a social protection measure, the government, in March, issued fuel subsidies and discount vouchers to public transport drivers, farmers, and fisherfolk to help them cope with rising fuel and production costs. Inflation is expected to decelerate to 3.5% in 2023 as global commodity prices moderate.

Although the overnight reverse repurchase rate was kept steady at 2%, the central bank, in its latest policy review meeting on 24 March, indicated the possibility of rate hikes to arrest second-round inflation.

The current account deficit is projected to widen to 3.2% of GDP in 2022 and marginally narrow to 3.1% in 2023, as faster economic growth boosts imports. Higher oil prices this year will also drive up import costs. Growth in merchandise exports will be moderate compared with imports. Rising remittances and services exports, including business processing outsourcing and tourism receipts, will help trim the current account deficit.

The main downside risks to the outlook stem from the unpredictable sequence of global events triggered by the Russian invasion on Ukraine. There is a significant risk that inflation could surge higher with second-round impacts, such as tightening credit markets and higher interest rates. Heightened and extended geopolitical tensions will dampen global growth, including in advanced economies, particularly Europe and the United States, which are among the Philippines' key export markets.

Policy challenge—supporting MSME competitiveness and long-term resilience

MSMEs have often been more affected than large firms by the COVID-19 crisis, which has exposed their considerable vulnerability to shocks. Since the pandemic's outbreak, the government has implemented financial support measures for MSMEs to tackle their liquidity challenges, including through loan payment deferrals, credit guarantees, and wage subsidies.

It is essential that policies are strengthened further to build the resilience of these firms and to enhance their capacity to respond to future shocks. Since MSMEs comprise 99.5% of businesses and employ 63% of the workforce, they have a key role to play in the country's economic recovery from the pandemic and in efforts to secure inclusive growth. Appropriate policies can complement ongoing government programs to harness the potential of MSMEs and help these firms grow and generate jobs. As well as recovering from the pandemic, MSMEs must be able to deal with long-term structural challenges and digital transformation. Here, priority policy areas should be on intensifying MSME support for digital transformation, business innovation, and skills development.

Emerging technologies offer a range of applications to improve the performance of MSMEs and overcome size-related limitations. Many firms in the Philippines have moved operations online and implemented smart working solutions to remain in business during COVID-19 lockdowns and to overcome disruptions to their supply chains. Online platforms are playing an instrumental role in connecting users to new markets, suppliers, and resources. However, a survey in September 2020 by the government showed a still low level of digitalization by MSMEs, with 51% of businesses surveyed saying that they only used basic digital tools and 23% not using these tools at all for business.

Digitalization is a major driver of competitiveness by reducing communications and transaction costs and providing better access to information. Given the digital profile of MSMEs, more targeted programs and incentives are needed to increase access to and the adoption of technology, which started during the COVID-19 pandemic.

A proactive approach to bring Philippine MSMEs to a point where they can successfully innovate and compete on a global scale, and stimulate economic growth, is the implementation of government-funded technology extension programs. These programs provide advice and expertise to MSMEs to improve technology use and innovation by expanding the absorption and adaptation of existing technologies. The services are provided by networks of specialists that conduct technology and problem-solving diagnosis, formulate improvement plans, and offer implementation assistance. The support can be delivered to individual enterprises or simultaneously to groups with common needs.

The experience of other countries supporting the competitiveness and resilience of small firms can help inform and enhance programs in the Philippines. Spain launched a program for small and medium-sized enterprises (SMEs) in the context of COVID-19 to support enterprises and the self-employed to rethink their business models and strengthen managerial and digital skills with tools such as assessments of digital maturity levels, advisory services, and training. Germany supports SMEs in digitalizing business processes and digital market development. German SMEs benefit from the expertise of consultancy firms that have been authorized for these programs and support businesses individually throughout the whole process.

Financial and technical support programs can be supplemented by strengthening management skills in SMEs through training and guidance on skill sets, and undertaking the organizational changes required to support technological change. Digital diagnostic tools combined with training, workshops, and more intensive approaches like management coaching can help identify management deficiencies.

In the Philippines, the COVID-19 pandemic has triggered a considerable reallocation of jobs across sectors. The hardest-hit ones have been those dependent on personal contact, which applies to most MSMEs (Figure 3.28.10). About half are in wholesale and retail trade, and 14% in accommodation and food services. In contrast, the sectors that are recovering quickly with positive job creation tend to be those that absorb lower shares of labor, such as communications and technology and higher-skilled services sectors.

Figure 3.28.10 MSMEs by industry sector, 2020

MSMEs are largely in trade, accommodation, and food services.

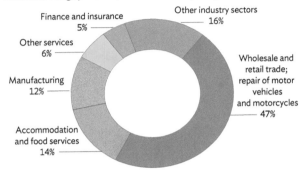

MSMEs = micro, small, and medium-sized enterprises.
Source: Department of Trade and Industry.

This divergence has widened skills mismatches in the labor market. Having workers with the right skills are key assets for companies to do business, adopt new technologies and innovative techniques, and to manage organizational changes. But unlike larger firms, MSMEs have greater difficulties in attracting and retaining skilled employees and fewer opportunities to provide skills development.

Massive reskilling is needed to retain and upgrade worker skills. Successful models to do this are industry- and employer-led skills training schemes to ensure that support is adapted to MSME needs. These programs provide annual grants to networks of enterprises (from a sector or locality) to fund the training of workers. The network is responsible for designing and implementing training programs suited to their needs, recruiting training providers, and obtaining certification for its workers. This approach is a cost-effective model to upskill and reskill workers and nurture a culture of workplace training and coordination across enterprises in an industry or locality. The government piloted this scheme with tourism enterprises in 2013. The Government launched this year enterprise-led skills training in more sectors, including construction, animation, and agribusiness, in addition to tourism, to assist with reskilling and job transitions.

SINGAPORE

GDP rebounded in 2021, propelled by domestic demand and exports. Inflation accelerated and the current account surplus widened. Growth should moderate in 2022 and 2023 as global growth slows. The inflation rate will rise in 2022 on higher oil and food prices, but ease in 2023. The current account surplus will narrow as imports grow. Sustaining an adequate labor supply during the recovery from the impact of the COVID-19 poses a policy challenge.

Economic performance

Singapore's economy grew by 7.6% last year in a strong recovery from 2020's contraction. All sectors of the economy expanded and domestic demand rebounded. Manufacturing grew by 13.2%, supported by higher output from electronics and precision engineering. Construction rebounded from 2020's stagnation, growing by 20.1% in 2021. Manufacturing and construction contributed 3.1 percentage points to growth. Services grew by 5.6%, contributing 3.8 points as all services subsectors expanded (Figure 3.29.1).

Domestic demand rebounded in 2021, growing by 8.9% and contributing 6.2 percentage points to growth. Private consumption rebounded on relaxed COVID-19 mobility restrictions, but government consumption declined to 4.5% on lower pandemic-related fiscal spending. Investment posted double-digit growth as construction works resumed. Exports of goods and services rose by 6.8% in real terms, supported by the recovery of the global economy and higher demand for electronics products. With imports of goods and services growing by 7.6%, net exports narrowed, contributing 0.9 points to GDP growth (Figure 3.29.2).

Figure 3.29.1 Supply-side contributions to growth

Manufacturing, finance, and trade remained engines of growth amid COVID-19.

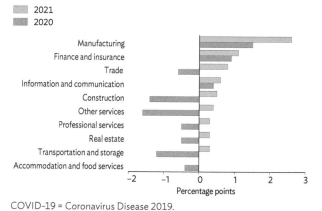

COVID-19 = Coronavirus Disease 2019.
Source: Ministry of Trade and Industry. *Economic Survey of Singapore 2021* (accessed 17 February 2022).

Figure 3.29.2 Demand-side contributions to growth

Total demand buoyed by the rebound in investment and private consumption.

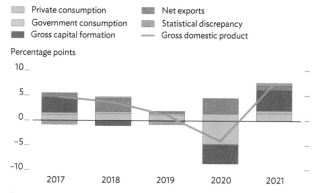

Source: Ministry of Trade and Industry. *Economic Survey of Singapore 2021* (accessed 17 February 2022).

This chapter was written by Shu Tian and Mai Lin Villaruel of the Economic Research and Regional Cooperation Department, ADB, Manila.

Headline inflation rose from 0.2% year on year in January 2021 to 4.0% in December on mainly higher food and private transport costs, averaging 2.3% after 0.2% deflation in 2020. Food inflation edged up, private transport costs rose on higher car and petrol prices, and higher rents increased accommodation costs. The Monetary Authority of Singapore's average core inflation index rose to 0.9% last year, primarily on increases in food and services costs (Figure 3.29.3).

Figure 3.29.3 Inflation

Core and headline inflation rose after deflation in 2020.

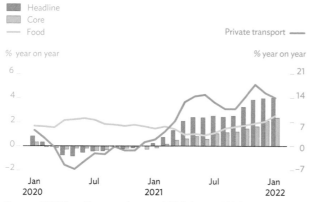

Source: CEIC Data Company (accessed 28 February 2022).

The Monetary Authority of Singapore maintained an accommodative monetary policy stance in the first 9 months of 2021, keeping the rate of appreciation of the policy band of the nominal effective exchange rate at 0%. But it tightened monetary policy in October 2021 and January 2022 as external and domestic cost pressures rose. The Singapore dollar depreciated against the US dollar in 2021 and was 1.4% lower year on year in February 2022, but the nominal effective exchange rate appreciated in 2021 and was 1.5% higher year on year in February 2022. The 3-month Singapore interbank offered rate remained stable at 0.4% (Figure 3.29.4).

Merchandise exports increased by 20.6% in US dollar terms last year, mainly on higher electronics exports. Imports rose by 22.8% on surging oil imports, but the trade surplus widened to 29.8% of GDP. Net service exports rose on higher receipts from financial services, but the net income deficit increased. Nevertheless, the current account surplus widened to 18.1% of GDP. The capital and financial account registered a net outflow

Figure 3.29.4 Exchange rate

The Singapore dollar weakened against US dollar in 2021.

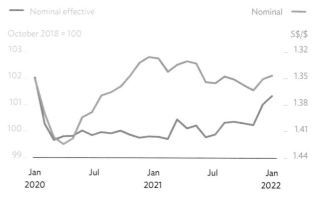

Source: CEIC Data Company (accessed 16 March 2022).

after a net inflow in 2020; this lowered the overall balance of payments surplus to 16.8% of GDP. Gross foreign reserves totaled $417.9 billion, equivalent to 8 months of imports (Figure 3.29.5).

Fiscal policy remained largely accommodative in fiscal year 2021 (FY2021, ended 31 March 2022). Total expenditure, including transfers, moderated to 19.9% of GDP on lower COVID-19 spending and delays in project implementation due to the COVID-19 pandemic. Budget revenue rose to 18.9% of GDP from 18.0% in FY2020 on higher receipts from stamp duty, asset taxes, and the vehicle quota premium. The overall budget deficit narrowed to 1.0% of GDP, a significant drop from FY2020.

Figure 3.29.5 Balance of payments

Overall balance-of-payments surplus narrowed as net capital flows reversed.

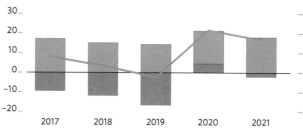

GDP = gross domestic product.
Source: CEIC Data Company (accessed 18 February 2022).

Economic prospects

Growth will moderate in 2022, but remain robust at 4.3% on the continuing economic recovery, both domestically and by major trading partners (Table 3.29.1). A high vaccination rate and the steady rollout of COVID-19 booster shots will facilitate the progressive easing of domestic and border restrictions, supporting recovery. Growth in 2023 is projected to moderate further to 3.2% on softer demand for semiconductors.

Table 3.29.1 Selected economic indicators, %

Growth will moderate, inflation will remain high, and the current account surplus ample.

	2020	2021	2022	2023
GDP growth	−4.1	7.6	4.3	3.2
Inflation	−0.2	2.3	3.0	2.3
CAB/GDP	16.8	18.1	17.0	17.0

CAB = current account balance, GDP = gross domestic product.
Sources: Ministry of Trade and Industry. *Economic Survey Singapore 2021* (accessed 18 February 2022); Asian Development Bank estimates.

Manufacturing will remain robust on rising demand for electronics. The manufacturing purchasing managers' index (PMI) edged up in February 2022 to 50.2 and the electronics PMI to 50.5, signaling expansion. Construction is expected to improve on the progressive easing of border restrictions on the entry of migrant workers. Services will be bolstered by the continued demand for information technology, digital solutions, and financial services, as well as a recovery in retail and food services. However, tourism's recovery will be hampered by the uncertainty and uneven mobility restrictions caused by the COVID-19 pandemic (Figure 3.29.6).

Private consumption will pick up on the gradual easing of COVID-19 restrictions, but fiscal spending on tackling the pandemic and defense will be moderate. Gross fixed capital formation will grow relatively slowly this year after 2021's rapid expansion, as investment commitments have fallen by 31.3% from their 2020 level. Still, there will be positive gains from the gradual resumption in construction.

Figure 3.29.6 Purchasing managers' index

Index in January 2022 continued to signal growth for manufacturing, especially for electronics.

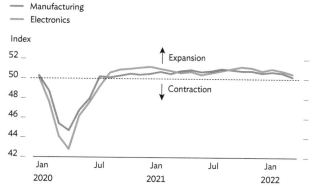

Source: CEIC Data Company (accessed 16 March 2022).

Rising oil and food prices, rents, service fees, and wage pressures have kindled inflation, with the rate reaching 4% in January and forecast to average 3% this year. Food inflation will remain high due to regional supply disruptions, and services fees will increase as private consumption picks up. The Monetary Authority of Singapore is expected to monitor its current policy stance to ensure inflation remains within its forecast 2.5%–3.5% range. Although the goods and services tax will increase from 7% to 8% in January 2023, inflation is expected to moderate to 2.3% next year on easing global and domestic cost pressures and the freezing of license and administrative fees for 1 year, starting 1 January 2023.

The latest trend in external demand suggests moderating exports and imports growth. Growth in merchandise exports slowed from 25.1% in December 2021 to 20.6% in February 2022; growth in imports moderated to 17.9% in February from 32.3% in December (Figure 3.29.7). The trade balance is expected to remain in surplus, which, together with rising net service receipts, will lower the current account surplus to a projected 17% of GDP in 2022 and 2023.

Fiscal policy in FY2022 will be accommodative. Government expenditure, including transfers, is forecast at 18.2% of GDP, lower than in FY2021, with health, education, and security accounting for the bulk of expenditure. Total revenue is expected to reach 17.3% of GDP on anticipated increases in corporate taxes and a higher vehicle-quota premium.

Figure 3.29.7 Trade indicators

The trade balance remained positive, buoyed by strong growth in exports and imports.

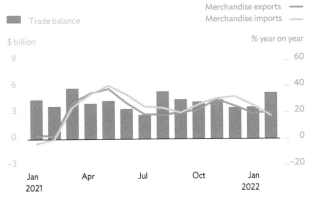

Source: CEIC Data Company (accessed 17 March 2022).

Figure 3.29.8 Unemployment and employment

The unemployment rate declined during the recovery, but the number of employed did not pick up.

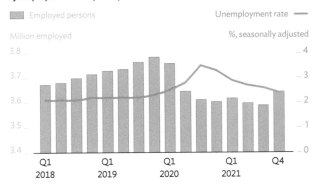

Q = quarter.
Source: CEIC (accessed 24 February 2022).

So, at a forecast 0.9% of GDP, the overall fiscal deficit will be narrower than in FY2021.

The main risks to the outlook continue to be uncertainty over the COVID-19 pandemic and the weaker-than-expected economic performance of major trading partners. Protracted supply disruptions alongside a stronger pickup in demand, and rising energy commodity prices, could lead to persistent inflationary pressures. Faster-than-expected monetary policy tightening in advanced economies could reduce liquidity in financial markets and put pressure on Singapore's financial stability because of capital outflows and spillovers of higher interest rates.

Policy challenge—sustaining labor supply for the recovery

Singapore's labor market strategy of building a high-skilled domestic workforce while tapping low-skilled workers from abroad has faced challenges since the outbreak of the COVID-19 because of restrictions on movement and cross-border mobility. The unemployment rate declined from 3.5% in the third quarter (Q3) of 2020 to 2.6% in Q3 2021 as restrictions on mobility and economic activity were gradually lifted. Even so, the labor market remains tight. In particular, despite a recovery in demand for workers, the number of employed, which fell to 3.6 million in Q2 2020, remained below the level in Q4 2019 (Figure 3.29.8).

When business activity began to return to normal, labor demand increased in all sector, but labor supply was slow to pick up. Job vacancies grew and the ratio of job vacancies to unemployed persons surged in 2021 (Figure 3.29.9). The increase in vacancies is partly due to the reduction in the foreign workforce, from 1.4 million in December 2019 to 1.2 million in June 2021, amid difficulties in coming to Singapore because of border mobility restrictions and relatively high travel costs. The vacancy increases are especially pronounced for the construction and information and communication technology (ICT) sectors—the only two sectors with increased shares in total vacancies. To sustain an adequate supply of workers during the recovery, the authorities need to address the reliance on foreign workers and improve the availability of a local labor force.

To tackle the labor shortage for low-skilled foreign workers, the government, in May 2021, raised the foreign worker levy rebate for employers in construction, marine shipyards, and processing to help them retain and bring in foreign workers. Nevertheless, the share of construction vacancies to total vacancies increased from 4.0% in Q4 2019 to 17.7% in Q3 2021. The impact of these rebates can be enhanced by flexibly allocating more work permits, reducing processing times, and extending or increasing the special levy rebate for sectors facing labor shortages.

Figure 3.29.9 Job vacancies by sector

Construction and ICT saw proportionally more job vacancies in 2021.

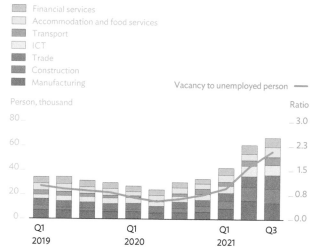

ICT = information and communication technology, Q = quarter.
Source: CEIC (accessed 24 February 2022).

As a structural solution to reduce the reliance on low-skilled foreign workers, the government should provide incentives for labor-intensive sectors to adopt labor-saving innovations, such as digital tools and modern machinery, and provide technical assistance for training workers to use new technologies.

To sustain the supply of ICT workers, the government has been advocating innovation and digitalization via various policy instruments, such as SkillsFuture, to help build a high-skilled ICT workforce in the medium term. Despite these efforts, from Q4 2019 to Q3 2021, ICT experienced proportionally more vacancies. This suggests that current education and upskilling programs cannot immediately meet the rapid surge in demand for ICT workers. Tailored support to equip the local workforce with needed ICT skills can help. For example, special training programs can be set up for skills with more vacancies in the market. Consideration could be given to attracting foreign workers with the needed ICT skills though targeted migration policies that are designed to take into account the high level of global competition for attracting this expertise.

THAILAND

A severe COVID-19 outbreak dragged the economy down in 2021, but the last few months of the year saw a gradual recovery and this is expected to continue into 2022 and beyond. Risks, however, remain tilted to the downside from the possibility of renewed COVID-19 outbreaks, especially of new variants, and the global economic impact of Russian invasion of Ukraine affecting the cost of living and production in Thailand. Reviving tourism—the hardest-hit sector since the start of the pandemic—is the priority policy challenge.

Economic performance

Thailand's economy remained mired in uncertainty last year because of the impact of COVID-19's Alpha and Delta variants. GDP growth was 1.6%, indicating the economy had just about recovered from its 6.2% contraction in 2020 (Figure 3.30.1). Growth started to gradually recover in the fourth quarter on robust merchandise exports, relaxed COVID-19 mobility restrictions, and fiscal stimulus measures.

Despite weak overall growth, exports of goods and services did well in 2021, with the US dollar value of merchandise exports rising by 14.9%. Export growth was underpinned by improved economic conditions in major trading partners, especially in the semiconductor sector. Services exports, however, contracted by 22.8% on the continued decline in international tourist arrivals. A mere 400,000 tourists visited Thailand last year, down from 6.7 million in 2020 (Figure 3.30.2).

Private consumption, which grew by 0.3%, perked up after COVID-19 mobility restrictions were eased from September as vaccination rates improved and on fiscal

Figure 3.30.1 Demand-side contributions to growth

The economy was primarily driven by merchandise exports and investment in 2021.

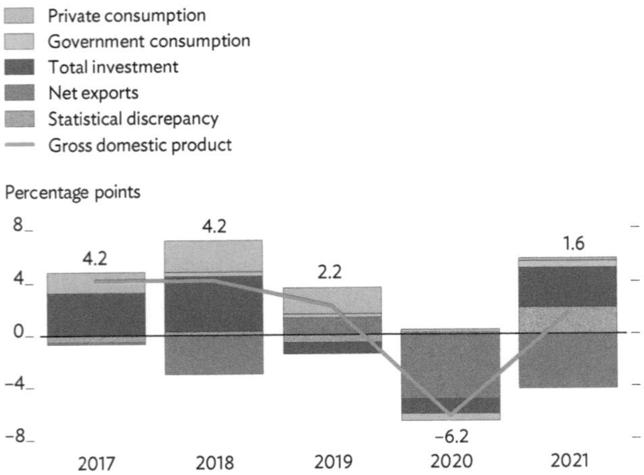

- Private consumption
- Government consumption
- Total investment
- Net exports
- Statistical discrepancy
- — Gross domestic product

Percentage points

Chart values: 4.2 (2017), 4.2 (2018), 2.2 (2019), −6.2 (2020), 1.6 (2021)

Source: Office of the National Economic and Social Development Council. *Quarterly Gross Domestic Product* (accessed 14 March 2022).

Figure 3.30.2 International tourists

Tentative recovery signs in late 2021 and early 2022.

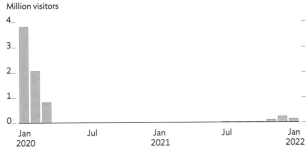

Million visitors

Source: CEIC Data Company (accessed 14 March 2022).

This chapter was written by Chitchanok Annonjarn of the Thailand Resident Mission, ADB, Bangkok.

stimulus programs. The government extended domestic tourism subsidies, copayment schemes, and cashback e-vouchers for domestic purchases, which helped to increase consumer spending. The government achieved its target of 70% of the population having at least a first COVID-19 vaccination shot by the end of 2021.

Private investment rose by 3.2%, underpinned by robust merchandise exports and recovering domestic consumption. Although the industry sentiment index has shown positive growth since September, businesses are concerned about the possibility of new COVID-19 outbreaks, especially from new variants, and worker shortages in the labor market.

Public consumption expanded by 3.2% last year, driven largely by increased medical spending on COVID-19. Public investment expanded by 3.8%. The government budget in fiscal year 2021 (FY2021, ended 30 September 2021) was in deficit, equivalent to 4.8% of GDP, albeit a lower one than FY2020's 5.2%. The disbursement of B1 trillion government emergency loans to mitigate the impact of COVID-19 on the economy accounted for 94.3% of the total budget by the end of the fiscal year. The bulk of this spending was assistance to help workers and entrepreneurs affected by the strict COVID-19 containment measures. In the third quarter of 2021, the government started to allocate budgets under a new B500 billion loan to tackle the effects of the pandemic. Consequently, the ratio of public debt to GDP at the end of FY2021 increased to 58.2% from 49.4% in FY2020 (Figure 3.30.3). In September, the government raised the public debt ceiling from 60% of GDP to 70%, enabling further borrowing to rehabilitate the economy.

Figure 3.30.3 Public debt

Public debt almost reached 2021's debt ceiling.

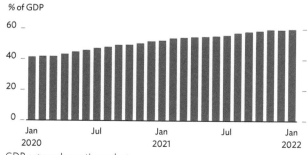

% of GDP

GDP = gross domestic product.
Note: Years are fiscal years ending on 30 September of that year.
Source: Public Debt Management Office (accessed 14 March 2022).

Imports of goods and services increased by 17.9% last year in line with the strong increase in merchandise exports and improving domestic demand. Imports of consumer goods rose in line with higher private consumption. Imports of medicines and pharmaceuticals rose on imports of COVID-19 vaccines. Capital goods imports expanded in tandem with rising investment in machinery and equipment. Raw material imports increased on stronger demand for inputs to the country's exports of intermediate and final goods.

Agricultural production, benefiting from favorable weather, grew by 1.4% last year. Industry expanded by 1.6%, and manufacturing by 4.9% on strong merchandise exports. Services grew by 0.7%, supported by the rising use of mobile applications. But within the services sector, accommodation and food declined by 14.4% in line with the drop in international tourist arrivals and the resurgence of COVID-19 (Figure 3.30.4).

Figure 3.30.4 Supply-side contributions to growth

Manufacturing led economic growth on strong exports of goods.

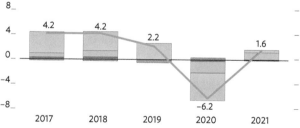

Source: Office of the National Economic and Social Development Council. *Quarterly Gross Domestic Product* (accessed 14 March 2022).

The current account turned a deficit of 2.2% of GDP last year on weaker receipts from international tourism. The capital and financial account had a net inflow. The overall balance of payments was in deficit, at $7.1 billion, reversing 2020's surplus of $18.4 billion(Figure 3.30.5).

Figure 3.30.5 Balance of payments

Balance of payments turned a deficit on weak international tourism.

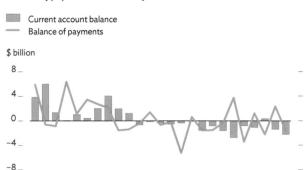

Source: CEIC Data Company (accessed 14 March 2022).

Prices rose by 1.2% in 2021 largely on higher energy and food prices after deflation of 0.8% in 2020. External stability remained strong. At the end of 2021, international reserves were ample at $246 billion. The baht depreciated by 2.1% on average against the US dollar in 2021 on tighter monetary policy in advanced economies and concerns over the sudden outbreak of COVID-19. The policy interest rate, at 0.5%, stayed low to support economic recovery (Figure 3.30.6).

Figure 3.30.6 Inflation and policy interest rate

Inflation remained low and the policy interest rate was maintained at 0.5% throughout 2021.

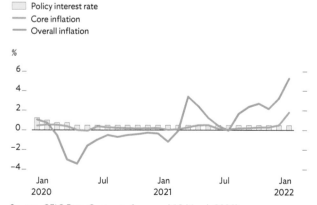

Source: CEIC Data Company (accessed 12 March 2022).

Economic prospects

The economy's recovery and particularly tourism hinges on whether there will be further COVID-19 outbreaks and whether these involve new variants. An encouraging sign is that the Omicron variant seems to be causing milder symptoms. The economy is expected to recover gradually in the second half of 2022—a forecast, however, that depends heavily on whether it will become necessary to reimpose movement restrictions. GDP growth is forecast at 3.0% this year and 4.5% in 2023 (Table 3.30.1 and Figure 3.30.7) .

Table 3.30.1 Selected economic indicators, %

Merchandise exports and investment to lead the recovery in the near term.

	2020	2021	2022	2023
GDP growth	−6.2	1.6	3.0	4.5
Inflation	−0.8	1.2	3.3	2.2
CAB/GDP	4.2	−2.2	0.5	4.2

CAB = current account balance, GDP = gross domestic product.
Source: Asian Development Bank estimates.

Figure 3.30.7 GDP growth

The economy is expected to gradually recover in the near term, driven by merchandise exports and investment.

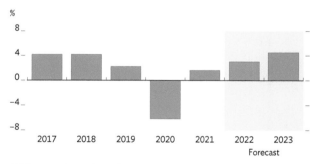

GDP = gross domestic product.
Source: *Asian Development Outlook* database.

The US dollar value of exports of goods and services is projected to grow by 6.1% this year and 9.4% in 2023 in line with the global economic recovery and easing supply chain disruptions in 2023. However, the Russian invasion of Ukraine could affect exports of several manufacturing goods produced in Thailand, including automobiles and parts, rubber products, and electrical appliances if there are prolonged supply chain disruptions. Tourism is expected to gradually recover. Thailand resumed its no-quarantine program in February after suspending it for a month as the spread of the Omicron variant was not as severe as expected. Relaxed entry measures for international arrivals continue. The Russian invasion of Ukraine will affect international tourist arrivals. Long-haul travelers, especially from Europe, may be less inclined to travel as there are now flight disruptions from Europe to Thailand, making it more difficult and costly to travel to there. The number of international tourist arrivals is expected to rise to 5 million in 2022 and to 12 million next year, still far below the pre-pandemic 40 million.

Private consumption could slow in the first half of 2022 due to the spread of the Omicron variant. A significant rise in oil prices would reduce consumers' purchasing power throughout 2022. Continued support from fiscal stimulus measures will, however, boost consumer spending, forecast to grow by 3.3% this year. In January 2022, the Ministry of Finance launched the fourth phase of a 50% copayment scheme, available from 1 February to 30 April, for buying products and services to reduce the cost of living and generate revenue for small businesses. Another stimulus to encourage spending was a tax deduction for individual taxpayers of up to B30,000 on purchases of goods or services from 1 January and 15 February, applicable for the 2022 tax year. In December 2021, the government extended property tax incentives, which include cuts in property transfer and mortgage fees from 2% and 1% to 0.01%, respectively, for units priced B3 million or less from December 2021 to December 2022 to stimulate the housing market. Private consumption growth is projected to slow to 3.0% in 2023 as several stimulus measures gradually wind down.

The impressive outlook for exports should encourage businesses to increase investments this year and next. Private investment is expected to grow by 5.0% in 2022 and 5.1% in 2023, despite higher costs of production from rising oil prices and delays in infrastructure investment projects caused by the spread of the Omicron variant and delays in selecting investors from the private sector.

Public consumption is projected to decline by 0.4% this year due to budget cuts in FY2022 that are likely to affect most ministries, reflecting the reduced need for emergency COVID-19 support measures. Public consumption is projected to increase by 0.6% in 2023. Public investment is forecast to expand by 3.8% in 2022 and 2.1% in 2023. Several Eastern Economic Corridor construction projects that were delayed by COVID-19 should resume this year and next. Imports of goods and services are projected to rise by 1.1% in 2022 and 3.5% in 2023 in tandem with increasing exports and domestic demand.

Agriculture production is expected to expand by 3.0% this year and 2.4% in 2023, supported by favorable weather, particularly buoyant rainfall. Industrial output is forecast to grow by 3.2% in 2022 and 4.0% next year on a continued strengthening in exports and domestic demand. Services output is forecast at 4.5% and 8.6%. Digital services will continue their upward trend on growing online platforms. Relaxed COVID-19 mobility restrictions, the tourism stimulus program, and accelerated vaccination should support a recovery in tourism. It is likely that domestic tourism will return to pre-pandemic levels by 2024. But international tourism, although gradually recovering, is unlikely to reach pre-pandemic levels in 2024. Digital services, especially in finance and telecommunication, will continue their upward trend in line with growing online platforms and the development of robotics to replace human workers in several segments in the services sector.

Inflation is expected to edge up on rising food and persistently high energy prices, with the rate forecast at 3.3% in 2022 and moderating to 2.2% in 2023 (Figure 3.30.8). If the global economic fallout from the Russian invasion of Ukraine is prolonged, this could contribute to rising commodity prices, particularly wheat and maize, in Thailand. A surplus in the current account is projected at 0.5% of GDP this year and 4.2% next year, with the surplus expanding on rising merchandise exports and a mild recovery in international tourism (Figure 3.30.9).

Several downside risks could delay Thailand's economic recovery. The emergence of new COVID-19 variants remains a major risk. Rising food and energy prices, as well as high production costs from disruptions to global and regional production networks and supply chains, would affect the country's manufacturing sector. A prolonged war could worsen Thailand's economic outlook in the near term.

Figure 3.30.8 Inflation

A sharp rise in oil prices is projected, putting upward pressure on inflation.

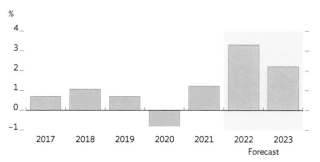

Source: *Asian Development Outlook* database.

Figure 3.30.9 Current account balance

The balance will return to a surplus in the near term.

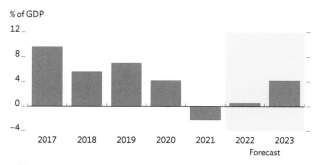

GDP = gross domestic product.
Source: *Asian Development Outlook* database.

Policy challenge—reviving tourism

Thailand's economic recovery depends largely on tourism. The sector's direct and indirect receipts accounted for about 20% of GDP before the outbreak of COVID-19, and tourism employs about a fifth of the work force. New COVID-19 variants would create uncertainty for domestic and international tourists. Although Thailand's higher vaccination rates will help reduce transmission and severe illness and deaths, an outbreak of a new variant would force the government

to reimpose mobility restrictions—a huge setback for tourism. The Test & Go quarantine waiver program, launched last November, that aims to attract fully vaccinated international tourists got off to a good start. Under the program, Thailand received 310,043 international tourists during November–December 2021, much higher than the 65,670 arrivals during July–October 2021.

But just 2 months into the program, the outbreak of the Omicron variant forced the government to suspend the Test & Go program in January. The program was resumed at the start of the following month after COVID-19 was assessed to be under control. But the respite did not last long: on 21 February, the government upgraded the risk of COVID-19 infections to level 4, the second highest level, as new Omicron cases rose nationwide. The private and public sector was encouraged to work from home, and nonessential interprovincial travel discouraged. Although the Test & Go program remains in place, rapid changes in the COVID-19 situation and health protocols will affect both domestic and international travel in the near term. Travel plans could be delayed or even suspended.

A future pandemic could widen the gap between large and small hoteliers as large hotels are likely to have adequate cash flow. Hotel workers who lost their jobs last year after the outbreak of the Delta variant are still finding it difficult to regain their jobs. Business travel is anticipated to face a slower recovery with companies encouraging remote working. Consumer behavior in the hospitality sector will also change on the increasing public awareness of health, hygiene, and personal wellness.

To revive tourism, hoteliers will need to upskill and reskill their employees on digital and data analytics for planning business. Policy makers should continue to help businesses in the tourism sector that are struggling with liquidity problems. Over the longer term, a push for sustainable tourism that reduces the sector's carbon footprint would be highly desirable.

TIMOR-LESTE

The economy made a weak recovery in 2021 due to a surge in COVID-19 infections and the impact of devastating floods, the worst in 40 years. The rise in international food prices stoked inflation. The economy is expected to gather momentum in 2022 with a planned rise in government spending, particularly capital expenditure. As growth will continue to be largely driven by government spending over the medium term, reforms to public financial management are the key policy challenge.

Economic performance

Timor-Leste's GDP grew a modest 1.8% in 2021 in an expansion constrained by twin shocks—a sharp rise in COVID-19 cases from March and the economic impact from the severe flooding caused by Cyclone Seroja in April. Private consumption was subdued, as consumer confidence and household income was hit by the pandemic and the floods. Government consumption was boosted by a record-high budget, further supplemented in April, totaling $2.0 billion. The 36% increase over the 2020 budget was originally to support the government's short-term COVID-19 measures and the medium-term economic recovery, but it was further

increased in response to the shocks. Public transfers nearly doubled in 2021 compared with pre-pandemic 2019. Despite the high budget ceiling, execution rates were low, particularly capital development spending, which only reached 24% of its budget allocation last year (Figure 3.31.1). Gross investment is estimated to have fallen by 20%.

Non-oil domestic revenue fell an estimated 12% in 2021 from 2020 due to the creation of two new public enterprises for power and water supply, which removed their revenues from nontax receipts. Tax collection

Figure 3.31.1 Cumulative recurrent and capital expenditure

Recurrent spending reached a record high in 2021, while capital spending was at its lowest since 2008.

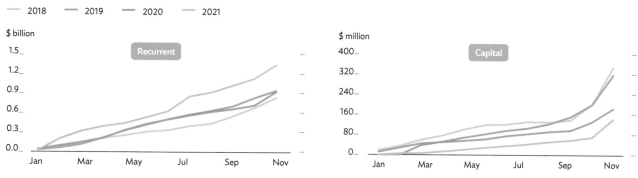

Source: Timor-Leste Budget Transparency Portal (accessed 28 January 2022).

This chapter was written by Kavita Iyengar of the Timor-Leste Resident Mission, ADB, Dili.

in 2021 is estimated to have been slightly lower than in 2020, particularly revenue from excise, sales, and withholding taxes due to the sluggish economic growth. Petroleum revenue rose to $718.8 million from $326.2 million in 2020 on rising oil prices. The fund's investment returns remain high, valued at $19.6 billion at the end of 2021, nearly 12 times 2021 GDP, the highest in its history (Figure 3.31.2). This translated to a fiscal surplus of 31% of GDP in 2021.

Figure 3.31.2 Petroleum Fund balance at year-end

The Petroleum Fund ended 2021 at its highest level, though forecast to decline as oil production in current fields ceases in 2023.

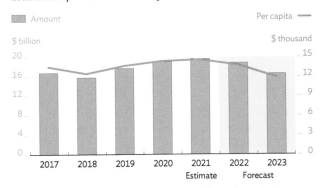

Sources: Ministry of Finance; Banco Central de Timor-Leste (both accessed 21 February 2022); Asian Development Bank estimates.

The US dollar value of exports of goods and services surged by 90% last year, reflecting the strong rebound in coffee exports, which grew 600% year on year (Figure 3.31.3). Imports of consumable products, particularly food, rose by 40% due to the COVID-19 pandemic and flood-related public relief spending, particularly under the Cesta Basica program, a household support scheme providing food and hygiene necessities. The rise in imports resulted in a substantial current account deficit, estimated at 39.1% of GDP in 2021 (Figure 3.31.4).

Higher global food prices caused consumer prices to rise by 3.8% in 2021 from 0.5% in 2020 (Figure 3.31.5). Poorer households were particularly hard hit by the spike. Mobility restrictions to contain COVID-19 and higher government spending added to the upward pressure on prices.

Figure 3.31.3 Coffee exports

Coffee exports rebounded significantly to exceed pre-pandemic levels.

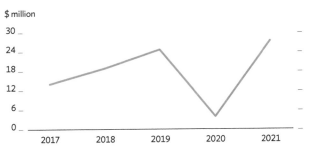

Source: General Directorate of Statistics (accessed 27 January 2022).

Figure 3.31.4 Current account components

Negative current account balance will continue with the rising deficit in goods and services trade.

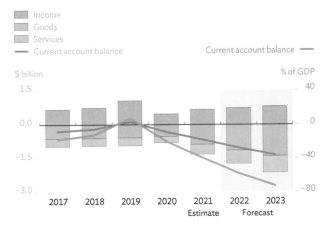

GDP = gross domestic product.
Sources: General Directorate of Statistics (accessed 28 January 2022); Asian Development Bank estimates.

Figure 3.31.5 Monthly inflation

Consumer prices rose rapidly in 2021, driven by higher global food prices.

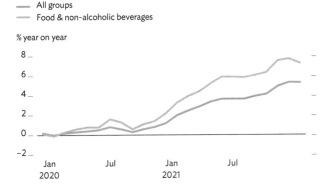

Source: General Directorate of Statistics (accessed 3 March 2022).

Economic prospects

The economy is forecast to grow by 2.5% in 2022 and 3.1% in 2023 (Table 3.31.1). Parliament approved a $1.9 billion ceiling for the 2022 budget, still large despite a 5% reduction on the final budget for 2021. Over a third of the budget is for transfer spending. Budget execution rates are expected to be higher in the near term, but real GDP will likely return to pre-pandemic levels only by 2024. Presidential elections this year and parliamentary elections scheduled for 2023 may have implications for future government spending plans if there are any structural changes.

Table 3.31.1 Selected economic indicators, %

Growth to recover on large government spending in the medium term.

	2020	2021	2022	2023
GDP growth	−8.6	1.8	2.5	3.1
Inflation	0.5	3.8	2.6	2.7
CAB/GDP	−19.3	−39.1	−58.4	−72.8

CAB = current account balance, GDP = gross domestic product.
Note: GDP refers to non-oil growth.
Sources: General Directorate of Statistics; Asian Development Bank estimates.

The government doubled taxes on tobacco products in early 2022 to boost tax receipts and discourage smoking. Timor-Leste has one of the highest rates of smoking in the world, with over a third of adults tobacco users. Further planned tax reforms include the expansion of the Standard Integrated Government Tax Administration System to digitalize the current system and introducing value-added tax, which is due to be discussed in Parliament this year.

Oil prices rose slightly in early 2022, but uncertainties in global financial markets, coupled with a projected decline in petroleum production, may lower inflows into the Petroleum Fund. That, in turn, could cause a deterioration in fiscal and current account balances, as well as dampen investor interest in developing new petroleum fields. The current account is expected to see large deficits in the medium term.

Inflation is forecast at 2.6% in 2022 and 2.7% in 2023. Timor-Leste's exposure to extreme weather events and natural disasters induced by global climate change makes it vulnerable to upward pressure on the prices of food products, especially if there is another bout of heavy floods. Agriculture is especially vulnerable to the high risk of geophysical and climate hazards as 66% of the population depends on the sector. The impact on food prices and supply chains due to Russian invasion of Ukraine will further affect inflation in Timor-Leste.

The 2022 budget includes $15.0 million for the creation of an emergency climate response fund and $3.9 million for equipment to respond to natural disasters. In addition to a third wave of COVID-19, Timor-Leste has had to grapple with a particularly severe dengue outbreak, with the death toll in first 2 months of 2022 higher than total dengue deaths in the past 2 years. Another health crisis or natural disaster on the scale of 2021's floods are the main risk to the near-term economic outlook.

Policy challenge—reforming public financial management

Timor-Leste has one of the world's highest levels of public expenditure, averaging 86% of GDP over 2008–2020, and government spending is the main driver of economic growth. The Petroleum Fund, which financed 81% of the state budget over 2016–2021, works as a fiscal buffer that allows the government to respond to economic shocks without the need to significantly reduce expenditure or increase the debt ratio (Figure 3.31.6). Despite a fiscal rule defining a sustainable yearly amount that can be withdrawn from the fund, the government has consistently approved "extraordinary" withdrawals since 2009.

The economic impact of the COVID-19 pandemic has been a stark reminder of the importance of a well-functioning public financial management (PFM) system during crises. System reforms will be critical for the Petroleum Fund's sustainability and the country's future—and they need to be prioritized to ensure that the basic requirements for sound fiscal

Figure 3.31.6 Petroleum Fund contributions
to government expenditure

*Total withdrawals from the Petroleum Fund to finance government
expenditure were 48% over ESI over 2016–2021.*

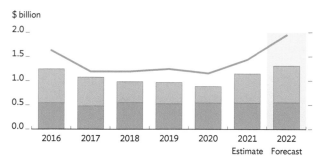

ESI = estimated sustainable income.
Source: Ministry of Finance (accessed 3 March 2022).

management and high-level budget allocations are implemented before addressing specific issues on operational and services efficiency. Timor-Leste has made some progress in PFM by, among other initiatives, creating a treasury single account and improving financial reporting. But key gaps remain. Improving fiscal forecasts, particularly domestic revenue and budget estimates, strengthening the public investment

management framework, and improving accounting and auditing capacities in line ministries and municipalities, should be the initial focus. A roadmap is needed to ensure a coordinated approach for PFM, both within the government and among donor agencies. Focusing on institutional development will facilitate the preparation for more advanced PFM reforms, including accrual accounting and fiscal risk analysis. Political buy-in and country ownership will be vital for the successful implementation of PFM reforms.

The Budgetary Framework and Public Financial Management Law, passed in February 2022, changes the structure of the budget cycle to limit upward pressure on the budget ceiling, which often occurs in the current annual process. It also created a new step in the budget, the Law on Major Planning Options, which enables the government to approve multiyear budgets, thereby supporting the process of medium-term budget planning. The new law confirms the move from line-item budgeting to program budgeting and aims to enhance financial reporting, both internally from public sector entities to the Ministry of Finance and through the timely publication of monthly budget execution accounts. Timor-Leste must continue to build on these reforms to ensure long-term socioeconomic development through the sustainable use of the Petroleum Fund.

VIET NAM

A resurgence of the COVID-19 pandemic tightened labor markets, disrupted supply chains, and slowed growth in 2021. The economy is set for a strong rebound this year and next, made possible by a high vaccination rate that enabled disruptive containment measures to be dropped, trade expansion, and continued monetary and fiscal accommodation. Risks to the bright outlook are a renewed COVID-19 wave and a slower-than-expected global economic recovery. A key policy challenge is ensuring the speedy and effective implementation of the economic recovery and development program to boost growth.

Economic performance

A renewed COVID-19 outbreak in April 2021 dampened Viet Nam's economic recovery, tightened the labor supply, and disrupted labor-intensive manufacturing and production supply chains. GDP growth last year slowed to 2.6% from 2.9% in 2020 (Figure 3.32.1).

The fast recovery of industrial output in the first quarter (Q1) and Q2 was erased by strict COVID-19 mobility restrictions in Q3, causing output to contract in that quarter. The easing of mobility restrictions in October on rising vaccination coverage restored growth, with output rising 4.0% overall in 2021. Services growth slowed to 1.2% from 2.3% in 2020. A 96% drop in foreign tourist arrivals last year offset rebounding health and financial services in Q4 (Figure 3.32.2). Agriculture grew by 2.9%, up from 2.7% in 2020, underpinned by revived food demand in the People's Republic of China (PRC) and elsewhere.

Figure 3.32.1 Supply-side contributions to growth

Growth in 2021 was still well below its pre-pandemic trend.

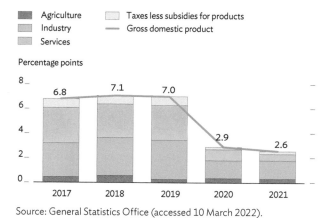

Source: General Statistics Office (accessed 10 March 2022).

Figure 3.32.2 Tourist arrivals

Tourism remained moribund in 2021.

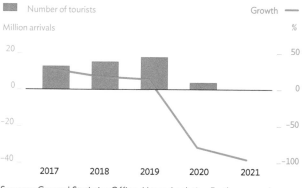

Sources: General Statistics Office; Haver Analytics (both accessed 10 March 2022).

This chapter was written by Cuong Minh Nguyen, Chu Hong Minh, and Nguyen Luu Thuc Phuong of the Viet Nam Resident Mission, ADB, Ha Noi.

The labor market suffered severe shocks from both the supply and demand sides as the economy weakened and workers left the labor force, which fell by 2.0 million workers ages 15 and over in Q3 from the previous quarter. Private consumption grew by 2.0% last year, up from 0.6% in 2020 but much lower than 2019's pre-pandemic growth of 7.4%. Rising unemployment and falling incomes constrained private consumption growth last year.

Public consumption declined to 2.9% from 6.2% in 2020 as the government cut current expenditure. Total gross capital formation was unchanged at about 4.0%, but still half the pre-pandemic level. Registered foreign investment increased by 9.2%, but fragmented central and local coordination held back disbursements of foreign direct investment, which decreased by 1.2%. External trade performed robustly despite COVID-19 headwinds.

Inflation decelerated to 1.8% in 2021 from 3.2% in 2020 on weak domestic demand; last year's inflation rate was the lowest since 2016 (Figure 3.32.3). With low inflation, the State Bank of Vietnam maintained its accommodative monetary policy, keeping record-low policy rates unchanged since October 2020, providing credit relief measures, and increasing credit growth limits for some commercial banks. Interest rate reductions and waivers totaled an estimated $1.5 billion. Revived economic activity since October 2021 restored high credit growth in the last months of the year, bringing full-year credit growth to an estimated 13.6%, up from 12.2% in 2020 (Figure 3.32.4). Money supply growth is estimated at 10.7% at the end of 2021, down from 14.5% in 2020.

Figure 3.32.3 Monthly inflation

Inflation decelerated in 2021.

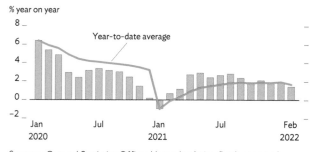

Sources: General Statistics Office; Haver Analytics (both accessed 10 March 2022).

Figure 3.32.4 Credit and money supply growth

Growth in monetary aggregates slowed somewhat in 2021.

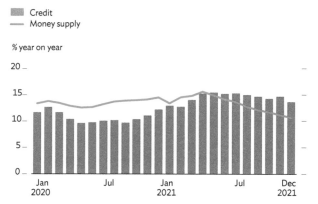

Sources: State Bank of Vietnam; Asian Development Bank estimates.

Financial stability risks were under control last year despite the economic impact of the pandemic. Accommodative monetary and fiscal policies fueled the rise of the Ho Chi Minh Stock Index to a historic peak in November 2021. Government bond issuance totaled the equivalent of $13.7 billion, up 32% from 2019's level. Vulnerabilities to financial stability are emerging. The growth of the corporate bond market was underpinned by private placements, largely unsecured and without a credit rating, causing concern about potential risks. Nonperforming loans (NPLs) may further rise once the loan restructuring and retaining category stalls.

Merchandise trade exports rose to 19% in 2021 from 7% in 2020. Shipments of mobile phones, computers and electronics, accounting for 32% of total exports, rose by 13.2%. The United States remained Viet Nam's biggest export market with a 28.4% share of the total value of exports, followed by the PRC. The PRC's zero-tolerance approach to the COVID-19 pandemic hindered exports to the PRC last year and in the first 2 months of 2022.

The merchandise trade surplus shrank to 4.9% of GDP from a record-high surplus of 8.9% in 2020. Rising imports were driven by the recovery in production and domestic consumption. The narrowing trade surplus, together with the decline of net receipts from services, turned the current account balance to a deficit, estimated at the equivalent 1.1% of GDP after a 4.4% surplus in 2020. Net capital inflows buoyed the surplus of the capital account, estimated at 8.5% of GDP, creating a balance-of-payments surplus of 3.9% of GDP

(Figure 3.32.5). At the end of December, foreign reserves were estimated to cover 3.9 months of imports, slightly down from 4.2 months at the end of 2020.

Figure 3.32.5 Balance of payments indicators

Capital inflows supported the external account in 2021.

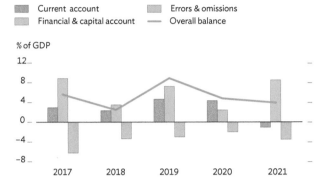

GDP = gross domestic product.
Sources: State Bank of Vietnam; Asian Development Bank estimates.

The budget deficit is estimated to have widened to 3.8% of GDP from 3.5% in 2020. Budget revenue increased slightly by 1% on increased tax receipts from external trade, up 22%, and oil, up 32%. These gains were offset by a 3% decline in domestic tax revenue caused by weaker economic activity. Government expenditure rose by only 3% year on year. But increased government COVID-19 spending offset the slow disbursement of public investment.

The pandemic slowed divestments by state-owned enterprises. In 2021, revenue from divestment and equitization from these firms was only 14.5% of the planned level. The quality of bank assets was affected by weak economic activity. The ratio of on-balance-sheet NPLs to total outstanding loans was about 2.0% at the end of last year, up from 1.7% at the end of 2020. All NPLs, including those warehoused at Viet Nam Asset Management Company and other high-risk loans held by banks, are estimated at 3.8% of total outstanding loans.

Economic prospects

GDP growth is forecast at 6.5% in 2022 and 6.7% in 2023—a rebound made possible by Viet Nam's high COVID-19 vaccination coverage, the shift to a more

flexible pandemic containment approach, expanding trade, and the government's economic recovery and development program (ERDP) (Figure 3.32.6 and Table 3.32.1). As of 22 March, 79.4% of the population above age 18 were fully vaccinated and 47.5% had received booster shots. The high vaccination rate allowed the government to abandon harsh and disrupting containment measures. This timely shift of the pandemic containment strategy helped restore economic activity and reduce uncertainty in the business environment. A General Statistics Office survey of business trends in processing and manufacturing shows that 81.7% of respondents believe the production and business situation will be better in 2022. The economy grew by 5.0% in Q1 2022, up from 4.7% in the same quarter last year.

On 11 January, the National Assembly endorsed combined monetary and fiscal measures estimated at $15 billion to implement the ERDP in 2022 and 2023. The program's $11.5 billion in fiscal measures include tax reductions; exemption policies; support for health

Figure 3.32.6 GDP growth

Strong recovery forecast for 2022 and 2023 on lifted COVID-19 curbs.

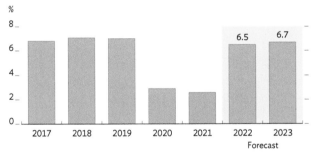

COVID-19 = Coronavirus Disease 2019, GDP = gross domestic product.
Source: *Asian Development Outlook* database.

Table 3.32.1 Selected economic indicators, %

Economy to rebound in 2022 and 2023 after soft growth in 2021.

	2020	2021	2022	2023
GDP growth	2.9	2.6	6.5	6.7
Inflation	3.2	1.8	3.8	4.0
CAB/GDP	4.4	–1.1	1.5	2.0

CAB = current account balance, GDP = gross domestic product.
Source: Asian Development Bank estimates.

care, infrastructure development, and social security; and an interest rate subsidy for firms and household businesses. The ERDP's monetary measures will provide additional liquidity to the economy through an expected reduction in the lending rate by 0.5%–1.0% by credit institutions over this year and next and the continued implementation of credit relief measures until the end of 2023. The State Bank of Vietnam set the 2022 target growth rate for credit at 14%. Reaching the target will be aided by interest rate cuts and revived credit demand from businesses.

A recovering labor market and other stimulus measures will spur industrial growth by a forecast 9.5% in 2022, contributing 3.6 percentage points to GDP growth. The sector got off to a strong start this year. The manufacturing purchasing managers' index rose to 53.7 in January (over 50 indicating expansion) and to 54.3 in February from 52.5 in December, the fourth straight month of growth (Figure 3.32.7). Agriculture output is forecast to grow by 3.5% this year, contributing 0.4 percentage points to GDP growth on revived domestic demand and rising global commodity prices. The government's tourism-reopening policy implemented in March and the lifting of pandemic controls are expected to boost services, with the sector forecast to grow by 5.5% and contribute 2.3 percentage points to GDP growth this year. Accelerated disbursements will drive construction and related economic activities.

The ERDP will speed up public investment, stimulating domestic demand. Improved coordination between the central and local levels of government and restored labor mobility will increase domestic and

Figure 3.32.7 Purchasing managers' index

Index recovered in January and February 2022.

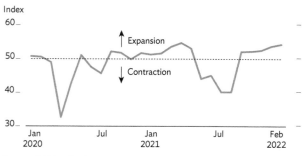

Source: IHS Markit (accessed 8 March 2022).

foreign investor confidence in Viet Nam's recovery. The European Chamber of Commerce in Viet Nam's business climate index in Q4 2021 showed European firms had a positive and optimistic view of the country's business environment after the government loosened harsh COVID-19 containment measures. Foreign direct investment disbursement in the first 2 months of 2022 increased by 7.2% over the same period last year (Figure 3.32.8).

Figure 3.32.8 Foreign direct investment

FDI should increase in 2022, implying the expansion of manufacturing.

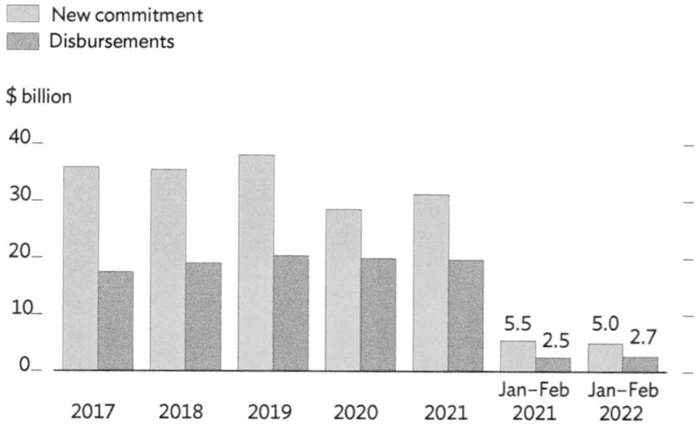

Sources: General Statistics Office; Haver Analytics (both accessed 10 March 2022).

External trade will remain robust this year. The Regional Comprehensive Economic Partnership, which came into effect 1 January, is expected to accelerate trade and the recovery once COVID-19 pandemic passes by forming stable and long-term export markets for Viet Nam and creating a legally binding foundation for expanding trade. Merchandise exports are forecast rising by 8%–10% this year. Imports will rise on increased demand for capital goods and manufacturing inputs, and rebounding domestic consumption. The recovery of tourism and sustained remittances will support a current account surplus, forecast at 1.5% of GDP this year and 2.0% in 2023.

Viet Nam's recovery is clouded by major near-term downside risks. High COVID-19 infections since mid-March could obstruct the economy's return to normalcy this year. A slowing global recovery and a surge in global oil prices from the Russian invasion of Ukraine would directly affect Viet Nam's external trade and domestic oil prices, which would affect inflation. Moreover, uncertainties in the global financial markets and the withdrawal of monetary and fiscal accommodation by advanced economies would weaken the dong, the local currency, rendering imports more costly and putting additional upward pressure on inflation. By the end of Q1 2022, average inflation increased to 1.9% from 0.3% in the same quarter of 2021. Inflation is forecast to accelerate to 3.8% in 2022 and 4.0% in 2023 (Figure 3.32.9). Slower growth in the PRC would slow Viet Nam's exports and recovery. Rising NPLs are another medium-term risk. Adding in the restructured loans that have retained the classification category, Viet Nam's potential gross NPL ratio is estimated at 8.2% of total outstanding loans. In addition to rapidly rising costs of construction materials, complex procedures for disbursing public investment could delay the implementation of Viet Nam's ERDP, diminishing its desired impact on growth, as discussed in the policy challenge.

Figure 3.32.9 Inflation

Inflation will rise in 2022 and 2023 in line with the global trend.

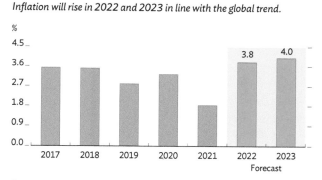

Source: *Asian Development Outlook* database.

Policy challenge—ensuring the ERDP's speedy implementation and effective coordination to boost growth

The government launched two fiscal and monetary support programs, in April 2020 to July 2021, to tackle the economic impact of the COVID-19 pandemic. In response to COVID-19's resurgence in 2021, the National Assembly, in January 2022, passed a resolution for new monetary and fiscal measures to accelerate the implementation of the ERDP this year and next. The program's effective implementation will be critical for Viet Nam to revive its growth momentum. But the ERDP's timely delivery faces several policy challenges.

Infrastructure development is one of the ERDP's most significant components and this has been allocated a D113 trillion budget (about $5 billion) for 2022 and 2023. The timely implementation of the infrastructure program may be at risk because Viet Nam has a systemic problem in project preparation, approval, and disbursement caused by complex and rigid public investment procedures. This is especially so for land acquisition, resettlement, and procurement. Timely implementation will require radical simplification and changes in public investment regulations and policy coordination.

Interest rate subsidization totaling D40 trillion (about $1.7 billion), a major fiscal component of the ERDP, is expected to spur aggregate demand. But because creditworthiness and capacity to recover are key conditions for firms to be able to tap these loans, small and medium-sized enterprises may not be able to meet the criteria because their balance sheets and capacity have been weakened by the COVID-19 pandemic. Another concern is that the interest rate subsidy program could be vulnerable to subsidized loans being misused for other purposes, including investing in risky sectors, such as stocks or property. This happened with a similar program in 2009. To guard against this happening again, clear guidelines and close coordination between concerned agencies will be crucial to strengthen the monitoring of the ERDP's implementation.

Another critical fiscal component of the ERDP is a 2% value-added tax (VAT) reduction for products and services in 2022, currently subject to a 10% VAT rate. The total value of the tax cut is approximately D49 trillion (about $2.1 billion). The VAT reduction could generate substantial pass-through and broad-based impacts if successfully implemented. But the eligibility criteria and procedures are complicated and could limit the access of firms to the VAT reduction. Clearer eligibility criteria and procedures are needed to support a speedy implementation of the VAT reduction.

THE PACIFIC

FIJI

The economy contracted for a third consecutive year in 2021, the latter 2 years under the COVID-19 pandemic. International border closures and other containment measures suppressed tourism before the border reopened in December 2021, providing hope for an economic turnaround. While necessary, safety nets and budgetary stimulus for affected businesses narrowed fiscal space despite increased grant financing from development partners. Remittances supported domestic consumption. Inflation remained benign, but recent structural and market movements may further erode purchasing power.

Economic performance

Hope of a recovery in 2021 was shattered as the spread of Delta and Omicron variants of COVID-19 caused the economy to contract by a further 4.1% (Figure 3.33.1). The service and primary sectors subtracted 5.3 percentage points from GDP as manufacturing and mining added 1.2 points. Improved mining efficiency raised gold production, and timber output remained strong as pinewood and mahogany production increased, but adverse weather affected cane harvest and sugar output.

Visitor arrivals shrank by a further 78.5% in 2021 (Figure 3.33.2). A quarantine protocol breach in April 2021 triggered a second community transmission wave of the Delta variant, generating one of the highest infection rates per capita globally. Nascent recovery in business expectations took a hit as a result. A third wave, this time of Omicron infections, occurred toward the end of the year.

Figure 3.33.1 GDP growth

Recovery is expected in 2022 as the border reopens.

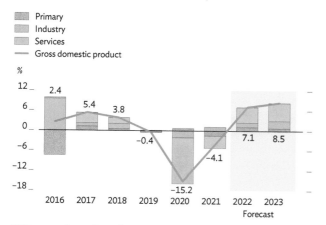

GDP = gross domestic product.
Sources: Fiji Bureau of Statistics (accessed 31 March 2022); Asian Development Bank estimates.

Figure 3.33.2 Visitor arrivals

Border closure wiped out visitor arrivals in 2020 and 2021.

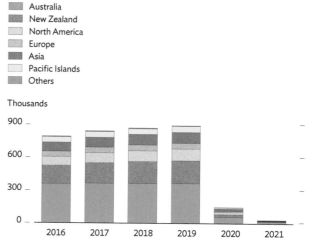

Source: Fiji Bureau of Statistics (accessed 31 March 2022).

This chapter was written by Isoa Wainiqolo of the South Pacific Subregional Office, ADB, Suva, and Noel Del Castillo, consultant, Pacific Department, ADB, Manila.

Border reopening to selected tourist markets on 1 December 2021 provided hope for recovery. This was possible after the authorities managed to keep hospitalization rates in check, supported by high vaccination rates in the adult population. By the end of 2021, 92% of the eligible population had been fully vaccinated. Visitor arrivals from Australia and the US in December 2021 were about half of arrivals from those markets in December 2019.

Consumption improved in 2021 from a low base, buoyed by government support packages and record high 14.6% growth in remittances. Sales of new vehicles rose by 20.9%. New commercial bank lending for consumption reversed 27.2% credit contraction in 2020 with growth by 17.2%, signaling renewed business confidence. New investment lending reversed a 24.9% decline in 2020 to increase by 7.8%, the bulk of it going to building and construction.

The fiscal deficit almost doubled to equal 10.8% of GDP in fiscal year 2021 (FY2021, ended 31 July 2021), with a 21.1% decline in revenue (Figure 3.33.3). While the government sustained its COVID-19 response stimulus, tight control on spending and lower interest costs under concessional debt terms lowered expenditure by 4.9%. As a result, public debt rose to equal 79.0% of GDP. Nontax revenue increased by 40% on one-off divestment proceeds from Energy Fiji Limited and high budget-support grants from Australia, New Zealand, and the European Union.

Figure 3.33.3 Fiscal deficit and public debt

The pandemic has widened the deficit and raised public debt.

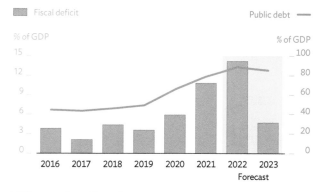

GDP = gross domestic product.
Note: Years are fiscal years ending 31 July of that year.
Sources: Fiji Ministry of Economy; Reserve Bank of Fiji.

Commercial bank liquidity improved further, benefiting from high foreign reserves. Private demand for credit, spurred by lower lending interest rates, reversed a 3% contraction in credit to the private sector in 2020 with marginal growth.

Deflation by 2.6% in 2020 yielded to inflation by a scant 0.2% in 2021 (Figure 3.33.4). Adverse weather early in the year drove up prices for domestically grown vegetables, while supply constraints and high fuel and food prices raised import costs.

Figure 3.33.4 Inflation

Rising global prices will drive domestic inflation.

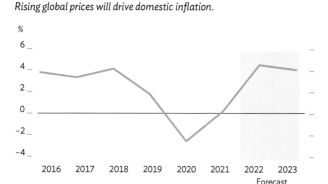

Sources: Fiji Bureau of Statistics (accessed 31 March 2022);
Asian Development Bank estimates.

Despite a wider deficit in goods trade, the current account deficit narrowed slightly to equal 11.9% of GDP as remittance inflows reached another record in 2021 (Figure 3.33.5). While exports increased by 5.2% with higher exports of mineral water and woodchips, imports increased by 11.7%, led by chemicals, machinery and transport equipment, and food. Tourism earnings remained depressed under prolonged border closure.

Economic prospects

The economy is projected to recover, growing by 7.1% in 2022 and 8.5% in 2023 (Table 3.33.1). Border reopening in December 2021 is expected to spur tourism, which remains key to a quick economic turnaround and restored employment, but international competition among travel destinations is likely to be intense.

Figure 3.33.5 Current account balance

Strong remittance inflow tempered a current account deficit worsened by a lack of tourist.

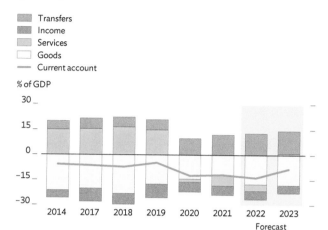

GDP = gross domestic product.
Sources: Fiji Bureau of Statistics (accessed on 31 March 2022); Asian Development Bank estimates.

Table 3.33.1 Selected economic indicators, %

Recovery is expected despite an uncertain global environment.

	2020	2021	2022	2023
GDP growth	−15.2	−4.1	7.1	8.5
Inflation	−2.6	0.2	4.5	4.0
CAB/GDP	−12.2	−11.9	−13.6	−8.3

CAB = current account balance, GDP = gross domestic product.
Source: Asian Development Bank estimates.

Since border reopening, the Government of Fiji has gradually eased travel restrictions, initially admitting travelers only from countries listed as travel partners but planning to reopen to all countries on 7 April 2022. Travelers only need to present negative COVID-19 test results (prior to departure and upon arrival in Fiji), travel insurance, and proof of vaccination. Fiji has a certification program for accommodation and tour operators to reassure travelers and better contain any imported COVID-19 cases. Monthly visitor arrivals since border reopening suggest that 2022 annual arrivals may reach half of 2019 numbers, rising by the end of 2023 to three-quarters. Recovery in Australian visitors is particularly important, but progress will differ by source location according to their travel restrictions.

Inflation is projected to surge to 4.5% in 2022 as the Russian invasion of Ukraine pushes up global commodity prices, most notably of oil and wheat, and consequently affects prices for other imported goods. Prices will remain elevated in 2023. Domestically, even regulated prices are likely to rise with pass through of higher import prices and shipping constraints. Sugar warehouse prices increased by about 60% year on year in the first quarter of 2022, and flour warehouse prices rose by 21% in the same period.

The government has budgeted a higher fiscal deficit equal to 14.2% of GDP in FY2022 and a deficit only a third as large in FY2023. As a result, debt is forecast to surge to 88.6% of GDP in FY2022 before subsiding to 85.3% in FY2023. This necessitates significant fiscal consolidation notwithstanding uncertainty surrounding the pandemic and, as always, any future extreme weather events. Revenue performance in the first half of FY2022 was on target, but less-productive public outlays may still need to be reviewed.

The current account deficit is projected to widen to equal 13.6% of GDP in 2022 on elevated prices for commodity imports and on high demand for goods and services that are inputs for tourism. While remittance income may counter the widening of the trade deficit, the current account in 2023 will depend as well on recovery in tourism earnings and global oil price movements.

Policy challenge—repairing the fiscal gap

Fiji's fiscal position deteriorated as the pandemic unfolded and its tourism-dependent economy was forced to close its borders. Revenue dropped substantially in 2020 and 2021, mainly reflecting contraction in tax revenue. As the government rolls out its economic recovery plan, starting with the gradual resumption of tourism, rebuilding the country's fiscal position will ensure its sustainability under future weather or external shocks.

The government needs to adjust its fiscal stance to address persistent deficits that predate COVID-19. According to the International Monetary Fund, the government could lift revenue as a percentage of GDP by 4.3 percentage points from FY2023 to FY2026 by rationalizing tax holidays, adjusting upward selected tax and excise rates, broadening the tax base, and improving revenue collection. Further significant deficit reduction could be achieved in the medium term by unwinding some pandemic-related tax relief measures.

On the expenditure side, as economic activity picks up the government can consider a measured phasing out of pandemic-response transfers, such as the unemployment assistance scheme, which would temper recurrent spending and narrow the deficit. New expenditure should be closely scrutinized alongside existing priorities, with reallocation favored over higher aggregate expenditure.

Regarding debt, a surge in contingent liabilities during the pandemic requires close monitoring. While the government has made important progress in reform to state-owned enterprises, a recent increase in sovereign guarantees held by some of them, particularly Fiji Airways and Fiji Development Bank, could pose fiscal risks, especially if recovery turns out to be slower than expected. The government should plan responses to contingent liabilities that threaten to drain public funds.

PAPUA NEW GUINEA

Growth returned in 2021 but was dampened by two COVID-19 surges worsened by a very low vaccination rate. Some relief came from strong commodity prices and fiscal stimulus sustained by development partners. Elections in 2022 will occasion additional spending, and higher mining output from the second half should accelerate growth. Rising commodity prices in 2022 will buoy the current account and inflation, both subsiding somewhat in 2023. An expanded revenue base would support economic recovery.

Economic performance

Following contraction in 2020, the economy returned to growth in 2021 but only at an estimated 1.3% (Figure 3.34.1). Two large surges of COVID-19 during the year significantly restrained economic recovery. The first was from February to July, and the second, attributed to the Delta variant of COVID-19, ran from September until late December. As of early March 2022, 41,533 cases of COVID-19 and 638 deaths had been reported. While no national lockdowns were imposed during the year, some regional lockdowns affected provinces whose health services had become overwhelmed. Travel restrictions were imposed, and for much of the year incoming travelers were required to quarantine for 2 weeks. The first vaccines were administered in March 2021, but the rollout was hampered by a weak delivery system and prevalent reluctance to be inoculated, such that less than 3% of the population of Papua New Guinea (PNG) was fully vaccinated by the end of 2021.

Having contracted by 21.1% in 2020, mining and quarrying contracted further by an estimated 12.5% in 2021. Porgera, the second-largest gold mine in the country, remained shut for all of 2021, having closed in April 2020 after its mining license was not renewed. Other big mines reduced production in the face of operational challenges, including COVID-19, among them the Ok Tedi gold and copper mine and the Lihir gold mine. Lihir is the largest gold mine in PNG,

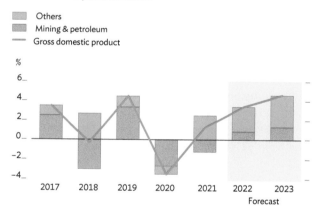

Figure 3.34.1 Gross domestic product growth

Growth was dampened by two surges of COVID-19, but is expected to accelerate to the forecast horizon.

Source: Asian Development Bank estimates using data from Papua New Guinea National Statistical Office.

contributing in 2019 about 40% of the country's gold production, but saw gold output fall by 14% from 2020 to 2021. Petroleum was broadly flat, with liquefied natural gas output in 2021 little changed from 2020 and oil production only slightly higher.

Agriculture, forestry, and fisheries expanded by an estimated 3.7% in 2021, largely reflecting recovery from a low base in 2020, when output was hampered by lockdowns and trade bottlenecks.

This chapter was written by Edward Faber and Magdelyn Kuari of the Papua New Guinea Resident Mission, ADB, Port Moresby.

Increased production of palm oil, cocoa, and coffee was stimulated by rising global commodity prices and the resolution of trade bottlenecks. Log and fish production changed little from 2020.

Growth in the rest of the economy was generally weak. Having contracted significantly in 2020, transport and storage services and accommodation and food services recovered only marginally in 2021 as COVID-19 continued to affect business travel and tourism and deter investment. However, construction, which had been hampered in 2020 by lockdowns and travel restrictions, picked up as government capital expenditure rose from the equivalent of 8.1% of GDP in 2020 to 8.5% in 2021.

The fiscal deficit in 2021 equaled 7.1% of GDP, according to a 2022 national budget document released by the Department of Treasury in November 2021. The final deficit may exceed this amount, however, considering a tendency to underbudget in certain areas, including public sector wages.

Inflation averaged 4.5% in 2021 but stood at 5.7% year on year in December 2021 (Figure 3.34.2). Transportation costs increased by 7.7% in the year to December, and education costs jumped by 20.0% as the government introduced tuition fees in public schools. Food prices increased by 5.2%, mostly reflecting higher prices for edible oils, led by cooking oil, which jumped by 35.6%. By contrast, rent slipped by 0.6% and, with greater competition in the marketplace because of new entrants, communication costs fell by 2.5%.

Figure 3.34.2 Inflation

Inflation remained high, driven by rising commodity prices.

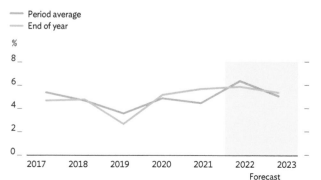

Source: Asian Development Bank estimates using data from Papua New Guinea National Statistical Office.

The current account surplus expanded from the equivalent of 20.2% of GDP in 2020 to 22.0% in 2021 (Figure 3.34.3). Exports saw gains with higher prices for palm oil, copper, and oil, which offset weaker mineral output, while imports decreased, reflecting weak investment.

Figure 3.34.3 Current account balance

Exports and imports alike fell in 2021 as percentages of GDP, but the large current account surplus was little changed.

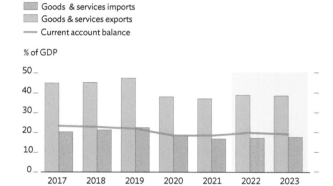

GDP = gross domestic product.
Sources: Bank of Papua New Guinea; Asian Development Bank estimates.

Economic prospects

Growth is expected to accelerate steadily to 3.4% in 2022 and 4.6% in 2023 as activity in mineral extraction picks up and more normal global economic conditions return (Table 3.34.1). The Porgera gold mine, which contributed about 28% of the country's annual gold production before it closed, is expected to reopen in the second half of 2022 and ramp up production only later. Its effect on GDP will therefore be greater in 2023 than in 2022. Papua LNG, a long-awaited liquefied natural gas project, is expected to proceed to its front-end engineering and design phase in the middle of 2022, but project expenditure within PNG during this first phase may not be large. A final investment decision should be made in the second half of 2023, when construction is expected to commence. Several other large resource projects are on the horizon. The P'nyang gas field project is a multibillion-dollar investment, as is the Wafi Golpu gold and copper mine, but its timing remains uncertain.

From the outset of 2022, however, the economy has been weighed down by the Omicron variant of COVID-19, which appeared in PNG in January. If experience elsewhere is a guide, its effects should dissipate fairly quickly, allowing a return to more normal conditions from sometime in the second quarter. In February, the PNG authorities ended quarantine requirements for incoming travelers who are fully vaccinated.

Table 3.34.1 Selected economic indicators, %

Growth is projected to gradually accelerate.

	2020	2021	2022	2023
GDP growth	–3.5	1.3	3.4	4.6
Inflation	4.9	4.5	6.4	5.1
CAB/GDP	20.2	22.0	26.5	22.1

CAB = current account balance, GDP = gross domestic product.
Source: Asian Development Bank estimates.

Uptake of COVID-19 vaccines in PNG is unlikely to improve significantly in 2022, so the vast majority of the population will remain unvaccinated. These conditions could discourage overseas arrivals, but commercial investors are unlikely to be deterred as they are already used to dealing with many challenges in PNG.

National and local government elections are scheduled for the middle of 2022. Significant expenditure will accompany the election period as spending is ramped up in provinces to improve services and infrastructure and as aspiring candidates fork out on rallies and other events to win votes. The government has pledged an additional K600 million for the election to cover security arrangements, logistics, and polling. Providers of accommodation and food services and of transportation services are expected to benefit.

Inflation is expected to gather pace in 2022 as the Russian invasion of Ukraine pushes up commodity prices and in particular oil prices. Inflation should moderate in 2023 as commodity prices cool and global economic conditions normalize.

The current account surplus is forecast to widen to the equivalent of 26.5% of GDP in 2022, driven up by rising commodity prices and reopening of the Porgera mine. Then it is seen narrowing somewhat to 22.1% in 2023 as import volume picks up to supply increased

investment and as, geopolitical events permitting, commodity prices cool.

The 2022 national budget forecasts a fiscal deficit equal to 5.9% of GDP in 2022 and 4.4% in 2023 (Figure 3.34.4). Raising sufficient revenue and other financing to execute the budget in 2022 will be a challenge. Revenue should, however, find support in higher oil and gas prices, particularly taxes and dividends paid by the PNG LNG project. The Department of Treasury forecasts that accumulated national debt will rise to equal 51.9% of GDP in 2022 and 52.5% in 2023.

Figure 3.34.4 Fiscal balance

Debt levels should stabilize if the government can meet its fiscal consolidation targets.

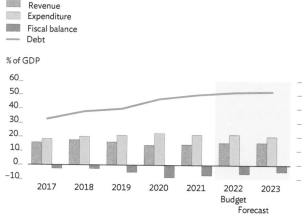

GDP = gross domestic product.
Source: Papua New Guinea Department of Treasury.

Policy challenge—expanding the revenue base to support economic recovery

The ratio of tax to GDP in PNG has followed a declining trend, falling from 18.6% in 2013 to 13.0% in 2019, before the pandemic, and then further to 11.5% in 2020 and 11.7% in 2021 (Figure 3.34.5). These ratios are well below norms in Asia and the Pacific, where the average ratio in 2019 was 14.6% in Southeast Asia, 14.9% in South Asia, and 22.9% in the Pacific. Compared with other low-income, resource-rich developing countries in 2019, however—11.5% in Gabon, 13.8% in Brazil, 9.4% in Angola, and 9.3% in Equatorial Guinea—the PNG ratio is fairly typical.

Figure 3.34.5 Ratio of tax revenue to GDP

The ratio of tax revenue to GDP is lower in PNG than in most other countries in Asia and the Pacific.

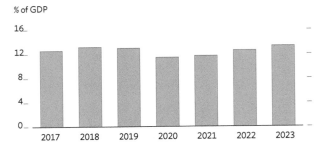

% of GDP

GDP = gross domestic product.
Source: Papua New Guinea Department of Treasury.

The PNG tax take from mineral and petroleum companies is notably low. Only 7.0% of all tax revenue in 2019, equal to 0.6% of GDP, came from mining and petroleum companies in the form of corporate taxes. This had fallen to 4.8% by 2021.

Aside from tax revenue, PNG benefits from nontax revenue, including income from state-owned enterprises, authorities, and investments, that averaged the equivalent of 1.4% of GDP from 2017 to 2021. It also receives grants, which annually averaged 2.0% of GDP over the same period.

A taxation review commissioned by the government and released in 2015 identified core taxation challenges for PNG: (i) too much reliance on personal income tax, (ii) too narrow a tax base and resulting reliance on high rates for corporate and personal income tax, (iii) outdated and unclear tax legislation, (iv) overused tax discretionary incentives, (v) overly generous use of stability contracts in resource development projects, and (v) a tax administration system ill-suited for business growth and development.

In response to these challenges, the authorities developed with support from the International Monetary Fund the Medium-Term Revenue Strategy, 2018–2022. It targeted three strategic reforms: (i) amend tax policy to broaden the tax base and address distortions, (ii) modernize and simplify tax legislation, and (iii) improve tax administration and compliance.

As a first step, a steering committee was established to lead the implementation of reform, starting with establishing the Revenue Policy Branch within the Department of Treasury.

To strengthen tax compliance and administration, an office for large taxpayers was created in 2018. PNG customs underwent several administrative changes to boost tax collection, notably through stiffer enforcement and a crackdown on trade in illicit goods. The Customs Act was amended in 2020 to increase penalties for traders evading tax.

The Tax Administration Act, 2017 was introduced to clarify tax laws and require taxpayers to apply for a tax identification number. Further, significant revision to the Income Tax Act intends to simplify tax compliance, in part by introducing a simple tax for small businesses.

It is important for PNG to sustain momentum toward tax system reform. A new medium-term revenue strategy, 2023–2027 is due for development to guide reform. Strong leadership is needed, both political and in the bureaucracy, to ensure that sufficient attention and resources are directed toward its development and implementation. Continued support from international partners is also essential.

Revenue collection can be improved and sustained by adopting international best practices and tax standards, including doing away with discretionary exemptions and tax concessions; expanding revenue agencies' investment in technology; and implementing effective revenue legislation and policy.

Finally, PNG must continue to consider carefully how best to tax mineral and petroleum companies, and it should seek the best international advice available.

SOLOMON ISLANDS

The economy contracted for a second year in 2021, buffeted by civil unrest and disruption to travel and trade from the pandemic. A weak economy brought deflation and expanded the current account deficit. Contraction is expected to deepen in 2022 as inflation returns and the current account deficit widens further, followed by modest growth in 2023. Forecasts assume continued easing of COVID-19 restrictions and implementation of major infrastructure projects. Financial sector development and inclusion could support long-term economic recovery.

Economic performance

Economic contraction eased from 4.5% in 2020 to 0.5% in 2021 as weak expansion in industry could not compensate for contraction in agriculture and services (Table 3.35.1). In industry, recovery in construction returned the sector to growth despite a decline in mining output. In agriculture, continued decline in logging output overwhelmed recovery in fish and crop production. In services, contraction was led by wholesale and retail trade and by transport.

Table 3.35.1 Selected economic indicators, %

Economic growth is expected to return only in 2023, after 3 years of contraction.

	2020	2021	2022	2023
GDP growth	-4.5	-0.5	-3.0	3.0
Inflation	3.0	-0.2	5.0	4.0
CAB/GDP	-1.7	-6.0	-12.0	-12.5

CAB = current account balance, GDP = gross domestic product.
Source: Asian Development Bank estimates.

In November 2021, political and socioeconomic tensions came to a boil in 3 days of civil unrest in which buildings in the wholesale and retail district of the capital, Honiara, were burned and three people died. Peacekeepers from neighboring countries flew in to help restore order. Physical damage from the unrest was estimated in the range of $66 million–$87 million, equal to 4.3%–5.6% of GDP.

Logging output fell by an estimated 14.0% to 2.0 million cubic meters in 2021 (Figure 3.35.1). This decline was even sharper than the 12.5% decrease in 2020. Despite output declines for 3 consecutive years, logging remained well above what is believed to be environmentally sustainable. The fish catch rebounded from a 40.4% plunge in 2020 with 18.3% growth in 2021.

Figure 3.35.1 Logging output and fish catch

A decline in log output continued, but the fish catch rebounded strongly in 2021.

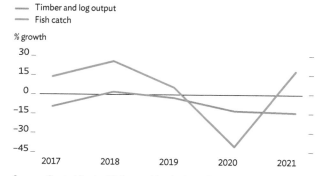

Source: Central Bank of Solomon Islands; Asian Development Bank estimates.

This chapter was written by Jacqueline Connell of the Pacific Liaison and Coordination Office, ADB, Sydney, and Prince Cruz, consultant, Pacific Department, ADB, Manila.

The fiscal deficit expanded from the equivalent of 2.4% of GDP in 2020 to an estimated 3.2% in 2021 (Figure 3.35.2). Expenditure was little changed from 2020, but revenue fell by an estimated 2.6%. The fall in export duties on logs deepened, from 18% in 2020 to a further contraction of 21% in 2021. The government implemented a freeze on hiring from the start of 2021, leaving the public wage bill almost unchanged from 2020. Public external debt rose from the equivalent of 8.4% of GDP in 2020 to 10.7% in 2021.

Figure 3.35.2 Fiscal balance by component

The fiscal deficit expanded in 2021 as tax and nontax revenue declined.

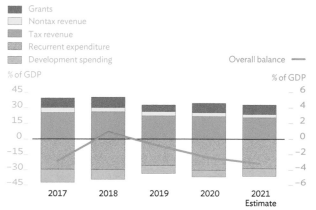

GDP = gross domestic product.
Source: Asian Development Bank estimates using data from budget documents and the International Monetary Fund.

Inflation of 3.0% in 2020 yielded to 0.2% deflation in 2021 (Figure 3.35.3). The consumer price index fell by 0.9% in the first 3 quarters as the weak economy dragged down demand. Prices for food and beverages, alcoholic beverages and tobacco, and health services were lower in 2021 than in 2020, while rates for domestic water, electricity, and gas utilities rose, as did transportation prices.

In its September 2021 monetary policy decision, the Central Bank of Solomon Islands maintained its expansionary stance adopted in March 2020. Money supply increased by 5.0% in 2021, while credit to the private sector rose by 1.7%, mainly on higher personal loans.

Lower exports of logs and minerals were mostly responsible for widening the current account deficit

Figure 3.35.3 Inflation

Inflation is forecast to rise in 2022 on higher commodity prices and COVID-19 disruption to supply chains.

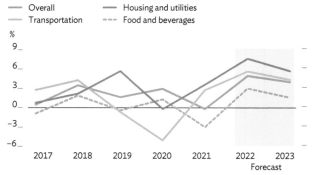

Sources: Solomon Islands National Statistics Office; Asian Development Bank estimates.

from the equivalent of 1.7% of GDP in 2020 to 6.0%. Imports rose on orders of machinery and transport equipment and manufactured goods, though imports of food, fuel, beverages, and tobacco declined. Remittances increased, and by the end of 2021 rising gross international reserves were sufficient to cover 14.2 months of imports of goods and services.

Economic prospects

After containment measures kept COVID-19 at bay for almost 2 years, community transmission of the virus broke out in January 2022. Even with vaccination mandated for frontline workers and public employees, including those of state-owned enterprises, only 8.8% of the population had received two doses by 4 January and only 27.0% one dose. The domestic outbreak that followed consequently strained the health-care system as the number of cases reached 10,204 by 22 March, causing 128 deaths. Yet, even with some improvement spurred by local transmission, the vaccination rate remained low at the end of February, with only 13.5% of the population having received two doses and 29.3% one dose. The government has set July 2022 for reopening international borders following efficient and effective vaccination rollout.

The economy is expected to contract again by 3.0% in 2022 because of restrictions on mobility and domestic transportation imposed in response to COVID-19 community transmission in the first quarter and lingering health impacts (Figure 3.35.4). While logging output is projected to continue to decline in 2023, fragile economic recovery by 3.0% is expected as COVID-19 restrictions ease, buoyed by higher construction, fishing, and mining.

Figure 3.35.4 Supply-side contributions to GDP growth

Community transmission since January and resulting restrictions will cause further economic contraction in 2022.

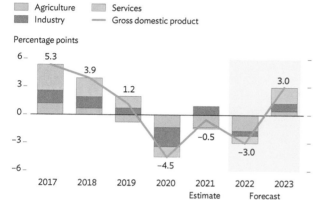

GDP = gross domestic product.

Source: Solomon Islands National Statistics Office; Asian Development Bank estimates.

The need to rebuild infrastructure damaged during unrest in 2021 extends the construction pipeline beyond development projects and infrastructure for the Pacific Games in 2023. However, protracted mobility and border restrictions could further stall large infrastructure projects that rely on foreign experts and workers and imported materials, posing a downside risk to the outlook.

The passage of the 2022 budget has been deferred from December to April, as was the 2021 budget. The proposed budget, formulated before COVID-19 arrived in the community, targets a 2022 fiscal deficit equal to 2.1% of GDP. It will likely go higher, though, with elevated government spending for health care, virus containment, and support for economic revival, combined with a trend suggesting weakened revenue because of COVID-19 disruption. Public debt is thus expected to rise over the forecast period to finance persistent fiscal deficits and infrastructure projects.

Inflation is expected to accelerate to 5.0% in 2022 on international prices for fuel and other commodities pushed up in part by the Russian invasion of Ukraine, before easing slightly to 4.0% in 2023. Supply bottlenecks arising from COVID-19 restrictions likely made the situation worse in the first quarter of 2022.

The current account deficit is forecast to widen to the equivalent of 12.0% of GDP in 2022 and 12.5% in 2023 as exports suffer under virus containment measures while imports accelerate, notably of health supplies and materials for construction projects (Figure 3.35.5). Strong remittance inflows are expected to continue with the expansion of seasonal worker programs in Australia and New Zealand. Higher grant inflows in 2022 in response to the pandemic will cushion the current account and keep the deficit from increasing even further.

Figure 3.35.5 Current account balance by component

The current account deficit is forecast to expand in 2022 on higher medical imports while exports fall.

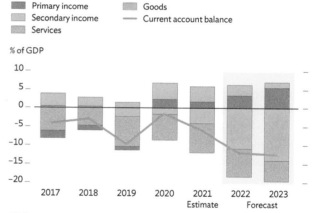

GDP = gross domestic product.

Source: Asian Development Bank estimates using data from the Central Bank of Solomon Islands.

Policy challenge—supporting financial service development and inclusion

Dispersed population in Solomon Islands poses challenges for financial services. Traditional banking measures, such as the number of commercial bank branches per person, are low compared with regional peers (Figure 3.35.6). Further, the central bank

Figure 3.35.6 Access to commercial banking services, 2020

Access to financial services is poor as the country has fewer than four bank branches and 15 ATMS per 100,000 adults.

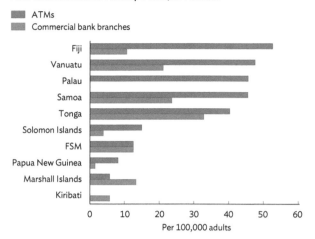

ATM = automated teller machine, FSM = Federated States of Micronesia.
Source: World Development Indicators (access 22 February 2022).

Figure 3.35.7 Commercial bank loans, 2020

Bank loans equaled only 16.5% of GDP in Solomon Islands, indicating an underdeveloped financial market.

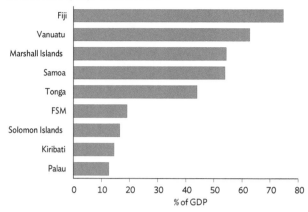

FSM = Federated States of Micronesia, GDP = gross domestic product.
Source: International Monetary Fund Financial Access Survey database (access 22 February 2022).

reported that more than two-thirds of the country's financial access points were in Honiara in 2020, while provisional census data show 82% of the population in 2019 residing outside of the capital, spread across nine provinces. This indicates a rural–urban divide.

Aside from physical access challenges, financial institutions are often reluctant to extend credit because of perceived high risk and the inability of most low-income households to meet loan requirements. The high cost of debt recovery and low recovery rates can induce lenders to demand highly liquid collateral, which is difficult for borrowers to provide. In 2020, commercial bank loans equaled only 16.5% of GDP, one of the lowest ratios in the Pacific (Figure 3.35.7). Growth in commercial bank credit averaged only 3.1% in the past 5 years. The 2021 International Monetary Fund Article IV staff report concluded, meanwhile, that stronger growth in private sector credit is needed to support post-pandemic recovery.

The government launched its third National Financial Inclusion Strategy in April 2021. The aim is to increase the number of adults with access to formal credit from 28,890 in 2020 to 48,000 in 2025. The strategy calls for policy and legal changes to extend the reach and improve the quality of digital financial

services by utilizing recent improvements in internet connectivity and mobile phone network coverage.

The government has begun to modernize its financial sector legislation with a bill on national payment systems that paves the way for digital payment infrastructure. This could especially benefit rural residents who must otherwise travel great distances to banks and government agencies to process transactions. By using digital technology, financial services can be extended to rural communities at lower cost, enabling bank branches to serve more customers and thereby improving financial inclusion. Further reform is needed to allow more efficient allocation of capital across the economy while minimizing risks to consumers and the financial sector.

To strengthen credit growth, continued efforts are needed to improve financial literacy alongside reform to enforce debt collection and make commercial and nonbank financial institutions more willing to lend. The government's reestablishment of the Development Bank of Solomon Islands and such public–private partnerships as youSave LoMobile could extend services to rural communities. Ensuring adequate governance arrangements and commercial orientation will be crucial, however, to minimize fiscal risk to the government.

VANUATU

Despite a rebound in agriculture and construction, the economy continued to contract in 2021, though less than in 2020. Inflation slowed as supply chain disruption was resolved, but the current account balance slipped into deficit as exports of services fell further. Recovery will be weak in 2022 as domestic COVID-19 transmission is likely to delay any reopening of international borders. The current account deficit is expected to persist as imports rise. Fiscal sustainability is needed to ensure resilient recovery.

Economic performance

After a sharp decline in 2020, the economy contracted by a further 1.0% in 2021 (Table 3.36.1). While some sectors recovered, the border remained closed, causing continued decline in tourism. This was reflected in exports of services, which have fallen from a peak equal to 40.3% of GDP in 2018 to 12.4% in 2020 and only 5.1% estimated in 2021 (Figure 3.36.1).

Agriculture expanded with better weather than in 2020, when Cyclone Harold pummeled the sector, and probably ample labor as tourism workers turned to farming and fishing. Cocoa output doubled as copra output increased by a quarter and beef production increased by almost a tenth. Sawn timber became the third largest export after kava and copra. Kava exports, which accounted for more than half of exports in 2018-2020, fell by 18% in volume.

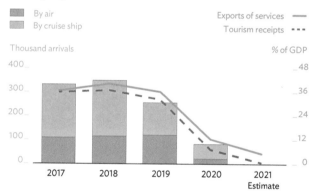

Figure 3.36.1 Visitor arrivals and exports of services

With international borders closed, tourism receipts dried up as visitor arrivals plunged.

GDP = gross domestic product.
Sources: Reserve Bank of Vanuatu; Vanuatu National Statistics Office; World Development Indicators; Asian Development Bank estimates.

Table 3.36.1 Selected economic indicators, %

Higher global fuel prices are forecast to push inflation and the current account deficit higher in 2022.

	2020	2021	2022	2023
GDP growth	-7.5	-1.0	1.0	4.0
Inflation	5.3	2.1	4.8	3.2
CAB/GDP	1.9	-7.0	-10.0	-7.0

CAB = current account balance, GDP = gross domestic product.
Source: Asian Development Bank estimates.

Despite continuing disruption under the pandemic, construction increased as the government allowed technical experts to enter the country to resume large infrastructure projects. Imports of machinery and transport equipment revived from 17% decline in 2020 to expand by 20% in 2021.

The fiscal deficit widened to the equivalent of 3.0% of GDP as expenditure growth outpaced a rise in revenue and grants (Figure 3.36.2). Current expenditure rose,

This chapter was written by Jacqueline Connell of the Pacific Liaison and Coordination Office, ADB, Sydney, and Prince Cruz, consultant, Pacific Department, ADB, Manila.

Figure 3.36.2 Fiscal balance and components

The fiscal deficit deepened in 2021 as nontax revenue fell while current expenditure rose.

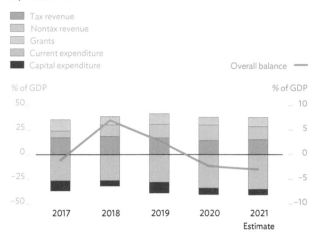

GDP = gross domestic product.
Sources: Government of Vanuatu budget documents, Asian Development Bank estimates.

Figure 3.36.3 Inflation

Inflation slowed in 2021 as food prices stabilized following a spike in the wake of Cyclone Harold.

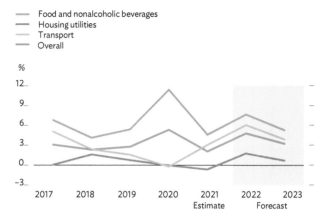

Sources: Vanuatu National Statistics Office; Asian Development Bank estimates.

led by employee compensation and then goods and services. Even with a second stimulus package— announced in May and comprising wage subsidies and small business grants—combined subsidies, transfers, and grants fell from their record in 2020. Increases in taxes and grants compensated for the drop in nontax revenue, mainly from honorary citizenship programs.

Inflation slowed from a 29-year peak of 5.3% in 2020 to 2.1% in 2021 as food supply constraints eased (Figure 3.36.3). Food inflation dropped by more than half from 11.4% in 2020 to 4.6%. Several items in the consumer basket registered deflation, including clothing, housing utilities, health care, and communication. Transport inflation revived, however, reversing 0.2% deflation in 2020 with a 3.1% rise reflecting higher global fuel prices.

The current account swung from a surplus equal to 1.9% of GDP in 2020 to a 7.0% deficit in 2021 as receipts from honorary citizenships fell and exports of services continued to decline with lower visitor arrivals. Exports of goods and services dropped by an estimated 35% while imports rose by 38%. In agriculture, higher export earnings from copra, beef, sawn timber, cocoa, and coconut oil offset the drop in the value of kava exports. Imports of goods rose on higher purchases of machinery and transport equipment, fuel, beverages, and tobacco. Remittances from participants in

seasonal worker programs in Australia and New Zealand continued to increase. At the end of 2021, international reserves provided cover for 12 months of imports, triple the 4-month target set by the Reserve Bank of Vanuatu, the central bank.

Economic prospects

Vanuatu reported its first community transmission of COVID-19 on 5 March 2022 and has since imposed containment measures, weighing on domestic demand and supply chains. With border reopening unlikely before the second half of 2022, the economy is projected to grow by only 1.0% in 2022, accelerating to 4.0% in 2023 with gradual revival in tourism and continued expansion in agriculture and construction (Figure 3.36.4).

Before the local outbreak, the government had targeted reopening borders when 90% of the adult population had received at least one vaccination dose and 70% two doses. While the target has been met in Port Vila, Luganville, and surrounding provinces, as of 13 March only 74% of adults nationwide had at least one dose and 53% two doses. With COVID-19 cases numbering 959 on 22 March, a state of public health emergency was scheduled to remain in effect until July 2022.

Significantly delayed border reopening would increase the risk of economic scarring as tourism businesses close and former employees shift to other pursuits.

Figure 3.36.4 Supply-side contributions to growth

Growth will be fragile in 2022 under indefinite border closure to contain COVID-19.

- Agriculture
- Industry
- Public services
- Other services
— Gross domestic product

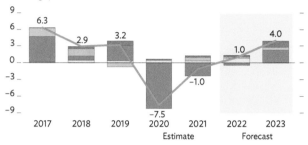

Percentage points

Sources: Vanuatu National Statistics Office; Asian Development Bank estimates.

While high vaccination rates and easing restrictions in the main source markets of Australia and New Zealand bode well for revived tourism, low health-care capacity in Vanuatu raises concerns, as do dim prospects for sustained business services during lockdowns. Only 17% of companies surveyed in October 2021 by the Vanuatu Chamber of Commerce indicated they would likely continue operating in a lockdown lasting 2 weeks, while 42% indicated that they would cease operations.

More positively, strong growth in beef and crop production and the fish catch is expected to boost agriculture. Kava exports are expected to rebound after Australia allowed commercial imports in late 2021.

Industry is expected to expand as construction gains momentum on public infrastructure projects that were suspended in 2021. The possibility of prolonged pandemic-related restrictions poses a risk to the outlook because the execution of Vanuatu's public infrastructure pipeline, which includes energy, roads, and post-cyclone reconstruction projects, hinges on the availability of imported materials and international project experts.

In its 2022 budget, the government planned a fiscal deficit equal to 4.5% of GDP, financed by cash reserves and loan drawdowns. Despite the deficit, the government expected external debt to remain below its targeted ceiling of 40% of GDP as it declines from 38.1% of GDP in 2021 to 36.4%

in 2023 (Figure 3.36.5). However, fiscal pressures could rise with lower revenue under a prolonged lockdown, any need to increase spending for health care and COVID-19 containment, or a recent Council of the European Union decision to suspend its visa waiver agreement for Vanuatu passport holders, which could reduce demand for honorary passports.

Figure 3.36.5 Government debt

External debt, equal to 38.1% of gross domestic product in 2021, is projected to remain close to the government's 40% threshold.

- External debt
- Domestic debt
— Total debt ceiling
--- External debt ceiling

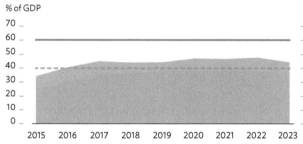

% of GDP

GDP = gross domestic product.
Note: Nominal debt figures (2015-2019 actual, 2020-2021 preliminary) and projections (2022-2023) are based on the 2022 national budget.
Sources: Government of Vanuatu budget documents; Asian Development Bank estimates.

With higher global commodity prices and supply chain disruption under the pandemic, inflation is expected to accelerate to 4.8% in 2022 before easing to 3.2% in 2023 (Table 3.36.1). Rapid increases in global fuel prices with the Russian invasion of Ukraine are expected to catalyze higher prices for food, which makes up 38% of the consumer basket; housing utilities, at 21% of the basket; and transport, at 7% of the basket.

Although remittances are expected to continue rising in 2022, falling revenue from honorary citizenships and more costly imports—including fuel, medical supplies and equipment, and construction materials—are projected to push the current account deficit wider to equal 10.0% of GDP in 2022. The deficit should narrow to 7.0% in 2023 as tourism revives (Figure 3.36.6).

Figure 3.36.6 Current account balance

The trade deficit will remain large in 2022, widening the current account deficit.

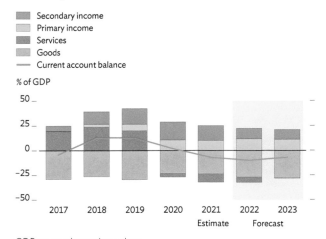

GDP = gross domestic product.
Sources: Reserve Bank of Vanuatu; Vanuatu National Statistics Office; Asian Development Bank estimates.

Figure 3.36.7 Revenue and grants, by source

Revenue from honorary citizenship programs remained the biggest source of revenue despite a decline in 2021.

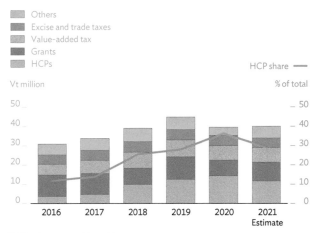

HCP = honorary citizenship program.
Sources: Government of Vanuatu budget documents; International Monetary Fund; Asian Development Bank estimates.

Policy challenge—ensuring fiscal sustainability for resilient recovery

Vanuatu entered the COVID-19 pandemic with significant cash reserves accumulated from fiscal surpluses in the 2 previous years. As taxes declined by 18.7% from economic contraction in 2020, receipts from honorary citizenship programs (HCPs), which offer passports in return for investment, offset lost revenue to some extent. HCPs have been the biggest revenue source since 2018, their contribution reaching 36% of total revenue and grants in 2020 before declining to 30% in 2021 (Figure 3.36.7).

A smaller HCP contribution in 2021 and the recent Council of the European Union decision raises concerns about HCP sustainability as a revenue source. The government has so far managed the volatility of HCPs by conservatively projecting revenue and then using any windfall to pay down debt, build cash reserves, and finance spending on disasters, including the pandemic. Beyond carefully managing revenue, efforts are needed to strengthen fiscal sustainability and support Vanuatu's economic recovery.

Expanding the tax base could help the government continue to achieve its fiscal target of a positive recurrent balance over the medium-term and reduce reliance on external revenue. In 2018, an increase in the value-added tax rate by 2.5 percentage points contributed to a 14.0% increase in tax revenue. In 2021, it appointed the National Revenue Governance Committee to develop policy options to broaden the revenue base. Further, it outlined a range of revenue options in its 2022 budget, including higher excise taxes on tobacco and sugary drinks. The International Monetary Fund estimates that the introduction of personal and corporate income taxes could increase government revenue by an amount equal to 2.5% of GDP, even with reduced collection of less efficient taxes. With careful design, any change to tax policy, including rates and the tax base, can minimize the burden on workers with low incomes and firms with low profit margins as the economy recovers.

As well as exploring revenue measures, it is crucial to ensure that government expenditure is efficient and well targeted, especially if the border closure is protracted and further stimulus is required. Developing a medium-term fiscal strategy could help the government to sequence reform and build capacity in the bureaucracy to administer the changes.

CENTRAL PACIFIC ECONOMIES

All three Central Pacific economies grew in 2021, supported by increased government spending and resumed infrastructure projects. Inflation was stable in Kiribati and Nauru but rose in Tuvalu because of a one-off adjustment following a new tax law. Growth is expected to be higher in 2022 in Kiribati and Tuvalu but decelerating in Nauru. Surging global oil prices will significantly affect inflation in these import-dependent economies. With very narrow economic bases, an enduring challenge is domestic resource mobilization for fiscal sustainability.

Kiribati

A return to modest growth at 1.5% in 2021 was supported by social protection spending equal to 31.5% of GDP (Figure 3.37.1). While nascent tourism had little to lose, business travel was curtailed by pandemic travel restrictions. Higher expenditure to mitigate impacts from COVID-19 lifted household income and domestic consumption. Economic activity increased with the resumption of smaller infrastructure projects that had been halted in 2020 by the pandemic.

The government's decision to keep its borders closed to visitors throughout 2021 prevented the entry of COVID-19 into Kiribati. The vaccination program currently under way has further mitigated risks. By 4 March 2022, over 70% of the eligible population had been fully vaccinated, with almost everyone else having received their first dose. However, an outbreak following border reopening on 10 January 2022 prompted the government to declare a state of disaster on 22 January, reimpose movement restrictions, and fine residents not adhering to prescribed public health measures to contain COVID-19. By 18 March, Kiribati had confirmed over 3,000 COVID-19 cases, 13 deaths, and 2,488 recoveries. Virus transmission in the community has slowed.

Economic growth is expected to accelerate to 1.8% in 2022 and 2.3% in 2023, supported by the government's vaccination program and incremental implementation of high-value infrastructure projects (Table 3.37.1).

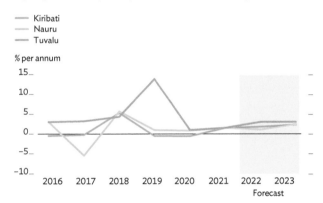

Figure 3.37.1 GDP growth in the Central Pacific

Higher government spending and investment sustained growth in 2021.

— Kiribati
— Nauru
— Tuvalu

% per annum

GDP = gross domestic product.
Note: Years are fiscal years ending on 30 June of that year in Nauru and coinciding with the calendar year in Kiribati and Tuvalu.
Sources: Kiribati budget documents; Nauru budget documents; Tuvalu budget documents; International Monetary Fund Article IV reports; Asian Development Bank estimates.

Downside risks to the forecast stem from the current COVID-19 outbreak or any future outbreak becoming unmanageable and jeopardizing the infrastructure pipeline.

Kiribati's fiscal surpluses in recent years were wiped out in 2021 as the country posted a fiscal deficit equal to 23.4% of GDP (Figure 3.37.2).

This chapter was written by Jacqueline Connell of the Pacific Liaison and Coordination Office, ADB, Sydney; Lily-Anne Homasi and Isoa Wainiqolo of the South Pacific Subregional Office, ADB, Suva; and Prince Cruz and Noel Del Castillo, consultants, Pacific Department, ADB, Manila.

Table 3.37.1 Selected economic indicators, %

Growth was steady in 2021 despite a surge in global prices for imports.

	2020	2021	2022	2023
Kiribati				
GDP growth	−0.5	1.5	1.8	2.3
Inflation	2.3	1.0	5.0	3.7
CAB/GDP	39.2	32.3	35.7	38.2
Nauru				
GDP growth	0.8	1.5	1.0	2.4
Inflation	0.9	1.2	2.3	2.2
CAB/GDP	2.8	4.1	...	...
Tuvalu				
GDP growth	1.0	1.5	3.0	3.0
Inflation	1.6	6.7	3.8	3.3
CAB/GDP	3.8	−1.8	−5.1	−1.2

... = not available, GDP = gross domestic product.
Source: Asian Development Bank estimates.

Figure 3.37.2 Fiscal balance

Increased spending on COVID-19 measures worsened fiscal outcomes in Kiribati and Tuvalu.

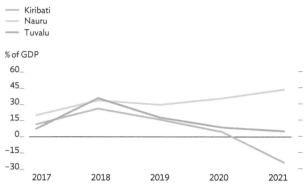

GDP = gross domestic product.
Note: Years are fiscal years ending on 30 June of that year in Nauru and coinciding with the calendar year in Kiribati and Tuvalu.
Sources: Kiribati budget documents; Nauru budget documents; Tuvalu budget documents; International Monetary Fund Article IV reports; Asian Development Bank estimates.

Figure 3.37.3 Fishing license revenue

Revenue from license fees and royalties dropped after the onset of the COVID-19 pandemic.

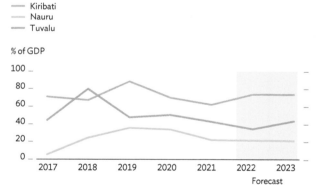

GDP = gross domestic product.
Note: Years are fiscal years ending on 30 June of that year in Nauru and coinciding with the calendar year in Kiribati and Tuvalu.
Sources: Kiribati budget documents; Nauru budget documents; Tuvalu budget documents; International Monetary Fund Article IV reports; Asian Development Bank estimates.

The government's COVID-19 response package saw spending on social protection jump by 128.9% as it continued to provide material support to residents while borders remained closed throughout 2021. Meanwhile, fishing revenue, bulk of which comes from fishing license fees, compounded an 18.7% contraction in 2020 with further decline by 10.1% in 2021. Insufficient numbers of I-Kiribati observers were available to verify the catch on each fishing vessel, and border restrictions delayed transshipment, depressing fishing receipts (Figure 3.37.3).

Tax revenue fell by 3.2% in 2021 with lower collection of personal income and excise taxes. While the government is expected to sustain its current spending for social protection, revenue from its principal source, fishing license fees, is forecast to bounce back in 2022, contributing to a fiscal surplus equal to 1.3% of GDP. A key need is to monitor fiscal risks posed by high social protection spending that depends on volatile revenue such as fishing fees, especially when tax collection is difficult and has a low base. Spending is currently high to support citizens affected by COVID-19 but is expected to decline as borders fully reopen.

Even as movement restrictions and supply disruption contributed to price increases for imported fuel, food and beverages, and alcohol and tobacco, inflation slowed to 1.0% in 2021 (Figure 3.37.4). It is expected to accelerate to 5.0% in 2022 as rising global prices affect prices for imported food, fuel, raw materials, and other commodities, then moderate in 2023 to 3.7% as supply chains normalize.

Figure 3.37.4 Inflation

Higher international prices for fuel are forecast to push inflation up in Nauru and Kiribati in 2022.

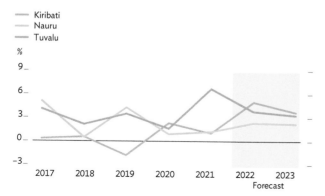

Note: Years are fiscal years ending on 30 June of that year in Nauru and coinciding with the calendar year in Kiribati and Tuvalu.

Sources: Kiribati budget documents; Nauru budget documents; Tuvalu budget documents; International Monetary Fund Article IV reports; Asian Development Bank estimates.

Figure 3.37.5 Current account balance

Current account surpluses fluctuate depending largely on grants and fishing license fees.

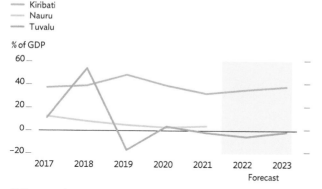

GDP = gross domestic product.

Note: Years are fiscal years ending on 30 June of that year in Nauru and coinciding with the calendar year in Kiribati and Tuvalu.

Sources: International Monetary Fund Article IV reports; Asian Development Bank estimates.

The current account surplus narrowed to equal 32.3% of GDP in 2021 with a higher trade deficit and lower fishing revenue (Figure 3.37.5). The surplus is expected to widen again in 2022 and 2023 as a rebound in fishing licenses outweighs higher imports for infrastructure projects.

Nauru

Growth accelerated to 1.5% in fiscal year 2021 (FY2021, ended 30 June 2021), supported by continued COVID-19 response measures (Figure 3.37.1). The resumption of construction projects, stalled by supply chain disruption and measures to keep out COVID-19, lifted economic activity in the fourth quarter. Growth is expected to ease to 1.0% in FY2022 as activity at the Regional Processing Centre (RPC) winds down, but activity related to infrastructure projects should reaccelerate growth to 2.4% in FY2023 (Table 3.37.1).

Border restrictions and quarantine measures have prevented COVID-19 community transmission. Businesses and public administration continue to operate without domestic lockdowns, while COVID-19 expenditure sustained regular air and sea freight and funded economic stimulus payments in FY2021. Following the achievement of near-universal adult vaccination against COVID-19 in 2021, boosters and first doses for adolescents aged 12 to 17 were rolled out in February 2022.

Despite domestic revenue falling by 5.3% in FY2021 as pandemic-induced disruption lowered inflows from fishing licenses, and visa fees tied to the RPC dropped, the fiscal surplus widened on higher grants from the equivalent of 35.7% of GDP in FY2020 to 43.8% in FY2021 (Figure 3.37.2). Most of the fiscal surplus was deposited in the Nauru Intergenerational Trust Fund, but the government also paid down significant long-standing liabilities, including defaulted bonds, having reached a settlement with creditors. This sharply lowered public external debt from the equivalent of 30.1% of GDP in FY2020 to 5.2% in FY2021.

The passage of two supplementary appropriation bills means higher projected expenditure in FY2022 than in FY2021. The increase is partly supported by additional revenue received under RPC extension. The fiscal surplus is forecast to narrow in FY2022, partly because of lower grants. External debt is expected to rise considerably in FY2022 as the government borrows to replace aircraft for its airline.

Inflation remained moderate at 1.2% in FY2021 (Figure 3.37 4). The government-owned airline and shipping line continued to supply goods to the country.

Inflation is expected to rise to 2.3% in FY2022 and 2.2% in FY2023 in tandem with higher global prices for fuel and other commodities. The current account surplus expanded in FY2021 with higher inflow from grants and exports of phosphate (Figure 3.37.5).

Tuvalu

Growth accelerated to 1.5% in 2021 as the country remained free of COVID-19 (Figure 3.37.1). Capital expenditure almost doubled, offsetting restrained consumption that saw tax revenue decline by a fifth. In the coming months, business travel and remittances are projected to return to their pre-pandemic levels in line with gradual opening of international borders, bringing GDP growth to 3.0% in both years (Table 3.37.1).

The fiscal surplus narrowed from the equivalent of 8.7% of GDP in 2020 to 5.4% in 2021 (Figure 3.37.2). As expenditure dropped by 13.0%, revenue fell by a similar magnitude, with fishing revenue contracting by 19.3% and tax revenue by 22.4%. The government has budgeted for a fiscal deficit equal to 9.7% of GDP in 2022, as 27.6% higher expenditure is expected to outweigh projected 10.6% higher revenue, mainly from license fees for the dot-TV web domain. Government staffing costs are budgeted to increase by 52.5%, after declining by 21% in 2021 with 69 new positions being filled and higher salaries for 177 civil servants.

Inflation is estimated to have surged to 6.7% in 2021 with the implementation of sin taxes at the start of the year (Figure 3.37.4). Passed in the 2021 budget, the taxes are designed to discourage consumption of alcohol, cigarettes, soft drinks, salted beef, lamb flaps, candy, and other consumables considered unhealthy, as duties on imports of goods such as fruits and vegetables are removed. An expected surge in global fuel prices is forecast to translate into 3.8% inflation in 2022, easing somewhat to 3.3% in 2023 as the impact from higher commodity prices lingers.

The current account slipped into deficit equal to 1.8% of GDP in 2021 as fishing revenue declined (Figure 3.37.5). Higher prices for imported goods with the surge in global oil prices are forecast to widen the current account deficit in 2022 before it narrows again in 2023.

Policy challenge—mobilizing domestic revenue sources

Government dependence on external revenue sources poses issues of fiscal sustainability, especially in light of their volatility in the Central Pacific (Figure 3.37.6). Regarding fisheries, for instance, the volatility of fish stocks makes it difficult to project license revenue from foreign fishing vessels and hampers efforts to produce a robust medium-term fiscal strategy. As government spending is a primary driver of economic activity in these economies, internal revenue sources need to be improved to more sustainably finance government expenditure.

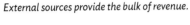

Figure 3.37.6 Revenue sources, average 2016–2020

External sources provide the bulk of revenue.

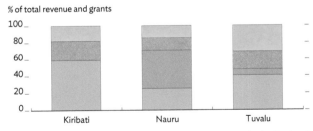

Notes: Other major sources of external revenue are primarily the Regional Processing Centre in Nauru (including reimbursement for operating expenses) and, in Tuvalu, dot-TV internet domain license fees and other commercial contracts. Years are fiscal years ending on 30 June of that year in Nauru and coinciding with the calendar year in Kiribati and Tuvalu.
Sources: Kiribati budget documents; Nauru budget documents; Tuvalu budget documents; International Monetary Fund Article IV reports; Asian Development Bank estimates.

As part of Kiribati's efforts to broaden its tax base, a bill amending the income tax law may improve revenue collection, as well as strengthening tax administration and compliance to plug tax leakage brought about by weak monitoring. Corporate tax revenue averaged only 3.8% of all revenue from 2016 to 2020. Sparse government tax audits of firms weaken its ability to enforce tax obligations and collect revenue. Higher tax compliance can be fostered by strengthening tax audit capacity and upgrading the tax monitoring and payment system.

Finally, the government should consider formulating a medium-term revenue strategy toward developing an overall framework for managing government revenue and supporting revenue mobilization.

In Nauru, the government has taken steps to broaden its revenue base, notably adopting a tax policy framework in 2014. An employment and services tax introduced in 2015 and a business profits tax introduced in 2016 together supplied 13.4% of all revenue in FY2016–FY2020. A tax-free threshold for Nauru citizens means that these taxes are collected mainly from RPC activity. The International Monetary Fund 2021 Article IV staff report on Nauru indicated that broadening the tax base could generate more reliable revenue. The government plans to upgrade its customs information system, and ongoing modernization of revenue administration promises to generate revenue more efficiently. Reform success depends critically on ensuring that tax changes and systems upgrades are appropriate and cost-effective in a microstate with capacity constraints.

In Tuvalu, where tax contributes little to revenue, a priority policy to increase the tax share would be to broaden the tax base and improve tax compliance, particularly from businesses. The 2021 Article IV staff report on Tuvalu found only 2 of 21 registered large taxpayers currently paying corporate tax.

From 2016 to 2019, corporate tax averaged only 1.9% of all revenue in Tuvalu. Broadening the tax base takes on additional importance in light of the Pacific Agreement on Closer Economic Relations Plus, which will lower earnings from import duties. Finally, capacity building and boosting staff resources will support tax audits, which are integral to the functioning and credibility of tax administration.

The vulnerable fiscal positions of these remote microstates are exacerbated by revenue sources that depend largely on external factors. Mapping domestic resource mobilization strategies can make revenue flow more predictable. Likewise, making expenditure more efficient and effective is vital to ensure healthier fiscal positions and improved implementation. Governments should look to phase out economic support measures as their situation allows and closely scrutinize how effectively spending priorities deliver core government services. Coupled with prudent spending plans, this will improve fiscal resources and support government efforts to address longer-term challenges from human development gaps and climate change.

NORTH PACIFIC ECONOMIES

These three island economies contracted further as travel and mobility restrictions continued to stifle tourism in Palau and trade in the Federated States of Micronesia and the Marshall Islands. Border reopening is expected to help catalyze recovery, though an ongoing wave of Omicron variant infections poses a significant downside risk. Inflation is forecast to pick up on higher commodity prices and economic recovery. Domestic resource mobilization is critical for generating fiscal resources to support resilience and sustainable recovery.

Federated States of Micronesia

Strict border controls and public health measures have effectively contained COVID-19 but strained the economy, with GDP shrinking by 3.8% in fiscal year 2020 (FY2020, ended 30 September 2020) and a further 1.2% in FY2021 (Figure 3.38.1). While borders remain closed, the government has provided fiscal support and gradually eased public health measures that until mid-2021 delayed public investment projects and economic activity.

The authorities have taken a cautious approach to the pandemic and conditioned any easing of border restrictions on vaccination progress. Despite an early start to vaccination and the implementation of vaccine mandates, expansion in coverage has slowed with the logistical challenges of rolling out vaccines to remote islands. As of 16 March 2022, nearly 55,000 residents were fully vaccinated, or 65.6% of the eligible population aged 5 years and above.

The private sector has borne the brunt of the pandemic as the hotel and restaurant industry contracted by 73% in FY2021 and the transport industry by 14%, but the small size of the private sector has muted the impact on the whole economy. Moreover, $75 million worth of government stimulus measures mitigated cumulative GDP contraction in FY2020 and FY2021 by an estimated 1.9 percentage points.

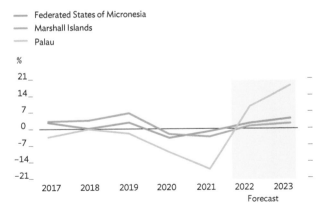

Figure 3.38.1 GDP growth in the North Pacific

Growth is expected to resume in FY2022 as borders reopen and business activity normalizes.

— Federated States of Micronesia
— Marshall Islands
— Palau

GDP = gross domestic product.
Note: Years are fiscal years ending on 30 September of that year.
Sources: Asian Development Bank estimates using data from the latest Republic of the Marshall Islands, Federated States of Micronesia, and Republic of Palau economic briefs and COVID-19 impact assessments.

In FY2021, inflation rose to 2.0% on higher fuel prices and supply disruption (Figure 3.38.2). The current account surplus narrowed further to the equivalent of 0.5% of GDP on account of deteriorating remittances and trade in services, particularly tourism receipts (Table 3.38.1). Meanwhile, the fiscal surplus fell to 9.0% of GDP in FY2020 and 6.3% in FY2021 under increased spending against the pandemic.

This chapter was written by Remrick Patagan, Rommel Rabanal, and Cara Tinio of the Pacific Department, ADB, Manila.

Figure 3.38.2 Inflation in the North Pacific economies

Prices are projected to rise more quickly, tracking international price trends.

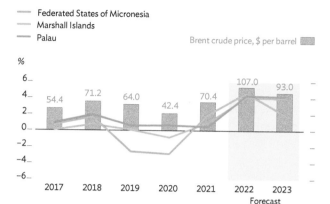

Note: Years are fiscal years ending on 30 September of that year.
Sources: Asian Development Bank estimates using data from the Republic of the Marshall Islands, Federated States of Micronesia, and Republic of Palau economic briefs.

Table 3.38.1 Selected economic indicators, %

Inflation is expected to rise sharply as the Russian invasion of Ukraine boosts commodity prices.

	2020	2021	2022	2023
Federated States of Micronesia				
GDP growth	–3.8	–1.2	2.2	4.2
Inflation	–2.9	2.0	4.6	2.0
CAB/GDP	7.9	0.5	–10.2	–8.8
Marshall Islands				
GDP growth	–2.2	–3.3	1.2	2.2
Inflation	–0.8	1.0	4.1	4.0
CAB/GDP	20.5	23.5	3.5	2.0
Palau				
GDP growth	–9.7	–17.1	9.4	18.3
Inflation	0.7	0.5	4.3	4.2
CAB/GDP	–48.2	–55.9	–51.3	–30.3

CAB = current account balance, GDP = gross domestic product.
Note: Years are fiscal years ending on 30 September of that year.
Source: Asian Development Bank estimates.

The economic outlook assumes that travel restrictions will persist until the middle of FY2022 and that economic activity will then normalize. Accordingly, the hospitality and transport industries are expected to return to growth, and construction will

benefit from easier materials availability and mobility of skilled personnel. Full recovery to pre-pandemic levels is not expected, however, until FY2023, which is also the last year of the amended Compact of Free Association with the United States (US).

The projected start of economic recovery in late FY2022 reflects slow vaccination progress and government caution on border reopening. In response to the spread of the Omicron variant toward the end of 2021, authorities suspended repatriation flights. The suspension was extended indefinitely on 7 February 2022, noting, among other considerations, the need to improve the country's vaccination rate, particularly by rolling out vaccines for children and boosters for adults.

Current restrictions have prompted the government to extend its economic stimulus package for businesses to June 2022 and augment its social protection program for low-income households. A downside risk to the outlook for FY2022 and FY2023 would be further delays in improving the vaccination rate sufficiently to reopen borders.

Inflation is projected to accelerate to 4.6% in FY2022 because of markedly higher import and commodity prices and improved domestic demand, before settling to 2.0% in FY2023 in line with expected inflation in the US. As commodity prices spike following the Russian invasion of Ukraine and the flow of pandemic response grants from development partners starts winding down in FY2022, the current account is expected to drop into a deficit equal to 10.2% of GDP and the fiscal surplus to narrow further to 5.1% of GDP. In FY2023, broader import recovery and elevated commodity prices are projected to keep the current account deficit at 8.8% of GDP, but recovery in government revenue will enable a higher fiscal surplus of 5.8% of GDP.

Marshall Islands

The economy continued to shrink in FY2021 (ended 30 September 2021), contracting by 3.3% as the country experienced its first full year of mobility restrictions under the pandemic (Figure 3.38.1). Containment measures prevented a local outbreak of COVID-19 but depressed economic activity, especially in fisheries and onshore fleet services, hotels and restaurants, and construction including public infrastructure projects.

Resulting tepid demand tempered inflation, which reached only 1.0% despite significantly higher international fuel prices (Figure 3.38.2). Imports remained low, driving—together with continued grant inflow from development partners—a current account surplus equal to 23.5% of GDP.

The fiscal surplus narrowed from the equivalent of 4.3% of GDP in FY2020 to 1.4%. Government spending increases to cope with the pandemic were dampened somewhat by low implementation capacity. Grants from development partners to support pandemic response boosted fiscal resources, offsetting slightly lower collection of taxes and fishing license fees. With access to grant financing, the government reduced public external debt from the equivalent of 25.0% of GDP at the end of September 2020 to 23.4% a year later.

The economy is forecast to return to growth in FY2022, expanding by 1.2%, with a slight easing in the strict quarantine requirements for registered inbound travelers allowing for some normalization in business activity in the latter part of the fiscal year (Table 3.38.1). Any further easing of restrictions will depend on the course of Omicron infections elsewhere in the subregion and on progress in immunizing the population. As of 15 March 2022, only 64% of those aged 5 and older were fully vaccinated (Table 3.38.2). Growth is expected to pick up to 2.2% in FY2023.

Table 3.38.2 Marshall Islands population fully vaccinated as of 15 March 2022, %

Vaccination is progressing more slowly as logistical challenges hamper rollouts to more isolated islands.

	Majuro	Kwajalein	Other Islands	National
Aged 5+	75	72	32	64
Aged 12+	89	90	46	79
Aged 18+	99	100	60	91

Source: Republic of the Marshall Islands Ministry of Health and Human Services.

Inflation is projected at 4.1% in FY2022 and 4.0% in FY2023, tracking international commodity prices, particularly of fuel, and buoyed by greater demand with resumed economic activity in FY2023. Imports are expected to pick up as fuel shipments become significantly more expensive under current geopolitical tensions and later as borders reopen and public infrastructure projects recommence in earnest. These developments and the winding down of COVID-19 grant inflows are projected to narrow the current account surplus to the equivalent of 3.5% of GDP and then 2.0% over the next 2 fiscal years.

The fiscal deficit is forecast equal to 3.5% of GDP in FY2022 and 2.5% in FY2023. Government spending is seen to fall in FY2022 against a larger reduction in revenues as previously received COVID-19 grants are drawn down. In FY2023, recovery in tax revenue and some improvement in fishing license revenue will help fund a slight uptick in expenditures. Public external debt is projected to be 20.4% of GDP in FY2022 and 17.5% in FY2023.

Palau

This tourism-driven economy, in which the industry's direct contribution to GDP averaged 23.2% before the pandemic, continued to languish under international travel restrictions. With virtually no inbound tourists during the first 6 months of FY2021 (ended 30 September 2021), annual arrivals collapsed by a further 91.8% to only about 3,400, from almost 90,000 just ahead of the pandemic (Figure 3.38.3). As a result, the economy contracted by 17.1% in FY2021, compounding a 9.7% decline a year earlier (Figure 3.38.1).

Palau's vaccination program started in January 2021, and in April a travel bubble with Taipei,China commenced but was suspended a few weeks later as case numbers rose in that market. In May, Palau opened its borders to fully vaccinated people from the US arriving via Guam. By July, sufficient immunization progress had been made to allow entry for fully vaccinated travelers and those registered to receive vaccinations on arrival. The travel bubble with Taipei,China also resumed in mid-August. These measures contributed the bulk of arrivals in FY2021, 90% of them from either Taipei,China or the US.

Figure 3.38.3 Visitor arrivals in Palau, by source

Arrivals collapsed by over 90% in FY2021, with virtually zero visitors in the first half.

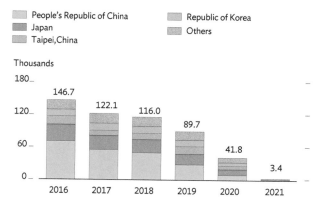

Note: Years are fiscal years ending on 30 September of that year.
Source: Palau Bureau of Labor and Immigration.

Figure 3.38.4 Supply-side contributions to growth in Palau

Economic recovery is expected to commence in FY2022 and accelerate in FY2023.

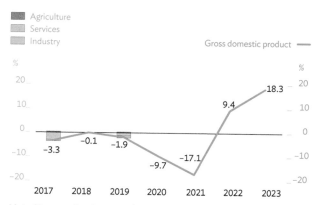

Note: Years are fiscal years ending on 30 September of that year.
Sources: Republic of Palau FY2019 Economic Review;
Asian Development Bank estimates.

Inflation remained low at 0.5% in FY2021 as subdued economic activity more than offset rising international commodity prices (Figure 3.38.2). The collapse of tourism receipts widened the current account deficit from the equivalent of 48.2% of GDP in FY2020 to 55.9%. Further, with declining tax collection from the economic downturn and additional spending to mitigate pandemic impacts on private businesses and workers, the fiscal deficit widened from 10.9% of GDP in FY2020 to 19.5%.

After 6 consecutive years of contraction, the economy is expected to return to growth in FY2022, forecast at 9.4% (Figure 3.38.4). Reopening measures begun in FY2021 continued to allow some recovery in visitor arrivals, to 1,900 in the first quarter of FY2022. However, as did many other countries, Palau recorded a sharp rise in COVID-19 cases at the start of 2022, increasing during January from just 13 border cases to more than 600, with local transmission first detected in mid-month. This popped Palau's travel bubble with Taipei,China again in late January.

Relatively low hospitalization and mortality rates—helped by Palau's high vaccination coverage—and rapid virus spread are consistent with patterns seen in other countries that grappled with the highly transmissible Omicron variant. A subsequent pattern of a sharp decline in cases seems to be holding true for Palau as well, with cases appearing to have peaked by mid-February. The nascent tourism recovery also

remained mostly unaffected by the outbreak, with 952 additional arrivals in January–February 2022, pushing arrivals during the first 5 months of FY2022 to 84% of the FY2021 total. Tourist arrivals are projected to recover to about 25,000 in FY2022, subject to downside risks from uncertainties globally.

Economic growth is then expected to accelerate to 18.3% in FY2023 (Table 3.38.1). An underlying assumption is the likely resolution of the pandemic by then, allowing for a return to near pre-pandemic numbers of international visitor arrivals. Despite the positive outlook over the near term, Palau's GDP in real terms will likely remain below its FY2019 value until FY2023.

Inflation is expected to pick up to 4.3% in FY2022 and continue at 4.2% in FY2023, in line with projected trends in international commodity prices. With gradual recovery in visitor arrivals and tourism receipts, the current account deficit is seen narrowing to the equivalent of 51.3% of GDP in FY2022 and further to 30.3% in FY2023. Similarly, as fiscal pressures gradually ebb with economic growth, the fiscal deficit is projected to narrow to 12.6% of GDP in FY2022 and 3.2% in FY2023. Public debt will likely peak at 90.3% of GDP in FY2022 and then decline steadily over the medium term. While this is relatively high, Palau's debt remains sustainable, and the public debt-to-GDP ratio can revert below the pre-COVID-19 level in about a decade with steady economic recovery.

Policy challenge—domestic resource mobilization to support sustainable recovery

While broad public financial management reform is important, improved domestic resource mobilization (DRM) remains particularly critical for the North Pacific economies because of their narrow economic bases, which heighten their sensitivity to shocks, and the looming expiration of grants under compact agreements with the US. These contribute to risks of debt distress being rated as high for the FSM and the RMI, while Palau's need for fiscal space is greater in view of debt servicing of substantial new borrowing necessitated by COVID-19.

In September 2021, Palau enacted comprehensive tax reform that promotes greater DRM through a system enabling more efficient tax collection with less distortion to the economy and more equitable sharing of the tax burden. The package (i) broadens the revenue base by replacing the general import tax with a value-added tax (VAT) that includes consumption of services; (ii) eliminates distortions by moving away from taxing gross revenue with no deductions for production costs to taxing business profit, while replacing import duties on alcohol and tobacco with an excise tax that also applies to local production; and (iii) promotes equity by adjusting wage and salary tax income thresholds and aligning net profit tax with the highest marginal tax rates for wages and salaries.

In the Marshall Islands, recent DRM efforts have improved implementation and administration. Momentum for tax reform waned with the 2012 implementation of a vessel-day scheme that significantly boosted collections from fishing license fees. However, the economic impact of the pandemic is forcing down revenue. Together with the expiration of the country's compact with the US, this development underscores the urgency of pursuing tax reform that revises income tax rates and replaces import, gross revenue, and local sales taxes with consumption, net business profit, and excise taxes. A reform coordination unit established under the Ministry of Finance has already identified institutional, system, and capacity upgrades needed to facilitate reforms to tax policy. Reform will be complemented by improved administration, including capacity building in the tax office and the implementation of new processes and a digital revenue management system.

In the Federated States of Micronesia, the importance of tax reform and enhanced DRM is underscored by fiscal pressures exerted by the pandemic and uncertainty surrounding the renewal of its compact with the US. Excluding FSM domicile revenues, tax collection is low at the equivalent of 14% of GDP on average in FY2016–FY2019 and hampers government capacity to respond to future fiscal shocks. Incentive to increase taxes is stymied nationally by high sovereign rents from fishing license fees (Figure 3.38.5) and corporate domicile revenue. Meanwhile, the practice of earmarking the bulk of tax revenue for state governments makes them cooler toward tax reform.

Figure 3.38.5 Fishing license revenue in the Federated States of Micronesia

Fishing license fees have become a strong and stable source of government revenue.

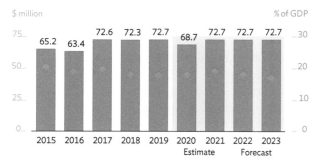

GDP = gross domestic product.
Note: Years are fiscal years ending on 30 September of that year.
Source: Graduate School USA. 2021. Economic Monitoring and Analysis Program (accessed 6 February 2022).

In July 2021, the government established the National Tax Reform Commission to expand and update the national revenue base and share revenue equitably among the federation's four member states. The International Monetary Fund welcomed the commission and suggested replacing gross revenue tax with VAT and implementing excise taxes on tobacco, alcohol, and fuel. The government pledged to prioritize revenue-neutral VAT reform and submitted to Congress legislation for excise taxes on tobacco and alcohol. Reform is expected to raise tax collection to about 16% of GDP.

SOUTH PACIFIC ECONOMIES

The Cook Islands, Niue, Samoa, and Tonga have only recently encountered COVID-19, with community transmission of the Omicron variant all but inevitable. In addition to other recovery challenges, fuel and other import prices have worsened inflation that was already trending up from disrupted supply chains, and the Russian invasion of Ukraine is likely to add further price pressure. With fiscal space constrained after 2 years of crisis management, economic recovery remains vulnerable to further shocks.

Cook Islands

The Cook Islands suffered the largest contraction among Pacific member countries in fiscal year 2021 (FY2021, ended 30 June 2021) and its largest on record. Fiscal programs equal to 20.3% of GDP benefited vulnerable people working in both the public and private sector but were insufficient to offset the impact of zero tourist arrivals in the first 10 months of FY2021 and delays to large infrastructure projects. GDP contracted by 29.1%, with accommodation falling by 81.3% and travel by 65.1% (Figure 3.39.1). With borders reopened to travelers from New Zealand on 13 January 2022, the economy is expected to rebound in the second half of FY2022. Including 1.5 months of open travel in and after July 2021, tourist arrivals in FY2022 are projected at 43,000, or 25.0% of FY2019 numbers, bringing GDP growth to 9.1%. Growth is expected to accelerate to 11.2% in FY2023, with over 80% recovery in arrivals from the primary tourism market in New Zealand (Table 3.39.1).

The positive outlook is supported by a vaccination rate at over 96% of the eligible population and the acceleration of infrastructure projects to enhance readiness to receive tourists. Downside risks pertain to a worsening COVID-19 outbreak in Rarotonga, traveler hesitancy to visit destinations with active cases, and competition from other international destinations.

Inflation increased to 2.2% in FY2021 largely on higher fuel prices, which raised costs for transportation and imported food and beverages (Figure 3.39.2).

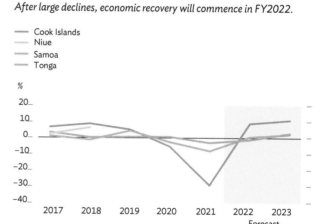

Figure 3.39.1 GDP growth in the South Pacific

After large declines, economic recovery will commence in FY2022.

— Cook Islands
— Niue
— Samoa
— Tonga

Note: Years are fiscal years ending on 30 June of that year.
Sources: Cook Islands Ministry of Finance and Economic Management; Statistics Niue; Samoa Bureau of Statistics; Tonga Department of Statistics; Asian Development Bank estimates.

Supply disruption and further fuel price increases from the impact of the Russian invasion of Ukraine are expected to continue to push up prices for goods and services. Inflation is forecast to accelerate to 4.3% in FY2022 before easing to 4.0% in FY2023.

The fiscal deficit widened to equal 23.1% of GDP in FY2021, with 33.0% growth in recurrent spending to support stimulus measures and a 41.7% fall in tax revenue as tourism receipts collapsed (Figure 3.39.3).

This chapter was written by Lily-Anne Homasi, Isoa Wainiqolo, and James Webb of the South Pacific Subregional Office, ADB, Suva.

Table 3.39.1 Selected economic indicators, %

Inflation is expected to rise sharply as the Russian invasion of Ukraine boosts commodity prices.

	2020	2021	2022	2023
Cook Islands				
GDP growth	–5.2	–29.1	9.1	11.2
Inflation	0.7	2.2	4.3	4.0
CAB/GDP	–6.0	–12.5	–7.0	5.1
Samoa				
GDP growth	–2.6	–8.1	0.4	2.2
Inflation	1.5	–3.0	8.9	3.2
CAB/GDP	0.0	–10.6	–10.0	–5.0
Tonga				
GDP growth	0.7	–3.0	–1.2	2.9
Inflation	0.2	1.4	7.6	4.2
CAB/GDP	–3.8	0.1	–1.8	–5.2

CAB = current account balance, GDP = gross domestic product.
Note: Years are fiscal years ending on 30 June of that year.
Source: Asian Development Bank estimates.

Figure 3.39.2 Inflation

Inflation has accelerated so far in FY2022.

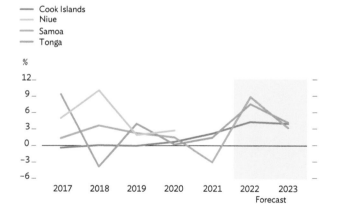

Note: Years are fiscal years ending on 30 June of that year.
Sources: Cook Islands Ministry of Finance and Economic Management; Statistics Niue; Samoa Bureau of Statistics; Tonga Department of Statistics; Asian Development Bank estimates.

Lower capital expenditure and increased revenue from fishing license fees prevented greater deterioration. An improved fiscal deficit equal to 11.2% of GDP is projected for FY2022, with tax revenue forecast to grow by 22.5%. A fiscal deficit equal to 6.6% of GDP is forecast for FY2023 as tax revenue continues to

Figure 3.39.3 Fiscal balance

Fiscal positions deteriorated across the South Pacific in 2021.

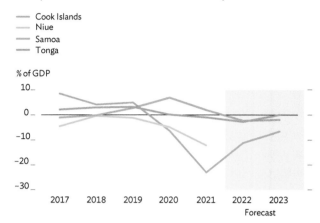

GDP = gross domestic product.
Note: Years are fiscal years ending on 30 June of that year.
Sources: Cook Islands Ministry of Finance and Economic Management; Niue Department of Finance and Planning; Samoa Ministry of Finance; Tonga Ministry of Finance and National Planning; Asian Development Bank estimates.

recover and spending normalizes. Debt is expected to increase from a low of 17.1% of GDP in FY2020 to a peak of 43.5% in FY2022, and decline thereafter.

The current account deficit doubled to equal 12.5% of GDP in FY2021 largely because of the decline in tourism. The deficit is forecast to narrow to 7.0% of GDP in FY2022 and revert to a surplus of 5.1% in FY2023 as tourism receipts recover.

Samoa

Economic contraction deepened by a further 8.1% in FY2021 (ended 30 June 2021) as closed borders continued to weigh heavily on tourism, which had contributed an estimated 24.2% of GDP in FY2019. Mitigating this, remittances rose by 6.7% to their highest level on record, supporting household consumption and expanding foreign currency reserves.

With no clear announcement from the government about reopening borders, GDP growth in FY2022 is forecast at only 0.4%, with risks to the downside (Figure 3.39.1 and Table 3.39.1). After a measles outbreak in 2019 and then 2 years of closed borders, the long-term scarring of the tourism industry is expected to contain growth at 2.2% in FY2023, despite assumed border reopening. The biggest risk to the economic outlook would be any escalation in community transmission of COVID 19 and consequent delay in restoring tourism.

Price declines early in the fiscal year brought deflation of 3.0% in FY2021 (Figure 3.39.2). Inflation is forecast to return in FY2022 and reach 8.9% on significant increases in food and transportation prices stemming from high global oil prices and imported food costs. It is expected to moderate to 3.2% in FY2023 as these effects dissipate.

Despite GDP and tax revenue contraction, Samoa recorded a fiscal surplus equal to 1.9% of GDP in FY2021 as nontax revenue rose and grants continued to flow from development partners (Figure 3.39.3). A fiscal deficit at 2.4% of GDP is projected in FY2022 as tax revenue continues to fall, this time without one-off nontax revenue gains. Public external debt is forecast to decrease from the equivalent of 49.3% of GDP in FY2021 to 43.0% in FY2022, but debt-servicing costs will still rise following the expiration of the multilateral Debt Service Suspension Initiative on 31 December 2021.

A current account deficit equal to 10.6% of GDP was recorded in FY2021. The deficit was driven by a 28.4% decline in exports as the collapse in tourism receipts outpaced continued growth in inbound remittances (Figure 3.39.4). Imports fell by only 3.8%. The deficit is expected to narrow slightly to 10.0% of GDP in FY2022 with continued strength in remittances and growth in export earnings other than from tourism, and then narrow further to 5.0% of GDP in FY2023 as tourism recommences.

Tonga

The economy contracted by 3.0% in FY2021 (ended 30 June 2021) with the suspension of all inbound travel. Partially mitigating this, remittances continued to grow to record levels, supporting domestic consumption and the accumulation of foreign reserves (Figure 3.39.1). The eruption of the Hunga Tonga–Hunga Ha'apai volcano and consequent tsunami in January 2022 are likely to cause agricultural production losses that will bring a further 1.2% contraction in GDP in FY2022. The delayed reopening of borders, competition for returning tourists, and losses from repeated disasters are likely to slow long-term recovery in tourism. However, with border reopening, growth is projected at 2.9% in FY2023 (Table 3.39.1).

Inflation is expected to accelerate from 1.4% in FY2021 to 7.6% in FY2022 as local supply constraints return, prices for fuel and other imports rise, and agriculture takes time to recover from the effects of the eruption (Figure 3.39.2). Price increases will moderate heading into FY2023 along with these effects, though local labor supply constraints, especially in construction, will keep inflation close to trend.

The fiscal deficit equaled 1.0% of GDP in FY2021 following a fall in revenue and increased expenditure in response to COVID-19 (Figure 3.39.3). The deficit will likely expand to 2.8% of GDP in FY2022. Emergency response to the eruption was facilitated by rapid financial and material assistance from development partners, which contained immediate damage to government finances. Capital investment will increase significantly in light of coastal damage and risks to infrastructure. External debt is expected to ease from 41.5% of GDP in FY2021 to 38.4% in FY2022.

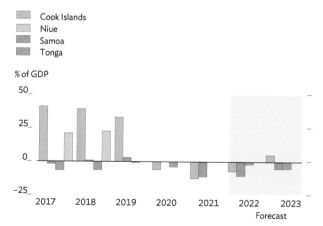

Figure 3.39.4 Current account balance

Current account balances will remain stressed into the medium term.

- Cook Islands
- Niue
- Samoa
- Tonga

% of GDP

GDP = gross domestic product.
Note: Years are fiscal years ending on 30 June of that year.
Sources: Cook Islands Ministry of Finance and Economic Management; Statistics Niue; Samoa Bureau of Statistics; Tonga Department of Statistics; Asian Development Bank estimates.

Reconstruction costs will impose a significant fiscal burden and require ongoing support from development partners, likely in the form of grants.

Growth in private remittances outweighed the loss of tourism receipts to create a current account surplus estimated to equal 0.1% of GDP in FY2021 (Figure 3.39.4). Increased imports in FY2022 will likely revert the current account to a deficit of 1.8%, despite large official transfers from development partners in the immediate aftermath of the eruption. With the return of tourism receipts likely to be slow, imports of reconstruction materials will widen the current account deficit in FY2023 and beyond, though growth in official transfers and remittances will avoid more serious deterioration.

Niue

The economy contracted in FY2021 (ended 30 June 2021) as prolonged border closure hobbled tourism and public investment projects. Fiscal outcomes in the first 7 months of FY2021 suggest broad decline across the economy despite there being no community transmission of COVID-19. One-way quarantine-free travel into New Zealand commenced in March 2021, but two-way quarantine-free travel with New Zealand has been interrupted several times following COVID-19 outbreaks in Auckland. Economic recovery will depend on the arrival of tourists in the coming months as restrictions ease.

Inflation accelerated to 2.3% in calendar year 2020 on higher prices for food and transport, but no data are available for 2021. Higher inflation is expected in FY2022 in the wake of retail fuel prices increasing by 14% in January 2022. This was their first increase since 2017 and came following the government's announcement that it was no longer economically feasible to subsidize fuel.

The fiscal deficit in FY2021 is estimated equal to 12.2% of 2019 GDP, deepening from 4.9% in FY2020 (Figure 3.39.3). Estimated growth in recurrent expenses outpaced the increased revenue from budget support. Grants cover 47% of government financing. The government is considering introducing user-pay terms for utilities and measures to raise productivity by reverting civil servants to a five-day work week from

the current 4 days. The government deficit in FY2022 and FY2023 is likely to be determined by recovery in the tourism industry and access to external financing, which is overwhelmingly funded by the Government of New Zealand.

The deficit in goods trade widened to equal 37% of FY2019 GDP in calendar year 2020, after a 23.7% decline in domestic exports, mainly noni juice, outweighed a 12.5% drop in imports. Prospects for tourism earnings in FY2023 depend on border reopening, following low arrivals in FY2022.

Policy challenge—managing the first COVID-19 wave

South Pacific populations were largely spared health impacts from community transmission of COVID-19 until recently. The delayed onset of the first wave of COVID-19 cases allowed time for near-universal vaccination coverage, which is especially important in populations with high comorbidities (Figures 3.39.5 and 3.39.6). In Niue and the Cook Islands, most people in high-risk groups have received booster shots, but vaccination supplies in Samoa and Tonga have been more constrained.

Figure 3.39.5 Prevalence of obesity in the Pacific, % of population 18 and older

South Pacific economies have some of the world's highest rates of obesity, a significant risk factor for COVID-19 complications.

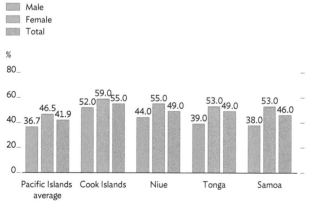

Note: The World Obesity Federation ranks the Cook Islands third, Niue eighth, and Tonga tenth for both genders, and Samoa thirteenth for males and ninth for females.

Sources: World Health Organization. WHO STEPS survey factsheets: 2013 (Niue and Samoa) and 2017 (Tonga); World Health Organization. 2018. *Noncommunicable Diseases Country Profiles (Pacific)*.

Figure 3.39.6 COVID-19 vaccination rates, % of eligible population aged 12 and older

Vaccination programs have been successful except for booster shots in Samoa.

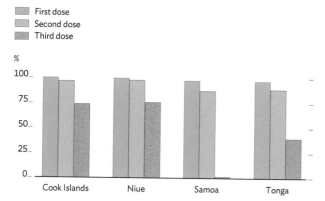

Source: Figures, provided by ministries of health in each country, are from 7 March 2022 for Cook Islands and Niue, 8 March 2022 for Samoa, and 4 March 2022 for Tonga. Third-dose figures for Samoa are from the World Health Organization.

Figure 3.39.7 Change in gross domestic product, FY2019–FY2023

At the end of FY2023, South Pacific economies will still languish below GDP in FY2019, most so in the Cook Islands.

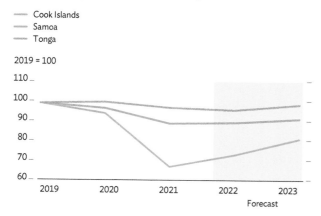

FY = fiscal year, GDP = gross domestic product.
Note: Years are fiscal years ending on 30 June of that year.
Sources: Cook Islands Ministry of Finance and Economic Management; Samoa Bureau of Statistics; Tonga Department of Statistics; Asian Development Bank estimates.

Economic recovery in the South Pacific remains fragile, reversible, and subject to extreme risk. Tourism and related businesses across the region have lost financial and human capital, which may delay the establishment of mature tourist destinations. Slower growth may have spillover effects on other retail and commercial services and on fiscal and economic recovery. As the eruption in Tonga has shown, the region is subject to natural hazards, the reconstruction costs of which need to be factored into long-term development financing needs. Fiscal positions are much weaker than when the crisis began 2 years ago, and contingent liabilities, especially in Samoa and Tonga, have risen steadily in state-owned airlines and the Development Bank of Samoa.

Further, a labor shortage in the Cook Islands means recovery depends on attracting foreign labor. Proactive immigration measures adopted during the COVID-19 crisis need to be expanded. In Samoa and Tonga, the reopening of borders and resumption of international activity are important to salvage tourism industries and resume public infrastructure programs.

Remittances, which have played a key role in supporting household incomes in Samoa and Tonga, may not be reliable over the longer term. Local agribusiness may provide a growth avenue and mitigate the high cost of importing food but is unlikely to create many jobs and may compete for labor alongside seasonal work programs. Samoa and Tonga should examine measures to improve the general business environment and the potential role of foreign investment.
In all four economies, fiscal consolidation should be accomplished through revenue recovery and close consideration of expenditure priorities, rather than through significant cuts to expenditure, to avoid weakening fragile private sector recovery, with GDP values languishing below FY2019 to the forecast horizon (Figure 3.39.7). Governments should be especially wary of measures that expand expenditure or further increase government contingent liabilities, which would delay the rebuilding of government balance sheets, the health of which will be essential in future crises.

4

STATISTICAL APPENDIX

STATISTICAL NOTES AND TABLES

The statistical appendix presents in 18 tables selected economic indicators for the 46 developing member economies of the Asian Development Bank (ADB). The economies are grouped into five subregions: the Caucasus and Central Asia, East Asia, South Asia, Southeast Asia, and the Pacific. Most of the tables contain historical data from 2017 to 2021; some have forecasts for 2022 and 2023.

The data were standardized to the degree possible to allow comparability over time and across economies, but differences in statistical methodology, definitions, coverage, and practices make full comparability impossible. The national income accounts section is based on the United Nations System of National Accounts, while the data on the balance of payments use International Monetary Fund (IMF) accounting standards. Historical data were obtained from official sources, statistical publications, and databases, as well as the documents of ADB, the IMF, and the World Bank. For some economies, data for 2021 were estimated from the latest available information. Projections for 2022 and 2023 are generally ADB estimates based on available quarterly or monthly data, though some projections are from governments.

Most economies report by calendar year. The following record their government finance data by fiscal year: Brunei Darussalam; Bhutan; Fiji; Hong Kong, China; Singapore; Tajikistan; Thailand; and Uzbekistan. Reporting all variables by fiscal year are South Asian countries (except for Bhutan, Maldives, and Sri Lanka), the Cook Islands, the Federated States of Micronesia, Myanmar, the Marshall Islands, Nauru, Palau, Samoa, and Tonga.

Regional and subregional averages or totals are provided for seven tables: A1, A2, A6, A11, A12, A13, and A14. For tables A1, A2, A6, A11, A12, and A14, averages were weighted by purchasing power parity (PPP) gross domestic product (GDP) in current international dollars (see Box). PPP GDP data for 2017–2020 were obtained from the IMF World Economic Outlook Database,

October 2021 edition. Weights for 2020 were carried over to 2023. For Table A13, regional and subregional totals were computed using a consistent sum, which means that if economy data were missing for a given year, the sum excluded that economy.

Tables A1, A2, A3, A4, and A5 show data on output growth, production, and demand. Changes were made to the national income accounts series for some economies to accommodate a change in source, methodology, and/or base year. Constant factor cost measures differ from market price measures in that they exclude taxes on production and include subsidies. Basic price valuation is the factor cost plus some taxes on production, such as property and payroll taxes, and less some subsidies, such as for labor but not for products. The series for Afghanistan, India, Myanmar, and Pakistan reflect fiscal year data, rather than calendar year data, and those for Timor-Leste reflect GDP excluding the offshore petroleum industry. Some historical data for Turkmenistan are not presented for lack of uniformity. A fluid situation permits no estimates or forecasts for Afghanistan in 2021–2023.

Table A1: Growth rate of GDP (% per year). The table shows annual growth rates of GDP valued at constant market prices, factor costs, or basic prices. GDP at market prices is the aggregate value added by all resident producers at producers' prices including taxes less subsidies on imports plus all nondeductible value-added or similar taxes. Most economies use constant market price valuation. Pakistan uses constant factor costs, and Fiji basic prices. Pakistan's national accounts data were rebased, and consistent series were available from 2016.

Table A2: Growth rate of GDP per capita (% per year). The table provides the growth rates of real GDP per capita, which is defined as GDP at constant prices divided by population. Nepal uses GDP at constant factor cost. Also shown are data on gross national income per capita in US dollar terms (Atlas method) for 2020, sourced from the World Bank's World Development Indicators online. Data for the Cook Islands and Taipei,China were estimated using the Atlas conversion factor.

Table A3: Growth rate of value added in agriculture (% per year). The table shows the growth rates of value added in agriculture at constant prices and agriculture's share of GDP in 2020 at current prices. The agriculture sector comprises plant crops, livestock, poultry, fisheries, and forestry.

Table A4: Growth rate of value added in industry (% per year). The table provides the growth rates of value added in industry at constant prices and industry's share of GDP in 2020 at current prices. This sector comprises manufacturing, mining and quarrying, and, generally, construction and utilities.

Table A5: Growth rate of value added in services (% per year). The table gives the growth rates of value added in services at constant prices and services' share of GDP in 2020 at current prices. Services generally include trade, banking, finance, real estate, and similar businesses, as well as public administration. For Malaysia, electricity, gas, water supply, and waste management are included under services.

Table A6: Inflation (% per year). Data on inflation rates are period averages. Inflation rates are based on consumer price indexes. The consumer price indexes of the following economies are for a given city only: Cambodia is for Phnom Penh, the Marshall Islands for Majuro, and Sri Lanka for Colombo. For Indonesia, a series break starts in 2019 because of a change in base year from 2012 to 2018. A fluid situation permits no forecasts for Afghanistan in 2022–2023.

Table A7: Change in money supply (% per year). This table tracks annual percentage change in broad money supply at the end of the period, M2 for most economies. M2 is defined as the sum of currency in circulation plus demand deposits (M1) plus quasi-money, which consists of time and savings deposits including foreign currency deposits. For Cook Islands; Georgia; Hong Kong, China; India; Kazakhstan; and Solomon Islands, broad money is M3, which adds longer-term time deposits. For Sri Lanka broad money is M2b, or M2 plus bond funds. A fluid situation permits no estimate for Afghanistan in 2021.

Tables A8, A9, and A10: Government finance. These tables give central government revenue, expenditure, and fiscal balance expressed as percentages of GDP in nominal terms.

Where full-year data are not yet available, GDP shares are estimated using available monthly or quarterly data. For Cambodia, Georgia, India, Kazakhstan, the Kyrgyz Republic, Mongolia, the People's Republic of China, and Tajikistan, transactions are those reported by the general government. From 2017, the series for Cambodia is based on the IMF *Government Finance Statistics Manual 2014* format. A fluid situation permits no estimates for Afghanistan in 2021.

Table A8: Central government revenue (% of GDP). Central government revenue comprises all nonrepayable receipts, both current and capital, plus grants. These amounts are computed as a percentage of GDP at current prices. For the Republic of Korea, revenue excludes social security contributions. For Kazakhstan, revenue includes transfers from the national fund. Grants are excluded for Malaysia and Thailand. Revenue from disinvestment is included for India. Only current revenue is included for Bangladesh.

Table A9: Central government expenditure (% of GDP). Central government expenditure comprises all nonrepayable payments to meet both current and capital expenses, plus net lending. These amounts are computed as shares of GDP at current prices. For Thailand, expenditure refers to budgetary expenditure excluding externally financed expenditure and borrowing. For Tajikistan, expenditure includes externally financed public investment programs. One-off expenditures are excluded for Pakistan.

Table A10: Fiscal balance of the central government (% of GDP). Fiscal balance is the difference between central government revenue and expenditure. The difference is computed as a share of GDP at current prices. Data variation may arise from statistical discrepancy when, for example, balancing items for general governments (central plus selected subnational governments), and from differences between coverage used in individual revenue and expenditure calculations and fiscal balance calculations. For Fiji, the fiscal balance excludes loan repayment. For Georgia, the fiscal balance is calculated according to the IMF *Government Finance Statistics Manual 2001* format, as is the Cambodia general government fiscal balance using the 2014 manual. For Thailand, the fiscal balance is the cash balance of combined budgetary and nonbudgetary balances. For Turkmenistan, the fiscal balance does not include off-budget accounts.

For Singapore, fiscal balance excludes special transfers (top-ups to endowment and trust funds) and contributions from net investment returns. For the Republic of Korea, it excludes funds related to social security.

Tables A11, A12, A13, and A14: Balance of payments. These tables show the annual flows of selected international economic transactions of economies as recorded in their balance of payments. A fluid situation permits no estimates or forecasts for Afghanistan in 2021–2023.

Tables A11 and A12: Growth rates of merchandise exports and imports (% per year). These tables show the annual growth rates of exports and imports of goods. Data are in million US dollars, primarily obtained from the balance-of-payments accounts of each economy. Export data are reported free on board. Import data are reported free onboard except for the following economies, which value them based on cost, insurance, and freight: Afghanistan; Hong Kong, China; Georgia; India; the Lao People's Democratic Republic; Maldives; Myanmar; Singapore; and Thailand.

Table A13: Trade balance ($ million). The trade balance is the difference between merchandise exports and imports. Figures in this table are based on the export and import amounts used to generate tables A11 and A12.

Table A14: Current account balance (% of GDP). The current account balance is the sum of the balance of trade in merchandise, net trade in services and factor income, and net transfers. The values reported are divided by GDP at current prices in US dollars. Some historical data for Turkmenistan are not presented for lack of uniformity.

Table A15: Exchange rates to the US dollar (annual average). Annual average exchange rates are quoted as the local currency per US dollar.

Table A16: Gross international reserves ($ million). Gross international reserves are defined as the US dollar value at the end of a given period of holdings in foreign exchange, gold, special drawing rights, and IMF reserve position. For Taipei,China, this heading refers to foreign exchange reserves only. In some economies, the rubric is foreign assets plus the reserves of national monetary authorities (the net foreign reserves of, for example, the State Bank of Pakistan) plus national funds for earnings from oil or other natural resources. A fluid situation permits no estimate for Afghanistan in 2021.

Table A17: External debt outstanding ($ million). For most economies, external debt outstanding includes short-, medium-, and long-term debt, public and private, as well as IMF credit. For Armenia, Cambodia, and Maldives, only public external debt is reported. Intercompany lending is excluded for Georgia. Data for 2021 are as of the end of March for Sri Lanka and the end of September for the Kyrgyz Republic, Singapore, and Thailand. A fluid situation permits no estimate for Afghanistan in 2021.

Table A18: Debt service ratio (% of exports of goods and services). This table generally presents the total debt service payments of each economy, which comprise principal repayment (excluding short-term debt) and interest payments on outstanding external debt, given as a percentage of exports of goods and services. For Armenia and Cambodia, debt service refers to external public debt only. For the Philippines, income and exports of goods and services are used as the denominator. For Bangladesh, the ratio presents debt service payments on medium- and long-term loans as a percentage of exports of goods, nonfactor services, and overseas workers' remittances. For Azerbaijan, the ratio presents public and publicly guaranteed external debt service payments as a percentage of exports of goods and nonfactor services. For the Kyrgyz Republic, 2021 data are as of the end of September.

New weights for aggregating economy-level data to developing Asian subregions

To generate aggregate data or forecasts for developing Asia and its subregions, weights need to be assigned to each economy. Until last September's *Asian Development Outlook (ADO) 2021 Update*, these weights were derived from gross national income (GNI) data, computed using the World Bank's Atlas Method that aims to reduce the impact of exchange rate volatility when comparing national incomes.[a] GNI, however, is conceptually distinct from gross domestic product (GDP), which is how national incomes are measured and forecast in the *ADO*. While GDP is the total value added generated in a specific territory, GNI is equal to GDP plus net capital and labor income received by residents. For consistency when aggregating GDP data and forecasts, the *ADO* has therefore moved to using GDP weights.

GDP weights using purchasing power parity also limit the impact of exchange rate volatility. The reason for using GNI over nominal GDP as weights was to limit the impact of exchange rate volatility on the weights attributed to each economy. This objective will also be achieved by using purchasing power parity (PPP) GDP as weights.

The impact of the new weights is generally limited, although they give slightly higher weightings to less advanced economies. The effect of using PPP GDP weights instead of GNI weights is generally limited, as box figure 1 shows. Because PPP conversion inflates the GDP of less advanced relative to more advanced economies, using PPP GDP weights generally gives a slightly larger role to less advanced economies. For the regional aggregate, for example, the weights of India and Indonesia increase by 7.5 and 2.3 percentage points, respectively. Conversely, the weights of the People's Republic of China and the Republic of Korea decrease by 12.0 and 2.4 percentage points.

Using 2019 data as an illustration, the new weights do not affect developing Asia's aggregate GDP growth, which remains equal to 5%. For Southeast Asia, the new weights increase subregional growth by 0.3 percentage points due to higher weights for fast-growing Indonesia and Viet Nam and lower weights for slower-growing Malaysia, Singapore, and Thailand, as box figure 1 shows. For the Pacific, the new weights decrease subregional GDP growth by 0.4 percentage points due to the higher weight for slower-growing Fiji and the lower weight for faster-growing Papua New Guinea.

1 *Asian Development Outlook 2019* weights[a]

PPP GDP weights slightly increase the weight of less-advanced economies.

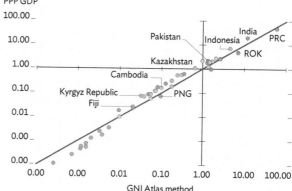

2 Regional and subregional GDP growth for 2019 computed using old and new weights

The new weights do not significantly alter aggregate growth rates for most subregions.

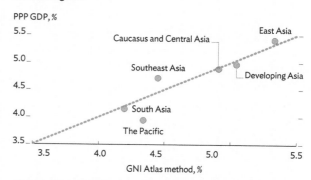

GDP = gross domestic product, GNI = gross national income, PNG = Papua New Guinea, PPP = purchasing power parity, PRC = People's Republic of China, ROK = Republic of Korea.

[a] Logarithmic scale.

Sources: International Monetary Fund. World Economic Outlook Database. October 2021 Edition; World Bank. World Development Indicators database (both accessed 9 March 2022).

[a] In practice, nominal GDP in local currencies is converted to US dollars using the average exchange rate for the last 3 years, adjusted for the difference between domestic GDP inflation and a weighted average of GDP inflation for five key global currencies.

This box was written by Jules Hugot of the Economic Research and Regional Cooperation Department, Asian Development Bank, Manila.

Table A1 Growth rate of GDP (% per year)

	2017	2018	2019	2020	2021	2022	2023
Developing Asia	6.2	6.0	5.0	−0.8	6.9	5.2	5.3
Caucasus and Central Asia	3.9	4.2	4.7	−2.0	5.6	3.6	4.0
Armenia	7.5	5.2	7.6	−7.4	5.7	2.8	3.8
Azerbaijan	0.2	1.5	2.5	−4.3	5.6	3.7	2.8
Georgia	4.8	4.8	5.0	−6.8	10.6	3.5	5.0
Kazakhstan	4.1	4.1	4.5	−2.5	4.0	3.2	3.9
Kyrgyz Republic	4.7	3.8	4.6	−8.4	3.6	2.0	2.5
Tajikistan	7.1	7.3	7.5	4.5	9.2	2.0	3.0
Turkmenistan	...	...	...	...	5.0	6.0	5.8
Uzbekistan	4.4	5.4	5.7	1.9	7.4	4.0	4.5
East Asia	6.4	6.1	5.5	1.8	7.6	4.7	4.5
Hong Kong, China	3.8	2.8	−1.7	−6.5	6.4	2.0	3.7
Mongolia	5.6	7.7	5.6	−4.6	1.4	2.3	5.6
People's Republic of China	6.9	6.7	6.1	2.2	8.1	5.0	4.8
Republic of Korea	3.2	2.9	2.2	−0.9	4.0	3.0	2.6
Taipei,China	3.3	2.8	3.1	3.4	6.4	3.8	3.0
South Asia	6.5	6.4	4.0	−5.2	8.3	7.0	7.4
Afghanistan	2.6	1.2	3.9	−2.4	...	...	...
Bangladesh	6.6	7.3	7.9	3.4	6.9	6.9	7.1
Bhutan	4.7	3.1	5.8	−10.1	3.5	4.5	7.5
India	6.8	6.5	3.7	−6.6	8.9	7.5	8.0
Maldives	7.2	8.1	6.9	−33.5	31.6	11.0	12.0
Nepal	9.0	7.6	6.7	−2.1	2.3	3.9	5.0
Pakistan	4.6	6.1	3.1	−1.0	5.6	4.0	4.5
Sri Lanka	3.6	3.3	2.3	−3.6	3.7	2.4	2.5
Southeast Asia	5.4	5.3	4.7	−3.2	2.9	4.9	5.2
Brunei Darussalam	1.3	0.1	3.9	1.1	−1.5	4.2	3.6
Cambodia	6.9	7.5	7.1	−3.1	3.0	5.3	6.5
Indonesia	5.1	5.2	5.0	−2.1	3.7	5.0	5.2
Lao People's Dem. Rep.	6.9	6.2	4.7	−0.5	2.3	3.4	3.7
Malaysia	5.8	4.8	4.4	−5.6	3.1	6.0	5.4
Myanmar	5.8	6.4	6.8	3.2	−18.4	−0.3	2.6
Philippines	6.9	6.3	6.1	−9.6	5.6	6.0	6.3
Singapore	4.7	3.7	1.1	−4.1	7.6	4.3	3.2
Thailand	4.2	4.2	2.2	−6.2	1.6	3.0	4.5
Timor-Leste	−3.1	−0.7	2.1	−8.6	1.8	2.5	3.1
Viet Nam	6.8	7.1	7.0	2.9	2.6	6.5	6.7
The Pacific	4.0	1.0	3.1	−6.0	−0.6	3.9	5.4
Cook Islands	6.8	8.9	5.3	−5.2	−29.1	9.1	11.2
Federated States of Micronesia	2.7	0.1	2.7	−3.8	−1.2	2.2	4.2
Fiji	5.4	3.8	−0.4	−15.2	−4.1	7.1	8.5
Kiribati	−0.2	5.3	−0.5	−0.5	1.5	1.8	2.3
Marshall Islands	3.3	3.6	6.6	−2.2	−3.3	1.2	2.2
Nauru	−5.5	5.7	1.0	0.8	1.5	1.0	2.4
Niue	2.4	6.5	5.6	...	...	...	...
Palau	−3.3	−0.1	−1.9	−9.7	−17.1	9.4	18.3
Papua New Guinea	3.5	−0.3	4.5	−3.5	1.3	3.4	4.6
Samoa	1.1	−1.2	4.4	−2.6	−8.1	0.4	2.2
Solomon Islands	5.3	3.9	1.2	−4.5	−0.5	−3.0	3.0
Tonga	3.3	0.3	0.7	0.7	−3.0	−1.2	2.9
Tuvalu	3.4	1.6	13.9	1.0	1.5	3.0	3.0
Vanuatu	6.3	2.9	3.2	−7.5	−1.0	1.0	4.0

... = data not available.

Table A2 Growth rate of GDP per capita (% per year)

	2017	2018	2019	2020	2021	2022	2023	Per capita GNI, $, 2020
Developing Asia	5.0	5.2	4.3	−1.3	6.5	4.8	4.8	
Caucasus and Central Asia	2.5	2.9	3.4	−3.2	4.3	2.3	2.8	
Armenia	8.0	5.6	7.8	−7.4	5.6	2.9	3.7	4,220
Azerbaijan	−0.9	0.6	1.6	−5.1	4.6	2.9	2.0	4,480
Georgia	4.9	4.8	5.2	−6.6	10.3	3.5	5.0	4,270
Kazakhstan	2.7	2.8	3.2	−3.8	2.7	1.9	2.6	8,710
Kyrgyz Republic	2.7	1.9	2.5	−10.5	1.9	1.0	1.5	1,160
Tajikistan	4.8	5.1	3.1	4.5	7.1	−0.1	2.0	1,060
Turkmenistan	...	...	...	...	4.0	5.0	4.8	...
Uzbekistan	2.5	3.5	3.9	0.1	5.6	2.2	2.7	1,740
East Asia	5.8	5.7	5.1	1.6	7.6	4.7	4.5	
Hong Kong, China	3.0	2.0	−2.4	−6.2	7.4	−1.2	3.1	48,630
Mongolia	3.7	5.7	3.7	−6.2	−0.2	0.5	3.8	3,740
People's Republic of China	6.3	6.2	5.7	1.9	8.0	5.0	4.8	10,550
Republic of Korea	2.9	2.4	2.0	−1.0	3.7	2.7	2.3	32,960
Taipei,China	3.1	2.7	3.0	3.3	6.4	3.7	4.0	28,794
South Asia	3.8	5.0	3.1	−6.2	7.1	5.9	6.3	
Afghanistan	0.0	−1.2	1.5	−4.8	...	...	...	500
Bangladesh	6.0	6.1	6.6	2.3	5.8	5.8	6.0	2,030
Bhutan	9.4	3.2	4.7	−10.9	2.5	3.5	6.7	2,840
India	3.9	5.2	3.0	−7.6	7.9	6.5	7.0	1,920
Maldives	3.0	3.8	2.5	−36.3	26.2	6.4	7.3	6,490
Nepal	7.6	6.1	5.2	−3.4	1.0	2.6	3.8	1,190
Pakistan	2.1	3.8	1.1	−2.9	3.5	2.0	2.4	1,270
Sri Lanka	2.4	2.2	1.7	−4.1	2.5	2.4	2.0	3,720
Southeast Asia	4.3	4.2	3.6	−4.0	2.5	4.0	4.3	
Brunei Darussalam	−1.6	−2.9	0.0	2.4	3.9	3.3	2.7	31,510
Cambodia	4.4	6.0	5.6	−4.4	1.5	3.6	5.0	1,500
Indonesia	3.9	4.1	3.9	−3.3	2.9	4.0	4.2	3,870
Lao People's Dem. Rep.	5.2	4.6	3.1	−1.9	0.7	1.8	2.1	2,520
Malaysia	4.5	3.7	4.0	−5.8	2.9	5.3	4.9	10,570
Myanmar	4.8	5.5	5.8	2.3	−19.0	−1.0	1.9	1,350
Philippines	5.2	4.7	4.6	−10.8	4.2	4.7	5.1	3,430
Singapore	4.6	3.2	−0.1	−3.8	12.2	4.2	3.1	54,920
Thailand	3.5	3.8	1.8	−6.5	1.1	2.5	4.0	7,040
Timor-Leste	−4.9	−2.6	0.1	−10.3	0.0	0.7	1.3	1,990
Viet Nam	5.7	5.9	5.0	1.7	1.6	5.2	5.4	2,650
The Pacific	1.7	−1.2	0.8	−8.2	−2.9	1.5	3.0	
Cook Islands	7.3	9.5	5.8	−4.7	−28.7	9.7	11.8	18,143
Federated States of Micronesia	2.8	−1.0	2.5	−4.0	−1.3	2.1	4.0	3,950
Fiji	4.9	3.2	−1.0	−15.6	−4.6	6.5	7.8	4,890
Kiribati	−1.4	4.0	−1.7	−3.8	−0.2	0.1	0.6	2,960
Marshall Islands	2.9	3.2	6.2	−2.6	−3.7	0.8	1.8	4,940
Nauru	−7.0	4.0	−0.7	−0.4	0.3	0.2	1.6	15,990
Niue	1.3	2.3	...	...	...	...	...	...
Palau	−3.4	2.0	−1.6	−9.4	−16.8	9.8	18.7	14,390
Papua New Guinea	0.4	−3.3	1.3	−6.4	−1.8	0.3	1.4	2,720
Samoa	0.2	−2.0	3.5	−3.4	−8.8	−0.4	1.3	4,050
Solomon Islands	2.6	1.2	−1.7	−7.0	−3.1	−5.5	0.3	2,300
Tonga	3.4	0.4	0.8	0.7	−2.9	−1.1	3.0	5,190
Tuvalu	3.6	1.8	14.2	−9.3	0.6	2.1	2.1	5,820
Vanuatu	3.9	0.8	1.0	−8.7	−3.2	−1.2	1.8	3,190

... = data not available, GNI = gross national income.

Table A3 Growth rate of value added in agriculture (% per year)

	2017	2018	2019	2020	2021	Sector share, 2020, %
Caucasus and Central Asia						
Armenia	−5.1	−6.9	−5.8	−4.1	−1.4	12.3
Azerbaijan	4.2	4.6	7.3	1.9	3.3	7.7
Georgia	−7.7	14.0	0.8	7.6	−2.5	8.3
Kazakhstan	3.2	3.8	−0.1	5.9	−2.4	5.7
Kyrgyz Republic	2.2	2.6	2.5	0.9	−5.0	15.2
Tajikistan	6.8	4.0	7.1	8.8	6.6	22.8
Turkmenistan	...	...	...	...	...	...
Uzbekistan	1.2	0.3	3.1	2.9	4.0	26.4
East Asia						
Hong Kong, China	−5.2	−1.8	−0.8	3.8	−3.0	0.1
Mongolia	−0.3	6.5	5.2	5.8	−5.5	14.3
People's Republic of China	4.0	3.5	3.1	3.1	7.1	7.0
Republic of Korea	2.3	0.2	3.9	−4.0	2.7	2.0
Taipei,China	8.3	4.5	−0.9	−1.6	−4.2	1.6
South Asia						
Afghanistan	6.4	−4.4	17.5	5.9	...	22.9
Bangladesh	3.2	3.5	3.3	3.4	3.2	12.4
Bhutan	2.9	4.2	1.3	4.6	3.6	19.8
India	6.6	2.1	5.5	3.3	3.3	20.0
Maldives	8.3	4.8	−7.6	7.0	−4.9	8.8
Nepal	5.2	2.6	5.2	2.2	2.4	26.2
Pakistan	2.2	3.9	0.9	3.9	3.5	21.9
Sri Lanka	−0.4	5.8	1.2	−2.2	2.0	9.1
Southeast Asia						
Brunei Darussalam	−1.6	−1.6	−1.4	14.4	46.8	1.2
Cambodia	1.7	1.1	−0.5	0.4	1.1	24.4
Indonesia	3.9	3.9	3.6	1.8	1.8	14.2
Lao People's Dem. Rep.	2.9	1.3	1.0	2.1	1.2	17.3
Malaysia	5.9	0.1	2.0	−2.2	−0.2	8.3
Myanmar	−1.5	0.1	1.6	1.7	0.8	20.9
Philippines	4.2	1.1	1.2	−0.2	−0.3	10.2
Singapore	2.9	3.3	6.6	−4.2	10.8	0.0
Thailand	4.8	6.1	−0.9	−3.5	1.4	8.7
Timor-Leste	−3.0	2.9	2.5	5.1	1.8	19.0
Viet Nam	2.9	3.8	2.0	2.7	2.9	13.6
The Pacific						
Cook Islands	2.5	0.0	−2.1	−8.6	−4.0	3.0
Federated States of Micronesia	−0.9	0.1	2.1	−2.2	−1.0	25.6
Fiji	10.8	3.7	4.4	4.4	−5.8	11.7
Kiribati	13.1	−2.6	2.5	−1.0	...	25.2
Marshall Islands	2.0	4.3	31.7	0.7	−0.6	21.4
Nauru	...	...	...	...	...	...
Niue	3.5	1.7	...	...	...	...
Palau	8.4	−5.2	−4.2	...	...	...
Papua New Guinea	2.4	4.6	2.3	0.1	3.7	19.4
Samoa	15.7	−7.8	−6.4	−1.2	0.8	10.3
Solomon Islands	3.6	2.1	−2.6	−4.5	−4.4	31.0
Tonga	−2.5	0.4	3.6	0.8	−1.4	23.7
Tuvalu	3.4	1.6	13.9	...	...	...
Vanuatu	0.2	0.9	6.2	1.3	2.8	25.2

... = data not available.

Table A4 Growth rate of value added in industry (% per year)

	2017	2018	2019	2020	2021	Sector share, 2020, %
Caucasus and Central Asia						
Armenia	9.0	3.7	10.5	−2.9	3.8	29.6
Azerbaijan	−3.1	−0.7	1.0	−5.7	2.8	45.8
Georgia	4.4	−0.3	2.3	−6.6	6.2	24.2
Kazakhstan	6.8	4.4	5.5	1.5	4.5	35.0
Kyrgyz Republic	8.6	5.9	8.0	−9.9	3.1	32.8
Tajikistan	21.3	11.8	13.6	9.7	22.0	35.1
Turkmenistan	...	...	...	...	...	...
Uzbekistan	5.2	10.8	5.0	0.9	8.7	34.4
East Asia						
Hong Kong, China	−0.7	2.4	−6.5	−11.4	2.0	6.4
Mongolia	1.4	8.5	3.1	−4.4	−2.8	40.9
People's Republic of China	5.9	5.8	4.9	2.5	8.2	45.3
Republic of Korea	4.2	2.0	0.7	−0.7	5.0	35.6
Taipei,China	4.7	2.6	1.4	7.0	12.9	37.1
South Asia						
Afghanistan	9.2	11.1	4.8	−4.6	...	29.4
Bangladesh	8.3	10.2	11.6	3.6	10.3	34.1
Bhutan	2.5	−5.0	2.0	−13.1	4.7	35.4
India	5.9	5.3	−1.4	−3.3	10.3	26.9
Maldives	13.0	15.5	1.9	−25.4	−1.0	13.1
Nepal	17.1	10.4	7.4	−3.7	1.7	13.4
Pakistan	4.6	9.2	0.3	−5.8	7.8	18.6
Sri Lanka	4.7	1.3	2.6	−6.9	5.3	27.8
Southeast Asia						
Brunei Darussalam	1.5	−0.4	4.2	2.9	−4.4	58.1
Cambodia	9.7	11.6	11.3	−1.4	7.4	37.0
Indonesia	4.1	4.3	3.8	−2.8	3.4	39.7
Lao People's Dem. Rep.	11.6	7.8	3.7	6.2	4.4	34.2
Malaysia	4.8	3.2	2.3	−6.6	6.0	33.4
Myanmar	8.7	8.3	8.4	3.8	−20.9	38.6
Philippines	7.0	7.3	5.5	−13.2	8.2	28.4
Singapore	6.9	5.6	−1.1	0.3	13.4	27.2
Thailand	1.7	2.9	0.0	−5.4	3.4	33.2
Timor-Leste	−26.5	5.3	4.8	−28.5	1.8	13.1
Viet Nam	8.0	8.9	8.9	4.0	4.0	40.5
The Pacific						
Cook Islands	11.1	11.7	25.6	−31.6	−17.9	8.4
Federated States of Micronesia	2.9	−7.3	−6.9	−0.5	2.0	4.4
Fiji	4.2	5.5	−0.5	−6.2	2.4	22.2
Kiribati	−15.2	−13.9	−9.9	−1.6	...	9.4
Marshall Islands	−0.7	7.9	15.2	−4.7	−10.9	12.6
Nauru	...	...	...	...	...	...
Niue	−4.7	90.4	...	...	...	...
Palau	−5.8	2.3	5.9	...	...	...
Papua New Guinea	4.7	−7.5	7.5	−6.5	−2.8	36.4
Samoa	−6.0	−12.4	10.2	−7.7	−10.3	14.9
Solomon Islands	10.5	9.1	5.2	−13.9	7.1	17.6
Tonga	9.7	−14.4	4.6	−2.9	−5.3	17.7
Tuvalu	0.0	2.2	5.6	...	...	...
Vanuatu	10.1	4.9	−8.3	0.7	9.5	11.0

... = data not available.

Table A5 Growth rate of value added in services (% per year)

	2017	2018	2019	2020	2021	Sector share, 2020, %
Caucasus and Central Asia						
Armenia	10.4	9.2	9.8	−8.8	6.8	58.1
Azerbaijan	3.1	3.8	3.8	−3.9	7.8	46.5
Georgia	6.4	5.6	6.4	−8.1	14.5	67.5
Kazakhstan	2.5	3.9	4.4	−5.3	3.9	59.3
Kyrgyz Republic	3.3	2.8	3.2	−9.8	6.5	52.0
Tajikistan	1.8	2.1	2.9	−2.6	7.9	42.1
Turkmenistan	...	...	...	...	...	...
Uzbekistan	6.3	5.6	6.4	−0.7	9.2	39.2
East Asia						
Hong Kong, China	3.5	3.1	−0.7	−6.7	5.7	93.5
Mongolia	7.1	5.1	6.4	−6.5	3.9	44.7
People's Republic of China	8.3	8.0	7.2	1.9	8.2	47.7
Republic of Korea	2.6	3.8	3.4	−1.0	3.7	62.4
Taipei,China	2.9	3.0	3.6	1.1	2.7	61.3
South Asia						
Afghanistan	−0.7	1.9	−1.4	−5.9	...	47.7
Bangladesh	6.4	6.6	6.9	3.9	5.7	53.4
Bhutan	6.7	8.9	13.2	−6.9	2.8	44.9
India	6.3	7.2	6.3	−7.8	8.6	53.1
Maldives	6.2	7.3	8.6	−34.3	36.2	78.1
Nepal	8.4	9.3	6.8	−4.0	2.5	60.4
Pakistan	5.6	6.0	5.0	−1.3	5.7	53.7
Sri Lanka	3.6	4.6	2.3	−1.6	3.0	63.1
Southeast Asia						
Brunei Darussalam	1.1	0.8	3.4	−2.1	0.4	40.7
Cambodia	7.0	6.8	6.2	−6.3	−0.4	38.6
Indonesia	5.7	5.8	6.4	−1.5	3.6	46.1
Lao People's Dem. Rep.	4.5	6.8	7.4	−5.5	0.4	48.5
Malaysia	6.3	6.9	6.2	−5.5	1.9	58.3
Myanmar	8.1	8.7	8.3	3.4	−26.3	40.5
Philippines	7.4	6.7	7.2	−9.2	5.3	61.4
Singapore	3.8	3.5	1.8	−4.7	5.2	73.0
Thailand	5.6	4.8	3.9	−7.0	0.6	58.0
Timor-Leste	2.7	−2.1	1.2	−7.1	1.8	67.9
Viet Nam	7.4	7.0	7.3	2.3	1.2	45.9
The Pacific						
Cook Islands	9.5	7.0	4.3	0.1	−26.8	88.7
Federated States of Micronesia	2.9	0.8	3.0	−4.5	−1.4	70.0
Fiji	3.6	1.7	0.2	−12.8	−2.6	66.2
Kiribati	4.8	2.0	3.4	2.0	...	65.4
Marshall Islands	5.1	3.2	1.2	−1.9	−2.9	66.0
Nauru	...	...	...	...	...	...
Niue	2.4	4.7	...	...	...	...
Palau	−2.8	9.3	0.6	...	...	...
Papua New Guinea	1.4	5.0	2.5	−0.6	2.7	44.2
Samoa	0.9	2.3	4.7	−1.7	−8.7	74.9
Solomon Islands	5.0	3.7	2.4	−2.0	−0.3	51.4
Tonga	1.8	3.3	0.8	0.9	0.3	58.6
Tuvalu	13.7	−8.5	77.0	...	...	...
Vanuatu	4.6	0.8	6.1	−14.6	−5.3	63.8

... = data not available.

Table A6 Inflation (% per year)

	2017	2018	2019	2020	2021	2022	2023
Developing Asia	2.6	2.7	3.3	3.2	2.5	3.7	3.1
Caucasus and Central Asia	9.1	8.2	7.3	7.7	8.9	8.8	7.1
Armenia	1.0	2.5	1.4	1.2	7.2	9.0	7.5
Azerbaijan	12.9	2.3	2.6	2.8	6.7	7.0	5.3
Georgia	6.0	2.6	4.9	5.2	9.6	7.0	4.0
Kazakhstan	7.5	6.0	5.3	6.8	8.0	7.8	6.4
Kyrgyz Republic	3.2	1.5	1.1	6.3	11.9	15.0	12.0
Tajikistan	6.7	5.4	8.0	9.4	8.0	15.0	10.0
Turkmenistan	8.0	13.2	13.0	10.0	12.5	13.0	10.0
Uzbekistan	13.7	17.5	14.6	12.9	10.7	9.0	8.0
East Asia	1.5	2.0	2.6	2.2	1.1	2.4	2.0
Hong Kong, China	1.5	2.3	2.9	0.3	1.6	2.3	2.0
Mongolia	4.3	6.8	7.3	3.7	7.1	12.4	9.3
People's Republic of China	1.6	2.1	2.9	2.5	0.9	2.3	2.0
Republic of Korea	1.9	1.5	0.4	0.5	2.5	3.2	2.0
Taipei,China	0.6	1.3	0.6	−0.2	2.0	1.9	1.6
South Asia	3.9	3.7	5.0	6.5	5.7	6.5	5.5
Afghanistan	5.0	0.6	2.3	5.6	5.2	...	...
Bangladesh	5.4	5.8	5.5	5.7	5.6	6.0	5.9
Bhutan	5.0	2.6	2.8	5.6	7.4	7.0	5.5
India	3.6	3.4	4.8	6.2	5.4	5.8	5.0
Maldives	2.8	−0.1	0.2	−1.4	0.5	3.0	2.5
Nepal	4.5	4.2	4.6	6.2	3.6	6.5	6.2
Pakistan	4.8	4.7	6.8	10.7	8.9	11.0	8.5
Sri Lanka	6.6	4.3	4.3	4.6	6.0	13.3	6.7
Southeast Asia	2.9	2.8	2.6	1.5	2.0	3.7	3.1
Brunei Darussalam	−1.3	1.0	−0.4	1.9	1.7	1.6	1.0
Cambodia	2.9	2.5	1.9	2.9	2.9	4.7	2.2
Indonesia	3.8	3.2	3.8	2.0	1.6	3.6	3.0
Lao People's Dem. Rep.	0.8	2.0	3.3	5.1	3.7	5.8	5.0
Malaysia	3.8	1.0	0.7	−1.1	2.5	3.0	2.5
Myanmar	4.0	5.9	8.6	5.7	3.6	8.0	8.5
Philippines	2.9	5.2	2.4	2.4	3.9	4.2	3.5
Singapore	0.6	0.4	0.6	−0.2	2.3	3.0	2.3
Thailand	0.7	1.1	0.7	−0.8	1.2	3.3	2.2
Timor-Leste	0.6	2.4	1.0	0.5	3.8	2.6	2.7
Viet Nam	3.5	3.5	2.8	3.2	1.8	3.8	4.0
The Pacific	4.5	4.3	2.9	2.9	3.1	5.9	4.7
Cook Islands	−0.4	0.1	0.0	0.7	2.2	4.3	4.0
Federated States of Micronesia	0.7	1.7	−2.6	−2.9	2.0	4.6	2.0
Fiji	3.3	4.1	1.8	−2.6	0.2	4.5	4.0
Kiribati	0.3	0.6	−1.8	2.3	1.0	5.0	3.7
Marshall Islands	0.0	0.8	0.1	−0.8	1.0	4.1	4.0
Nauru	5.1	0.5	4.3	0.9	1.2	2.3	2.2
Niue	5.0	10.1	1.9	2.7	...	...	...
Palau	0.9	2.0	0.6	0.7	0.5	4.3	4.2
Papua New Guinea	5.4	4.7	3.6	4.9	4.5	6.4	5.1
Samoa	1.3	3.7	2.2	1.5	−3.0	8.9	3.2
Solomon Islands	0.5	3.5	1.6	3.0	−0.2	5.0	4.0
Tonga	9.4	−3.8	4.0	0.2	1.4	7.6	4.2
Tuvalu	4.1	2.2	3.5	1.6	6.7	3.8	3.3
Vanuatu	3.1	2.3	2.8	5.3	2.1	4.8	3.2

... = data not available.

Table A7 Change in money supply (% per year)

	2017	2018	2019	2020	2021
Caucasus and Central Asia					
Armenia	18.5	7.4	11.2	9.0	13.1
Azerbaijan	9.0	5.7	20.0	1.1	18.7
Georgia	14.8	14.7	16.7	23.3	11.3
Kazakhstan	−1.7	7.0	2.4	16.9	20.8
Kyrgyz Republic	17.9	5.5	12.8	23.9	19.1
Tajikistan	21.8	5.1	17.0	18.4	12.3
Turkmenistan	11.4	8.4	12.9	11.8	15.6
Uzbekistan	41.0	13.2	13.8	17.9	30.3
East Asia					
Hong Kong, China	10.0	4.3	2.7	5.8	4.3
Mongolia	30.5	22.8	7.0	16.3	15.0
People's Republic of China	9.0	8.1	8.7	10.1	9.0
Republic of Korea	5.1	6.7	7.9	9.8	12.9
Taipei,China	3.6	2.7	4.5	9.4	7.3
South Asia					
Afghanistan	4.1	2.6	5.7	12.1	...
Bangladesh	10.9	9.2	9.9	12.6	13.6
Bhutan	17.4	6.5	13.1	27.7	...
India	9.2	10.5	8.9	12.2	8.7
Maldives	5.2	3.4	9.5	14.2	26.6
Nepal	15.5	19.4	15.8	18.1	21.8
Pakistan	13.7	9.7	11.3	17.5	16.1
Sri Lanka	16.7	13.0	7.0	23.4	13.2
Southeast Asia					
Brunei Darussalam	−0.4	2.8	4.3	−0.4	2.7
Cambodia	23.1	26.6	18.2	15.3	16.3
Indonesia	8.3	6.3	6.5	12.5	13.9
Lao People's Dem. Rep.	12.2	8.4	18.9	16.3	24.0
Malaysia	4.9	9.1	3.5	4.0	6.4
Myanmar	18.0	18.6	15.4	15.0	9.5
Philippines	11.9	9.5	11.5	9.6	7.3
Singapore	11.1	3.2	5.5	12.7	7.8
Thailand	5.0	4.7	3.6	10.1	4.6
Timor-Leste	12.1	3.1	−7.1	10.2	28.7
Viet Nam	15.0	12.4	14.8	14.5	10.7
The Pacific					
Cook Islands	12.3	14.8	7.3	14.8	−6.6
Federated States of Micronesia	...	...	...	...	...
Fiji	8.5	3.1	2.5	0.9	11.9
Kiribati	...	...	...	...	...
Marshall Islands	...	...	...	...	...
Nauru	...	...	...	...	...
Niue	...	...	...	...	...
Palau	...	...	...	...	...
Papua New Guinea	−0.7	−4.0	4.7	7.0	...
Samoa	7.8	16.5	9.9	−0.9	...
Solomon Islands	3.5	6.8	−3.1	6.6	3.4
Tonga	11.3	10.6	1.8	1.1	19.3
Tuvalu	...	...	...	...	...
Vanuatu	9.3	13.1	7.0	−0.7	7.2

... = data not available.

Table A8 Central government revenue (% of GDP)

	2017	2018	2019	2020	2021
Caucasus and Central Asia					
Armenia	22.2	22.3	23.9	25.2	24.1
Azerbaijan	23.4	28.0	29.5	34.1	28.4
Georgia	26.8	26.5	26.2	25.2	25.7
Kazakhstan	21.3	17.5	18.3	20.6	19.5
Kyrgyz Republic	28.2	26.6	27.0	25.3	29.0
Tajikistan	30.6	29.1	26.7	27.2	28.5
Turkmenistan	14.9	13.5	12.9	13.3	12.3
Uzbekistan	24.1	27.7	27.7	26.9	27.7
East Asia					
Hong Kong, China	23.3	21.2	20.8	21.1	23.9
Mongolia	28.3	30.9	31.5	27.8	33.1
People's Republic of China	20.7	19.9	19.3	18.0	17.7
Republic of Korea	18.7	19.7	19.4	19.2	22.3
Taipei,China	10.8	11.0	11.0	11.0	11.0
South Asia					
Afghanistan	27.1	30.6	26.9	25.7	...
Bangladesh	8.7	8.2	8.5	8.4	9.3
Bhutan	28.0	31.9	24.3	31.2	33.0
India	9.1	8.8	8.7	8.5	9.4
Maldives	27.7	27.2	26.9	26.4	25.6
Nepal	20.8	22.2	22.4	22.1	24.2
Pakistan	13.9	13.3	11.2	13.2	12.4
Sri Lanka	13.8	13.5	12.7	9.1	8.6
Southeast Asia					
Brunei Darussalam	22.7	32.7	26.4	12.5	21.1
Cambodia	21.6	23.7	26.8	24.5	21.4
Indonesia	12.3	13.1	12.4	10.7	11.8
Lao People's Dem. Rep.	16.1	16.2	15.7	12.9	14.2
Malaysia	16.1	16.1	17.5	15.9	17.8
Myanmar	18.6	19.2	18.2	18.4	15.7
Philippines	14.9	15.6	16.1	15.9	15.5
Singapore	19.1	17.7	17.8	18.0	18.9
Thailand	16.3	15.5	17.0	17.1	16.9
Timor-Leste	128.4	77.1	81.3	159.2	127.4
Viet Nam	25.8	25.9	25.7	18.9	18.1
The Pacific					
Cook Islands	43.8	45.9	42.3	44.8	42.5
Federated States of Micronesia	78.3	80.0	75.4	72.1	69.8
Fiji	26.4	28.5	27.0	25.1	22.1
Kiribati	129.0	111.9	121.0	129.5	117.3
Marshall Islands	68.3	62.5	61.9	69.4	72.4
Nauru	121.8	129.3	148.7	170.2	179.3
Niue	58.0	69.3	81.0	50.1	107.5
Palau	40.3	44.5	44.5	47.4	46.3
Papua New Guinea	15.9	17.7	16.3	14.2	14.7
Samoa	29.3	30.6	31.7	37.6	39.1
Solomon Islands	39.2	40.2	32.7	34.4	32.9
Tonga	42.4	42.6	41.7	34.3	36.6
Tuvalu	114.2	168.5	131.7	124.4	101.4
Vanuatu	35.6	38.8	41.7	38.1	37.9

... = data not available.

Table A9 Central government expenditure (% of GDP)

	2017	2018	2019	2020	2021
Caucasus and Central Asia					
Armenia	27.0	24.0	24.9	30.6	28.5
Azerbaijan	25.0	28.4	29.8	36.5	29.5
Georgia	27.6	27.2	28.3	34.5	32.2
Kazakhstan	23.9	18.8	20.2	24.5	22.6
Kyrgyz Republic	28.8	27.7	27.1	28.6	29.3
Tajikistan	35.7	31.9	30.4	31.6	30.5
Turkmenistan	17.8	13.7	13.3	13.5	12.6
Uzbekistan	25.2	29.5	31.4	31.2	33.5
East Asia					
Hong Kong, China	17.7	18.8	21.4	30.5	24.4
Mongolia	32.2	28.3	30.2	37.3	36.3
People's Republic of China	24.4	24.0	24.2	24.2	21.5
Republic of Korea	20.7	21.4	23.7	26.8	27.6
Taipei,China	10.9	10.9	10.9	12.4	12.5
South Asia					
Afghanistan	27.7	28.9	28.0	27.9	...
Bangladesh	11.6	12.2	13.3	13.3	13.0
Bhutan	32.8	34.5	25.5	33.1	39.1
India	12.5	12.2	13.4	17.7	16.2
Maldives	30.8	32.5	33.6	49.9	42.2
Nepal	23.6	28.0	27.3	27.4	28.4
Pakistan	19.1	19.1	19.1	20.3	18.6
Sri Lanka	19.3	18.8	20.6	21.9	19.8
Southeast Asia					
Brunei Darussalam	35.7	32.5	31.9	32.2	47.3
Cambodia	22.4	23.0	23.8	28.0	25.5
Indonesia	14.8	14.9	14.6	16.8	16.4
Lao People's Dem. Rep.	21.6	20.9	19.0	18.3	15.7
Malaysia	19.0	19.8	20.9	19.4	18.4
Myanmar	21.5	23.2	22.3	23.4	21.7
Philippines	17.1	18.7	19.5	23.6	24.1
Singapore	16.8	17.1	17.7	28.8	19.9
Thailand	17.9	17.5	20.9	28.8	29.5
Timor-Leste	83.4	81.5	81.2	82.1	96.5
Viet Nam	27.1	25.9	25.3	22.4	21.9
The Pacific					
Cook Islands	35.4	41.8	37.3	51.1	65.6
Federated States of Micronesia	64.0	55.7	56.3	63.0	63.5
Fiji	28.5	32.9	30.6	31.0	32.9
Kiribati	117.3	85.6	104.9	124.8	140.7
Marshall Islands	63.9	60.0	63.7	65.1	71.0
Nauru	101.8	95.6	118.9	134.5	135.5
Niue	62.6	69.7	82.2	55.0	119.8
Palau	35.5	38.2	44.1	58.3	65.8
Papua New Guinea	18.4	20.3	21.3	22.7	21.9
Samoa	30.3	30.8	29.0	30.7	37.2
Solomon Islands	42.1	39.3	33.5	36.8	36.1
Tonga	40.3	39.7	38.5	34.2	37.7
Tuvalu	106.6	132.6	113.7	115.7	96.1
Vanuatu	36.8	31.8	39.0	40.5	40.9

... = data not available.

Table A10 Fiscal balance of central government (% of GDP)

	2017	2018	2019	2020	2021
Caucasus and Central Asia					
Armenia	−4.8	−1.8	−1.0	−5.4	−4.4
Azerbaijan	−1.6	−0.4	−0.3	−2.4	−1.1
Georgia	−0.8	−0.7	−2.1	−9.3	−6.4
Kazakhstan	−2.7	−1.3	−1.9	−4.0	−3.1
Kyrgyz Republic	−0.6	−1.1	−0.1	−3.3	−0.3
Tajikistan	−5.1	−2.8	−3.8	−4.4	−2.0
Turkmenistan	−2.8	−0.2	−0.4	−0.2	−0.3
Uzbekistan	−1.1	−1.8	−3.7	−4.4	−5.7
East Asia					
Hong Kong, China	5.6	2.4	−0.6	−9.4	−0.6
Mongolia	−3.9	2.5	1.3	−9.5	−3.1
People's Republic of China	−3.7	−4.1	−4.9	−6.2	−3.8
Republic of Korea	−2.0	−1.8	−4.2	−7.5	−5.3
Taipei,China	−0.1	0.1	0.1	−1.4	−1.5
South Asia					
Afghanistan	−0.7	1.6	−1.1	−2.2	...
Bangladesh	−2.9	−4.0	−4.7	−4.9	−3.7
Bhutan	−4.8	−2.6	−1.2	−1.9	−6.1
India	−3.5	−3.4	−4.7	−9.2	−6.9
Maldives	−3.1	−5.3	−6.7	−23.5	−16.6
Nepal	−2.8	−5.8	−5.0	−5.3	−4.2
Pakistan	−5.2	−5.8	−7.9	−7.1	−6.1
Sri Lanka	−5.5	−5.3	−8.0	−12.7	−11.1
Southeast Asia					
Brunei Darussalam	−12.9	0.2	−5.6	−19.7	−26.3
Cambodia	−0.8	0.7	3.0	−3.5	−4.0
Indonesia	−2.5	−1.8	−2.2	−6.1	−4.6
Lao People's Dem. Rep.	−5.6	−4.7	−3.3	−5.3	−1.5
Malaysia	−2.9	−3.7	−3.4	−3.5	−0.6
Myanmar	−2.9	−4.0	−4.1	−5.0	−6.0
Philippines	−2.1	−3.1	−3.4	−7.6	−8.6
Singapore	2.3	0.7	0.2	−10.8	−1.0
Thailand	−2.6	−2.4	−3.9	−11.7	−12.5
Timor-Leste	44.9	−4.5	0.1	77.2	30.9
Viet Nam	−1.2	−0.1	0.4	−3.5	−3.8
The Pacific					
Cook Islands	8.4	4.1	4.9	−6.3	−23.1
Federated States of Micronesia	14.3	24.3	19.1	9.0	6.3
Fiji	−2.1	−4.4	−3.6	−5.9	−10.8
Kiribati	11.7	26.2	16.0	4.7	−23.4
Marshall Islands	4.4	2.5	−1.8	4.3	1.4
Nauru	20.0	33.7	29.8	35.7	43.8
Niue	−4.6	−0.5	−1.2	−4.9	−12.2
Palau	4.8	6.3	0.4	−10.9	−19.5
Papua New Guinea	−2.5	−2.6	−5.0	−8.6	−7.1
Samoa	−1.1	−0.2	2.7	6.9	1.9
Solomon Islands	−2.9	0.9	−0.9	−2.4	−3.2
Tonga	2.1	2.9	3.2	0.1	−1.0
Tuvalu	7.6	35.9	18.0	8.7	5.4
Vanuatu	−1.2	7.0	2.8	−2.3	−3.0

... = data not available.

Table A11 Growth rate of merchandise exports (% per year)

	2017	2018	2019	2020	2021	2022	2023
Developing Asia	11.9	9.0	−2.4	−0.9	30.5	11.2	8.6
Caucasus and Central Asia	23.0	24.4	4.5	−16.2	29.6	28.3	6.1
Armenia	26.2	14.1	20.7	−19.2	10.5	3.5	6.0
Azerbaijan	14.7	37.2	−4.5	−36.6	80.1	18.1	−10.1
Georgia	24.0	22.4	12.2	−12.4	25.2	12.1	14.9
Kazakhstan	33.3	26.5	−2.8	−18.7	27.2	38.2	0.7
Kyrgyz Republic	14.4	4.2	6.6	−3.4	15.9	5.0	5.0
Tajikistan	9.4	−10.4	9.3	19.8	52.8	15.0	10.0
Turkmenistan	3.6	49.6	−4.7	...	...	...	...
Uzbekistan	17.5	12.0	22.1	−6.8	8.8	27.0	23.0
East Asia	11.5	8.5	−2.3	3.5	28.9	9.1	5.9
Hong Kong, China	7.8	5.1	−4.4	−0.3	24.6	5.7	4.8
Mongolia	21.4	12.4	9.6	−2.7	18.0	1.3	14.5
People's Republic of China	11.4	9.1	−1.3	4.6	29.0	9.0	5.0
Republic of Korea	13.4	7.9	−11.1	−7.0	25.5	10.9	15.7
Taipei,China	10.8	0.8	−4.3	3.6	34.0	8.2	5.8
South Asia	8.9	9.2	−3.3	−8.5	37.0	10.4	13.7
Afghanistan	27.6	11.6	−1.3	−10.1	...	...	...
Bangladesh	1.7	6.7	9.1	−17.1	15.4	26.2	8.1
Bhutan	12.0	5.9	13.1	−5.4	30.0	16.5	18.4
India	10.3	9.1	−5.0	−7.5	42.5	6.8	12.5
Maldives	24.3	6.6	6.3	−28.6	12.4	10.8	−2.6
Nepal	9.8	15.8	12.5	−7.6	31.0	25.0	27.5
Pakistan	0.1	12.6	−2.1	−7.1	13.7	28.0	30.0
Sri Lanka	10.2	4.7	0.4	−15.9	24.4	5.0	2.8
Southeast Asia	15.5	7.9	−2.5	−3.3	27.5	17.1	11.0
Brunei Darussalam	13.8	18.2	11.4	−9.4	61.6	15.8	8.9
Cambodia	9.3	15.5	15.6	23.6	5.1	15.5	14.0
Indonesia	16.9	7.0	−6.8	−3.0	42.5	26.0	8.9
Lao People's Dem. Rep.	14.8	18.6	2.8	8.1	20.6	4.7	5.8
Malaysia	12.5	10.4	−4.1	−6.2	27.5	29.3	22.2
Myanmar	10.5	7.4	−6.8	−4.1	−13.0	4.2	5.5
Philippines	21.2	0.3	2.9	−9.8	12.4	7.6	8.0
Singapore	11.8	10.4	−3.9	−5.6	20.6	6.5	7.5
Thailand	9.5	7.5	−3.3	−6.5	18.8	6.3	12.8
Timor-Leste	−17.4	48.6	5.5	−33.0	123.1	12.9	10.0
Viet Nam	21.2	13.9	8.4	7.0	19.0	8.0	10.0
The Pacific	16.3	4.3	6.3	−17.4	7.0	19.5	2.0
Cook Islands	−16.4	91.6	−56.3	110.6	...	...	...
Federated States of Micronesia	11.2	−14.7	5.9	−26.6	1.4	4.2	3.6
Fiji	7.1	1.9	2.2	−20.4	4.7	5.0	5.0
Kiribati	45.9	−44.9	46.9	−20.1	39.9	−11.4	12.8
Marshall Islands	16.0	4.9	8.1	3.6	...	...	...
Nauru	−45.4	−14.8	17.0	−61.5	125.0	9.1	−16.0
Niue	29.0	−5.3	...	...	...	...	...
Palau	9.6	6.2	−13.5	−54.5	42.6	16.1	37.6
Papua New Guinea	21.6	5.4	8.8	−18.6	7.9	27.0	0.3
Samoa	2.9	−4.6	38.0	−9.5	−23.1	15.2	0.7
Solomon Islands	8.3	14.5	−14.0	−17.7	−5.7	−12.2	−1.9
Tonga	−17.3	−31.2	9.9	14.3	31.4	−4.4	29.8
Tuvalu	−14.3	−51.6	152.5	−78.1	14.2	52.6	7.0
Vanuatu	20.3	4.4	−27.8	1.2	13.3	3.8	8.0

... = data not available.

Table A12 Growth rate of merchandise imports (% per year)

	2017	2018	2019	2020	2021	2022	2023
Developing Asia	16.2	14.8	−3.6	−6.8	36.2	12.5	10.4
Caucasus and Central Asia	9.5	16.4	12.6	−9.7	14.4	6.7	4.0
Armenia	32.0	17.4	12.8	−20.0	6.0	6.5	8.0
Azerbaijan	0.4	21.2	3.5	−11.1	16.2	−10.3	−4.8
Georgia	9.3	15.1	1.8	−13.5	26.7	8.0	9.6
Kazakhstan	16.5	12.0	16.9	−7.5	6.3	8.4	2.4
Kyrgyz Republic	12.1	17.9	−5.7	−20.3	49.8	5.0	5.0
Tajikistan	−8.5	13.5	6.3	−5.9	33.6	33.3	20.0
Turkmenistan	−22.7	−47.8	9.6	...	...	...	...
Uzbekistan	12.1	47.5	16.1	−10.1	20.7	9.1	8.0
East Asia	15.7	15.8	−2.7	−1.3	34.3	11.1	9.0
Hong Kong, China	8.7	6.6	−7.0	−2.1	22.9	6.4	5.6
Mongolia	25.2	35.5	2.4	−13.1	32.7	10.2	7.6
People's Republic of China	16.0	17.1	−2.1	−0.6	34.6	11.0	8.5
Republic of Korea	18.0	10.6	−7.6	−8.3	31.2	13.8	16.3
Taipei,China	9.7	6.5	−1.9	−2.1	37.9	9.6	6.4
South Asia	18.2	11.9	−6.8	−16.0	47.7	12.0	14.2
Afghanistan	8.2	−1.4	−7.0	−4.6	...	...	...
Bangladesh	9.0	25.2	1.8	−8.6	19.7	24.3	2.5
Bhutan	4.2	0.2	−4.6	−12.6	18.0	14.8	16.7
India	19.5	10.3	−7.6	−16.6	54.3	8.2	13.3
Maldives	6.3	24.2	−0.4	−37.9	42.2	16.5	0.5
Nepal	29.4	27.9	5.2	−18.9	26.5	7.3	4.3
Pakistan	16.4	16.0	−6.8	−15.9	23.3	36.0	35.0
Sri Lanka	9.4	6.0	−10.3	−19.5	28.5	6.2	2.3
Southeast Asia	15.5	15.4	−4.5	−12.3	30.3	18.5	10.9
Brunei Darussalam	15.5	33.7	21.8	3.5	57.8	9.3	12.1
Cambodia	9.8	21.3	18.3	−5.3	45.9	−7.7	10.3
Indonesia	16.2	20.6	−8.8	−18.1	39.9	30.5	9.7
Lao People's Dem. Rep.	7.9	6.1	−0.9	−10.8	12.3	12.9	6.1
Malaysia	12.9	11.4	−5.7	−9.1	28.2	32.1	24.1
Myanmar	9.3	2.9	−13.8	5.9	−23.0	1.0	8.5
Philippines	17.6	11.9	−0.2	−20.2	31.7	16.3	10.0
Singapore	11.6	12.7	−3.3	−8.8	22.8	9.0	8.0
Thailand	13.2	13.7	−5.6	−13.8	23.4	1.8	7.0
Timor-Leste	11.4	−2.9	−3.4	−11.0	71.2	31.1	21.7
Viet Nam	22.3	12.2	7.0	3.7	26.5	7.0	9.0
The Pacific	33.4	13.0	5.0	−18.1	−8.7	18.2	12.6
Cook Islands	11.4	15.2	−4.7	−5.3	...	...	...
Federated States of Micronesia	9.6	0.1	−0.3	−5.0	2.9	24.6	20.5
Fiji	7.9	11.4	−13.6	−25.9	−6.4	26.1	9.7
Kiribati	5.8	−11.6	5.9	1.1	0.8	6.2	0.8
Marshall Islands	12.5	11.4	58.6	−37.2	...	...	...
Nauru	−5.9	33.3	0.7	4.8	24.0	−4.2	−1.9
Niue	30.0	7.8	...	...	...	...	...
Palau	4.0	−1.0	3.0	−1.7	−18.3	21.9	21.0
Papua New Guinea	47.9	14.7	12.1	−16.5	−11.3	17.0	14.0
Samoa	0.4	6.7	6.2	−9.5	0.9	−4.8	4.2
Solomon Islands	10.2	14.7	−6.2	−18.6	4.1	13.8	11.7
Tonga	7.0	5.2	2.2	−5.5	−3.2	8.4	8.3
Tuvalu	2.7	−8.3	95.1	4.4	−1.9	3.4	5.1
Vanuatu	−1.4	−4.2	6.1	−21.2	10.8	13.6	10.1

... = data not available.

Table A13 Trade balance ($ million)

	2017	2018	2019	2020	2021	2022	2023
Developing Asia	581,284	403,003	427,649	701,905	669,715	664,236	574,736
Caucasus and Central Asia	7,492	22,038	14,318	–2,773	9,891	34,879	32,808
Armenia	–1,401	–1,724	–1,728	–1,356	–1,318	–1,492	–1,672
Azerbaijan	6,115	9,841	8,533	2,512	10,968	16,283	14,079
Georgia	–5,311	–5,982	–5,721	–4,709	–5,831	–6,119	–6,457
Kazakhstan	16,728	25,579	18,131	10,286	20,836	40,517	40,120
Kyrgyz Republic	–2,383	–3,034	–2,626	–1,746	–3,911	–4,107	–4,312
Tajikistan	–1,639	–2,104	–2,165	–1,671	–1,953	–3,010	–3,868
Turkmenistan	–2,401	6,328	7,186	...	...	...	...
Uzbekistan	–2,215	–6,866	–7,291	–6,088	–8,900	–7,193	–5,082
East Asia	649,376	525,594	516,251	667,061	724,805	710,564	639,455
Hong Kong, China	–22,909	–32,276	–15,381	–5,327	2,775	–1,767	–7,568
Mongolia	1,494	676	1,158	1,756	1,302	700	1,335
People's Republic of China	475,941	380,074	392,993	515,000	554,400	550,944	474,855
Republic of Korea	113,593	110,087	79,812	80,605	76,207	68,000	75,000
Taipei,China	81,257	67,034	57,668	75,028	90,120	92,687	95,833
South Asia	–221,862	–259,165	–228,323	–163,082	–265,703	–306,494	–352,870
Afghanistan	–5,932	–5,721	–5,294	–5,101	...	...	...
Bangladesh	–9,472	–18,178	–15,835	–17,858	–22,799	–27,619	–25,610
Bhutan	–462	–431	–304	–216	–177	–190	–205
India	–160,036	–180,283	–157,506	–102,152	–192,753	–214,872	–247,127
Maldives	–1,908	–2,425	–2,392	–1,451	–2,140	–2,510	–2,533
Nepal	–8,434	–10,882	–11,382	–9,186	–11,510	–12,119	–12,284
Pakistan	–25,998	–30,903	–27,612	–21,109	–28,188	–40,386	–56,162
Sri Lanka	–9,619	–10,343	–7,997	–6,008	–8,136	–8,798	–8,950
Southeast Asia	141,755	110,205	120,416	196,687	195,361	218,229	248,987
Brunei Darussalam	2,403	2,365	2,211	1,359	2,395	3,301	3,307
Cambodia	–4,278	–5,844	–7,255	–2,544	–11,257	–5,884	–5,658
Indonesia	18,814	–228	3,508	28,301	43,806	46,689	48,807
Lao People's Dem. Rep.	–2,108	–1,635	–1,411	–151	352	–227	–264
Malaysia	27,233	28,405	30,112	32,999	41,083	47,728	53,434
Myanmar	–4,696	–4,362	–2,978	–4,204	–2,239	–1,982	–2,424
Philippines	–40,215	–50,972	–49,312	–33,775	–53,781	–67,303	–75,199
Singapore	101,066	104,137	98,162	103,648	118,213	116,255	122,872
Thailand	32,581	22,388	26,725	40,856	39,955	52,940	73,208
Timor-Leste	–615	–589	–566	–510	–864	–1,140	–1,392
Viet Nam	11,570	16,540	21,221	30,708	17,697	22,299	27,938
The Pacific	4,523	4,332	4,987	4,012	5,362	7,058	6,356
Cook Islands	–107	–114	–121	–102	...	...	...
Federated States of Micronesia	–120	–129	–125	–130	–134	–169	–168
Fiji	–1,077	–1,293	–958	–653	–522	–838	–961
Kiribati	–98	–92	–94	–98	–95	–103	–102
Marshall Islands	–53	–62	–131	–54	...	...	...
Nauru	–34	–55	–53	–68	–77	–71	–73
Niue	–11	–12	...	...	...	...	...
Palau	–139	–136	–143	–148	–117	–143	–172
Papua New Guinea	6,888	6,973	7,465	5,998	7,099	9,312	8,877
Samoa	–270	–293	–299	–271	–284	–264	–277
Solomon Islands	6	6	–36	–26	–64	–165	–227
Tonga	–185	–202	–206	–191	–179	–197	–208
Tuvalu	–20	–18	–36	–38	–37	–38	–40
Vanuatu	–256	–240	–276	–207	–228	–265	–293

... = data not available.

Table A14 Current account balance (% of GDP)

	2017	2018	2019	2020	2021	2022	2023
Developing Asia	1.3	0.1	0.8	2.1	1.3	0.9	1.0
Caucasus and Central Asia	−0.9	−1.0	−3.0	−3.6	−1.8	0.0	0.2
Armenia	−1.5	−7.0	−7.4	−3.8	−2.7	−4.5	−4.7
Azerbaijan	4.1	12.8	9.1	−0.5	12.9	20.2	16.9
Georgia	−8.1	−6.8	−5.5	−12.4	−9.5	−10.0	−7.5
Kazakhstan	−3.1	−0.1	−4.0	−3.8	−3.0	−0.1	0.5
Kyrgyz Republic	−6.3	−12.1	−12.1	4.8	−7.0	−10.0	−10.0
Tajikistan	2.1	−4.4	−2.3	4.3	2.6	−1.5	−2.5
Turkmenistan	...	...	...	...	0.6	1.2	2.4
Uzbekistan	2.5	−7.1	−5.8	−5.0	−6.6	−7.0	−6.5
East Asia	2.5	1.1	1.5	2.7	2.8	2.4	2.1
Hong Kong, China	4.6	3.7	5.8	7.0	11.2	6.0	5.5
Mongolia	−10.1	−16.7	−15.2	−5.1	−13.0	−16.3	−12.7
People's Republic of China	1.5	0.2	0.7	1.9	1.8	1.5	1.2
Republic of Korea	4.6	4.5	3.6	4.6	4.9	3.8	3.5
Taipei,China	14.0	11.6	10.6	14.2	15.0	15.2	15.2
South Asia	−1.9	−2.5	−1.2	0.5	−1.6	−3.0	−2.1
Afghanistan	7.6	12.2	11.7	11.2	...	...	...
Bangladesh	−0.5	−3.0	−1.3	−1.3	−0.9	−2.7	−1.8
Bhutan	−23.6	−20.9	−13.9	−13.8	−11.0	−10.6	−10.5
India	−1.8	−2.1	−0.9	0.9	−1.6	−2.8	−1.9
Maldives	−21.6	−28.4	−26.6	−35.6	−18.0	−19.5	−17.5
Nepal	−0.3	−7.1	−6.9	−0.9	−8.0	−9.7	−6.1
Pakistan	−3.6	−5.4	−4.2	−1.5	−0.6	−3.5	−3.0
Sri Lanka	−2.6	−3.2	−2.2	−1.3	−4.2	−4.3	−2.8
Southeast Asia	2.4	0.7	1.7	2.7	0.6	1.2	1.6
Brunei Darussalam	16.4	6.9	6.6	4.5	12.5	16.0	12.0
Cambodia	−8.1	−11.8	−15.0	−8.7	−45.7	−21.5	−16.1
Indonesia	−1.6	−2.9	−2.7	−0.4	0.3	0.0	−0.5
Lao People's Dem. Rep.	−15.1	−13.1	−12.2	−5.4	−5.0	−6.0	−6.5
Malaysia	2.8	2.2	3.5	4.2	3.5	3.3	3.0
Myanmar	−5.5	−4.7	0.4	−2.5	−1.1	−0.8	−1.3
Philippines	−0.7	−2.6	−0.8	3.2	−1.8	−3.2	−3.1
Singapore	17.3	15.2	14.5	16.8	18.1	17.0	17.0
Thailand	9.6	5.6	7.0	4.2	−2.2	0.5	4.2
Timor-Leste	−17.5	−12.1	7.8	−19.3	−39.1	−58.4	−72.8
Viet Nam	2.9	2.4	4.6	4.4	−1.1	1.5	2.0
The Pacific	13.8	13.5	13.6	10.9	11.5	13.8	12.3
Cook Islands	41.1	39.3	33.2	−6.0	−12.5	−7.0	5.1
Federated States of Micronesia	10.3	20.4	23.1	7.9	0.5	−10.2	−8.8
Fiji	−6.4	−7.2	−4.7	−12.2	−11.9	−13.6	−8.3
Kiribati	37.3	38.9	48.5	39.2	32.3	35.7	38.2
Marshall Islands	6.4	5.0	−24.4	20.5	23.5	3.5	2.0
Nauru	12.4	8.1	4.9	2.8	4.1	...	...
Niue	14.9	15.7	...	...	...	...	...
Palau	−19.4	−15.6	−31.1	−48.2	−55.9	−51.3	−30.3
Papua New Guinea	23.5	22.9	22.1	20.2	22.0	26.5	22.1
Samoa	−2.0	0.8	3.0	0.0	−10.6	−10.0	−5.0
Solomon Islands	−4.2	−3.1	−9.8	−1.7	−6.0	−12.0	−12.5
Tonga	−6.7	−6.3	−0.8	−3.8	0.1	−1.8	−5.2
Tuvalu	11.5	54.0	−16.9	3.8	−1.8	−5.1	−1.2
Vanuatu	−4.2	12.9	12.8	1.9	−7.0	−10.0	−7.0

... = data not available.

Table A15 Exchange rates to the United States dollar (annual average)

	Currency	Symbol	2017	2018	2019	2020	2021
Caucasus and Central Asia							
Armenia	Dram	AMD	482.72	482.99	480.45	489.01	503.77
Azerbaijan	Azerbaijan new manat	AZN	1.72	1.70	1.70	1.70	1.70
Georgia	Lari	GEL	2.51	2.53	2.82	3.11	3.22
Kazakhstan	Tenge	T	326.00	344.71	382.75	412.95	425.91
Kyrgyz Republic	Som	Som	68.87	68.84	69.79	77.35	84.64
Tajikistan	Somoni	TJS	8.55	9.15	9.53	10.32	11.31
Turkmenistan	Turkmen manat	TMM	3.50	3.50	3.50	3.50	3.50
Uzbekistan	Sum	SUM	5,140	8,069	8,837	10,065	10,623
East Asia							
Hong Kong, China	Hong Kong dollar	HK$	7.79	7.84	7.84	7.76	7.80
Mongolia	Togrog	MNT	2,439.30	2,472.60	2,663.70	2,813.40	2,849.25
People's Republic of China	Yuan	CNY	6.75	6.62	6.90	6.90	6.40
Republic of Korea	Won	W	1,131.00	1,100.16	1,165.36	1,180.27	1,143.96
Taipei,China	NT dollar	NT$	30.41	30.13	30.90	29.45	27.93
South Asia							
Afghanistan	Afghani	AF	68.03	72.08	78.40	76.80	83.55
Bangladesh	Taka	Tk	79.12	82.10	84.03	84.78	84.81
Bhutan	Ngultrum	Nu	65.10	68.40	70.42	74.11	73.94
India	Indian rupee/s	Re/Rs	64.45	69.89	70.88	74.20	74.00
Maldives	Rufiyaa	Rf	15.41	15.41	15.38	15.40	15.40
Nepal	Nepalese rupee/s	NRe/NRs	106.21	104.37	112.88	116.31	117.80
Pakistan	Pakistan rupee/s	PRe/PRs	104.70	109.80	136.10	158.00	160.02
Sri Lanka	Sri Lanka rupee/s	SLRe/SLRs	152.00	162.48	178.78	185.52	198.87
Southeast Asia							
Brunei Darussalam	Brunei dollar	B$	1.38	1.35	1.36	1.38	1.34
Cambodia	Riel	KR	4,045.08	4,044.83	4,052.00	4,077.42	4,067.58
Indonesia	Rupiah	Rp	13,381	14,237	14,148	14,582	14,310
Lao People's Dem. Rep.	Kip	KN	8,245.34	8,401.38	8,679.85	9,049.00	9,737.25
Malaysia	Ringgit	RM	4.30	4.04	4.14	4.20	4.14
Myanmar	Kyat	MK	1,355.69	1,381.92	1,525.82	1,429.05	1,490.40
Philippines	Peso	P	50.40	52.66	51.80	49.62	49.25
Singapore	Singapore dollar	S$	1.38	1.35	1.36	1.38	1.34
Thailand	Baht	B	33.94	32.31	31.05	31.30	30.01
Timor-Leste	US dollar	US$	1.00	1.00	1.00	1.00	1.00
Viet Nam	Dong	D	22,370	22,603	23,050	23,209	23,160
The Pacific							
Cook Islands	New Zealand dollar	NZ$	1.40	1.40	1.49	1.57	1.44
Federated States of Micronesia	US dollar	US$	1.00	1.00	1.00	1.00	1.00
Fiji	Fiji dollar	F$	2.07	2.09	2.16	2.17	2.17
Kiribati	Australian dollar	A$	1.30	1.34	1.43	1.45	1.33
Marshall Islands	US dollar	US$	1.00	1.00	1.00	1.00	1.00
Nauru	Australian dollar	A$	1.30	1.34	1.44	1.45	1.34
Niue	New Zealand dollar	NZ$	1.41	1.45	...	...	...
Palau	US dollar	US$	1.00	1.00	1.00	1.00	1.00
Papua New Guinea	Kina	K	3.19	3.30	3.39	3.46	3.46
Samoa	Tala	ST	2.54	2.57	2.62	2.70	2.57
Solomon Islands	Sol. Islands dollar	SI$	7.89	7.95	8.17	8.21	8.02
Tonga	Pa'anga	T$	2.21	2.19	2.27	2.31	2.28
Tuvalu	Australian dollar	A$	1.30	1.34	1.44	1.45	1.33
Vanuatu	Vatu	Vt	107.82	110.17	114.73	115.38	109.75

... = data not available.

Table A16 Gross international reserves ($ million)

	2017	2018	2019	2020	2021
Caucasus and Central Asia					
Armenia	2,314	2,259	2,850	2,616	3,215
Azerbaijan	5,335	5,628	6,258	6,369	7,074
Georgia	3,000	3,300	3,500	3,900	4,200
Kazakhstan	30,997	30,927	28,958	35,638	34,378
Kyrgyz Republic	2,177	2,155	2,424	2,808	2,978
Tajikistan	1,272	1,211	1,385	...	...
Turkmenistan	...	...	...	...	...
Uzbekistan	27,700	27,081	29,172	34,900	34,500
East Asia					
Hong Kong, China	431,370	424,670	441,350	491,775	496,867
Mongolia	3,008	3,549	4,349	4,534	4,366
People's Republic of China	3,235,895	3,167,992	3,222,933	3,356,529	...
Republic of Korea	389,267	403,694	408,816	443,098	463,118
Taipei,China	451,500	461,784	478,126	529,911	548,408
South Asia					
Afghanistan	8,211	8,273	8,573	9,763	...
Bangladesh	33,407	32,916	32,717	36,037	46,391
Bhutan	1,184	974	1,214	1,491	...
India	424,545	412,871	477,807	576,984	629,947
Maldives	587	712	754	985	791
Nepal	10,494	10,084	9,500	11,646	11,753
Pakistan	16,145	9,765	7,285	12,132	17,299
Sri Lanka	7,959	6,919	7,642	5,665	3319
Southeast Asia					
Brunei Darussalam	3,488	3,407	4,273	3,997	4,557
Cambodia	12,201	14,629	18,763	21,334	20,265
Indonesia	130,196	120,654	129,183	135,897	144,905
Lao People's Dem. Rep.	1,016	873	997	1,319	1,263
Malaysia	96,421	103,978	102,376	102,830	117,489
Myanmar	5,370	6,307	7,244	8,528	8,528
Philippines	81,570	79,193	87,840	110,117	108,794
Singapore	279,900	287,673	279,450	362,305	417,904
Thailand	194,929	206,318	217,632	247,579	256,812
Timor-Leste	17,344	16,467	18,337	19,647	...
Viet Nam	49,233	55,263	78,517	95,149	109,439
The Pacific					
Cook Islands	...	...	...	...	...
Federated States of Micronesia	...	...	...	...	...
Fiji	1,100	964	1,027	1,011	1,476
Kiribati	...	...	...	...	...
Marshall Islands	...	...	...	...	...
Nauru	...	...	...	...	...
Niue	...	...	...	...	...
Palau	...	...	...	...	...
Papua New Guinea	1,736	2,215	2,313	2,686	2,560
Samoa	114	155	187	220	282
Solomon Islands	575	627	576	647	694
Tonga	192	214	213	235	314
Tuvalu	78	86	89	91	91
Vanuatu	394	434	510	572	643

... = data not available.

Table A17 External debt outstanding ($ million)

	2017	2018	2019	2020	2021
Caucasus and Central Asia					
Armenia	5,495	5,536	5,785	6,059	6,643
Azerbaijan	9,398	8,927	9,091	8,822	8,136
Georgia	14,363	14,634	15,324	17,043	17,839
Kazakhstan	167,218	159,797	159,154	164,156	...
Kyrgyz Republic	6,998	6,828	7,008	7,367	7,271
Tajikistan	3,179	2,925	2,922	3,247	3,015
Turkmenistan	...	...	...	...	...
Uzbekistan	17,235	18,750	26,331	36,333	41,619
East Asia					
Hong Kong, China	1,575,303	1,694,817	1,675,364	1,789,289	1,878,975
Mongolia	27,493	28,715	30,702	32,362	33,190
People's Republic of China	1,757,958	1,982,800	2,070,810	2,400,790	...
Republic of Korea	412,020	441,153	470,736	544,917	628,468
Taipei,China	181,938	191,161	184,659	189,873	213,592
South Asia					
Afghanistan	1,258	1,212	1,147	1,482	...
Bangladesh	28,337	33,512	38,475	44,095	...
Bhutan	2,672	2,504	2,741	2,990	...
India	529,290	543,112	558,437	573,736	614,919
Maldives	1,202	1,403	1,536	1,976	2,046
Nepal	4,013	4,781	5,366	6,745	7,777
Pakistan	83,477	95,237	106,348	113,014	122,210
Sri Lanka	51,604	52,412	54,811	49,212	...
Southeast Asia					
Brunei Darussalam	...	...	...	...	...
Cambodia	6,669	7,022	7,597	8,810	9,493
Indonesia	352,469	375,430	403,563	416,935	415,065
Lao People's Dem. Rep.	15,766	16,732	17,073	17,957	...
Malaysia	217,927	223,035	231,506	238,760	256,290
Myanmar	9,800	10,100	11,100	12,900	13,000
Philippines	73,098	78,960	83,618	98,488	106,428
Singapore	1,447,359	1,541,608	1,560,539	1,602,542	1,710,157
Thailand	155,949	163,103	171,885	190,713	189,914
Timor-Leste	107	146	192	218	281
Viet Nam	...	...	...	...	...
The Pacific					
Cook Islands	56	61	62	55	115
Federated States of Micronesia	80	76	71	65	59
Fiji	663	698	674	788	1,091
Kiribati	43	39	37	35	39
Marshall Islands	78	73	68	61	56
Nauru	38	38	34	35	7
Niue	...	...	...	...	...
Palau	86	92	93	150	175
Papua New Guinea	2,001	3,026	4,228	5,185	6,706
Samoa	402	426	399	372	389
Solomon Islands	95	94	94	126	167
Tonga	178	198	197	181	196
Tuvalu	4	4	5	3	3
Vanuatu	313	337	360	345	368

... = data not available.

Table A18 Debt service ratio (% of exports of goods and services)

	2017	2018	2019	2020	2021
Caucasus and Central Asia					
Armenia	5.1	6.2	6.2	10.7	8.7
Azerbaijan	5.8	6.3	4.5	8.1	5.7
Georgia	18.8	19.2	19.3	27.8	...
Kazakhstan	69.0	75.6	56.2	64.8	...
Kyrgyz Republic	35.3	32.8	36.6	44.4	24.8
Tajikistan	13.0	16.8	13.9	15.9	...
Turkmenistan	...	...	...	...	...
Uzbekistan	15.3	15.6	15.7	23.3	17.1
East Asia					
Hong Kong, China	...	...	...	...	...
Mongolia	48.6	50.1	40.8	44.5	...
People's Republic of China	5.5	5.5	6.7	6.5	...
Republic of Korea	8.2	8.8	...	...	...
Taipei,China	2.0	2.3	4.8	2.3	2.1
South Asia					
Afghanistan	...	...	...	...	...
Bangladesh	3.0	3.5	3.4	4.4	...
Bhutan	4.5	18.8	47.1	138.7	...
India	7.5	6.4	6.5	8.2	...
Maldives	2.6	2.9	2.7	4.9	...
Nepal	10.8	8.3	8.2	10.9	4.6
Pakistan	29.2	24.5	38.3	52.1	42.6
Sri Lanka	23.9	28.9	29.7	33.5	...
Southeast Asia					
Brunei Darussalam	...	...	...	...	...
Cambodia	1.3	1.4	1.5	1.8	1.9
Indonesia	25.5	25.1	26.9	27.7	21.6
Lao People's Dem. Rep.	22.7	21.8	24.6	32.9	...
Malaysia	13.6	11.3	12.8	14.2	10.9
Myanmar	4.5	5.2	4.2	5.4	5.3
Philippines	6.2	6.6	6.7	6.7	7.2
Singapore	...	...	...	...	...
Thailand	5.8	6.2	6.9	8.9	6.1
Timor-Leste	1.6	2.6	6.1	16.7	12.3
Viet Nam	...	...	...	...	...
The Pacific					
Cook Islands	4.4	5.6	4.5	7.5	...
Federated States of Micronesia	6.1	5.2	5.7	7.8	7.3
Fiji	1.8	1.7	1.9	0.3	0.2
Kiribati	3.4	4.2	4.5	8.4	7.6
Marshall Islands	9.7	8.2	8.4	7.8	...
Nauru	0.0	2.3	0.9	0.9	0.7
Niue	...	...	...	...	...
Palau	5.2	5.9	7.9	16.1	39.4
Papua New Guinea	0.8	0.8	1.2	1.4	1.7
Samoa	8.1	9.5	8.4	11.3	25.6
Solomon Islands	1.0	0.7	1.1	1.5	1.6
Tonga	6.2	6.0	8.2	14.0	23.3
Tuvalu	11.6	12.4	...	...	...
Vanuatu	5.6	9.4	4.7	16.9	30.2

... = data not available.

Lightning Source UK Ltd.
Milton Keynes UK
UKHW050727190822
407482UK00004B/124